THE HUMANITARIAN GENE
1891-1922

Letters and Diaries by Ernest C. Partridge,
Winona G. Partridge, Mary L. Graffam, Edward G. Partridge

Priscilla L. Partridge, M.S.

ISBN 978-0-9908155-0-1

Library of Congress Control Number 2014953562

Book design by Nancy Barnes, StoriesToTellBooks.com

Published by Oak Hollow Press, California

Contents

Preface

I began this book to share with family and friends the innate trait of humanitarianism that is present in successive generations of Partridges born in New York, Vermont, Turkey, and Ohio. I believe that it is important for people, and family most importantly, to know that the Partridges and Mary Graffam were genetically programmed–it was part of their DNA–to promote education for all, practice gender and racial equality, share religious beliefs while showing respect for differing views, and encourage hard work and self-reliance.

Members of this family exhibit a commitment to this particular set of values as though they were contained in a "humanitarian" gene that has been passed down from parent to child. This humanitarian gene has been expressed through public service given by family members to fellow humans in need. This gene was present in the Partridges and Graffams as early as the 1800's when this story begins and contains a collection of traits that brought these two families together. Social concerns including providing physical and spiritual comfort, sharing of education, the value of religious beliefs, and gender and racial equality are some of the traits passed down to the succeeding generations, although the traits were not always activated to the same intensity in every descendant.

Two generations embarked on adventures as missionaries, three generations produced ordained ministers, and a member of the generation sandwiched between the ministers (and he loved peanut butter and jelly sandwiches!) was a practicing Congregationalist who regularly stepped up to lead religious services at his home church and at a summer camp for boys. His generation also had early inclinations to continue in the missionary field, but focused on research and teaching instead. In this tale I include two sisters, born to uneducated parents of modest means who valued education, and were fortunate to have an uncle willing and able to aid them in financing their educations at Oberlin College in the 1890's where they joined with the Partridges in the commitment to missionary service and humanitarian causes.

The lives of the generation of Partridges educated in the late 19th century was played out on a world stage. Mary Louise ("Louise") was killed in 1900 while serving as a missionary in China during the Boxer Rebellion. Ernest and Winona Partridge and Winona's sister, Mary ("Polly") Graffam, were living in Turkey at the outbreak of World War I where they were eyewitnesses to the Armenian genocide of 1915. Mary died in Turkey after six years of grueling work assisting the victims of war and the genocide survivors, many of them orphans. Ernest and Winona lived to watch the destruction and death of a people and culture they embraced. Statements from people who knew Ernest before and after the genocide inform us that he never truly recovered from the events in Turkey.

Partridge Family ca 1917, Oberlin, Ohio. Top row: Ernest; middle
row: George, Winona, Edward, Frances; bottom row: William,
Alfred. Courtesy of the Partridge Family Collection.

The scope of this book is not to present complete biographies of these individuals, although collecting that information in one place would be a worthwhile endeavor. It is to address the personalities of Ernest and Winona and Polly in the context of their ancestry and through their personal writings that have been safely preserved over the years.[1]

Ernest and Winona were prolific writers. Both kept daily diaries although Ernest tended not to write in his when he was not actively involved in education, industrial work, religion, or public speaking. Ernest primarily logged his "work" activities in the diaries—sermons, public speaking engagements, places he went, miles traveled, number of people present, names of people with whom he met, public events, sightseeing trips and art/museums visited. His entries of a personal nature involved the children's grades, the first time the boys wore long trousers, major medical events, and sporting or tennis scores.

Recently, I re-read letters that my son sent home from the United States Naval Academy during his plebe year. He mentioned attending Friday evening Jewish services for reflection and quiet; relaxing at the Sunday night gathering put on by Academy chaplains; joining the Catholic choir for a time; attending Baptist outings off The Yard; and attending meetings of the Italian Club. I was reminded of Ernest who regularly attended services and gatherings of differing faiths as well as visited art museums and historic buildings and sites throughout his travels. I observed similarities of character although their purposes may have been different—a young mind trained in scientific method above any religion yet seeking relief from the intensity of military training and a religiously trained individual seeking to learn from and about different beliefs. Both respected the differences.

Winona's entries certainly focus on her life as a "single mother" of five children and several "adopted" Armenian girls. Although Winona was very much married, Ernest traveled frequently and extensively during their marriage. His trips ranged from a single overnight to an entire year away, leaving her to manage the family alone. However, she had an active social life with the missionary families, the church, Oberlin College and as a public speaker during the first years after the genocide. Her diary recounted the weather, the foods they ate, and the difficulty of keeping her household clothed and fed on a tiny budget, all while tracking politics and women's right to vote. She was a strong supporter of Ernest, their missionary work, and the Armenian people. In 1922 as a Near East Relief employee in Leninakan, Winona once again forged new ground as a woman working with men in operating and managing orphanages and industrial schools.[2] These skills were acquired by necessity and represented quite a contrast to her pre-marriage employment as a teacher and her formal education in reading, writing and speaking classical languages. Winona's diaries provide insight into the cultural and societal changes of the World War I period (washing machines, telephone, automobiles, movies), as well as holding appeal to those interested in the Oberlin community and Oberlin College events, fellow missionary families and their activities, and their beloved Armenian friends.

A family friend gave Ernest and Winona's oldest son, Edward, a diary in 1914 when he was twelve and living in Sivas, Turkey. Edward recounted the life of a pre-teen boy in a foreign country prior to the deportations of the Armenian people of Sivas and the family's return to the States. Edward spent a lot of time playing, caring for a diverse collection of family pets, and going on outings with various adults and, occasionally, with Papa or Mama. By March 1915, Edward had recorded in his daily entries the death of family pets, the death of people he knows or has heard about, the taking and releasing of prisoners, "the government," and the departure of "our people."

Part II of this book contains the transcripts of these letters and diaries held by family members for over 100 years. The earliest is a letter written by Polly to her family in 1891. Letters written by Winona to her sister and her fiancé span her last college year (1894) through 1898 when she was an American Missionary Association teacher in Macon, Georgia. Winona's diaries from her first 15 years as a missionary with the American Board of Commissioners of Foreign Missions were lost on the trip out of Turkey in 1915, but she resumed daily entries in January 1916 upon receiving a 5-year Line A Day diary from Ernest for Christmas in 1915.

Ernest also carried a *Line a Day* diary with him throughout his travels from 1916 until 1934. After the evacuation from Sivas, Ernest traveled continually throughout the United States and made two trips to Turkey. On the first, he went westward across China in the fall of 1917 to Armenian settlements on the border of Turkey and Russia. His second trip was eastward from New York as a leader of the Pensacola Party in 1919 to provide relief to the Armenians and Syrians. His diaries during 1919-21 serve as a window into Near East Relief activities in American Board/Near East stations of eastern Turkey in post World War I period, particularly since communication among stations was poor or non-existent at that time. Ernest's letters home to his wife and sons during his travels to Constantinople in 1922 provide more depth than his diary entries for that year and enable us to experience Ernest more fully.

Nineteen-twenty-two was not the end of the diaries. Ernest continued his diaries until 1934 when he retired from overseas missionary work for the last time. Winona kept her diaries until 1955 when Ernest passed away. However, closing this volume in 1922 seemed a natural stopping point—we have heard first hand from Mary, Winona, and Edward. So, we close with Ernest's voice as he expresses his hope to return to Sivas with his family by his side to rebuild community for their Armenian friends—to honor "Our People."

Winona and Ernest's diaries are presented in side-by-side format in order to use each other's entries to better understand their activities—family life, friends, coworkers, missionary work and travels. Since we are approaching the century mark for the time covered in this book, a summary of the history of Armenia and events leading up to the Partridge's departure from Turkey are included for the reader to better understand the lifestyle and concerns of the Partridges and Mary Graffam. The information presented here is by no means a complete history and readers are invited to review the bibliography and pursue topics of interest in more depth through their own research.

Priscilla L. Partridge, M.S.
August, 2014

Part I

Partridges and Graffams: Humanitarians

Chapter 1

An Introduction: Who Were Ernest, Winona, and Mary?

Who were Ernest Partridge, Winona Graffam Partridge, and Mary Graffam? Born in the last third of the 19th Century, these three were descendants of colonists who arrived in New England shortly after the Mayflower. They were devout young people–Ernest was the oldest surviving son of a Wesleyan Methodist and Congregational minister; Mary, "Polly" as she was known by the family, and her younger sister Winona, who would become Mrs. Ernest Partridge, were the daughters of a Civil War veteran who toiled in the slate quarries of Maine. Their paths intersected at Oberlin College in Ohio, a school known for progressive causes such as abolitionism and women's rights. Armed with degrees they began a life of service, Ernest as a minister, Mary and Winona as teachers, but were shortly drawn to accept the challenge of posts as missionaries to the Armenians in Sivas, Turkey.

Teachers and graduates of Sivas Teachers' College posed in front of the Swiss Orphanage, Sivas ca 1907. Rev. Ernest C. Partridge (middle row, left).
Courtesy of the Partridge Family Collection.

For fifteen years they lived lives of blissful and dedicated service building schools and training teachers in Turkey while building interest and support back home for their growing educational program. Under Ernest's guidance the Sivas Normal School flourished and became the Sivas Teachers College. The school's graduates became teachers in towns throughout Turkey. Many became lifelong friends of Ernest, Winona and Mary. They built friendships with the residents of this distant land and immersed themselves in the existing community.

But outside forces destroyed this lifestyle and made Ernest, Winona, and Mary eyewitnesses to the 20th Century's first genocide committed by the Young Turk government against the Armenians in 1915. The "catastrophe," as the deportations were called by many people, was a turning point in the lives of the Partridges and Mary as well. Unable to stop the atrocities perpetrated against "our people" as they called the Armenians of Sivas, they dedicated the rest of their lives to attempting to make up for the tragic events they had seen close up. Ernest and Mary documented what they had experienced and collected the experiences of survivors. The three of them told the story to all who would listen. They raised money for the refugees and orphans in the wake of the disaster and helped rebuild industries to reduce the poverty and misery, all the while reconstructing an educational system for the victims. The deportations and senseless deaths impacted the Partridges and Mary Graffam tremendously and permanently changed the directions of the trio and of pre-teen Edward.

The joining of these two families carrying the humanitarian gene began as a chance meeting, however common values brought the two families to that single place. The commitment to basic education, gender and racial equality, support of Christianity, and concern with helping to provide food and shelter to those in need are family traits that became career and lifetime goals for the three adults.

Meeting at College

A boarding house at Oberlin College in Ohio was the setting for the meeting of a determined minister's son and a forthright, independent daughter of a quarry worker. He waited tables; she was a dishwasher. The following year, the more traditional but equally lively sister of the dishwasher arrived at Oberlin to create a trio of human energy! They were conscientious, hard-working and frugal, having come from poor families, but life was not all business—they each had a sense of humor and they had fun at college.

Ernest Partridge, a native Vermonter, was raised in upstate New York and central Florida, attended the Oberlin Academy along with his siblings prior to enrollment in Oberlin College where he worked for his room and board. His life plan was to attend Andover Theological Seminary—the place to go for young men interested in ministry and the "work of Foreign Missions"—to become a minister and missionary like his father.[3]

Mary Graffam, graduated from Punchard High School in Andover, Massachusetts where she took the classical course that included Greek and Latin in preparation for college. Mary, without immediate funds for college, taught school in Baldwinville, Massachusetts for a time before returning home to care for their ill mother. Mary eventually financed her college education with income from a combination of selling books door-to-door, tutoring, loans, and regular gifts from her Uncle Rufus Goodell. At Oberlin College, she studied mathematics, Greek, and Latin and received her BA in 1894 and an honorary MA in 1917. Upon graduation, Mary taught in schools in Massachusetts and New Jersey before accepting a position at the new National Cathedral School for girls in Washington, DC.[4]

Winona was one of several young ladies who studied the classical course at Punchard High School, where she earned valedictorian honors. Winona continued in the classics at Oberlin where she earned money by tutoring younger girls and eagerly anticipated each check from Uncle Rufus. She and Ernest began dating during their later years in college. Winona often mentioned Mr. Partridge in her letters to Mary.

Upon graduating from Oberlin College in 1895, the happily, betrothed Ernest and Winona began their engagement by heading in separate directions—he to Andover as planned and she to the South. Winona took a position with the American Missionary Association (AMA) to teach negro children in the Ballard School of Macon, Georgia.[5] Here she dealt with racial discrimination and inadequate teaching materials while learning the customs of a southern state. Even though she was a white woman she was not welcome at the white people's church. Ernest stayed in New England carrying out his studies and serving as guest minister at New England churches until he was ordained in 1898. Winona moved north to marry the Reverend Ernest Croker Partridge and began her life as a minister's wife in Shoreham, Vermont.

By the turn of the nineteenth century, the three college graduates were settled in comfortable, respectable occupations.

The Missionary Call

After two years of church work, Ernest was called upon by the American Board of Commissioners of Foreign Missions (ABCFM/American Board/ "the Board")[en:] to continue the work of Reverend Albert W. Hubbard who had been in service for 26 years at the Sivas Station in Turkey and had passed away in 1899.[6] American Board missionaries had been in service in Turkey for over 50 years so that the conditions would not be nearly as uncomfortable and unfamiliar as an assignment to China. Furthermore at that time, "Armenia resonated with Americans, and Armenian civilization held a place of fascination in the Western mind because it was an ancient culture of the Near East and the first Christian nation in the world."[7] The

Partridges on furlough to Massachusetts in 1908. Left to right: Edward, Winona, George, Ernest, and Zuzu. Courtesy of the Partridge Family Collection.

Armenian communities at that time were dealing with hunger, lack of clothing, inadequate shelter as well as a tremendous number of orphans.

Ernest and Winona and their baby boy, Robert, "were welcomed with great joy."[8] Ernest assumed the position of principal of the Sivas Normal School which offered education to Armenian boys to a level equivalent of a college freshman. These young men would then go to small towns in Turkey to teach basic education in common schools. Several of these men went on to American colleges—some returned to Sivas to teach. Several others became lifelong friends of the Partridges.

Immediately, Ernest and Winona were determined to have Mary join them in the work by filling an opening at the Girls' School. Mary's position at National Cathedral School had not been entirely satisfactory for Mary—whether she had ideological issues with staff or an inability to identify with the girls of wealthy upper class Washington upbringing—which made it easy for her to leave their father and join Winona in Turkey. As much as Winona and Ernest wanted Mary to join them, they were careful not to crush the hopes and intentions of a childhood friend from Maine who had been considered for the vacant position. Soon after arriving in Sivas, Mary was made principal of the Girls' School.

The Partridges were determined to provide quality education to the students. "Though embarrassed by lack of room and equipment, the school made progress and won the appreciation of the people. All the Armenian communities wished to improve their schools, and made application for teachers, but the supply never equaled the demand."[9] Ernest and Winona and their next two boys, Edward and George (Robert died in the first year), returned to the United States in 1907 for a year's furlough. Ernest received permission from the American Board to make "special appeals for the school, and returned the following year with fair success."[10]

During Ernest's tenure, Sivas Normal School was elevated to the Sivas Teachers College and land was purchased and buildings built to move the college to a 15+ acre campus outside of town. Reverend Joseph K. Greene reported in his 1916 publication *Leavening the Levant* that by 1912 the college served roughly 375 students, some of them boarders, had a faculty of 12 teachers, at least one a graduate of Oberlin, and instituted a music department. By 1914, the year before the "catastrophe," Sivas Teachers College successfully made the move to the new campus on Hoktar Hill.[11] Winona and Ernest's diaries from this 15-year growth period of the Sivas station have not survived, but a sense of their lives can be gleaned from Reverend Henry Holbrook's vivid and detailed tour of Sivas written in 1912 and the diary their son Edward kept from January 1914 to July 1915 in which he mentions the progress of the buildings, visits and activities with missionaries, teachers and townspeople.[12] (See Part II)

The new Sivas Teachers' College building ca 1914. Courtesy of the Partridge Family Collection.

While the educational aspect of the mission grew steadily, Ernest had to respond to personal problems of students, staff, and friends, student discipline and delinquent pupils. "Scarcely a day passes that the Partridges do not arise from the breakfast or dinner table to find a motley collection of complainants or beggars or 'poors' awaiting them in the hall."[13] Their responsibilities extended beyond the mission to the larger community.

Winona was the perfect helpmate to Ernest in the

early years in Turkey. She raised their children while carrying out ancillary duties to Ernest. Winona was also superintendent of the lower, middle and boarding schools, taught classes in the normal school, and was lunch supervisor while the teachers ate their lunches.[14] The Partridges encouraged a happy and intellectually stimulating social life by participating in a "College Club" on six Tuesdays each year. This club performed plays and other recreational pursuits as there were no movies or television. The members were missionaries, teachers of college rank, including some from the nearby Sanassarian Academy faculty, and a few people not connected to the schools. All were expected to dress in their best clothes and the men had to shave! "One of the rules for members was that they should dress in their best – so to give the club an air of distinction. We ran up against a snag when we said that the [male] teachers must shave for the occasion. They protested that they shave Saturday nights only but the ladies won and the teachers came clean shaven."[15]

The Partridge family occupied the front half of the second floor of this building in Sivas.
Courtesy of the Partridge Family Collection.

Family album photo labeled "At Camp" by Winona (seated in the center).
Courtesy of the Partridge Family Collection.

On Monday nights the teachers gathered at the Partridges' for informal discussion and relaxation and Thursday night was the mission station meeting. A community-wide church prayer meeting was held on Wednesday evening, a teacher lecture course was regularly held on Friday nights, alternating with a travel club or some event to entertain the boarding boys and girls. And, finally, Saturday night offered choir practice, "a good stiff drill under Miss Graffam's direction for the Sunday morning anthem.[16] Hoktar Hill was a bustling place.

Winona's memories of her sister, Mary, written in 1944 and her own 1947 autobiography (both unpublished) contain insight into the lives of the trio in Sivas. The missionaries went on hikes and went camping with their families. The Partridges frequently had guests for dinner or ate meals at the homes of other missionaries. The children went on outings with adults of varying nationalities and occupations— American, European, Armenian, Turkish, carpenter, teacher, cook, and doctor. Ernest, Winona, and Mary made special friendships with many Armenians in Sivas. The entire family cultivated respectful relationships with Turkish governing officials such as the Vali, local and regional religious leaders like the Apostolic priest Grigoris Balakian and the Armenian business community in addition to those involved with the schools and missions.[17] These relationships are evident in the diaries. Thirteen-year-old Edward's diary provides a first hand account of life in Sivas prior to the deportations.

Armenia - Beginnings to 1915[18]

A brief history on Armenia is necessary to begin to understand the political environment that was brewing when Ernest and his family arrived in Turkey in 1900. American Board missionaries had been sent out from Boston, Massachusetts to western Asia in the 1820's to bring their religious beliefs to the Jews and Muslims. Missionaries soon learned that Turks who expressed interest in Protestantism were violently harmed or killed, and that the Jews showed little interest in Christianity.[19] When the early missionaries made their way into the interior they found Christianity already established in the Armenian Apostolic Church. The Apostolic Church was not happy with the arrival of Protestantism. It used techniques such as shunning and excommunication to keep its members from straying.[20] However, legal status was given to the Protestant religion in 1850 under a term called Prote.[21]

Many Armenians did not know how to read and write and were thus amenable to the missionaries' teachings. Founding schools provided a way to teach basic reading, writing, and math while gradually and inconspicuously introducing the Protestant religion to the Armenian Christians and at the same time to the Turkish population. Education was broadly based and extended to females something that had not been a primary goal but was appreciated. "Educating women was a goal for many missionaries," like the Graffam sisters, who had college degrees from Oberlin College and who believed in thorough education for women.[22]

Historically, Armenia emerged in the sixth century B.C. as a culture that with Hebraic origins, exhibited a tight-knit family structure of craftspeople, entrepreneurs, and farmers. Armenians had both written and spoken language. In 300 A.D. Armenia became the first nation to claim Christianity as its official religion.[23]

Over the centuries, Armenia and its people were repeatedly conquered but continued to exist under the assorted rulers. Cilicia, the last independent Armenian kingdom, came to an end in 1375. By 1453, the Ottoman Turks, who were Muslim, made Constantinople the center of the Ottoman Empire and absorbed the nation of Armenia. For a time, measures were taken to enable the non-Muslim residents of the Empire to be somewhat self-administering along religious lines. A system of "millets" was established under which the leaders of various religions were the formal representatives of their people, thereby creating a number of subject governments. As time passed, the Armenian people along with Greeks and Assyrians were deemed inferior and made to follow oppressive social and political rules. An extreme example was the requirement that nomadic Kurds and Turks, and their livestock, must be accommodated in Armenian homes during the winter. The nomadic lifestyles of the Kurds and Turks in the eastern provinces were a dramatic contrast to the more settled lifestyle of the Armenians who permanently occupied small dwellings. The groups clashed over their respective religious practices as well.

Gregorian priest and George L. Partridge, ca 1907. Courtesy Partridge Family Collection.

This situation gradually deteriorated until the late nineteenth century when Addul Hamid II was Sultan of Turkey. Hamid II has been described as "the most notorious despot known to the Western world."[24] The Sultan was not happy with the presence of Armenians, their exposure to western ideas, and the pressure put on him by foreign interference. Hamid II began to eliminate the word "Armenian" from the public vocabulary along with words like "liberty" and "revolutionary." The first massacres of Armenians took place in 1894, and again in 1895 and 1896.[25]

In this environment of dramatically unequal cultures and violently suppressed religious persuasions, strict censorship of books and newspapers, restricted public displays of intellectualism, oppressive acts against minorities, along with espionage, surveillance, and paranoia, a group of progressive Muslims and educated Turks created new political and nationalistic goals. Corruption in government and the army allowed these men, known as the Young Turks, to assume power in 1906. The Young Turk revolution of 1908 forced the return of the Constitution and presented hope for all minority peoples of the Empire.[26] Then in 1909, the Armenians in the region of Cilicia, who believed that they were equals in the eyes of the authorities, were attacked and killed. The Christian section of Adana was looted and burned, and the surrounding towns and villages were ruined. Despite official inquiries, no consequences were meted out for the massacre of Armenians "The concept of Armenian massacre with impunity was hammered into the social psychology of Turkish society."[27] It was a deeply entrenched mentality.

The Ottoman Empire aligned with Germany during 1912-13 as Talaat Bey, Enver Pasha, and Djemal Bey took control of the government. These Young Turks and the Union and Progress Committee (CUP) were nationalists and not interested in the minority communities. In February of 1914, Armenians persuaded Russia and the European countries to then prevail upon the Ottoman Empire to agree to reforms for the Armenians. Unfortunately, the outbreak of World War I in July of 1914 created a distraction that allowed the nationalistic Turks to embark on the annihilation of the Armenians–their final solution to the "Armenian Question."[28] The Turks stepped up Turkish-only nationalism within the country and among the ruling bureaucracy. The geographic area of the Ottoman Empire had shrunk in the years of Abdul Hamid's reign thereby encouraging Enver Pasha (Minister of the Army) to expand Turkism by eliminating the Armenian threat and by envisioning the reclamation of the lands of the Caucasus and Central Asia that had been lost to Russia during the Russian-Turkish war of 1878.[29]

By early 1915, Armenian men were required to join the army but were not given weapons–they were primarily a labor source. All Armenians were required to surrender any and all weapons they had acquired since the re-instatement of the Constitution. On April 24, 1915 the "final solution" began with the removal of Armenian writers, artists, teachers, political activists, church and city leaders. These cultural leaders were arrested, imprisoned, tortured, and eventually killed–the voices of Armenia were silenced.[30] With no evidence to support the charges, many Armenians were accused of being revolutionaries. A new form of massacre was enacted–the use of deportation or relocation to inhospitable areas that held no possibility of survival. The Turkish ruling party appropriated or destroyed the wealth and property of Armenians through legal and violent methods. The remaining old men, women and children were then systematically deported–marched from their hometowns to remote areas of desert to be killed if they made it that far. Many died along the way of thirst, hunger, and violence.

Mary Graffam, having no family of her own and holding high regard and love for the Armenian people of Sivas, decided to travel with "our people," the Sivas Armenians, from the mission compound when they

Sivas Station members 1912. Sitting, left to right: Mrs. Partridge, Miss Zenger, Miss Graffam, Mrs. Clark, Miss Fowle, Miss Rice. Standing, left to right: Miss Ash, Mr. Holbrook, Dr. Clark, Mrs. Perry, Miss Stuckey, Mr. Partridge, Dr. Perry.
Courtesy of the Partridge Family Collection.

were ordered to depart on July 7, 1915 for the town of Mosul over 400 miles away. Mary believed that they would be treated well as long as she was present. Mary traveled with them to Malatia, approximately 100 miles, at which point she was removed from the refugee caravan by the authorities, escorted away from the Armenians, and eventually returned to Sivas.

Ernest and Winona had been caught up in helping their Sivas friends and associates prepare for the deportation and hadn't thought about their own plans. The family was shocked and saddened by the emptiness of the mission compound and the school. Regrettably, there was nothing Ernest and Winona could do in Sivas at this time, so they decided to take furlough and return to the States.

Mary chose to stay in Turkey, although she may not have been allowed to leave anyway. Her knowledge of Turkish and other languages gave her an advantage when dealing with people and her strong-willed, stubborn personality demanded that basic human needs be provided to all. Mary's presence provided safety to Armenian girls and helped them acquire medical skills to ensure their value to the Turkish government. Communication was cut off both to and from the Armenian provinces making it difficult to get news out of the country. Hence, Mary Graffam was not able to share her experiences as they happened, and she could not let her family know she was alive. Six years later, and six months before Winona returned to Turkey, Mary Graffam succumbed to a heart attack following a cancer operation, never having seen her father and sister again.

Armenian Extirpation and World War I 1915-1922

Meanwhile, America debated whether or not to enter the war. News of the horrific treatment of Armenians and Greeks in Turkey did reach America but there was conflict in the United States over taking action. Some missionaries were concerned that the ability to provide humanitarian aid would be jeopardized if Americans were not neutral. Other entities were concerned about the loss of property and possibility of missing out on involvement in the oil industry if the United States declared war on Turkey.[31] Meanwhile, the Bolshevik Revolution in Russia (March 1917) affected the eastern lands of Turkey where many Armenians had escaped to safety. The Turkish army invaded these Russian lands and the seemingly "safe" Armenians were massacred.

President Woodrow Wilson, who aimed to restore Armenia to the status of an independent nation suggested a mandate system until Armenia could resume governing by itself. Henry Cabot Lodge proposed in the U.S. Senate that Armenia be an independent state that would include the historic Armenian homelands. Various organizations formed and worked together toward this independent future, raising funds, making political contacts, and using media outlets to bring awareness to the Armenian plight. In April 1917, the United States declared war against Germany and sent troops to Europe, but did not join the Allied Powers. After the Armistice, the United States negotiated separate treaties with Germany and its allies.

Unfortunately, in March 1918, the Treaty of Brest-Litovisk between Russia and the Central Powers put surviving Armenians once again under Turkish rule in an unstable political area. As this meant continued violence against Armenians, a group of Armenian residents of that region declared independence creating a small land-locked area containing starving refugees and resident Armenians.

The Turks surrendered to the Allies as part of the Armistice in November 1918 (the Treaty of Compiègne ended the war with Germany) but were allowed to keep troops near the Russian border. As they retreated from Alexandropol, the Turkish army continued violence against the Armenians and sabotaged humanitarian relief efforts.[32] Delays in signing the Treaty of Sèvres (1920) allowed a new Turkish nationalistic effort to grow strong under Mustafa Kemal and the commitment to destroy Armenia was renewed. The word "America" became hated as much as "Armenia."[33]

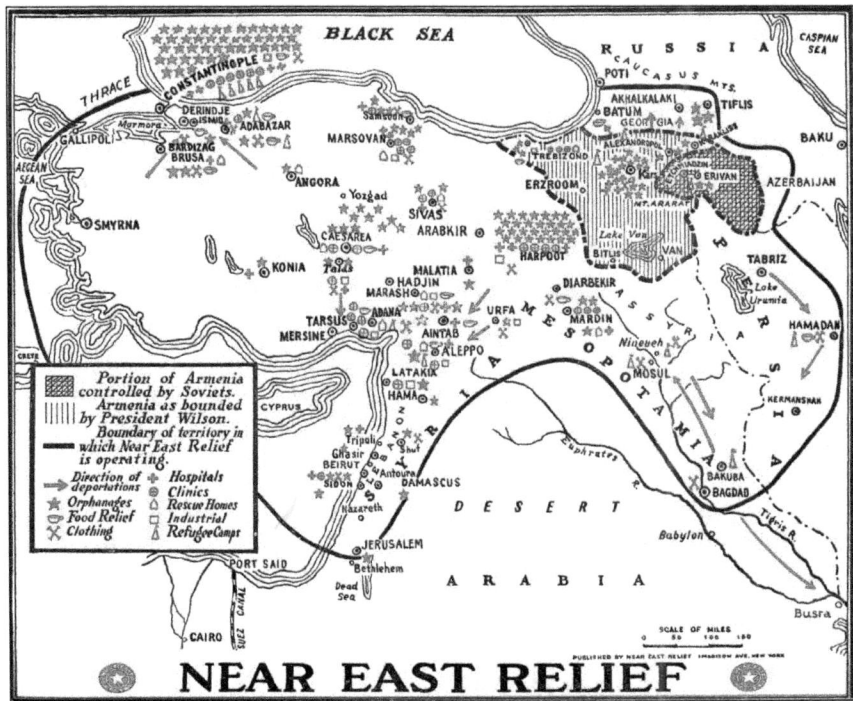

Map of Turkey after World War I. Courtesy of Abraham D. Krikorian and E.L Taylor.

President Wilson sent two American fact-finding commissions to Turkey in 1919 to gain an American perspective from the parties involved on what would be best for the region and the Armenians. The King-Crane Commission recommended that the overall geographical entity or borders of Turkey should be retained but that an independent Armenian state with Black Sea access should be set aside and supervised by the United States under a mandate system.[34] Mary Graffam told the commission that it would be "impossible for Turks and Armenians to live together."[35] The Harbord Mission was also investigative but it had a military focus. General Harbord spoke with Apostolic Armenians (usually referred to as Gregorians by the Protestants) in Etchmiadzin, "Mustafa Kemal and his nationalistic officers" who were located in Sivas Turkey, representatives of governments in the region, and private individuals of numerous nationalities.[36] The commissioners met with Mary Graffam and reported on her heroic work with orphans. The end result of the report was to also strongly recommend that the United States support a mandate system. It concluded that the Turks would continue killing Armenians without outside supervision. The final treaty (The Armistice of Mudanya) to end the conflict between the Allies and Turkey was signed at the end 1922 but no mandate or protection for Armenians was in place.

American Ambassador Henry Morgenthau believed that the stationing of the German military in Turkey meant that Kaiser Wilhelm intended to absorb the Turkish army into his own army.[37] At one point, Talaat Bey, Minister of the Interior, outright told Ambassador Morgenthau that the Union and Progress Committee (CUP) had carefully planned the deportations.[38] The United States had no post war power but the British were influential in demanding that Talaat, Enver, and Djemal as well as Wilhelm II of Germany be tried for war crimes.

The number of Armenians killed from 1915 through 1922 was between one million and one and a half million people.[39] In spite of the significant losses, the surviving Armenians had no formal representation in any of the peace talks. Even when the various commissions and westerners traveled to Asia Minor to gather information, little attempt was made to gain perspective from those who had borne so much of the inhumanity—the Armenians. Those who survived were literally sick, injured, starving or on the verge of death from starvation. The majority of survivors were children, now orphans. As a result, other people—including Mary Graffam, Ernest and Winona Partridge—had to speak for the Armenians. Throughout all the negotiations to end the conflicts of World War I, the Armenians were not present and had no real say in the arrangements that were made regarding national boundaries and governments. When the decisions were made concerning Armenia, the noble reasons for the war such as helping wronged minorities like the Armenians gain independence from their oppressors were forgotten.

By 1923, a small landlocked area surrounding Lake Sevan and tucked up against Georgia and Azerbaijan became what remains today of the various Armenias of history. The independent state was short-lived and Armenia was incorporated into the Soviet Union under whose government it existed until the dissolution of the USSR in 1991. Armenia became the independent Republic of Armenia at last. The towns of Alexandropol/Leninakan (now Gyumri) and Erivan (now Yerevan) are within the nation's borders but the highly important geographical and historical feature, Mount Ararat, lies outside of Armenia yet wholly visible on a clear day from its capital, Yerevan.

After the Catastrophe

The Partridges and three young Armenian women quickly packed up and left Sivas on July 13, 1915, six days after the Sivas deportations. Ernest and Winona resumed their diary entries and these are transcribed in Part II of this book. In a red address book Winona recorded the names of all the people they could remember from Sivas–Armenian, European, American–along with family relationships and status–exiled, imprisoned, killed, America, Switzerland. Survivors of the Armenian extermination plan of 1915 called what had happened "the catastrophe." The term "genocide" was not created until 1944 in the aftermath of The Holocaust. Ernest and Winona were anxious for Armistice. Like so many people in America they believed it would help the Armenians to resettle and all would be well again.

Winona and the children settled in Oberlin where she gave talks on the Armenian catastrophe, continued her education, attended to the needs of her husband, their five children, and the young Armenian women they brought over to America with them.

Ernest's resumé for the lecture circuit in 1920 best describes his activities after the war. He traveled ceaselessly for two years working with the Layman's Missionary Movement and the American Committee for Armenian and Syrian Relief which quickly became the American Committee for Relief in the Near East (ACRNE) and then Near East Relief (NER).[40] Ernest was State Secretary in charge of the Relief Committee work in Ohio. Ernest's post-war mission was to provide education and economic skills to the many orphans and few adults who survived the deportations and massacres. He desperately wanted to return to Sivas. In 1917 he was sent to the Trans-Caucasus as leader of a party of relief workers–he was in charge of creating industrial work in Alexandropol where 3000 women were eventually employed. Because of the Bolshevik Revolution, the work was cut short and Ernest had to evacuate through Russia to Peking. In 1919 Ernest sailed on the US transport Pensacola as head of a party of 42 relief workers with 6000 tons of food and clothing to be distributed to the refugees of Asia Minor.[41] He spent several months of that trip in Sivas learning first hand from Polly about her experiences since he and Winona had departed Sivas. Ernest went east again in 1922 under the auspices of the American Board, but was assigned Near East Relief work in Erivan where Winona and the younger children joined him.

Upon going overseas again, there were a variety of openings where Winona was qualified to teach in Turkey, but she and Ernest decided that they wanted to be together. She actively worked with Ernest outside the family arena as Assistant Director of Education for the Caucasus and Acting Superintendent of Education at Polygon putting her in charge of schools and teachers in the Alexandropol/Leninkan area. While Ernest was waiting for his permanent assignment in 1922, he was approached to teach at the holy site of Etchmiadzin. It was a great honor for a Protestant to be considered to teach there. He resumed a missionary role under ABCFM in 1926 to continue educational work in Aleppo, Beirut, and Smyrna (now Izmir) until his retirement from missionary work in1933.

As always, Ernest's first goal was to provide education for teachers who would then teach in locals schools spreading knowledge; as his father had done in the southern mountain schools of the United States and as his siblings had in the local school districts of Wilmington, New York.

Ernest, Winona, and Mary were not self-serving people–they acted on their values, beliefs, and morals without expectation of recognition or fame. Ernest wrote articles about the genocide and he often neglected to put his name on these typed accounts. He did claim authorship of a biography of Mary Graffam and her experiences of the deportations written in 1917 and later in an article about Mary in the *Armenian Affairs*

Presented "To Most Excellent Miss Mary Graffam" by Archbishop Zaven, Patriarch of
Armenians in Constantinople, September 13, 1919. Author.

(1949-50).[42] Ernest recounted his experience as leader of the first party of relief workers who accompanied
the shipment of relief materials on the steamer *Pensacola* which was also published in *Armenian Affairs*
(1950).[43] The Archbishop Zaven, Patriarch of Armenians in Constantinople, presented Mary with a
proclamation in 1919–a beautiful document written in Armenian and a companion document in English–
recognizing her support of the persecuted Armenians of Sivas. The Reverend Holbrook offered a terrific
tribute to Winona, the least mentioned of the three, regarding the myriad of tasks she undertook daily in
Sivas.[44] On April 24, 2009, the trio was publicly honored and remembered by the Armenian community
of the San Francisco Bay area in their Commemoration program. The keynote speech by Richard Kloian
was titled *Unsung Heroes of the Armenian Genocide*. One daughter-in-law plus assorted grandchildren,
great-grandchildren, and great-great grandchildren were present at this very special remembrance of Ernest,
Winona, and Mary.[45]

 The following chapters in Part I of this book provide a look into the humanitarian and socially-conscious
natures of these three people, who spent their lives trying to make a difference for the friends who survived,
and to honor the friends who perished. The *Prologue* describes the genetic, cultural, and social history of
the Partridge family starting with a successful farmer who grew up during the Second Great Awakening and
developed a deep commitment to the education of his children. Separate chapters for each of the trio
demonstrate the importance of humanitarianism, social consciousness, gender and racial equality, and the
importance of education using examples from family writings. Ernest and Winona had a strong personal,
professional, and spiritual bond lasting 57 years of marriage which is discussed in *The Work Together*. And
finally, the *Epilogue* shares the legacy of the "humanitarian gene" as it appears in succeeding generations.

Part II of this volume reveals the personal writings of these sensitive, caring individuals connected by family relationships and common beliefs. The documents span the years of 1891 through 1922–beginning with the youthful, joyful and productive energy of three college students, passing through the shock and anguish of the First World War, and closing with the hopes and expectations for the rebuilding after the Armistice. The letters and diaries are presented in their entirety allowing readers to pursue topics of interest to themselves–world history, genealogy, family ties, sociology, and geography.

HIRAM PARTRIDGE (PATRIDGE) FAMILY

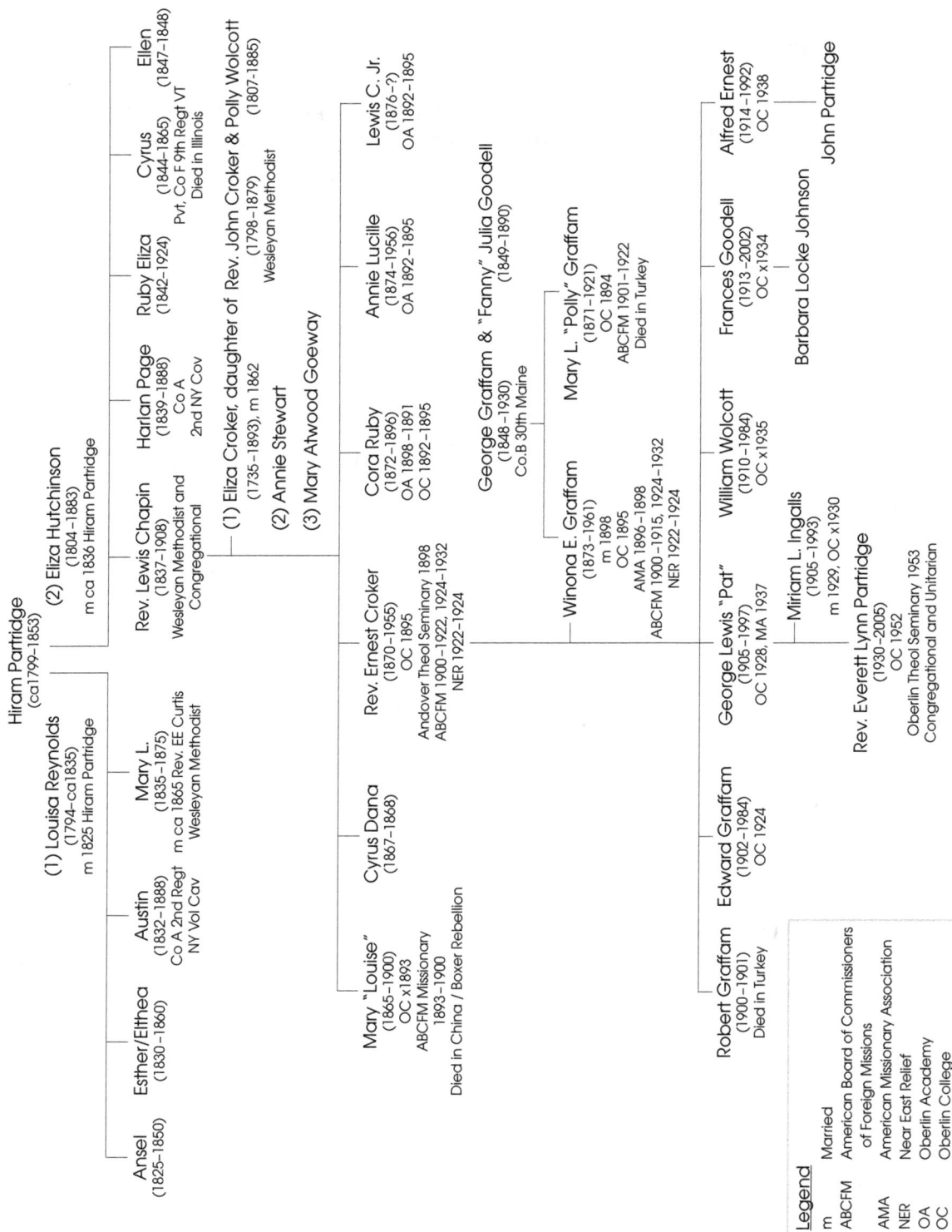

Hiram Partridge
(ca1799–1853)

(1) Louisa Reynolds
(1794–ca1835)
m 1825 Hiram Partridge

(2) Eliza Hutchinson
(1804–1883)
m ca 1836 Hiram Partridge

Ansel
(1825–1850)

Esther/Elthea
(1830–1860)

Austin
(1832–1888)
Co A 2nd Regt
NY Vol Cav

Mary L.
(1835–1875)
m ca 1865 Rev. EE Curtis
Wesleyan Methodist

Rev. Lewis Chapin
(1837–1908)
Wesleyan Methodist and
Congregational

Harlan Page
(1839–1888)
Co A
2nd NY Cov

Ruby Eliza
(1842–1924)

Cyrus
(1844–1865)
Pvt, Co F 9th Regt VT
Died in Illinois

Ellen
(1847–1848)

(1) Eliza Croker, daughter of Rev. John Croker & Polly Wolcott
(1735–1893), m 1862
(1798–1879)   (1807–1885)
Wesleyan Methodist

(2) Annie Stewart

(3) Mary Atwood Goeway

Mary "Louise"
(1865–1900)
OC x1893
ABCFM Missionary
1893–1900
Died in China / Boxer Rebellion

Cyrus Dana
(1867–1868)

Rev. Ernest Croker
(1870–1955)
OC 1895
Andover Theol Seminary 1898
ABCFM 1900–1922, 1924–1932
NER 1922–1924

Cora Ruby
(1872–1896)
OA 1898–1891
OC 1892–1895

Annie Lucille
(1874–1956)
OA 1892–1895

Lewis C. Jr.
(1876–?)
OA 1892–1895

George Graffam & "Fanny" Julia Goodell
(1848–1930)   (1849–1890)
Co.B 30th Maine

Robert Graffam
(1900–1901)
Died in Turkey

Edward Graffam
(1902–1984)
OC 1924

Winona E. Graffam
(1873–1961)
m 1898
OC 1895
AMA 1896–1898
ABCFM 1900–1915, 1924–1932
NER 1922–1924

Mary L. "Polly" Graffam
(1871–1921)
OC 1894
ABCFM 1901–1922
Died in Turkey

George Lewis "Pat"
(1905–1997)
OC 1928, MA 1937

William Wolcott
(1910–1984)
OC x1935

Frances Goodell
(1913–2002)
OC x1934

Alfred Ernest
(1914–1992)
OC 1938

Miriam L. Ingalls
(1905–1993)
m 1929, OC x1930

Rev. Everett Lynn Partridge
(1930–2005)
OC 1952
Oberlin Theol Seminary 1953
Congregational and Unitarian

Barbara Locke Johnson

John Partridge

Graphic by Caitlin J. Low

Chapter 2

Prologue: The Humanitarian Gene

Ernest, Winona, and Mary embodied conscientious, compassionate, empathetic, and dedicated souls. The career and lifestyle choices these three made were a result of their genetic makeup, a humanitarian gene, shared by each of them and expressed through strong family values held by both the Partridges and the Graffams. The families that produced this trio supported Christian beliefs and teachings, the importance of basic education, equality in gender and race, and humanitarian concerns. Self-reliance, hard work, and putting basic human needs over extravagance are character traits that caused them to be in Turkey at that pivotal time of the first genocide of the twentieth century. Ernest, Winona, and Mary were not destined to lead lives of wealth and social indifference. This chapter seeks to provide an insight into the people who preceded the Partridges and the Graffams described in this book and shows how the humanitarian gene manifested itself in successive generations.

The majority of the ancestors of the Partridges and Graffams arrived in America shortly after the Mayflower in search of religious and economic opportunities. Many served in the conflicts that created this country; their descendants fought in our Civil War to maintain the integrity of our country. Through the centuries, these descendants left settled Massachusetts behind for the wilds of northern New York and Vermont or headed northeast to the frontier of Maine, many of them settling new lands and forming new towns. Farming had been a common occupation over the generations but a shift to more worldly and expansive interests, such as education, religion, and abolitionism, began to appear in the family.

The Successful Farmer

Born at the beginning of the nineteenth century, one of these farmers, Hiram Patridge, owned and farmed land on both sides of Lake Champlain during his 50+ years.[46] Both Wilmington, New York and Lincoln, Vermont are mountain communities with harsh winters and rocky lands. In the slightly over 15 years after he returned to Wilmington with his second wife Eliza, Hiram proved to be a successful farmer and in 1848 bought property on the Ausable River called "the Old Partridge Farm."[47] The New York Agricultural Census of 1850 and the New York Population Schedule of 1855 show that Hiram lived in Wilmington in a framed house on 140 acres having a cash value of $2000, owned an array of livestock including a flock of sheep, and harvested 180 bushels of grains.

Hiram's will of 1853 demonstrated the importance of education to this farmer. "Secondly I give and bequeath to my beloved wife Eliza Patridge all my property both real & personal during her natural life subject to & charged with the obligation on her part & duty to maintain & educate the children of the said Hiram & Eliza Patridge until each shall arrive to the age of twenty one years."[48] The 1850 federal census shows that Hiram's six children living at home all attended school within the year. This commitment to education led Hiram's oldest son, Ansel, to attend the State Normal College in Albany and then to teach school in Plattsburg, New York before his death at age 25. The Wilmington School records show that both Harlan and Mary taught at a district school in Wilmington for a time before moving away.[49]

Wilmington Methodist Episcopal Church, late 1800's.
Courtesy of the Wilmington Town Historian.

Hiram grew into adulthood during the period known as the Second Great Awakening, a time of renewed interest in Protestantism. Locally, in Wilmington, Hiram's uncle Reuben Partridge and wife Diademia were active in the start of the Methodist Episcopal Church by holding prayer and Bible study sessions at their home until the church building was completed in 1834.[50] Reuben became one of the first trustees of the Methodist Episcopal Church. He chose Prindle as the name for his second son, born in 1820, five years before his brother Hiram was married by the local minister Reverend Cyrus Prindle. Prindle's brother Lyman was the minister of the Wesleyan Methodist Church in Waitsfield, Vermont.

Religion certainly played an important part in the life of young Hiram. Reverend Prindle, at various times was pastor at Vergennes and Ferrisburg, Vermont as well as Jay, New York, the predecessor town to Wilmington. Reverend Prindle wrote numerous sermons and books discussing sinfulness and illegality of slavery and compiled the missionary experiences of a young man from Essex County New York by the name of Reverend Daniel Meeker Chandler, who went among the Indians of Michigan in 1834. Reverend Prindle broke from the Methodist Episcopal church over slavery to promote the Wesleyan Methodist Church and was then elected first president of the Champlain Conference of the Wesleyan Methodist Connection. Cyrus's younger brother Lyman also followed a religious path as a boy, becoming another of the "pioneer preachers of the Wesleyan Methodist church" along with Cyrus and served as pastor of the Wesleyan Methodist Church at West Chazy, New York.[51] Cyrus had moved to Cleveland, Ohio by the time of his death in 1885. Numerous ministers in addition to the two Reverend Prindles would have crossed paths with Hiram as a boy, and later as a married man with a family.

Another person who influenced the Partridges was an Irishman, Reverend John Croker. Reverend Croker was minister of the Methodist Protestant Church of Pawlet, Vermont when he attended the first meeting of the Champlain Conference of the Wesleyan Methodist Connection where he met with other ministers including the Prindles. Croker served as president of the Champlain Conference in 1845 and again in 1865 and became father-in-law to Hiram's third son, Lewis in 1862.[52] Lewis took his turn as conference president in 1871-72.

Another active participant in the religious revival of early nineteenth century was John Jay Shipherd who had ties to New York and Vermont and may have had an impact on the spiritual inclinations of the Partridges. After a harrowing fall from his horse, he turned to the Lord and a life without sin that included preaching about the wrongfulness of slavery. After another accident caused damage to his eyes, Shipherd spent several years in Vergennes and New Haven, Vermont sharing his religious views before focusing on becoming a minister. Beginning in 1828, Shipherd traveled around the state of Vermont founding and inspecting Sunday Schools and spreading his publications—quite likely passing through Lincoln while the Partridges lived there. In 1830, Shipherd was assigned a missionary pastorate in Ohio where he formulated plans for a "Christian colony and manual-labor school" which resulted in the creation of the Oberlin Collegiate Institute (later Oberlin College).[53] He traveled again through New York and Vermont to promote the opening of the college possibly providing an introduction to Oberlin to the Partridges.

Although Hiram was raised in Wilmington, New York, along with various uncles and cousins, he married Louisa Reynolds from across Lake Champlain (Panton, Vermont, 1825) and began married life in Lincoln, Vermont, another mountainous community, and one where many of his neighbors were Quakers. The union was officiated by Reverend Cyrus Prindle, the circuit minister and well-known antislavery proponent.

Later, Hiram and his second wife, Eliza Hutchinson, displayed the importance of religion by naming their son born in 1839 after Harlan Page of Coventry, Connecticut who had died five years earlier. Page had been a painter and craftsperson with a strong religious ethic and who wrote a religious magazine for youth and distributed religious pieces for the American Tract Society. He is credited with starting the first Sunday School in Coventry, Connecticut.[54] Sunday Schools became an important focus of later Partridges. Hiram and Eliza named their third son, Cyrus, most likely in honor of the minister. Records of the Methodist Episcopal Church of Wilmington list Hiram, Eliza, and three children as members in 1851—Hiram was deceased—but all had left this church by 1857.[55]

Hiram's son Lewis Chapin's interest in religion and human rights may have stemmed from the visits of the itinerant and Wesleyan ministers during his childhood and throughout his studies at Keeseville Academy, New York. Lewis came of age during the Third Great Awakening of 1850-1900's. His father's will requested that Lewis stay at home with his mother until age 21, but the family farm was left to another of Hiram's sons, Harlan, suggesting that Hiram did not expect Lewis to be a farmer. Hiram's oldest son, Ansel, had already left town to attend the State Normal College to become a teacher. At age 23, Lewis was ordained and became a minister of the Wesleyan Methodist Church serving Waitsfield, Vermont,

Rev. Lewis Chapin Partridge ca 1893.
Courtesy of the Partridge Family Collection.

succeeding the Reverend Lyman Prindle. Sometime after 1865 and when she was past 30 years old, Hiram's oldest daughter, Mary, married Reverend Enoch E. Curtis, a Wesleyan minister who served churches from Hague, New York, westward to Lake Ontario.

When the War Between the States broke out, Hiram's sons enlisted. The young Partridge men of this generation had grown up in the presence of vocal opponents of slavery and worshipped in spiritual halls where the concept of owning another human being was condemned. It is not surprising that they joined the cause. Austin and Harlan represented New York in cavalry units and the youngest brother, Cyrus, joined Vermont's 9th Regiment infantry.[56] Young Cyrus died in 1862 in Illinois while in service to our country.[57]

The Young Minister

The year 1862 brought big changes and challenges for Lewis C. Partridge, although it appears that he did not go to war. Lewis was listed as farmer and preacher in the New York Military Census of 1862. His role during the war was to remain on the farm—caring for his mother and sisters and to follow his career as a minister—providing the spiritual support to the families in his community. Early that same year, Lewis married 27-year-old Eliza Ann Croker, a fellow Wesleyan minister's daughter—not the love of his life Mary Lenore Atwood. George Partridge wrote the following on the back of a 1985 photo of his grandfather's headstone: "Lewis and Mary were childhood sweethearts. Her father denied permission [to marry]—'A minister can't support a wife.'" Each married someone else. Late in life, spouses having died, at long last, they married each other." Lewis is buried with Mary and her first husband in the Goeway plot in West Chazy, New York, where he served his final church and lived out his last years with his sweetheart.[58]

Eliza, it seems, was well-suited to the life of a minister's wife. Her parents, an Irish-born Wesleyan minister and the daughter of a Vermont family with colonial Connecticut origins, moved the family throughout Vermont to accommodate Reverend Croker's church appointments. Eliza attended high school at the Literary and Theological Institution of Fairfax, Vermont. Her oldest daughter, Mary Louise, wrote soon after her mother's death: "It is so real to me that she is with Jesus, her dearly loved Saviour." Years later Mary wrote:

"When I remember the tears mamma shed in prayer, and the almost agony of pleading which often possessed her, I feel sure that she had that anxiety for souls, which is as rare as it is fruitful. I think I scarcely ever heard her pray, that she did not shed tears. It seemed strange to me, but I can understand it now. 'He that goeth forth and weepeth bearing precious seed, shall doubtless come again with rejoicing bringing his sheaves with him.' She used often to repeat those words, and I so often think of them in connection with her. It seems to me that no one will be more surprised than she at the number of stars in her crown."[59]

Since his ordination as a Wesleyan minister in 1860, Lewis had been servicing Congregational and Wesleyan Methodist churches across northern New York and Vermont. Periodically, Lewis met both Cyrus and Lyman Prindle and his father-in-law John Croker at conferences. Sometime in 1884, Lewis and family headed south where Lewis served churches in Florida, Georgia, and Alabama. The eldest children, Mary and Ernest, were enrolled as charter students for a brief time at Rollins College in Winter Park, the first college in the state of Florida. Rollins College was modeled after New England Congregational colleges.[60]

Beginning in 1892, Lewis joined with the American Missionary Association (AMA) and took the pastorate of a Congregational Church in Jellico, a coal-mining region on the Tennessee/Kentucky border to serve as a teacher and minister. The AMA was founded "by a network of nineteenth century abolitionists" and strongly supported abolitionist principles unlike the American Board of Commissioners for Foreign Missions, which saw abolitionism as a distraction from the organization's worldwide mission.[61] "The Association's primary concern was to provide a liberal education among African Americans…when public opinion ran strongly in favor of vocational training for the race."[62] Mrs. L.C. (Eliza) Partridge and her daughter Miss Annie L. Partridge were also mentioned in AMA reports for their work in the community.[63] Several years later, a young college graduate named Winona Graffam, began her teaching and missionary career in an AMA school in Macon, Georgia.

The Oberlin Tradition Begins

After his initial support of Rollins College, in 1889 Lewis began a multi-generational tradition by sending his older children to Oberlin College in Ohio. The Oberlin Colony and School were founded in 1833 by two men—John Jay Shipherd, a Presbyterian minister who had been a missionary to the Choctaw Indians of Mississippi and Philo Penfield Stewart. The men had been schoolmates in Pawlet, Vermont.[64] The founding colonists committed to live a pious life—eat and dress plainly, avoid vanity in general, work diligently for the community, refrain from alcohol, coffee and tea—much like the New England Puritans. The primary goal of the Collegiate Institute was to prepare "gospel ministers and pious school-teachers" through manual labor and education. Shipherd and Stewart intended for the Institute to offer the best possible education for ministers.[65] The colony schools would also educate females in a manual labor program. Fortuitous timing brought the first seminary students and several teachers from Lane Theological Seminary in Cincinnati, Ohio to Oberlin. The Lane students were active against slavery and wanted freedom of speech, which the school's trustees were loath to give them. The Collegiate Institute (Oberlin College after 1850) became the first coeducational institution to educate African-Americans (1835) and to award bachelor's degrees to women (1841).

Miss Mary Louise Partridge ca 1893 prior to missionary service in China.
Courtesy of the Partridge Family Collection.

The underlying beliefs of the founders and faculty made Oberlin a strong community, and Oberlin College and the associated Academy, an appropriate choice for the continued education of Lewis' five children. Ernest Croker began at the Academy and then followed his older sister Mary Louise to the college. The three younger siblings also attended Oberlin Academy and Cora Ruby went on to Oberlin College (1892-95). Thus began a legacy of consecutive generations educated at Oberlin College or the preparatory school and of multiple families joined in marriage after meeting at this educational institution.

Lewis and Eliza certainly developed an affinity for Oberlin as "her remains were taken to Oberlin for burial, services being held at Stewart Hall and in the Chapel of the First Congregational Church" rather than burial in her hometown of Colchester, Vermont with her parents and sister.[66] Eliza rests in Westwood Cemetery in Oberlin, Ohio along with her oldest son and daughter-in-law and a great granddaughter.

Lewis's oldest child, Mary Louise, decided to discontinue her college studies and instead joined with the American Board of Commissioners of Foreign Missions (ABCFM) to carry out missionary service. Several years later, Ernest and his wife, and later his sister-in-law, entered into missionary service with the "Board" as the family called it. Louise, as she preferred to be called, headed to the Shansi Province of China to join the Oberlin Band.[67] She lived in Shansi for seven years before being killed in the Boxer Rebellion in 1900. Lewis was still serving the community of Jellico as a Congregational pastor and teacher when he learned of the death of his oldest child at the hands of the Boxers. "Rev. L.C. Partridge of Hague has just received a white silk banner lettered in gold, that was used in the re-burial of his daughter Mary, in China." The *Ticonderoga Sentinel* also reported that Louise's diary had been recovered and was to be sent to Mr. Partridge.[68]

After her death, Lewis wrote a memorial to his daughter and dedicated it to his deceased wife and Mary's mother, Eliza. He related that Mary's parents and her grandparents were interested in missions at home and abroad but that he and Eliza did not urge the children into this work, "...glad as they were to have them go, and the children were the first to announce the divine call."[69] Furthermore, Lewis recalled that Mary, at six years old, had told her grandfather Reverend John Croker, "an aged minister," that she was going to be a missionary. Whether the telling, or retelling, of the visit by Father Jenkins when Mary was one day old and his prayer that tenderly and solemnly dedicated her to God, contributed to her career choice is not likely to ever be known. Nevertheless, at the farewell meeting in Oberlin, Mary stated that the life of her parents influenced her to become a missionary.[70]

After the massacre of the Oberlin Band in Shansi, China, the Oberlin Shansi Memorial Organization (OSMA) was established in 1909.[71] Surviving missionaries Lydia Davis and Alice Williams, friends and colleagues of Louise, were active in this endeavor to support the educational work begun by Oberlin graduates in China in the 1880's. The OSMA, or the Shansi program, sent representatives for two to three-year commitments to perform teaching assignments or carry out extra-curricular activities. After 1928, both men and women were eligible to be Shansi representatives.[72]

For over seventy years Lewis served the communities around him—his family, his congregations, the students and families of his missions. Reverend Lewis Partridge's skill at bringing people together was described in a tribute published in the *South Ticonderoga* section of The *Ticonderoga Sentinel* on March 20, 1902.

Three generations of Partridges and Graffams in West Chazy, NY, 1907.
Standing: George H. Graffam, Winona G. Partridge, George; wagon backseat:
Rev. Lewis C. Partridge; Mrs. Mary Atwood Goeway Partridge; wagon
frontseat: Rev. Ernest C. Partridge, Zuzu (Armenian nursemaid), Edward.
Courtesy of the Partridge Family Collection.

"Owing to the stormy weather a small, but appreciative audience gathered at the Valley View
Chapel to hear our beloved pastor, Mr. Partridge, of Hague, preach. 'Twas a trying time for him,
but nobly he did his part. It had been noised about that he who had come to us in all kinds of
weather, notwithstanding his feebleness, old age and the fact that he had administered to the sick
and dying, regardless of denomination, was about to be repaid for the said office by being "voted
out" and a YOUNGER man chosen. Knowing all this, yet did this Spartan preacher face the
storm of Sunday and drive from Hague, his heart doubtless filled with sorrow that people should
be so thankless. Yet never by word or deed did he betray his emotion, except to a close observer,
like myself, who could see the sadness in his fine old face, that is usually lit up by sunny smiles.
He said that after the service there would be a business meeting; then he silently withdrew. Had
he but stayed he would have gone home with a much lighter heart, for he would have found that
the South Ti. people, taken as a whole DID appreciate the sacrifices he had made in their behalf."

The author continued to comment that when Brother Partridge first arrived in their community the different
denominations were at odds; brothers were not speaking to each other, and old soldiers who had fought
together behaved as strangers. Rev. Partridge's "patience, tact and hearty goodwill" had smoothed many
ruffled feathers.[73]

Thus, we have gained perspective on the emergence of theology, equality, education, and humanitarianism in the Partridge family of upstate New York. It sounded the call to serve—our country, our people,
and people of the world—and nurtured the roots from which Ernest sprang.

The Graffams Arrive

Winona Estelle Graffam followed her older sister Mary Louise (class of 1894) to Oberlin College starting in the fall of 1891. She graduated in 1895. In turn, Mary followed her younger sister to a post with the American Board in 1901, serving in Turkey.

Their father, George H. Graffam, was descended from many generations of Maine residents. He enlisted in the Union Army on December 18, 1863. He was 16, but gave his age as 18. "They wanted to make him a cooks' assistant but he made himself so useless that they finally acceded to his request and put him into the regular army until the war was over."[74] Young George served as a private with Company B 30th of the Maine Regiment. Winona related "The night Lincoln was assassinated my father was in Washington, ready to be mustered out of the army. He was just unfastening his belt, getting ready to go to bed when the alarm was sounded and the soldiers were alerted. My father was one of the guard who conducted Lincoln–who was still alive–from the theater to the drugstore where he died. He may not have been one of the special body guard but one of the company stationed along the route. I don't know."[75]

George H. Graffam.
Courtesy of the Library of Congress collection Portraits of Civil War Enlisted Men of the Union Army.

After the war, George Graffam returned to Maine where "the most beautiful girl in Monson" waited table at his boardinghouse. Frances "Fanny" Julia Goodell was "very pretty with big, brown eyes and a lovely complexion" so George married her and remained in Monson! Winona recalled that "my father was a good dancer, very fond of a good time, but my mother had no sense of rhythm."[76] George worked in both the Penebscot Mill and the slate quarries. One day a faulty blast sent a slate shard into his eye eventually causing the loss of that eye. When Mary was five, the family moved to Andover, Massachusetts where George worked as groundskeeper at Andover Academy. The girls attended Punchard High School and were successful students. "Our father and mother had very little education but were both intelligent and gained a great deal from their contacts with educated people in Andover...Our parents were very indulgent but very strict in regard to honesty."[77] After Fanny succumbed to years of illness and both his daughters had left for Oberlin College, George remarried (another Frances!) and returned to Maine. Fanny's half-brother, Rufus Goodell, sent money to help the girls attend college and continued to assist Winona's family financially for many years.

Frances 'Fanny' Julia Goodell (Graffam) ca 1870. Courtesy of the Partridge Family Collection.

Friendships Begin

Ernest Partridge and Mary Graffam met in the boarding house at Oberlin College where manual labor afforded them the opportunity to follow their dreams. Winona joined them the following year and her goals fit in with those of her sister and Ernest. At this time we begin to see the three personalities emerge in the letters and diaries that remain in the family. The presence and importance of the humanitarian gene are treated in separate chapters for each of these individuals. We know that Mary wrote regular letters to her parents and sister, although very few were found in the family collection, and no mention of diaries has been found. Her independent spirit shows through in the college letter, but it appears she did not find recording daily events as a priority in her life, a decided contrast to her sister and brother-in-law.

Whereas there are many direct quotes about Mary in both Ernest and Winona's writings, the reader has to look for inferences and subtle expressions of Ernest and Winona's personalities because they rarely wrote about themselves, their feelings or inner selves. The following chapters seek to share the unique characteristics and dedicated, caring natures of these three individuals who were caught up in a human crisis that tested their humanitarian values.

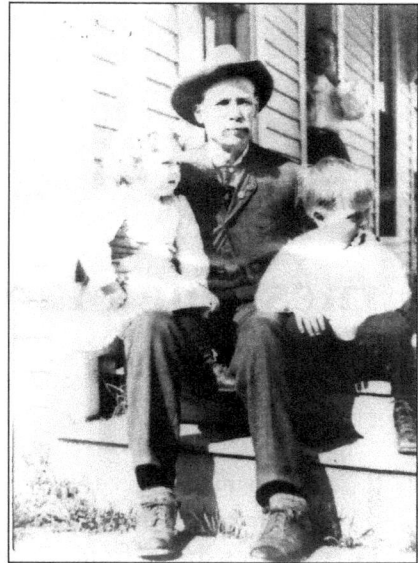

George, George H. Graffam, Edward 1907. Courtesy of the Partridge Family Collection.

Chapter 3

Ernest the Man: Survivor's Guilt

The humanitarian gene was not merely present in Ernest Partridge's personality–the gene dominated the direction of his life. Ernest Partridge's unique character is demonstrated in this chapter through examples, drawn from family writings, of the traits passed down by his forebears that express the humanitarian gene. It was this genetic inheritance that caused Ernest to suffer intense distress at the deportation of his Armenian friends and his inability to remedy the situation to his humanitarian standards.

Rev. Ernest C. Partridge, ca 1925.
Courtesy of the Partridge Family Collection.

Minister and Missionary

Ernest decided early on to follow his father's and grandfather's footsteps into the ministry, and envisioned a life as a missionary in the tradition of his father and older sister Louise. That single-minded purpose is evident in his choice of theological schools. Andover Theological Seminary was the logical place to pursue his ministry education–a primary goal of the institution was to educate ministry students for missionary work.[78] "The missionaries who have gone from this Seminary into different parts of the world, have as a body acquired a high reputation, not only in the places where they have labored, but among the friends of missionaries generally, both in American and Europe. Their intelligence, zeal, and persevering fidelity, have given character to the missionary enterprise in this country, and have had a powerful influence in awakening the missionary spirit, and advancing the missionary cause."[79] Winona often discussed Ernest's dedication, directness, and drive to be a missionary in letters to her fiancé during their courtship.

But, Dear, let me warn you not to talk about it to the theologues and other people too much, because they will get tired of it and it may have just the opposite effect to what you intend. I wish some of them could go with you and we could establish a new mission. If your sister and mine and three or four more could go with us we should be able to start a mission all by ourselves. But I speak to the housekeeper and let the rest do the preaching. I do not think you intended it that way but it might sound a little conceited to anyone except me for you to say that the reason that you were going to stay in the Sem[inary] next year was that they needed to be waked up in the subject of missions. It is all right to say that to me but it would be likely to sound a little self-righteous to those who were not in sympathy with you.[80]

Winona went on to propose a group of people going on a mission together similar to Louise and the Oberlin Band in China.

Later in the same letter, she teased Ernest about his determination to be a missionary and her lack of equivalent drive. "I bought a book yesterday for five cents, written by Charles Kingsley, but I shall not tell you the name of it, because you would laugh at me. It was not about missions."[81] And, finally, she closes with: "Well, my Dear, here it is after eight o'clock and I haven't read my missionary book today. But I have one right here and shall read it as soon as I finish this. Remember, dear, that I am not so very bad and I do love you even if I do not enjoy Miss[ionary] books as much as I might."[82] According to plan, Ernest received his Bachelor of Divinity (DB) from Andover Theological Seminary in 1898 and was hired to be minister of the First Congregational Church in Shoreham, Vermont.

A family story that Ernest decided to become a missionary after his sister Louise was killed in China, and largely because she was killed in service, is actually a myth. Ernest was well on his career path of minister and missionary when her traumatic death occurred. The following excerpt from Ernest and Winona's correspondence shows he had already decided to become a missionary but his intention had been to join her in China.

"I do not care to take back what I said about going to China, thank you. I am not sorry that I did and should do it again under the same circumstances. Polly says a great many things that she does not mean and I should not be surprised if she went with us some day. I do not yet look forward with pleasure to going to China except as it means that I shall be with you all the time then, but then I am willing to go in order to be with you. I do not think that I have the real missionary spirit for I am afraid that my motive for going is a selfish one, but you seem to think I am improving so perhaps I shall make quite a decent missionary sometime."[83]

Winona's letters continued their on-going discussion of missionary work, her current work in Georgia, and their future work together in a foreign land.

Spiritual Upbringing

Religion and spirituality were most certainly visible and influential during Ernest's childhood. He and his siblings experienced a number of church communities throughout Vermont, Tennessee, and Florida. As a small child, Mary Louise made a declaration of piety and as an adult she chose missionary life over the completion of her college degree. Ernest, the next child, followed a lifelong calling as minister and missionary. Ernest's niece, Edna, wrote about choosing a headstone for her mother, Annie: "We chose a marker with an open Bible. It seemed right for mother as she was truly one of the finest Christians I ever knew." Although Annie did not choose missionary work as Louise and Ernest had, she was a selfless, caring individual. Annie's "church group in Redondo, sent an underprivileged girl to summer camp and named mother as donor. This was done in lieu of sending flowers and I know it would have made her happy. She truly loved to give, as she asked so little in return."[84] Ernest's sister, Cora, died in her early twenties–her short life did not offer her as much opportunity to share her spirituality publicly, yet she cared for her father as best she could after her mother's death, and in that way showed her compassion and family loyalty.

Although their father was a minister and his influence was prominent and public, the words and actions of Louise, Ernest, Annie, and Cora also embody the nature of their mother Eliza–a faithful worker in church, Sunday school, missionary duties, and temperance.[85] Sunday School was important to the Partridges and Winona recalled that Ernest had been a Student Volunteer in Oberlin.[86] Ernest continued his interest in Sunday Schools throughout his life by holding classes wherever he was stationed or when he was just passing through–undoubtedly a legacy from his mother.

Renaissance Man

Ernest was an active person and pursued a variety of hobbies and interests. As an officer of the Class of 1895, Ernest chronicled for the forty-year reunion the many competitions, athletics, musical events, and pranks he and his classmates participated in during the college years. The Oberlin yearbooks, *The Hi-O-Hi*, show Ernest as majoring in Classics and belonging to the Prohibition and Dude Clubs.

World's Sunday School Convention at Haifa. Courtesy of the Partridge Family Collection.

The invention of cars and their eventual affordability for ordinary citizens created a time-consuming, and possibly relaxing, pastime for many men including Ernest. Ernest enjoyed cars–both driving and repairing them! One time he performed a tune-up on a host's car in exchange for using the vehicle. By 1922 he didn't see how he could properly do his work in Armenia without a Ford! Ernest's diaries recount final scores of numerous basketball and football games and tennis matches. He liked playing sports as well as watching his sons play. Ernest followed college sports, particularly his alma mater Oberlin, and surely he became an avid fan once the National Football League began in 1920 and the National Basketball Association when it was launched in 1946.

Ernest was always on the move; but when not, he could spend a full day in reading and studying. He traveled on horses, steamers, ricksha, motor cars, trains, flatbed cars, boxcars, and subchasers! The diverse places he slept included train stations, opium refuges, homes, hotels, khans, and offices. Always the educator, he gave English lessons to random soldiers on a train in Turkey and regularly spoke to groups about the Armenians–including some missionaries he visited in China in 1918. Ernest would hike large mountains to experience the grandeur of nature on earth–its plants, animals, and geography–and he gladly shared what he observed. Ernest was an experienced horseman and, like his sister Louise, often traveled on horseback to conduct his work before cars became available.[87]

Ernest was very interested in the arts–paintings, architecture, music and literature. "My hobbies have been vocational education, religious education and religious art. In the interest of my work in the former I have visited Hampton Institute and Tuskegee, and Berea, and of the later have spent time in most of the art galleries of London, Paris, Milan, Naples, Rome, Florence and Venice, as well as in Brooklyn, New York, Boston, and Cleveland."[88] When traveling, he would fill any spare time not necessary to his work with visits to museums, historic sites and churches. Music was important to Ernest and was something to be shared

George, Rev. Ernest C, and Edward Partridge ca 1909.
Courtesy of the Partridge Family Collection.

and participated in by all. *The Missionary Herald* describes Mr. Partridge's enthusiasm and pride at the audience's appreciation of *The Messiah* performed at the Sivas Normal School in 1912.[89]

The diary entries of Ernest's oldest son, Edward, written at ages 12–13, provide a view of Papa as a very creative, hands-on, Renaissance man. Frances, the only daughter, remembered visiting her father's first church in Shoreham, Vermont after Ernest had passed away. "George and I visited the church (a lovely red brick building) and the rectory where Papa had built a long wooden tunnel for the cats to use as an exit, but preventing the cold winter winds from blowing into the house."[90] Frances reminisced about her father: "He was a man of many parts and abilities all of which throughout his life he devoted to the welfare of others....he was not a very easy man to know. He was a Vermonter and didn't reveal much about his inner self, but enjoyed telling about his work and travels, etc. and filled his stories, and sermons too, with humor. He loved to laugh and saw the funny side of things."[91]

That sense of humor shows through humorous anecdotes and poems Ernest wrote. Some of these pieces ended up in newsprint and were found in the family collection. In reviewing for the forty-year class reunion, Ernest came across a poem he had written about a classmate during college. "This started my train of thought on my dear departed roommate of my senior year, and the train went as follows:

> There was a grave senior named Mike
> Who never had studied his psyc
> He passed thro our college
> With too little knowledge
> And gained the professors dislike."[92]

Ernest remembered that nearly all members of the senior class participated in at least one of the five literary societies on campus. The class of '95 may have been fun-loving but they knew how to interpret the written word!

Rev. Ernest C. Partridge (center) and Armenian teachers and students ca 1904 by Encababian Bros.
Courtesy of the Partridge Family Collection.

Ernest was extremely social, particularly for the "cause" of Armenians–attending meeting after meeting, tea after tea, dinner after dinner, trip after trip, to raise awareness and funds for the Armenians who had survived the genocide. His son George described him as "a combination travelling salesman and globetrotter."[93] Together, Ernest and Winona made lifelong friends in college with whom they kept in touch through Round Robin letters. Several of these college friends sent condolence letters when "Pat" died.[94] The Partridge family participated in letter circulation and exchanges as well. Ernest and Winona were close to the missionary community, both in Oberlin and worldwide, and developed tight friendships with several missionary families as well as with the Armenian teachers and their families during the years of service in Sivas.

Oberlin and President King's Influence

The Oberlin College community contributed much to Ernest's maturation from teen to manhood as it did for many young Oberlinians. Henry C. King was a Professor of Latin, Mathematics, and Philosophy during Ernest's preparatory and undergraduate years, and because the number of men attending Oberlin was small compared to the women, the two men became acquainted during this period.[95] Upon King's return from study abroad, he focused on teaching, "his main course being history of philosophy. A good part of the class were 95ers and 8 of our men were in his Philosophy Club."[96] King was appointed Professor of Theology in 1898 and then became the president of Oberlin College in 1902, holding that post while the Partridges lived in Oberlin.[97] President King filled a mentor's role for Ernest.

This association with President King certainly influenced Ernest's education and quite likely the ideals and morals that directed Ernest's life. Many similarities exist between King and Partridge. Both men had intended to go to China as missionaries yet circumstances took them in other directions–President King was persuaded by President Fairchild to dedicate himself to Oberlin and Ernest was directed towards Turkey. King and Partridge both had strong foundations in theology, but chose education as their dominant life missions. Ernest then expanded his personal mission to the establishment of industries (lacework, rug making) as a means for the Armenians, mostly orphans, to earn money to feed and clothe themselves after the genocide. President King carried a pocket memorandum book to record his lectures and appointments, and wrote long letters to his wife (a fellow Oberlin graduate) when he was away from Oberlin. President King held his wife in high regard and valued her contributions to Oberlin and his professional duties and most certainly her role as mother and director of their household. Ernest also valued and respected Winona (a fellow Oberlinian) as a professional partner and a life mate. Family life was important to both men particularly the handling of boys; they each raised four!

Ernest's relationship with President King progressed from student and teacher to respected colleagues. In pursuit of his Master of Sacred Theology (S.T.M.), Ernest took several classes and lectures from King and was allowed to finish these classes independently when he was called away on the Pensacola Expedition. Ernest met King in Turkey in 1919 and then the following year "talked Turkey situation over with Pres. King."[98] After both had returned to Ohio, Ernest continued to follow King's lectures–"Heard Pres. King on Asia Minor."[99] Occasionally, the two men would share a podium.

Family Ties

During their courtship, Winona commented on Ernest's lack of family attachment, certainly in comparison to hers. "Really, dear, I do not think that you are attached to your folks and friends as much as ordinary people are. Tuesday morning. Perhaps that last sentence that I wrote last night does not sound very complimentary but I did not mean it that way at all. You know yourself that you can go away from your friends and still be happy, even away from me."[100] Clearly, the Partridges cared for each other: sister Cora visited Ernest in August of 1896 when he was preacher at Woodford, Vermont.[101] A few months later brother Louis accompanied an extremely ill Cora on her trip to Florida to see her father and finally sister Annie was care-giver to Cora for her final days.[102] Ernest's diary entries show that he nearly always made a point of visiting Partridge and Graffam relatives when he passed through their towns—whether in Maine, Boston, New York or Los Angeles.

The Partridge definition of family was, however, broader than the solid sisterly relationship between Winona and Mary. In a May 1922 letter home to his wife, Ernest wrote, "Our regular family at present consists of Miss Shane, Mr. Maynard, Sister Bodil (a Norwegian nurse here to start a small orphanage on her own hook) and myself."[103] Ernest considered his fellow missionaries and current housemates to be "family" showing that the relationship was not restricted to biological or marital ones.

Winona's observation on family may be attributed more to a gender difference or the facts that she had one sibling and her mother died young. Shortly after assuming his first position, *The Ticonderoga Sentinel* announced in the news section for Hague, New York, that "Rev. Mr. Partridge is to exchange with his son, Rev. E. C. Partridge, of Shoreham, Vt., next Sunday."[104] These churches were 17 miles apart and required crossing Lake Champlain to complete the journey. Not quite twenty years later on the return from Ernest's first relief trip to Turkey after the genocide, he made a side trip to Taiku, Fenchow, China to see where Louise had lived, worked, and died. He visited the graves of his sister and the other Oberlin missionaries who perished in the Boxer Rebellion. The members of Ernest's family extended beyond his biological relations—church people, missionary coworkers, anyone in need.

For all his travels and focus on the missionary work, he was a family man. Ernest recorded personal family events—each time his sons were bought their first pair of long pants, the boys' sports successes, the children's illnesses and operations. He often took daughter Frances with him on his travels in the United States and to various towns in Armenia. In 1922 Ernest sent Billy a postcard of a clock in St. Marks Square, Venice and, in a letter he explained how the clock worked.[105] Ernest's diaries show him to be a caring and dedicated father and spouse.

It was important for Ernest to have his family and his wife with him while he carried out his missionary work. He wrote to Winona nearly daily during his third trip to Turkey in 1922 and encouraged her to join him. Even before embarking on that trip, Ernest wrote to Winona urging her to get to Constantinople by the end of August. In February he wrote, "I think you ought to make yourself get out more," recognizing her need to take time for herself and to have outside-of-family interactions.[106]

Rev. Ernest C. Partridge and Frances, ca 1916. Courtesy of the Partridge Family Collection.

Humanitarian Focus

The humanitarian aspect of Ernest's nature was regularly evident in his actions. When the Partridge's were forced to return to America in 1915, they brought an Armenian teenage girl and two Armenian young women along with their five children. Since Nazeli Muradian [Mouradian; immigration record: Muradias] was 15 years old and not traveling with her own family, she was held for special inquiry at Ellis Island. Baidzar Jamoozian [immigration record: Jamozian] stayed by her side until the emigration approval was received from Washington and Nazeli was released to the Partridges. Seven years later, when Ernest left Boston for Turkey, Nazeli, then in her twenties and living with family members, came to the boat to see him off. Armen [Armenoohi Sharigian Varbedian] lived with the family in Oberlin while she obtained her education at Oberlin College. She married and had a daughter, Alice; both were always considered part of the Partridge family. The expression of humanitarianism was not just professional—it was personal for Ernest.

Ernest was extremely dedicated to the welfare of the orphans that resulted from the deportations. Winona describes in her diary how Ernest went to Stepanavan with the intention of resting, but did not rest at all!

"Merry Christmas from Your Nazeli, Adelaide, and Nina." Nazeli Muradian, Adelaide, Miss Nina Rice, 1956. Courtesy of the Partridge Family Collection.

"December 12 Sat. Mr. P. and Arsen went to Stepanavan in the Cadillac. Mr. P. went for a little rest & Arsen to show moving pictures.

December 13 Mr. P. showed or explained pictures to the orphans for four hours.

December 14 Again he showed pictures for two hours & then attended a banquet until midnight. Some rest!

December 17 Sunday. Mr. P. sick all day, nervously and physically tired out."[107]

Ernest's innate social consciousness allowed him to see the complete needs of the orphans—children needed entertainment and physical activity in addition to food, medical care, housing, and education. His own physical needs were often put aside.

Ernest had a further personal connection with those orphans and survivors suffering from tuberculosis, one of the many physical and health problems that plagued the 16,000 orphans in Leninakan. Winona "spent nearly all the afternoon at the hospital and defective schools, visiting classes, vocational works and the very sick tubercular children, very pitiful."[108] Knowing these sick children, and knowing that his sister, his father, and possibly his father's first two wives, had died from tuberculosis, probably influenced Ernest to actively work with public health officials and tuberculosis organizations in Florida after permanently returning to the United States.

Humor as a Release

Ernest dealt with his disappointment and anger with humor. He developed a strong emotional attachment and dedication to the Armenian people of Sivas. Watching and learning the details of the deportations and massacres by men he had known was a crushing blow. Edward mentions in his diary that in April, 1914 Zeya Pasha (Enver's brother) came to the Partridge's house and in January, 1915 Enver himself came. These visits to Sivas took place during the period that Talaat and Enver were creating an "empire dominated by Turks and in which minorities would have nominal rights" and Armenians would no longer be protected by religious differences.[109] The "black eagle insignia, an honor very rarely given to non-Germans" was given by Kaiser Wilhelm to Talaat after he escaped to Berlin to avoid criminal proceedings.[110] This honor bestowed on the murderer of his friends was understandably an added insult, causing further anguish to Ernest inciting him to write a humorous poem about hating the Kaiser as an emotional release.

"My Tuesdays are meatless
My Wednesdays are wheatless,
I'm getting more eatless each day.
My home it is heatless.
My bed it is sheetless
They're all sent to the Y.M.C.A.
The barrooms are treatless,
My coffee is sweetless;
Each day I get poorer and wiser.
My stockings are feetless,
My trousers are seatless,
My: How I do hate the Kaiser!"[111]

Life After the Catastrophe

Letters and memoirs written by people who knew Ernest before and after the Armenian genocide confirm that Ernest never truly recovered from the events in Turkey. A young resident of Gurun and former boarding student at the American College in Sivas recalls the respect and admiration he had for Mr. Partridge and the Americans. "I admired their ideals, their humanitarian efforts to serve, to help and to uplift."[112] John Minassian was told by Mr. Partridge that he was one of their best students and had high hopes for him. Thus, during the catastrophe, Minassian was eager to see Mr. Partridge when by chance they were both in Konia. "He [Mr. Partridge] recognized me instantly and inquired about my father and family. He was shaken by the news, then asked me about the boys from Gurun…My last glimpse was of him waving his hand and saying over and over, 'Take care of yourself.' He was returning to Adana to reorganize a school of returning Armenian deportees." Ernest was in Turkey as part of the 1919 Pensacola Expedition to provide relief materials. He then went to the interior before seeing Minassian again in Constantinople.[113] Upon reaching the safety of Constantinople, John Minassian again made a point of meeting Mr. Partridge when he learned that Mr. Partridge was staying at Roberts College.

"When the door opened, he jumped up and greeted me. I noticed he had lost his old jovial smile. In fact, he was not responding to my conversation. He stared at the floor while I was talking, and he looked very sad. He reminded me that he was tired and needed rest. On his return to the interior, he had been tortured by the drama of a vanishing race and its manifold tragedies. Hopelessly, he had struggled to help these unfortunate people, but in vain. His heart could not take it anymore. He had lost his faith in humanity."[114]

Ernest's diary confirms that he was at Roberts College in August of 1919. He was additionally sad that he had not been allowed to go to Sivas with Polly to continue in the rebuilding work there. Instead, Ernest returned to America and the arms of his family where he regained his strength to continue work for the Armenians. Minassian "learned later that he never recovered from that melancholy. The sadness had been too much for so sensitive a soul."[115]

Another young man, Samuel Boyagian, had a friendship with Ernest and Winona that began in Sivas and spanned 50 years. Samuel left Turkey in 1914 and settled in Detroit. He visited the family in Oberlin often. After learning of Ernest's death in a letter from Mrs. Partridge, he wrote that he had not been notified by his family and had no chance to attend the funeral or send flowers. "Mr. Partridge was a nice person, everybody like him [sic] loved him, respected him and that it [sic] all a man can do in his life… None of us are going to live forever, life for him after that stage was surely a misery. I am sorry He is gone, but I am glad it is over."[116]

Letters, cards and telegrams came from across the United States and Turkey in remembrance of Ernest and his dedication throughout his life to people worldwide. This one was typical, "Often in the discouragements of school work here the thought of the tremendous problems he faced in his educational work in Alexandropol has made me realize the pettiness of my problems. Georgie and I extend to you our sympathy and want you to know we share in your feeling of loss. We here are only building on the work that you and he and the other[s] who went before us have done."[117] A condolence card from Miss Nina E. Rice remembered, "Mr. Partridge was not just a colleague but a real brother –'not looking only to his own things, but also to the things of others.'"[118]

Edward, George (on wagon) and Ernest loading hay, 1920, Monson ME.
Courtesy of the Partridge Family Collection.

Ernest's tireless, determination to help the Armenians suggests he suffered from survivor's guilt and possibly even a general disappointment in mankind. Throughout his life he repeatedly reached out to friends, colleagues, and associates from Turkey. In 1929 when he was passing through Europe, Ernest made a point to stop in Marseille, France to visit with Girgoris Balakian, the Archbishop of the Armenian Apostolic Church.[119] Balakian, a high ranking priest, had survived the terrors and Ernest, true to character, certainly wanted to honor him with a visit.

Taking priority over all his strongly held beliefs—religion, education, industry, and concern for the mission buildings and property—was the love of family. Ernest had a wife, five children and three young Armenian women whose safety he needed to ensure by leaving Turkey when they did. In response, Ernest embarked on a lifelong quest to improve the lives of the survivors as his compensation for leaving "our people," the Armenians of Sivas, behind. Those people had truly touched his heart.

Chapter 4

Winona the Woman: Faithful, Loving, Dependable

The same inherent qualities of intelligence, family values, spiritual beliefs and social causes drew Winona to Ernest and a life of humanitarian service. From her parents and uncle, Winona, and her sister as well, received a genetic gift of faith in their religion, belief in basic education for all, support for racial and gender equality, self-reliance and concern for fellow humans. Winona was a social being, very caring and compassionate. She acted to ease suffering and provide basic human needs. She formed strong loving attachments. Expression of the humanitarian gene and examples of her loving relationships are gleaned from the many letters she wrote to her sister and fiancé, years of diary entries, and the memoirs she was prompted to write by her family.

The Formative Years

The Graffams were not financially well off and were members of the South Church, the Congregational church in Andover, thereby sharing fundamental religious beliefs and a frugal lifestyle with the Partridges. The Graffams valued education, including college level, for both boys and girls. Winona was a determined and capable student, graduating as valedictorian of her high school class in the pre-college major. She was elected vice-president of her sophomore college class, and elected secretary her senior year. Several of her female classmates, including college roommate Annie Fish, held

Winona E. Graffam in her wedding dress made by Mary L. Graffam, 1898. Author.

offices. Winona, like Ernest, was a lifetime chronicler of the events around her and the activities she participated in. Her letters and diaries provide much insight into her personality and life. Winona did not seek accolades; she did what she believed needed to be done.

Her son George summed up his mother's personality: "Mama certainly deserves as much space (as much 'publicity') as Papa, but she won't get it. This is mostly because her achievements were more subtle, and less noticed. For example: In Turkey, she was merely principal of one school, while Papa was President of Sivas Teachers College. Of course, on the side, Mama was bearing and bringing up five children (six, if you count Bobby)… Again, in America, while Papa was traveling all over, she merely stayed in Oberlin. Actually, 'merely' is a masterpiece of understatement, and is a word that doesn't fit Mama at all. She was never 'merely' anything!"[120]

Winona G. Partridge, March 16, 1908, Massachusetts.
Courtesy of the Partridge Family Collection.

Winona's earliest letters in the family collection were written from Oberlin College in 1894 and reveal a great deal about her young self. Winona was very interested in fashion and did not want to look "shabby," yet she was extremely conscious about expense and careful to avoid being wasteful. At some point in most of her letters to her sister, Winona discusses clothing–flannels, dresses, waists, coats with capes, hats. "Now I want to have a little interview with you about a winter coat. Of course I do not expect to get it now but you know it is a tendency of mine to always want things settled early… It would be nice for me to have a fur cape but that is out of the question, of course."[121] She so much wanted a coat with a cape even though they were going out of fashion. In probably one of the last letters received from Polly, Polly asks Winona about the waists she sent from Turkey. The sisters maintained a close, clothes connection.[122]

Compassionate Concerns

Winona was very attentive to how other people felt. "Don't you think I am a self-sacrificing room-mate? Miss Fish hasn't got her Winter hat fixed yet and today it was too winterish to wear a straw one so I let her take my best hat and I wore my old sailor. She would have worn my sailor but it was too small for her."[123] Winona was conscientious about others. She did not want to hurt people's feelings nor did she want to appear vain and self-absorbed.

Winona was compassionate and focused on the comfort of people around her. Ernest's sister Cora stopped in Macon in October of 1896 on her way to Florida. Winona was distressed by Cora's sickly condition when she arrived and her caring, nurturing nature was put on alert. In her letter to Ernest she wrote, "I presume she has not said more than a half dozen sentences today. She just lies there perfectly exhausted. Oh dear, I wish we could be married and settled somewhere and take care of her as long as she lives."[124] Soon after, Cora returned to Vermont where she died the day after Christmas. Although Winona often had kitchen help when she was overseas, she learned to make dishes that made her family happy and content. Winona's children and grandchildren loved Mama's special comfort food—homemade doughnuts.

Winona had high expectations of herself and was often self-critical. She wrote to Ernest of her feelings and insecurities regarding her teaching position at the southern missionary school. "[One of the parents] said that Minnie said that I was the best teacher that she ever had, that she didn't like me, she loved me. Now wasn't that encouraging? I tell you it did me lots of good, because she has had lots of Northern teachers and is about the first scholar I have had here. I guess she is the best. If that sounds too conceited, forgive me, for I am not conceited about my teaching. I do not think that I am a good [teacher]."[125] Winona intended to do well by her students.

In another letter, Winona again expresses disappointment in herself. "All my energies lately have been directed toward teaching grammar but I am afraid that I am not making much of a success of it now. We have a miserable book anyway and the scholars do not 'take fast' to language anyway. They make such ridiculous mistakes. I cannot help laughing but I do sometimes feel like knocking their heads together. If I didn't like them I do not know what I should do. But I have just fallen in love with some of them and that makes it interesting. It is nothing serious I assure you, but what should we do if we couldn't like folks in this world."[126] Winona was unhappy with herself, frustrated with the students' abilities, but truly enjoying and respecting her students' unique personalities.

Ernest was aware of her tendency to be harsh on herself and wrote words of encouragement to Winona in response to her words of self-deprecation. She responded, "I was just reading the next to the last letter I had from you, in which you say that I am always trying to help everyone around me. Where did you get your information. I do not

Winona G. Partridge skating in Millbury, MA, 1907.
Courtesy of the Partridge Family Collection.

know of anyone whom I have helped I am sure. I am afraid that I am willing to help people if it happens to suit my [unreadable] the time so to do, but I am selfish even in the help I give."[127] She was not always willing to accept the praise and encouragement offered to her.

Early Missionary Experience

Winona acted on her belief that education was important for all children by accepting a position teaching black children in Georgia. In actuality she became a missionary before Ernest, immersing herself in a culture quite different from the New England states and Ohio. In January of 1896, Winona "went to Macon, Ga. to teach in Ballard School, an American Missionary Association (AMA) school for negroes. I had a very happy time the rest of that year and the two succeeding years."[128] Winona dedicated herself to the education of her students, but was unhappy that her students did not have the same quality of educational materials she was used to.

She wrote to Ernest in quest of reading material for her class. "Oh, dearie, what standard novels have you? I am in deep distress about what to have my Literature class read. I want them to read something that is interesting and at the same time helpful toward giving them a taste for good reading... How I wish I had a good library containing books from all the good authors, but I fear that my library will have to be composed mostly of nine-cent or five-cent books."[129] Several days later Winona is still looking for books and wishing for a generous benefactor. "I should like to have money enough to buy all the books I want to teach Literature, but then I suppose it would be a nuisance to carry them around. It would be nice if someone would present the school with some books, but people send down here books that they do not want themselves and of course they are of no use to us."[130] She carried on, making do with the materials on hand.

While in Macon, Winona experienced racism from white residents. Her strength of character allowed her to support her students and their families by attending their church.

"We attended the negro church of which Mr. McLean was minister, very black, very able. He had nine children who attended our school. We were not received socially by the white people. The only white callers we had were the minister of the Presbyterian Church and a Methodist woman who came to evangelize us. We finally told the minister, a Mr. White (a northerner) that he'd better not associate with us as it would hurt his influence with his people. I had many friends among the colored people and even now fifty years later we have more or less association. I visited Macon and stayed at the house of Mr. & Mrs. Martin, the negro principal of Ballard school which had grown tremendously."[131]

She believed education was important for all people regardless of skin color and was not going to be intimidated by others.

A Ballard School student, Truman Gibson, told in his memoirs how he had been accused of being a troublemaker by the principal and then in a moment of hurtful pride and anger spoke disrespectful words to the principal. Winona believed that Truman was one of the school's better students and that he deserved another chance. At the faculty meeting she voted against the principal and expulsion. The result was that Truman was punished but got to stay at school. Later on he learned she was not rehired for the next year. "That hurt me. Mrs. [sic] Graffam was a friend now, and because of me, she'd lost her job." Winona told him it was not his fault but Truman knew it was.[132] Winona recognized the potential of her students and was willing to take risks to see an injustice overcome. She understood that people, especially children, make mistakes and should get second chances.

Many of her students in Georgia lived in poor conditions, and they didn't even have a warm classroom in which to learn. This compassion shows through in letters to Ernest and Polly. She regularly expressed concern for her students' welfare:

"Fri. morning:- Another cold morning, dear. The scholars will be just frozen up. They do not have proper clothing and so they just shiver.... I know how to sympathize with them for I am cold myself."[133]

"I do think a lot of the scholars here. I just enjoy them immensely almost all of them. They are not all bright but are well-disposed."[134]

In addition to her desire to provide a worthwhile education with meager resources, she is distressed at the uncomfortable condition of her student's classroom.

Spiritual Self

Winona taught Sunday school classes in Macon as a way to express her spirituality and to share the importance of her faith. She had also been a Student Volunteer at Oberlin. "I came home from Sunday School this morning and did not stay to church and am using the time to write to you."[135] At that time, it was normal for Congregationalists to attend church twice on Sundays. Winona continued this commitment when she returned to Oberlin with her family. She clearly respected Henry Churchill King and was a regular attendee at President King's Sunday morning Bible class; she often chose his class if she was not going to attend both morning and evening church.

Winona lists the titles of King's sermons in her daily entries. "Heard an address by Pres. King on 'Mother and Son.' The subject was: 'I will conquer that boy no matter what it costs him, but I will help that boy to conquer himself no matter what it costs me.'"[136] The King influence extended to Sunday activities in the Partridge family which frequently included less church and more outdoor exercise—walking to the Oberlin arboretum and water works, or to nearby rivers and farms when the family was overseas. These allowances on Sunday were strikingly similar to the childrearing philosophy of the Kings who allowed their boys to take walks into the country on Sunday.[137] The health and physical well-being of Winona's children superseded the sedentary nature of church.

Winona G. Partridge and George (10 months),
October 1906, Sivas.
Courtesy of the Partridge Family Collection.

Gender Equality, Politics, and Social Causes

Obtaining equal rights for women was important to Winona. She was an early supporter of the League of Women Voters (LWV), marched in parades representing the LWV, and attended meetings in Oberlin.[138] "October 26 (1916) Wed. League of Women Voters meeting at Mrs. King's. Mrs. Martin presided. Mrs. Fullerton & Mrs. Andrews & Mrs. Peabody spoke."[139] Winona noted in her diary when the 19th Amendment passed and in October of 1920 she "attended a political meeting to find out how to vote."[140] On Tuesday November 2, 1920, she wrote in her diary: "I voted for President etc. I voted for Cox & Roosevelt. For the four coming Presidential elections I shall have a boy casting his first vote. I hope they will all have more worthy candidates for their first vote than I had." She may not have been happy with the selection of candidates for president, but she cast her ballot as soon as she received that right. She often mentioned important political events worldwide as well as election results. She modeled loyalty to our country to her family; they regularly attended Memorial Day and Fourth of July parades and other patriotic activities.

As she matured, Winona increasingly wrote of civil and political interests in her diaries. Winona joined with Mrs. King and Oberlin professors' wives in the pursuit of mutual causes. Winona demonstrated dedication and respect for the causes of Oberlin College and the early colony.[141] The college's early emphasis on philosophical and theological thought was carried out in Winona's daily piety, her temperance, and her respect for gender equality and racial tolerance.

Winona viewed college President King with high esteem; she mentions King in her diary more than thirteen times in 1916. In fact, she started off her new year in Oberlin after fifteen years as a missionary with a visit to discuss Armenian students. "January 7 Fri. Called on Pres. King. He promised to take two Armenian young men free into the college to train them for work in Turkey. I had in mind Yerevaut Hurian and Karekian Vartanian." She was already doing her part to help the people she had lived with and loved for fifteen years.

Winona G. Partridge, ca 1932.
Courtesy of the Partridge Family Collection.

Lifelong Loving Relationships

In spite of her personal misgivings, Winona certainly had a big heart and generous personality. She made strong friendships and maintained them for life. Her college roommate, Elizabeth (Annie) Fish, clearly adored Winona and was glad her parents approved of Winona. "I read your letter to the folks and somehow they seem to be laboring under the impression that you are a 'mighty' fine girl, and they speak very tenderly of you. Of course this pleases me and I never try to dissuade them from their erroneous opinion in regard to you."[142] Further on in the letter, Miss Fish joked about Winona's vacation with high school friend Jo Beard in Old Orchard, Maine as a period of "convalescing" after finishing college. What Miss Fish did not know was that while Winona was visiting, Mrs. Beard went berserk and attacked her daughter and Winona one night when they were sleeping. Winona was smashed in the head with an object that caused bleeding.[143] Ironically, Winona had to return to the safety of her father's home to recuperate from her convalescent trip, but her memories of the event demonstrate her resilient character!

In addition to a lasting friendship with the principal of the Ballard School, Winona maintained contact with one of her students, Preston Stubbs. He was the brother of Minnie and came to Vermont while Ernest and Winona lived in the parsonage in Shoreham. Preston "was helping us while I helped him with Latin etc. to get ready for Middlebury College where he graduated later." Winona recalls that she called Preston north to "get him away from the girls to whom he was inordinately devoted." Stubbs finished his medical course and practiced in Philadelphia "giving his life to help the negroes of that section to a better condition of living."[144]

Preston was very attached to Winona and transferred that affection to Polly. From Sivas in 1900, she wrote to Polly: "Preston seems to feel very much grieved because you have not written to him. I do not quite know why he should expect you to but I presume he feels a little lonesome now that he has no regular house. He writes to us very regularly."[145] Twenty-two years later, Preston visited Winona in Oberlin. "Preston Stubbs visiting us. Armen & Mrs. Clark very much impressed by him & I am quite fond of him."[146] Even Ernest kept in contact with Preston and called on him during his speaking tour to Philadelphia in 1930.[147] Winona recalled the "last time I saw him was once when we were leaving for Turkey and he met us on a street corner and I talked with him for a while. That must have been in 1931 and he died before we returned from Smyrna in 1933."[148] Winona was genuinely caring and interested in other people and as a result made lifelong friends.

Winona maintained a close relationship with her father and sister. These attachments may have been intensified by the years her mother was ill and the grief Winona felt at her passing. She was emotionally close to her sister and enjoyed being near her at college. In the fall of 1894 after Mary had graduated, a wave of homesickness passed over Winona. "Before I forget it I want you to find out if Edwin cannot stop to see me on his way West. I should like to see him so much and it is so lovely to have company here. The folks here at Baldwin are always having company, mothers or brothers or friends or something and I want somebody."[149] She was a social being and craved family. Fortunately both were qualities in common with her new lifelong partner, Ernest Partridge.

Partner for Life

While at Oberlin, Winona met "Ernest Partridge who was a classmate and boarded in the same house" and he already knew her sister.[150] Ernest and Winona became engaged, and after six years, they married. Ernest filled the most important family relationship for Winona, closely followed by her relationship with Polly. Winona was fully supportive of Ernest, intending to go with him wherever his missionary duties took him, but did not hesitate to speak her mind about situations and circumstances.

"But I do not think that you are quite fair to me when you keep hinting that I always do just the opposite of what you say. Just now I can think of four great questions that I have had to decide since I know you. 1. to promise to marry you. 2. to agree to go to China if you were bound to go. 3. to go to Patchogue. 4. to come down here, and I should like to know how far I have departed from your wishes or advice in any one of those, and I will also add that I have not regretted following your advice in any case, so there now I do not think that you realize how much weight your opinion has with me."[151]

Gender equality was important to Winona and figured regularly in her relationship with her husband. She was willing and determined to go with him on his travels, but not without expressing her views. Winona's outspokenness was a new concept for the times, although not so unusual in the liberal, highly educated environment of Oberlin, Ohio. Several days later she continued in the same vein:

"My dear Ernest:-
Your missionary letter came today but I do not feel constrained to answer it tonight. I have spent so much time visiting and drinking lemonade with the teachers that I haven't time to discuss such a weighty subject and then I do not know what to say anyway. I don't want to go a bit more than I did but there is really nothing to decide because where you go I shall go, but I shall not promise to go without protest. I am not so much of the clinging vine kind that I just submit myself to you and let you do what you please with me and I know that you do not want me to do so either."[152]

Winona then suggested to her betrothed that she should study medicine. Polly would help, but that money was tight, and that getting married would be a way to support her study.

Continuing her education was an important goal for Winona, but she was determined to have a family life of her own with Ernest. "My dear, to go back, there is no question at all about leaving my father and my mother and cleaving to my husband, it is simply a question as to whether I shall cleave to him in this country or China and I prefer to cleave to him in this country. I love you with all my heart and should be miserable without you wherever I might be, so you see you are destined to be in my charming society wherever you are."[153] Winona intended to be supportive, but her personality would not let her yield fully to the male half of the relationship. She would not be a subordinate wife!

Winona was both anxious and determined to participate in a missionary life with Ernest. "I intend to read some Missionary Literature today but my afternoon is broken up because I have to read to the scholars here in the house this afternoon. You think that I am not at all interested in missions and I presume you have reason to think so but I am interested, dearie, and I told my S.S. class this morning about the lepers and the missionaries who gave their lives for them. I never shall think you are a 'bore', sweetheart, but I do think you are a crank on the subject of missions."[154] She berated herself for not reading all the missionary books, but cautioned him to not be singly focused. Even though Winona was working under the AMA, she didn't seem to consider her work equivalent to the kind of missionary work for which Ernest was preparing.

Passion and Romance

Winona, as a healthy, strong, young woman, most definitely had romantic feelings and desires and, in spite of her logic and practicality, craved some display of affection from her fiancé. She often wrote to Ernest that she wished for more expression of feeling, and more courtship actions from him. "I love you lots, dear, and if I were there I should probably ask you if you love me. I know you do but I like to have you say so once in a while. You do better in letters than you do when I am there."[155] She was clearly a romantic yet showed strong protective, motherly behavior toward Ernest. "With ever so much love to my dear faithful devoted little boy. These adjectives were very carefully selected. Love, Winona"[156] She regularly addressed him in correspondence as "My dear precious boy," "My dear little boy," "My dear little twenty-six year old."

In an obvious romantic gesture, Winona made an outward gift of herself to her fiancé for his 26th birthday. Winona wrote to Ernest: "There is something else that I should like to present to you or rather re-present. It may not be as valuable in money as those little things I sent, but it is more valuable to me and I hope will please you more. I am delighted to make you a birthday present of myself and all I am and hope to be."[157] She has a woman's heart and gives it away in entirety, but pines for more open affection from Ernest.

Winona was very tolerant and understanding with Ernest. Daughter Frances recalled, "I know Papa went to Boston on their wedding day to buy a wedding ring and was very late getting back for the ceremony, but they just waited calmly. Mama was not one to get angry or criticize."[158] Winona firmly believed in their partnership and common goals. "After Ernest Partridge and I were married we went to Shoreham, Vt. where Ernest had a pastorate. The parsonage was lovely in summer but the winters were very severe and the parsonage was heated by a coal stove in the parlor and wood stoves in the kitchen and back kitchen."[159] She was already embarking on a life of discomfort and encountering the everyday challenges of a minister's wife.

Family Life

And then, the romantic young woman began a family of her own. Her first son, Bobby, was four months old when the missionaries traveled to Turkey on their first American Board assignment. Bobby struggled with digestive problems and died after one year on the third anniversary of his parent's marriage. Bobby was buried in Sivas and left behind when the deportations began. Five more children were born at the Sivas Station. Winona proudly brought her two older boys, Edward and George, home to visit their grandparents and relatives in upstate New York and Maine. Photos of mother and sons, father and sons, and assorted family groups were taken during their furlough visit in 1907–1908.

Adding to Winona's family were the three young women from Sivas and several young Armenian men who were already in America or who had escaped the massacres. So Winona, like Ernest, had a broad view of family. These young men and women filled roles of "adopted children" and were important family members for life; her door was always open to them. Winona was careful not take advantage of Baidzar, Nazeli, and Armen and focused on getting them a proper education. After 45+ years, these women continued to be a part of

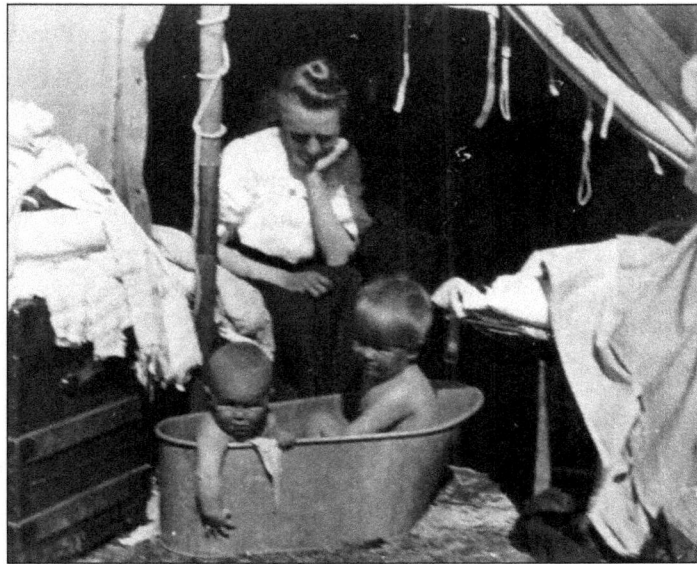

Winona G. Partridge, George, and Edward camping near Sivas, ca 1906. Courtesy of the Partridge Family Collection.

her life and the lives of all the Partridges. In 1956, Winona received a photo of Nazeli with Miss Nina Rice, who was also "family." And several years later, Armen sent Winona a valentine addressed to "Mom" and she began her note with "Dear Mom."[160] No one could dispute that Winona was devoted to each one of her children. Her diaries abound with anecdotes and accountings of the family activities along with facts of life—grades, illnesses, heights and weights.

Winona and children, 1920, Oberlin, Ohio. Back: Edward, George, Winona; front: Alfred, Frances, William. Courtesy of the Partridge Family Collection.

Winona "supported [Ernest] in his 'unretirements' in Rootstown, Gentry, and Valparaiso," even though these jobs took "Mama" away from her family.[161] The strong partnership between Winona and her husband is explored in a separate chapter. For her remaining years after her Ernest's death, Winona had no home. "Mama" lived among her grown children and their families, reaching Massachusetts in October to see the fall colors and arriving in California for the winter.

Without a doubt Winona loved her family and liked to have as many of them as possible nearby. She loved all her children including the young Armenian women they brought over from Turkey. Family was probably the most important value to her. The close bond between Winona and Mary was the motivator for enticing her older sister to join her in Turkey. More of this relationship is revealed in the following chapter.

Chapter 5

Mary: Polly the Take-Charge Caregiver

"These things are never so bad as they seem to be and after you go off and get up a little cheek you are all right." June 31, 189[1][162]

We now turn our attention to the final part of the trio—Mary Graffam. She also inherited the family commitment to basic education for all, gender equality, humanitarian and social concerns and solid religious beliefs—the humanitarian gene. Mary acted from the strength of her character and the depth of her personal values, and as a result of that inner strength, she often took risks. Mary was driven by her humanitarian beliefs, her belief in the importance of education, and the belief that she should help to provide basic human needs to all people she encountered. She shared her sister and brother-in-law's values and was a partner in achieving their life goals.

Mary's life was of shorter duration than Winona and Ernest; she died at age fifty—yet it was a full life. Winona loved her sister, depended on her and was proud of her accomplishments. These feelings show through in the letters and diary entries quoted in this chapter. In the 1940s, Winona wrote a biography of her sister from which we learn much about Mary. Ernest was a good friend to Mary and respected her professionally. Ernest wrote numerous articles, before and after Mary's death, broadcasting her strength of character, humanitarian nature, and commitment to a greater good. Both Winona and Ernest were grateful for Mary's dedication to the Armenians of Sivas.

Mary L. Graffam and Winona E. Graffam, ca 1878. Courtesy of the Partridge Family Collection.

Go For It

The opening quote sums up Mary's character in one sentence—just get up and go for it. A young and vibrant Mary wrote this sentence in a letter home to her dearest younger sister and father after completing her first year at Oberlin College. Even as a twenty year old, she was full of spirit and the independence of youth. Her feisty personality showed through as she declared that she would ride in a car with two young men which was against school rules, and she closed with a promise to be on her best behavior with their father's intended wife if she could get home for Christmas. Winona acknowledged that independent spirit nearly ten years later, when she advised Mary not to travel to Turkey with another single woman. "You would like it better to come with a man and his wife because you would be more independent."[163] Mary Graffam could not be described as shy![164]

Mary, like her sister and brother-in-law, had a sense of humor. She and Winona probably developed their quick wit and emotional resilience in response to their father's teasing nature.[165] Prior to teaching at the National Cathedral School, Mary was invited to dinner by two principals who she suspected wanted to test her table manners. Mary did not order the corn-on-the-cob but the teachers did. "These two principals had a terrible time with that corn, scattering it on the table and even on the floor. Afterwards when she was a teacher in the Cathedral School, the dinner in Middlebury was mentioned and Polly remarked that she had never seen anyone eat corn like that. 'Neither did we,' they said."[166] In spite of the horrors she had seen in Turkey, her optimistic, cheery self persisted. J.C. Linn, Jr. visited with Ernest and Mary in Sivas in the spring of 1919 and wrote: "After the strain of loneliness and danger in which she has lived for four years, Miss Graffam is as cheerful and happy as any woman in America who has never known sorrow. Most of the people among whom she worked for fourteen years are dead, but she can still be cheerful because she has unwavering confidence in the recuperative power of the Armenians."[167] As we saw with Ernest, humor had a powerful, healing effect on Mary.

Her actions might suggest a fearless human being. Mary experienced horror and terror but said she recalled being fearful only once during the years of extirpation of the Armenians.[168] More often, Mary's actions caused other people to be uncomfortable, compliant, and maybe even fearful. Winona wrote shortly after her sister left Sivas with the deportees, "'Winona,' she must have said, 'show me quickly the largest and brightest hat that you have. I want to borrow it to wear it on the road.' 'Why?' I must have exclaimed, heartbroken that she was determined to go with the deportees, knowing that once she set her mind on something there would be nothing to stop her."[169] Mary responded that an American, and particularly an American woman in a big hat, would be less likely to be murdered on the road, and that the Turks were afraid of foreign women. This contention guided Mary during the deportations and the subsequent war years.

Self-Reliance and Hard Work

The Graffams and Goodells believed that learning was an important use of their daughters' time. "Our father and mother had very little education but were both intelligent and gained a great deal from their contacts with educated people in Andover, Mass."[170] Winona described Mary: "She was always a good student, very quick to understand."[171] And, unlike some of the other Andover families, Mary's parents supported her choice of pre-college classes and her goal of attending. Mary and another female classmate, Josephine Beard, were the only students in high school "to study the classical to prepare for college."[172] Both girls took the examination to attend Smith College in the fall when "Miss Annie Davis, secretary to Prof. George

Frederick Wright in Oberlin, visited her house in Andover and pictured Oberlin College so pleasantly that the two girls went to Oberlin the next fall."[173] Mary was an excellent student with a knack for languages. She studied Greek, Latin, Hebrew, and French. This ability served her well during her travels in Europe and her years in Turkey.

Additional defining characteristics of Mary Graffam were her leadership skills and the capacity to undertake any task and fulfill it superbly. In an early letter to Polly and the folks from Sivas, and even though Winona was more than five thousand miles away from her sister, Winona was counting on Mary's help. "I forgot to say, Polly, that it will be necessary for you to be out here next year because I have to have Thanksgiving dinner then and of course I shall have to have you. Mrs. Hubbard thinks it will be lonely for you to spend the whole year here. I really think you would enjoy it very much."[174] Winona desperately wanted her sister to join her in Sivas and appealed to Mary for her organizational and planning skills to help prepare such a large meal!

In 1917 Ernest wrote that missionaries all have odd jobs to do and some are less pleasing than others. "One of the characteristic things about Mary Graffam's life in Turkey has been her willingness to do odd jobs, of which she has had her full share, and her success in doing them."[175] Soon after arriving in Sivas to be a teacher, Miss Brewer contracted typhoid early on and never recovered—Mary was promoted to supervisor of the Girls' School.[176] "The striking quality of Mary Graffam was her versatility. She did well anything she undertook. She was a successful teacher and a capable administrator."[177] Mary was a reliable and responsible leader and did what was required in the moment.

Mary L. Graffam (bottom row, fourth from left), missionaries, and nurses, Sivas. Courtesy of the Partridge Family Collection.

Mary loved music. She participated in and led musical groups regularly throughout her life. Letters, diary entries, and mission reports show that Mary involved herself in musical activities yet her abilities appeared to be functional and from enjoyment rather than from any superb talent. At Oberlin, "She was a member of the First Church Choir and the Musical Union. She sang alto, had not [an] extra-fine voice but could sing correctly."[178] Winona continued on the subject of her sister and music. "She was no musician but when she taught in Wolfeborough, New Hampshire, and was asked to teach the singing, she did it but felt hardly prepared to lead the chorus and orchestra, which she had to do because the orchestra leader could not come. I was present at the Commencement Exercises and shall never forget the vigorous way she beat time for chorus and orchestra. One of the members of the orchestra did all in his power to help her for which she was very grateful."[179] For a time in Sivas, she led choir practice every Saturday night. "It [the choir] does very creditable work" but the soloists for one program were imported and performed by the phonograph.[180] All reports lead to the same conclusion—she would not have been in demand as a performance vocalist or musician! Mary believed in the music as an activity that brought people together and possibly as a way to share religious beliefs.

Inclination to the Mission Field

Mary, also, felt a calling to participate in a life of service to encourage education and spiritual growth. The Congregational church supported missionary lifestyles and she was an active member in Andover and then in Oberlin. In 1920, the Rev. Bigelow of the South Congregational Church, Andover, spoke about Mary's missionary interest. "No one who knew Mary Graffam in her childhood days could fail to notice the budding flower of the missionary spirit in her heart. In her home she spent much time in singing missionary hymns to piano accompaniment by her sister, with a fervor that was most inspiring."[181]

Missionary work may have been a topic in common with Ernest when they first met. "Early in her college course Miss Graffam had become a Student Volunteer, but when it seemed probable that her sister would go to the foreign field, she felt for a time called to remain at home and declined invitations from educational institutions in Africa and Japan."[182]

After graduation from Oberlin, Mary considered missionary work. Winona shared this idea with a mutual acquaintance and wrote to Mary, "I told Mrs. Johnston about the circumstances the other day and she said she thought it was a splendid opportunity and then she repeated the following sentence again and again, 'I think she would make a capital missionary, a capital one.' etc. ad infinitum. Then the next day she saw me again and said the same thing over and told me to tell you she said so."[183]

Putting her missionary leanings aside, Mary resumed her teaching career in stateside high schools. The mission statement of the National Cathedral School for Girls in Washington, D.C. matched her views on female education so she accepted a post there in 1900. "The founding curriculum was daring and liberal for its time," and it was a school dedicated to "preparing young women for the intellectual, ethical, and emotional challenges of life."[184] But "it was a new experience for Polly to teach girls from rich and prominent families. Theodore Roosevelt's daughter was a pupil. One day Polly took the girls to some entertainment and on the way back to the school it started to rain so the girls got a little wet. One of the principals was very much wrought up and said, 'These girls will get cold and have pneumonia and die and you'll be the murderer.' I don't think Polly worried very much about that. She had often been wet, and never contracted pneumonia."[185] The social customs were more genteel, affluent, and protective at this school than those

Mary was used to. Therefore, it is not surprising to learn that Mary eventually followed the Partridges into missionary work when both Ernest and Winona repeatedly urged Mary to join them in Sivas.

Fiscally Conscientious

Like her sister and Ernest, Mary was conscientious about money having grown up in a home where every penny counted. Her concern with finances was illustrated by an 1891 letter: "I suppose there is a letter in Oberlin with some money in it. I shall need about ten dollars but if you don't send it all I suppose Mrs. W. can wait a week or two for the other five I owe her. I feel awfully mean to take so much money but I hope to earn my own after a while and when I get through college I hope I can do something for you people."[186] She worked several jobs and borrowed money to pay for her college education. In order to get the most out of her money, Mary learned to sew clothes; she was able to make new items or revamp existing pieces to look stylish and new.

This talent made Winona's wardrobe fashionable on a tight budget. In her 1891 letter to the family, Mary cites Winona's dress as a distraction from her studies. Clothing was a common topic in Winona's correspondence with her sister from Oberlin, from her teaching years in Georgia, and from Sivas before Mary arrived. In October 1894 Winona wrote to her sister in great length about clothes.

> ... Now I want to have a little interview with you about a winter coat. Of course I do not expect to get it now but you know it is a tendency of mine to always want things settled early. You have of course seen any number of those heavy capes which they call golf 'capes' and know that they are all the go now, do you think that it would be a good scheme for me to have one of those instead of a coat? It would serve two uses you see, as a coat & a cape to wear over any party dress & a nice one of those would not be as expensive as a coat... If you do not think you'd better try to make one, I can get one in Cleveland in the Christmas vacation. It would be nice for me to have a fur cape but that is out of the question, of course. I started to say that my grey skirt looks fine and it will be a real pretty suit when I get the waist to it. Please make it as soon as you can so that you can fix the blue one for my black skirt is fast giving out and I shall soon not have anything to wear to school. Never mind about the light waist. I can get along without that.[187]

Even Winona's college roommate depended on Mary for her sewing skills.

> Miss Fish says to tell you that you have a little home missionary work to do before you go abroad and that is to come out here and help us fix up our room, make us some long muslin curtains, some cushions for our window seats, etc.[188]

In possibly the last letter that Mary ever wrote to Winona, she mentions her latest contribution to her little sister's wardrobe. "I am glad you liked the waists. I have some others now that are just as good for me and fit me better."[189] Mary always looked out for her sister.

Mary's skill as a seamstress was put to use in ways other than keeping herself clothed and her sister even more fashionably clothed. Her knowledge of clothing construction enabled her to teach an Armenian tailor how to make clothes suitable for the missionary women. American and European clothing was not readily available in Sivas in 1901. This talent along with her leadership abilities was critical for the safety of the girls that were left behind when their mothers and siblings were deported. Mary supervised these girls in occupations, like sewing and knitting, which would enable them to be needed by the military and government.

Always the Care-Giver

As the oldest daughter and the child of a sickly mother, Mary developed nurturing tendencies. Frances "Fanny" Graffam was sick for many years, and Mary assumed nurturing responsibilities when their mother could not care for them. After graduating from high school and going away to teach, Mary returned home from a teaching position to nurse her mother until death took her away. Many years later Winona remembered, "Although she was only two and a half years older [Polly] always felt that she must take care of me. That feeling lasted until the end of her life."[190]

A surprise opportunity for nurturing resulted after Winona graduated from Oberlin and took a restorative trip to visit Mary's friend Jo Beard in Maine. One night Mrs. Beard went berserk and attacked her daughter Josephine and Winona in their beds. The next day, as soon as she was able, Winona hurried home to Andover sporting a gash on her head. "Polly took wonderful care of me so that I should not be frightened for I was in such a nervous state that I was afraid to be with people and at the same time afraid to be alone."[191] Mary provided a comforting presence for her sister.

The empathy Mary held for people in pain and discomfort encouraged her to learn nursing "on the job." She never had formal training, but through her friendships and professional collaborations with the missionary doctors and nurses, Mary learned basic nursing procedures and became a competent nurse and effective administrator. During the winter of 1914-15, the war between the Turkish army and the Russians was raging east of Sivas near Erzroom, but no doctors were present near the battlefront to help the wounded. Mary could speak some Turkish so she went along with a small group of medical people from Sivas to assist in a Red Crescent hospital. "Here for four months she acted as matron and head nurse. Her executive ability, unlimited nerve and a disposition to have her own way, because she believed it the best way, enabled her to do successfully a very difficult piece of work...When the cooks objected to giving milk to patients, she got the physicians to write 'milk' on every chart, so that she could give it as she deemed best."[192] She used her Yankee ingenuity to deal with the irregular conditions and shortages of supplies to ease the discomfort of patients. Her patients were grateful and wrote letters of appreciation. Later she explained her motives for aiding the Turkish army. "I did not go to help the Turks particularly, but as I told someone, I went to

Mary L. Graffam (left) and teachers, Sivas. Courtesy of the Partridge Family Collection.

work with the Turks, thinking that possibly I could get on the good side of some of the pashas, and it might help us later on, for I felt the time was coming when we would need such help."[193]

In spite of this effort, Mary was unable to stop the deportation and massacre of Armenian people, but she felt adequately informed to attempt to accompany the teachers and students from Sivas as they were deported. Once she was stopped in Malatia and sent back to Sivas, she turned her attention to the young girls who remained. She taught many of them nursing skills in order to give their lives value to the Turkish army. "Today a postal from Nishan Bekhian in Geneva says that Polly writes Nov. 4th that she hears more or less from this one and that one but none of our people write. They are supposed to be in Haran (Oorfa) or near there. She is very, very busy, cannot describe all her labors but is mostly engaged with sick soldiers.[194] Mary used her nursing skills and innate desire help to ease the suffering of any human beings she encountered.

Family Ties

Mary valued her extended family connections, as did her sister and Ernest. As children the girls often visited their mother's family in Maine. Mary continued those vacations as an adult, resulting in a nickname that stuck. After her graduation from college, while visiting her mother's sister, Mary Esther Goodell, and her husband Roderick Burt, Mary became known as "Polly."

Another Mary, a granddaughter of the Burt's, was visiting at the same time "so Uncle Roderick to distinguish them called them Molly and Polly; so Mary Graffam was 'Polly' to the end of her life."[195] The nickname surely came in handy once Winona married Ernest Partridge, whose sister was also named Mary Louise. She became "Aunt" Polly once the nephews arrived.

Rather than take a post overseas as a missionary, family ties kept Mary in America to look after and be near her father. When the invitation came from the Women's Board of Missions in 1901 to go out to Sivas, Turkey to be associated with Miss Brewer, Mary took the opportunity to fulfill her missionary intentions. Mary's college training and teaching experience gave her excellent qualifications to teach in Turkey. It meant leaving her father behind, but Mr. Graffam was then remarried, and Mary would be stationed with her sister and brother-in-law. "After Mrs. Partridge's departure for Turkey, her father decided that if one of his daughters was to be abroad, he was willing to have his two daughters together and so, in 1901, Miss Graffam responded to the invitation of Sivas Station."[196] Her father gave his blessing for her career change to educational missionary.

Aunt Polly was actively involved with the lives of her nephews. Prior to the family's departure from Sivas in 1915, the backs of Aunt Polly and 13 year-old Edward were captured in an open forest. Their heads are bent down. In Edward's handwriting on the

Edward and Aunt Polly examining trees, Sivas, 1915. Courtesy of the Partridge Family Collection.

back of the photo: "Polly and I examining a dendrological specimen (a twig from a tree)."[197] And, Edward's diary mentions Aunt Polly frequently. They went to market, worked on arithmetic problems, went visiting together, and she gave him money. Edward kept track of her comings and goings in his diary. He recorded that the family bought Aunt Polly a team of horses and ox cart "to go to Mosool [Mosul] with."[198] Aunt Polly was only allowed to go as far as Malatia.

Winona recalled in 1944 that "[Polly] lived with me 36 of her 51 years and used to say, 'I have all the advantages and none of the disadvantages of a family. I have my sister's children to enjoy and when I want rest from that I can just give them back to their mother or nurse and I have a brother-in-law to quarrel with so I do not need a husband.'"[199]

Friends and coworkers were family for Mary as well. When Mary was allowed to stay in Sivas, after the Partridges returned to America and the remaining missionaries were ordered to Constantinople, fellow missionary Mary C. Fowle was allowed to stay as well. Mary Fowle died before the close of 1915 so her companionship was brief. Miss Nina Rice, herself a daughter of missionaries to Turkey, became a lifelong friend of Mary, the Partridges, and the young Armenian girls, Nazeli, Baidzar, and Armen.

Like Winona and Ernest, Polly also made personal and emotional ties with the Armenian people. They worked closely with Dr. Hekimian from their early years in Sivas and their American friend Mrs. Sewny was married to an Armenian doctor. Mary coordinated the financing of Yeranouhi Kevorkian's education at the Girls' College in Constantinople, as she had been very helpful to the missionaries and it was not yet safe for her to live in Sivas. In her last letter in the family collection, Polly wrote of "my friend…his son knows English…I think Mr. Partridge knows him…" –although this man's identity is not known.[200]

Responsibility and Leadership

Mary's professional and humanitarian values and deep friendships kept her in Turkey after the war ended and travel became more reliable and safer. Mary explained to Winona why she couldn't leave Turkey yet–"… those few who know the language are like tools which cannot be dropped just now."[201] Mary would not leave her friends, her adopted family and their culture, just then. Nina Rice attended to Mary during and after her surgery for cancer in 1921. It had been difficult to authorize the transportation of surgeons to Sivas and Mary would not leave her work to go to Constantinople. Miss Rice wrote to Dr. Peet in Constantinople: "She had all along been unwilling to leave her work here under present conditions, and by this time she also felt unequal to the journey…We all feel the confidence in Dr. Hekimyan and the N.E.R. nurses, and Miss Graffam insisted that they perform the operation."[202] She continued by saying the operation itself was successful, but Mary's heart just gave out–she was exhausted. "Indeed she should have had her vacation years ago, but circumstances have never been such that she felt justified leaving."[203] Mary was conscientious and gave her self and soul to her friends.

Mary L. Graffam.
Courtesy of the Partridge Family Collection.

Mary's decision to go with the Sivas people on their deportation march in order to attempt to assure their safety was a bold move and demonstrated her commitment to human rights over her own security. She took it upon herself to travel with "the Protestants and our teachers and pupils" from Sivas when the deportation order was given in 1915.[204] Winona recalled, "Watching her go was one of the hardest things I had ever had to do. As I stood and saw her disappear, the memories in my mind's eye of our warm, safe, loving and happy childhood began to cascade into my mind's eye."[205] Edward wrote that the Partridges donated a wagon. Mary traveled nearly 100 miles protecting her adult friends and students from vicious attacks from villagers along the way, until she was noticed by police and sent back to Sivas. She remained throughout the war to aid and assist the victims and to visually record the events to share at later time. Communication out of interior Turkey was rare or non-existent and caution was necessary when writing to avoid causing problems for surviving Armenians or harm to herself. Her experiences on the road to Malatia were related in a letter to a friend in Constantinople and published in *The Missionary Herald*.[206] When Ernest reached Sivas in 1919, she recalled the events to him and he recorded and wrote about her experiences.

Ernest perfectly and completely described Mary's personality in 1917. "The qualities of character in Miss Graffam's life, which have made possible whatever of self-denial and service she has shown...are: a spirit of optimism based on faith in God and the certain triumph of right; a determination to win...; an elasticity of nature...a versatility... and a willingness to help which makes her unselfish and ready to serve others."[207] In contrast to the piousness of Ernest's sister Louise Partridge, Mary began her adult life and professional career as an educator and ended it as a humanitarian pragmatist. She was a person—a woman—who got things done particularly when basic human needs of food, shelter, health, employment and education were not adequately met.

Chapter 6

The Work Together: "Our People"

The teamwork exhibited by Ernest and Winona Partridge throughout their lives requires separate mention. Ernest and Winona worked together as an affianced couple, a married pair, as dedicated parents, as committed humanitarians and educators, and as active members of their personal, professional, and residential communities. These two people shared mutual respect for each other and for the goals they had in common as well those held individually. As a team they dedicated themselves to expressing the humanitarian gene that brought them together and caused them to spend their lives in service to other people.

Winona was a "single" mother for months and years at a time, yet she maintained her connection to her husband, partner, and the father of her children through letters and daily diary entries. The diaries served the role of the daily update that couples living together would share. Ernest was a "modern" father in that he attended his children's school and athletic events and he was an active participant in the home—varnishing floors, packing boxes, repairing autos and household equipment, occasionally preparing a meal, and frequently taking his children with him on his travels.

Together, Ernest and Winona attended many social events—at their church or at the homes of friends—as well as informational and educational lectures at Oberlin College and local missionary meetings. The way Ernest and Winona carried out their married and professional lives was similar to that of President and Mrs. King of Oberlin—blending marriage, family, and the sharing of spiritual and educational beliefs through social interaction and writing.

Rev. Ernest C. Partridge and Winona G. Partridge, 50th anniversary, 1948.
Courtesy of the Partridge Family Collection.

As a young married couple with a newborn, they eagerly embarked on their first assignment as missionaries with the American Board (ABCFM) traveling to the interior of Turkey in the fall of 1900. Within a month of arriving in Sivas, Winona was already writing Armenian words—writing "I have love to you" in a letter to her sister thereby displaying her ease with languages.[208]

The early years of their missionary work are described in Winona's letters written in the last few months of 1900, family photographs from Sivas before their furlough and during the 1907-08 furlough, and updates published in *The Missionary Herald*. In a small notebook, Winona wrote of accidentally leaving her diaries in a khan on the family's journey to Constantinople in 1915 and went on to describe her family's first few months back in the United States. She resumed her *Line-a-Day* diaries in 1916 and continued them through 1955 when Ernest passed on. (The years 1915-1922 are printed in Part II of this book.)

Unlike some of the American missionaries and ambassadors who spent time in Turkey, Ernest and Winona formed a particularly strong attachment to, even love for, the Armenian people of Sivas, and this affection remained throughout their lives. They kept in close contact with the Armenian girls they brought back to the United States with them in July of 1915, as well as many students and fellow teachers who had either lived in other countries, escaped to safety, or who had miraculously survived the genocide. Winona's compassion and concern are evident in this entry. "Now it is three months since our people left Sivas and I am afraid there is nothing left by this time. We wait for news all the time but we know that probably we shall get no good news for a long time. After months perhaps we shall begin to hear of one or another who managed to live through the long journey but not many, I fear."[209]

Winona again expressed her concern for the Armenian people and wondered if they would be honored centuries from now.

"October 11, 1915 Last night we attended a lecture by Prof. Shaff of Western Theological Seminary on John Huss, it being the 500th Anniversary of his martyrdom. The Armenians are being martyred by the thousand, and perhaps 500 yrs. later the world will honor them."[210]

At the close of the same year, in December, she again wrote of her emotions at what had happened in Turkey to the people she and Ernest loved.

"December 31, 1915 Such a year as this has been, war, typhus, fear, hanging, torture, imprisonment and deportation to the desert of our best friends, people whom we have known and loved for fifteen years, people whom we know and love more than most of our relatives, refined, educated, honorable, lovable friends. How can we bear the thought that they are enduring such suffering and we cannot help them…About five months of our furlough is past. I wonder if in seven months it will be evident what we shall do for the rest of our lives. The outlook is very discouraging. The war seems likely to continue indefinitely."[211]

As a record of the horrible fate of many of their friends and the survival of others, Winona and Ernest created the Red Book, an alphabetical list of all the people they knew and could recall from their fifteen years in Turkey. They recorded where these people were in 1915, and, if they knew or when they found out, what fate befell them.

From the left, the third seated woman is Winona (white blouse with black tie, no hat). Edward is seated slightly behind her to the left. Mary Graffam is the fifth seated woman (wearing black, no hat). George is seated on the man's lap to the left. Ernest is the fifth man from the right, sitting cross-legged and wearing a light-colored cap. Courtesy of the Partridge Family Collection.

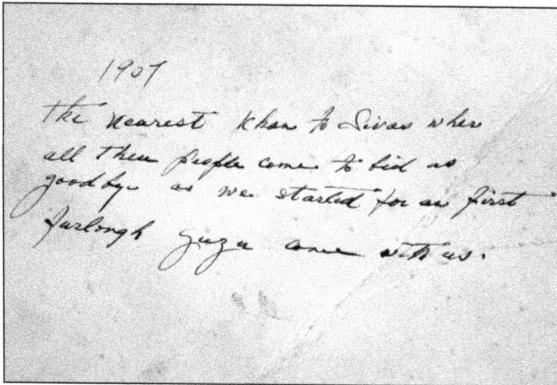

"The nearest khan to Sivas where all the people came to bid us goodbye as we started for our first furlough. Zuzu came with us." Winona G. Partridge wrote this on the back of the photograph, 1907, Sivas.
Courtesy of the Partridge Family Collection.

In 1922 after seven years in Oberlin, Winona and the three youngest children returned to Turkey to be with Ernest. She noted in her diary how the times had changed and commented on how they were treated with a big reception 22 years ago when they arrived in Sivas; but in Erivan no one met them. Even though they were working with orphans on the Turkish/Russian border, far to the east, Winona still remembered Sivas with affection and interest.

"November 13, 1924 Twenty four years since we arrived in Sivas and we received a letter from Dr. Clark telling of his visit to Sivas and of plans to rent the building for a while and then start missionary work."[212]

And two years later on their travels from Leninakan to Beirut, they sailed on the Black Sea to Constantinople. Winona again reminisced: "August 9 Mon. Arrived early in Samsoun…We left in the evening. It seemed very near to Sivas where we saw the wagon road that we used to travel."[213] Samsoun is a coastal town on the Black Sea located approximately 150 miles north of Sivas where on earlier trips they would have disembarked for the land journey to Sivas.

The Partridges left Sivas six days after the residents and the remaining teachers and students of the missionary schools were deported in July 1915. Upon landing in America in August, Ernest carried out 74 public speaking engagements before the year ended. Ernest and Winona decided to settle in Oberlin, "at least Mama did, with her five children. Papa became a combination traveling salesman and globe-trotter."[214] While Winona took on some public speaking engagements on the new home-front, Ernest undertook a grueling tour, traveling mostly by train across the United States, speaking to assorted groups about the plight of the Armenians and raising money for the American Committee for Relief in the Near East (ACRNE). During that time he also represented the Layman's Missionary Movement—a men's organization dedicated to educating and interesting people and churches in the concept of foreign missions.

As soon as it was possible to return to Turkey, Ernest headed a relief party of eight people traveling westward across the United States, the Pacific, China and Russia to reach the Armenians in eastern Turkey. Ernest focused more on "the work" as he called the building up of "industry" for the orphans and survivors of the genocide. He felt that it was critical that in order to ensure their future, the children had a skill resulting in a product to sell in addition to basic education. Ernest was ahead of many on this need for industry and was frequently put in charge of building renovations and repairs.

Ernest and Winona kept each other informed of their activities. Ernest wrote frequently during the nine months he was separated from Winona in 1922. (These letters are printed in Part II.). He numbered the 37 letters he had written to his wife by mid-May. In these letters to Winona who was still in Oberlin, he shares with her the political situations in Turkey, the possible places they could be stationed, and general American Board business. He wrote in detail of his February 7 meeting with Dr. MacLaughlin at

Gathering of Armenians to honor Winona and Ernest Partridge (seated).
Courtesy of the Partridge Family Collection.

Mrs. JohnStewart Kennedy's house where they discussed Turkey, the Allies, armistice, Sivas, and Kemal. He told her of his discussion with Dr. Clark, Dr. Barton, Mr. Riggs and himself about the future work: evangelistic, educational and medical. He went on to tell Winona that, "I am convinced of one thing and that is that if things politically settle down so there is safety of life and freedom of work, we are going to have some very vital and interesting problems to help settle."[215] Ernest wanted to be located where he could apply his missionary beliefs and skills.

Following through on his commitment to family—blood, marriage, or otherwise—Ernest visited numerous people in Northeast cities before setting sail for Europe. On his travels around the United States, Ernest made sure to call on the Graffams and Goodells as well as any Partridge relations he passed near. These visits were in addition to his many work-related appointments. Yet, he was often saddened that he had not been able to see everyone and wanted Winona to know that he had done his best. Ernest wrote to Winona of his stopovers in Venice and Milan where he visited museums, classic art pieces, churches. "I had forgotten, in my plans for this trip that the great Armenian Monastery is at Venice. I shall certainly want to go there."[216] Ernest shared with his wife his good fortune at being able to fulfill his personal interest in art, history and architecture.

On the topic of their professional lives, Ernest told Winona that he planned to take language classes until he got a permanent assignment and that the Armenians he had talked to were pessimistic about missionary opportunities in Asia Minor. More importantly he wanted them to be in the same place—not separated for a school year if she were to teach in another village. In setting up his missionary plans Ernest always kept Winona in mind. He told his associates "That you were a teacher and preferred that kind of work to housekeeping and that I should be very glad next summer to get you out here where you could keep a servant and do some school work."[217] Later in the same letter he wrote: "The difficulty is the same as you had about Berea, we do not want to be tied for a school year when the possibility may open up of getting together."[218]

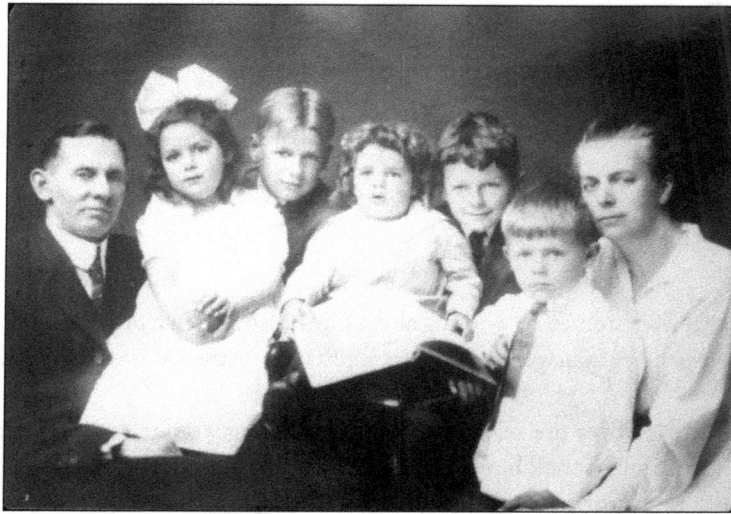

Family group: Rev. Ernest C. Partridge, Frances, Edward, Alfred, George,
William, Winona G. Partridge, ca 1916, Oberlin, Ohio.
Courtesy of the Partridge Family Collection.

Ernest valued their marriage and was respectful and understanding of the challenges Winona faced raising their brood of children. On February 12, 1922, he wrote in a personal tone: "I suppose you are having a 'quiet Sabbath.' Do [not] take your kids too seriously and make them do something for their selves and each other. I think you ought to make yourself get out more. Lots of love to all Ernest." In another demonstration of the importance of their marriage and family life he wrote: "I have accumulated about five dollars-worth of pictures suitable to hang about; two that I liked the best in each gallery which will help to decorate a house if we ever have one again that we want to fix up."[219]

Upon his arrival in Constantinople in 1922, and his subsequent assignment as Director of Education for the Near Ear Relief in Russian Armenia, his daily entries record the towns he visited and the various people he met with in pursuit of economic advances and basic education for the 16,000 orphans of the region. Once Winona arrived in Leninakan in late 1922, her diary entries portray the substance of the relief work they performed together.

"May 2 Wed. Mr. P. was busy with Com. business all day. We sat up until midnight & could not get the school problems settled.[220]

August 16 Thurs. I finished writing the teachers papers for the Personnel Department. Several disagreeable room questions came up."[221]

And three years later she was still filling a professional role in association with Ernest. "June 11 Thurs. Very busy all day trying to learn about Mr. P's work."[222] Winona performed Ernest's duties while he went to Constantinople on business and to meet their son George who was coming to Leninakan for a year. It was a lengthy journey to Constantinople and Ernest would be gone several weeks.

As a white woman in a Near East country, Winona had her share of obstacles in carrying out her partnership with Ernest.

September 5 Wed. A long, rather disagreeable talk with Baron Nishan about the vocational work .[223]

October 22 Mon. Very cold, water frozen in the yard. Baron Nishan came over to see Mr. P. He does not like to do business through me.[224]

Local men were not at all accustomed to working along side of women in a professional capacity. Six months later Winona demonstrated her management skills as well as her distress at the reality of life for the residents.

June 19 Thurs. I turned over the selection of the ten sewing women to be sent to Mr. Rankin's shops to the Mestkom and it took him three hours. It is like a death sentence to those not chosen, they are so poor & need work."[225]

Winona successfully delegated the duty to a male colleague!

Upon his return to the United States for the last time after 34 years of missionary service, Ernest accepted positions as part-time pastor at churches in Ohio, Arkansas, and Florida. While serving the Valparaiso Community Church in Valparaiso, Florida, Ernest took on a new agenda–the education, prevention, and relief of tuberculosis (TB)–the disease that ended the lives of Ernest's father Lewis, at least one of Lewis' wives, and Ernest's sister Cora. Ernest was a member of the Florida Public Health Association and was active with the Okaloosa County TB and Health Association.

Winona continued by his side as wife, mother and grandmother, keeper of their home, and undoubtedly as a supporter if not participant in his new passion for the eradication of TB. In 1953, the Partridges celebrated their fifty-fifth wedding anniversary. Ernest, just two years before his death, honored their union by writing a poem titled *Needles and Pins*. Winona continued to make entries in her diaries until 1955–the year her companion and her partner in life passed on. One condolence card from a college classmate tells Winona: "Words are so futile. But I'm sure you know how deeply I feel for you & your family. God gives us strength & courage to go on faithfully. He will comfort you as I too have been comforted."[226] And another tribute to Ernest written by college friend Reverend C. Rexford Raymond describes the work that Ernest, and Winona, accomplished together.

Ernest had a full life with larger success as a servant of Christ than most Christians have accomplished; Sivas, with his school for teachers; his service to the uprooted in Russia as they fled from Armenia; his further service in Smyrna; and his refusal to quit his service for Christ after his age made it necessary for him to return to America. Preaching and work for the Red Cross in Florida rounded out a remarkable career for Christ and the Church. You and all the family have every reason to rejoice in his abundant service.[227]

Winona and Ernest developed and maintained a strong friendship and partnership. They depended on each other in many ways. The first time Ernest journeyed out of the country leaving the family behind

NEEDLES AND PINS

When love was rife in student life in 1895,
A passion burning with labor and yearning
Took fire and came alive.

A black cravat and a derby hat hid an Ernest Latherio,
And a bosomed shirt with a flowing skirt
Tried to "Win" this dashing beau.

A billet deux in the chapel pew, or a touch at the dark church door,
was about the height of dalience light
Where cupid seemed to score.

But they made the goal by remote control and
And two were finally one.
And a life began, for wife and man like nothing under the sun.

From Beersheba to Dan, and back again, they taught both
chapter and verse.
They suffered and strove in thier mission of love
But never found time to curse.

They replenished the earth, with many a birth,
had children both here and abroad.
And in spite of the Turks, and their own little jerks,
They still believed in God.

Through a hectic life, of trouble and strife
they lived by the rule of love.
They made friends galore, on every shore
And gave credit to Him above.

Oh long its been,since Ernie and Win took flight in their mad career,
And its past the date when they celebrate
Their fifty-five married years.

But even the Lord, for all of his hoard,
of angels a million strong.
Couldn't stand the life of man and wife
Anywhere near that long.

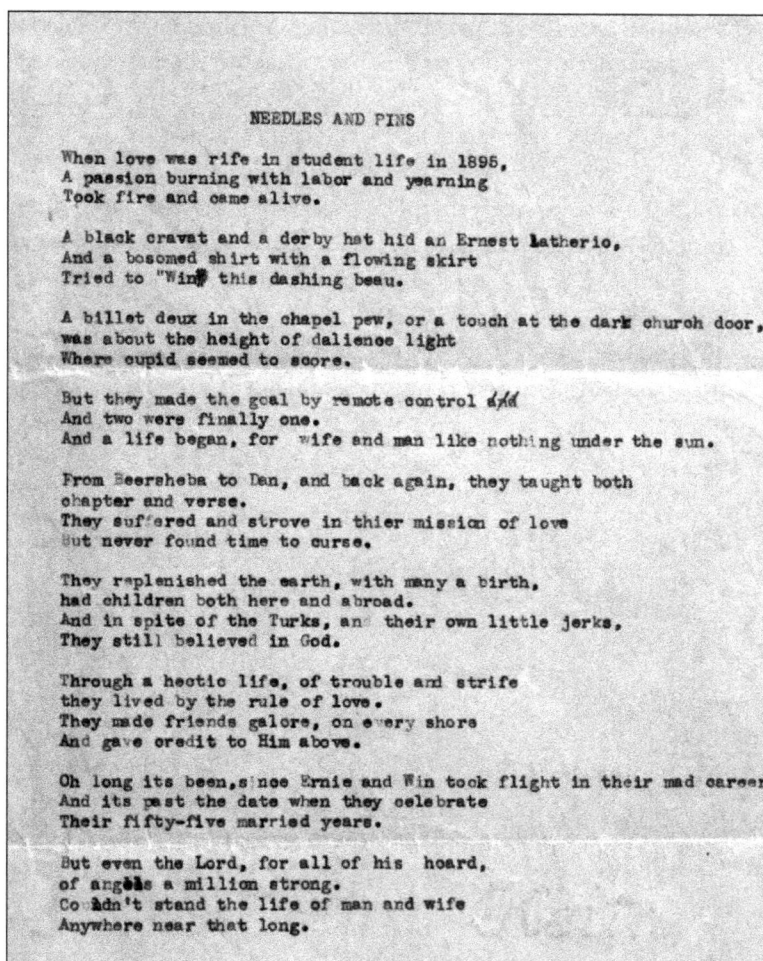

Needles and Pins was written by Rev. Ernest C. Partridge in honor of his and Winona's 55th anniversary. Courtesy of the Partridge Family Collection.

in Oberlin in 1917 Winona was very sad and melodramatic. She wrote on July 13, I am "lonesome, more lonesome, most lonesome" and again on July 14 she wrote: "ECP… wrote from Chicago…doesn't seem as though he was dead."[228] Theirs was not an overtly affectionate, loving relationship. Winona mentions in the diaries about preparing rooms for Ernest when he returned home, but love and respect and commitment to common goals and family connected them for over sixty years. "Mama" and "Papa" are the terms of endearment their children and grandchildren used. Winona recalled:

Papa died at Stow, after a short illness or more general decline…He became unconscious and I was in the yard for a breath of air when the nurse called me and then he was beyond recognizing me. His death was painless to him but what a blow to us. We had been married 57 years. He had been away in his work more or less without the family. Once he was two years in Aleppo while I stayed with the children…Roy Bowers, a classmate, and Lynn, our grandson, conducted the ceremony at graveside. They paid wonderful tributes to a man who had lived a good and useful life with no thought for his own glory but with a great desire to serve others, in his case the Armenians. He had a host of Armenian friends who remember him with affection. [229]

The unity of this partnership and the strength and clarity of Ernest and Winona's personal goals are illustrated in the following words written by Winona immediately after Mary left on the road to Malatia. "We knew then that our friends, teachers and loved ones were to be deported. Life as we knew it would change forever. Little did we know how much the blissful but difficult existence we had found in the interior of Turkey would turn upside down. It should not have been a shock as these orders to leave had occurred before in history for the Armenians even as recently as 1895. I called the life as we had known it blissful because we had chosen to follow our careers as teachers, missionaries, helpers and therefore considered it our calling."[230]

Chapter 7

Epilogue: The Humanitarian Legacy Continues

The descendants of the Partridges and Graffams have continued to express the values which comprise the humanitarian gene. The gene's theological component was not as prevalent in Ernest and Winona's children; none went into the ministry or service as missionaries. The children demonstrated religious beliefs in more diverse ways or even set them aside, however Ernest and Winona's first grandson followed the call to ministry. Education continued to be of primary importance in the family and all five children attended college as did many of the grandchildren. Marriages brought spouses with similar values into the family. The legacy of the humanitarian gene, including commitment to social concerns of food and shelter, gender and racial equality, tolerance and respect for differing religious beliefs, basic education, and self-reliance and hard work, has been evident in the succeeding generations.

The Offspring

Ernest and Winona's oldest son, Edward Graffam Partridge, was given a diary for Christmas in 1913 by an Armenian family friend in Sivas. For a twelve-year old boy, he wrote diligently in his diary for one and a half years (January 1914–July 1915). Edward's words provide a valuable view into the family's life in Sivas and an eyewitness account of the confusing events that took place prior to the deportation orders. Certainly, seeing his friends imprisoned or marched away was disturbing for the boy, but learning that most of the family friends went to their death at the orders of people he had met was a great shock for Edward.

Edward G. Partridge, ca 1922, Oberlin, Ohio.
Courtesy of the Partridge Family Collection.

65

After the family returned to Oberlin, Edward played sports, succeeded academically, and showed his patriotism and loyalty to the United States in high school. He was "made Corporal of his H.S. Company" in April of 1917.[231] Edward grew into a quiet, reserved man.

During his senior year at Oberlin (1924), Winona mentioned in her diary that Edward was coming out to Leninakan. "Edward is appointed to come out here but he had not decided between that and the University of Illinois."[232] His inclination to enter mission work was fleeting although his commitment to education was well established and long lasting. Edward chose the scholarship to University of Illinois where he received his doctorate in chemistry in 1927. He became an inventor and consultant specializing in rubber for the tire industry and did not return to Turkey or Russia.

As a parent, Edward carried on the Partridge/Graffam commitment to the importance on education with a family ritual. His daughters recalled that their father received three weeks of vacation every year. Ann and Ellen "got educated for two weeks and got one week at the lake!"[233] Although the words Edward wrote in his diary evoke a confident, happy boy, the events he recorded in Sivas prior to the deportation orders most certainly affected the young boy; Edward's response was to lock those memories away. Like most of the other grandchildren, Ann and Ellen were raised on lamb pilaf and madzoon (yogurt), but "our father never spoke about living in Turkey or the events that took place."[234] His daughters recalled a vacation during their high school years. "We took grandma with us on vacation to Erie. Our mother was hoping that grandma would talk to us girls about Sivas," but the conversation never took place.[235]

Although Edward followed a career in science rather than service in a missionary field or the ministry, his family was associated with the local community church. Yet, he was a compassionate man—opening

George L. Partridge, ca 1960, Keewaydin Camp, Salisbury, VT. Author.

his home to his parents in their later years and caring for his father until his death. The tragedy that Edward experienced as a young teen caused him to keep his feelings within and his humanitarian gestures close to home.

Edward shared with his father and his brother George the family trait of appreciating and displaying humor. Many of the descriptions in his high school photo album are plays on words. Younger brother George showed his sense of humor in the form of quietly delivered puns. George's grandchildren would continue the tradition with puns of their own.

Second son George Lewis Partridge did not receive degrees in religion either, but his spirituality and humanitarianism were evident in his lifetime activities. He was an active member of the Trinitarian Congregational Church of Northfield, Massachusetts and was often called upon to perform Sunday Services and various Chaplain duties at Keewaydin Camp in Vermont where he was a counselor for 42 summers. Education was also an ever-present part of George's life and being. George was a science teacher for over 50 years, retiring from The

George L. Partridge with Polygon staff, 1925, Leninakan.
Courtesy of the Partridge Family Collection.

Northfield School for Girls and he often took on extra duties as coach and class advisor.[236] After "retiring," he taught at a school for disadvantaged boys and substituted at the local public high school. At Keewaydin he became "Mr. Pat" where he worked with boys of all ages in the roles of counselor, chaplain, and head naturalist. Coincidentally, letters written by George's father's college friends referred to Ernest as "Pat"!

Ernest and Winona thought for a time that their older sons would take up the missionary calling. Winona wrote in 1924: "Two letters from George and one from Edward. George says he is about decided to take a pre-medic course and prepare to be a medical missionary."[237] In fact, George did return to Turkey after the genocide in a brief role as missionary. He joined his parents and younger siblings in Leninakan in 1925 for a year to run a recreational program for the orphans, but ended up in charge of an orphanage.[238]

While at Oberlin College, following in the tradition of his parents and Edward, George met his life partner—Ohio native Miriam Ingalls—and they married in 1929. "Mim" was the spiritual and professional partner to George for 54 years. Together they were house parents of boys at Suffield Academy, class parents of girls at The Northfield School and raised a son of their own. As camp mother, "Mrs. Pat" mended scores of clothes damaged by active young Keewaydin campers.

Clearly, compassion and spirituality had been part of Miriam's childhood. Her brother, Harold Ingalls, served as a Shansi Representative to China during his college years at Oberlin before turning to the ministry. Harold became chaplain at The Northfield School and had notified George of an opening in the chemistry department. George relates in his autobiography that the truck that took Harold's household from Northfield to New York returned to Northfield carrying his and Miriam's household belongings from Connecticut. During college, Harold had encouraged George to become involved with the YMCA, the organization that had employed Miriam and Harold's father as a young man.[239]

George carried on the family tradition of sending Round Robin letters. In one letter to the family written while attending summer school on Long Island, New York, he shared his continued connection with the young Armenian women who lived with the family. "Got a letter from Baidzar, our nurse. She is in a camp in Freeport, N.Y., not far away. We'll try to see her tomorrow. Also will try to see Nazeli."[240] George's grandchildren eagerly looked forward to visits with Pat and bedtime stories of Partridge family life in Sivas and Leninakan.

And The Next Generation

Rev. E. Lynn Partridge ca 1960.

George's son, Everett Lynn Partridge, grew up in small private schools of New England. Lynn, as he was known, was an active and athletic boy and used those qualities to work outdoors in a camp setting with teenage boys during his high school years and early twenties. At Keewaydin Camp his counselor duties included leading the older campers on two or three-week long canoe trips into the wilderness. Since his father taught at the Northfield Girls School, Lynn attended the associated boys school when he was old enough. At Mount Hermon School for Boys, the students were expected to perform work on the farm or in the dormitories and classrooms, and attend religious instruction.[241] Manual labor and religious study were goals in common with Oberlin College.

Upon his 1948 high school graduation from Mount Hermon, Lynn represented the third generation of Partridges to attend Oberlin College. The theological gene was activated in Lynn and he embarked on the family calling of minister. Oberlin Graduate School of Theology (the Seminary) had been preparing ministers for a century, although Lynn's class was one of the final classes to receive a theological degree from this institution. Following Oberlin and family tradition, Lynn met and married Judith Griswold, another Ohio native whose parents and sister attended Oberlin. Judy participated in Shansi Program activities as did her mother-in-law's brother, Harold Ingalls, 25 years before. Coincidentally, Judy's father Courtland Griswold had been a boarding student at Mount Hermon (1919-1923) prior to attending Oberlin College and was a minister's son as well.

Lynn's first pastorate was in the hamlet of Pittsfield, Ohio in a church founded by Reverend John Jay Shipherd of Oberlin. Early Oberlin Student Volunteers frequently visited the Pittsfield community because of its nearness to the college. Mrs. May Channon wrote to Winona in 1955, "I hear through our Seminary student-pastor, Reverend John Bruce, of your grandson preaching at Pittsfield."[242] Tragically, all the buildings of this community including the church were destroyed by a tornado in 1956 just months after Lynn and his family moved on to Michigan. Lynn, as minister and first grandchild, shared comforting words at his grandfather's burial in Westwood Cemetery, Oberlin.

In spite of more lucrative career opportunities, Lynn felt a strong pull to serve a spiritual community. In 1958, the Fountain Street Church of Grand Rapids, Michigan, reorganized, leaving Lynn without a position. George wrote to his mother of his disappointment at not seeing his grandkids that summer since Lynn and Judy's "plans are indefinite, for Lynn is being dropped at Fountain Street Church. It is an economy move in which Lynn and the Director of Religious Education are being replaced by one man. At the moment, as far as we know, he has no definite church prospects. Strangely, he has had several excellent offers, with high salaries, in advertising and insurance, but he wants to stay in church work, if he can get a living salary at it."[243] Lynn's talent as a carpenter supported his wife, four children, and numerous pets until he was chosen to become the first minister of the newly formed First Unitarian Society of Rockland County, New York.[244] While leading worship services and carrying out church work in a nearby YMCA, Lynn physically constructed the new church building as well as built up the congregation.

Rev. E. Lynn Partridge, Miriam I. Partridge holding Douglas, George L. Partridge, Jeffrey, winter 1954, Pittsfield, Ohio. Author.

Years later, Lynn served four churches on Long Island, New York as a circuit minister much like his grandfather Ernest, great-grandfather Lewis, and great-great-grandfather John Croker. He then directed his attention to education by teaching science to teenagers in a challenging high school environment. At his memorial service, Reverend Julia Older said this: "Lynn was, I know, from his sermons, a humanist, someone who hoped that life could be changed for the better and that we could improve our caring for the world…Commitments would be to a grander purpose and small mindedness would be left behind."[245]

Lynn's first cousin, Barbara Locke Johnson, is the daughter of Ernest and Winona's only daughter Frances. Barbara was born in Smyrna (Izmir, Turkey) and lived with her grandparents off and on during her childhood. Barbara feels that she is very much like her grandmother in personality. She certainly shares with both her grandparents an interest in art and compassion for humanity. Barbara graduated from the University of California Berkeley with a major in art history but ultimately trained to be a nurse in order to provide quality hospice care.[246] Winona's Red Book holds special meaning for Barbara as it represents her grandmother's love and respect for the Armenian people of Sivas.

While Lynn was raising a family and ministering to his congregation, a younger cousin, John, who was born the middle child of Ernest and Winona's youngest son Alfred, began to explore his spiritual beliefs. In spite of being raised in a home by parents who did not practice religion, John recalls a *Bible* present in the house and that his father would quote the *Bible* on occasion. John debated his personal view of religion for many years even considering becoming a clergyman and was eventually baptized at age 30. Ultimately, John chose to use his "musical talents for the good of the church" believing that his talent "is the best thing I have to offer in service to God."[247]

The musical gene was evident in John's family. John recalls that his father, Alfred, loved to sing. John began piano lessons at age five and as a teen began writing music and working as a church musician which gave him the opportunity to write church music. To date, John has written several large choral works and dozens of songs and anthems, but does not limit his musical writing to religious works. To this day, John and his siblings, their spouses and offspring gather annually with extended family members to sing for enjoyment and camaraderie.

John shares many traits and values with his missionary grandparents. "I can certainly see that my religious bent is along the same lines as my grandparent's in the sense that I am more interested in the social justice aspect of religion than in things like the afterlife. Feeding the poor, helping the helpless, encouraging reconciliation and healing among people are the things that are central to my understanding of my faith."[248]

The Legacy

This exploration of the causes, concerns and accomplishments of multiple generations of Partridges and Graffams, through the lens of the lives of Ernest, Winona and Mary, demonstrates the presence of a humanitarian gene present for greater than a century and a half in both families. Successive generations have lived and worked to encourage human rights, interpersonal understanding and acceptance, to increase access to education, and to share the positive aspects of religious beliefs at home and worldwide. These values did not disappear with generations—they carry on in the descendants of these remarkable people through a genetic legacy that continually activates these traits.

Part II

Personal Writings by Family Members

Statement of Editorial Method

Throughout these primary documents the editors comments or notations have been placed in []. A bracket containing a question mark [?] represents an unreadable word. A question mark after a word represents a best guess at a somewhat readable word (ex. word[?]).

Names of cities, countries, places are left as written in letters and diaries. Current names and spellings may be included within []. Most names are spelled as written even if misspelled, unless it was clear that the same person was being referred too.

Language has not been adjusted to current social standards (ex. "darkies," "black imp").

Dates/headings are as written with varying uses and combinations of periods, commas, and dashes (;– :– ,–).

The flow of text in the letters is as written, although minor spelling errors and letter reversals have been corrected, and occasional punctuation inserted to aid in reading.

In the diaries, some punctuation and capitalization have been added to improve flow of text. Ernest did not use punctuation after titles (Mr, Dr, etc.) and they have been left as such. He often ran his appointments together, therefore, periods or semicolons and capitalization were added.

Ernest recorded the miles he traveled and numbered his lectures within the body of the entry, particularly in 1916 and 1917. Sometimes this information was written at later times in different ink. I have placed the numbered lectures in parentheses () and the number of miles in parentheses (m) or (mi) using his abbreviations. Note: Miles was abbreviated as "m" or "mi" although in current abbreviation standards "m" refers to meter.

Also toward the end of 1917, Ernest began numbering letters to Winona and these numbers have also been placed in ( ). However, these notations are placed at the end of the daily entry and often include names or initials of other people written to on that same day.

M.E. typically refers to Methodist Episcopal. S.S. refers to Sunday School.

Letters of Mary L. Graffam 1891 and 1921

[M. L. Graffam]
Kipton, Ohio
June 31, 189? [1891]

Dear folks.

I suppose you see I have left Oberlin. Miss Sheffield wanted me to come here and spend Sunday and so I did. I have been having a fine time. I haven't felt very well. The strain of exams last week about used me up but I guess I will survive. I got a dreadful cold at the quarterly the other night and am still so hoarse that I can hardly speak aloud so I think I shall not go to Fremont until Saturday for I couldn't converse any if I did. I have a letter of introduction to some folks in Fremont who I think will help me about getting a boarding place and I am going to try get Dr. Brand to give me a letter to the Pastor of the Cong. church there etc. I am going to canvass on recommendation as much as I can and not go to every house for the place is too big for me to work the whole of it in two months and I might just as well take the cream. I am quite anxious to see how I shall come out. Everyone says I am cut out for a book agent and I really expect to enjoy it. There was a teacher from Elyria here yesterday to see the folks who gave me the letter & she is going to visit Fremont soon and she says she will try to have me get acquainted with some of the young people there. She has canvassed some and she says it is very pleasant work.

Well it seems impossible that I can have gone through the last weeks and think of it as a mere matter of course now. I studied last week early and late and conquered. I got every question on the exam but possibly made a mistake on part of one question while everyone else that I know got about half of it. They all think that I did the best in the class. I hope so anyway. I deserve it for I crammed. Josie did better than I did in Greek and she is delighted. I didn't look at my card but she did and she said I had mostly fives but there were some 2's & 2.5's. Those are the evil effects of your dress. There were a few days there that I didn't study it anyway. This is her only victory and she would better make the most of it for we won't be together next term for we will take different studies. I am going to take Chemistry, Hebrew and French next term I think. Oh Miss, I just wish you were going to be here next term but it is impossible, I suppose. Now Miss, about next year, I wish I were in your shoes and you in mine for I know [how] it seems to go away from home the first time and how much I dreaded that Baldwinville school and a year ago I couldn't have been persuaded to get off in a strange place to sell books but now I don't dread it a bit. These things are never so bad as they seem to be and after you go off and get up a little cheek you are all right.

Yes, I think if I were you I would try to get a school. Very likely you won't get one but I would apply I think. Talk to Mr. Baldwin about it and ask his advice. Then I would look around for something else to do. Who works in the bookstore now a days? If you feel well enough you might go with Josie and see what you could do at canvassing. I advise you so strongly to try to do something because I want you to come to college as soon as you can get $200 even if only for one year. I am here and realize what it is and I would do anything to be here for I am thoroughly in love with Oberlin even if I am going to stretch the rules most awfully this afternoon. There is the strictest rule possible about riding with boys through commencement and I am under rules until Tuesday night but Mr. Pennock & Mr. Skidmore are coming out here after noon today (10 miles or more) and I am going to ride with them as far as the edge of town and then walk in. "How's that?"

The people here are fine well to do farmers with plenty of money, horses, cows, and all. Cream plenty. Mrs. Sheffield is a middle aged woman, an old teacher but, strange to say, a model housekeeper. Mr. Sheffield, when he is well, a good farmer, good looking, generous, full of fire, and a general favorite, but for the last seven weeks he has been laid up with Rheumatism in one hip and leg so that he can't walk a step nor go to bed nor hardly move but he sets in a chair or on the lounge with his foot up right and day but he gets only 2 hours of sleep or so in all. His foot pains him all the time but he is just as patient and pleasant all the time and only groans when he is asleep. I wonder how Parf would stand it. I think Mr. is a Christian if ever any one cares. They say when he is well he is just such a teaser as Parf is.

Last night Mary and I went to ride about 5 miles I guess. They have five teams, four horses all young and spirited & two colts not broken. I suppose there is a letter in Oberlin with some money in it. I shall need about ten dollars but if you don't send it all I suppose Mrs. W. can wait a week or two for the other five I owe her. I feel awfully mean to take so much money but I hope to earn my own after a while and when I get through college I hope I can do some thing for you people. I should like immensely if I could go home next Christmas and see you all. I am quite curious to the new head of the house. I think I could behave for a week or two so that I should not disgrace myself. I think I will stop now and rest your weary brains.

Love M. L. Graffam

Fabrica, Sivas
May 14, 1921

My dear Sister:–

Doctor and two of our personnel and I are spending this Saturday afternoon in Mr. Hawkes's room and while I am waiting for some tea I will practice on his Corona and write a letter to you.

Some incoming personnel brought a lot of letters from you beginning in October. Mr. Hawkes also had a letter from Mr. Partridge. I certainly wish there were some way for you to get a rest and you will be all right here as things are now, but on the whole I think we shall have to admit that the Board is right in its decision about families.

I am glad you liked the waists. I have some others now that are just as good for me and fit me better. The Unit gave me a navy blue silk dress as a Christmas present which is just made up. On my fiftieth birthday we had an afternoon reception and they presented me with a blue silk handkerchief containing fifty gold liras as a present. They also had fifty candles burning in a pyramid. I blew them out as soon as the law would allow for candles are a scarce article and kersosene is very expensive.

I was sorry you did not finally go to Trebizond, for it seemed a good plan to me, but you there know much better than I do what is best to do. There seems to be nothing ahead here and we live from day to day. The relief work is the only bright spot in life and the need was never greater even at the beginning of it. The way people continue to give is splendid.

We have a new man for the accounts which will make my work much lighter. I have been doing them myself since Miss Scribner went a way. Perhaps you know that we have a new and complete system of accounting now and that our accounts are audited by the official auditor up to Nov.1. I wish someone were here to go over the Mission accounts with me. I have the balance sheets all made out as far as the statements from Constant go but the details need to be thoroughly analyzed.

My one and greatest desire in life is to see you and also the family. The only reason that I don't go is that I feel that I can't. Dr. Dodd came here with the purpose of persuading me to go and then changed his mind. Miss Allen was on her way home only to turn back to the interior. She passed through here this week on her way to Angora. We who know the language are like tools which cannot be dropped just now.

The place here is beautiful and I certainly did enjoy sleeping on the sleeping porch last night. Last Summer I did not stay here a single night but I came out one night this Spring only to be hastily called back to the city. Today I am going back this afternoon anyway. Someone has to be in that office all the time. My staying there so constantly is the reason I outgrow all my clothes. I weigh one hundred ninety pounds if not more. When you write to the Clarks, give them my love, also to Mrs. Sewny. I wonder if she is coming back. She could be very useful here, more so than Talas, it seems to me, but I do not insist upon anything as I must say the different ways of looking at things have passed my comprehension of late. That also is not strange when the world has gone crazy. I have not seen my friend since he came back from London, but I hope to perhaps this summer. He passed through here when he was on his way there and we had a very fine afternoon tea with him and his companions. His son knows English and was very agreeable to the younger set. I think Mr. Partridge knows him. He has always been a true friend to us here.

I must send my love and take this out of the typewriter.

Affectionately, your sister,
Mary L. Graffam

[Handwritten along the side]
June 2. P.S. This letter was delayed and I will only add that all is still well even better than two weeks ago. Love to all, Polly

Letters of Winona E. Graffam 1894-1898

Oberlin, O.
Oct. 14, '94

My dear Polly:–

I have just returned from the Y.W.C.A. and instead of going to church I will write to you and Papa. I went to church this morning and Mr. Bosworth preached. I like him very much and I believe his sermons are more within the range of my intellect or perhaps my interest than Dr. Brand's. The choir sang "Hosanna in the highest, hosanna, hosanna, etc." Mr. Savage led it, the first time he ever led a choir in his life. Mr. Sweet's father died today and he was very suddenly called away and Mr. Spear is not in the choir this time so it devolved upon Mr. Savage to lead. Mr. Spear's voice has given out at least partly. I do not know whether he cannot sing at all or whether he is afraid to. I suppose he is quite a loss to them but they have Mr. Savage & Mr. Penniman in his place.

Now I want to have a little interview with you about a winter coat. Of course I do not expect to get it now but you know it is a tendency of mine to always want things settled early. You have of course seen any number of those heavy capes which they call "golf capes" and know that they are all the go now, do you think that it would be a good scheme for me to have one of those instead of a coat? It would serve two uses you see, as a coat & a cape to wear over any party dress & a nice one of those would not be as expensive as a coat. Sara and I looked at some for her when we were in Boston and my impression is that we could get a real nice one for twelve dollars. Now you cannot get a real nice coat for that amount, you know. I do not know but that you could get a pattern and make one if you wanted to and have it pressed at the tailors. Mrs. Johnston has a beauty, a very expensive one too, I suppose. Hers is quite long and has a shorter outside cape over the shoulders instead of a hood. I like that kind pretty well but it takes more cloth, I suppose. If you do not think you'd better try to make one, I can get one in Cleveland in the Christmas vacation. It would be nice for me to have a fur cape but that is out of the question, of course.

I wore my silk waist and gray shirt to church today. My blue skirt is so short that it does not cover my shoes. And my foot is so sore that I have to wear my old shoes. I am waiting for that agent to come before I get any new shoes and then I do not know as I shall be able to wear them. But I shall have to get some that are large enough and soft enough to be comfortable. I started to say that my gray skirt looks fine and it will be a real pretty suit when I get the waist to it. Please make it as soon as you can so that you can fix the blue one for my black skirt is fast giving out and I shall soon not have anything to wear to school. Never mind about the light waist. I can get along without that. And another thing, sometime when you haven't anything else to do, I wish you would make me some of those crocheted slippers. I haven't anything comfortable to wear in my room and I go around in my stockings all the time which does not look well and does not keep my stockings clean. But I am not reckoning on you doing anything for yourself at all. I do not know how much money Mr. Partridge intends to pay us but a little will be quite acceptable now. At any rate he will save me quite a good deal in taking me to places, I guess, for he has started in well. He has tickets to all the games for nothing and I guess he has a chance to earn some for most of the entertainments. He has invited me to go hear Prof. Clark of Chicago next Friday night. I am so anxious to hear him again. In this connection it may be appropriate to mention that Kate Ely has at last succeeded in teasing her mother to let her have two little kittens named respectively "Pittypat and Tiffytoe." Kate seems quite happy with her new pets. I am up there every week, sometimes two or three times. It seems so good to have a place to go where I know they will be always glad to take me & Mrs. Ely is very lovely to me. I do hope she will take me in vacation. Miss Mirch is visiting here as is also Mr. Vorhees, Miss Bushnell, a niece of Mrs. Johnston's & her little boy and one of the boys' mother. When the tables are all full, they bring in a little table just big enough for two and put two folks there. I am going to send this letter to Thorndike although you may not be there, but instead you are coming within a day or two I suppose they will send it to you. I expect you will want your union suits before long and I will send them and I will send them when I send my blue dress if you can wait until then. If not I will send them now. I do not know what I shall do about flannels yet. I suppose I ought to wear some although I do not want to. Well, I suppose I must stop writing to you and write to Papa, but it is lots easier to write to you. Sophie and I are quite chummy this term. She is lots nicer than she used to be. I think Mr. Fritts has called on her only once and you should see him grin at me. I think he is getting stuck on me. Do you think it is possible that he is?

Give my love to Edward and Belle and Marion and that blessed baby. I do think she is so sweet. I should think they would get along without a girl while you are there, you'd better suggest it.

With lots of love, Winona.

Oberlin, Ohio
Oct. 18, '94

My dear Polly:—

Your good long letter came this afternoon just before Thursday lecture. I am awfully busy tonight and afraid I shall not have time to write a very long letter. We have had to write out our parts in Greek for the last two days and it takes such a long time. In my two morning courses we are taking selections from Plato and we are reading now the Apology and Crit. by assigned parts. They have all had the Apology and part of them the Crit. but I have had neither. Prof. Martin said that if I couldn't get it all to get as much as I could, but of course I would acknowledge that I couldn't get it so I just dig it out. He gave Sophie and me a dialogue together in the Crito so she helped me some this P.M. The three hour course in Greek is that Aristophanes that you took. We are reading the clouds now and it is a fine course I think. Your interlinear translations are quite helpful. I suppose you read in class out of a text edition as we do so it wasn't wicked.

Did I tell you that Sophie and I are the only ones in the Latin class? We have great times. I enjoy Sophie very much this year.

I went up to Mrs. Ely's this evening until seven o'clock. (What a bright sentence!) She sent her love to you, also Mrs. Hall and Mrs. E. told me to tell you that I was looking very nicely this term. I suppose she thinks I am growing fat and I do not think I have lost any flesh. I do thrive so well in milk and cream. We had some of the loveliest waffles tonight and I was fortunate enough to be sitting at Mrs. Curtis' table and she just wants us to eat "a genteel sufficiency" or other words, etc. But really I am in a horrid place this week between a Freshman and a Prof., both of whom have some one very interesting on the other side. But the Freshman, the worst one, is going away to spend Sunday and then I shall get along better. I had two Reviews last week because mine went to Talcott and Mr. Callender brought me another one so I will send it with this week's and then if the other one doesn't come you will miss nothing.

When our electric light was a novelty we did study by it but our eyes began to hurt so now when we get ready to study we turn it out & light the lamp or rather in the other order. Oil is furnished and our lamps are filled for nothing. So you see it is just as cheap to have both. Our room is very pleasant especially when we are in it, for we are anything but a sober pair this term. Before I forget it I want you to find out if Edwin cannot stop to see me on his way West. I should like to see him so much and it is so lovely to have company here. The folks here at Baldwin are always having company, mothers or brothers or friends or something and I want somebody. I haven't seen Edwin since I came to college and I do wish he would stop here. I would try to make him have a good time. Now be sure to invite him very cordially.

We went to an Artist's Recital by the Detroit Philharmonic Club last night and did not like it at all. I will send you the announcement about the first recitals. We are going to hear Clark tomorrow night. As I remember it Mrs. Johnston's cape is not lined but I will notice it again. Hers is of very heavy dark gray cloth with a double cape. I think I would like the double cape, but I am going in to Johnsen's to try some on and I will write about it later. I took my blue hat down today to be trimmed & all I had put on extra was a silver buckle a real pretty one, which cost .50. I think that is all I want. It does seem good not to have any dishes to do and it gives me lots of time. I most always walk around until one o'clock outdoors and then go to studying. I think that teething necklace must be working like a charm for in the letter I got Tuesday you said that Charlotte had two teeth, in this one three, only two days apart. I must stop now and write to Papa and then go to studying.

With love to all,
Winona.

I wish I had time to write all I could think of to say but time is precious & tempus fugits. W.E.G.

Oberlin, Ohio.
Nov. 4, 1894.

My dear Polly:--

Your letter came Saturday and it was just as I expected it would be. I did hope that you could find some good reason why you should not go but I couldn't myself and I see that you couldn't. As far as the money is concerned I think that will be all right whether you have any money left from your salary or not. I shall be able to pay it in time and then I think you will have some left anyway for it probably does not cost very much to live there. I think Mary Partridge has sent home about one hundred dollars this year. If you did that it would not take very long for us both to pay it up. I am so anxious to know definitely whether you are going or not. If you do go when do you suppose you will go? Not before commencement will you? You mustn't for you must be here then. You asked me who I had talked with on the subject. With no one of importance, only the girls and they said, "How nice?" I thought to myself, "I guess you would not think it very nice if she was your sister." I tried to see Mrs. Johnston about it, jut to tell her a little about it, but I haven't had a chance. By the way, she asked me the other day if you had a position and said there was a school here five miles out in the country, which wanted a teacher and they would give $35 a month. But she said she supposed it wouldn't pay you to come way out here, because it would probably be for only four or five months, a winter school, you know. Miss Mary Pinner is boarding at Mr. Daniels on West College, the next house to Prof. Churchills'. I do not know the number, but if just directed to W. College, she would get it, of course. I think she would be lovely to go with, but I did not know that she was a Missionary Volunteer. My roommate has written six letters today and now she is reading the Bible.

Oh, you should have been here yesterday. We had more fun than a little. Oberlin and Case played football in Cleveland yesterday and O. beat 20–6. Well, every boy except one from Baldwin went and he went to Munsen's to supper, so we had no one but girls he[re] until after study hours in the evening. We pulled taffy, danced the figurine Reel and did everything we could think of. The boys sent five telegrams telling us how the game came out, and when they came we went out in front of the Cottage and gave the College yell two or three times. But the worst thing of all was that when the boys got home about 7:30 they came up here and got their supper and although we begged and entreated Mrs. J. wouldn't even let us go down and look at them. We had to stay about on the 2nd or 3rd floor. After the boys went Mrs. J. came to the 3rd floor and Dr. Hanna to the second and told us a little about it but they couldn't tell it very well. Mr. Partridge got me some candy in Cleveland & sent up a note with it telling me a little about it but I am just crazy to get him long enough to hear all the particulars. Of course the boys could not stay to talk about it and at table this morning we had only one boy and he was a quiet one so we have not heard a very satisfactory account, at least I haven't. About all I know is that Boothman and Billy Miller distinguished themselves. They said that Boothman would run way out around and leave the others so far behind that they would hardly seem to move. There will be an account of it in the Review I suppose so you can see it. Mr. P. is chief cook & bottle washer in regard to the games for Mr. Jamieson is president and he is Sec. and Mr. J. hasn't got hustle or voice enough to keep things stirring. I tell you Mr. P. is about the biggest toad in the puddle this year. I think he is better liked by both girls and boys than anyone in the class. He is a jewel I tell you only you do not know how to appreciate him. You asked me how well off I was for money. I think I am in debt to every storekeeper in town, at least a few cents.

Mr. Partridge has let me have ten dollars but I intend to pay him back for he is dreadfully hard up.

Miss Fish says to tell you that you have a little home missionary work to do before you go abroad and that is to come out here and help us fix up our room, make us some long muslin curtains, some cushions for our window seats, etc. Well, I must stop & write to Papa. With love to all, Winona.

Monday morn.- I want to say a little about my coat. I have an economical scheme on hand. You know long coats with capes are not the style any more but lots of folks have them & they say they are very cheap. Now I think it would be a good scheme for me to get a dark blue one & wear it this year all the time and next year keep it for a storm coat. You know Grace Gilletto had a real pretty one and I think it would be the most useful thing I could get and don't you think I'd better send for my money in two or three weeks and go down to Cleveland and see what I can do?

Love, Winona.

❧

Oberlin, Ohio.
Nov. 8, 1894.

My dear Polly:—

Miss Fish is waiting very expectantly for Mr. McClure and seeing she does not like to have me go away until he comes I will write a letter to you. Your letter came this afternoon and I was a little surprised for I supposed that you had told him that you wanted or was willing to go. I told Mrs. Johnston about the circumstances the other day and she said she thought it was a splendid opportunity and then she repeated the following sentence again and again, "I think she would make a capital missionary, a capital one." etc. ad infinitum. Then the next day she saw me again and said the same thing over and told me to tell you she said so. What do Edward and Belle think about it? I wish that this opportunity could be put off or kept open for two or three years until I get started at something. I shall hate dreadfully to have you go but of course as you say five years will not be very long. You would get back in time to just about attend my wedding. It will settle my plans about library work of course but I presume it would be foolish for me to spend any more money when I do not expect to work more than four or five years. Of course I may work all my life but it does not look that way now.

I want to know whether you have been looking onward so much that you have entirely overlooked the things of the present or are you still waiting to go to Springfield to get my dress fixed. I am very sure that I can get some silk here if that is what you want & you will tell me how much to get. I do not like to put on my gray dress because I catch it so often & it will very soon look shabby & my black dress already looks that way. I am not scolding but I wonder why you haven't mentioned it. I learned today that at dinner on Thanksgiving day the girls dress in full evening dress. Where shall I come in? I should have to wear my white silk waist and get a rose to wear with it, I guess.

I am afraid you will think that I shall have a large sum to send to Uncle Rufus for however economical I may be. Lets see I will reckon up the big bills.

Coat $12 probably
Tuition 12
Shoes & slippers 5
Books 5
Mr. P. <u>10</u>
          44

You see that is $44 and then there are other little things that I have not reckoned, that umbrella cover, etc. And then if you do not teach next term that is if you go as a Missionary I shall have to have money for all of next term. Please write to me in your next letter just what to do about a coat. I am perfectly at sea. I am thinking of going to Cleveland to get it next Sat. or rather one week from Saturday to see what I can do. I can get the money for two or three weeks from Mr. Partridge and I really do need a coat for we have had some real cold weather and are likely to have some more. Of course a long coat will not be at all stylish to wear to church etc. but if I get a nice one which I probably can for twelve dollars, it will do anyway and next year I can have something new. Oh, dear, I cannot bear to think that you will not be here next year. If it were not for having such a good opportunity to go now I should say that it would be lots better for you to wait until you are a little older and until we get our debts paid and I get settled somewhere. Papa sent two papers to me, the first one of Oct. & the first one of Nov. I guess I will send you the last one. We have pretended to get our Greek lesson for tomorrow and I have neglected my other lessons to write to you. But then French is easy and I am home tomorrow and in Latin I can get along all right. Last time I read a page and a half at sight and Prof. Magorin finally asked me how far the lesson went and when I told him that it stopped a page and a half back, he said he thought I was reading the advanced. I told him I did not think that was much of a compliment but he thought it was. You know Sophie and I are the only ones in the class and we say just what we please. Mrs. Ely and Mrs. Hall have agreed to let me come there in vacation. I am afraid I shall not want to leave when I get back there. Of course things are a great deal more convenient here than there but Mrs. Ely isn't here and no one as good as she is. By the time you get this letter I suppose Edward and Belle will be home. I should think you would be lonesome there. When is Edwin going? Now be sure to air your views freely on the subject of a coat.

[no closing]

❦

Oberlin, Ohio.
Nov. 13, 1894.

My dear Polly:–
    Your letter came this morning and I was very glad to hear your views on the subject of cloaks, but still I am afraid a cape would not be warm enough. I have asked several people who have capes and none of them think they are warm enough especially when it is windy or when you have to hold an umbrella. I just asked one of the girls here in the house who has one of those long lovely fur capes what she thought about it and she said that when she got her cape she expected to wear it all the time but afterwards her mother

got her a coat because she did not think she would be warm enough. Miss Fish's sister just sent her a cape, a very pretty one, which she will wear all winter. Hers cost $12. I think they are rather pretty but almost everyone in town has had one this fall and they are very common. I wish I could have a coat and a cape to wear to concerts but that would cost too much of course. I do not want a light opera cape because you need a very swell dress to wear under it. By the way what shall I do with my party dress? You know it has no collar and nothing around the bottom of the waist. Would one of those ribbon collars be all right? And I suppose those plaits will need to be pressed, won't they? Please be as spry with my blue dress as possible because my black dress has a hole through each elbow and I have to wear this black silk waist and it is not very warm. I saw a dress the other day that was made about like my old gray one and it had some satin puffs on the sleeves evidently to make them look modern and I wondered if I couldn't have some black silk or satin puffs put on that gray dress. You see my black dress is about gone up and I thought if I could have that gray one fixed to wear in unpleasant weather it would keep my blue one looking fresh longer. I should think the waist could be cut off just to meet the skirt. If you would like the job of fixing it I will send it to you.

I got permission to go to Cleveland next Monday but I know that I shall not know what to get after I get there. I wish I could find someone to go with me. Miss Fish could go if I would pay her fare but I cannot afford that. My heart turns toward a long coat although they are so dreadfully out of style. I do not know what I shall do but what I do I must do quickly for I shall freeze to death. This is purely a business letter as you see and I must stop. Sophie has come to read Latin.

With love, Winona.

Oberlin, Nov. 18. [1894]

My dear Polly:–

On an accompanying piece of paper I send all the information that I think you will need about that piece of music. I hope I got the right one. Louis Church brought it home to me from church and told me that I might get what information I wanted from it. I copied all I think you can possibly use except the place in Boston where Q. Ditsan's establishment is and it didn't tell that but I guess you can manage without it. I have been practicing the Alto solo this afternoon much to the disgust of my roommate who began to howl as you used to when I tried to read to you. What was it I used to want to read that made you yell so? I have forgotten. I quoted or rather copied that measure or two of the music so that you could be sure whether that was the one you wanted or not.

No, I do not think your mittens are here. I have not seen them since I came back and I hunted for them yesterday and could not find them. But I do not see where they can be. I will hunt some more. If I do not find them I will send you one pair of mine. They need a little mending but you are welcome to them if you will mend them. I will also send you a dollar to buy stamps with. Miss Fish and I are going to Cleveland tomorrow morning at half past six. I wish you were here to go too. I was up to Mrs. Ely's yesterday and she invited me to come up there to Thanksgiving dinner. Wasn't that lovely of her? And she and Mrs. Holbrook have been talking about me and Mrs. Holbrook wants me to come down to live with her next term if she can possibly arrange for me to have a room. She wants me for company and to help the girls a little in their lessons. They are both in the Academy. It would not cost me anything only just what little I could help her. They think it would be good for the girls to have some one like me to tone them down a little by my bright and shining example. Hmm. Just think of earning your board by your example. I suppose you would advise me to go if I get a chance. The only objection to it is that I suppose I should have to room alone and you know how I dislike that. I wish you could do something here and come live with me. It would certainly be quite a saving in the money line. You know they live where Prof. Morrison did, a lovely house with all the modern improvements. I really hope I can go. It would not break my heart at all to leave Baldwin. Folks are too clicky here altogether.

Uh, I must tell you about the box that came up to me last night. Someone of the girls brought up a box all nicely done up which was apparently a box of flowers, which it proved to be, but such flowers! There were two roses which were quite a good deal faded so that the leaves began to drop when I first put them on this noon and then there were two Chrisanthemums [sic] which looked as though they had been through the war. There was no card with them. The only thing I can think of is that Mr. Partridge left word before he went to Ann Arbor with Fred White to send up some roses and that he forgot them until they were all gone except those he sent up. Fred White works in Burgess's now and they keep cut flowers there. I am anxious for Mr. P to get home so that I can find out about it.

I have thought several times when I haven't been writing to you that I never said anything about those night-dresses that you made. They bind just a little around the sleeves but then they do all right and I like to have them long so much because we run around the halls a good deal at night and in the morning after water. I shall be so glad to get my blue dress for I do hate to have to put on that gray dress any time except Sunday for I catch it so much. Don't you think I am a self-sacrificing room-mate? Miss Fish hasn't got her Winter hat fixed yet and today it was too winterish to wear a straw one so I let her take my best hat and I wore my old sailor. She would have worn my sailor but it was too small for her. I must close now.

With love, Winona.

Cannot get a dollar of change, nothing less than a thousand. Will send it later.

❧

290 Elm St. [Oberlin]
May 14, 1895.

My dear Polly:–
    Your letter came tonight and I must say that it seems a little more like a letter than those you have been writing lately. But Polly I never dreamed of such a thing as you getting my lawn waist and you making it. I thought I could buy it here in town and have it made. Of course it is very much better, but you must stop doing so much. Do not think of making any shirt waist for me. I do not know as you had any idea of it but I cannot tell what crazy thing you will do next. With my two shirt waist and my lawn waist I shall have enough to last until school is out anyway. I have gone back to winter clothes now, flannels and coat. I

think I shall need a new felt hat or a hood. I haven't decided which yet. I think you are the most energetic girl I ever saw. I did not know that you did your own washing. I paid my wash-bill for this term or so far this term and it was $1.50. You see my bill is not so bad as when I had to have my own bedding washed. That doesn't count in my handkerchiefs which Miss Schwarz does, but that doesn't amount to much. For my part I think you are rather foolish to make any shirt waists because I am sure you can buy them that are good enough for a dollar and a half and I think your time to rest is worth more than that. Did you purposely not tell me what kind of a dress you got for me? I am glad that it is going to have a ribbon sash. I hope it is going to tie in the back. Now it has been so long since I have bought anything in the way of footwear that I really do not know what size I want. I could not wear a 5 ½ AA though it would have to be wider than that and I do remember now that those slippers that I bought in Cleveland were 6 ½. Just think of it! They are not a bit too long but are too wide of course since I got them to wear in my room. You might send a pair of 6A and 6 ½ AA and then let me bring the pair that I do not keep when I come. I do not yet like the idea of having white but if you say I must I suppose I must. I can keep them for my wedding. There is such a difference in shoes that you cannot tell much by the size. The shoes which I wear are 5 and my slippers are 6 ½ so you see they do not agree. If possible do not get those real high heels. They are not only uncomfortable but awfully hideous I think. Do you think I shall need a fan? Did you wish you had one last year or didn't you want one. If you could find a common fan there that looked delicate for a quarter I think I should like it. They have none but bright colors here.

Grace is bothering me to death with her Algebra. I have to stop every minute and correct some silly little mistake that anybody who had ever studied algebra would not make. She cannot multiply at all and as for subtracting that is out of the question. She just asked me if she might depend upon me to help her get her Caesar in the morning. I told her that I didn't know because I wanted to do something of my own. But I must stop tonight.

Miss Fish's sister sent her an organdy but she is going to have it made over cotton. Bertha is not going to have a wash dress. I am so glad I haven't got to decide how to have it made. Oh what a time I should have! I will try to get that lining made and sent to N. Y. by Sat. but perhaps I shall not be able to. The pictures have not come yet. I cannot get all my recommendations. I got one from Mrs. Johnston today. As I remember it m[ine] is almost like yours, word for word except the experience. Well, I must stop and go to bed. If I have to get up in the morning to translate Caesar I shall need more sleep.

With lots of love, Winona.

Wed. morn. – I do not quite understand about the N. Y. arrangement. Where are we going to get money to pay for food and gas and fuel, etc.? It costs so much to run an establishment you know. Perhaps Papa would contribute a little but we couldn't ask him to do very much of course. If one of us or both of us could get some tutoring to do that month to keep us going wouldn't it be fine? I should think Mrs. Y. F. might get you some to do anyway. I have only one class today and I guess it is lucky for I have a headache and I had one yesterday too. I got some of that preparation of iron that Dr. Noble gave me before and I am going to try that. I hope our pictures will come today. I am anxious to see them. Mr. Prentiss told someone that I, just think of it, I, was the best girl in '95 and he had heard lots of folks say so. Just think what an enviable reputation, ahead of Susan Lord. But I thought Mr. Prentiss liked Miss Fish and Bertha and some others better than he did me. Well, I must do something beside write letters to you. I spent every bit of last evening reading the paper and writing to you and helping Grace do Algebra. Oh, I could teach Latin and Algebra now without the least difficulty. Well, I must stop. The breakfast bell has rung.

Love, Winona.
Bess is fine.

❀

806 Pine St. Macon [GA].
March 27, 1896.

My dear Ernest:–

Your good long letter just came with the one from Mary enclosed. I do not like it at all to have her speak so impersonally of your wife just as though you were going to hunt up someone to go with you. Perhaps she thought that probably I would not go and that you would get someone anyway. You wouldn't would you, dear? Oh dear, if you should die I think I would get Polly to go off to China or somewhere and I would work so hard that I should not have time to think, but then Mary says it is dreadful to go single, so I hope I shall not have to. My dear, I did not send you that clipping because I thought you were particularly lacking in any of those qualities for I do not think that you are even in the one that you think that you are deficient in because you have not had a fair trial, since I asked you to settle those things which no one except me can settle. I think when the time comes that it will be your place to settle things for me or help me settle them that you will be right there and equal to the occasion. But I do not think that you are quite fair to me when you keep hinting that I always do just the opposite of what you say. Just now I can think of four great questions that I have had to decide since I know you. 1. to promise to marry you. 2. to agree to go to China if you were bound to go. 3. to go to Patchogue. 4. to come down here, and I should like to know how far I have departed from your wishes or advice in any one of those, and I will also add that I have not regretted following your advice in any case, so there now I do not think that you realize how much weight your opinion has with me.

I am glad Mr. Raymond has the opportunity to earn some money and I wish you could have an opportunity too but I do not regret that you haven't just the qualities to make you a good one to travel for a college. It requires the same qualities that it does for a book agent and we know that you haven't those, and I am glad of it. I suppose Mr. Raymond is with Miss Landon now then. I wonder if he will be able to see her next Summer again. I suppose he will. I hope they will get married if they want to before he gets through the Sem. but that is one thing that I do not intend to do. I do not think it is best at all and I hope you won't urge me to do it, because I am afraid I shouldn't yield and I do not think that I ought to. Much as I should like to spend another year in Oberlin I do not want to be a theologue's wife there. I am sure it would not be best for you for I am sure you would not be able to study so well. You say that you are sure that I would be "reasonable." I suppose of course that you do not use the word in the sense that you did that day going into Boston because that would be the height of unreasonableness surely, but perhaps that would be a good way to keep from going to China for of course we couldn't go under those circumstances. I hope that you will not feel it necessary to stay out next year and then we shall run no risk of being rash and getting married before you get through school. We ought to be strong minded enough to do the best thing anyway but if one of us should happen to take the notion I am afraid the other one would yield.

You may give my regards to Mr. Cressy and tell him that I am glad that someone appreciates that Madonna for I am sure you do not. I am anxiously waiting for the time to come when I can educate you on those subjects.

We had a glorious time this morning but I have a headache to pay for it. Six of us, Mr. and Mrs. B., Miss Chesley, Miss Woodruff, Miss B. and I went to ride for four hours way out in the country with a fair. It was so novel and interesting. I thought of you so much of the time and wished that you were along. I hope we can take another drive to Mr. Van Howe's before you go away. We have a little social for the teachers tonight and I must get ready. I intended to write you a nice long extra letter but I have tried to do so many things and I presume you will get this one and my last one together. I will enclose a letter from Grace which tells about her wedding. Mine is not going to be like it, though.

With ever so much love to my dear faithful devoted little boy. These adjectives were very carefully selected.

Love, Winona.

❁

806 Pine St. Macon.
March 30, '96.

My dear Ernest:—

Your missionary letter came today but I do not feel constrained to answer it tonight. I have spent so much time visiting and drinking lemonade with the teachers that I haven't time to discuss such a weighty subject and then I do not know what to say anyway. I don't want to go a bit more than I did but there is really nothing to decide because where you go I shall go, but I shall not promise to go without protest. I am not so much of the clinging vine kind that I just submit myself to you and let you do what you please with me and I know that you do not want me to do so either. However I intend to go where you do if it is to the middle of Africa. Are Daisy Doane and Mr. Bigelow going abroad as missionaries? She is the last person that I should think of as being a missionary. I think it would be a good scheme for me to study medicine and Polly is willing to pay all the debt only it cannot be paid fast enough. If she had to support me and pay the debt too it would take her forever. Besides Uncle R. has Aunt Mary to support and he has lost so much money that he has had to sell his own horse. He wrote to us that when we had $5 to spare to send it to Aunt M. And that would be a great help to him. So you see the poor man needs it. The only way we can ever get my study in is to be married so that you can support me. I had a letter from Polly today and she is talking about leaving Westfield and has been after Mr. Kellogg to get a place for us to be together. If she should do that I suppose that I would be in the North next year and perhaps we could pay our debts faster, but I should rather hate to leave this place after all.

My dear, to go back, there is no question at all about leaving my father and my mother and cleaving to my husband, it is simply a question as to whether I shall cleave to him in this country or China and I prefer to cleave to him in this country. I love you with all my heart and should be miserable without you wherever I might be, so you see you are destined to be in my charming society wherever you are. Really, dear, I do not think that you are attached to your folks and friends as much as ordinary people are.

Tuesday morning. Perhaps that last sentence that I wrote last night does not sound very complimentary but I did not mean it that way at all. You know yourself that you can go away from your friends and still be happy, even away from me. I hope you could not always stay away from me and be happy and I do not think you could. I am all dressed up in a shirtwaist this morning prepared for hot weather and I guess there is no doubt but that we shall get it. I expect we are just going to roast down here. I must stop now dear, and go to school.

With ever so much love, Winona.

After school. Your letter came but I cannot answer it but I love you just the same.

❧

806 Pine St. Macon.
Oct. 4, 1896.

My dear precious boy:–
We are in Macon at last and I guess Cora is very glad indeed to get here. She got through the journey but she has been in bed all day today and feels dreadfully. I do not know what to do about her. She certainly cannot go to Florida alone and I do not believe it would be possible for her to get along without someone whose business it was to take care of her. I realize now more than ever how very sick she is and I am afraid that it was not wise to bring her down here. The doctor, the best one we know of, was here yesterday and he said that she ought not to be in a city where there was so much dust and smoke. He said that very soon she would be a very decided care for someone. It certainly would not be right for her to board and think of taking care of herself. Why, my dear, she cannot comb her hair herself. Mr. Burrage and all the rest are lovely. We shall keep her here until you or your father either comes for her or tells us what to do. I do not know what I can do about taking care of her. I am nearly dead now with nothing else to do and tomorrow school commences. Of course, they will make my school work as light as possible for me, but that is my business & I must do it. She feels as though she could not travel any more at present. Mr. Burrage said that he would excuse me from school long enough to take her down there to Longwood and get her settled but, dearie, I am sure those folks there would not take her for a boarder if they knew in what condition she was. I do not feel that I can decide what to do and Mr. Burrage does not think that I ought to but if she continues to grow worse for the next day or two before I hear from you further I think the best thing I can do is to take her to the hospital which is the next door to us. I know that you will think that I might know what to do myself once in a while but it is quite a responsibility outside the family. Miss Scobie thought

she perhaps would not live a week. I think that she probably will but I am afraid not very long. I presume she has not said more than a half dozen sentences today. She just lies there perfectly exhausted. Oh dear, I wish we could be married and settled somewhere and take care of her as long as she lives. I haven't time to write about myself or the school, only that I am still alive but awfully tired. I intend to see the doctor tomorrow. He gave her some medicine and told me to slip out and come over to see him in a day or two. He thinks there is no hope for her, because he told Mr. Burrage as much. Now I think that if you can suggest anything that you think should be done you should write to your father immediately about it. I am dreadfully homesick and discouraged tonight and I do wish I could see my dear little boy, but I can't. You couldn't teach carpentering to the boys, could you? They want an industrial teacher here. I will write better letters after this. I do not think that Cora ought to spare any of her money to send Louis [Lewis C. Jr.] north as her father wants her to. She will need it all I am sure. If you know of anybody that you can borrow money of, you'd better do and you or your father come down here and take charge of Cora. You would not be the one I suppose, although I would like to have you come. But, sweetheart, I must stop. I love you with all my heart. Please do take good care of yourself for you may have inherited the tendency to consumption. Don't wet your feet and do be careful. I must stop.

With lots of love to my dear little boy, Winona.

❀

806 Pine St. Macon.
Nov. 29, 1896.

My dear little boy:–

Your letter came Friday and I got none from Polly yesterday so I got no mail at all, but I am getting along nevertheless. You speak of the poor unfortunates who could not go away from Andover at Thanksgiving time. What do you think of us who cannot go away until May and in the meantime have no society at all except what we can find among ourselves. Just think what a privilege it is for you to go to Prof. Ryder's. You must have had a fine time. I wish I could have been with you. You'd better be thankful as I presume you were that I wasn't there because you would have had to take dinner at our house [with father George Graffam and stepmother Frances] and you would not have enjoyed that very well and I should not blame you either.

Dearie, I do have little outside work to do compared with what I did last year, that is I do not have to work so many Algebra problems, nor study history so much but there is a great deal of reading that I should like to do in connection with my Literature, but I always have some sewing or mending on hand which takes all my spare time. I came home from Sunday School this morning and did not stay to church and am using the time to write to you. I intend to read some Missionary Literature today but my afternoon is broken up because I have to read to the scholars here in the house this afternoon. You think that I am not at all interested in missions and I presume you have reason to think so but I am interested, dearie, and I told my S.S. class this morning about the lepers and the missionaries who gave their lives for them. I never shall think you are a "bore", sweetheart, but I do think you are a crank on the subject of missions. That is a compliment I think, though for it is said and I believe it is true that a man has to be a crank in order to succeed. But, Dear, let me warn you not to talk about it to the theologues and other people too much, because they will get tired of it and it may have just the opposite effect to what you intend. I wish some of them could go with you and we could establish a new mission. If your sister and mine and three or four more could go with us we should be able to start a mission all by ourselves. But I speak to the housekeeper and let the rest do the preaching. I do not think you intended it that way but it might sound a little conceited to anyone except me for you to say that the reason that you were going to stay in the Sem. next year was that they needed to be waked up in the subject of missions. It is all right to say that to me but it would be likely to sound a little self-righteous to those who were not in sympathy with you. You may think that I imply that you do not know what you ought to say but a person cannot always tell himself how anything will sound. I should enjoy attending a Missionary Convention, but in March of '97, I expect to be still teaching the young idea how to shoot and could probably not get away unless I should be teaching with Polly and she could teach my classes. But that is a long way ahead. We might have a fortune left to us and be married before that time. You speak of getting someone interested enough to support you, what is going to be done with me? I am afraid no one would ever be interested enough in me to support me.

I bought a book yesterday for five cents, written by Charles Kingsley, but I shall not tell you the name of it, because you would laugh at me. It was not about missions. By the way, I should like to suggest that you give me a calendar for Christmas and you can make that correspond to your pocket book. And will you please look up the subject of fountain pens and decide which is the best and tell me the price. I think I shall get Polly one for Christmas and I presume you can get one better than I can.

I want to tell you something that one of my last year's scholars said about me. We had the tenth grade over here Friday night and the mother of one of these came too, and she is the aunt of this other girl that I had last year. She said that she had wanted Annie, her daughter, to be in my class because she had heard so much about me from Minnie, her niece. She said that Minnie said that I was the best teacher that she ever had, that she didn't like me, she loved me. Now wasn't that encouraging? I tell you it did me lots of good, because she has had lots of Northern teachers and is about the first scholar I have had here. I guess she is the best. If that sounds too conceited, forgive me, for I am not conceited about my teaching. I do not think that I am a good [teacher?] and especially not for these folks, because I haven't the patience to drill them enough on one thing.

Later – I have just returned from Christian Endeavor where Miss Chesley allowed me to go after considerable discussion. I thought I was all well, but she thinks that if I do not improve I am likely to have quick consumption or something of the kind but I think that she is more scared than she needs to be. It seems that she and two other teachers consulted together about my case today and decided that I must be looked after. I feel pretty well, but there is something wrong, I know. I wish I could take a good rest until I get entirely well, but that won't do for me.

Well, my Dear, here it is after eight o'clock and I haven't read my missionary book today. But I have one right here and shall read it as soon as I finish this. Remember, dear, that I am not so very bad and I do love you even if I do not enjoy Miss. books as much as I might.

Love, Winona.

806 Pine St. Macon.
Dec. 1, 1896.

My dear Ernest:–

This is the kind of a night when you like to hover around your own fireside with those that you love most, for it is cold and rainy, a very disagreeable night. I hope not many more Decembers will pass before we shall have a fireside of our own if it is nothing more than a little rusty wood stove. Let me see, there will be probably be two more Decembers before that happy time, but never mind, we should be happy enough then to make up for all the waiting. Some of these days when I feel too tired to get up and go to work I wish that it was nearer and then again I get interested in these little black imps ad don't mind so much. These two days have been rather drags than anything else, for it has been so cold and rainy that ever so many of the scholars have been absent. And then those that are there want to sit around the stove and bake, which makes lots of confusion and disorder.

I had a letter from Josie yesterday in which she invited me to spend my Christmas vacation with her and she said that if I could get a round trip ticket for fifteen dollars she would gladly buy half of it. I should like to go ever so much but I cannot afford it unless Polly and Papa give me money instead of buying me any Christmas presents. I do not know what I shall do but I should like to go ever so much. I want someone to decide for me as usual. "The Rivals" came today and I am much obliged. I do not know as we shall be able to do anything more than read it. We are reading "The Mystery of [?]" by A. Conan Doyle, and it is mysterious I tell you.

Thanks for the quotation from the Greek. It does my heart good to read some Greek once more, but I am sorry that that word is fem. but that doesn't make any particular difference. I guess perhaps Mrs. Obenauer does know what she is talking about but I am very glad that we have changed seats at the table so that I don't have to hear her clack all the time. She is awfully tiresome to me. When you get to see Miss Norton, as I suppose you will soon, please give her and her sister my love. I think they are ever so nice and I hope that I shall see them again sometime.

I hope you may get a chance to preach there in Wolfeborough. Wouldn't that be fine. If you do not get anything else, are you obliged to give up your Boston work?

Oh, dearie, what standard novels have you? I am in deep distress about what to have my Literature class read. I want them to read something that is interesting and at the same time helpful toward giving them a taste for good reading. We have read some from Irving, Longfellow, Whittier, and we are on Hawthorne now. Have you anything written by Holmes? or Lowell? or Bryant? How I wish I had a good library containing books from all the good authors, but I fear that my library will have to be composed mostly of nine-cent or five-cent books. But then if they have all the reading in them, that is sufficient. I enjoy my Lit. class very much and feel as though I were learning something if they are not. I am sorry that I have to put you off with a short letter tonight but I have several things I want to do and I must get to bed early. For I am not very well lately and must take care of myself. I love you just the same as though I wrote fifty pages. I am ever so glad that you went to see Polly so often. I think I told you that I had a letter from Sara but perhaps I did not. I wrote a letter to Aunt Fannie yesterday. I wonder if they are buried in snow up there. I should like to hear how Mrs. Easton is. I hope to visit Woodford again sometime. But I must not write any more to you, sweetheart. With ever so much love to my own dear little boy.

Love, Winona.

806 Pine St. Macon.
Dec. 3, 1896.

My dear Ernest:–

I received no letter from you today chiefly because we did not get the afternoon mail, as I presume it would come on that as usual. I wonder if you folks are not all frozen up up there. It has been quite winterish here. Snow which fell yesterday did not all melt today, that is there is some on the shady side of the houses, etc. I have been cold all day today. I was telling Miss Chesley tonight that I guess I do not have blood enough to go below my knees for my feet are like icicles all the time. I wish I did have more blood to circulate. But then I feel ever so much better these cold days. The school has been almost demoralized though. Yesterday there were only a third of the scholars there.

I have just been to S. S. teachers' meeting at which I was quite late, owing partly to its commencing earlier than I expected and partly to Miss Chesley carrying off the key so that I could not get in to get my things. I went down to the depot this P. M. and found that I can get reduced rates to Nashville, but I do not know whether I shall go or not. I am afraid that I ought not to afford it when I am so hard up. There doesn't seem to be very much to write about tonight. All my energies lately have been directed toward teaching grammar but I am afraid that I am not making much of a success of it now. We have a miserable book anyway and the scholars do not "take fast" to language anyway. They make such ridiculous mistakes. I cannot help laughing but I do sometimes feel like knocking their heads together. If I didn't like them I do not know what I should do. But I have just fallen in love with some of them and that makes it interesting. It is nothing serious I assure you, but what should we do if we couldn't like folks in this world. The boy who brings our kindling up is just as nice as he can be. I just wish he could be educated and brought up well. But he acts now as though he had been well brought up.

You made a good suggestion about teaching the S. S. lesson, and I guess I needed it. I am not a good S. S. teacher yet but I guess I shall improve. I enjoy it ever so much. I have the S. S. Times now. So I am a little better off than I was. We are to have a S. S. concert during the holidays so I presume we shall practice most of the time now. If you go to Woodford you will miss hearing the Christmas music there in Boston, but then John Cushman will furnish you with any amount and then you might get up a concert in Woodford. I should like to go north at Christmas time but I guess I won't this year. I am ever so sorry about Sara's face. She had quite a narrow escape I should think. I intend to write to her just as soon as I get time. Although I do not seem to accomplish much I do keep busy. Tomorrow is Friday and I am glad, but the weeks do skip past so fast. Just think this makes nine weeks, more than a quarter of the whole time, and it seems as though we had just come down. The time doesn't drag a bit and I am quite happy, and should be very happy if you were only here. You couldn't teach carpenter work, could you? We need a carpenter very much. Oh well if we wait just a little longer we shall be happy. I had a letter from Miss Dole, the preceptress here last year, and she became acquainted with Mr. and Mrs. Dawson this summer in Illinois. Do you know where they live in Oberlin? Well, dearie, I must stop and retire.

With ever so much to my dear little boy, Winona.

Fri. morning:– Another cold morning, dear. The scholars will be just frozen up. They do not have proper clothing and so they just shiver. Miss Chesley thinks it is just foolishness but she has so much blood and vitality that she doesn't mind the cold. I know how to sympathize with them for I am cold myself. I should like to go farther south now, but then this won't last very long. There is the first bell for breakfast. Dearie, I love you with all my heart even if it is cold.

❁

806 Pine St. Macon.
Dec. 5, 1896.

My dear little twenty-six year old:–

I wish you many happy returns of this day and I hope that before it returns many times I may be there to help make them happy. I mailed this afternoon a very slight token of my regard for you, but I assure you that a great deal of love went into every stitch. The white one is a bureau scarf made plain purposely so that it be easy to wash. The red ribbon thing is for photographs. Take four photographs and put the ribbons over the tops and bottoms. Then stand them up as you would a screen. It is a very simple thing but I have one which holds three photographs on my bureau and like it very much. I wish I could have sent you something very nice but you will have to take the will for the deed, dear.

There is something else that I should like to present to you or rather re-present. It may not be as valuable in money as those little things I sent, but it is more valuable to me and I hope will please you more. I am delighted to make you a birthday present of myself and all I am and hope to be. I do not care to take back what I said about going to China, thank you. I am not sorry that I did and should do it again under the same circumstances. Polly says a great many things that she does not mean and I should not be surprised if she went with us some day. I do not yet look forward with pleasure to going to China except as it means that I shall be with you all the time then, but then I am willing to go in order to be with you. I do not think that I have the real missionary spirit for I am afraid that my motive for going is a selfish one, but you seem to think I am improving so perhaps I shall make quite a decent missionary sometime.

You do not own "The Daughter of the Revolution" do you? You must have a "feast of reason and flow of soul" at your Literary Seminar. What can you do with Browning?

I was just reading the next to the last letter I had from you, in which you say that I am always trying to help everyone around me. Where did you get your information. I do not know of anyone whom I have helped I am sure. I am afraid that I am willing to help people if it happens to suit my [self at?] the time so to do, but I am selfish even in the help I give.

I do not know whether I shall be home next Thanksgiving or not even if I am in Wolfeborough but I do know that I shall either go to Andover or you will come to Wolfeborough. I am not sure but that the latter would be pleasanter and it certainly would be cheaper because there are two of us. But I will not count on it because most likely I shall not be in Wolfeborough anyway.

I was very glad to get your letter this afternoon containing the poetry, pen, and postal card from your folks. I am writing with the pen now and I do think that it is remarkably good. I enjoy the pieces of poetry that you send me very much, principally perhaps because they sound as though you would appreciate a home when you have one and appreciate me too, because I shall be there, you know. I have faith that you will like home better than any other place, although you do not seem to have been so inseparably attached to your own home. I do not worry about that at all however. I am sure that we shall both be so happy that we shall want to stay there.

I hope it was a false alarm about Mrs. Easton. I am thankful every time I think of it that Sara got home. How lonely and hard it would have been for her down here.

Sunday P. M. – I have gotten into my wrapper and have settled myself to my letter-writing. Miss Woodruff and I went down to the Episcopal Church this morning, now that is a lie and I do not know why I wrote that unless I just read Mr. Palmer's name in the paper & Miss Gage and I were talking about the Episcopal Church. Well, Miss W. and I went to hear Mr. White and we had a good sermon on the Golden Rule. I wonder how many people in the world live up to that.

Dr. Barton is a very prominent man in Boston, isn't he? I read his name in the paper very often. I just read it in connection with that statue that they are protesting against in The Library there. What a shame it would be to have anything there that is at all questionable. I want very much to spend some time in that library next summer. I am already commencing to wonder where you will be next Summer. I want to stop in Oberlin when I go back, but I don't want to do that unless I shall be able to see you during the summer. If you could only get in there at Wolfeborough you could probably stay there during the summer and then I could surely see you. But then no such good luck as that would ever come to us.

I wish, dear, that you would keep your eyes open for cheap editions of Lowell's and Holmes's works. I presume that you can get one of those household editions quite reasonable anywhere. I have to teach both of those and I should like to get them cheap so that I shouldn't mind lending them. I should like to have money enough to buy all the books I want to teach Literature, but then I suppose it would be a nuisance to carry them around. It would be nice if someone would present the school with some books, but people send down here books that they do not want themselves and of course they are of no use to us. They will send the second volume of a book or something of that kind.

If you have the last Congregationalist for Dec. 3rd or the week before, will you please cut out that article about Israel Putnam in the conversation corner and send it to me? I was glad to hear such good reports from Louis [Lewis C. Jr.]. I do think that he is more of a man than he was. I do wish he were strong enough to do something. He would be so much better off if he were busy, don't you think so? Milton doesn't seem to be amounting to very much. He is janitor of the public school building but I should think he might take some studies in college. Perhaps he is not afflicted with a great desire to study anymore than Louis is. But I liked his appearance very much and he was good to Annie. I am glad that Louis has him to go with but it seemed to me that he lacked ambition.

Oh, my dear little boy, do you realize that you are growing old and that pretty soon you will be an old man of thirty. How old I shall feel when I get to be thirty! I wanted to write you an extra letter for your birthday but I think it will not be worthwhile to spend the stamp and stationery, so I will send this a little earlier than usual. I love you lots, dear, and if I were there I should probably ask you if you love me. I know you do but I like to have you say so once in a while. You do better in letters than you do when I am there. Please remember me to James when you write. No, you needn't either because I sent my regards to him through Aunt Fannie the other day and I am afraid he will think that I am too fond of him. I must stop, sweetheart, and write to Polly.

With ever so much love to the best boy in the world, even if he does think he isn't.

Love, Winona.

❀

806 Pine St. Macon.
Dec. 8, 1896.

My dear Ernest:–

I came near disgracing myself today when I received your letter and read that there was a probability of your going to Wolfeborough wouldn't that be fine? I suppose you would stay there through the summer and then I could come up there and stay with Polly and have a fine time. Is it possible that any such good luck as that could come to us? Then if you kept it next year and I should teach there, how blissful that would be! But I am afraid that it is too good to be true and that you will not go after all.

I am glad that you are having such good musical opportunities. I remember that Dr. Torrey used to play on a flute when he was a theologue. What are you going to do to amuse the company? I should rather hear you talk five minutes than to hear all the musical talent there is in Andover or Boston either for that matter.

You have been doing a good deal of reading, dear. I wish I had done as much. We teachers have all joined together for a few nights to read "As You Like It." Have you ever read it? I haven't got head nor tail out of it so far. My Literature class is reading "House of Seven Gables."

Mrs. Obenauer interpreted that feminine this way. "Upon this rock (of truth) I will build my church," because the word for truth is feminine. I think it is rather far-fetched but then I presume I was the only one in the house that gave it a second thought, as I am the only one who has studied Greek, except Mr. Burrage, who has studied a little by himself.

The question uppermost in my mind just now is, "Shall I go to Nashville?" On one side is my debts, all the books I might buy etc., and on the other is the change, seeing Josie, visiting Fisk, etc. I am just as undecided as ever, but I presume that I shall not go. I wish I could go if in truth. But just think, sweetheart, this is our tenth week, over a fourth of the term gone, of the year, I mean. The time goes very fast. I can hardly realize it.

It has warmed up here quite a little now, so it is quite summerish now. We had a little fire in the school room but I let it go out as soon as it would, and opened the windows. I think I will send you a history paper that one of my boys handed in to me today. I wrote the questions on the back of his paper. It is hard to see what connection the 5th has with the Continental Congress but this is it. When Ethan Allen demanded the surrender of Ticonderoga, the British officer asked him in whose name and Allen said, "In the name of the Great Jehovah and the Continental Congress." That is more connection than some of their answers have with the questions, but in this case Willett has left out the all important words. That was really the most ridiculous one that I had but they are all bad enough. That boy is a darkie of the deepest die, good but oh so funny. I guess he comes to my desk six times a day to ask a question and it takes him so long to get it out! He gets right up close to me and just grunts so I can hardly understand a word.

Well, dearie, this is your birthday and I wish I could quote a real appropriate verse but this is the only one I remember now: "As sure as the vine grows around the stump, so nice you are my sugar lump." I love you, dear, with all my heart, but I do not know as I should express it just that way. I hope that before twenty-six years more pass over your head we shall be living peacefully together. I trust it will be peaceably if at all.

You must get up a real good sermon and do your best if you go up to Wolfeborough. And, dearie, let me give you this advice, stand behind the pulpit. It is ever so much nicer I think. Well, I want to study my Sunday School lesson a little so I think I must stop.

With ever so much love to my dear little boy, Winona.

[missing pages: Ernest was temporary pastor at Union Church in Woodford, VT at this time.]

...Vermont with you. You have a nice long vacation don't you? We have from the night of Dec. 24 to the morning of Jan. 2 just as little as possible and take in both Christmas and New Years. Well it will be a little longer than that too because Jan. 2 is Saturday.

One of our poor teachers here is threatened with appendicitis. The doctor cannot tell until tomorrow, but he is very anxious about her. I am just as sorry for her as I can be. I am feeling quite spunky lately. I get dreadfully tired every day but not tired enough to keep my spirits down. Although I am just pining away to see you I manage to bear up under it pretty well. Now, in my mind, I can just hear you say "Is that so?" I wish I could hear it.

❈

806 Pine St. Macon.
Dec. 10, 1896.

My dear Ernest:—

I have had only one letter from you this week but quite often your letter comes Friday, so I shall expect it tomorrow.

School went pretty well today and I thought that I was going to get through without being vexed with anyone, but near the close of school I was explaining something to a girl and had my back to the class, or most of it and when I turned around I found a girl taking advantage of her opportunities and whispering behind my back. Nothing makes me so provoked as to have them do things on the sly. I try not to scold, that is sputter, which is one of my besetting sins. You know, but unless you show a proper amount of spunk they pay no attention to you. I am bound that school teaching shall not make me cross and sour, if I have to overlook some whispering etc. for I am cross enough already and it won't do to get any worse. I think that you would have a right to break your engagement if I should get to be like some school teachers I know. We have one down here who is very nice and pleasant as long as you agree with her, but if you disagree with her she takes it as a personal offense. She is just painfully sensitive, applies everything that is said right to herself and then if it doesn't fit she says, "I don't think I do that" when no one ever supposed she did. But I am also trying not to talk about people and here I go right at it. But then I don't call it when I talk to you about anything anymore there [then] you do when you promise not to tell anything and then come and tell me. You see that I am really trying to get to be an angel right straight off, but you need not be afraid of losing me right away for I have a horrible disposition naturally and

I do not see where I got it either.

I had a letter from Annie the other day. She said that Cora seemed to be growing weaker, but I presume you hear from there quite often so that I do not need to tell you. I am ever so sorry for the poor girl and I do wish that Mary were here with her. It is pretty hard for Mary to lose her mother and her sister while she is away. When I think of such things as that it makes me feel almost sick when I think that in two or three short years I shall go myself. Oh no, dear, I am not trying to back out. I don't want to stay at home if you are going, and I hope we can take Polly with us too.

I haven't decided about Nashville yet, but hope to soon. I went downtown today and saw so many pretty Christmas things that I wanted to buy that I want to spend my money for those instead of railroad fares. There are so many nice books and pictures that I want to buy for you. But what can I buy for Papa? You are a man, can't you suggest what would be good for a man? He is not literary

[no closing]

❊

806 Pine St. [Macon]
Dec. 15, 1897.

My dear Polly:—
    Your letter came today and I am certainly glad to hear that you are getting along so nicely in school. I do hope that you will like well enough to stay there next year. I should like to be with you wonderfully well but I am afraid the discipline would be hard for me. Sometimes I think that I do not want to come back here and then again it seems as though I just must. I do think a lot of the scholars here. I just enjoy them immensely almost all of them. They are not all bright but are well-disposed. One place where we called, the sweetest little woman came in and little by little we got her story. Her husband is a drunkard and she allows him to have a room in the basement and will not let him come upstairs. She has five children and she keeps four of them in school by washing. She says that sometimes she irons all night and doesn't go to bed at all. I do not see how she can do it, do you? Her oldest daughter is in the High School and she doesn't do anything in school. She tries but cannot do it. You don't do any calling of course so you do not get interested in their homes as I do.

    We made fudges the other night and they were fine I tell you what. But there is something else I want now and that is some marshmallows to toast. We bought 5 cents worth and now I have got the taste of them I want some more.

    I have your Christmas present all bought. I do not know whether you will like it or not but I do and I should like to keep it. It did not cost much which is its chief charm.

My head feels horrid tonight and my throat is sore. I have taken cold and so I have all sorts of troubles this week you see. Next week I shall be better and the week after we have a vacation for a whole week. If I had thirteen dollars that I did not know what to do with I should like to go to Fisk to spend that week. Prof. Andrews of Oberlin is to give three organ recitals there on their new organ. When do you go home and how long a vacation do you have? This is Minnie's night to recite but she did not and I am very glad.

We are reviewing Arith now and I find that they cannot do an example in addition and get it right. Only two succeeded in getting three examples in addition right. Of course they were long ones but then they had considerable time to do them in, and as for notation and numeration they know nothing about it. Well, my dear, I hope you are a good girl and are saving your money. I am getting so penurious that I use the same match to light my lamp and my fire. Do they keep your room nice and warm? I think a furnace isn't all that could be desired in the way of heat and your room is not very sunny.

Well, I must say "goodnight," with lots of love, Winona.

806 Pine St. Macon.
Dec. 29, 1897.

My dear Polly: -

Your letter came today but the samples must have been stolen on the way because I could not find them. Of course you put them in. If I had a skirt to wear with it, I should like the waist made to wear Junior Ex. which comes sometime in April I think.

Thurs. morn. I did not get this finished last night as you see. Miss Gage came in to read for a while and then we went down to Miss Farlin's room to have chocolate cake. I am afraid I shall eat enough to make myself sick this week. The calendar came and I think it is beautiful, too pretty to keep out a minute in this coal dust. I am glad that the frame can be used after this year when I shall be in a cleaner place perhaps. Did you buy the calendar? I will enclose a note to Louise. I do not know her address. I am glad that you have a grip. I hope it suits you. Is it as large as mine? Mine is just right for me. It couldn't be better.

Did the Blounts have a Christmas tree for the children? You must have had a good time up there and you must have had a jolly time when Mr. Merriam [Junius Merriam; lifelong Oberlin friend, '95] was there. I have a very soft place in my heart for Mr. Merriam. I have heard Mr. Raymond [also class of '95] recite those two pieces and I think he does them very nicely only I am conscious all the time that he thinks so too. It was delicate in you to leave out Mr. P. when you were comparing Mr. Merriam with the others only I should like to know what you think of him in comparison with other boys. I think he is real nice, don't you?

We had a very select five o'clock tea the other night at half past seven. We dressed in light clothes as far as possible. I put on my pink dress. For refreshments we had fruit salad, wafers, cake, coffee, and later candy. We had our best manners out and had a genteel time generally. We have had some kind of a spread or party every night commencing with Friday, so we are quite giddy, you see.

I have run myself short in money, so that I have about a quarter to last me until the middle of January.

If you have a dollar to spare until then it would be a great favor to me. I expect to send you the ten dollars I owe you then unless you would rather have me put it in the bank until summer. You did not say whether you got the money order or not. I hope you did I am sure.

Miss Gage and I are reading Quo Vadis. It gives a good idea of the state of society at the time of Nero but it is dreadful nevertheless. I expect to wash my hair this morning and I must get my room ready to be cleaned. We are having perfect weather. We visited the white blind asylum yesterday. It was very interesting.

With lots of love, Winona.

❈

806 Pine St.
Macon, Ga
Feb. 12, 1898.

My dear Polly;—

Do you realize that this is Lincoln's birthday? You don't think so much about Lincoln as we do I suppose. The colored people do not celebrate his birthday as they might I think.

Well, I went down to the doctor's to let him look at my arm and he said it was working all right. I should think that it was by the feeling only it is not going to be nearly as bad as it was when I was a child. We have vaccinated one hundred and forty one at school and lots of the others have been vaccinated somewhere else so we are a vaccinated crowd now.

I hope Jenne Morrison will get that position I am sure. I shall be ever so glad of a picture of the snow to see myself and to show the scholars. Surely those teachers could say nothing against you after you took them to dinner. I wish you could have gone home yesterday to cook Papa something decent to eat. It is a shame to have to pay so much for yarn with but I do not see as it can be helped. I am afraid mine are past fixing, that is, the back ones. I dread having them fixed, dreadfully. The time is not far distant now when I shall be turning my steps homeward. I think I shall be glad when the time comes only I do think lots of my nice girls and boys. They are ever so nice. You don't know of anyone who would like a nice girl to take care of children or do housework just through the vacation, do you? One of my nice girls would like to go north just for the experience of it. I could heartily recommend her to anyone in want of a girl.

Well, Miss Farlin is ready for bed and I must go. There is nothing to write hardly for we do not go calling or anywhere on account of the small pox.

With lots of love, Winona.

Sunday P.M.

What a perfect day this is, like June! It occurred to me that when I get a new dress I'd better get one of such a color that I could wear it with that silk waist that Mr. P. gave me. I shall have to have something to wear to things there in Andover at Commencement time. I wish that striped lavender dress of yours were made up so that I could wear it Junior Ex. here. How much work does it need on it?

There was a woman in church this morning who just shouted when they sang "Is My Name Written There?" She thought her name was written there and she wanted everyone to know it. It is said that that same woman was so ugly to her husband that he could not live with her. I know she does not live with him, but I do not know the reason.

My arm is just having a good ache today. It is taking all right I guess. The doctor said that today or tomorrow would be the worst day for me.

I wish you were here today.

With lots of love, Winona

Letters of Winona G. Partridge 1900

Straits of Messina.
Oct. 23, 1900.

My dear Polly,–

We are just passing between Scylla and Charybdis and I ran down to write a line to you in this historic spot. I must go back up and see but will write more later. The mountains on both sides are very plain and I should think we were within a quarter of a mile from each side but perhaps it is really farther. – Well, I got back up on deck and found that we were going through the Lifari Is. and haven't got to the Straits yet. We are very near one rugged island on the north and we can see a little white village on an island on the south. We are delighted to see land again. We have brought baby [Robert Graffam] upstairs and baby is sleeping here beside me. We think we are just passing Stromboli and the volcano is smoking. Can you realize that your little sister is way off here? Don't think of it. I cannot bear to. It is very warm. I am sitting on deck with your pink shirt waist on and I am warm now.

But to go back. I intend to write at least a card in Marseilles but was misinformed about when the boat was to start so did not get it ready in time. We started from London last Friday morning about nine o'clock, I think and went in three or four hours to Dover and then crossed the English Channel to Calais. The boat rocked a good deal but none of our party was seasick. Our tickets indicated that we were to go by–

(We are now passing between Sicily & Italy's toe and are having a strong wind from the whirlpool. Is it Scylla or Charybdis?)

(Passing Rhegium)

To resume, our tickets indicated that we were to go by New Haven, crossing there to Dieppe but that would take five hours or more so we exchanged for the others. From Calais, we went in an apartment car, second class, to Paris. The apartment cars are very nice if you have enough of a party to fill the apartment. The baby filled up pretty well so we had an apartment all by ourselves, that is Mr. and Mrs. Peet, and Willie, and we three. Some apartments hold eight and some six. They are very nice, at least these were. There is a walk along the side and each apartment opens into this vestibule. Some of the poorer ones have no corridor and so you are entirely isolated from every one else in the car. We reached Paris late in the afternoon and left there about nine o'clock Friday night, in a regular car, much more comfortable than our common cars but still not a sleeping car. We took pity on a young lady who was traveling alone and let her come into our apartment. That made just six beside the baby. The cushions and springs on the seats are to be pulled out so that you can slip down and put your feet on the cushions on the other side and there are headrests at the side of each seat. We got out our steamer rugs and spread them along our laps and steeled down for a comfortable night. The baby was just as good as gold but I had to hold him, at least let him rest on my arm to keep him safe. I sat next to the window and there was so much of a draught that I did not dare to change the baby to my left arm.

As my right arm and side was nearly paralyzed sitting in position, Mr. Partridge offered to change but he had some cold and I did not dare to let him sit by the window. In some ways it is a disadvantage to be so little troubled by irregularities. I can ride backwards, sit in a draught where I nearly freeze, am never car sick, never sea-sick, do not mind noise, nor jolting, so I am always able to take care of the baby or do anything else that needs to be done. I have one weak spot. I cannot eat everything and I really suffer from that in traveling.

Well, after that diversion I will continue on. We slept some that night. By the snoring I should judge that the others slept most of the time. We took a bottle of water on the train and used our alcohol lamp and fed the baby regularly. By the way, the baby seldom varies ten minutes from the regular three hour feed during the day and very seldom has more than one feed from ten or so until six. But he is often awake until midnight with colic and cries much worse than I ever heard him in Shoreham. But he was lovely that night and in the morning the Peets voted him a first class A No 1 baby and he certainly is. After that night of sleeping under difficulties we felt pretty well tired out so at Marseilles we went to a hotel and hired a room and got a little rested. Mr. Peet knows just as much about French as I do so you can imagine how funny it is when we try to order dinner or do anything in fact. If it weren't for the agents of Cook's Tourist Agency I do not know what people would do but they are everywhere at the stations and steamers etc. If you have one of their tickets you are all right. He expects a fee but so does everybody else who does even a little polite thing for you. It is dreadful.

We went on the boat at Marseilles on Saturday afternoon and the boat was to sail at four o'clock Sat. P.M. but did not sail until the next morning. My heart sank when I got on the boat. In the first place we had to go to it in a row boat and then climb over boxes and other things to get on board. We went down into the cabin and found a dark and gloomy place. The others found their staterooms all right but they could not find the key to the one they had assigned to us and when they did find it and opened the room it was dirty and horrid. It was a room that had belonged to the man who had charge of the supplies of dishes etc. perhaps and was fitted up for only one person, but the stewardess made a long hard bed up on the lounge and scraped around a little. There are some great advantages in it and for us is better than our ordinary stateroom for it is a two goodsized rooms opening into each other and the room where the bed is not has a desk and two tables and together the rooms have three port holes so we have more air than most people and a place to put our trunk and dry things. We were on board, you see, one night before they started and that night they turned the electricity off so I had to feed the baby in the dark or with what light the alcohol lamp gave. It was a terrible night, I tell you. Now we have a light.

We are in a great predicament because we cannot ask for anything. One of the sailors understands English and counting us there are eight people aboard who speak English. A young man sits by us at the table and acts as interpreter. But the way the food is served one cannot get along very nicely without talking. They pass each course and you can take it or not as you please. We nearly starve for they bring us coffee and bread into your stateroom about seven, then breakfast is served about half past ten or eleven and dinner at half past six. The time between breakfast & dinner is endless almost. Then when the food comes it is mostly drenched in olive oil. So I can hardly stand the smell of it. I have thought of Miss Blackwell a great many times. Things are growing a little better in the way of cleanliness. They are gradually cleaning up. By the time we get to Constantinople we shall be quite clean, I think. But when you go up stairs your troubles vanish if the baby is good. It is warm as summer and the water is beautiful, so there. We have been following along the coast of Italy about half the time today. It is very interesting. I cannot think that it is really I who is doing all this.

It is very calm now but night before last and one day it was very rough. Mr. P. had a little touch of seasickness and I could hardly manage to feed the baby the boat rolled so. I had to put the bottles around under pillows and manage every way to keep things from breaking. When I would get out of bed I would just shoot across to the other side of the room. Fortunately Bob was good and did not have much attention. It is against the rules of the boat to have an alcohol lamp but I have to use mine. I do not know whether they know it or not but if they did they could not make us stop because we cannot understand what they say. It is sometimes amusing though, when they are talking about the baby and his parents and I do understand. I know enough French to follow it if they do not speak too fast. But it does seem queer not to be able to talk with people. We stop tomorrow afternoon at Patras, Greece, on the Gulf of Corinth and I hope to get this mailed there. If I have time I will write some tomorrow.

Wednesday – Oct. 24– We are passing through the Ionian Islands now. We went between Cephalonia and Zante. Cephalonia is still beside us. It is quite large and high. Its K € Ø a lamda z' [6 greek letters for mtn or peak] is above the clouds and it is a very pretty sight. How I do wish you were here to enjoy this with us. I want to make the trip with you sometime. They want these letters very soon so I must stop now. Little Bob hasn't seemed so very well but I think he is a little better this afternoon. He sleeps pretty well. There is an English nurse on board, very pleasant, 28 yrs. old who is going to Athens to be a sister in a children's hospital. She has given me some points about the baby. I got a doctor's book in London, perhaps I told you. Well, I must stop for this time. I am afraid these letters are not very interesting, but nothing very exciting happens. We are mostly excited about whether we shall get enough to eat or not. I get woefully homesick sometimes. Shoreham looks very attractive to me, I tell you. How I have longed for my little rocking chair out there in the kitchen! I hope some few of the people will remember us until we come back. I try to think that it won't be very long. This will be mailed at Patras. We do not lose sight of land again, I think.

With lots of love, Winona.

❖

Patras, Greece.
Oct. 24, 1900.
10-15 P.M.

My dear Polly,–

We are stopping in the harbor of Patras for a few hours to unload freight. Patras is on the Gulf of Patras, a part of the Corinthian Gulf and is the largest city in Achara, a city of about fifty thousand. We got in before dark so had a chance to see the town. It is not a very attractive looking place but is quaint. There is a church with two towers and two clocks on it and ruins of some old castle or other. Those are the most interesting things. Mr. P. went ashore and got some fruit and stuff and a plate for a souvenir. He tried to find something to send you but couldn't. I am sorry. If you look in your map you will see that we go way out of our way. We find that we do not stop at Peiraeus [Piraeus] but go way up to Salonica, way out of our course. Our next stop is Syra, an island in the Aegean Sea or the Grecian Archipelago.

Now I want to turn from these historical places to Bobbie. He has grown two inches and a half since he was born and now measures 24½ in. He is growing out of his clothes already. Those two little jackets, one of which Mrs. Bushnell made, are really too small and the sleeves of his flannel slips and those Gertrude dress are hardly long enough. He has a new trick of running his tongue out and it amuses him very much. He evidently thinks it is very cute, and it certainly is. If it weren't for the colic he would be a perfect baby. He is getting a little nervous so that he wants someone near to put her hand on him once in a while. He wakes up frightened quite often and if I put my hand on him and hum a little gently he will go right back to sleep. Of course he is a wonderful baby. We are taking pictures of him along which you will receive in time. I try to make him look at the scenery but he won't even deign to glance at Greece and Italy. He'll be sorry that he did not some day. You will hardly believe that he sleeps without a thing over him but a sheet and is as warm as toast. He sleeps on deck in his basket with just that little knitted shawl thrown over him. He stays on deck nearly all day. You see he is not as delicate and cold as he was. I do wish you could see him. Perhaps that is enough of a dissertation on the baby tonight and I will go to bed.

Thursday P.M.– Just imagine seeing the sun rise on the little hills of Greece! I never expected to see it. We left Patras very early and came out of the gulf, turned south and passed between the coast and Zante, so we have been on two sides of Zante. That island is noted for currents. There has been a young man on board who is on his way to attend the British School of Research in Athens. He is very pleasant, speaks English, as well as French and so often acted as our interpreter. He left us at Patras, but gave us his card and invited us, or any of our friends to call on him. He is to be there several years so when you come if you stop at Athens he will help you to see what you want to. Don't you forget it if I do.

It seems that in Turkey they have a different time every day for they call sunset twelve o'clock no matter what time it really is. In Constantinople they have two faced watches, one for Turkish time and one for European time. There is about seven hours difference in time between Sivas and Boston, I think. Mrs. Peet says that Thanksgiving Day is a great holiday for missionaries. I hope we shall be in Sivas by that time. It seems as though we got along very slowly. The southern trip from N.Y. is a very nice one, Mrs. Peet says and I think it would be fine for you to come that way. You can leave N.Y. by the North German Lloyd line and go to Naples, then by train to Trieste and there take a steamer to Constantinople. I am getting anxious for you to start already. I must confess that I am somewhat homesick. I hope either you or Tavie and will come next summer. If you do not come next summer, of course you will come the summer after. It seems a long time to wait but it will pass quickly.

Friday evening. – I must close this letter and go to bed, because I lost lots of sleep last night. Bob was not feeling very well and was therefore wakeful. He seems better tonight. We haven't cereal milk enough and have changed to malted milk. You see we have been much longer than we expected to be.

Today we stopped at the island of Syra, at the city of Syra, in the Aegean. It is a queer city built o the slopes of hills and the city seems to be built in these sections like pyramids with some important building like a church at the apex. We have been near land almost all day. I haven't been on deck as much as I wanted to be because Mr. P. was taken sick last night, on account of eating too much truck that he bought in Patras and the baby was fussy all the forenoon. Between the two I have been quite busy. We expect to be in Salonica in the morning and that means we shall be in Turkey tomorrow. Just think of it! I shall probably not be out of Turkey for several years. But I mustn't think about it. I never cried so easily since I was a baby, I am sure. I am afraid I shall be a real cry-baby after a while. I excuse myself on the plea that I am tired and nervous. I suppose I shall get rested sometime but it looks like a long time before we can settle down anywhere. I think the Peets have a little idea of advising us to stay in Constantinople this winter. If it is very cold we might or if I am absolutely so tired that I cannot go on, but we shall go clear through if we can, of course.

That old dress of yours is just fine. The baby has vomited all over it but of course it isn't injured any. I shall have to have a dress before very long I think. Mr. Peet thinks we are to have $880 salary until Bob gets to be more of an expense to us. He says he guesses they will let us take our first furlough in less than ten years, so you will see us in America before very long. Before that a good while I expect to see you in Turkey.

But I must stop and go to bed. I shall probably not write any more until after we leave Thessalonica. Just think of going to the town where Paul preached!

Yours with lots of love, Winona.

❁

Sea of Marmora.
Oct. 28, 1900.

My dear Polly,—

We have had so many interesting things the last two or three days that I have not spent any time in writing. I believe the last letter was mailed at Patras, no Salonica, I guess. Well, we had a fine time at Salonica. We were there six or seven hours. Mr. Peet had sent word to the missionaries that we were coming so they were all ready for us. Dr. House, Mr. Baird, and Edward Haskell, with their families, and Miss Stone are there. Dr. Buckley, a dentist who expects to settle in Constantinople was there too. He wants to be a missionary dentist but of course will not be employed by the Board, so proposes to pay his expenses by working for other people, do missionaries' work for nothing and then work among sailors evenings and Sundays. Isn't he a missionary? Poor man, his wife is cranky and does not want to come so he may have to give up and go back.

(Constantinople) I wrote that first page and then stopped until now, Wed. Oct 31. I will proceed with Salonica. Mr. Haskell and family are in America so we did not see them, but the others are all lovely. As soon as I entered the door one of the House girls took the baby and I hardly touched him all day. We went around the city some in a tram car and carriage. We walked through the street where Paul walked, sure because the old city gate was there and he had to go through that. The street has been filled in so we walked several feet above where he walked. We visited two Turkish mosques which were formerly Christian temples dating back surely to the third or fourth centuries and probably to the time of Christ. In one, Mosque of

St. George, Theodosius was baptized and buried. There is nothing very beautiful about them but they are interesting. They put slippers on our feet to keep us from profaning the place. To be sure, we would lose one off and walk several feet before we discovered it but then that was all right.

Everything could be seen on the streets in the way of people and costumes and dirt. It is customary to walk in the street with the donkeys and that day it was muddy so we had a time of it. But it was all very interesting and foreign. The most interesting part was the dinner. We had been living on two meals a day with a little bread and poor coffee thrown in in the morning, and when we sat down to a good American meal, it did seem good. All the missionaries were invited to Dr. House's, sixteen of us in all. They have everything very nice in their house, not luxurious but comfortable. After dinner we went over to Miss Stone's little house and to the boat. Everyone in the mission rowed out to the boat with us and stayed as long as possible. We had a most royal reception and Mr. Peet says that we shall be treated just like that everywhere and I guess we shall.

Dr. Barnum met us here and insisted upon our coming to their house to stay. They have things more than comfortable. They gave us a room, no two rooms on the third floor and they are supplied with everything anyone could think of wanting. I think I never went to a house where there was nothing in the way of conveniences to be desired. There is a desk in each room furnished with everything for writing and everything else is well furnished. I said yesterday that the only thing I had wanted that I had not found was a stove hook and I found that later in the closet. Speaking of our welcome, we found letters here from Marsovan and Sivas telling us how glad they were to see us. Mr. Perry is to meet us in Samsoun. They say here that it is not nine days' trip. Mr. Perry expects to make it in six and a half but he will go faster than we shall I presume. Miss Ellsworth of Sivas married the English Consul last week. They were married here and may go back with us. That leaves a vacancy there now. I am trying to get Tavie to take it as I suppose you won't. You would be fine for that position. I think she looks after the girls' school and the boarding department. I cannot decide whether I'd rather have you come next summer or the summer after next. Mrs. Barnum said she ran over to America just for the summer. Her niece married Charles Riggs in Middlebury and her son graduated from college. Miss Brewer's sister spent the vacation with her last summer here in Constantinople. It doesn't seem as far from here to America as it does from there here. I am afraid you will not have money enough to come next summer. Perhaps by the next letter I shall know just how much it will cost. I think $150 each way would cover it but that wouldn't leave you any money to buy anything with. If you think of coming really you want to get every bit of French that you can. You can go anywhere with French. This is sort of a diversion.

I just cannot describe the sail through the Aegean, Dardanelles, and Sea of Marmora and they say the Bosphorus far surpasses them all. We have a beautiful view of the Sea of Marmora from this house.

It did seem so good to get a letter from you here. We found quite a package of letters but of course we read yours first. We did not get yours in London. I was sorry that I had not told you to write there. I presume Mr. Perry will have mail for us in Samsoun. We got letters here from Hattie, Carrie, Chester Greene, Josie, Uncle Gene, Aunt Jen and Essie. Some were from Shoreham and some were to late for the steamer so Mr. Swett forwarded them. Mabel Goodell is married by this time. She had to go where he was to get married, because if he left he would lose his position. I think I should wait until he had a vacation. I am going to try to get something to send her from here.

Will you please send me patterns of short clothes for Bob? And also send me a pattern of some kind of a dress for myself, not too fancy, sort of a loose waist that I can make myself, if necessary. Mrs. Hubbard has just had a silk dress made here and I guess I have to have clothes even in Sivas. I have got to put new sleeves into all Bob's dresses just as soon as I get there. He grows like a weed. I send you a detail from that group picture that we had. I am sorry Bob and I moved. The rest are good. We took several in the boat but it is so hard to get a good picture of the baby. He cannot stand the bright sun and he cannot stay still long enough for a time exposure. When he gets old enough to sit up and hold his head up we can take a good picture of him. He would be absolutely perfect if it weren't for the colic. It seems to be lower down now in his bowels. Barnum thinks it will be over very soon now. Mrs. B. has had six children but lost all but one. Mrs. Hubbard wrote that they were glad for Mr. Perry but sorry for themselves that we were not to be with them this winter. It is very unsatisfactory to ask questions but after you have been here you will understand things better. I do not know whether you have been sending my letters to Shoreham or not, but anyway you need not send this one because I have just written to one of the ladies which contains a good deal that this does.

Mrs. H. is going to send a bundle of diapers to Samsoun but I do not expect to need them. He got reduced to his best dress but I am having a good big washing done here. I may not be able to write any more while here but will try to mail something in Samsoun.

With lots of love, Winona.

❁

Sivas, Turkey.
Nov. 16, 1900.

My dear Polly,—

This is mamma's birthday and I wish I might write to her but it would be only one more to leave behind and it would be still harder to leave America. Bob is on the couch beside me amusing himself but I am afraid he has about exhausted his resources. He hasn't many, you know, although he notices more every day. He hasn't been very well since he got here but he is getting better. Such a journey is enough to kill any baby and I do not know how he ever got through alive, but here he is and as near as we can figure on these scales weighs fourteen pounds. That is gaining only two pounds in six weeks but it is a wonder that he could gain anything on such a trip.

Let me see, I believe I wrote about things until we got on the Black Sea. I worried a little about getting off the boat at Samsoun because we gave Mr. Perry a pretty short time to get there and I thought if we could not speak to the officials on the boat nor on the land we should be in a mess. When the boat stops there is a perfect rush of row boats from the shore and the men come aboard and bargain for people to go ashore with them. We decided to wait as long as we could on board the boat and see if the counselor agent at Samsoun or Mr. Perry did not arrive. We waited quite a long time and finally saw a very imposing looking company coming towards the boat, a tall nice looking man dressed in citizen's clothes, a man in a uniform nearly covered with gold braid, with a sword, revolver etc., then one or two lesser lights. We made up our minds before they got to the boats that they were after us and so it proved. Mr. Perry arrived in Samsoun just as our boat was coming in. Wasn't that fortunate! We stayed in Samsoun that night at a Greek hotel, a miserable place, but what is called fancy in this country so it proved. Bob got stung on the head there and you can imagine how he cried. Fortunately, I brought some soda along to wash the bottles with and I put some of that right on. It was not long before the inflammation was all out.

Tuesday morning we began our memorable land trip. We started at or a little before sunrise, that is had no breakfast, got Bob ready and actually started about six o'clock. That was our program almost every morning and one or two mornings we started earlier. We rode all day until sunset or a little after, stopping an hour for lunch, perhaps. I think I can send you a picture of our araba in this letter. I am sorry we did not get one of us but everything was so rushed that it wasn't convenient. Our araba is really a very comfortable wagon when it is properly equipped with quilts and pillows. If we hadn't had Bob we should have rested a great deal. I think but it is rather hard taking care of a baby all day lying down in a wagon. He slept most of the time but did want to kick and get his arms out. It was too cold for that most of the time. At noon and night we topped at "khans" for the most part and I will try to describe them. They are built around an open court which sounds rather hightoned, but the wagons were kept there and the horses around underneath the rooms. We drove into this court and then mounted the stairs to our room. Oh, horrors, the dirt! I should much prefer to sleep in anybody's barn. The hay would be paradise as far as cleanliness is concerned. Nominally they were empty but Bob and I have marks which show that they were far from empty. I counted ten bites on one little foot not counting his ankle. I am in the same condition only I make more fuss about it than he does. Well, those rooms had an old husk mat usually and a dirty couch and once or twice we found a bed which we did not occupy. The only way of heating the rooms was by means of a pan or brazure of coals just set into the room. It was so cold that there was ice all around the watering troughs and on the streams. Just imagine getting up at three o'clock or four at the latest, bathing the baby, eating your breakfast, and starting out in the cold at daybreak. Don't you think Bob must be tough and his mother too? The hardest part was getting up nights to feed him when we had no coals even and the windows are loose and everything is cold. But we got through it and in a way enjoyed out trip. The way to enjoy that trip is to go when it is warm and camp in a tent. Mrs. Jewett said that was [what] they did. You had to have a soldier to watch in case of robbers or bad men. I wasn't at all prepared for the sights that I saw, long trains of camels, perhaps fifty in a row. When Mr. Perry was coming for us, he counted 2500 camels and got tired and stopped. Then, there are any number of little donkeys carrying freight. They put two boxes the size of ours on those little creatures no larger than the Mathews' ponies and some not so large. We saw also a great many horses loaded in that way. Our train consisted of three two-horse arabas, one with springs for us, one without springs for Mr. Perry and the cook and one for the trunks etc. There are three mountain ridges to cross but we do not go straight up and down here but wind around. The roads are very good for the most part, all macadamized.

We had a little experience the night we reached Marsovan. We had got ahead of Mr. Perry so that we were out of sight but our wagon and the goods wagon were together. We did not know whether our men knew where we were going or not but concluded from their stopping to consult as often that they did not and were wondering what they should do with us. We could not understand a word of their language nor they a word of ours and there we were with darkness coming on fast. Well, they kept on and followed around a wall, mistook the way once or twice, stopped to inquire, but finally came to a large gate at which they knocked. Then the jabbering began. There seemed to be quite a number inside talking and they talked back and forth with our drivers some. Finally the gate was cautiously opened and we drove in. We did not know whether to jail or the poor house. As soon as we were inside a regular flock of young men surrounded us and walked along beside us all jabbering a foreign tongue. Finally we stopped at a house and to our great delight Dr. and Mrs. Tracy came out and greeted us. The crowd around us was the students welcoming us to Turkey but we, poor things, didn't know it. We stayed only over night and the next forenoon because if we stayed longer than that we would have to stay over Sunday and that is risky at this time of year. But we had a beautiful time there. The people are lovely. We saw Dr. & Mrs. T. and two boys, Mr. and Mrs. White and children, Miss Cull, Miss Susie Riggs, Dr. & Mrs. Carrington, Mr. and Mrs. Charles Riggs, Miss Ward, Miss Barnum of Harpoot, Mrs. Smith and son, Mr. Getchel and two English nurses. We did enjoy them all, although the baby wasn't very good. Every time we stopped he seemed to be all upset. He seemed all right as long as we kept going, but I suppose it shook him up too much and he got tired and nervous. Everybody thinks he is a perfect wonder and he is a darling too. I do wish you could see him.

The next place of importance where we stopped was Tocat, an outstation of Sivas, but quite a city. We expected to stay at the khan there but a colporteur lives there and wanted us to go to his house so we did. We took our beds and bedding along and also our wok and some provisions. They gave us the sitting room and did everything they could for our comfort, but it was dreadful. Not one of the family could speak a word of English and Mr. Perry did not stay there nights. I stayed there with the baby Sunday while the two Mr. P's went to church. We had callers most of the time. They want us to move to Tocat very much but we do not expect to do so.

The next place where we had new experiences was at the last stop before reaching Sivas about three hours' ride away. It was cheerless enough when we arrived because we were very cold and they could furnish us no fire. But pretty soon the people began to arrive from Sivas and made it a little more cheerful. Mrs. Hubbard, Miss Zenger and Miss Lena Zenger (Swiss), Miss Brewer, Mrs. Jewett, about twelve native teachers, the Hubbard children, and I do not know how many students. They gave up school and made a regular holiday of it. Dr. Jewett, the consul, sent his regards out to meet us and called the next morning. I was over there yesterday. They are very nice and interested in the mission work. They want us to be very neighborly and we are. Mr. P. and Mrs. Hubbard ran in there this afternoon.

The missionaries were invited to the French Consulate last evening to a reception in honor of the vali pasha, the governor general of this whole province. He is very friendly and quite interested in Mrs. Hubbard. She played last night. They tried to get her to play for the dancing but she would not. The vali sent them home in his new carriages. It seems strange to hear Mr. Perry, this veteran missionary, talking about people being graceful on the floor. They never got home until one or two o'clock. They go just as little as they can and not give offence. It is too hard work to work all day and be out all night. They had not met us so we were not invited. It is fortunate for I have nothing to wear to such a place. They do not dress in party costume but my blue dress is getting a little rusty or quite a good deal rusty. I found I should have to have another dress for a standby so I bought one today. I think it is very pretty. I [will] send samples. The plain is the waist. There is a tailor here who does fairly well at dressmaking and I shall have him make the skirt right away and I wish you would send a pattern of a pretty wool shirt waist. He cannot make fitted waists. I should like a couple of fancy ribbons suitable to wear with this or my black silk waist. This cloth is very wide and the plain cost a little less than a dollar a yard and the other about sixty-five cents. We can buy about everything that we want here. Next time I will tell you about the family etc. I cannot send you things by mail very well because they are very likely to be confiscated. We get mail Thurs. and Sunday. It came yesterday and there was not a thing for me. I will try to send a letter to you every Saturday.

With lots of love, Winona.

Please send the pattern as soon as possible. I'd like it tucked or something a little fancy.

❀

Sivas, Turkey.
Nov. 23, 1900.

My dear Polly,—
    This is purely a business letter in which I will enclose a letter to Kate Goodell Sturgis. I do not know her address.
    Please send the patterns I asked you to send by mail, a pattern of a dress, something simple, a pattern of a woolen shirt waist with plaits or tucks and one of a cotton shirt waist. I tried on my skirt today and it is going to be very pretty. I am going to get enough cloth for a jacket and have it wadded. It will make a good winter suit. The man who is making it is a regular tailor but did not have trade enough or something so took up the trade of making ladies' things for the foreigners. They have taught him. He can make anything if he has a pattern for it. I guess you'd better send patterns for baby's short dresses by mail too. There is no knowing how many months the other things will be coming. I wish you would also put in with the other things a pair of No. 2 shirts like those patent ones he has and a pair of No. 3's. He has almost outgrown the sleeves of these now. How he does grow out of his things. Please put in three bottles of Hollis' Compound Essence of Ginseng, a little sulphur, a homeopathic bottle of Belladonna, epicac (?), Mercurius. We do not want the regular old fashioned yellow sulphur but some preparation of it. Mr. P. keeps having boils and he needs something for his blood. Please also put in some coffee. If you can get some tin cans of coffee ⅔ Java & ⅓ mocha, I wish you would send tens pounds, unground, if you think it will keep a few months. The regular coffee here is poor. They prepare Turkish coffee which is very nice to serve in little tiny cups after dinner or when callers come. I cannot think now of anything more that I shall want but you can put in anything you think it would be nice for us to have.
    Mrs. Perry is in America, you know, and she is going east soon. You'd better inquire at the Board Rooms where she is. She might be there in Boston so you could see her.
    Please give my love to the Harmons. I ought to have written to them after we were entertained there but I do not know as I shall ever have time. With studying Armenian and looking after Bob I have about all I want to do.

[Armenian words] (I have love to you)

Winona G. Partridge

❀

Sivas, Turkey.
Nov. 25, 1900.

My dear Polly,–

I am writing this at the official request of Mr. Partridge. He has taken a notion that he is very anxious to have you come out here to settle and he has great faith in my powers of persuasion, and really I can think of no one that I ever knew that could fill the bill out here except you. Your letter containing the account of your trials with Miss Whiton just came today. It was written just after you got over being sick and I do think they were very unjust. Miss Bang's speaking to you so about the salary was dreadful, I think. Of course she knew what your salary was to be. This diversion is all – I do not know what this diversion is all for, as I have had quite a time with Bob. He has a stomach ache. Dzmroughd, the nurse, has him now and he is quiet. He doesn't have the stomach ache as much as he used to, I am glad to say.

To return to my first subject – As I have probably told you several times Mrs. Perry is in America and she writes that some Wisconsin people are quite enthusiastic to send some one out here to take Miss Ellsworth's place, so I think they will probably send some one next summer. I wrote to Tavie she would be good one only they are very anxious to have someone who can sing and play. That sounds big but it needs someone with a pretty strong voice to help sing and play hymns and do a little with music in the schools. You would be sent to take Miss Ellsworth's place but if Mrs. Hubbard leaves as she is talking of doing you would naturally take her place for she is the one who has ideas about everything and to whom everybody goes. She is capable in every way, just like you. Ahem, now won't you come? Mr. P. has decided very firmly that you would be just the one and he thinks he would much prefer to have you here than at Marsovan. I told him you would ruin Bob and me but he thinks it will be all right. I really do not think you will find your right place until you get out here. You are really needed and I think the Board will send you if you apply. Now, please go in to see Dr. Smith when you go back from your vacation. I am going to send this to Pejebscot so that you will be sure to get it so you can talk it over with papa. If you do not apply, you'd better plan to take a vacation next year and come out here. It will not cost you any more than to come for the summer for you will not need to spend a cent here. It will be altogether too short a time to come for the summer. I will say good night now but will probable add more.

With lots of love, Winona.

❀

Sivas, Turkey.
Nov. 30, 1900.

Dear Folks and Polly,–

They tell me this is the time to write a Christmas letter and I am going to take it for granted that you will be together.

We had a great day yesterday for Thanksgiving. In the first place Mr. Perry invited Mrs. Hubbard and her two children and Miss Brewer and two Swiss ladies, Miss Zanger and Miss Lena Zanger over here to breakfast. Then at two o'clock we had a service at the other house for the Americans, Swiss & Consul's. At that meeting and at dinner there were present ten Americans, five missionaries, five children, American Consul and his wife and the wife of the English Consul, the English Consul, five Swiss people, two Greeks, one the interpreter for the Am. Consul, and the other the cashier of a bank. The baby did not go to the service nor to dinner but he did go in the evening. At dinner the Kavass and waiter from the American Consulate waited on the table. Let me see if I can enumerate the courses.

1. Soup, 2. Toast and Sardines and stuffed eggs 3. Meat patties 4. Chicken pies made by Mrs. Jewett 5. Two large turkeys 6. Some kind of a pudding 7. Mince pie 8 Plum steamed pudding 9. Apples, nuts and candy of various kinds and somewhere we had salad but I do not know where. It was the best dinner that I ever had, I think. Mrs. Hubbard had charge of it but Mrs. Jewett helped her a great deal and the rest of us more or less. After dinner we had music, games, and sociability. It isn't everybody who can play "going to Jerusalem" with American and English Consuls and their wives. They are all very pleasant indeed and we did have a nice time. After the games and sociability they had tea and cake and popcorn. I had to come home and tend the baby then, but Mrs. H. sent me some cake. I haven't been very well for a day or two because I have lost so much sleep. The baby has a great deal of trouble with his stomach and he keeps us up a great deal. He is living on malted milk now waiting for his other food to get here from Samsoun. Just think, it left America middle of September and we hear that it is on the way now. It will probably arrive next week. Perhaps he will be better when that comes. We will hope so.

Sat. morning. – Such a night as we had of it. I sat up with Bob until two o'clock and then his father got up. Until two o'clock he slept about five minutes at a time and then woke up with a cry. I have sent to Dr. Carrington for some medicine for him and I hope it will come soon. When you get this he will probably be all right so do not worry about him.

I forgot to say, Polly, that it will be necessary for you to be out here next year because I have to have Thanksgiving dinner then and of course I shall have to have you. Mrs. Hubbard thinks it will be lonely for you to spend the whole year here. I really think you would enjoy it very much. There is no doubt, I think, that we can help you to get back at the end of the year. We shall have about nine hundred dollars for just living expenses and that is a good deal here. Of course we shall be just settling up housekeeping but we shall get things gradually. It will do you worlds of good to come out here and ride horseback. Mrs. Hubbard has a horse that all the ladies ride and you can always get one in market for a few cents. There is a horse that belongs to the station but no woman would dare to ride it.

I am going down town this morning to get a few things that I need. I am very sorry that I cannot send things from here safely. I shall just have to take my chances and send things when someone is going. There will probably be someone going from here or Harpoot every year.

This mail day and I have lots of letters to write and lot of other things to do. This note is just to wish you all a very Merry Christmas. I wish I could be with you, but I guess I shall have to wait a little while.

With lots and lots of love, Winona.

✤

[ca Dec 1 1900]

Now, Polly, I am very much stirred up about your coming out here. Perry has got on the track of someone and you must apply at once to get ahead of her. It is none she knows but she has heard of. It is sure to be someone from the N. E. Evangelical Alliance or someone of that stamp and we do not want her. Mr. P. is very much stirred up because he is afraid you will not come. You are just the one for it, I am sure. You would have to work under Miss Brewer for a while but she would soon give it to you. She reminds us both very strongly of Annie so you can imagine that having charge of all these schools is not her forte. She is a treasure in some ways, though. The schools are not all here but some are in outstations. It would be very different from anything you have ever done but it would be more worthwhile. You could live with us and so get away from it.

[pages missing]

all ears. Bob is just now demolishing and chewing up the envelope that belongs on your last letter. Everything goes straight into his mouth. He eats about half a pound of his food in a day, that is one of those big bottles lasts him about ten days. He ought to grow, hadn't he? Dr. Jewett vaccinated him again the other day, but I do not think it will take. Did I tell you that the pictures we took on the way out are no good? I do not know whether it was the fault of the camera or the people who took them or the man who finished them. But isn't it too bad? I want you to get a camera for us some time but we haven't the money to pay for it now. If you want one there in Washington you can buy one and then we will buy it of you later. They have a camera with which you can use a film or plates. We want one of that kind or a film camera. It is much more convenient when you are traveling.

We hear that our books are on the way from Samsoun so I suppose they will be here next week. I wish the rest of the things would come.

I must not write a long letter because I want to leave room enough for a picture of Bob if it comes. You shall [have] the first one, of course. Isn't he a dear? Mrs. Jewett thinks he will talk when he is nine months old. Of course that means only that he may say two or three words. He is as bright as a dollar.

I must write to papa & go to bed. We do not lose much sleep with Bob now. Last night he woke up once to be changed and once to be fed. I do not mind it as much as I did and we take turns now so I have him every other night.

With heaps of love, Winona.

Please write to Dr. Daniels. He remembers you.

✤

Sivas.
[ca Dec 4] 1900.

My dear Polly,

You'd better see Tavie if you think of coming out here. I do not want to treat her shabbily. I have not heard from her but do not think she will come and now that I know more about it I do not think she is the one for the place.

Please send me some of the smallest size of safety pins.

I cannot write much tonight.

With lots of love, Winona.

If you send a racket and net put in a half dozen balls. ECP

❁

[written across the top by ECP]
I enclosed a letter which I have just copied for Mr. Perry about our new school house. It is not very clear because I did not make this until some hours after the others. They were on two sheets and so too bulky to send in this letter. ECP

Sivas, Turkey.
Dec. 8, 1900.

My dear Polly,–

This is Mr. P's birthday and the band is playing and the flags are up all over the city. It happens also to be the Sultan's birthday. We are invited over to Mrs. Hubbard's to dinner and they at that house presented him with six little coffee cups and an Armenian hymn book and sweet chocolate etc. The make quite a little of people's birthday's in the station here. I wish you would keep your eyes open for pretty little after dinner coffee cups. It is the style here to serve Turkish in those little cups to all callers and sometimes they come in crowds and you need a good many cups. I like odd ones and I should like American ones.

I have not written much about the baby lately because he has not been well and I did not want you to worry about him. He has had a cold and a cough ever since he has been here and his bowels have been very much out of order. We have changed his food two or three times to find something to agree with him as his own food did not come. We used malted milk, Nestles food and sterilized milk and still he fussed a great deal, kept us awake nights right along so we might about as well have taken turns sitting up as to try to go to bed. We have divided the nights in taking care of him. We doctored him for his stomach and one morning I found that a lot of matter had run out of his ear, showing the poor fellow had had an abcess gathering. Now he is much better and last night we all slept eight hours. You can imagine that it has been hard work studying Armenian in the daytime and sitting up with the baby at night. But Bob is beautiful now. I wished this morning that you were here to give him his bath. He is cunning and it is such fun. I always do it myself. I have a little bath tub of Mrs. Hubbard's and I lay him right down in it, just putting my hand under his head. He just likes it but he does not want the water hot any more. He wants it just barely luke warm. He is growing very fast and you must come next summer. Save every bit of money you can and if you do not come under appointment come any way and we will help you get back. If you cannot go back after the first year, you can after the second perhaps. We will keep you and pay your expenses as long as you want to stay. You can help us in a great many ways. It is possible that Mr. Perry will go to America next fall and that will leave Mrs. Hubbard a great deal to do. You could teach her children and relieve her of that and do lots of things.

But I do want you to come to stay. The Woman's Board of the Interior in Chicago has taken the contract to send a woman to take charge of the schools and it is the very place for you. Please apply at once and see Tavie or write to her. I just must have you. I think papa would about as soon have us together as to have us so far apart.

The land has been bought for us and now we must raise the money for a house. The Board has made no grant for it and we have to raise the money extra. We shall fix a place for you in our house. Can't you raise some money for it? Out plan is to ask people or different groups of people to furnish the money for building one room and have it sort of dedicated to them. We are making our plan now with no money in sight. We have faith to believe it will come, though.

Our first shipment of goods, except the books, has just arrived, and very little is broken. The cook stove is broken in two or three places and the glass in that largest picture. That is pretty good in view of the fact that everything has to be unpacked and packed over in Samsoun. I tremble for the China dishes. There is one other thing that did not come, the cask with our wash bowls etc. The cask was broken so they kept it to pack it over. The Consular Agent looks after things as well as he can. I am anxiously waiting got the second shipment to get some more clothes. One of our union suits is there and my black skirt and wrappers etc. You knew that I did not get a single wrapper in my steamer trunk and only that old red wrapper in this shipment. Fortunately, I do not need a wrapper as much as I did.

We want you to bring us an American flag about six feet long or so. Today we have an American flag out between the Turkish flags.

Just now Bob is talking right along and kicking up both feet. He feels fine today. By the way, it is a mistaken idea to have such short dresses. It is very nice in the summer or in steam heated houses but it is just impossible to keep his feet warm. I should never advise anyone to have them so short. I write it to you so you can advise anyone that needs advice. Have them long enough to keep his feet warm.

Next week I hope to have some photographs to send you. The photographer has them now.

With lots of love, Winona.

❈

Sivas, Turkey.
Dec. 14, 1900.

My dear Polly,–

Mr. Perry wants to have his pen exercised and I will do it while my patience holds out. You deserve a good scolding for writing such a little bit of a note last time. It is very extravagant to pay five cents for such a brief note. I am sorry that these things I sent from Constantinople weren't all for you. If I find that Mrs.

Marden is glad to sell them to missionaries I will send some more. She sells them to me for just what she pays the native women for them.

Dr. Norton arrived here today on his way to Harpoot. He is to be the American Consul there if the Turkish Government recognizes him. We are invited to Dr. Jewett's tonight to meet him and over to the English Consul to take tea with him tomorrow night. Tonight I am going to leave the baby with the nurse but tomorrow night I think I shall take him along with the nurse. Mrs. Anderson asked me to bring him. I wish you could see the nurse playing with Bob. He found out yesterday that he could squeal and he squealed all day long. I should think his throat would be sore. He has some cold yet he was up only twice last night. I fed him once and the other time I had to walk the floor with him he cried so. He is really spoiled and I do not know as he will ever get over it. The nurse likes to play with him and walk him so she does just what he wants. He is just squealing now at the top of his lungs. He laughs a great deal now. He is not handsome yet.

When we were in Constantinople we sent a sofa pillow cover to Hague to be sent to you a Christmas time. I hope you got it all right. It was made in Oorfa under the direction of Miss Shattuck. I thought it was very pretty. Mr. P says to tell you that he is unable to find anything suitable to send by mail. It is very hard to send any thing from here. We cannot go to market alone because we do not know the language and the people here send by their servants. Mr. Perry's man is a young man and is not very efficient. I will keep my eyes open and when I do find anything that I can send in a letter I will.

Saturday morning – We went over to the Consul's last night and had a very pleasant and informal time. By the way, Dr. and Mrs. Jewett expect to go to America next summer to be gone four months and if you decide to come out here for good or to spend next year, it would be fine for you to travel with them. They would be able and glad to take you under their wing. Of course they would not be coming back until September but if you came to stay you would probably want to spend the summer there, anxious as I am to have you get here. The Riggs will be coming in the spring probably to Marsovan. You'd better try to please come with somebody. Miss Willard of Marsovan will be coming sometime. You would like it better to come with a man and his wife because you would be more independent. I shall be dreadfully disappointed if you do not come next summer but I do not see how you can if you are just going to spend the summer. If you come for next year you would have a fine opportunity to earn to speak French with these Swiss people. It is probable that they will not be here very much longer perhaps not more than two or three years. The orphans are getting old enough to take care of themselves. I wish I could import some of them to America for servants. The Swiss are very particular and they are well taught. Dzmroughd, Bob's nurse, is well trained. It is a new experience to have someone right around after us to clean spots off our clothes, pick up your things etc. She makes herself useful in a great many ways. Mr. P. said yesterday that he should like to have her with no special business and let her just keep herself busy. She would like to have some sewing always ready to pick up. She sits on the floor always except when she is holding Bob. They prefer that way.

Preston seems to feel very much grieved because you have not written to him. I do not quite know why he should expect you to but I presume he feels a little lonesome now that he has no regular house. He writes to us very regularly.

Our little alcohol lamp has given out and we're using one of Mr. Perry's which has a regular wick. It is much better. We want one of our own and when you find a good one, buy it. We want one on which you can set any kind of a dish. Your chafing dish will be useful, if you want to bring it. We do not need it especially. They have all kinds of arrangements here for heating things with coals.

By the way, did I tell you that we think we have found out why Bob had the colic so much? We have tried boiling his food and he hasn't had colic since. We think that we did not get it thoroughly dissolved, so when you recommend canned milk which I do heartily, advise them to boil it if the baby has colic. Please also recommend the homeopathic preparation of chamomilla for colic instead of peppermint or castor oil. Anise seed is good for wind in the stomach such as Bob used to have but it makes no impression on those dreadful pains in his bowels from which he has suffered so much. I write this to you because you will be giving advice from your wide experience, no doubt, and I want it to be good. Recommend boracic acid for everything in the way of a sore. I have used it with a little ear syringe for Bob's ear a great deal. The sore in his hand still discharges some but I do not think that it pains him any more. We feed him only once from seven or eight until six or seven in the morning. He does wake up at other times but we do not feed him. It seems too bad for you not to live with your only nephew, especially when he is so cunning. I wish you would send by mail some little white stockings, the smallest size, and the next size, two pairs each, and some of those little moccasins. He does not need them now but he will before long. He is very active and strong and I think he will learn to walk early if we let him.

Mr. Partridge went down to the boys' school this morning and has not returned. I hope nothing has happened to him. I live in constant fear of something happening all the time, although I suppose there is no danger at all. I hope you are happier than you were and that school goes better. You would find it quite a change from the way the girls live there to the way they live in this boarding school. They sleep on the floor. There is a matron who looks after them but Miss Brewer has to have a general oversight of everything. She is a very capable person in many ways but rather unfitted for school work.

I must stop and write to papa.

With lots of love, Winona.

If you can find anything made of rubber for Bob to play with so that he wouldn't hurt himself, I wish you would send it.

Sivas, Turkey.
Dec. 16, 1900.

Dear Folks at Home,–

This is mail day and I must be sure to get it in a letter to you. The mail travels the first one hundred and fifty miles by wagon and it takes three days and nights for it to get to the coast. After that it goes quite quickly. Now it will not be as regular because it is getting to be winter and the roads will be bad. We had just a little snow the other day, but only enough to whiten the ground. The mountains around are covered and look very pretty. We were invited to the American Consul's house last night to meet Dr. Norton, an American who is stopping a few days here on his way to Harpoot. We had a good time but when I go out in the evening and then have to be up with the baby, I do not get sleep enough and so feel very tired the next day. I have quite a hard cold in my head now so that makes me feel all the worse. The houses here are not built for warmth a much as the American houses and there are so many draughts that we all have a cold most of the time.

Bob has just found out that he can squeal and he squeals most of the time, now. It is too bad to have the only grand child grow up without any of his grandparents near him. You see, he is the only one on either side, and seeing we are the only married ones there isn't much prospect of a large number of grandchildren.

You know didn't you, that Mr. Partridge's sister Mary was one of the people killed in China. They have no very definite news but everything looks as though they were all killed where she was. It is dreadful. I am very sorry for her father. It must have been hard for him to lose her and have us go away about the same time.

We are invited over to the English Consul's to dinner tonight. Here and in Europe it is almost the universal custom to have lunch at noon and dinner at night. I rather like it.

We are studying hard on Armenian now. Let me write just a little and let you see how it works. [Armenian letters crossed out] I made a mistake. [more Armenian letters] It means, "I love my father and mother." It looks hard but it is not so very hard. Of course we hear it spoken all the time and that will make it easier for us to learn. I talk with you when I come home. It won't be so very long before I shall be coming home.

I must close,

With lots of love, Winona.

❁

Sivas, Turkey.
Dec. 28, 1900.

My dear Polly,

This is probably the last letter I shall write to you this century. Your letter came the day before Christmas with one from papa, one from Mrs. Northrup, and company letter from two of the Shoreham ladies. It was lovely of them to write me a Christmas letter. I think three more came by the last mail. The package of which you spoke has not come. It was all right for you to send that one but the missionaries seem to think that he would not like it if many were sent that way. Mrs. Hubbard has her Independent come in his name and Mr. Perry his Missionary Herald, but our Cong. and Outlook have come all right so far to us.

Christmas day we had a company breakfast for the missionaries here. Dr. & Mrs. J. were not invited because if we invited them we would have to invite others and there was not room but when we came into the dining room they were there. They had come over to breakfast and brought us each something. They brought me a very fine linen handkerchief & a card with Sivas flowers pressed on it. We had dinner with Mrs. Hubbard, a very nice turkey dinner. We hung up our stockings the night before and all went over to Mrs. H's before breakfast and looked at our presents. I was very generously remembered. I had a white gauze thing to put around my neck, an immense Turkish towel, a hand lamp, a box of English crackers, a beautiful bureau from Mr. P. and Mr. Perry is going to give us a rug.

Bob had two pretty pairs of socks, a string of white bone beads to bite on, a gold piece, a fine sponge.

We had callers all day long, Armenians, Turks (Dr. J's kavass and our guardsman), Greeks, English, Syrian, Americans. We had a very pleasant day but I should liked to have been with you or have you with me. Bob seemed to enjoy his Christmas very much. He is very well now indeed & gaining all the time. I hope to have a picture of him to put in this letter. It was taken in one sitting room just in front of the organ on top of which is his donkey which Mr. Peet bought at the Dardanelles of a peddler and gave to Bob. Bob is small for five months' old baby but he is not small for a baby that has been through all he has.

This picture makes him look more helpless than he is, I think but still he cannot manage his head very well. That day it was way past his feed time and the photographer fooled around a long time with him until he got tired. I am sorry his hands do not show, they are so very cunning, but he moved one hand and hid the other one. He has on his best dress, the one that you made for him. The pictures do not do him justice, of course. He is beautiful when he smiles.

I wonder if you had charge of that ten year old girl this vacation and if you did how you got along. I am glad people are beginning to see that you are of some account and that they appreciate you a little. This is my love to Aunt Polly. Robert [scribbly by Bob]

He had the pencil all himself.

He started out very well, but failed at the end.

Yes, please do send a pair of our pictures to Rev. Benjamin Swift, Orwell. Thanks ECP

[no closing]

Diary of Edward G. Partridge 1914-1915

[Inside cover] A Happy Christmas to Edward Partridge 1913 Sivas R.S. Racoubian

1914

January 1 Thursday. "Success comes in "cans"! Friends' Calendar [adult handwriting; probably Racoubian] We had 135 callers among whom were the Vali, Cipulian and two pêres.

January 2 My lesson today was Harrison. I cleaned part of the yard. A man from the Turkish Normal named Stepan came to ask to teach in our school.

January 3 Today the desks came and we thought they were our boxes. This evening the boy's had a debate about whether money is more needed or knowledge.

January 4 I did not go to church today. It was a warm day and it snowed a little. Badvelly [Badvilli] Kevorks wife came last night and today us called on her.

January 5 I began my arithmetic lessons again today. We went to the ladies room to tea and had peanut butter sandwiches.

January 6 George and I ate at the Clark's house and had plump pie. Mama is reading "Pollyanna" to me.

January 7 I went with Aunt Polly to market and I got a new electric-light. The gas exploded and tore up some of the boards.

January 8 This morning I started to trace the map of the United States. I went sleigh riding with Papa, Billy and George.

January 9 Today we bought a big dog whose name is Gurnush and payed two medjids. Once he ran away and we caught him.

January 10 I went to market with Georgie and got a coller and a chane for Gurnush. We made candy and put it into boxes for the bazaar.

January 11 We played the Sunday school game today in Sunday School. Frances got her first tooth and she is a little sick.

January 12 Papa and George and I bought a little mat, an apron, a face cloth and a big tablecloth trimmed with brown.

January 13 I bought a jar for money. I went to the first Messiah practise that I have been to. We went to the boy's school for gaghas.

January 14 Mugrditch and I made the runners of a sled. One of the runners of the sleigh broke. I went to the "Merchant of Venice" practice.

January 15 The boxes came but not the dishes. Papa ordered some irons for our sled.

January 16 Billy and I slid, I lay down and he rode on me. We had the "Merchant of Venice" and forgot our parts. I was Salerinia.

January 17 I went to the Kohoonians house and saw the boys. I sang in the Messiah concert.

January 18 They let Gurnush go without a chane. We had the Messiah again tonight. I was soprano.

January 19 Papa, George, Nazaret and I went to skate, but the snow was on it. George and I went to the school to play games.

January 20 Aunt Polly and I went to the Avazanian's to call. I played snowball with Mugerditch.

January 21 Billy, George, and I went to the Kulygian's house. Billy got tired and came home. Gurnush was out-of-doors all day.

January 22 I went to market and bought a pocket book like papa's only smaller. I payed a quarter for it.

January 23 We went to the school to see some plays. They lighted the lights of the school for the first time.

January 24 Aunt Polly finished the sum for my bicycle by giving a lira. Papa and I went out to the skating pond on horseback.

January 25 I ate at the school today. Ruth and Stephen have chicken pox. Papa made some puffed rice brittle.

January 26 Gurnush took our bag to school with us. He also brings a hat if you throw it. Papa ordered my bicycle. Aunt Polly taught the teachers better Halva.

January 27 George and I ate at the Myrigs house. Papa, and George, and I went to the ice pond but there was no skating.

January 28 George and I went to school and Gurnush came after us. Mama, Nishan eff., Aunt Polly and I worked on an example.

January 29 Papa vaccinated Billy, George, himself, and me. We went to the Dedeyan's house to tea.

January 30 Papa and George and I went skating, it was my first time. Mrs. Dedeyan and a teacher were there.

January 31 Papa, Mama, George and I went to skate this morning. In the after-noon Nishan eff., George, and I went. I can skate a little.

February 1 Miss Rice taught me this in S.S. I didn't write the purple cow; I do not know who wrote it, But this I'll tell you anyhow, I'll kill you if you quote it.

February 2 Yesterday was Zabel's George's Birthday but we celebrated it today.

February 3 We went skating but there wasn't any good ice. Tonight we went to a Parent's reception.

February 4 Mugerditch and four other boys went skating with me. The ice was the best we have had this year.

February 5 Papa, George and I went some distance on the road to the pond but turned back. There is some water I think will freeze.

February 6 Today there was a great fire in the market. We had ice.

February 7 There was good ice. Tonight we had the "Merchant of Venice" for the boys.

February 8 I went to Church today. There was ice but we couldn't skate because it was Sunday.

February 9 We skated today. George learned pretty well. The Governor of Kara Hissar died.

February 10 We put some water on the ice. Frances's hair is curling. We are preparing a play for Lincoln's birthday.

February 11 We went skating to the pond. My horse ran away. We are reading "Martha By the Day."

February 12 Today we celebrated Lincoln's birthday. We had some poems and a play.

February 13 Our ice was not good today. I played nat danag. It was a cold day today.

[February 14 no entry]

February 15 I went to Church today. Gurnush is sleeping out-of-doors.

February 16 I went to market with Mama. I got a notebook. We looked for some cordiroy.

February 17 I went to market in the stone wagon.

February 18 The two Levons and I went to skate at the pond.

February 19 I went again on the stone wagon to the skating pond.

February 20 We practiced a play about Washington. I have learned how to cross my legs on the ice.

February 21 The two Levons and I went to the pond. Parts of the time I skated [with the Levons] and part [of the time with] George. I had a music lesson.

February 22 Frances put on her short dresses today. I went to Church and to the Sunday School. I bought a "New Testament."

February 23 Today was the day of Krare[?] for Colleges. Our dishes and the school dishes came. The heifer had a calf.

February 24 In the night it rained and it is very muddy. We ate at the boy's school because they ate out of the new dishes for the first time.

February 25 Today we have a vacation. We went to a musical at the chapel. They sold things to eat.

February 26 My new trousers came. Billy has some new cloths too. We went to the boy's school to a celebration of Vartan's.

February 27 The boy's have a swing and I swing every day. We went to Rupen eff.'s house to a party.

February 28 Papa and Mama went to the concert of the Senecherinian but I played the phonograph to the boys.

March 1 Sun. I went to church. It was very rainy.

March 2 Mon. I was going to have school today but got a vacation. Papa and Nishan eff. went to Kara Hissar. We went to the orphanage.

March 3 Tues. After school I went to market and bought a pair of rubbers. Garabed eff. sent me some stamps by post.

March 4 Wed. I swung a lot today. The weather is pretty good.

[March 5]

March 6 Fri. I spilt [split] some of our new wood and in the afternoon some boys and I threw it in. I swung some too.

March 7 Sat. Levon and I ordered some stamps.

March 8 Sun. Today it hailed a lot. We are reading "T. Tembaron" [Frances Hodgson Burnett].

March 9 Mon. Some boxes came but still are in market. Our rubber boots are in them.

March 10 Tues. The boxes came to our house but we did not open them. We went to the "College Club."

March 11 Wed. I opened the boxes. Our rubber boots were very nice. I went to the market and got a ball full of rubber.

March 12 Thur. The boys were going to the feilds [fields] today but they were naughty. I finished my grammer book. I have begun on the 2nd.

March 13 Fri. I went to the yard with Hovsep and got some clothes from Miss Fowle. Our hen's are laying almost every day.

March 14 Sat. We went to the Clark's house to Mrs. Clark's birthday and ate ice cream and cake. It rained almost all day.

March 15 Sun. A letter came to the boys from Nishan eff. saying that he is in prison with the other prisoners. It is drying.

March 16 Mon. I had a examination in history on the Revolutionary War and got 86. George had one in arithmetic and got 88.

March 17 Tues. I learned some things to do in the rings. I think Dicran took his hens and roosters home.

March 18 Wed. I got a new bag for my books. Aunt Polly went to Enderes.

March 19 Thur. The pens didn't come. Georges hen was lost. It rained. We bought a feild [field] by the windmill for 190 liras.

March 20 Fri. Halil got four hens. I took one, George two and Billy one. Halil, George and I went to the horse-race.

March 21 Sat. Mikiel eff. brought his bicycle here and I went to the city. He left it here today.

March 22 Sun. I did not go to church. A telegram came and we think Nishan eff. is out of prison and is coming.

March 23 Mon. Our pens came today but only three came. I am writing with mine now.

March 24 Tues. The boys and I went to the fields. I played a lot.

March 25 Wed. We had a telegram saying, "Let Mister Wingate come."

March 26 Thur. The Wingates came but I did not go to meet them. I wrote a letter to Papa. Noemzar made a kind of bread just now.

March 27 Fri. Mr. Wingate came here today. Halil, George, and I went to the horse-race. I wrote a letter to Nishan eff.

March 28 Sat. I counted some money in the treasury. One of my waists was finished. Mr. Heck is coming here Tuesday morning.

March 29 Sun. Mr. Wingate preached at church today. Aurthor came to Sunday School.

March 30 Mon. I wore my new rubber boots for the first time. I played the violin with Nishan eff. [Nishan Bekhian, music teacher].

March 31 Tues. Mr. Heck came. Mr. and Mrs. Wingate and Aurthor came here this morning.

April 1 Wed. I didn't fool anybody. Mr. Heck thinks that Nishan eff. will get out of prison tomorrow.

April 2 Thur. I had a written lesson in history and got 90. The trial is put off until April 18. Our black cow had a calf.

April 3 Fri. I finished my history today. I went to the horse-races. Nishan eff. got out of prison.

April 4 Sat. I had a music lesson. We went over to the boy's school to a play.

April 5 Sun. I ate at the school tonight. George and Bardev found some of my stamps.

April 6 Mon. Bizar [Baidzar] found my snikers. Garabed eff.'s mother died.

April 7 Tues. We went to teachers meeting and ate ice cream and cake.

April 8 Wed. They cut down some of the trees in the yard. We went to a play of the Y.W.C.A.

April 9 Thur. I had malaria. The girls went to the fields today and I went on the horse with Halil and George.

April 10 Fri. Today is the last day of school. We are going to have Easter vacation. I went to the races.

April 11 Sat. We had ice-cream for supper. I played the phonograph to the boys.

April 12 Sun. Mr. Heck went to church. Today was Easter. I didn't go to Sunday school.

April 13 Mon. We put some eggs under my hen. I got a letter from Papa and Nishan eff. I went out to ride.

April 14 Tues. I finished making a list of my stamps. I have 80 countries and 373 stamps.

April 15 Wed. Nishan eff. is coming Friday. I played the phonograph to Mr. Heck.

April 16 Thur. We went to meet Miss Zenger and Mr. Hopf. I drove some on the road.

April 17 Fri. We went to meet Nishan eff. and Aunt Polly. He came and is very well.

April 18 Sat. Rupen eff. and Hagopos eff. planted my garden.

April 19 Sun. I did not go to Sunday School. I worked the sterioptacum for the boys.

April 20 Mon. Hamparsoon eff. had a boy whose name is "Miran."

April 21 Tues. A telegram came saying Papa is coming Thursday. I went to market but the stores were closed.

April 22 Wed. Today was Frances's birthday. We went to Yeni-Khan in a snow-storm.

April 23 Thur. We waited for Papa and he came. He went to Sivas. We went to the Church and School.

April 24 Fri. We came to Sivas in a Yaila. Aunt Polly had her party. Papa gave me a cravat.

April 25 Sat. We went to meet Mickial eff. in the pitone[?] but he didn't come. We went to a play at the school.

April 26 Sun. I didn't go to church. Papa opened George's drawer and we counted the stamps. He has 41 countries.

April 27 Mon. We had a vacation today. Zeya Pasha came to our house.

April 28 Tues. Today was my birthday. Papa gave me two neckties and a pair of cuff buttons.

April 29 Wed. Mama gave me a "lovers knot"! It is very cold.

April 30 Thur. Levon's and my stamps came. Some of them are very nice. I played football.

May 1 Fri. I went to the horse-races.

May 2 Sat. I got my stamps from Levon. I have 88 countries. We went to a play at the boy's school.

May 3 Sun. I made stamps lists. I wore my new necktie and pin.

May 4 Mon. The chickens didn't hach today. I played football with the boys.

May 5 Tues. We hitched my horse to the shovel and I drove him. I sat on his back. We worked on the tennis court.

May 6 Wed. I played football and worked on the tennis court.

May 7 Thur. I rode my horse. One of the trees has leaned out some others haven't little.

May 8 Fri. Halil and I went to the races on horseback. A horse ran away. We worked on the tennis court.

May 9 Sat. The other pasha came here today; he had a very pretty horse. We ate ice-cream tonight. It rained a lot.

May 10 Sun. I didn't go to church because I had a sore foot. I went to sunday school.

May 11 Mon. I played football. We went to Rupen eff.'s house to Monday Club.

May 12 Tues. The boys went to the fields and I went. The boxes came.

May 13 Wed. Bodvely and Miss Fowle went to Monchuluk. Nishan eff. gave me a tuning fork.

May 14 Thur. The girls went to the fields and I went. It rained.

May 15 Fri. We went to school with my horse. I went to market and I bought a watch chain and some samples for pants.

May 16 Sat. We went to hkonergooder. The Varabeds and the Vashoohi's were there. We went to "Othello" at the boys school.

May 17 Sun. Five of our "Buff Orphingtons" hatched and two are going to today.

May 18 Mon. I had a violin lesson today. We had brought the chickens up here. They are very nice. They are only six. Halil went to Khanshkal.

May 19 Tues. I had a letter from W. V. Field and he sent me some stamps. Miss Fowle came.

May 20 Wed. Halil came back. Frances walks when I make her go to Mama. She takes about three steps.

May 21 Thur. Our new cook came. She is Solakian's mother.

May 22 Fri. It rained almost all day. We went to the Sewny's house to tea. We saw their colt.

May 23 Sat. We played football in the house because it was muddy. We plastered part of the barn with the left-over carbiad.

May 24 Sun. Mickael eff. preached. Consul Davis came. It rained all day.

May 25 Mon. Consul Davis didn't go today. He ate at our house today.

May 26 Tues. We helped papa make a hen yard.

May 27 Wed. One of the chickens was lost. The first class and the second class had a match game in football. The first class beat.

May 28 Thur. We had a vacation today. We took Biazar out to ride. Papa and I went to Y.M.C.A. picnic.

May 29 Fri. Papa and I fixed some wire on top of the chicken yard. Papa, George, and I played parcheesy. Papa beat and George second.

May 30 Sat. Georgia got a lash for me. My new pants came. I had a music lesson. Another chicken was lost.

May 31 Sun. Another one of our chickens was lost. We brought a kitten from Miss Fowle's room.

June 1 Mon. We brought the Sewny's dogcart up and rode some.

June 2 Tues. We went to school in the dogcart. We put the chickens in the barn.

June 3 Wed. We went to school in the dogcart and we came home in the rain. Two of George's chickens were hatched. One out of three died.

June 4 Thur. I brought Stephen up here to ride. Nishan eff. changed the bridge and strings of my violin. We practiced my peace [piece].

June 5 Fri. We played in the water. They put in the new seats but they are not nailed. I lost my pen.

June 6 Sat. Hagonig found my pen. I played my peace [piece] in the concert. I did not succeed very well. It was kena butel.

June 7 Sun. Frances was sick today. There were nine soldiers at church.

June 8 Mon. We took the dogcart to the Sewny's house. Avni Pasha's son came and I rode horse-back with him.

June 9 Tues. I played with a tennis ball and it went into the boy's W.C.

June 10 Wed. The prep class was going to have a picnic in the garden but it rained and they had it inside. I went to it.

June 11 Thur. We invited the Armenian soldiers to a entertainment. They had a very good time.

June 12 Fri. Today was our last day of school.

June 13 Sat. I jumped 4 ½ feet poles. George put some ducks eggs under my hen. The Pierces came. They have a 19 month old baby.

June 14 Sun. The horse-races took place today and we watched them with a spy-glass. Mikiel eff. went to them.

June 15 Mon. The Pierces went. It was James's birthday.

June 16 Tues. I jumped 4 ft 8 in. We went to the girls party and play.

June 17 Wed. I went to the boy's class day.

June 18 Thur. I went to the girls class day. They had "everyman."

June 19 Fri. I went to commencement and sat by Avni Pasha's boy.

June 20 Sat. I jumped with a pole. Avni Pasha's boy came up on horse-back.

June 21 Sun. The camels came with shingles.

June 22 Mon. My bicycle came. It is small but very nice for me. Nishan eff. is being engaged to Navart.

June 23 Tues. Aunt Polly went to Constantinople with the two Nishans. My tan shoes came.

June 24 Wed. Billy got washed without crying. Muggurditch went to Enderes.

June 25 Thur. Beloian brought a bicycle and I rode with him.

June 26 Fri. I went to the Armenian hospital on my bicycle and got some quinine. Today the girls cornerstone was laid.

June 27 Sat. I rode the bicycle and played football almost all day.

June 28 Sun. Iris caught a mouse for the first time.

June 29 Mon. I went to ride with Papa, he rode his horse and I rode my bicycle.

June 30 Tues. We went to a party at the Clark's house. They gave Haiganoosh a diploma. She is going to Beyrout.

July 1 Wed. I went to Chermoog with Mikiel eff. and George.

July 2 Thur. Hovsep and I went to the yard and brought the Clarks things.

July 3 Fri. Rupen eff. went to Constantinople. I bought some fire-works.

July 4 Sat. I bought some more fire-works. We celebrated tonight.

July 5 Sun. Miss Rice came here for a lesson and she ate here too.

July 6 Mon. I wrote a letter to Muggerditch. We used the rest of the fire-works and ate ice-cream.

July 7 Tues. Today I went to Kkonoogoodoor with Michiel eff., Levon eff., and George. This evening my horse was sick. They laid the orphanage corner stone.

July 8 Wed. They took the carriage shed down and made another one. My face was swollen and I was sick.

July 9 Thur. I went with Michiel eff. to send Krikore eff. but missed him. I went on my bicycle. I bought a pump for my bicycle.

July 10 Fri. Dr. Clark did an operation on my horse. Some of the ducklings were hatched.

July 11 Sat. One of the ducklings died.

July 12 Sun. It was very hot today.

July 13 Mon. We watered the garden. I rode the bicycle with Beloian.

July 14 Tues. Mr. Young came here today. I ate in the market. I brought Encabians horse for Papa to ride.

July 15 Wed. I went to see Miss Loughridge and Miss Dwight on my bicycle. Papa went on his horse. We came home in the dark.

July 16 Thur. Mrs. Sewny, Dr. Levon Sewny], Miss Loughridge, Miss Dwight, and Miss Rice called on us. Arozian and Asghig were married.

July 17 Fri. I rode my bicycle with Armenag Beloian and his tire tore open. I went to ride with Papa and George on my bicycle.

July 18 Sat. One of the ducklings died.

July 19 Sun. We ate at Miss Rice's house. James, Stephen, Ruth, Billy, George and I. Papa showed pictures in the English meeting.

July 20 Mon. Michiel eff. and I spent all day in market. We ate cababs. We watched some government horses sold.

July 21 Tues. I went to Yene Khan with Sabel and her children and Michiel eff.

July 22 Wed. We got to Tocat and saw Aunt Polly and Nishan eff. A baby boy was born I had a baby brother born in Sivas.

July 23 Thur. We went to Yene Khan. They were wrestling there and I watched them.

July 24 Fri. We got to Sivas and I saw the baby.

July 25 Sat. Barkev and I made a kite with the help of James and George. It flys very nicely but it broke and we mended it.

July 26 Sun. A young man from Visa-Cupry I think, preached. We did not have Sunday School.

July 27 Mon. A box of fruit came from Muggerditch. We flew the kite. We went out to camp in the wagon.

July 28 Tues. We went out to camp on horseback and bicycle. There are Miss Loughridge, Miss Dwight, Miss Rice, Mrs. and Dr. Sewny.

July 29 Wed. We went to camp. Armenoohi [Armen Sharigian] is coming Saturday.

July 30 Thur. Barkev got a lantern for the kite but there wasn't any wind.

July 31 Fri. Barkev and I made a kite out of pieces of curtains.

August 1 Sat. We went to meet Armenoohi and she came. My bicycle tire tore.

August 2 Sun. We went to church and I wore my new necktie that Nishan eff. gave me.

August 3 Mon. The government gave orders that all the men from 20 to 45 yrs. should go to be registered. And were to take five days food.

August 4 Tues. Again today the government registered soldiers.

August 5 Wed. Halil went as a soldier. We almost bought a horse for me. Miss Kendall came. She has a dog.

August 6 Thur. Michiel eff. came from Tocat. Perhaps we will give the horse back because his legs are bad, three of them.

August 7 Fri. We went to Khonoorgoodoor. Michiel eff., George and I went in the wagon with my white horse.

August 8 Sat. I took a bath myself for the first time. Pilibos wants my horse for seven liras and seven liras beside horse. The government took the wagon.

August 9 Sun. The Government took Nishan eff., Michiel eff. and Dr. Levon as soldiers.

August 10 Mon. The vali called on Miss Kendall. Alabash beat Miss Kendall's dog Jack.

August 11 Tues. Pilibos sent the black horse up here. Miss Kendall went to Talas.

August 12 Wed. The Government took more than fifty wagons from Percurik. I wrote a letter to Muggerditch.

August 13 Thur. The black horse goes nicely on the wagon.

August 14 Fri. The Varbed fixed my bicycle. Pilos's men thrashed some of the wheat.

August 15 Sat. Michiel eff. came up here with a tent. The government is taking horse very strictly today.

August 16 Sun. Avni Pasha came here this morning and his boy came in the after-noon and I had to ride horse-back with him.

August 17 Mon. The ladies came down from camp.

August 18 Tues. Avni-Pasha's son came and I rode horse-back with him. His name is Muinver.

August 19 Wed. We brought the yonja in. The orphans brought some in, and we brought the rest.

August 20 Thur. We took some boards from the Orphanage to the school with the wagon.

August 21 Fri. There was an eclipse of the sun today.

August 22 Sat. Avni-Pasha's boy came and I rode Papa's horse with him.

August 23 Sun. We had Sunday School today.

August 24 Mon. Hrant and I turned the yonja so that underneath will dry.

August 25 Tues. Dr. Clark and the children and I worked on the tennis court. We had some lime brought to mark it with.

August 26 Wed. We finished the tennis court.

August 27 Thur. I learned how to play tennis some. Nishan eff. got free by being asistent pastor.

August 28 Fri. We took the yonja to the gal to thrash it.

August 29 Sat. I played tennis four times besides once with George.

August 30 Sun. I went to Church. We had Sunday school after Church. Zea-Pasha's wife is Anver Pasha's Sister.

August 31 Mon. I played tennis twice today. I got a letter from Muggerditch.

September 1 Tues. We stayed at the Mill some with our wheat. The government is going to take our workmen. They wrote their names today.

September 2 Wed. We thrashed yonja some today. I wrote a letter to Mugerditch.

September 3 Thur. We watered the tennis court and we are going roll it tomorrow.

September 4 Fri. We rolled the tennis court and marked it again. I played with Nishan eff.

September 5 Sat. I played tennis almost all day.

September 6 Sun. We had afternoon tea. The bank people came here.

September 7 Mon. Michiel eff. and I went to Yeldas Khan to meet Rupen eff. We went to Chernoog and bathed.

September 8 Tues. We found out that Rupen eff. had gone before. We caught up with them at Chiftlick.

September 9 Wed. I wrote a letter to Muggerditch.

September 10 Thur. Avni-Pasha's son came and a soldier. Halil, Muinver, George, and I went out to ride. I played tennis with him.

September 11 Fri. It was very windy. We smoked cornsilks.

September 12 Sat. I played tennis with Avni-Pasha's son.

September 13 Sun. I took Billy to Sunday School. George, Armen, and I ate hadig in our little house.

September 14 Mon. We made some bricks so to make our house bigger.

September 15 Tues. It rained almost all day. I began to read "The Adventures of Tom Sawyer."

September 16 Wed. We rolled the tennis court. I played four sets with Nishan eff. I got two and Nishan eff. two.

September 17 Thur. We took some wood from the school with the wagon. I played tennis three times.

September 18 Fri. We were going to go to Chernoog but we did not succeed. Ardashes eff.'s father died.

September 19 Sat. Michiel eff., Levon and I went to the Chiftlick on bicycles.

September 20 Sun. Meserobe and Maxood eff. had supper with us.

September 21 Mon. We were going to Chernoog but we didn't go.

September 22 Tues. We went to meet Toros. We met Miss Gage and Toros. Muggerditch came.

September 23 Wed. I went to market and got a knife for Billy and a knife for Papa and one for me. Miss Gage and Mr. Burger had supper with us.

September 24 Thur. The Varbed put chains on our knives. We played tennis Papa and I and Sanekerim eff. and Nishan eff. We beat.

September 25 Fri. I had a lesson in Algebra with the third class.

September 26 Sat. I took some wood from the school to our house. I rode the bicycle with Narbey.

September 27 Sun. It rained very little.

September 28 Mon. Toros eff. is learning to play tennis.

September 29 Tues. We had an Algebra lesson with the third class. Vorperian had supper with us.

September 30 Wed. I went to the yard for my lesson to begin. Frances has two new teeth.

October 1 Thur. It rained and was muddy. I went to study hour with the boys and learned my algebra. Miss Zenger moved to the city.

October 2 Fri. I began my history lesson with Papa. It is Monroe's Administration.

October 3 Sat. Muggerditch learned how to ride the bicycles some. We went to camp and ate cababs and grapes. I went on my bicycle.

October 4 Sun. Billy went to church for the first time. He was very good. Frances fainted away.

October 5 Mon. I had my first real Armenian lesson from Armenoohi. Billy and I ate at the girl's school. George brought a box of pansies from the Clark's house.

October 6 Tues. The Varbed and I went out on the rode with Mr. Hopf on bicycles.

October 7 Wed. George and I rose horse-back. George rode on my horse and I on Papa's horse.

October 8 Thur. Papa rode his horse around the yard and I rode my horse some and George rode some. I went to the school to study-hour.

October 9 Fri. Mama went to market and bought a clock for the kitchen and some chocolates.

October 10 Sat. Antwerp was taken by the Germans.

October 11 Sun. Nothing of importence happened.

October 12 Mon. The Wheeler Orphan money came.

October 13 Tues. George and I brought the duck home from Yeva's house. We had college club at our house.

October 14 Wed. We went out to meet Shouzian eff. but he did not come.

October 15 Thur. We went to the fields with the boys. Yegisha eff. came.

October 16 Fri. George went to market and bought two ducks. Perigian was taken to the hospital, he has tisfoyed [typhoid] fever.

October 17 Sat. It rained.

October 18 Sun. I wore my winter suit and my red necktie.

October 19 Mon. We went to Monday Club at Michiel eff's. house.

October 20 Tues. George wrote his first composition, he wrote about "ducks." I wrote one about "Traveling in Turkey."

October 21 Wed. I had my first Algebra Examination. I got 80. I went to the fields with the girls.

October 22 Thur. I rode horse back. Alfred is 3 months old today. He weighs 10 pounds and Mama took his picture with me.

October 23 Fri. I had a examination in Algebra. They tried to shoe Michiel eff's horse and he ran away. Garabed, George and I went to bazaar but came back empty.

October 24 Sat. The old teachers were invited to a picnic by the new teachers. The boys went to the fields too. It rained.

October 25 Sun. We went to the school to hear the phonograph.

October 26 Mon. George and I didn't go to school because Miss Rice is sick. The type for the printing-press came.

October 27 Tues. I found my Sheffield knife. It was in the pocket of my cordiroy pants. It was very muddy.

October 28 Wed. It rained.

October 29 Thur. I rode horse-back some. Georgie brought some slippers but they did not do for me.

October 30 Fri. We went to bazaar but there were not any ducks.

October 31 Sat. George and I went to the school to some games.

November 1 Sun. Today they had cumunion service. Tonight Senechirian eff. read "the Love Watch" in Armenian and Papa had the Steriopicon.

November 2 Mon. I took Alfred in front of me on the horse for the first time. Yeghia Perigian is better this morning. His temperature was 106.

November 3 Tues. Nishan eff. Mama and I went to market and got samples for George and me and others. I am going to have a blue suit.

November 4 Wed. I had an examination in Algebra and got 98. My horse had a stomach ache almost all day.

November 5 Thur. Nishan eff. is sick.

November 6 Fri. Yehia [Perigian] died. They had a service in the school and another at the mother church.

November 7 Sat. The post office will not take any letters that are not either French or Turkish.

November 8 Sun. Biadzar had a proposal from a Tocat man.

November 9 Mon. We had Monday Club at Michiel eff's house.

November 10 Tues. It snowed a little this morning. Biazar had a tooth pulled.

November 11 Wed. Rupen eff. took my picture splitting wood. The Varabed is having a dump cart made.

November 12 Thur. We had the childrens pictures taken. One with Frances alone and one with Billy. They were weighed too. Frances weighed 27 pds and Billy 43 ¼ lbs.

November 13 Fri. Miss Gage came from Harpoot on her way to Marsovan.

November 14 Sat. The school had a debate on whether the war is worthwhile or not. And in the evening the boarders and wether knowledge was more needed or language.

November 15 Sun. Miss Gage, Miss Rice, Miss Fowle and Mrs. Sewny ate supper with us. Miss Gage spoke at the English meeting.

November 16 Mon. I dressed Frances. She calls me ada. The English counsel of Erzuroum came here on his way home.

November 17 Tues. Major Lange ate supper with us. He is German in the Turkish army. He is going to the front. Today the College Club was at the school.

November 18 Wed. I went to market and got two watches to get one for George's birthday.

November 19 Thur. We decided one of the watches for George. Frances had her picture taken again.

November 20 Fri. Nishan eff. Mama and I went to hunt for a duck for George's birthday but we did not find it.

November 21 Sat. Our clothes came. My suit is dark blue and my over-coat is green and many colors mixed. George's suit is brown. We went to the school for games.

November 22 Sun. I wore my new clothes today.

November 23 Mon. The Clark's had a baby born. They are going to name it David. We found the duck we were looking for and are going to give it to George on his birthday.

November 24 Tues. Georgie brought some chains and I took one for George. I wrote a composition on George Rogers Clark.

November 25 Wed. Today is George's birthday. He got presents, a watch and chain from us, two geese from Apig and the Varbed and Georgie, five ducks from the teachers and one from us, two ducks from Miss Fowle, a knife from the Clark children and a knife from Miss Zenger.

November 26 Thur. Today was Thanksgiving and we ate goose and turkey at the Clarks house. The boys had some games and we went to them.

November 27 Fri. It snowed quite a little in the night. We put the geese in the calve's place and made a place for the calves.

November 28 Sat. A blacksmith came and I helped him make a iron for the dumpcart.

November 29 Sun. It was so muddy that when I came home from Sunday school I took off my rubbers and walked with my shoes.

November 30 Mon. The Monday Club was at the school.

December 1 Tues. The Varbed finished the dumpcart and we hauled some wood.

December 2 Wed. Some boys and I hauled dirt with the dumpcart.

December 3 Thur. We hauled some more dirt.

December 4 Fri. We did not have school. We finished the dirt in the corner of the front-steps.

December 5 Sat. Papa and Dr. Clark went to the Vali to see about going to Ezeroum.

December 6 Sun. We had a memorial service for Mr. Holbrook to dedicate his library.

December 7 Mon. The teachers gave a reception to the people that are going to Erzeroum.

December 8 Tues. Aunt Polly, Mrs. Sewny, Harutune Kizirian and Ardashes eff. went to Erzeroum.

December 9 Wed. Miss Zenger and Dr. Clark went to Erzeroum. We finished hauling the wood. We bought a dove.

December 10 Thur. We had a Algebra Examination in factors yesterday and I got 80. Muggerditch got 78. The government men asked for the tenth of the yondja.

December 11 Fri. I ironed my neckties. James and George and I are practising a song for Christmas.

December 12 Sat. We bought a mate for the dove.

December 13 Sun. The new dove flew away but we caught it again. A telegram came from Aunt Polly saying that they started from Enderes yesterday.

December 14 Mon. We went to the ladies room to drink tea.

December 15 Tues. Alfred was sick today.

December 16 Wed. I had a sience class with the second class. Papa is taking it.

December 17 Thur. We received Christmas cards from Nishan eff. and Krikor eff. from Switzerland.

December 18 Fri. Mama had us do as many Algebra examples as we could. I did the most, too.

December 19 Sat. Papa, George, and I went to market for Christmas. We cleaned the yard.

December 20 Sun. We got a telegram from our folks that they are going to start for Erzeroum tomorrow.

December 21 Mon. George's new shoes came. Nishan eff. gave a lecture on Mohammed.

December 22 Tues. I ate at the ladies house. I have got a bad cold.

December 23 Wed. We did up some presents for Christmas tonight.

December 24 Thur. We went to look for some doves at Hagop Varbed's house for me to give to George on Christmas.

December 25 Fri. A telegram came from the people at Erzeroum saying Merry Christmas. Tonight we fixed some ladders for a tree. We got a rabbit.

December 26 Sat. The boy's had English rhetoricals and I went to them. Our piano came from the school.

December 27 Sun. Biazar and Elmon saw David [Clark's new baby]. They like him very much.

December 28 Mon. The bank people came and called on us. Muggerditch and I fixed the holes in the tyre of my bicycle.

December 29 Tues. Halil and I went outside of the yard to ride, the first time in months.

December 30 Wed. I went to the 708 aniversity [anniversary] of the independence of the Turkish Empire. Our boys sang a song and Toros eff. spoke.

December 31 Thur. I rode the bicycle and the horse.

1915

January 1 Fri. We had about 120 or 130 callers. The vali, Savarsh Vartabed, and the Sivas bishop came.

January 2 Sat. Hagop Varabed brought the doves. They are very pretty.

January 3 Sun. We had a service at the college and Savarsh Vartabed spoke.

January 4 Mon. I heard of Sahag Vartabeds death. He was shot near Enderes. We made a cage for the doves.

January 5 Tues. The little dove died. Alfred twists his nose up when he laughs and looks very funny. I am reading Yeghisha Vartanans in my lesson.

January 6 Wed. We had a test in Algebra.

January 7 Thur. We got word that Dr. Levon died of tifus in a village near Tortoom[Ezeroum]. Mrs. Sewny and Aunt Polly took care of him.

January 8 Fri. Alfred slept seven hours today.

January 9 Sat. Michiel eff. and I developed some films in the bathroom.

January 10 Sun. Papa preached today.

January 11 Mon. I rode Michiel eff's horse. He ran but I tried to stop him and one ring broke bit I stopped him with one rein.

January 12 Tues. The school and our house made pakkarch.

January 13 Wed. We went to the school to celebrate Gaghant. We had candy and I passed some pictures around to the boys.

January 14 Thur. George bought five doves that we are going to give to the sons of the servants. Nazeli, Biazar, George and I went to the girls school for Gaghant.

January 15 Fri. We had a reception for the servants and gave them presents. We gave some doves for presents. I fell down from a pen in the stable and cut my hand pretty badly.

January 16 Sat. I went to the hospital and had my hand done up. We had the messiah for the boys of the lower schools.

January 17 Sun. I played the phonograph at the messiah consert. My hand aches some. Our small cow had a calf. It is a female.

January 18 Mon. Enver Pasha came. We had games at the school.

January 19 Tues. Today was the Armenian Christmas. Only Papa went calling. We played football.

January 20 Wed. The government is going to take from 33 to 40 as soldiers. I played football almost all day. I went to the Hospital for my hand.

January 21 Thur. The police took some horses from Hoktar. Yeva came to wash clothes. It was two months since she came last.

January 22 Fri. We had our horses shod. My horse kicked Garabed's hand while he was being shod.

January 23 Sat. The government is going to take from 20 to 45 as soldiers. The second class came to our house and Michiel eff. explained about light. We had coffee and cake.

January 24 Sun. I did not go to church. Some villagers brought boulghour from their villages for the army.

January 25 Mon. We began school. They are putting wire on the lower end of the field.

January 26 Tues. Today was Miss Rice's birthday. We had a surprise party for Miss Rice.

January 27 Wed. Hagopos eff. came up here.

January 28 Thur. We got a letter from Aunt Polly.

January 29 Fri. Almost all of the bretheren went to be nurses to get away from soldier duty. We are going to take the house by the hospital to put sick soldiers.

January 30 Sat. I played football in the moonlight. Yetvart brought their colt up here and I rode it.

January 31 Sun. It rained a little.

February 1 Mon. I finished Geography today. It snowed some.

February 2 Tues. A man came from market and fixed my bicycle.

February 3 Wed. We were invited to the Clark's house to eat dinner.

February 4 Thur. I am writing a composition about Raphael. The closet in the lower hall fell on Billy and bruised his head and leg.

February 5 Fri. A cernel [colonel?] came to put his son in our school I think. They are cleaning the new building that is going to be a hospital.

February 6 Sat. Mushegh Arabian and Stavak had a fight together and the Facalty is trying to decide a punishment for them this evening.

February 7 Sun. I lost my lovers-knot.

February 8 Mon. Some soldiers came to the new hospital. I found my lovers-knot in the kitchen.

February 9 Tues. Muggerditch and I rode the bicycle some.

February 10 Wed. We got a letter from Aunt Polly. She writes that she is alone in the hospital with 80 sick officers. We made pagharch.

February 11 Thur. Today they took the bandage off of my hand. The boys celebrated Vartan's day.

February 12 Fri. We played football almost all day. Michiel eff's horse ran away but he went into the barn.

February 13 Sat. We danced with the boarding school boys for para gentan [Poon Paregentan, the last Sunday before the beginning of Great Lent]. We played football some.

February 14 Sun. Mushegh Arabian went to Gurun because his father is going to be a soldier.

February 15 Mon. We went to supper at the badvelly's house and after supper we stayed to Monday Club.

February 16 Tues. School began today. The water in the stable was left open and it ran to almost the horses places. The doves got wet too but we dried them.

February 17 Wed. We went to the river to skate. The ice was not very good. We saw some guinea-pigs at the new hospital stable.

February 18 Thur. George wrote a letter to Aunt Polly in lesson time, and James wrote to his father.

February 19 Fri. It rained a little. Zahre Levonian died. He had typhus and threw himself out of the window in the Armenian hospital.

February 20 Sat. George's chicken with a top knot laid its firts [first] egg today. The thing that Michiel eff. was going [to] send came. It is a young pig.

February 21 Sun. We watched the pig some.

February 22 Mon. I rode horse-back some. The Varghbeds and badvelli and the ladies and Mrs. Clark and her children came to and ate supper here for Washington's birthday.

February 23 Tues. I went to market but did not buy anything.

February 24 Wed. I went to market again today and I got a knife for myself and one for Mama and also a pair of suspenders. Miss Zbinden and a nurse came.

February 25 Thur. Twelve new pens came form America, George took one of them and Papa took another one. George's white dove laid an egg.

February 26 Fri. One hen began to lay today but we don't know which one it is.

February 27 Sat. The doves laid the second egg today. I rode horse-back with Papa some. Some Russian prisoners came here.

February 28 Sun. We got news that Boghos has died, and also that Meserob Vartanian has been taken prisoner by the Russians.

March 1 Mon. Today was day-of-prayer for Colleges. Toros eff. and Rupen eff. spoke at the big meeting in the College. Mama rode my horse a little. George brought the pedometer.

March 2 Tues. A man came to see Biadzar that has been to the war. He is wounded in four places he says. Papa rides his horse outside of the yard now.

March 3 Wed. My Buff Orphington laid its first egg today. We found some inside tyres for my bicycle in market.

March 4 Thur. The Varbed and I went to market and bough the tires.

March 5 Fri. One of George's ducks died.

March 6 Sat. The bicycle Varbed came and put a tire in the outer tire. I rode my bicycle some.

March 7 Sun. I made some fudge with the help of Biadzar and George and it turned out very nice.

March 8 Mon. Papa made an incubator but we have not tried it yet. The black cow had a calf. It is male.

March 9 Tues. Two of the men nurses resigned and are going to pay bedel.

March 10 Wed. I had a test in Algebra and I got 100.

March 11 Thur. I went to the yard twice on my bicycle.

March 12 Fri. It was very windy. We rode horse-back.

March 13 Sat. One of the geese laid an egg. It is very large.

March 14 Sun. We had an English service with the sterioptacun.

March 15 Mon. Six men were hung today.

March 16 Tues. Frances was sick today.

March 17 Wed. Today the geese laid an egg but I dropped it and it broke.

March 18 Thur. I am reading a book which is called "Don Quixote." We invited three doctors to supper but one did not come.

March 19 Fri. Some Turkish boys came under the wire and papa whipped them. I took Frances on the bicycle. A telegram came from Aunt Polly. She is at Erzinjan.

March 20 Sat. The little doves were hatched today. The boys bathed in the new bath in the cellar.

March 21 Sun. One of George's ducks died.

March 22 Mon. The Russia-Armenian doctor died.

March 23 Tues. Another one of the Russians died. A boy came and I rode the bicycle a little with him.

March 24 Wed. We got a telegram from Erzinjan saying that Miss Zenger has died.

March 25 Thur. The Russian prisoner with a big mustach died. We got a letter from Aunt Polly.

March 26 Fri. Toros eff. and Rupen eff. went to Enderes to bring Aunt Polly.

March 27 Sat. I rode the bicycle with Muggerditch and some with George. We put the goose to hatch on eight eggs.

March 28 Sun. I made some fudge.

March 29 Mon. Frances was sick today. One of the little doves died.

March 30 Tues. A telegram came that Aunt Polly is starting from Erzinjan today.

March 31 Wed. Easter vacation began. It rained some today.

April 1 Thur. We played in the cellar of the school. We took a bath in the boys bathroom. It is very nice.

April 2 Fri. We let the doves out and they flew some. I have a very bad cold.

April 3 Sat. A telegram came saying that Aunt Polly is going to start from Enderes today.

April 4 Sun. Aunt Polly is coming tomorrow. We sang an Easter song at the English service.

April 5 Mon. Michiel eff. the Varbed, Muggerditch, Narbei and I went to meet Aunt Polly on bicycles. Muggerditch and Narbei stayed at Gavra.

April 6 Tues. Miss Rice and Miss Fowle took supper with us. Muggerditch did not come from Gavra today.

April 7 Wed. The Vali promised Papa two vesicas for horses.

April 8 Thur. The Vali came to call on Aunt Polly.

April 9 Fri. We had a test in Algrebra.

April 10 Sat. A dove came by our doves but we made it go away.

April 11 Sun. We ate ice-cream.

April 12 Mon. I went to market with Toros eff. and also to parts of the government. There was a lecture today. Yeghishe eff. spoke.

April 13 Tues. We went to meet Dr. Clark. There were 15 horsemen, 2 Yiaylas, one bicycle and one donkey. I rode my horse.

April 14 Wed. We chalked out a game on the floor and played. The big calves were lost but they found them.

April 15 Thur. We went to market and bought some clothe for trousers. The blind duck died.

April 16 Fri. Papa made junket. It rained some. We changed the place of the doves. We made some nests for the hens.

April 17 Sat. I got the bicycle from Varbed's house and rode it some.

April 18 Sun. I had an Examination in Sunday-school.

April 19 Mon. They almost put Toros eff. in prison.

April 20 Tues. The boys went to the fields and George and I went on bicycles.

April 21 Wed. This evening Dr. Kazakos died in our hospital.

April 22 Thur. Today was Frances's birthday. She is two years old. It rained some. The doves laid one egg.

April 23 Fri. Papa and George put my old hen to set on 9 Buff Orpington eggs and 5 of her own.

April 24 Sat. The doves laid the other egg. Mrs. Sewny ate supper with us.

April 25 Sun. Michiel eff. and Armen who are newly engaged ate supper here. They had a memorial service for Miss Zenger and Dr. Levon Sewny at the College.

April 26 Mon. Halil's small son died. He was 1 ½ years old. It rained a lot.

April 27 Tues. We had a holiday because of the Sultan's birthday. The boys had a holiday too.

April 28 Today was my birthday. I got three liras from Papa, Mama, and Aunt Polly. Rupen eff. gave me Arabian nights. Papa also gave me a saddle.

April 29 Thur. Yesterday Miss Rice and Miss Fowle gave me an Armenian Bible but I didn't know it till today. The missionaries took supper here.

April 30 Fri. I gave Apig four of the Buff Orpington's eggs.

May 1 Sat. The Varbed bought a bicycle for me for 5 liras.

May 2 Sun. The little white Constantinople hen laid its first egg and Papa set the big white hen.

May 3 Mon. The goose is hatching chickens. Alfred got his first tooth and we celebrated it in Monday Club.

May 4 Tue. The white cow had a calf. The gosling died.

May 5 Wed. Senecherim eff. and I worked on the tennis court to fix it. Two chickens were hatched.

May 6 Thur. Five more chickens were hatched. It was offal cold.

May 7 Fri. One of the ducks died.

May 8 Sat. We took a bath today.

May 9 Sun. I was sick and did not go to church or Sunday-school. Mrs. Sewny took supper here.

May 10 Mon. We went to the ladies to tea. Billy and I went on horseback. I found a hole in my bicycle.

May 11 Tues. I was sick all day. Mama made some fruit cake.

May 12 Wed. One of the little doves was hatched. Senecherim eff. and I marked the tennis court.

May 13 Thur. I played tennis a lot. It was a holiday on account of Hampartsoom.

May 14 Fri. Twelve chickens were hatched today.

May 15 Sat. We hatched a chicken but we are afraid that it will die. My horse ran away with the dumpcart.

May 16 Sun. A kitten was born. The other little dove is going to hatch I think because it was cracking the shell. The chicken is still alive.

May 17 Mon. I had a violin lesson with Yervant eff. Michiel eff. tried to fix the tennis racket but it is not very good.

May 18 Tues. I played 88 games of tennis.

May 19 Wed. I played two sets of tennis with Nishan eff. and beat him in both. We had a test in Algebra and I got 85.

May 20 Thur. I played two sets of tennis with Nishan eff. and I got one and he got one. I played a lot besides that.

May 21 Fri. We played tennis with Dr. Clark and Armen.

May 22 Sat. Papa fixed the racket that had a hole in it and we helped him. The brown duck died.

May 23 Sun. Two of the white hen's chickens were hatched. It hailed some and rained some.

May 24 Mon. Seven more of the white hen's chickens were hatched. Three doves came by our doves but we made them fly away.

May 25 Tues. The dogs ate two of the older chickens.

May 26 Wed. Nishan eff. beat me two sets. One of the setting hens died of lice.

May 27 Thur. Papa hatched eight chickens.

May 28 Fri. Mama played tennis.

May 29 Sat. It rained all day so we couldn't play tennis.

May 30 Sun. It did not rain any today.

May 31 Mon. We played tennis but in the evening it rained.

June 3 Thur. The hawk took two of our chickens.

June 4 Fri. I played tennis some.

June 5 Sat. Papa set the topknot hen on some eggs. I played two sets of tennis with Nishan Eff. I got one and he got the other.

June 6 Sun. Miss Suroohi and Miss Zbinden ate here.

June 7 Mon. The boys had a concert.

June 8 Tues. The boys went to the [?] and I went too. I played some tennis too.

June 9 Wed. Papa taught me to play Croquet a little.

[June 10]

June 11 Fri. Dr. Maksood came and said that he was going to be engaged.

June 12 Sat. I hauled the Clarks things up here as they are going to come here.

[June 13]

June 14 Mon. Swarms of flying grasshopper came here. The government gives six piastres an oke for collecting them.

June 15 Tues. Today was James' birthday and George gave him a knife.

June 16 Wed. Today the government took almost everybody to prison. They took Michiel eff. too.

June 17 Thur. We got word from Michiel eff. that he is well.

June 18 Fri. Mama and I beat Papa and Armen a set.

June 19 Sat. I played tennis almost all day.

June 20 Sun. Only a few old men, some soldiers and some women went to Church.

June 21 Mon. The doves hatched one or two little ones but we do not know how many.

June 22 Tues. We had our hair cut.

June 23 Wed. The girls began their vacation. We had an examination in Algebra.

June 24 Thur. The Varbed put a new tyre inside George's bicycle's front tyre so we can ride with one another.

June 25 Fri. I played two sets of tennis with Nishan eff. but I got beaten.

June 26 Sat. They put gendarmes at the gate. They caught the Varbed and took him to prison.

June 27 Sun. They let the Varbed go.

June 28 Mon. The teachers bought some cherries and I ate some with them.

June 29 Tues. We saw a pretty good bull.

June 30 Wed. The German nurses from Erzinjan came up here.

July 1 Thur. We got word that the Armenians of Harpoot have been exiled.

July 2 Fri. The government is going to exile the Armenians of Sivas. Everybody is bringing his money and jewelry to us.

July 3 Sat. We bought some donkeys for the exiles.

July 4 Sun. We celebrated the fourth in Sunday school.

July 5 Mon. The first exiles started.

July 6 Tues. Everybody bring their chickens to us. We bought a team of horses and a ox cart for 29 liras for Aunt Polly to go to Moosool with.

July 7 Wed. The protestants, the teachers and all our people went.

July 8 Thur. There is hardly nobody on the place and we are lonesome.

July 9 Fri. We are getting ready to go to America.

July 10 Sat. Roofat is going to buy my bicycle for three liras.

July 11 Sun. This is my last day in Sivas. We are going tomorrow at ten o'clock. We have three yialas and a common wagon.

July 12 Mon. We were going to go today but the versicas were delayed. I went to the prison and saw Michiel eff.

July 13 Tues. We started today for Khanba.

July 14 Wed. We stayed at Gamareg khan.

July 15 Thur. We came to Doozlasar khan.

July 16 Fri. We reached Talas and some of the Missionaries came to meet us. They took us to the Wingate's house.

July 17 Sat. We stayed in Talas today. We went to a party at the Compound.

July 18 Sun. We stayed at the Wingate's house today also.

July 19 Mon. We started from Talas. Mrs. Sewny started for Sivas.

July 20 Tues. We came to a very bad khan and we slept on the roof.

July 21 Wed. We came to a khan that was full of fleas.

July 22 Thur. We got on a train at Tchai-Havi. It was Alfred's first birthday.

[last entry in the diary]

Diary of Winona G. Partridge 1915

[Handwritten inside front cover]

June 16 Michael Eff imprisoned

July 5 Deportation began

July 7 Our people sent

July 13 We left Sivas

July 17 Reached Talas

July 19 Left Talas

July 24 Reached Constantinople

July 29 Left Constantinople

Aug. 1 Reached Athens

Athens, August 7, 1915

My other diary was left in a khan. Mrs. Sewney was going to try to find it but of course I cannot hear whether she did or not.

We left Sivas July 13, six days after our people were deported. We had made almost no preparation because those last days were taken up with changing money, receiving jewels etc. etc. We were so tired and sleepless that we could hardly do anything anyway.

We found three spring wagons with Turkish drivers and also one load wagon.

The khans were dreadful, hot, buggy, etc. The first two days my knee was so lame I could not move without a great deal of pain. The next day my knee was all right but I had lumbago in my back. When we got to Talas it seemed best for us to stay two days to get rested. We were royally entertained at the Wingate's and the ladies too did everything possible for us. Mrs. Sewny was there but started back to Sivas the day we left Talas.

On Monday we left Talas and traveled three days and a half to the railroad. We had difficulty all the way getting milk for the baby but we had a little condensed milk that we got from the orphanage and we used that when we were obliged to. Alfred ate any kind of milk that was given to him, but Frances refused entirely to drink anything. The last day at the khan the drivers brought us about six okes [one oke equals 0.75 liters] of milk thinking that we could not use so much but we gave them a cup apiece and used every bit of it.

146

The train was dreadful. We traveled night and day at the rate of about seven or eight miles an hour changing cars twice at midnight. We had one apartment for five grown people and five children so that when we got the children laid down there was hardly room to sit-up. We learned to sleep pretty well sitting up straight.

At last we reached Constantinople and as they had received no news of our coming and had provided no place for us we went to the Hotel Bristol. It was quite a comfortable hotel, only our rooms were on the fourth floor so the climbing stairs was difficult. We had a great many callers, Armenians who wanted to ask about people in the interior. We told the story of the imprisonment and the deportation an endless number of times. What a sad story!

We left Constantinople July 29th in the morning and arrived at Dedeaghadj [Dedeagach; renamed Alexandroupoli, Greece in 1920] early the next morning. There was not a single hotel where we could get in but one hotel keeper very graciously allowed us to sit out in front and make ourselves as comfortable as possible. We went in the steamer "Byzantium" just after noon, where we had lunch. The food on that steamer was very good but we could not stay in our stateroom even half an hour on account of the heat. It was infested with rats too, besides being dirty. We stayed on deck day and night. We managed to get hold of three steamers chairs, so that Mr. P., Edward, and Armen slept in them. Then we put the four other children on the sofas in the ladies sitting room and Nazeli and Baidzar lay down there and went to sleep. I was obliged to stay by the baby and there was no place to lie down so I was obliged to sleep sitting up for two nights more.

All went pretty well the first day and night and the next day we were stopped by an English Cruiser. An officer came aboard and investigated our cargo, then sent a wireless to a higher officer so we had to wait several hours for the answer. When it came the orders were to take us two hours distance to a fort where there were two torpedo boats. There a higher officer came aboard and after due investigation decided that we were innocent and let us go. On account of this delay, we reached Athens in the evening of August 1st instead of the morning.

Here we came to the Hotel Alexandra where we are quite comfortable. There is one man who speaks English and is very kind to us. On the steamer we became acquainted with an Armenian woman, Mrs. Bashbazirgian and her two daughters, and a young Armenian man, Mr. Nasibian, who are also going to America.

Our greatest difficulty is that Frances eats almost nothing and we cannot tempt her with anything.

We have been so tired out here that we have done almost no sightseeing. Edward and George and Armen went with Mr. P. to the Acropolis, the stadium, etc. Tomorrow perhaps some of us will go to the Museum. We expect to sail Tuesday on the Greek Steamer, Constantine the Great.

Here we met Dr. Bliss, President of the American University in Beyrout and Dr. Christie of Tarsus came with us from Constantinople. He is going to America but by way of England.

On the journey here, the three Armenian girls were sick and also our three youngest children, vomiting constantly. Edward and his father were a little affected but George and I were all right. Only the problem was how to take care of three sick babies at once. We lived through that. Now let's see what the next stage will be.

Auburndale, Mass Sept. 5, 1915.

From Athens we came to New York without accident. We had a good journey in some respects. The sea was not very rough and the children were not sick. Only Baidzar was a little sick but she did not stay in bed. We met some pleasant people on the boat, Mrs. Bashbazirgian and her daughters, Mr. Nasibian and at first several Americans were with us but afterwards changed to first class, Mrs. Wilfred Post, Mrs. Bedell, Mrs. Roundal, Dr. Young.

The steamer was very poorly managed but we stood it for fourteen days. Nazeli and Baidzar were third class but stayed with us all day. They would not let them get off with us but took them to Ellis Island. There, much to our surprise, they would not let Nazeli out because she was only fifteen and the law is that they cannot be given to anyone but a near relative and we were not relatives. They kept Baidzar to take care of Nazeli and were going to send them back. We appealed to the emigration department in Washington and after five days they released them without a bond which is unprecedented, they say.

When we landed Mr. Partridge and Edward stayed in the custom house to get the trunks out but Mr. Nasibian took us to the Park Ave. Hotel. We were dirty and tired, not fit to go to the table or to go to a restaurant so we ordered a lunch brought to our room. We had shredded wheat biscuit, cream, bananas, rolls, coffee and cocoa and our bill was $3.00. We understood from that that we could not afford to take any meals in the hotel, and after that we went out in two divisions to a restaurant, usually to the "standard lunch," on Fourth Ave. near the hotel which was a very good place.

We stayed there until Friday and during that time we saw Miss Wheeler and her mother and a good many Armenians, Mariane and Horcbaden[?], Berghosian, Rebecca and Antaran Racoubian, Harootune Raphaelian and his wife, Dicran Der Hachadoorian and his sister, Hovhannes Jedidian, and lots of others whom I do not remember by name.

From New York we came to Auburndale to stay in the Missionary house a few days. We are very comfortable here in four rooms on the third floor. Quite a number of missionaries from Turkey are here, Mrs. Browne, Mrs. Hoover, Mrs. Emrick, Mrs. White and two daughters and George. Dr. and Mrs. Scott are taking charge of the Home. Everything is very nice. The food is tasty, there are plenty of kinds but the amount is very small. I do not see how these girls and boys can live on so small an amount of food.

We have found a house in Oberlin and expect to go there this week. We have had a good many callers here, mostly Armenians, Levon Jarelezian and his sister, Sahag and Zarek Sahagian, Nichan Tonmagian, Kevork Vartenarian and others whom I do not remember so well.

Mr. Partridge and Edward went to Wellesley Hills this morning and this afternoon to Andover, and Armen went to an Armenian picnic in Boston. George went with her.

Oberlin, Sept. 26.

We came to Oberlin about two weeks ago where we were met by Capt. Garland who conducted us to the Irving Metcalf Bungalow as our new home. It is a most attractive little house, having six rooms down stairs and one upstairs. It is lighted with electricity and gas both, has a gas range and even a gas furnace.

Our neighbors are Mrs. Wilmot Metcalf, Mr. Todd, Mr. Husted and a little farther away, Prof. and Mrs. Lyman. I was invited there to supper last night with Mr. James and his mother and Mr. Cady and his sister. Mr. James and Mr. Cady have both been tutors in Marsovan. So far my callers have been Mr. and Mrs. Irving Metcalf, and Mrs. Wilmot Metcalf, Prof. and Mrs. Root, Mrs. Prince-Shaw, Mrs. Giles

Brown and Miss Lewis, Miss Marion Metcalf, 1st Church visitor, Miss Hosford, 2nd Church visitor, Mr. Williams, former missionary to China, Mr. Louis Lord, Mrs. Haskell, Dr. Greene, and perhaps others whom I do not remember.

Edward has entered the High School and is in the Freshman class. George entered the third grade but was promoted to the fourth. Billo goes to the kindergarten. I do not know how he gets along with the little English he knows but he does some way.

We had a letter from Polly saying that she could only go as far as Malatia with the deputation or the deportation and then she was turned back. It seems that the teachers were separated from the crowd and I do not where they went. Michael Eff. has been sent away from the prison but we do not know were. When shall we have definite word?

Oberlin, Oct. 11, 1915.

Other letters from Turkey confirm the suspicion that the teachers and servants and at least some of the other men were separated from the crowd at Hockin Khan, except Nishan and Toros who in some way stayed with the women. Now it is three months since our people left Sivas and I am afraid there is nothing left by this time. We wait for news all the time but we know that probably we shall get no good news for a long time. After months perhaps we shall begin to hear of one or another who managed to live through the long journey but not many, I fear.

Alfred is very independent in walking now. It is about two weeks since he really began. Of course he falls a good many times a day but he is so fat that he seldom gets hurt. Billo is learning quite a little English, but he is crazy over a velocipede that belongs to the boy next door, and he goes and gets it and rides off every chance he gets without saying anything to anyone. I think we shall have to get him one in self defence.

Last night we attended a lecture by Prof. Shaff of Western Theological Seminary on John Huss, it being the 500th Anniversary of his martyrdom. The Armenians are being martyred by the thousand, and perhaps 500 yrs. later the world will honor them.

Dec. 31 – The last day of the year.

We hoped by this time that some good news would come from Turkey but nothing good yet. Today a postal from Nishan Bekhian in Geneva says that Polly writes Nov. 4th that she hears more or less from this one and that one but none of our people write. They are supposed to be in Haran (Oorfa) or near there. She is very, very busy, cannot describe all her labors but is mostly engaged with sick soldiers. We are hoping every day for direct news from her, have had nothing for six weeks.

The Talas Protestants who with the Catholics were left when the others were deported are now being deported to Aleppo, or that is the report from Mr. Wingate, who wrote to Hranosh Boyagian's brother.

Such a year as this has been, war, typhus, fear, hanging, torture, imprisonment and deportation to the desert of our best friends, people whom we have known and loved for fifteen years, people whom we know and love more than most of our relatives, refined, educated, honorable, lovable friends. How can we bear the thought that they are enduring such suffering and we cannot help them.

Our children are in good health. Edward is doing very well in the High School, in the Freshman class, marks, Latin 99, English, Manual Training, Physiology. He is better in health than he has ever been before, but I wish he were a little more thoughtful with the other children. He has made some friends among the boys, Hubert Giles, Arthur Martin, Sidney Gulick, Paul Delaforte, and Norman Metcalf. There were others, I suppose, but these are the ones that I hear most about. He goes sliding with the boys and is very much amused that the boys want to take girls with them. We ordered skates for both Edward and George for Christmas but they have not come so they could not skate in vacation, but they have three sleds so they can slide.

George is doing well in the fourth grade. His best friend is Carroll Shaw. They were invited by a college student who has been teaching their Sunday School class to go on a hike today but afterwards he changed his mind and took them sliding and then invited them to his house to eat doughnuts and drink cocoa. We got up early to get George off on the 7:28 car and then when it was given up I thought George would be very much disappointed but he made the best of it and had a good time. He has a very happy disposition but rather a fiery temper.

Billo is just dear little Billo, as usual, naughty often but lovable always, very shy with strangers, very fond of his mother, very loving with Frances and Alfred, although often getting into spats with Frances. His best friend is Robert Todd who lives next door and also goes to Kindergarten. His father and I went to a Christmas tree in the Kindergarten and Billo had made a paper candy basket and candy for me and a clay dish for his father. His teacher, Miss Haynes, is very sweet and lovely.

Frances, the little girl is a treasure, but likely to be spoiled, although Alfred is so near her that she did not have her share of babyhood. She is still a baby and often shares my lap with Alfred. She is learning English with Billo.

Alfred is the pet of the household as the baby always is. He is saying words like [Armenian](give) [Armenian](milk) etc. He is very quick to learn and very, very cute. His grandfather and grandmother who are here think he is about perfect. He has seven teeth, having just cut his first double tooth. He is very fond of his bath and when we speak of a bath or he hears the water running he begins to smack his lips and go towards the bathroom.

My father is seventy years old but is very well, would not seem old at all if he could see better. I want him to be fitted to far seeing glasses. They both [stepmother Frances Packard] seem to be very happy and we are glad to have this long visit with them.

About five months of our furlough is past. I wonder if in seven months it will be evident what we shall do for the rest of our lives. The outlook is very discouraging. The war seems likely to continue indefinitely.

Diary of Ernest C. Partridge 1915

Ward's Trade Mark A Line A Day, Samuel Ward MFG Co Boston

Flyleaf:

  Ernest C. Partridge
  94 South Cedar,
  Oberlin, Ohio
  Sivas, Turkey

[January 1–June 15: No entries. Diaries prior to leaving Turkey were lost.]

June 16 Michael Eff imprisoned.

July 1 Armenians told they are to be deported.

July 7 Polly went out on the road with the Protestants, teachers, pupils, etc.[to Malatia]

July 13 We left Sivas for America taking with us Armen, Nazeli & Baidzar.

July 15 Reached Talas. Guests at the Uringater.

July 20 Reached Ooloo Kishla about 9AM and took the train at 3PM for Constantinople.

July 21 Elizabeth Curtiss 8yrs. July 21/17

July 22 Reached Constantinople about 5PM. Went to Bible House, no word recd from us to Hotel Bristol in Pera to stay. Memoranda: S[ivas]–OK[Ooloo Kishla] 235m OK–Con 600 Cosa[Constantinople]–NY

August 1 Left Constantinople for Athens about this date.

August 25 Reached New York on "Constantine" [Joseph Constantine Shipping Co had many ships.] from Piraeus. Staying at Park Ave Hotel.

August 26 New York. Armenians at Gotchnag Rooms.

August 29 Went to Auburndale for a few days till we decide where to settle.

August 31 Watertown Armenians (1) [first of numbered speaking engagements].

September 5 Morning Wellesley Hills church (2), Evening Andover Union Service at Old South (3).

September 11 About this date went to Oberlin to settle in Metcalf bungalow.

September 15 Evening train Oberlin to Chicago. Got in about 7 and went at once to Conference. (323m)

September 16 Training Conference Chicago Beach Hotel (4) Evening Cong supper twelve Miss[ionaries] (6).

September 17 Continue (5).

September 19 A.M. Wellington Ave (7) (8). Evening 3rd Oak Park (9).

September 20 Cong. Minister Meeting (10).

September 22 Woman's Meeting Maywood Church (11), Evening Wilmette Ch (12).

September 24 W.B.I. Meeting (13).

September 26 La Grange (14). PM 500 [attendees] Armenian Chicago Commons (15). Evening Berea Ch (16).

September 27 Lunch with Chicago Com of 60.

September 28 Riverside Rally Pres. Exis Mch (17).

September 29 Morgan Park (18).

September 30 Washington Park (19).

October 3 AM 2nd Oak Park (20) 12:10 1st Oak Park Naris[?] classes (21), 7:30 Brookfield (22).

October 5 South Side Assoc Auburn Park (23).

October 6 Heard Dr David at Sem Opening.

October 7 West Side Association (24).

October 9 Dinner & Evening with Prof Walker 5223 Dorchester Ave.

October 10 Hinsdale (25). Evening 52nd Ave Austin (26).

October 11 Visit to Gary schools.

October 12 Visit to Swift Stock Yards. Evening N.W. Union Volunteers (27).

October 13 New First Church PM (28).

October 14 Chicago Convention Blu M. (29).

October 17 New England Ch Men's club (30), Austin (31).

October 19 Oak Park Com. Sch of R Ed "Bible bands outside of Palestine" (32).

October 20 Oak Park 1st ch (33), Sleeper for Oberlin (323 m)

October 21 Reached Oberlin at 9:28.

October 22 Left on 4:55 for Brooklyn & New Haven.

October 24 AM South Church Brooklyn (34), PM Flatbush (35).

October 26 Board Meeting (36).

October 27 Left New Haven for Oberlin via Springfield Sleeper.

November 4 1915 Second Church Oberlin (37).

November 5 Started Cleveland Campaign Conneaut [Ohio] (38).

November 7 2nd Asthtabula (39), Geneva (40), 1st Ashtabula (41).

November 8 Congregational Union Cleveland (42).

November 9 Andover Union Meeting 16° (43).

November 10 Elm St. Youngstown (44).

November 11 Jefferson (45); guest of Goodrichs.

November 12 Austinburg (46); Guests at Academy dinner with Mooney's mother and sister.

November 13 Madison (47) guest over night at parsonage.

November 14 Painesville Morning Service (49), alone SS (48), dinner at parsonage. Evening Dennison Ave Cleveland (50) to Oberlin.

November 15 Burton, pastor away (51). Night at Mrs Smith's.

November 16 Chardon (52).

November 17 Hudson (53); guests at parsonage.

November 18 Tallmadge (54); guests at parsonage.

November 19 Kent (55).

November 20 Cuyahoga Falls (56).

November 21 Ravenna (59), SS (58). Evening West Akron (59) with Bauer.

November 22 Kent Normal School (60), Evening Canton (61), Night at Hotel, Niles.

November 23 Garrettsville (62); guests at parsonage.

November 24 Euclid Ave Cong Ch (63). Home to Oberlin.

November 25 Thanksgiving 1st Ch Oberlin (64).

November 26 Chagrin Falls (65).

November 28 Highland, Cleveland (66) Hough Ave (67).

November 29 Archwood Men's League (68).

November 30 Amherst Union Club (69).

December 1 Grace Ch Cleveland social at parsonage (70).

December 3 Mt. Zion Cleveland (71).

December 5 Lakewood (72). Dinner at Whipples. Jones Road Welsh (73).

December 8 LMM [Layman's Missionary Movement]. Cong Conf Cleveland Medical Missionaries (74).

Diaries of Winona & Ernest Partridge 1916

Flyleaf:
>*"Winona G. Partridge,*
>*Christmas, 1915.*
>*Oberlin, Ohio"*

January 1 Sat. Samuel Boyagian alias Painter came. George was sick with some cold. We called Dr. Thatcher, soon recovered. Our cellar had 18" of water from melted snow.

January 2 Sunday. I stayed in the house all day. Frances and Alfred played very nicely together, she taking care of him. I put on a little suit of pantaloons and waist-fastened together, blue & white. It had a pocket in the trousers and he was delighted. I hate to lose the baby, but he will grow. Mrs. Bohn's baby died of pneumonia.

January 3 Mon. Neither Edward nor George was able to begin school in the morning. Marian Hagopian Boghosian sent neckties to the boys and a box of candy for the little ones.

January 4 Tues. Called on Mrs. Lyman and her new adopted baby, eight months old. She is sillier than I am over it.

January 5 Wed. Spoke to the Ladies Missionary Society here about Turkey of Today, read Polly's letter from Malatia, met Mrs. Edith Whiting Thatcher. Rained, no, poured.

January 6 Thurs. Met with a company or club of Seminary student's wives, spoke to them about what a missionary's wife does. Went with Mrs. Wilmot Metcalf, called on Miss Brand. Mr. P. left for Duluth.

January 7 Fri. Called on Pres. King. He promised to take two Armenian young men free into the college to train them for work in Turkey. I had in mind Yerevaut Hurian and Karekian Vartanian. Alfred has learned "No" but does not know what it means, only knows that it is English, and when any one addresses him in English, he answers "No," no matter what he says.

January 8 Sat. Edward and George went skating on Gayters rink and came home very late for dinner. Mr. Fred Bridgeman came to call. Armen and Edward and I went to pay the December bills, gas, electricity etc. Gas $42.26, electricity $2.16, milk, $13.86, groceries $25.86. Three boys went to see a six-legged cow. Postals from Mr. P. from Chicago, just starting for Ashland, Wis.

Ernest C. Partridge

January 1 Samuel came for a visit. 18 inches of water in cellar. George was sick.

January 2 Edward had malaria. Samuel went back.

[January 3–4]

January 5 Cleaned things up and went to Elyria for Union Meeting of Women (75). Missed train for Detroit so returned to O and gave up Detroit for present. 18m.

January 6 Spent day at home & took evening train for Chicago.

January 7 Reached Chicago from Oberlin at 7AM Spent day at Rooms, routes to Tacoma etc. Spoke in W.B.I. meeting (76).

January 8 Reached Ashland, Wis at 8:05AM. Mrs Jordan met me at depot. Visited Northland College in PM.

January 9 Sunday. Armen and I went to Pres. King's Bible class as usual. He is discussing the conditions for a permanent peace. He deplores mostly that the Germans have given up their own ideals, seeming to think that everything is justified in time of war. Thinking that Germany will have to make plans for lack of food.

January 10 Mon. I took Armen to Prof. Lehman today to have her voice tried for the choir. He accepted her and she is going to begin this week. Letters from Mikran Eff. and Susie Clark. The paper says that the Allies have entirely abandoned the Dardanelles expedition. Edward is sick, probably has grippe. Gave him quinine and rhinitis[?], put him into a room alone with me.

January 11 Tues. Word came that Dr. Shepard had died. Mrs. Martin and Mrs. Gulick called. U.L.A. lecture by Frederick Palmer, Armenian war correspondent, moving & still pictures. No awful pictures but the awfulness and seriousness of war impressed upon us. The business of Europe is war and it is carried on as deliberately and scientifically as trade. Edward and Frances both sick. George willing to sleep anywhere or do anything for the good of all.

January 12 Wed. Rainy. This morning at 3 o'clock Billo woke up nauseated and the electricity was turned off. Then we found that all the children except George were sick. It reminded me of the Greek Steamer where four children and three girls became sea-sick at once. George there was the only well one. Edward and Billo did not go to school. Armen made potato soup.

January 13 Thurs. Cold. None of the children were worse, rather better. Edward went to school in the afternoon, but coughs very badly tonight, so does Billy. The November copy of the "Ararat" (published in London) came today. It says that 20,000 Armenians from Ezroom and Sivas have arrived in Aleppo. Oh, if we could only get relief to them!

January 14 Fri. Very cold. Edward went to school, not Billo. Went to Mrs. Greene's house for a few minutes. Walked back with Mrs. Haskell. Had a letter from Erevaut Hurian saying that he thought he would keep on working & so would not study in Oberlin. I think he intends to be a dentist. Also a letter from Yeranoohi Kullydjian say that she is not going to visit us at present.

Ernest C. Partridge

January 9 Address in SS (77). Address Cong. Church morning service (78). Address YMCA Northland College (79). Address Evening Cong & Res Union Service (80).

January 10 Ashland to Mellen (26m) Spent day at Parsonage with Merritt; sick with grip. Evening informal talk at church (81). Night at Hotel.

January 11 Back to Ashland (26 m). Talk at College "The Foreign Call" (82). Supper and evening at home of Prof Bobb of College with younger faculty. Harold and Margaret.

January 12 Very cold. Over to Washburn for meeting. 13 m. Meiths came in. About 65 [people] out in storm (83); [?] Louise Smith.

January 13 Thermometer 33 below at 7AM. Train to Duluth. Called on Sec Roark at YMCA (79 m). Came out to Dr Thorpe's. Spoke (84) in evening on Medical Missions & Irwin's work.

January 14 A quiet day visiting and writing. Down town PM. Willard & Margaret. Evening went with Dr and Mrs Walker & the Thorpe's to hear Frederic Palmer. A splendid lecture and pictures.

January 15 Went to L.M.M. prayer meeting at YMCA. Wrote & read. Evening with Mr & Mrs Thorpe to hear Forbes-Robertson in Passing of Third Floor Back. Fine.

January 16 Morning service Superior, (85) C.J. Armstrong. Vesper service (86) Pilgrim, Duluth, both very satisfactory services. Took train for Tacoma at 7:30PM.

January 15 Sat. Sunny. Mrs. Wilmot Metcalf took Edward and me to see a basket ball game. The first game that I ever saw proved to be a glorious defeat for Oberlin. Oberlin, 21 Case, 47. But it was very exciting and interesting. The Case men did play finely. Edward and Armen went to Orchestra Concert in the evening, N.Y. orchestra, Walter Downsorch, leader. Light, hurdy-gurdy time.

January 16 Sunday. Pres. King's class. Finished his talk about programs & forecast for peace. Thinks America ought protest to some purpose about Lyatavia, Aneona and Armenia. Disapproves of Wilson's plan for Armenians, not even a remnant, I am afraid.

January 17 Mon. Very cold. Too cold to venture out. Mrs. Lyman donated four quilts and two blankets to keep the Partridges warm. George's school was closed on account of the cold. Two letters from Mr. P. He is on his way to Tacoma now. Edward had his first half year exams today English, Physiology, and Manual Training.

January 18 Tues. Very cold and below 0. Baidzar is sick but the others are all better. I was invited to Mrs. Greene's with the other Turkey people but could not go as I was expecting a telephone message or a call from the doctor for Baidzar. Edward had no school today and Billy did not go. Letter from Nazeli and Samuel Aramian of Sierra Madre, Colorado.

January 19 Wed. Very cold, but a little warmer. Dr. Thatcher came to see my mother and Baidzar who have the grip. I had a sick headache but slept it off just after supper. Edward had his exam in Latin today. He has a vacation for the rest of the week. Letters from Mr. P. en route to Tacoma, from Uncle Gene and Samuel. Wrote four letters. Boys tried hard to be quite when I was sick, almost worth being sick to see them try to be good.

January 20 Thurs. Warm & rainy. Mr. Smithkous and Mr. Auten called. Edward and I went down town, got shoes for Alfred, material for work aprons and a gingham waist. My mother not much better, Baidzar better. George got 45 in music test. The others have learned music in the lower grades.

January 21 Fri. Warm as summer. No fires. Papa had his eyes examined. Letter from Beth Partridge appreciating the children's picture, wants to adopt George. Sent them five dollars to buy something with. Armen and I took a long walk with the two babies in the carriage and Billo on the velocipede.

January 22 Sat. Mild & pleasant. Went to a moving picture show at Finney Chapel, Antartic Continent by Marvlson, quite interesting, Penguins very funny. Billy's first show.

January 23 Sunday. Mild. Attended evening service, saw Armen in choir. Mr. Spence preached on "Thy statutes have been my song though all my pilgrimage." Fine preacher.

January 24 Mon. Warm. Invited to speak to the Y.M.C.A.

Ernest C. Partridge

January 17 A long tiresome day in a very hot Tourist Sleeper across North Dakota.

January 18 Ditto across Montana gradually losing time. Four hours and three quarters behind.

January 19 Reached Tacoma at 2:30 (1911m) from Duluth. Took taxi to 1st Church. Dr Dyer took me to Womens Meeting 'Heroines." Stopping at Bonneville. Evening 1st Church Social (87).

January 20 Visited Dr Dyer at his office. Lunched with Cong. Convention Com. Read awhile in Dyer's study. Evening w Dyer & Jacks Mason. M. E. Church Brotherhood (88).

January 21 Called on Sec. Jacks and spent most of forenoon conferring with him & J Bauer. Lunch at Commercial Club. Cong. Com 2:30–3:30. Moved down to YMCA.

January 22 A rather quiet day writing and preparing for Sunday.

January 23 Sunday, Tacoma. 11 AM 1st Church The Pentecost of (89) Calamity in Turkey. Dinner at Dyers with Jacks. 5PM Pilgrims (90) Present Conditions. Supper Livingston. 7:30 East Destruction of a (91) Xu Role. 2 Auto rides.

January 24 Met with Tacoma Committee & Kelsey & Mathews & Jamison. Returned to Seattle with them. Visited Bakers. Mr & Mrs McCome over in evening. 12 years Frank "Apr 1/16." Saw Mather of '95.

January 25 Spent forenoon at Cong. Headquarters. Back to Tacoma (40m). Down to Roy for evening. Return to Tacoma (40m). A small crowd but interested (92).

at Ann Arbor, by Mr. Tinker. Dr. Greene came and read a letter from Mr. Camp giving information from Miss Frearson. Only 213 from 5,000 who started from Harpoot arrived in Aleppo, naked. Where are our people, not a word from them or about them. Letters from Miss Wheeler, E.C.P.

January 25 Tues. Mild. Letter from Miss Rice quoting postal from Sivas saying they had found a former pupil in a Turkish orphanage & also their chief work was finding clothing for the soldiers. They tried to have a union communion service, but others were not as interested as they hoped. Letter from Mr. P. from Karekian Vartanian. Called on Mrs. Miller about Armen's music.

January 26 Wed. Very warm. Saw Dr. Jamieson about glasses for papa. He says he can make him see twice as well. Let's see. First word of a definite Sivas person who arrived at Aleppo, Mrs. Yergainian, wife of Karekeen Teghnazian's brother-in-law. The husband is evidently a soldier in Sivas. We are thankful for one who has reached any place.

January 27 Thurs. Warm & rainy. Miss Marion Metcalf and Mrs. Whiting called. Letters from Melikoff Setigian & Mrs. Hubbard.

January 28 Fri. Colder. Got permission from Prof. Morrison for Armen to take what Mrs. Miller thinks best for the conservatory. Went to the Women's Club and heard Miss Nast read Middleton's "On bail" and "Waiting." In the evening went to a church social at First Church. George was a valentine. Letters from Mikran Eff. & Mr. Putnam & Mr. Bell & Mr. Camp's letter from Cairo. Annie Riggs died.

January 29 Sat. Rainy. Armen & Baidzar spent most of the day preparing Turkish food for a Turkish supper for George White, Eva MacNaughton, Mr. James, Miss Cady, Mr. Cady and his fiancée, Mr. Compton, and I do not know who else. Letters from Mr. Tinker and Hranoosh Varzhoohi.

January 30 Sunday. Mr. Spence's morning sermon on Jacob's wrestling with the angel. Evening: Christ's treatment of sinful or unsuccessful men, like Peter.

January 31 Mon. Rainy. Letters from Polly dated Nov. 26 and Dec 15, also boys had postal from Miss Rice of Dec. 7. Maksood Eff. & Dr. Kailenian & Dr. Vartamian have evidently been shot. Aramanoosh is just alive. Ara & Garabed Ibekjian are there. Polly suggests that they take the remnant of the Armenians to Cyprus. She speaks of Knell Episco- for talking it over with her.

February 1 Tues. Colder. Went to Elyria with Baidzar to buy her a coat. Bought one for $1. Copied Polly's letters on Mr. Metcalf's type-writer. Took them down to read to the Greenes in the evening. Letters today from Hovnian and one from Josephine Beard urging me to visit her in Detroit. Mr. P. was to leave Tacoma today, but not for home. He is going to Sacramento.

Ernest C. Partridge

January 26 Spoke briefly following Bauer at 1st Cong Church (93) Tacoma. Spent night with Mr. & Mrs. Ells.

January 27 A ride with Jones in auto. Spoke at noon meeting to N.P. Shops (94). Evening train to Chehalis. 1 hour late for Union meeting 5 denom 25 people (108m).

January 28 Last night at Methodist Parsonage, Chehalis, E.J. Smith. Train to Tacoma. Wrote for papers all PM. Supper at Booster's at 1st Xu World vision (96) 180 men out.

January 29 Spent day writing and conferring. 5:50 train to Olympia. Met at train by Pastor Edmonds. Entertained at parsonage. Retired early.

January 30 Sunday. Morning service at Olympia (97). Returned to Tacoma after dinner (66m). Evening Plymouth Church (98) Sterling Studio, Tacoma.

January 31 Got up late. Worked on typewriter all day. Lunched at YWCA with Committee. Evening social at Dyer's. Talk on Sivas (99).

February 1 Left Tacoma at 9:35 for South Bend (111m). 3–7 PM Visited with Mills. Men's Club Supper. Spoke an hour on Turkey (100). F.E. Hazeltine OC [Oberlin College] '89. Night at Fred Bond's.

February 2 Left South Bend at 7:15 from Centralia on bad snow, 4 hours late at Portland. Went to YMCA. Found J.K. Browne who cashed check. Sleeper South. (151m)

February 3 Reached Roseburg, Oregon in heavy rain (10m). Brand met me & we came out 5 miles to Overland Orchards. A pleasant afternoon and evening visiting. (198m)

February 2 Wed. Cold. Word from Varsenig that Asghig has come to America, from Hranoosh Var. that her mother has arrived in Aleppo, Dr. Patten that they are trying to keep 6,000 apples in Sivas during the winter. Attended Missionary meeting and went to chicken supper as guest of Prof. & Mrs. Root. Prof. and Mrs. Hutchins were also there.

February 3 Thurs. Cold. Postal from Varsenig Alexanian to Armen saying Asghig has come to America, also word through Mrs. Fowle that Armenoohi Demirgian has gone to Switzerland, also Bad. Kavme. Wrote five letters but am very far behind. Went with Armen to Mrs. Miller and Miss Whipple to get piano lessons started.

February 4 Fri. Cold. Letters from Mikran Eff. & Youths Companion about motors. Am to speak three times in Ann Arbor. Went to library, to Secretary's office, paid gas, electricity and telephone bills. Capt. Garland, Mrs. Cummings called, also Dr. Greene. Alfred has learned to say "Up" in Armenian and "No" in English.

February 5 Sat. Milder. Made out a list of all the things I had to do and did not do half of them. Letter from Susie Clark saying they had heard from Sivas, also from Mr. P. from Tacoma. Alfred said "see" today apparently understanding its meaning.

February 6 Sunday. Snowy & cold. Heard Mr. Spence twice, once on Moses not entering the promised land. Most people do not accomplish what they learned but it is good to undertake so big a job that you hope to leave a part for someone else to finish. Tonight the text was Let the dead bury their dead but go thou and preach the Kingdom of God.

February 7 Mon. Cold. Cosmopolitan Club, Bohemian Night. Alfred noticed how much Frances enjoyed sucking her thumb, so he tried his fingers one by one to see if he could find a sweet one.

February 8 Tues. Cold. Went to the library to work for an hour, writing a speech, appallingly quiet. Bought valentines with George for his father, teacher, and Nazeli.

February 9 Wed. Took tea with Dr. & Mrs. Greene at the tea Rooms on College Place. Letters from Mr. Ambrookian, Mrs. Riggs, Mr. P.

February 10 Thurs. First Church prayer meeting on "Blessedness of growing old." Called on Prof. Wightman to ask about attending a French class. Several letters and card of various dates from Mr. P. He has reached Sacramento.

February 11 Fri. Bought gloves and shirts. Got ready to go to Ann Arbor.

February 12 Sat. Cold. Went to Detroit, train late. Edith and Louise & Floyd Clawson, Samuel, Krikor Ansoorian, Ardashes Jimlegian and Yervaut Hurian met me. Went to the Clawson's. Josie Beard Heywood met me there and took me home with her. Saw her two boys Horace and Erwin.

February 13 Sunday. Cold. Went to Ann Arbor with Samuel and Krikor Ansoorian. Mikran Eff. met us and took me to a hotel. We went to the Church, saw Mr. Tinker. Fannie Berny, Judith and her husband. Went home to dinner with Fannie, then to the hotel, spoke to the Y.W.C.A. & Y.M.C.A. and then to an Armenian house, then to the hotel.

Ernest C. Partridge

February 4 Spent the day visiting. Went into town early and had dinner at Hotel. Evening train south.

February 5 Whole day down California. Upper part of the state in deep snow. Reached Sacramento in rain. Put up at YMCA. Dr Patten came in to call. (484 m)

February 6 Sunday. Out to Loomis on early train. Morning (101) service Cong Church. Evening drove 3 miles to Rocklin. Spoke in evening (102). (56m)

February 7 With Dr Briston & Ex Sec McConoughey to Marysville (103) for a Union meeting of pastors & laymen. Back to Sacramento. (104 m)

February 8 Rented a typewriter & spent day writing letters & press stuff.

February 9 Wrote till 10:30. Car out (70m) to Oroville. Put up at hotel. Visited Ehmann's Olive factory. Evening a business meeting, reception of 5 Chinese members. I spoke, a Social.

February 10 Rose early, took 6:30 car to Sacramento (70m). Found Bauer & decided to leave work to him. Took PM train for Fresno; arrived 11PM Hotel. (171m)

February 11 Fresno. Spent day with Dr Tracy & Mr Papazian. Evening spoke in Parehordznagan Meeting. Sleeper for Los Angeles. (278 m)

February 12 Reached L.A. 8:25. Went to Dr Day's house. Rested and visited.

February 13 Sunday. Spoke SS Armen's class (106). Judge Wilbur's Young Men (107). Out to Pasadena to see Goodells. 1st Ch C.E. (108) "Native Ministry" Armenian service (109). (50m)

February 14 Night at Dr Day's. Morning Cong Ministers Meeting. Lunch with Dr Edwin Harwood. Out to Upland (35m). (110)

February 14 Mon. Very cold. Back to Detroit & Josie, train two hours late. Visited Mrs. Eberle with Samuel & Krikor Ansoorian's brother. Some Armenians from Goodon & Khanzar came in. After they went sat up till two o'clock taking with Josie.

February 15 Tues. Milder. Called on Ovsarma Kohanian-Kouyomyian, and Asghig Arozian. Came home. Found three letters from Polly, two from Mr. P., others from Carrie Day Baker, Chvooshian, Yervant Chadurgian, Ambrookian.

February 16 Wed. Mild. Slept three hours. Little children have colds. Letter from Mr. Tinker & Hagop Tandorijian.

February 17 Thurs. Melting. Frances sick with bad cold. Called Dr. Thatcher. Alfred said "all gone." Letter from Mrs. Sewny from Constantinople. Erzroom taken by Russia.

February 18 Fri. Snowing & colder. Lecture by John Morefield on English poetry. Frances better. Alfred sick. Letters from Mr. P. Am. Board bulletin request for pictures for stereoptician lecture on Turkey.

February 19 Sat. Milder. Edward went skating. I called on Mrs. Haskell. Edward & George took me to a basket ball game between Oberlin & Reserve. O.34. R.31. First time escorted by my sons.

February 20 Sunday. A little colder. Was quite dissipate, attending church three times, and Bible class, where Dr. Greene spoke on "Turkey." Mr. Spence preached his last evening sermon on "Minister's in the World." Alfred said "Armen" many times with the children.

February 21 Mon. Cold & pleasant. Letter from E.C.P. today from Los Angeles, saying that Prof. Hagopian has written from Beyrout. We thought he was dead. Package of clothing from Central Church, Prov.

February 22 Tues. Warm. Washington's birthday, no school. My father and mother started for home, their first ride in a sleeper. Mr. Riggs (blind) & his wife called.

February 23 Wed. Cold & cloudy. Thunder shower last night. Took Edward & George to see moving pictures. Alfred's diapers were coming off and he found a big black button & wanted me to sew it on. He was 19 mos. old yesterday.

February 24 Thurs. Rainy. Went to the library and wrote ten letters to Mikran Eff., Mr. Wiggin, Mr. Peet, Polly, Mr. Ambrookian, Nazeli, Mr. P., Vahan, Mrs. McClure, & Garbis, one to Mr. Tinker at home & four postals.

February 25 Fri. Cold & slippery. Letter from Mr. P. saying that Uncle Rufus gave him $40 for cigarettes and was going to deposit $2000 to furnish Polly & me for money. Letters also from Mrs. Enid Brown & Samuel.

Ernest C. Partridge

February 15 Called on Barkins of Cong Church Ontario. Dr T.O. Douglass to dinner. Went to Claremont with Rices. Dined & visited with Mrs Renwick, Helen G. (14m)

February 16 Motored over to Claremont. Visited Pomona College, Chapel, Address "Native Workers" (111). Lunch at Dr Harvey Harwood. Conference (112). 1st Ch PM 272 Pentecost of C. (113). (35m)

February 17 S.M.M. Noon Rally I spoke on "World Vision A China" (114). Visited with Giles Brown, wrote some, dined with Mr Yeretzian and spent evening at Frengulian's.

February 18 Called on Ex. Secretary. Saw Hinman, Gammon[?] & Fisher. Out to Pasadena. Dinner with Stewart Goodell's. (10m)

February 19 Spent the day at Pasadena. Took a 40 mile drive with Uncle R, Stew & his children. Over to Upland where the ladies met me at train. (30m)

February 20 Sunday Upland Pres SS (115). Ontario Cong SS (116), church (117). Dinner at Blackies. Pomona College Volunteers "World Vision" (118). Venice Cong Church (119). (82m)

February 21 Forenoon Minister's Meeting. Called on Max Burke. PM Funeral of Carson. Long drive with Dr Day on Mt Holley. (201m)

February 22 A long visit with Giles Brown. Oberlin Reception at Mrs Betts. Saw Bob Cowley & wife, Prof Hall, Brown, Mrs Renwick, Max Burke (120).

February 23 Temple Baptist 12:30 (121). Dinner with Goodell's. 1st Baptist Pasadena (122). Back to Day's. (30m)

February 24 7:25 Train to Nordhoff High School (123). Visited Thacher Private School supper, spoke (124). 7:30 Pres church pastor Marsh (125). (103m)

February 25 Early train to Ventura where Daveson met me. Went to Santa Barbara. Lectures on Eggs studio. A good visit. William, Giles, Barbara (41 m)

February 26 Sat. Snowing & cold. George had a stomach ache and used the hot water bottle, Alfred watched him and later when he saw the hot water bottle he began to hold in his stomach & cry. Edward, George & I went to the Denison basket ball game, standing room only, O. 24, D. 21. Stephan Simonian from Cleveland, brought madzoon, oranges & candy.

February 27 Sunday. Windy & cold. Mr. Spence's last sermon. I think he is the best preacher that I have ever heard. Union Lenten service this evening. Mr. Luce preached, does not compare with Mr. Spence. I asked Edward to repeat one of the stories Mr. Luce told and he said he would tell it in English but not in Armenian, what a change! How hard we tried to have them speak English

February 28 Mon. Bright and cold. Called on Mrs. Martin & Mrs. Garland. Mrs. G's 51st birthday. Began a dark red sweater for Billo. Got eleven snapshots that took since Christmas with Michael Eff.'s camera. Very good but George cut off.

February 29 Tues. Pleasant. Called on Mrs. Husted & Mrs. Williams. Rec'd cable from Mr. Favre about moving the orphanage to Cyprus.

March 1 Wed. Went to hear Miss Cold of Hadjim, Miss Rice and Mrs. Frost of Berea at Missionary meeting, then with Mrs. Metcalf to hear Pres. Frost, then with her again to chicken supper at the Methodist church. Letters from Mr. P. and Dr. Gabuilian, and papa. Alfred pretended to read today, knew he must read in English so kept repeating "No" & "All gone."

March 2 Thurs. Snowy & warmer. Day of Prayer for College. Went to hear Raymond Robins at the chapel. He was very fine. Frances has a cold. Billy came home form school with headache, Alfred has hives, Edward has a stomach ache & George is sneezing his head off.

March 3 Fri. Cold. Shansi meeting, raised $3663. Dinner at tea rooms with Brewer[?] Eddy, Dr. & Mrs. Greene, Prof. & Mrs. Wright, Mrs. Haskell & Mary Cole. Call from Mrs. Martin & Miss Cold. Raymond Robins in.

March 4 Sat. Pleasant & cold. Rumor that Turkey wants to make peace. Went with Edward and George to the High School–Academy basket ball game. Score Acad. 17, High 9. Received bond for $58 a year until 1849 from Uncle Rufus.

Ernest C. Partridge

February 26 Train back to Los Angeles. Met Yeretsian at 5PM. Out to Frengulian's for night. (104 m)

February 27 Sunday 1st Church Armenians (126). McNaughton lunched at Day's. PM opening meeting of Convention 5150 delegates Glendale night (127). (30m)

February 28 Second day of Convention Went out to Univ of S.C. to speak at Chapel (128).

February 29 Convention growing in numbers & power. Spoke to ladies of WBP (129). Spent night with Traceys.

Memoranda page: Last day of Los Angeles L.M.M Convention. A great meeting P.M. Cong Conference in 1st Church. Night at Upland. (40m)

March 1 10:28 Santa Fe train East from Upland. A very good roadbed. To Williams (520m). Ione to Canyon. (63m)

March 2 Reached Grand Canyon 6:50AM. Drove with James family of St Louis over Rim Road 15miles. Spent afternoon looking at scenery. Lecture on canyon. (64m)

March 3 Took sleeper 7:40 last night. Waited at Williams for Santa Fe train 4 hours late. A tedious day thru Arizona & New Mexico.

March 4 Journey continued. Pres Eaton of Beloit and wife & daughter on train.

March 5 Reached Colorado Springs. Train 3 hours late. (839m) Continued to Colby 7:55 PM. U P train 12:05-1:30 to Hoxie [KS]. Slept at hotel. (222m)

March 6 Went to Annie's [ECP sister Annie Lucille Wellman] before breakfast. Spent day and evening visiting. Called on the Meth minister. Robert July 19, 1903 Edna Sept 11, 1906 Otto Feb 1, 1909 [Wellman children's birthdays.]

March 5 Sunday. Pleasant, cold. Pres. King's Bible class on some lessons from Raymond Robins's meetings. Edward, Armen, & I called on Miss Nellie Cole and Miss Mary Cole at Dr. Greene's. Met Miss Dean and Miss Brugger of the Kindergarten.

March 6 Mon. We went to Stewart Walker's portmanteau theatre. They played "Triumplet," "Nonetheless" and "Six who pass while the lentils boil." Very unique & fine.

March 7 Tues. Warm. First Haskell lecture by Prof. Scott of King's College, Canada. It was on St. Paul, probably very good but I was very sleepy. (This should be Tuesday.)

March 8 Wed. Warming, cold. Did not go out except to sweep the walk. Alfred a little sick & very fussy. Baidzar and I took turns working & tending baby. Had postals from Mr. P. from Grand Canyon, Arizona.

March 9 Thurs. Very windy. Invited to Mrs. Todd's house from 3 to 5. Met there, Mrs. Williams, Mrs. Thayer, Mrs. Lyman, Miss Peck, Mrs. Ohly, Mrs. Thatcher, Mrs. Horner, Mrs. Miller. Fine time. Refreshments, lettuce sandwiches, cake, coffee, tea, fudge. Mr. P. came home on the 7:20 car, had been gone 2 months. Letter from Mrs. Sewny from N.Y. Says Polly has relapsing fever.

March 10 Fri. Warmer. In the house all day, slept two hours in P.M. Alfred very fussy, perhaps has earache.

March 11 Sat. Warm. Basket ball, Oberlin & Ohio State. Oberlin 20, State 22. Also Knights of King Arthur & Berlin Heights H.S. former 19, latter 7. Mr. Manavian came & took dinner with us.

March 12 Sunday. Rainy. Went to Cleveland to an Armenian meeting where Mr. P. and Mr. Manavian spoke. Realized how much better the Armenians are in Turkey than here.

March 13 Mon. Pleasant & warm. Called on Mr. & Mrs. Chas. Riggs, and in the evening on Prof. and Mrs. Wright. Alfred took a bent wire and used it for a telephone. When we asked him what he was going to order he said "bananas."

March 14 Tues. Cold, blizzard. Attended a lecture by Mr. Forbush of Swathmore College on the "Dramatic Instinct."

March 15 Wed. A little warmer. Lecture by Mr. Dacko on Albania. Lecture by Pres. King on Panama Conference of Latin America. Made a chocolate cake, first time in years.

March 16 Thurs. Fair & Cold. Called on Mrs. Barnard, met Charles Gianque, and went with her to attend the Talcott-Huckins basket ball game. Huckins won.

March 17 Fri. Cold. Called on Mrs. Rogers and Mrs. Jameson. Went in evening to Men's Class social at Mrs. Richard's. Saw his curios, ate African refreshments.

March 18 Sat. A little warmer. Mrs. Ohly called. Y.W.C.A. circus with its ducks, monkeys, clowns, etc.

Ernest C. Partridge

March 7 Spoke at County High School Hoxie (130) History class (131) Union of Pres & M E. at Meth. church (132) Night train to Colby. (33m)

March 8 Trip Colby to Chicago in Tourist Sleeper.

March 9 Reached Chicago at 8:30 AM. Spent an hour with Dr Hitchcock & Mrs Lee 10:45 train to Elyria (323m). Re[turned] on Trolley (9m).

March 10 Rested and wrote and visited. Scott lecture on "Mystery Religions."

March 11 A visit from Manavian. Oberlin–State Basket Ball 20–22.

March 12 Sunday. Winona and I went to Cleveland to speak to Armenians (133). (74 m)

March 13 Called on Chas Riggs and Prof G.F. Wright.

March 14 Chapel Prof Scott lecture by Dr Forbush "The Dramatic Instinct in Religious Education."

March 15 Attended three lectures at Council Hall. Dako of Albania "Independence is a Necessary to Peace." Pres. King Report of Panama Conference. Prof Scott "The church of the Sects."

March 16 Spent day writing & reading. 4PM Talcott–Harkness [Oberlin dormitories] BB game. Evening 1st Church. PM Prof. Fiske "The Community Church."

March 17 Worked on MLG [Mary L. Graffam] leaflet. Spent an hour at gym. A 1st church reception in evening at Richards.

March 18 Indoor Inter-class track meet. Very successful, 1919 won.

March 19 Sunday. Heard two fine sermons by Dr McElveen, morning Union of 2 churches, evening Union Lecture.

March 19 Sunday. Fair & cold. Mr. McElveen of Evanston, Ill. Preached morning & evening in the chapel. Subjects, "The Complete Christ," and "Growth." Made some stuffed dates that were fine.

March 20 Mon. Mr. P, Baidzar & the boys went to an entertainment of the Cosmopolitan Club.

March 21 Tues. Warmer. Mr. P., Armen & Edward went to hear Maud Powell. Billy was a little sick & I stayed at home with him. Attended Mr. Jamieson's French class.

March 22 Wed. Thunder showers in the night. Colder. Mrs. Edward Riggs arrived. Attended French lesson. Alfred is 20 months old. Speaks Armenian by saying the first syllable. (Ha, head, ga, milk, pa, open etc.)

March 23 Thurs. Warmer. Mrs. Sarah Riggs took supper with us. Prof. Fiske spoke on the Community Church. Edward was elected one captain of the spelling match.

March 24 Fri. Warm. Mr. P. went on the 12:28 car to Cleveland to take the sleeper for N.Y. on his way to Hartford. Lecture on Child training by Mrs. Steiner. Went to the Greene's to see Mrs. Riggs, Mr. & Mrs. Chas. Riggs, Mrs. Martin, Mr. James, Miss Cady were also there.

March 25 Sat. Warm. Armen, Baidzar Edward had a headache. It was warm but wet and the little ones just splashed in the water. At night we were worn out with the noise and confusion. Alfred is not willing to spend one hour in the house. His first sentence was "[Armenian words]." He sticks a hat on his head at any angle, says "goodbye" and starts. Letter from M.L.G.

March 26 Sunday. Warm & rainy. Prof. King's Bible Class. Last Lenten service, Prof. Bosworth preached on "Submit yourself unto Christ."

March 27 Mon. Warm & rainy. Cellar flood 8 or 10 inches. Mrs. Roy Bowers and Miss Corning called. Postals from Miss Rice & Miss Fowle, saying Polly is better, five boys have returned or been heard from, no girls.

March 28 Tues. Warm. Yale–Princeton (girls) basket ball. Billo, Armen & I went. BIllo enjoyed the ice-cream which he ate dish & all & popcorn as well as the game. He tried all day to be good in order to go.

March 29 Wed. Warm & pleasant. Called on Mrs. Todd and Mrs. Roy Bowers. Armen had a lett card from her mother. She and Hrant are safe but in straightened circumstances, I judge.

March 30 Thurs. Warm. Prayer meeting in First Church led by Mr. Charmion of Micronesia, on "Public Opinion."

March 31 Fri. Warm. Ladies thimble party at First Church with Mrs. Greene. When we ask Alfred where his eyes are, he shuts them, his nose, snuffs, mouth, opens it wide, ears, sticks his fingers into them, teeth, shuts them together, tongue, runs it out. Hair curls even to his forehead.

Ernest C. Partridge

March 20 Finished & sent in MLG Heroines to W.B.M. [Woman's Board of Missions]. Went in evening with Baidzar, Ed & Y to International Night.

March 21 With Armen & Edward to hear Ward Powell play.

March 22 Snowed all day. Met Mrs Edward Riggs at noon train and took her to Chas Riggs. Mrs P and I called on her.

March 23 Had answer from Dr Barton and Ananibian and decided to go to Hartford. Mrs Riggs for supper. I took her to 1st church PM.

March 24 Went in to Cleveland at noon to get ticket to New York. Left on 8:41 Nickel Plate fare $6.55 (33m) Cleveland–Buffalo (184m)

March 25 A good night on sleeper. Reached city at 3:40PM. Evening at Oberlin Banquet. Wonderful opportunity. Telephone to Los Angeles. Buffalo–New York (410m)

March 26 Spent night with Raymonds. Morning to Scarsdale (134). Dinner with Hubbards. Visited Crescen's family. Heard Dr Coffin. (50m)

March 27 Spent forenoon in Board offices. Went to Ministers lunch as guest of Dr Smith to hear Dr Morganthau. Train to Hartford. Room 32 (109m)

March 28 Went to Turkish class of Misses Kinney and Greene, too rapid. PM class with Nilson, Islam class. Volunteer Band LMM (135)

March 29 Went to Prof Dawsons class Psyc of Religion. Visit with Dr Reynolds. A conversation lesson with the ladies.

March 30 Elementary Turkish lesson. Lecture on Islam. Conversation. 1st St John lecture.

March 31 Lessons till noon. Train to New York (109m). Spent night at Raymonds. Evening heard a magnificent lecture on Preparedness by Dr Cadman.

April 1 Sat. Cooler. Took Edward, George & Billo to the movies, Mary Pickford in "Such a little green."

April 2 Sunday. Cold. Pres. King gave report of "Pan American Congress." Vespers, Mr. Williams spoke on "Happiness."

April 3 Mon. Colder. Rec'd allowance from Mr. Wiggins and paid some monthly bills.

April 4 Tues. Warm. Children bought base ball, two mitts and bat. Went to see Mrs. Greene and Mrs. Martin. Left my light coat to be dyed.

April 5 Wed. Warm. Missionary meeting, Mrs. Fiske on Korea, Josephine Walker on China. In the evening went to Mrs. Greene's to meet Mrs. Bostwick of Upper Montclair.

April 6 Thurs. Cold. French lesson. Called at four places and found noone at home. Alfred dances a double shuffle, gives us many sailor kisses. Chicago paper says that the French made some progress at Verdun, English conquered the Turks in Mesopotamia & the Russians constantly advancing in Armenia.

April 7 Fri. Cold. Attended a lecture by Dr. Ulrich in Finney Chapel on the "Sexes," very sensible & good.

April 8 Sat. Cold, 5 in. of snow. Attended "Hansel & Gretel" presented by German Club. Hansel was Eva MacNaughton, Gretel, Miss Royce. Bought Billo shoes & rubbers.

April 9 Sun. Melting. Billo went to S.S. for the first time. Much impressed by putting his penny in the basket, brought home a paper and had me teach him the song, "Jesus loves me this I know."

April 10 Mon. Warm & pleasant. Called on Mrs. MacNaughton, took supper with her at Dr. Greene's, attended a lecture by Dr. Ulrich.

April 11 Tues. Warm. Called on Mrs. Gulick, who is not well. Attended another lecture by Dr. Ulrich and a U.L.A. lecture by Mr. Houseman on "Adornment and Use."

April 12 Wed. Another lecture by Dr. Ulrich on "Love & Marriage."

April 13 Thurs. Called on Mrs. Greene & Mrs. Martin to get a price on a piece of Turkish embroidery for Prof. Martin.

April 14 Fri. Had dictation in French, very interesting. I could understand quite a little.

April 15 Sat. Warm. Edward & George went to the shack, stop 98. The rest of us had a picnic lunch at water works. I took Billo & Frances to see Mary Pickford in Cinderella. Miss Lettle invited all the missionaries to her house. Letter from Mrs. Holway.

Ernest C. Partridge

April 1 After a leisurely start went to Board Rooms, there to see Miss Sewny. Brunch with her. Called on Ambrookian, dinner with Racoubian sisters.

April 2 Sunday morning at (136) Raymond's. Did not go to church. Dined with the Wheelers. Four o'clock Armenians of New York. Supper with Marian. Night train to H. (109m)

April 3 Studied hard all day and went to bed early.

April 4 Overslept and missed breakfast. Volunteer meeting. Mr Kelsey of Palestine spoke. Making good progress in reading Arabic.

April 5 Busy all forenoon with the lessons. PM practiced baseball with HTS team. Studied till supper. Leap Year Party at Reed Hall.

April 6 A busy day, 5 lessons or lectures. Baseball practice. Worked 3 hours in evening on Turkish.

April 7 Psyc of R lecture, conversation, Turkish study, baseball practice. Night heard Dr Adams & HW Hicks speak.

April 8 Three lessons forenoon. Studied Turkish all PM. Evening to Schultz house for a Social for Dr Jeffrey of China.

April 9 Sunday. Heard Dr Potter in morning. Rest of day read & wrote.

[April 10]

April 11 A busy forenoon of lessons. Caught behind bat some innings. Hurt my foot a little.

April 12 Went with Dr Capen to Noon lunch in City where I spoke on "World Vision" (137).

April 13 Heavy day for lessons. Five periods.

[April 14]

April 15 Worked hard till noon. Visited with Webster 1–1:45. 2–4:00 caught in 6-inning game 10–6. Besselive pitched. Evening Turkish 2 hours.

April 16 Sunday. Warm, showery. Having been up late & awake with the baby I got up at 10:30. Went to Pres. King's Bible Class. Took a walk with the children. George & Baidzar sick with colds.

April 17 Mon. Went to Mrs. Beford's house to see some samples, ordered a gray skirt for Armen $3.75, $1.50 a yard.

April 18 Tues. Pleasant. Mrs. MacNaughton called. George sick with tonsillitis, had the doctor. Went to hear Mrs. Smith of Cleveland on "Parent-Teacher Congress." Flat.

April 19 Wed. Pleasant. Trebizond has fallen to the Russians. Attended French lesson, took care of babies.

April 20 Thurs. Warm, showery. All of us quite miserable, partly from the weather. George better!

April 21 Fri. Showery. Stainer's Crucifixion sung by the Methodist Choir. Mr. Haroun and Mr. Adams soloists.

April 22 Sat. Rainy, cold. Frances three years old. Her Papa sent her a chain & heart. We gave her various small things, had ice-cream & cake. Carroll Shaw came in. Setrak Karolamian came to ask for Armen.

April 23 Easter Sunday. Cold, rainy. Dean Bosworth in the morning preached about Saul and Paul, his vision of Christ. In the evening special musical program.

April 24 Mon. Cold, rainy. I weigh 143 lbs, Edward 85.

April 25 Tues. Cloudy. Alfred speaks a queer jargon when he pretends to speak English. He speaks Armenian by first syllables.

April 26 Wed. Rainy. Finally the postponed track meet took place and the Freshmen won the honors. I did not see it however.

April 27 Thurs. Cloudy & Cold. Usual program, except that the washing was omitted. Alfred wore some rompers that were very cute.

April 28 Fri. Pleasant. Edward's fourteenth birthday. He had a memory book, a Bible, tennis balls from George, two candy eggs from Billo. I went to a public schools' concert which was very good.

April 29 Sat. Pleasant & warm. A real spring day. Edward, George, Armen & Baidzar went to the track-meet. I bought shoes for Billo and porshirt[?] underwear for the oldest boys.

April 30 Sun. Warm. First real spring day, everybody out walking in their bright spring clothes. I attended only Pres. King's Bible Class. Billo enjoying S.S. very much. Billo

Ernest C. Partridge

April 16 Sunday. Spoke at 9AM at City YWCA on "Some Modern Heroines of Missions" (138). Heard Dr Potter preach. PM Mrs Parkhurst on "Starving Service."

April 17 A day of hard work. 6:30 dinner at Dr Capen's with White & Wharton. Visited till 10 PM. light 159 lb [weight]

April 18 Spoke in Volunteer Meeting (139). Was elected member of Oriental Society. Prof McDonald read paper on Mohammedisms & the Wars. Very fine.

April 19 A lesson in history on the Selpike. Played tennis for the first time this year with Parker.

April 20 A busy day with five recitations and lots of time on Turkish.

April 21 Good Friday, a quiet day. A morning service at the Sem. A fine musical service at 4. Asylum Hill church [Hartford]. Called on Dr Reynolds & Prof A.

April 22 Spent afternoon and evening writing, reading & studying Turkish.

April 23 Easter Sunday. A morning service at 6:45. Heard Dr Potter with splendid music.

April 24 Spent day studying & reading. Played three sets of tennis after dinner.

April 25 First lesson in Turkish stories, very interesting.

April 26 A very interesting hour in History preaching, Mrs A on Sivas Early History. I spent 7½ hours today on T. Ball practice 1½ hours.

April 27 Four periods in classroom and 4 hours of work on Turkish, some general reading. Two sets of tennis.

April 28 Two Turkish lessons. Lecture on [blank]. A long walk with Kingsbury & Wharton. Studied with Miss Hazeltine.

April 29 Regular forenoon lessons. Watched some match tennis. By trolley to Longmeadow [MA]. Visit with James & Mrs Dr Ward. (30m)

April 30 Sunday in Springfield Mass. 9am spoke at College (140). (78m) 10:30 1st Res Church (141). Guest speaks English more than Armenian. Frances speaks English after a fashion. Alfred pretends to speak English but really knows only "No" & not the meaning of that.

May 1 Mon. Rainy. Went to the library with Edward to look up the times when Oliver Twist was written.

May 2 Tues. Called on Mrs. Greene & Capt. Garland. Coat came back dyed an awful color and torn across the front.

May 3 Wed. Cold & rainy. Spoke in Fairport Harbor [Ohio], made my first after dinner speech also. Went at 6 o'clock & returned at 5:30P.M.

May 4 Thurs. Pleasant. Called on Mrs. Anderegg with Mrs. Martin. Prof. A. has sciatica. Letter from Mr. Favre.

May 5 Fri. Showery. Lorain CO. S.S. Convention. I heard Mrs. Lydia Lord Davis define a missionary with examples. Mr. Williams spoke of "Amusements in the S.S."

May 6 Sat. Showery. Attended base-ball game, Oberlin-Miami, 7–9, first one in 21 years. Mr. Metcalf gave us a ticket and I went with Mrs. Barnard & Edward & George.

May 7 Sunday. Pleasant, warm. Pres. King's Class. Saw Mrs. Milton Norton. Went to walk with four children to foot ball field.

May 8 Mon. Pleasant, cooler. Called on Mrs. Martin, Mrs. Greene and Mrs. James. In the evening attended lecture, illustrated, America by Mr. Clunn. Took Armen & 4 kids.

May 9 Tues. Beautiful day. Went to hear Mrs. Parkhurst on "What Women are doing in the war." She was very interesting. Armen & Edward went with me.

May 10 Wed. Cloudy, sultry. Called on Mrs. Whiting, Mrs. Ingraham and Mrs. Lydia Lord Davis.

May 11 Thurs. Cool & pleasant. Polly's 45th birthday. Should like to see her. Attended session of the Eleven Club at Mrs. Martin's. (Leaven)

May 12 Fri. Cool. High School Concert with Edward. It was very good indeed.

May 13 Sat. Cool, pleasant. Had a picnic dinner in the Arboretum, dinner at night. Cooked pork chops in the oven, fine. Mrs. Barnard's way. Mrs. De la Forte & her daughter called.

Ernest C. Partridge

at College. Called on Goddard & Lees. 7pm St John Church (142) To Longmeadow.

May 1 Left Longmeadow early to Hartford for 9 o'clock class.

May 2 Played a set of tennis before breakfast. Umpired Senior-Junior game and worked hard rest of day.

May 3 Same old story. Turkish.

[May 4]

May 5 Psyc of R, 2 Turkish lessons & conversation. A Volunteer Picnic with supper cooked in woods and games.

May 6 Usual lessons. Wrote several letters. Umpired Sem–Dumney game. Went to Brattleboro. Guest at Robert Clarks. (97m)

May 7 Morning service at West Brattleboro "MedWork" (143). Taught SS class (144). Called on Aunt Mary & Macy. Evening Center Prof C in T. (145)

May 8 Went up to N. Bennington by trolley. Guest at parsonage. Called on Mr Mills and Whites. Evening several people came in. Mrs Hinsdale, Mrs Cole, Mrs Ed Welling, Hattie Welling. (74m)

May 9 Early car to Stockbridge, Mass via Bennington & N. Adams & Pittsfield. Livery team 8 miles to West Center. Spoke on P of C (146). Back to Lee in auto. Trolley to Pittsfield. Train to Worcester. Guest of Crooks. (185m)

May 10 Breakfast and a visit with the Crooks. Train to Gardner (147). Dinner at church. (92m) Spoke in Association Meeting, train to Boston "Midsummer Nights Dream." Ross.

May 11 Spent day at Board Rooms. Lunch with Manavian & Kalaidjian. Out to Hartford on evening train. Chinese social. Late evening. (125m)

May 12 A full day of lessons til 4 o'clock. Then went to see our team play Berkeley Divinity School. Got beat 7–3.

May 13 Coming down with a bad cold contracted on the road.

May 14 Sunday. Showery. Met Mr. Ryan after Bible Class. Baccalaureate sermon of the Seminary by Dean Bosworth. Choir sang "Unfold, Ye Portals."

May 15 Mon. Rainy warm. Picnic supper at water works. Evening, May Festival Concert. Beethoven Ninth Symphony & New Life. Soprano Miss Mabel Garrison, Alt. Margaret Keyes, Tenor Kingston, bass Warreviath.

May 16 Tues. Rainy. Nothing doing for us. Verdi's Requiem was given but we could not afford to go. Alfred and Frances were talking English together in their play.

May 17 Wed. Cold. Went to Mrs. Wright's with other missionary ladies to meet Miss Warfield who loves missionaries.

May 18 Thurs. Cold. Theological Commencement. Bishop MacConnell gave address. Was invited to banquet, Mr. Cady graduated.

May 19 Fri. "As You Like It" by High School Seniors. Called on Mrs. Haroun with Mrs. Lyman.

May 20 Sat. Pleasant. Capt. Gianque gave us two tickets to the ball games and Armen and I went. Ohio State beat 19 to 2. Max Ryan took dinner with us.

May 21 Sunday. Pleasant. Treasurer Severance died. Heard Sec. Burton of Home Miss. Society. Pres. King's last class this year, closed with comparison of Von [der] Goltz Pasha's work for Turkey & that of missionaries.

May 22 Mon. Rained all day. I slept about three hours, accomplished nothing but the washing.

May 23 Tues. Fireworks in honor of nomination of Roosevelt in mock Convention.

May 24 Wed. public school pageant on the campus. George danced "heel & toe." Elizabeth Crafts was May queen. High School girls wound the May pole.

May 25 Thurs. Warm. Called on Mrs. Martin. Had a picnic at the Water works.

May 26 Fri. Warmer. Stereoptician lecture on the Panama Canal. We had strawberry shortcake for supper.

May 27 Sat. Very rainy. French Play and Patriotic songs, managed by Prof. Jamieson.

May 28 Sunday. Stephan and Mariane Simonian and their boy, Henry, came to call on us today. Prof. Hutchins preached "Cleanse the inside of the cup & the platter."

May 29 Mon. George spelled down his whole grade.

Ernest C. Partridge

May 14 Sunday. Slept late and did not go out at all till evening. Turkey supper at Dr Snider's East Hartford. (8m)

May 15 Nearly sick with a cold but improving.

[May 16–17]

May 18 Rose at 4. Studied Turkish an hour, walked out to Goodwin Park 3 miles for India breakfast. Dinner & visit with Englishs. (10m)

May 19 Forenoon of lessons till 4. I umpired a ball game with Insurance men 4–3. Read paper in Dawson. Supper at Kelseys.

May 20 Forenoon busy as usual. Afternoon wrote letters, cleaned up & went to Wellesley Hills. (111m)

May 21 Sunday "Pent of C" Wellesley Hills church (148). SS (149). Men's class (150). Supper at Auburndale. Called on Miss Gage. Night at Ross. (20m)

May 22 Spent day in Board Rooms & at Merrill's office. Lunched with Dr Patton. Talked over their plan. Evening train to Hartford. (125m)

May 23 Last lecture in Islam. Last lecture in Hodja stories. Last lecture in Sociology.

May 24 Another Turkish lesson. Practice for Turkey scenes.

May 25 Wrote a number of letters, packed my box & cleaned up things preparatory to leaving.

May 26 I had a last lesson in Turkish alone, worked an hour fixing curtain. Sch of M. Banquet. "Intimations" Program. Graduation Exercises in evening.

May 27 Rose early, finished packing. Train after breakfast to Ashfield [MA]. Shelburne F[alls] to A 9 miles by stage. Visited from 1:30 to bed time. (81m)

May 28 Sunday. Ashfield, Mass. Morning service (151). Boy's class (152). PM Spruce Corners (153). Evening C.E. (154). (8m)

May 29 Stage down to Shelburne Falls. Train to Albany and Elyria, trolley to Oberlin. Saw Jack Kingsbury in Albany depot. (597m)

May 30 Tues. Colder. Memorial Day. George was in the parade. Mr. P. came from Hartford and we took the other four children to see the parade.

May 31 Wed. Cool & pleasant. Faculty-Senior ball game. Score Faculty 6, Seniors 14. Gianque, a senior, caught for faculty. Miss MacNaughton, Mr. James, Miss Cady & Mr. Nielsen took supper with us. Billo fell into the water works reservoir.

June 1 Thurs. Pleasant. My last French lesson with Prof. Jamieson's class. We finished "La Poudre aux Yeux." Called on Mrs. Greene & Mrs. Martin.

June 2 Fri. Showery. Did not go anywhere all day because we were washing and cleaning house. We had very heavy thunders showers.

June 3 Sat. Rainy, then clear. Another defeat for Oberlin – O 4 & Wesleyan 6. But in tennis Oberlin Beat Syracuse. Billy went to his first ball game but was more interested in the popcorn and the peanuts than the game.

June 4 Sunday. Pleasant. Children's Day. George and Billo took part. We took the whole family, when Alfred saw Billo on the platform he wanted to climb over the seats to go to him.

June 5 Mon. Pleasant & cool. Today we walked past the house where we get milk, quite a distance from our house & Alfred recognized it although he had been there only two or three times.

June 6 Tues. Cool & rainy. Called on Prof. & Mrs. Horner. Edward finished his examinations and so his first year of school in America except sub-primary seven years ago.

June 7 Wed. Rainy. At missionary meeting Mrs. Brown, of Ceylon, and Mrs. Delaforte and Mrs. Channon of Micronesia spoke. Billo finished his first year of school, K-9. Frances went to school with him. He translated for her.

June 8 Thurs. George's school closed.

June 9 Fri. More or less rainy. High School Commencement, very good. We knew only Norman Metcalf among the graduates. Senior Chapel.

June 10 Sat. Showery & cold. Conservatory Commencement, one third of it, very fine. Armen & I went.

June 11 Sunday. Rainy. Baccalaureate Sunday. Pres. King preached on "Citizenship in the New Civilization." Missionary meeting. Mr. Bridgman spoke about South Africa.

June 12 Mon. Pleasant. Wauseda game (Japanese) 4 to 1 in their favor but a good game. Conservatory Commencement. Armen & I got only standing room but a little Charnon girl & another girl gave us their seats.

Ernest C. Partridge

May 30 Reached home on first car in the morning Memorial Day. Went to see parade. George marched.

May 31 Nilson came. Went to Sr–Fac game 6–14. James & Mrs Cody & Miss McN to supper.

June 1 1916 Last day of regular High School. Called on Greenes & Mrs Martin.

June 2 Rained most of the day.

June 3 Wesleyan beat Oberlin 6–4. Oberlin won tennis with Syracuse.

June 4 Children's day. George and Billo took part. Alfred went.

[June 5]

June 6 Edward's last exam & first year in H.S. gen av 90 Latin 97–98. Called to Horners.

June 7 Rained. Last day at kindergarten Billo. Took Frances.

June 8 George's school closed.

June 9 Senior Chapel. High School commencement. Norman Metcalf in class.

[June 10]

June 11 Morning 1st Church Mr. Spence. 2:30 Baccalaureate Sermon. 7:30 Missionary Service. Address Fred Bridgeman. I made the prayer.

June 12 Oberlin vs Waseka Union baseball game 1–4. Conservatory Con evening. Winona & Armen went. Saw Newcomb and Eldred.

June 13 Tues. Pleasant. Alumni day. Meeting presided over by Prof. Ryder of Class of '66, the 50th Anniversary. Ivy Orathin, evening processional.

June 14 Wed. Pleasant. Commencement, address by Dr. Carasthen of Cambridge. Alumni banquet, Dr. Morgenthau spoke of Polly as a great heroine, and afterwards said to me, "She is the best." Alumni-varsity ball game 9–14. Evening reunion Glee Club concert, Ben Siddall, Basset, Pansy Metcalf, Bob Millican, Hatch sang.

June 15 Thurs. First day of vacation. Went to prayer-meeting and heard Mr. Fiske of the S.S. Society, no good.

June 16 Fri. Rained, rained. Nothing doing but house cleaning.

June 17 Sat. Cool. Called on Mrs. Greene and the new Beach baby. She is the prettiest little baby that I ever saw, I think. Her name is Elsie Bliss Beach, I believe.

June 18 Sunday. Pleasant, no rain. Heard the Sec. of the Baptist Convention preach a sermon about the early Christians.

June 19 Mon. Pleasant & cool. Two letters from Polly, dated Jan. 12 & March 1. Speaks of hearing from Annas & Yeghizafet & Manoog Minassian, but thinks our nearest friends are dead.

June 20 Tues. Pleasant & cool. Had a picnic dinner at the arboretum and picked about two quarts of wild strawberries. Went to see Mrs. Lyman's little adopted daughter, 8 wks. old.

June 21 Wed. Cold & rainy. Called on Mrs. Grace Millikan Behr and Mrs. Metcalf. Alfred said today, "Mama, train [Armenian words] choo, choo."

June 22 Thurs. Cool & pleasant. The boys & their father picked four quarts of wild strawberries. Billy picked faithfully to the end.

June 23 Fri. Warmer. Concert by the Conservatory faculty or part of it, Mr. Haroun, Mr. Goerner, Mr. Currie, Mr. Crain, Mr. Shauffer. Frances has the "squeaks."

June 24 Sat. Hot, with very heavy showers. Letter from Mrs. Sewny saying that the Americans have been sent out of Turkey, but Polly & Miss Fowle have remained in Sivas.

Ernest C. Partridge

June 13 Alumni Day. Prof Ryder presided. Ivy oration. Illumination and class Parade Prize to 1906 ['06].

June 14 Commencement address by Dr Crothers. DD to Bridgeman & Beard. LLD to Morganthau & Major Morton. Reunion Concert fine.

June 15 First day of vacation. Tennis. Yish of SS. Soc in evening.

June 16 Rained as usual.

June 17 Called at Greenes & Beach's.

June 18 Pentecost of C 1st Cong church Elyria AM (155). Evening attended union service at 2nd church. (18m)

June 19 Bought 2 tennis tickets & Edward & I played. Letters from Sivas.

June 20 A picnic dinner at Arboretum & picked two quarts of strawberries there.

June 21 Played tennis. Called on Grace Millikan-Behr & Mrs Metcalf. Bought a tennis net.

June 22 With the three boys picked 4 quarts wild strawberries Played tennis.

[June 23]

June 24 Letter from Mrs Sewny giving word that all Sivas but MLG & MCF [Mary C. Fowle] in Const. Also all Marsovan station. Picked 3 quarts berries.

June 25 Sunday morning Communion at 1st church. Prof Lyman in charge. Voted on Union 200 to 80. Evening Williams at Meth.

June 26 Wrote some letters. Played tennis, picked strawberries.

June 25 Sunday. Pleasant, cool. Union meeting, Dr. Williams preached. First time I ever heard Edward try to sing bass. Alfred wanted to change carriages with Frances. He came to her, called her by name, "Pacis," in his most winning tones, showed her the carriage. But Frances was perfectly indifferent to him. Very funny sight.

June 26 Mon. Pleasant, warm. Washed, ironed, sewed a little. Alfred is not feeling very well and is fussy. If Baidzar says "[Armenian] Alfred" he says "[Armenian] Baidzar."

June 27 Tues. Cloudy. Made morning calls on Mrs. Martin & Mrs. Beach, with Frances & Alfred & George, so that they could get out before it rained, but it did not rain. Mr. Auten brought beautiful peonies.

June 28 Wed. Pleasant, cool. Bought a ton of sand for the children to play in. Alfred came to me and said "Mamma, [Armenian words]" the first time he has joined his brothers' chorus. Frances is not as bad.

June 29 Thurs. Pleasant, warmer. Mr. Partridge & Edward, George & Billo went to Ringling's circus in Elyria, had a fine time but got very tired. Frances has a stuffy cold again.

June 30 Fri. Warm. Went strawberrying, called on the Martins about summer plans & saw the Beaches off. They are going to Michigan, thence to China. From the Chicago Tribune: 'The Russians won't stay beaten. The English don't know they're beaten. The French can't be beaten."

July 1 Sat. Hot. Letter from the Board Rooms saying that Polly and Miss Fowle were given a week to get ready to leave. We think they are probably out now. What a pity that the girls whom they have kept until now have to be left to the Turks finally!

July 2 Sunday. Hot & showery. Mr. P. & Edward went to Cleveland, the former to preach for Mr. Newcome. After telegraphing and telephoning Samuel came to Oberlin, having three days vacation. Alfred & Frances were afraid of him especially his bone ribbed[?] spectacles, but afterward got to be friends. Frances calling him Samuole.

July 3 Mon. Cool. Edward and his father went to a league game between Cleveland and Detroit. Spenker played with Cleveland. We went to five trolleys and a train to meet them & they finally came at 10:10.

Ernest C. Partridge

June 27 Got a tennis ticket for George. Call from Auten.

June 28 Alfred said "[Armenian word]" for first time.

June 29 Went with three boys to Elyria to Ringling Bros Circus. (18m)

June 30 Went strawberrying. Call on Martins & Beachs.

July 1 Letter from Rooms that Polly & MCF allowed to stay in Sivas.

July 2 Sunday to Cleveland. Guest of Newcombs P of C (156). S.S. PM (157). Edward went. Robinson 14 yrs Theodore 11 (14m)(66m)

July 3 Spent day in Cleveland. Saw Cleveland–Detroit 6–4. Supper at Whipple's.

July 4 Samuel came & returned by trolley. Kids had a great day.

July 5 Called on Mrs Martin.

July 6 A picnic dinner at the Arboretum.

[Jul 7–9]

July 10 Supper out of doors at Prof. Wrights. Miss Davis's last night before going to Andover.

July 4 Tues. Warm. Celebrated with firecrackers, torpedoes, sparklers etc. etc. with Carroll & Mr. Husted. Samuel went home by trolley.

July 5 Wed. Missionary meeting. Mrs. Lydia Lord Davis spoke about 13 women supported by the Ohio Branch as Missionary heroines, very interesting.

July 6 Thurs. Warm. Sewed on a 10 ct. gingham dress. Picnic dinner in the arboretum, potato chips, fish & peanut sandwiches, coffee, cheese, cherries.

July 7 Fri. Hot. Stayed at home. & worked all day. Letters from Karekeen Vartanian. He was thrown out of the National Guards on account of heart trouble.

July 8 Sat. Hot. Washed, ironed, sewed and took care of children.

July 9 Sunday. Cool. Took care of the children all day, going out on long walks, making candied pop-corn etc. to amuse them.

July 10 Mon. Hot. Had supper out doors at Prof. Wright's in honor of Miss Davis who went to Andover this morning. The auto-vacuum freezer came.

July 11 Tues. Hotter. Went to learn how to put up fruit from Mrs. Channon. Took a snap shot of Billo with his bobbed" hair, (then he had it cut), also one of the three & me and one of Alfred & Billo.

July 12 Wed. Hottest. 90° in our bedroom. Letters from Mrs. Clark and Miss Rice who had arrived in America. Ed. & Geo. & their father went to Henrietta to pick cherries. Alfred asked the blessing, understood Thank Him as "You."

July 13 Thurs. Very hot, showers. Canned thirteen quarts of cherries.

July 14 Fri. Hot. Our wedding day, 18th anniversary, and the fifteenth of Bobbie's death, no celebrations of one on account of the other. Heard a lecture in valesque[?] by Prof. Martin. Miss Cummings gave the children an auto ride.

July 15 Sat. Very hot 90°. Drudged away at housework but had ice-cream to eat and lemonade to drink. Finished a 10 ct. gingham dress & put it on. Alfred screamed for a tennis racket even after he was ready for bed.

July 16 Sunday. Hot. Alfred eats dirt occasionally and his face becomes perfectly black. Baidzar let him look in the glass and see it the other day. Today when he saw a picture of a man with a black beard he said, "[Armenian words]." We are reading "Rudder Grange" [by Frank Richard Stockton]. George & Edward enjoy it very much.

Ernest C. Partridge

July 11 Mrs P and I called on Mrs Channon.

July 12 Edward, George & I went to Henrietta to pick cherries. Got about 40 quarts.

July 13 Put up 13 quart cans of cherries.

[July 14–16]

July 17 Made coffee ice-cream, began to address for Polly's leaflet.

[July 18–30]

July 31 Hot wave broke and a fine breeze towards evening.

July 17 Mon. Hot. Slept most of the afternoon. Had coffee ice-cream. Bought a revolver for Billo. Alfred put one knee in the cart & pushed with other foot, like big boys.

July 18 Tues. Hot. Letter from Dr. Clark asking about houses in Oberlin.

July 19 Wed. Hot. Edward & his father and Arthur Martin called on the Roots at the Lake. I called on Mrs. Siddall, a friend of Miss Rice's mother, saw her niece Rita Candee.

July 20 Thurs. Slightly cooler. Dr. White came at half past five and went at 8:27. Miss Noyes came to supper. Mrs. Martin & Miss Webb and the Metcalfs called.

July 21 Fri. Miss Rice came on the noon train and we talked continuously about Turkey & our friends there. It is so sad.

July 22 Sat. Hot. Were invited to a piazza supper at Prof. Wright's. Mrs. Martin and Miss Webb were also there.

July 23 Sunday. Hot. Mr. Pyl preached but I did not go. Called on them, also went to the missionary yard.

July 24 Mon. Very hot. Miss Rice went. Mrs. Siddall and Miss Candee came & took all the children, except Edward, and me for an auto ride.

July 25 Tues. Very hot. Had a lame hip all day, so I limped around. Mrs. Shaw & Carroll started for Port Huron. Mrs. Barnard called.

July 26 Wed. Extremely hot. Have just sweltered all day. Bought material for night dresses. Must try to sew some.

July 27 Thurs. Still hotter. Too hot to do anything but I ironed and sewed nearly all day. Mr. P. was sick with a headache.

July 28 Fri. Very hot. Lecture by Prof. Louis Lord on Comparison between the present war and the Pelopennesian War.

July 29 Sat. Hot beyond description. Washed and ironed & melted. Had a picnic supper at the arboretum.

July 30 Sunday. Hottest. Went nowhere except for a little walk with the children.

July 31 Mon. Cooler towards night. Washing as usual. 100 people died of heat in Chicago. For three days about two hundred horses a day died in that city.

Memoranda. Last September (1915) weights were as follows. E.C.P. 137, W.G.P. 127, Edward 76, George 63, Billo 40, Frances 30 ½, Alfred 20.

August 1 Tues. Cooler. All weighed. E.C.P. 150 ½, W.G.P. 144, Ed. 83 ½, George 66, Billo 44, Frances 37, Alfred 28, Baidzar 114. Had Alfred's pictures taken again.

August 2 Wed. Hot. Missionary meeting on Dr. Bosworth's lawn. Miss Webb and Miss Noyes spoke. A letter from Amy Bridgman Cowles was read, very interesting.

August 3 Thurs. Hotter. Billo had an auto ride with Miss Willie & the Todds, then wanted to go down town and get some "All day suckers," candy on a stick.

August 4 Fri. Very hot. Mrs. Lydia Lord Davis called, also Prof. G. Frederick Wright.

August 5 Sat. Very, very hot. Invited to Mrs. Martin's for an hour or two in the afternoon to see Miss Cold. Miss Morley came before we left.

August 6 Sunday. Still hot. Pres. King preached on "All in the day's work." "My mother looked into my heart, found it brave, ready for the day's work, without shameful hope." Went to Prof. Wright's to meet Miss Maltbie, a friend of Miss Kendall's.

August 7 Mon. Hot. Billy & I went to Elyria to buy a skirt for me but did not find one. Got a 50 ct. racket for Alfred & he is supremely happy.

August 8 Tues. A little cooler, showers last night. Called at the Wright's, bought some blue cloth for a skirt. Miss Morley & Miss Noyes called.

August 9 Wed. Cool. Cut out and partly made a blue serge skirt, but it made my shoulder ache very hard. Alfred has hardly let his tennis racket out of his hand.

Ernest C. Partridge

August 1 Began to study Turkish again.

August 2 Read at library. Played tennis with Edward 8–6 6–3. Studied T 2 hours.

August 4 Calls from Mrs L.L. Davis and Prof Wright.

August 5 Call at Martins to see Miss Cold. Miss Morley came from Cleveland.

August 6 Winona went to church. We called on Miss Meltbie at Prof Wright's.

[August 7–10]

August 11 Winona went to Lorain to speak to ladies of 1st church.

August 12 Made potato chips & coffee ice cream. Read in library a while.

August 13 Sunday. Had a little lumbago. Read part of Froemer's Leull [?].

August 14 Sent second batch of Exercises to Anah to correct.

August 15 Made preparations to go to Lake for two weeks. Had a bad cold & grew worse toward night.

August 16 Was sick all night so could not go to the Lake. Edward & Arthur went on wheels, & the Martins by car.

August 10 Thurs. Warmer. Finished my skirt and bought a silk waist and gloves.

August 11 Fri. Hot. Spoke to the Woman's Association in Lorain. Mrs. Eva Hills met me and looked after me, 222 Fifth St.

August 12 Sat. Hot. Sick headache, was on the bed all the afternoon.

August 13 Sunday. Cool, almost cold. Had the quietest Sunday in a year. The three little children had a long nap and were pretty good the rest of the time.

August 14 Mon. Cold. Cut out and partly made a seersucker dress for Frances to wear at the Lake. Mrs. Martin and Miss Webb called.

August 15 Tues. Warmer. Got ready to go to the Lake. Mr. P. not very well. Mrs. Root and her sister, Mrs. Metcalf called.

August 16 Wed. Still warmer. Could not go to the Lake because Mr. P. was not able. Edward went on his wheel with Arthur Martin. Got ready to go again.

August 17 Thurs. Came to the day Shack in Lorain. It is rough and inconvenient but plenty of trees and water. Alfred was crazy about riding on the electrics.

August 18 Fri. Bathing, eating and bathing again.

August 19 Sat. Mrs. Martin went to Oberlin and I went to Lorain to buy a few things. The same program for the others.

August 20 Sunday. Mr. P. spoke in the 1st Church of Lorain on the Armenians. I went to church. It was almost unbearably hot.

August 21 Mon. Mrs. Martin came back and Capt. Garland called on us. Six went blackberrying & got about twenty quarts in an hour.

August 22 Tues. Mrs. Martin made blackberry jam. Same program, bathing, eating. bathing. Alfred is very fond of the cold water & all the others are.

August 23 Wed. Cold. Martins went home. I was teaching Alfred English today. I took hold of Edward's hair and asked him what that was. He said "Edward curl." He thinks all hair is curls because his is, I suppose. There was no bathing today, too cold & rough.

August 24 Thurs. Alfred repeats what the other children says, just by sounds, without understanding. He says, "I want 'ap(lap)" "I want bed" often" [Armenian words]," "bed [Armenian words]."

August 25 Fri. Mr. & Mrs. Day left their horse and carriage with us so we went out near their farm and turned the horse loose & had a picnic, picked 6 or 7 qts of blackberries, fine time.

Ernest C. Partridge

August 17 Got up and went to lake. A rather hard day but I made it. (12m)

August 18 Got well settled & everyone seems happy. I swim twice a day, the kids 3 times 2 hrs each.

August 19 Miss Martin went home for over Sunday. Winona went to town. Have done 3 exercises this week.

August 20 Sunday. Winona & I went into Lorain to 1st church where I spoke (158). Met a number of people of the church.

August 21 In PM 6 of us went to Mr Day's farm 4 miles to get blackberries. Picked 20 quarts and made jam.

August 22 A pleasant day with lots of bathing till night when had violent rains. All slept in house.

August 23 Martin's went home. Quite cold all day. Billo & I went to town.

August 24 Continues cold so that little bathing [is done].

August 25 Whole family drove over to Day farm for a picnic. Picked blackberries etc.

[August 26–September 18]

August 26 Sat. Went to town to find cream for "jello," finally found ½ pt., took Billo, gave him ice-cream in a cone, two for 5 cts. Got Edward's bicycle tire.

August 27 Sunday. Did not go to church, took several walks, too cold to bathe, read, little ones slept some.

August 28 Mon. Weather cool, lake rough. Little ones did not bathe, three older ones a few minutes with their father. Played in the sand.

August 29 Tues. Cool. Alfred collected fares & pulled the curtain. Returned to Oberlin, bag, baggage & children. Baby, Alfred, has been with me so much at the lake that now he wants me every minute.

August 30 Wed. Warmer. Began on the accumulated washing, bought material for two suits for Billo. Took Frances and gave her an ice-cream cone, much to her delight.

August 31 Thurs. Warm. Washed, ironed, sewed on a "middy" suit for "mamma," so I had to leave my sewing & take him for a walk. His mouth is very sore. Alfred says "Edard" "Geo" "Bro" "Pancis" and "Afet." His language is about half and half. Frances and Billo speak English almost entirely.

September 1 Fri. Announcement of Miss Douglas's marriage. She wrote that Mr. Barnum says he is going to keep well and strong, because noone knows when the matrimonial bug will strike. Also Will Peet's wedding announcement.

September 2 Sat. Dr. Marden called. Bought shoes for George, Frances & Alfred, trousers for George, belt for Billo. Mrs. Riggs came to Oberlin.

September 3 Sunday. Heard Mr. Hsu on China "The effect of Christianity on the civilization of China," not very interesting. Afterwards went to Mr. Irving Metcalf's house with Dr. Marden.

September 4 Mon. Labor Day & Gala day in Oberlin. Dr. & Mrs. Marden called.

September 5 Tues. Schools commenced. Edward, Sophomore H.S., George 5th Miss Wilkinson, Billo 1st Miss Brady.

Ernest C. Partridge

September 19 Began investigation of subject of study in Seminary.

September 20 Attended Prof Lyman Ethics class.

September 6 Wed. Hot. Missionary meeting. Mrs. Ryan spoke and Mrs. Williams read a paper on the Moslem World.

September 7 Thurs. Very hot. Letter from Polly, dated June 17 & some snap shots of her & Miss Fowle, with a German Doctor & officer and German consul[?] & another with Dr. Tasqiaris wife & daughter.

September 8 Fri. Rainy. Took the babies, Alfred & Frances, down to Tank Home, saw Mrs. Garland, Mrs. Martin, Mrs. James & Mrs. Ryan.

September 9 Sat. Cooler. In the morning Frances had a bad dream & got frightened. I lifted her and my back went to pieces, so that I could hardly move all day.

September 10 Sun. Cool. Back a little better, but did not go to church. Ernest, Edward & George a little sick with colds, apparently from the change in the weather.

September 11 Mon. Armen & Garbis came from Detroit. Also John Greene came on the same train to enter College.

September 12 Tues. Garbis left for Columbus where he is to be partly tutor & partly student in Ohio State University. He is a very modest, pleasant young man.

September 13 Wed. Baidzar left us with much weeping. She is going to her uncle in Brookline [MA].

September 14 Thurs. Hot & muggy. Frances's first day in the Kindergarten. She and Alden Ryan were put into the same class alone. She would not allow me to get an inch away from her, but she enjoyed it. Alfred has been very fussy, has missed Baidzar. First lecture in the Seminary given by Dr. Ian Hanna on "America's New Position in the World."

September 15 Fri. Cool. Invited to Prof. Bosworth's with the Seminary students & faculty. Frances said, "I wasn't afraid of my teacher and I said something to her." Edward took her & left her.

September 16 Sat. Cold. Was hardly able to accomplish anything because Alfred just clung to me. Now that Baidzar is gone he clings to me.

September 17 Sunday. Cool. Attended church twice for a wonder. Prof. Bosworth preached on "Sabbath Keeping" and Prof. Hutchins on "Bridge-building." The children have colds.

September 18 Mon. Cool. Frances was sick with the "squeaks." Dr. Thatcher came. Billo & Alfred also had colds. Two awful nights. Miss Morley & Miss Noyes called.

September 19 Tues. All better but Billo & Frances did not go to school. Attended Mrs. Cowdery's French class. I had her in solid geom. 24 years ago. Word that Baidzar reached Brookline.

September 20 Wed. Attended Home Miss. Meeting at the First Church. In the evening Mr. P. & I went to a recital at Warner Hall. Mrs. Adams & Mr. Haroun sang.

September 21 Thurs. Miss Webb & Miss Peck, both from Adana, called especially to see Armen because Miss Peck is a friend of Mr. & Mrs. Coos, Michael Eff.s friend.

September 22 Fri. Rainy. Regular routine, housework, French lesson, taking care of children.

September 23 Sat. Pleasant. At home all day. Saturday and Sunday are strenuous days.

September 24 Sunday. Attended church. Prof. Bosworth preached, also President King's class. Called on Miss Morley with Mr. P. & four children.

September 25 Mon. Miss Julia Patton and Annie Fish MacClure called this afternoon for a few minutes, also Mrs. Andrews.

September 26 Tues. Warmer. Attended French Composition class, very good and interesting. Mrs. Martin & Jessie called. Jessie is about to start for Smith. I called on Mrs. C.B. Martin to inquire for Prof. Martin who was hurt by an express train.

September 27 Wed. Hot. Went to Elyria to speak to the Women's Society of the 2nd Church. Mr. P. & all the children met me at the car. Edward was examined in violin & entered the Junior Orchestra.

September 28 Thurs. My birthday. I made a chocolate cake that looked as though I had begun to decline, but it tasted good. Dikran Eff. sent ten dollars to get me a birthday present. Asaghig Arozian & her baby came for a visit. A letter from Miss Rice. She had a letter from Sivas dated July 9.

Ernest C. Partridge

September 21 The Seminary faculty seem willing to allow 3 lessons a week of Turkish to count toward a post-grad year.

[September 22–25]

September 26 Three lectures. King, Bosworth & Heyman. Read 3–4 hours.

[September 27]

September 28 Winona's birthday. Had cake & ice cream for supper. D.K. gave her a field glass. Ashig came.

September 29 Prof Fiske says I can get credit for 2 lessons a week in Turkish if Mr. Ananibian will supervise my work.

September 30 Played 2 sets of tennis with Edward. Lectures 10 to 12. Got class cards. Heidleberg game, Oberlin lost 33–3.

October 1 Dr Harmeh preached at 1st church. I spoke to 1st ch training class (159).

[October 2–13]

September 29 Fri. Miss Morley & Miss Webb invited us down to their home with the other Turkey missionaries, Dr. & Mrs. Greene, Mr. & Mrs. Riggs, Mr. & Mrs. James, Madame James, Miss Noyes, Mrs. Martin.

September 30 Sat. Washed from morning until night except just long enough to go down town and buy shoes for Armen & George, we had four children with me. Alfred uses mostly English nouns and Armenian verbs. He says "(l)ap [Armenian]," "down town [Armenian]," by [Armenian]." He prefers a buster car to his baby carriage.

October 1 Sunday. Attended vespers with Asghig.

October 2 Mon. Mr. P. & I went to a Seminary picnic out on the Wellington road. Had a very interesting time.

October 3 Tues. French Composition class.

October 4 Wed. Warm. Miss. Thank Offering Meeting. Miss Morley spoke. $116 raised. Whole year $900 raised. Billo came home from school very happy because he could read to me. He had learned 3 words, "and" "to" and "come" which he could sometimes find correctly.

October 5 Thurs. The Husteds moved to Cleveland. Have taken care of children nearly all day. Alice Arozian & Alfred attracted great attention in the carriage together.

October 6 Fri. Calls from Mrs. Farnsley and Mrs. Miller about Asghig. She will go to the latter place, I think.

October 7 Sat. The day's work did not end until 11:30, when the ironing was finished.

October 8 Sunday. Went to vespers and sat with Mrs. Andrews. After the service Dr. Andrews explained the organ to us, to Edward and me.

October 9 Mon. Rainy. George was praised for his composition on "The Rubber Tree" by Mr. Rawdon, the superintendent. Miss Morley, Mrs. Martin. and Miss Webb called. Edward got A- in an English Composition.

October 10 Tues. French Composition class.

October 11 Wed. Ohio Branch meeting in Cleveland but I did not go because I was too sleepy to attend meetings. Began attending Prof. Jamieson's class.

October 12 Thurs. Movies, Mary Pickford in "The Foundling." Edward, George, Billo and I went.

October 13 Fri. Regular routine, washing, children, French lesson, housework, ironing.

October 14 Sat. Always a hard day. Ernest went to Toledo on the evening train. I did not get out of the house.

October 15 Sunday. At home all day, trying to keep the children within bounds and not succeeding.

October 16 Mon. Nothing doing.

October 17 Tues. Same as yesterday only French lesson.

October 18 Wed. Went to see Mrs. Greene, Mrs. Ryan, and Mrs. Martin. Mrs. Buddington called.

October 19 Thurs. Rainy. Mrs. Martin called. George had a story about "Rubber" printed in the "Oberlin News." Edward went to an enthusiasm meeting at the High School.

October 20 Fri. Went shopping in Cleveland with Mrs. Martin & Arthur. I took Edward & George. Bought a coat skirt & waist for myself, suits for George & Edward & a mackinaw for Edward.

October 21 Sat. Missionary reception at Mrs. Williams's to meet Mrs. Sheffield of China.

October 22 Sunday. Did not go to church. Special Sunday for Armenian & Syrian Relief. Prof. & Mrs. Miller took us out for an auto ride.

[October 23]

October 24 Tues. Mr. Partridge went to Toledo for the Board Meeting.

October 25 Wed. Bought a winter coat, blue, loose, at Yocani's for $18.50.

October 26 Thurs. Went to Toledo with Billo expecting that he would come back with his father that night, but they decided to stay.

Ernest C. Partridge

October 14 Evening train to Toledo. Stayed at Boody House.

October 15 Morning had church Lenthi (160). S.S. class (161). Mass meeting Trinity (162). Wash St Cong (163).

October 16 Spoke at Minister's meeting (165). Commerce Club (164).

[October 17]

October 18 Spoke to Woman of First Church Elyria. Geog & Pop of Turkey (166). (18 m)

[October 19–20]

October 21 Oberlin play Ohio Union. Got beat 13–7 but a fine game.

October 22 Armenian Relief Sunday (167). Morning at Berlin Heights (40m) [with] Cady. Evening, Sec Bell, Miss Morley & I spoke at a Community Service in (168) Finney Chapel collection $1000.00.

[October 23]

October 24 First day of Board meeting at Toledo. Quite a party from Oberlin. Guest at Mr & Mrs Bradley's. Dr Atkins preached a fine sermon.

October 25 A very full day. Listened to 16 addresses.

October 26 Winona and Billo came to Toledo and spent the night. Had a fine drive in the PM.

October 27 Fri. Mr. & Mrs. Andma called. Mr. Hargazoon Arrazian, a Marsovan graduate, invited all Turkey missionaries to dinner at the hotel. Returned to Oberlin. Mr. Giles Brown took supper with us.

October 28 Sat. Samuel came. Mrs. Chamberlain called. Also Miss Webb & Mrs. Robert Chambers. Masquerade Party at Tank Home. Edward dressed up as a village Armenian or Turk. Noone recognized him.

October 29 Sunday. Samuel went on the noon train. Called on Mr. & Mrs. Charles Riggs. They have each gained thirty pounds since coming to America.

October 30 Mon. A postal from Hampartsoom Kaloyan saying that he had escaped & had passed Erzroom going towards Tiflis. Mrs. Chambers, Miss Webb & Mrs. Chamberlain called.

October 31 Tues. Asghig and Alice came over. French lesson. Halloween. We had punkins. George, Carwell & Billo dressed up with masks etc. Alfred very much frightened.

November 1 Wed. Two letters & card from Hampartsoom Kaloyan from Tiflis. The Armenian soldiers in Sivas have been mostly killed.

November 2 Thurs. Called on Dr. & Mrs. William Chambers from Adana.

November 3 Fri. Asghig and Alice came back from Prof. Miller's. Senator Burton speaks in the chapel.

November 4 Sat. Mr. P. & Edward went to Cleveland to see the Reserve-Oberlin football game & enjoyed a glorious defeat for Oberlin 53 to 3.

November 5 Sunday. Went to vespers. Mr. Williams spoke on the "Fraternal Bond."

November 6 Mon. Called on Mrs. Buddington, Mrs. Moore, Mrs. Todd & Mrs. Bohn. Saw Mrs. Bohn's new baby, her brother's baby whom they have adopted.

November 7 Tues. Went to a tea party at Mrs. Buddington's. There were present Mrs. Williams, Rogers, Thurston, Moore, Lutz, Reed, Misses Reed, and Mrs. Buddington's mother & sister-in-law.

November 8 Wed. Went to the library after my lesson & wrote letters & then visited Sperry's bargain day. Edward & George went to John Westervelt's birthday.

November 9 Thurs. Called on Mrs. Wright.

November 10 Fri. Alfred says "where going?" "That all?" "I going down town." "What you want Mamma?" He speaks Armenian better still but it is changing fast.

November 11 Sat. Warm weather. Mrs. Bosworth called. Samuel sent $100 for Hampartsoom's traveling expenses. Edward & I went to the Latin play, "Mernaechmi" by Plantus.

November 12 Sunday. Mr. P. went to Columbus on his way to Dayton. Edward, George & I went to vespers. Helen Blanchard called.

November 13 Mon. Sixteen years today since we reached Sivas. Not one of the people that met us that day is there now unless perhaps Haleel and very few are living.

Ernest C. Partridge

October 27 Last Session of Board. Haigazin Asvazian gave a dinner to all Turkish miss. Home on PM train. Giles Brown dined with us.

[October 28–November 1]

November 2 Called on Dr & Mrs W. H. Chambers at Frank House.

November 3 Heard Senator Burton speak in Finney Chapel for Hughes.

November 4 Edward & I went to Cleveland to see Reserve game. Got beat 53–3.

[November 5–11]

November 12 Went to Columbus on noon train. Heard Dr. Gladden in evening. Home with Harry Marshall for night.

November 13 Early train to Dayton. Spoke at ministers meeting to 55 men on Armenian Relief. Then back to Oberlin via Cleveland.

November 14 Tues. First snow. As soon as Alfred woke up he sat perfectly still in bed and looked out the window & said "Flour [Armenian words]." William Marden died.

November 15 Wed. Mrs. Martin called to see about going to Mentor [Ohio] to attend little William Marden's funeral.

November 16 Thurs. Went to Mentor. It was a real uplift to see all who attended, I believe. Such self control and faith I have seldom seen.

November 17 Fri. Leaven Club at Mrs. Fullerton's. Prof. Wright spoke about the early days in Oberlin, Pres. Finney etc. Went to a telephone exhibition in the chapel where Pres. K. spoke to Alumni gathered in N.Y. Chicago, Omaha & San F.

November 18 Sat. Called on Mrs. Greene, Mrs. Holway, and Mrs. Ryan. In the evening went to the movies with George & Edward supposing that Marguerite Clark was on but it was not, a sad play.

November 19 Sunday. Billo & his father went to speak at Euclid Ave. S.S. in Cleveland. In the evening heard Prof. Hutchins on "Thee was no word from God."

November 20 Mon. Alfred and Frances were playing and Frances cried for something Alfred did. He sat back and said, "You 'faid of me?" He really is to be feared for he has no conscience about what he does or where he hits. Frances has a bad cold and is beginning to wheeze.

November 21 Tues. Called on Miss Morley who came back to pack up her trunk to go East with Dr. & Mrs. Marden. Frances had one of her bi-weekly colds and had to be held or wheeled all day. Her father took care of her until 2 o'clock last night & I the rest of the time.

November 22 Wed. Warm. Frances is better today but Alfred and Edward & Billo & George all have it. I spoke in Miss Morley's place at a Baptist Women's Association here.

Ernest C. Partridge

November 14 First snow of season. News of William Marden's death.

[November 15]

November 16 Winona & Mrs Martin went to Mentor [Ohio] to William Marden's funeral. I stayed with the kids.

November 17 Telephone demonstration Finney chapel. 2000 persons. New York, Chicago, Omaha & San F Alumni Associations on wire.

November 18 Last regular football game of season. Mt Union beat us 49–0. Team did not do as well as we expected. Martin starred.

November 19 Went in to Cleveland with Billo to speak at the SS of Euclid Ave Cong church (169). (74m)

[November 20–24]

November 25 Took noon train west via Toledo, spent night at a hotel Elkhart Ind. And took early morning train for Constantine, Mich.

November 26 Stevens met me at 7AM train. Spoke church morning adult class SS. Evening Union Service. Took night train back to Elkhart and on to Cleveland.

November 27 Reached Cleveland at 4AM and out to Oberlin by 1st car.

November 23 Thurs. Supper at the church, beans, macaroni, cabbage salad, raw fruit pudding, cookies, sandwiches, coffee. When the team went by Alfred called out "Oberlin, Oberlin."

November 24 Fri. Cold. Principal excitement, the gas gave out and we burned boxes in the fireplace to keep warm.

November 25 Sat. George's eleventh birthday. We invited Mr. Doolittle, S.S. teacher, Lee & Fred Comings, George and John Westervelt, Carroll Shaw, Arthur Martin, Almand Wilder. Served sandwiches & cocoa, ice-cream & cake, 11 candles. If we can judge by the noise they must have had a good time. Mr. P. went to Constantine, Mich. to speak for Urbinot.

November 26 Sunday. Today the gas did not give out as it had for two days. Did not go to church, worked & tended babies all day. Tired out.

Novemebr 27 Mon. Mr. Partridge returned. I went to Elyria and bought Musser stockings for the three oldest boys, also black & white waist for myself.

November 28 Tues. Dr. White came. We went to a party of the Senior class in the Seminary to celebrate the marriage of Mr. Robertson. It was at Mr. Thurston's house.

November 29 Wed. Getting ready for Thanksgiving. Alfred asked me to sing "Camafinda," which being interpreted is "On the Road to Mandalay," dawn comes up like thunder.

November 30 Thurs. Warmer. Thanksgiving. We invited Mikran Eff., Samuel and Garbis to eat dinner with us, but noone came, so we cooked it and then sat down and ate it. Even Edward agreed that it was very "[Armenian]." Our minds and hearts were in Turkey, though.

Memoranda. Money for Hampartsoom Kaloyan. $60 from Samuel Boyagian, $15 Mrs. Wright, $16 from Haigoohi, $40 from Samuel Boyagian's roommate, $25 from Mr. Irving Metcalf, $20 from Mr. Shipman. Sent $150 to Tiflis.

Ernest C. Partridge

[November 28–December 9]

December 8 Had a birthday cake and a little celebration.

[December 9–22]

December 1 Fri. Edward and George played football with a scrub team. Edward came home covered with mud and blood, but the blood was only from a nosebleed. Heard Mr. Salter on "Niche and the War."

December 2 Sat. Went to the "Movies" in the evening and saw Marguerite Clark in Heléne of the North. Much shooting, few fatalities.

December 3 Sunday. Rainy, warm. Went to an Anti-Saloon League meeting. Mrs. Richards, Pres. of the W.C.T.U. of Ohio spoke. Ex. Gov. Patterson was to speak later but Edward & I came home.

December 4 Mon. Word came of Miss Fowle's death at Tanagenia, Nov. 22. We are greatly puzzled about where it is and why she was there & wonder where Polly is.

December 5 Tues. The children went to sleep early and I had almost a whole evening to write letters. I wrote five.

December 6 Wed. Warm. Billo's birthday, six years old. We invited Robert Todd, Robert Crafts, Ralph Ormusky, Ralph Williams & Allen Buddington. Gifts: overalls, gloves, candy, tiddlede winks, book, jumping jack. Refreshments: ice-cream & cake.

December 7 Thurs. Warm. Last night was Seminary banquet and today we are sleepy.

December 8 Fri. Warm. Mr. P.'s birthday, 46 yrs. old. Did not celebrate much. I gave him a book of "Cathchwords," small angel cake, six candles & "40" on the cake. In the evening was parents reception in H.S. All the teachers praised Edward to the skies.

December 9 Sat. Cold & windy. Children in the house nearly all day and three other boys spent the afternoon here. A few more or less does not make much difference.

December 10 Sunday. Heard Pres. Allen of Doane College in morning and in the afternoon Prof. Fiske on the House of John Frederich Oberlin. Alfred is just beginning to use "her" & "him." Usually wrong, Billo said "I love you [Armenian]" as he used to long ago.

December 11 Mon. Mrs. Martin and I went to see Mary Pickford in "Poor Little Peppina." We took Edward and George and Billo. It was very good. I had a picture taken of Alfred & Frances to put on a calendar.

December 12 Tues. Snowy & cold. Bought a few Christmas presents. Attended Parent-Teachers association meeting where a Mr. Corey spoke about "Thrift."

December 13 Wed. Very cold. Billo was sick with a cold so I spent all of my spare time with him. The gas nearly gave out again.

December 14 Thurs. Very cold. After my French lesson I attended a lecture by Prof. Martin, given to Edward's class in the High School, his first lecture in Peters' Hall & by Prof. Martin.

December 15 Fri. Very cold. Leaven Club at Mrs. Booth's. Read some chapters from a theology which I did not understand very well. House was cold.

December 16 Sat. 10° below 0. Did some Christmas shopping. Went to Dr. Greene's. He told the story of an Abyssinian girl Banda and a Hindoo Singh, a Prince. Very interesting.

December 17 Sunday. Cold. Sacred Concert at Vespers. Very fine indeed.

December 18 Mon. Did Christmas shopping with Armen, George, Edward & Billo, not altogether.

December 19 Tues. Primary & Cradle Roll Christmas Party at James Brand House. Billo & Alfred went. Frances had a bad cold. Alfred's first début in society. Quite successful.

December 20 Wed. Colds, colds, colds, day & night. Frances wore her new dress or one of the four that Mr. Hosmer bought, light-blue. She looks so much older.

December 21 Thurs. In the house all day with my cold.

Ernest C. Partridge

December 23 Made up special Ethics Exam with Prof Lyman.

[December 24–29]

December 30 Studied and did housework. Dr. Dyermenjian came in the PM for a visit. Had three Martins to supper.

December 31 Sunday. Armen went to Detroit for Hranoush Boyagian's wedding. Community meeting in Evening.

December 22 Fri. Edward very much elated over his marks, all ninety or above. Visited Billy's & George's schools. Billy has trouble recognizing a &, called it "6."

December 23 Sat. Getting ready for Christmas.

December 24 Sunday. Samuel came. Children, George, Billo, Edward & Frances took part in a Christmas entertainment. Frances was only ornamental. She did not say a word.

December 25 Mon. Christmas. Stockings in the morning, tree in the P.M. My largest present was an electric iron from Mr. P., except $100 from Uncle R. We gave the boys a Meccano spring Newton & a "radio Junior." The others had leggings, toys, mittens, etc. Samuel sent beforehand $10 for presents for the children, and Baidzar $2. Rec'd word that Miss Fowle died in Sivas. The telegram was repeated.

December 26 Tues. Day after Christmas. Samuel went home. Everyone is tired, the weather is warm & rainy. Mrs. Martin & Arthur called.

December 27 Wed. Took supper, Mr. P. & I, with Mr. & Mrs. James and Madame James. Edward & George went to Tank Home & Miss Traion and Miss Santikian took supper with Armen & children.

December 28 Thurs. Frances is just at the contrary stage. Her favorite expression is "Anyway. I can't have any for never."

December 29 Fri. Went to Elyria & got a sweater for Billo. He has done up all sorts of things to put in the Christmas tree for presents every day since Christmas. Today we got each a real present.

December 30 Sat. Mikran Eff. came. Mrs. Martin & Arthur and Isabel came to supper. We had scalloped potato, tuna fish salad, sauce cake, coffee & tea. The boys showed pictures with the reflectoscope in evening.

December 31 Sunday. Armen went to Detroit to attend Hranoosh Varzhoohi's wedding. Mr. P. & I did housework nearly all day. Village Improvement Society meeting in evening which I did not attend.

Memoranda.
Jan 1st $50 sent to Aleppo for Haigayoon, Suchdorgian & Yester Kudishian. Of this $25 from Miss Rice, $12 for handiwork (also sold by Miss Rice) $10 from Haigoohi written also Dec. 1

Diaries of Winona & Ernest Partridge 1917

January 1 Mon. Mikran Eff. was visiting us. He took the children and me to the Movies. We saw "The Kid," not much of a play. After supper we had a Christmas tree for Billo's benefit, the fourth or fifth since Christmas but this time we had real presents on it. In the evening Mikran & Mr. P. went to call on Dr. Greene.

January 2 Tues. I stayed in the house all day. Frances and Alfred played very nicely together, she taking care of him. I put on a little suit of pantaloons and waist fastened together, blue & white. It had a pocket in the trousers and he was delighted. I hate to lose the baby, but he will grow. Mrs. Bohn's baby died of pneumonia.

January 3 Wed. Mrs. Martin came up to make a party call and show me her new dress. It is very pretty trimmed with Chinese embroidery. We expected Armen but she did not come. Mrs. Todd called with William Henry. She brought some of their outgrown clothes but they were mostly too small for Frances.

Ernest C. Partridge

January 1 Mon Dr. Mikran & the rest of the family went to Movies. Billo had another Xmas tree. Called with Mr D on Dr Greene.

January 2 Took Mikran Eff to library & museum and he took Interurban to Detroit.

[January 3–5]

January 6 Worked on lessons all day till 4:30. Winona & E & I went to 1st Basketball game Baldwin U. We won 43–1. The rest went to a concert.

[January 7–8]

January 9 Went to U.L.A. lecture by courtesy of Metcalfs. SS. McLure spoke 1 ¼ hrs on Editing a Magazine & 1 hr on the War.

January 4 Thurs. Mrs. Martin came (written by mistake for yesterday). Armen came at half past five. She had missed the train on Wednesday. Kindergarten opened and Frances went with her new blue & white checked dress.

January 5 Fri. Went to French class again. Prof. Jamieson is a fine teacher. I am surprised at the amount of cheating the boys in the class do. They deliberately open their books & hide them when he says to close them. I am hoping they will flunk.

January 6 Sat. Went to a Basket-ball game between Oberlin & Baldwin-Wallace score 43–1. After that went to a concert given by the Musical Union. It was a collection of folk songs which they gave this year in place of the Messiah. This was a repetition. Eva MacNaughton & Mr. Haroun sang solos, very fine. Rec'd $50 from Wellesley Hills Church for Yester.

January 7 Sunday. Attended vespers. Dr. Williams spoke on "The Challenge of the New Year," to be honest and right in every part, to be ready for great crises if they come. Wrote to Mr. Smith of Wellesley Hills & to Baidzar. Baidzar is very happy.

January 8 Mon. Attended a Committee meeting of the Women's Club to plan for Turkish part of a program. They decided to ask Armen & Miss Santikian to sing. I sent Rebecca for Paklava & to Samuel for costumes. Mr. Richards and Mr. Hill called, representing the cradle roll of which Alfred is a member. Nearly sick-a-bed all day. Miss Metcalf called.

January 9 Tues. French class. Prof. Alexander gave a stereoptician lecture to the sophomore History classes in the H.S. on the Roman Forum & Pompeii. I attended.

January 10 Wed. Went to a missionary meeting in Wellington to speak about Turkey. Mr. Emery is the pastor. They kept me speaking about two hour, a very appreciative audience. Had my picture taken for 50 cts. and bought a pair of shoes by trying them on. The first in fifteen years.

January 11 Thurs. French lesson. In the evening the Portmanteau Theatre under the direction of Stewart Walker. They gave "The Birthday of the Infanta" "The very naked boy" and "The Gods of the Mountains."

January 12 Fri. French lesson. Frances says "Ring around the roses, Pocket full of poses, Hush, hush, hush, hush, Aferdown."

January 13 Sat. At home all day as usual on Saturday, washing, ironing, etc. etc. We had four tickets offered us for the Artists Recital, the New York Symphony Orchestra. We could use only one as Armen had one anyway and Edward had to prepare for examinations.

January 14 Sunday. Very, very cold. Billo got up before seven, before his father and the boys, got dressed, put on his wraps and shoveled the paths, sweeping off the piazza and steps and making a place for the milk bottles etc., then had a fine time in the deep snow. Frances got very cold coming from S.S. Prof. Lyman preached.

January 15 Mon. Worked all day but loafed with the children all the evening. Edward, George & Billo went to the movies to see Romeo & Juliet. Armen went to Woman's Club to the supper & foreign evening. Mr. P. went to the library. I had a fine evening with the children in groups.

January 16 Tues. Armen & Alfred had their pictures taken. Mrs. Martin called, also Mrs. Garland. Went to Miss Cowdery's French class. Armen & I went to see Romeo & Juliet at the "Movies." The scenery was beautiful and the acting pretty good. I did not like Romeo. It is very cold & growing colder.

January 17 Wed. Cleaned house with Mrs. Metcalf's vacuum cleaner. It cleans rugs and carpets well. Edward had his last half year exam today and has now a vacation until Monday. George is having exams too but does not finish until tomorrow. Account for the paklava came $3 for four tins, 64 pieces regular price $4.

January 18 Thurs. The gas went down before noon today and did not come up at all during the day, so we had a cold house and poorly cooked food. Our last French class for this semester. Alfred tells where everyone goes, Kindergarten, H.S., 1st grade, 5th grade, etc. Mama goes to church and he himself to "my Oberlin."

January 19 Fri. Edward was sick with malaria all day. Mr. Partridge got his [Edward's] semester marks. English 91, Geometry 95, Latin 94, History 93 all above 90. I went to see Mrs. Wright about what Armen would better do. She ought to help her mother but wants to study. She will probably study and we will try to find help for her mother.

Ernest C. Partridge

[January 10]

January 11 Went to Senior PM in Sems[Seminary]. After that both Winona and three boys to Portmanteau Theatre. Very good indeed. Thur lect by E H Grigg, World War & Ethics.

[January 12]

January 13 Worked hard all day. Wrote part of Prof B's 2nd paper. Evening went to N.Y. Symphony Orchestra Concert; very fine.

January 14 Have a bad cold & so did not go out at all. Winona went to church in the evening.

January 15 Spent some time writing a paper for Prof Bosworth's. King's Class PM. Most of evening at library studying.

January 16 Three classes and reading between times. Spent evening working over Phil of R [Philosophy of Religion] notes for examination.

January 17 Went to two classes. Spent most of forenoon cleaning with vacuum cleaner. Edward & I went to a reading at Sem by Bells.

January 18 Worked some of N.T. paper; have 3 lessons.

January 19 Edward got his Semester marks: Eng 91, Geom 95, Latin 94, Hist 93. I have had a cold for some days. Finished N.T. second paper. George & I saw O.H.S. beat Glenville & Federals beat Elyria team.

January 20 Sat. Billo and I cleaned up the cellar. He picked up nearly everything on the floor and I swept it. I called on Mrs. Wilder, one of our new neighbors. Edward was better but not able to go out. He does not have any strength. Armen went to see Hansel & Gretel. This is a sample of Alfred's use of the reflexive verb. "Mama, I want you to dress yourself to me," which means "I want you to dress me."

January 21 Sunday. Did not go out except to go after some cream with Alfred. Mrs. Greene called. Lt snow in the morning and all last night and now it is raining. Alfred sings this way. "Onward Christian Soldiers marching on to war, with the cross of Jesus loves me." When he gets to Jesus he thinks it is the other song. His words are very indistinct and babyish but very cute.

January 22 Mon. George's half year marks 5th grade. Miss Wilkinson, teacher. Health E, Conduct E, Effort E, Read & Lit. 88, Spelling 93, Penmanship 81, Arith. 92, Lang. 84, Geog. 91, Music 76, Drawing 83. Went to movies, Mary Pickford in "Less than the Dust."

January 23 Tues. Letter from Polly, dated Nov. 12, during Miss Fowle's sickness. Speaks of Dr. Khosrov. Tells about her clothes, that her salary is not enough to live on. She had received a letter from me & children's pictures. Also I had a letter from Sarah Blunt. Alfred has been calling me "Mrs. P." today. I took him down town & he cried all the way home to go "down town."

January 24 Wed. Armen had a post card from Zabel Vahan dated Nov. 19, the very latest from Turkey. The College Secretary decided to allow Armen to be classed as a Freshman but take special studies this semester. Alfred has learned "just a minute" and he says it on every occasion.

January 25 Thurs. A package of letters from Mr. Peet and Mr. Case reported a telegram received in Con. from Polly

Ernest C. Partridge

January 20 Two classes. Worked all PM and evening at library and at home on Durkheim [probably Emile Durkheim, sociologist] for exam.

January 21 Sunday Dr Ozora Davis preached AM. Winona went in evening. Dr & Mrs Greene called.

January 22 George got his half-year marks. Good. Went to see Mary Pickford in "Less than the Dust."

January 23 Exam in Phil of R.

January 24 Called on Wirkler and arranged Armen's credits so she could be classed as a Freshman.

January 25 Exam in Evol of R on Durkheim's Book. Winona & I went to the Annual Supper & bus. meeting of 1st church.

January 26 Exam in Christian Ethics.

January 27 Worked all day for Phil of R Exam and in evening saw two basketball games. Case beat Oberlin 28–12 and OHS beat Mansfield 34–27.

January 28 Went to church in the AM. Prof Hutchins preached a fine sermon. Winona went in the evening.

January 29 Worked most of the day on Phil of R exam.

Jan. 15 saying she was well and busy. At night we attended the annual church supper of the First Church. The supper was good but the business meeting was long drawn out.

January 26 Fri. Went down town this morning. In the afternoon attended the Woman's Club with Mrs. Shaw. They had a musical program. Someone from the conservatory, a girl, sang. Miss Heacox played a cello solo. The High School girls Glee Club sang. Prof. Lutz read a O'Henry story.

January 27 Sat. Mrs. Wright came to give me some money for Armen's mother. In the evening Armen & George went to the picture show to see Marguerite Clark in "The Prince & the Pauper." Mr. P and Edward went to the Basketball game & I stayed with the babies. I cut out a skirt, brown plaid.

January 28 Sunday. Prof. & Mrs. Miller took Edward & me for an auto ride. We went to Elyria and Lorain & enjoyed it very much. The weather is warm & the snow is melting. In the evening Edward & I went to Church & heard Prof. Hutchins on "What doth the Lord require of thee but to do justly, love kindness & to walk humbly with thy God."

January 29 Mon. I took the two little ones out for a walk and I wished I had not. They went through the puddles and Alfred stood in the middle and stamped his feet. I met Mrs. Martin and she came with me. Billo & George went to a church social without any grown person & got along all right.

January 30 Tues. Armen did the washing and I worked on my skirt what time I could get. Mrs. Moore called. She is one of my nearest neighbors but has not called before. Alfred has learned "Help, mercy!" and today he was talking about his "[?]." Mrs. Moore spoke of our "jolly family."

January 31 Wed. Almost finished my skirt. Mrs. Barnard called. Attended a supper by the "Leaven Club" at Mr. Shaw's house. There were present Mr. & Mrs. James, Snyder, Reille, Booth, Freeman, Rooman, Christian, Boeher, Robertson, Madame James, Miss Brooks, Mr. Shaw's father & mother.

February 1 Thurs. Armen had lessons morning and afternoon, so did Mr. P. I was busy. Alfred says that his name is Alfred Mister Partridge. I wonder if he understands that his father's name is Ernest. He is learning very fast, can say almost everything in English.

Ernest C. Partridge

January 30 Worked on Phil of R Exam and did some other reading. In evening took exam at Prof Lyman's house.

[January 31]

[February 1–16]

February 2 Fri. Very, very cold & no gas. We had corned beef for dinner and French toast for supper which Armen cooked in the fire place like a Turkish "ojah." In our warm room Allen & Robert and Carroll came to play.

February 3 Sat. Cold as Greenland's icy mountains and no gas until evening. Down cellar there so we could warm up a little soup & some canned beans. Pres. Wilson broke off relations with Germany and told Count Bernstoff to go home and called Gerard from Germany. Oberlin beat Ohio U and High School beat Chaquin Falls.

February 4 Sunday. Cold & snowy. We had gas all day until about supper time. Dr. Greene has pneumonia. They have found a trained nurse. I hope he may recover. I went to vespers. Alfred did not go to sleep until half past nine, because he slept a little at noon. Edward made an elevator with his Meccano. War seems probable.

February 5 Mon. Very cold. No gas, no school for George on account of the cold. We were crowded up in front of the fireplace again. No letters and no callers except two boys to play with George. Billo has a cold but is not very sick. Dr. Greene no better. America not at war yet.

February 6 Tues. Warmer, good gas. Dr. Greene no better. Mr. Irving Metcalf gave us tickets to the U.L.A. lecture, Bliss Perry on "The Youth of Napoleon," very fine. He told the story of his youth but incidentally brought in all the important things in his after life.

February 7 Wed. Warmer. Gas fine. Dr. Greene no better. Mrs. Wright called in the afternoon. George and Armen and I went to see Silas Maruer at the "Movies," very good indeed. Edward went to the matinee. Letter from Mrs. Fowle.

February 8 Thurs. These days the newest stunt in our family is to wiggle the scalp. This morning Alfred shook his head and his curls wiggled. He said, "My curls wibble just like George's doos." War seems probable as Germany continues her U-boat campaign. Dr. Greene seems a little better.

February 9 Fri. Cold. Gas low again in spite of repeated assurances that hereafter it would be all right. Alfred fell with his buster car in the cellar and cut his head. He cried more for the blood than the hurt. Mr. P. went to a men's supper at 1st church, beans, ham sandwiches, pumpkin pie, coffee.

February 10 Sat. Cold, gas low. Dr. Greene died at 6 A.M. His sons Fred and Theodore are here and two others are coming. I attended a meeting of the "Leaven Club" at Mrs. Alice Williams. Miss MacConnaughey of Shansi spoke very informally and interestingly. Bought valentine's & materials for making them. Moving picture show Seven Sisters.

February 11 Sunday. Cold but good gas. The children made valentines, played basket ball, ate popcorn balls, chocolate. Our regular Sunday dinner is pork chops, potato etc. jello or gelatin jelly and whipped cream. Supper, macaroni with cheese. First Union Lenten Service in the Chapel. Pres. King spoke on "Our duty in these times."

February 12 Mon. Very cold, gas low. Dr. Greene was buried here in Oberlin. Dr. Hutchins conducted the funeral. Pres. King read two letters from the Board or rather a letter & telegram. Mr. P. spoke for the missionaries. Armen and Miss Santikian went, so I did not. It seems less likely today that we shall have war.

February 13 Tues. Warmer, more gas. The great event of the day was banging Alfred's hair. He is much is much improved we think. Before his front curls came down into his eye. Mrs. Ryan called. Weather is fine and the roads are fine for sleighing.

February 14 Wed. Valentine's day. All the children had plenty. Billy gave one to his teacher composed by his father, thus, "A Valentine to a lady, Please don't think me silly, My dear teacher, Miss Brady, Her loving pupil, Billy." Mrs. Martin & Mrs. Gammon called.

February 15 Thurs. Warm, gas low until suppertime. Washed the cellar with Billo's help. After dinner gave the little ones baths and washed their hair. The Board bulletin says that they have not been able to get word from Ambassador Elkus for a week.

Ernest C. Partridge

February 17 Lessons forenoon. Read 2 hours PM. Evening basketball Oberlin 28 Reserve 21. OHS 29 Wooster HS 7.

February 18 Auto ride to S. Amherst. Morning Cong ch. PM ME ch. Evening Cong ch. Night at parsonage, Lester Woods.

February 19 Breakfast early; to Oberlin on Ramsay.

[February 20–23]

February 16 Fri. Most important event, a call from Susie Zearing. I enjoyed her very much. We called on Mr. & Mrs. Eastman this evening. Letters from the Board, nothing from Sivas. Need in Turkey increasing but no very recent news.

February 17 Sat. Called on Mrs. Kur and Mrs. Greene and Mrs. Haskell. Mr. P. contributed 10 cts., George 10, & Edward 15 to by a ticket for me to go to the basketball game. Reserve beat Oberlin and Oberlin High School beat Wooster H.S. I bought Billo some rubber boots for $1.75 and some gray trousers for $1.00.

February 18 Sunday. Colder. At home all day. Mr. P. went to speak in Amherst or No. A. The children all went to Sunday School except Alfred. Billo wore his rubber boots most of the time although it was not much wet.

February 19 Mon. Mild. At home all day except that I took the babies to meet Edward and then "around Reamer." I found a quarter which I dropped Saturday night on the street. Alfred's rompers came from Mr. Hosmer, 79 cts. apiece. Also Billo's middy blouses came but they are too large.

February 20 Tues. Mild. Edward & I went to the Colonial Exhibition at the Second Church. It was very interesting but most of the things were a hundred years old or less. In the evening I went to the Parent-Teachers Association meeting at the Prospect St. School. Mr. Rawdon answered a few questions about vocational education etc. Came home with Mrs. MacClennon.

February 21 Wed. Mild. Red letter day, a letter containing snap shots of herself and Miss Fowle, from Polly. Polly looks well. One picture was taken with Dr. Hekimian. In the evening Mr. P. & Edward went to the father & son celebration, stunts, speeches, food. Mrs. Koos [or Coos], Michael's friend, was here. Armen took dinner with her.

February 22 Thurs. Mild. Dr. Ian Hanna addressed the students and others on "If George W. were here today," in place of Sen. Burton who could not come, very fine. Went to Elyria in the afternoon and bought me a striped blue silk waist, wore it to the faculty reception in the evening. Reception brilliant, talked mostly with Mrs. Jarrett, Miller, Moore, Prof. Martin Hall.

February 23 Fri. Mild. Leaven Club at Mrs. Rooman's. Tagore was the subject. Refreshments were cocoa, three kinds of cookies & peanut candy. Read "Georgina of the Rainbows" to George. Letter from Mrs. Clark. Alfred's great sentence now is "I want to show you something" or "I want to come in your lap for minute."

February 24 Sat. Mr. P. & I took four children, all except Alfred, to Glee Club Concert, very fine. It was repeated for the school children & their parents. In the evening George went to a "feed" at Mr. Doolittle's room. Edward and his father and Armen to a basketball game. Oberlin 26, Dennison 26. Alfred said he had a headache. I said, "Where?" He said, "I have a headache in my pants." He has a stomach ache.

February 25 Sunday. Warm. Had coffee ice-cream. Third Union Lenten Service. Mr. Barbour, Pres. of Rochester Theo. Sem. preach[ed] on "life" and "Eternal Life", very fine. The Musical Union sang.

February 26 Mon. Warm & damp. Letters from Dr. Clark and Mr. Hosmer. Susie Clark has been visiting them, is much better in health. We called on Mr. & Mrs. Shaw in the evening. Alfred fell down in the water and mud twice today. It distresses him very much, also his mother.

February 27 Tues. A little cooler or colder. Washed, ironed, cooked, swept, mended stockings, bathed the three little ones and was all tired out.

February 28 Wed. Fine cool weather. Heard Mr. Mott three times today. He is fine. Tonight spoke about "Atrophy of Moral & Spiritual Faculties." It was Allen Buddington's sixth birthday. George & Billo were invited over. They played games & ate ice-cream and cake. We got Alfred's pictures, the first in little trousers & banged hair.

March 1 Thurs. Pleasant. Day of Prayer for College. Mr. Mott addressed the meeting in the College. Armen & Mr. P. went and I got dinner. Went to call on Miss Zearing in the afternoon but she was not at home. In the evening I heard Miss Burton, Nat. Sec. of Y.W.C.A. on Christ's feeding the multitude with 5 loaves & 5 fishes.

March 2 Fri. A letter and photograph from Polly dated Dec. 6, the Photograph of a group containing Dr. Fazil Bey, Polly, Miss Fowle and the girl nurses. Hagopos Eff. is not among them but I hope that is not significant. She says she can hold out until she sees us again. I hope she can. Shansi Day, Rev. Dan Bradley spoke, raised $3764.

Ernest C. Partridge

February 24 Worked all the forenoon. PM all but Alfred & Armen went to Glee Club Concert. Evening Dennison BB game; a fine one but got beat 31–26.

February 25 Sunday. AM Prof Lyman on the War. Met my Mission Study class, Social Aspects. Evening Pres. Barbour of Rochester at Union Lenten Service; fine.

February 26 Only one lesson, King. Studied most of the day. Winona & I called on the Shaws.

February 27 Took Billo to the gym to see a basket ball game.

February 28 Mott gave Monthly lecture. I did house work & sent Winona. He spoke to Volunteers at 4:30 and to public at 7; "The Atrophy of Moral and Spiritual Faculties."

March 1 Mott spoke morning and evening. A large bunch of men signed cards.

March 2 Shansi Day. Dr Dan Bradley made the address. Pledged $3664.00.

March 3 Worked all day excepting 10-12, lessons of Phil of R Exam which I took in the evening. Last back work with Prof Lyman.

March 4 Communion at 1st church. Prof Lyman in charge. Had Mission Study class. Evening Hugh Black on Prayer.

March 5 Called on James in the Evening.

March 3 Sat. I called on Miss Burton, National Secretary of the Y.W.C.A. She is a very pleasant and capable young lady, resembles Helen Bacon, Vahan's sister. I heard her speak once. Alfred and Frances played with Betty Johnston today. They also had a fine time with buster cars. The older boys went skating. Nazeli's marks for the term ending Dec. 6 at Springfield were, Intermediate Arith 70, Word Class II 68, Elementary Comp. 84, 1st yr Citizenship 75-80

March 4 Sunday. Cold & stormy, almost a blizzard in the evening. Mr. P., the two boys and I went to the evening Lenten service to hear Dr. Hugh Black, the great preacher. I did not appreciate his preaching, I am afraid. It was a very good sermon on prayer, but not so remarkable as I expected.

March 5 Mon. George, Billo & I went to the Apollo theatre to see Dicken's Christmas Carol in the movies. The story is fine but the acting was dreadful. It was much better done in Sivas when Sennecherian Eff. was Scrooge, Toros, Marley, and Hurian, Bekhian, & Khalarian were the spirits.

March 6 Tues. Warmer. Worked all day but went to call on the James's in the evening, but after I came home I had to iron until after eleven. Then Alfred woke up at five so my night was short. He is a dear but has been the worst one about sleeping. He doesn't take a nap any more either.

March 7 Wed. Much warmer, rainy. The snow, about a foot, is melting. Mr. P. skipped his class & I went to Missionary meeting. Mrs. Martin also came down to stay with the children so I could go. So we went together. Edward got his first shirt, that is outside one, a few days ago. Until now he had worn waists.

March 8 Thurs. Windy & cold. As last year, did not go out except to take Frances to Kindergarten & bring her back. When I went for her, I took Alfred and they stopped to embrace each other on the steps. Alfred has been insisting upon calling him "Baby" today!

March 9 Fri. Warm & melting, snow nearly gone. Usual round of dishwashing, sweeping, dusting, making beds, cooking, washing, ironing, mending stockings, and especially looking after children, putting on & taking off rubbers, mittens etc. etc. Received Polly's picture, no writing in it.

March 10 Sat. Y.W.C.A. circus. Armen & I took the three small children. They enjoyed it immensely, eating popcorn, ice-cream cones. Mrs. Crafts and her daughter Elizabeth were with us. Afterwards I left Armen with the children and went to the Leaven Club meeting at Mrs. Williamses. She spoke to us.

March 11 Sunday. A thunder shower in the night and warmer today. Mr. Ryan called in the afternoon. In the evening we attended the last of the Lenten services. Prof. Hutchins preached about Matthew's follow Jesus. Then we called at the Adamses to talk about '95 reunion.

March 12 Mon. Went with Mr. P. to Whitney's to buy a suit of clothes. He bought a gray suit for $25. How easy it is for a man to be decently dressed!

Ernest C. Partridge

[March 6]

March 7 Cut my Ethics class so Winona could go to the Miss. Meeting.

March 8 Worked hard on paper for Prof Bosworth.

[March 9]

March 10 Y.W.C.A. circus PM. Winona and children went. Last basketball game of season. State beat us 28–20 in a good game.

March 11 A call from Ryan. Last of Lenten Services. Prof Hutchins on Mathew's call. '95 business meeting with Mr & Mrs Adams.

March 12 Bought a new gray suit of clothes at Whitneys.

March 13 Cleaned things up and started for New York on 4:55 for meeting of Relief Com.

March 14 Reached N.Y. City at 10:20. Got breakfast and visited with GG Brown till meeting time. Met Vickrey, Dr Barton & Drs Dodd, White, Chambers, Elmer & Prof Xinedes.

March 15 Spent night with Raymond. Spoke in P.M. Thursday. Visited Emily Wheeler & lunched there; talked with Vickrey. Dinner with Browns & Bauminga's & night at Mrs Hubbard's.

March 16 Went to New York and spent some time with Vickrey. 6:30 PM last train for Cleveland.

March 13 Tues. For the first time since this semester began and Armen began to attend college, I got to the bottom of the stocking basket. How dreadful it is to have it the height of your ambition to get the stockings mended! Mr. P. started for N.Y. to attend a meeting of the Relief Committee. I attended a Com. meeting at Mrs. Clarke's on So. Park St.

March 14 Wed. Colder, windy. Did not go out, except to bring Frances home from Kindergarten. Mr. Todd called in the evening. Read to George & Billo from "Alice in Wonderland." I enjoy it very much, although I have read it so many times. Billy was naughty & sent to bed. He went to sleep so could not get to sleep in eve.

March 15 Attended a lecture in the evening by Prof. H.H. Powers on France, Italy & Portugal, their reasons for entering the war, France to hold and improve the position she has been struggling for, Italy to defend herself from Austria, & Portugal as a loyal handmaiden of England.

March 16 Fri. Prof. Powers spoke about Great Britain, her unselfishness, her benevolence towards her colonies etc. In the evening he spoke about America, her condition and her danger, especially from Germany and Japan, who needs more room.

March 17 Sat. Usual Saturday drudgery. Mrs. Martin called, found me washing, so came down cellar. Mr. P. came home. He has to go right into relief work without finishing his course. Edward was a delegate, for the first time in his life, to a Boys' Confederation, meeting here.

March 18 Sunday. Heard an address by Pres. King on "Mother and Son." Not "I will conquer that boy no matter what it costs him, but I will help that boy to conquer himself no matter what it costs me." In the evening Mr. Stockdale of Toledo, Ohio spoke on "Three great secrets of life." They were a deep look within, a long look ahead and a steady look on high. Edward sat with the delegates.

March 19 Mon. Mrs. Martin and Mrs. MacNaughton called, also Mrs. Metcalf. In the evening George and I went to the picture show after the babies were asleep. It was a play to show the dangers of unpreparedness. Billo spent the afternoon with Ralph Williams.

March 20 Tues. Warm. Armen washed today so I had a little time and strength for washing floors, making pies and such things. Alfred and Frances played outside nearly all the afternoon. She takes good care of her little brother, calling him away from dogs etc. Mr. P. & I called on Mrs. Greene.

March 21 Wed. Called on Susie Zearing in the evening. It seemed like old times to be talking with her, although she has changed a good deal since she and Miss Fish used to be always together.

March 22 Thurs. Warm & springlike. Alfred took a long walk with Mrs. Bohn. Since a year ago he has learned Armenian to speak fluently, has forgotten it, now using only two or three words, [Armenian words], and has learned English pretty well, so that he can converse with strangers.

March 23 Fri. Tried to go to Elyria with Billo and his father but missed the car. I was invited to attend the Alumnae reception to the Senior girls but did not go. Receptions are so stiff and such dressy affairs that I thought I did not care to go especially alone.

Ernest C. Partridge

March 17 Reached Cleveland at 11:55 and Oberlin on 3:15 car. It is decided that I shall drop studies and get to work on Relief Organization in Ohio.

March 18 Prof Fullerton preached AM. My Mission study class and lesson on Russia PM. Pres King on "Mothers & Boys."

March 19 Talked over my work with Profs Bosworth & Lyman. Both agree to my making up the last two months work later if I can.

March 20 Attended Pres King's class and got his consent to finishing up his course later. Also MacClemmons in evening.

March 21 Spent the day in Cleveland. Talked with Wright, Rothrock, Royce, Fisk, Fraser etc. Found a room in same building. (66m)

March 22 Wrote some letters. Dictated some to a Business College girl. Went to Pres King's class.

March 23 Wrote more letters. Went to Cosmopolitan Club Annual Entertainment.

March 24 Went to Elyria with Winona on F.S.W. to shop. Evening spoke to Exec Com of Elyria Ch Fed. (18m)

March 25 Took care of the kids & let Winona go to church. Called on James.

March 26 Went to last lesson of Pres King's on Haering.

March 24 Sat. Went to Elyria for a suit for Billo and a coat & hat for Frances, Billo's first suit and France's first real hat, old rose straw. Frances was just a dear little girl, not fussing about anything. She tried on hats and every time she would look in the glass and begin to laugh.

March 25 Sunday. Beautiful weather, warm. Prof. Fiske preached on "Does God take a hand in making history?" I did not enjoy it for a sermon. As Prof. Anderegg said, "I can read that in the [Cleveland] Plain Dealer any day." Tonight he was to speak on Russia but I did not go.

March 26 Mon. Warm. Mr. P. & I called on Mrs. Martin and Mrs. Greene. The boys played base ball all day. A supposed burglar came to Mr. Cuming's house. Marie, the nurse was the only one awake. He did not get anything. I wonder if it was not someone trying to frighten Marie.

March 27 Tues. Cold, snow, rain. Had a postal from Hampartsoom Kaloyan, a letter from Mr. Favre, too. Mrs. [?] Johnston and Susie Zearing called. We washed Frances's and Alfred's hair. Frances was lovely but Alfred howled.

March 28 Wed. Rather cold. Went with Mrs. Haskell to Elyria to attend the Pre-Jubilee Mass Meeting. They gave A Day at School with the W.B.M.I. I meet quite a number of people whom I had seen before, from Lorain, Wellington, Cleveland & Elyria.

March 29 Thurs. I was invited to lunch at Mrs. Johnston's, where Susie Zearing is visiting. The others present were Mrs. Williams, Mrs. MacDaniels, Mrs. Shurtleff, May Shurtleff of Story, Mrs. Burton, Miss Barton, Mrs. Andrews. I called afterwards on Mrs. Fullerton.

March 30 Fri. Internation. Cafeteria supper at the James Brand house. Mrs. Martin, Mr. P. & I went over to prepare the Turkish booth in the morning. In the evening Armen, dressed up as a village girl, and Margaret Haskell in Turkish costume, served the coffee & sold locoom.

March 31 Sat. Nothing unusual except that I tried to do a little sewing. The boys' last day of vacation and they played all they could, although it was rather wet. George was going on a hike with Carroll & his father but they could not go on account of rain.

April 1 Sunday. Mr. P. & I started to church but found we were late, so turned back. In the afternoon heard Mr. Bennett of Lorain. When we got home Billo met us with the news that Frances had cut off her hair. We found that she had cut off a lot from the front. It looks dreadful.

April 2 Mon. Nothing doing for me. The public schools commenced.

April 3 Tues. Pleasant & warm. Armen and I cleaned house, mostly beating rugs, while Pres. Wilson and Congress were preparing to decide whether Germany & U.S. were in a state of war. Pres. Wilson made a masterly address that will be one of the great documents of all times, they say.

Ernest C. Partridge

March 27 Took 7:28 car to Cleveland. Conference with Pres Thuring. Home on noon-train. PM went to Lorain & talked to Bunnet & Kinney about Relief. (78m)

[March 28]

March 29 Spent 5 hours with James reviewing Haering. Went to Lorain for a Supper-Conference. Organized a Relief Com. (24m)

March 30 Helped make a Turkish booth at James Brand House. Went to Cleveland for a Com meeting. Had a conference with Pres Thuring. (66m)

March 31 Dictated 15 letters. Wrote some myself. Called on Ryan.

April 1 1917 Sunday. A rainy day. Was late to church so turned back. 1st Ch called Mr Van Der Pyl. Heard Bennett of Lorain PM.

[April 2]

April 3 Spent 6 hours with James going over Haering for paper. A letter from Vickrey authorizing Cleveland office.

April 4 U.S. Senate voted 82 to 8 that we are in a state of war with Germany.

April 5 The House after an all night session voted 373–50. News that MLG decorated by Sultan.

[April 6]

April 7 Helped house work forenoon. Took Billo & Allen to H.S. Carnival. Evening worked on Haering paper.

April 4 Wed. Warm & pleasant. Congress again met but took no action or we have not heard of some, as yet. A great mass meeting in the chapel, led by Mayor Yocum. Uncle Rufus sent me one hundred dollars.

April 5 Thurs. Cold & rainy. The Senate decided 82 to 8 that the U.S. is in a state of war with the Central Powers.

April 6 Fri Today the House of Representatives 373 to 50. The fire whistle blew and all the bells rang just after noon when the news was received. Miss Rice sent $6 ½ in payment of handiwork. Word came through Mrs. Bowen from Geneva that Polly has been decorated by the Sultan for "humanitarian work."

April 7 Sat. Leaven Club at Mrs. Shaw's. Miss Brooks told of her summer work preaching in Dakota [and] Mrs. James her experience in Fairmount. High School Carnival, Edward was one of a quartet who were supposed to sing but they turned around and there was s-e-l-l on their backs.

April 8 Sunday. Easter, cold & wintry. I attended vespers at the Second Church with Mr. P. and Edward. It was very good but I was too sleepy to enjoy it. My side ached all the time. The church was packed. In today's paper we read that it was not allowed to send mail to any of the enemy countries.

April 9 Mon. Cold like winter. Mr. P. went to Cleveland. Armen went out to look at birds from 4:30 to 6 A.M. I went with Edward to get a pair of new shoes, rubber soles, price $3.50. I made "hard tack" by Mrs. Shaw's recipe. 1 cup each of chopped nuts, dates, flour, sugar, a pinch of baking powder & salt, 2 eggs. Very good.

April 10 Tues. Warmer. My bicycle came, very fine. Went down town with Ernest to buy a cut away suit. Mr. Whitney did not have any to fit so he gave him his own to take to N.Y. Then he will get him another. In the evening heard a lecture by Mr. Kelman on the war, about the trenches, character development, ways to help allies, etc.

April 11 Wed. Warm & pleasant. Ernest went to New York. Frances fell down from a bicycle & hurt her head. The hurt did not seem to be so bad but she vomited four times and slept a great deal. Armen tried to ride the bicycle.

April 12 Thurs. Edward & Arthur played tennis, the first time this year. Arthur took supper with us. Frances was better and went to school.

April 13 Fri. Cold. Mrs. MacNaughton and Eva called. I went down town with Alfred to deposit some money and get a draft to send to Mr. MacGann but I forgot his initials. Had a postal from Ernest. He found Dr. Clark in N.Y. What a fortunate happening!

April 14 Sat. A day of dissatisfaction. Took all the children except Edward to see the puppet theatre, which was given under the direction of the German Club. I did not like it, lack of practice, too evidently mechanical. In the evening took George and Edward to Key Theatre. Saw a monkey play which was fine.

April 15 Sunday. Went to vespers. Dr. Williams preached on "Endure hardships as a good soldier of Jesus Christ." We

---

Ernest C. Partridge

[April 8–9]

April 10 Attended lecture by Prof F C Porter on "Religion of Jesus."

April 11 11:28 to Cleveland and 3:00 train to New York for FNI Education Conference & Relief Committee. Spent time till 10:00 PM reading.

April 12 Reached N.Y. 7:50AM. Three sessions of conference. More Board people present, Drs Burton & Strong. Night at Raymonds.

April 13 Spent free day calling. Lunched with Louie. Dinner with Dr Clark & Stephen at Racoubian sisters. Night with Raphaelians.

April 14 First day of Relief Conference. A very good day, full of work & fellowship. All lunched together. Night Billy Sunday, Arlington Hotel.

April 15 Morning at South Church, Brooklyn. PM & evening Conference. Night with LCP [brother Louie].

April 16 Spent the forenoon at Relief Headquarters, with Tagley Flammer, Vickrey & Barton. With James & Compton took [?] 2:00 train for Oberlin.

April 17 Reached Cleveland at 7:30 and Oberlin at 10:10. Dr Barton proposes that in company with Mr & Mrs James & Mr & Mrs Compton I start for Tiflis. [Several decades later, the Ruth and Carl Compton were neighbors of George Partridge in Northfield, MA.]

April 18 Spent the day in Cleveland fitting up office and trying to get a stenographer.

---

have got interested in Bible games lately, something like "20 questions" and "beast, bird or fish" thus "man, book or story."

April 16 Mon. Little warmer. Mrs. Freeman of the island of Banka, and Mrs. White of India called together and then Miss Marian Metcalf. Armen went to her first lesson in First Aid to the Injured.

April 17 Tues. Mr. P. arrived from New York. He had a good time, saw Dr. Clark, Stephen, Rebecca, Antaram, Raphaelians, Lewis [brother Lewis C. Jr], etc. etc. Dr. Barton proposes that Mr. P. and Mr. & Mrs. James, Mr. & Mrs. Compton start for Russia about the first of July. Mrs. Martin called.

April 18 Wed. Warm as summer. The little children lightened their summer underwear, also George. George got sat on in a game yesterday, literally, and his head ached very badly yesterday & today. He did not go to school but is better now.

April 19 Thurs. Very Warm. The most important event in our family was the appointment of Edward as Corporal in his military company in the High School. It rained more or less and twice Alfred played in the wet sand and was just covered with mud.

April 20 Fri. Warm. Went to Cleveland, took Billo, bought three dresses with bloomers for Frances, sport waists and caps for the boys, visited Mr. P's new office.

April 21 Sat. Went to picture show with George & Edward and Almond Wilder.

April 22 Sunday. Warm. Frances's birthday, four years old. She received roller skates, new dresses, hair ribbons, marshmallows etc. We went down to the waterworks but did not celebrate with ice-cream & cake because her father was not here. He spoke at North Dover.

April 23 Mon. Colder. Mr. & Mrs. Eastman & their two children called. Dr. Tracy's death reported.

April 24 Tues. Mrs. Greene and her sister called. The boys went to see Mary Pickford in "The poor little rich girl." I made a belated birthday cake for Frances. It was pretty good.

April 25 Wed. Showery. A busy day. Mr. P. went to Medina Conference and Armen had school work all day. We had a heavy thunder shower. The children are not much afraid but the little ones like to be near their mother.

April 26 Thurs. Cold, rainy. I worked hard all day except a half hour when I mended stockings and about the same in the evening when I read the children to sleep.

April 27 Fri. Pleasant. Edward's birthday according to American time as he was born at 12:30 A.M. April 28 in Sivas, attended a half hour or less later by Dr. Jewett & his wife & Miss Powers, besides Polly & Mr. P. Today he received a "Wilding" tennis racket, a fountain pen, Conklin's racket press, cover, balls, baseball, Bible game, some chocolate marshmallows. Frances sick with a cold.

Ernest C. Partridge

April 19 Lunched with a group of Elyria men talking over plans for Relief Organization. Edward made Corporal of his H.S. Company.

April 20 Made a long day in Cleveland.

April 21 Worked at home on lecture with slides and [went to] athletic field PM.

April 22 Took an early car to North Dover where I had a pleasant day with the Machs T & T in T. Slides evening. (55m)

April 23 Early car to Lorain for Minister's Meeting. Back to Cleveland. Still trying to get stenographer. Dictated in evening to Mrs Ormsby.

[April 24]

April 25 I went to Medina for Conf meeting. Spoke 5 minutes on Relief Work. Had a headache & returned before evening service.

April 26 Spent the day in Cleveland.

April 27 Worked on speeches and publicity material. Celebrated Edward's birthday (15).

[April 28–29]

April 30 Finally got a stenographer and got to work in Cleveland office. Called on Ryans, Greene, Martin etc.

[May 1]

April 28 Sat. Pleasant but cold. After dinner Armen went at 1:10 to Birmingham with a crowd of girls to spend Sunday. Edward went at 1:15 to a military drill, Mr. P. and Billo went to a triangular track meet, in which Oberlin won over Wooster & Case. George went to Rawdon field to play ball & the little ones & I stayed home. Mrs. Martin called.

April 29 Sunday. Cloudy & rainy. A miserable day for the four older members of the family. We all felt "pepless" as Fred Martin said, with headache, sore throat, bowel trouble and general "disheartening of the soul" as Edward said. He has the same kind of a headache every Sunday. Mr. P. went to Lorain, so we were only six at supper.

April 30 Mon. Warm but rainy. Mr. P. & I called on Mrs. Ryan, Mrs. Martin & Mrs. Greene & Mrs. Haskell, all Turkey people. The conscription law passed last night & now they are discussing whether it shall be from 19 to 25, 19 to 40 or 21 to 27. George's article on "Why I want to be a Millionaire" was printed in "Everyland."

May 1 Tues. very cold, like December. May Day. Allen hung May baskets for Billo & George. Billo had another but we do not know who hung it. Then Billo & George hung baskets to Ralph and Allen and Carroll.

May 2 Wed. Attended Missionary Meeting which was addressed by Mrs. Jones of India, her daughter, Mrs. Freeman of the Island of Banka, Mrs. Terbogh about her brother in Africa, and a Japanese young woman. Miss Telford & I were to speak but didn't have time. In the evening went to Prof. Fullerton's house to attend a reception to the Senior Class in the Seminary.

May 3 Thurs. At home working all day.

May 4 Fri. Sarah Blunt's birthday. I bought a Japanese flute to send her. The Leaven Club had a picnic supper but I did not feel able to go. I was again "pepless."

May 5 Sat. A rainy Saturday is a terrible experience in a family of four active boys but we survived. I went down town with Edward and bought a few things, but forgot my most important errands.

May 6 Sunday. Cold & cloudy. The first Sunday of the new minister, Mr. Van der Pyl, but I did not hear him. Everyone seemed to like him. I gave the first talk with the stereoptician that I ever gave. Mr. P. was to speak in Grace Church in Cleveland but was not able to go.

May 7 Mon. Rainy & cold. Mrs. Martin came to call. Mr. P. did not go to Cleveland. He did not feel able to, although he was not very sick.

May 8 Tues. Pleasant in the morning & rainy in the afternoon. Mr. P. went to Cleveland. I took a picture of Frances & Alfred in the pussy willow tree in the back yard. Alfred has heard the boys complain against Ralph Cooley & he sat at the window & muttered "dinged boy" whenever he appeared.

May 9 Wed. Mrs. Wright called.

[May 10]

May 11 Fri. Went to a High School Concert with Edward. It was very good. Miss Holton does sing beautifully. I made a birthday cake for Aunt Polly in her absence. We had lemonade with it because she likes it.

Ernest C. Partridge

May 2 Spent day in city. Evening Social at Prof Fullertons.

May 3 Spent whole day in Cleveland working on letters.

May 4 Most of day in City.

May 5 Did not go to Cleveland but worked at home on plans for Relief work.

May 6 Heard Mr Van der Pyl's first sermon at 1st church. Sick so Winona went to Grace Church Cleveland for lantern lecture.

May 7 Sick with lumbago and cold. Did not go to Cleveland.

May 8 Spent several hours in Cleveland dictating letters.

May 9 Plug to Cleveland, return on 23. Talked work over with Bohn and James.

[May 10–11]

May 12 Spent forenoon in Cleveland. Billo went with me. PM Oberlin beat Case 8–2. Tea at Prof Lyman's with a missionary crowd.

May 13 Attended Com Service at 1st church. Spoke in ME ch, Oberlin. Bac[calaureate] Sermon of sem. Evening Pres King.

May 14 Went early to Cleveland. 11 AM train to Columbus for Huntington State Conference. Reached there at 10 PM. Guest of Frank Peck, Kenova [WV].

May 12 Sat. Mr. P. & I went to Prof. Lyman's to supper. We had a tray supper, fruit salad, dutch cheese, stuffed olives, salted almonds & cocoa, then ice-cream & cake. There were present Mr. & Mrs. Christian from China, Mr. & Mrs. Anderson from Russia, the Jameses & Mr. [?]

May 13 Sun. Pleasant, not very warm. We went to the waterworks, the children, Armen & I, and had a little lunch. It was baccalaureate Sunday for the Seminary. Pres. King preached on "Good thoughts in a bad time." There are 12 male & 1 female graduate, Rachael Brooks, the second woman graduate.

May 14 Mon. Went to call on Mrs. Greene who was to go to the hospital Tuesday but I found that she had changed her mind. I took Alfred with me & she kept exclaiming "Isn't that a picture?" It is his mop of curly hair that makes him a picture.

May 15 Tues. Mr. P. went early to Cleveland, thence to Kenyan College on relief business, then to Huntington, W. Vir. to the Ohio Cong. Conference. In the afternoon, I went to Whitneys and bought George two pairs of blue trousers, very pretty.

May 16 Wed. The greatest event of the day was a long letter from Mesrob Vartamian, written in March. He is in Urban, having been taken prisoner while in the Turkish Army. Nazeli also wrote a nice letter saying that she wanted to spend the summer & next year with us.

May 17 Thurs. Frances was sick with one of her squeaky colds. It was Seminary Commencement but I did not go. Mr. James, Mr. Beam & Mr. Rooman graduated also Miss Rachel Brooks. Frances seemed a little better in the evening. I went to the banquet.

May 18 Fri. Frances seemed absolutely well. Her father came home in the afternoon.

May 19 Sat. I was sick all over, sore throat, back ache, bones ache etc. Mr. P. went to Cleveland and did not return because he was to preach in Ravenna & Cuyahoga Falls. Alfred took the camphor bottle & said "Take this out & you will be well." I took it out and rubbed some on my throat. Then he said, "Now are you well? Come & get me some water."

May 20 Sunday. I was no better but no worse. Armen did all the work, staying home from church to do it. Sunday is a hard day at best and harder when you are sick, although the children tried to be good.

Ernest C. Partridge

May 15 A pleasant day at Conference. I had ten minutes to present Relief work.

[May 16–17]

May 18 Reached Cleveland from Columbus at 9:30AM. Spent day in city, writing and working in Baptist Convention.

May19 To Cleveland in morning. Lunched with Dr Hapgard. Oberlin–Reserve BB game PM. Evening to Ravenna.

May 20 Guest of Mrs C.C. Canfield; address SS and church. Prayer at Christian church PM. Evening lecture at Cuyogha Falls.

[May 21–25]

May 26 Down to Columbus morning. PM to Big Six meet. Martin & Fall did finely. Stopped at Curtiss's.

May 27 Sunday morning. North church SS. Service. Called on Garbis. Evening South Ch. A group of Armenians took me home in a car.

May 21 Mon. I am better today but not able to wash, so I washed windows. I called on Mrs. Wirkler, Mrs. Merrill and Mr. Rooman. Mrs. Haskell called here. The paper has an article on the fact that Germany has already what she is fighting for, that is the road to Bagdad.

May 22 Tues. Terrible thunder, lightning, hail & rain, so that places in the streets were too deep for automobiles to pass, without great difficult. An item in the Boston Transcript says that Mr. Peet & Mrs. Marden have arrived in Berne. Poor people of Turkey! What can they do without Mr. Peet?

May 23 Wed. Mrs. Andrews and Mrs. Frank Warner called, the latter to say that she must see me to tell Mrs. Hubbard that she had seen me. Mrs. Ryan & Mrs. Martin also called, all four of these while I was still in my washing clothes.

May 24 Thurs. I visited Billy's and George's schools. Billy is slow and so does not keep up when quickness is required. He writes & draws miserably but he is all right, bright as a dollar. A letter came from Mrs. Sewny in which she seems to say that Maksood Eff. is alive. It is surely the day of miracles.

May 25 Fri. Called on Mrs. Lyman and saw her two adopted babies.

May 26 Sat. Ernest went to Mansfield & Columbus. I went to the Senior H.S. play, "The private secretary." Edward was an usher for the first time in his life and Arthur went with a girl, but not the first time in his life.

May 27 Sunday. Mr. & Mrs. Whipple called. In the evening Edward and I went to the Memorial Day sermon, preached by Mr. Van der Pyl on The gospel for a torn world. It was the first time I had heard him & I liked him very much. He is somewhat like Mr. Spence.

May 28 Mon. Mrs. Martin and Miss Webb of Adana called. In the evening I wrote some letters as the clothes were not dry enough to iron. Had a letter from Hampartsoom from Vladivostok. He is on his way to America.

May 29 Tues. Mr. P. came home in the afternoon. Called on Mrs. James, went to the library. Mrs. Chamberlain called to ask me to speak at the missionary meeting about Polly and the other women who had remained in Turkey.

May 30 Wed. Memorial day. Armen, Mr. P. and the children went to the parade and Mr. P. & I to the address, delivered by Prof. G. F. Wright. He reviewed the experiences of the 7th regiment Co. C. Met Mrs. Woodside of Africa.

May 31 Thurs. Mr. P. spoke in the Chapel about Armenian relief. In the afternoon we went to a pageant given by the Prospect St. School. After three or four numbers the rain began to pour down and we got soaked. The street near us was a river.

June 1 Fri. We were invited to Mrs. Jessie Hill's to supper with Mr. & Mrs. Richards and their children. They are Methodist Missionaries (retired) from Africa. We had chicken on biscuit, rice (!) croquettes, fruit pudding & cake.

June 2 Sat. Mr. P. went to Cleveland, then came back and attended a ball game, Oberlin-State, and then went to Columbus to speak.

June 3 Sunday. Children's day. Alfred received his diploma from Cradle Roll. The babies were supposed to go up on the platform. I went to the steps with him and then he walked right over to Frances. She hugged him & loved him as though she had not seen him for a long time. Billo also went through the same performance with him. He wore a blue Russian blouse suit the first time. Emery laughed at him & his curls.

June 4 Mon. Attended a "Seminary Survivors" social at Prof. Hutchins's house. We played a new kind of game, finding answers to questions in the papers (see copy). Refreshments were ice-cream and strawberries.

Ernest C. Partridge

May 28 Called on Brownlee & Dr Patton & lunched with the latter. Called on Sibley Pres State C.E. & Mr Copeland banker. Sleeper to Cleveland.

[May 29–30]

May 31 Did not go to Cleveland. Compton & I spoke in O.C. Chapel. I made a report to 1st church of State conference.

June 1 Meeting of Relief Com in Cleveland. Decided to appeal for our work Children's Day. Supper at Mrs Jesse Hill's.

June 2 Forenoon in office. PM Oberlin State ballgame and O. We got beat. Evening train to Columbus. Night at Deal house.

June 3 Sunday morning Eastwood Cong ch. Supper at Curtiss's. Dinner at Evan Walters. Evening first church. Night with Marshalls.

June 4 Spoke 5 min. at General Minister's Meeting, Columbus. Noon train to Cleveland. Evening Prof Hutchins.

June 5 Registration day. Took a vacation.

[June 6]

June 7 Stayed in Oberlin till noon to get some letters from Bus[iness] Col[lege]. Evening Madison. Night Lake Erie College.

June 8 Spoke to Lake Erie College students at Chapel. Day in Cleveland.

June 5 Tues. Warm & muggy. Tremendous thunder showers in the night. The lightning struck a tree on the next street. The rain was terrible, just flooding the streets. The drainage water backed up into the cellar.

June 6 Wed. Missionary Meeting. Again hot, and again thunder & lightning & rain. Mrs. Lydia Lord Davis spoke on the book that they have been taking in the Mission study course. I told about the women left alone in the stations in Turkey.

June 7 Thurs. I went to call on a Bulgarian girl who has been teaching in Ballard School, Macon this last year. I heard about some of my former friends, Mrs. Sutton, Clara Jones, Lizzie Jones, Dr. Greene etc. Ballard has been moved outside the city. Billy finished school, was "retained."

June 8 Fri. Nazeli came. Edward took his first journey alone, to Cleveland on the trolley. I was going but Frances was sick with the "squeaks." The boys got their marks. George, 5th, for the semester: Reading 88, Spelling 93, Penmanship

81, Arith. 92, Language 89, Geog. 91, Music 76, Drawing 83. Edward, soph in H.S., 2nd semester Eng. 93, Latin 94, Math. 97, European Lit 92. On Edward's card for the year there are 24 weeks, all 90 or above.

June 9 Sat. Nothing much exciting. Armen & Nazeli went to the Conservatory Commencement.

June 10 Sunday. Baccalaureate Sunday. Sermon by Pres. King. Admission by ticket. Edward went on my ticket. I went to the Missionary meeting in the evening. Dr. James L. Barton spoke about the Missionaries in war time.

June 11 Mon. Mr. P. & I went to see Dr. Barton in the morning. It was definitely decided that Ernest is to go to Tiflis, starting in July by way of Japan. He is to take Mr. McCallum's place in doing relief work.

June 12 Tues. Alumni meeting. I did not go. Ernest & I went to Mr. Adams's to dinner. Met there Miss Hughes & Mr. Fred Loomis, also a pupil of Mrs. Adams & her mother. Dell Close & Edith Roberts reuned with us at supper. The Art Building was dedicated. We did not go. Parade, ditto. Alfred a little sick, feverish.

June 13 Wed. Commencement. Hugh Black, speaker, Polly was given the degree of M.A. for distinguished services in the foreign field. Alumni dinner. Glee Concert, reunion club. It is very full day and very interesting.

June 14 Thurs. Went to the station to meet Mrs. Greene who was returning from the hospital. I made a mistake and went down by Eastern time then the train was an hour late. I had the three little children me. They had a pretty good time but I did not.

June 15 Fri. Called on Harry Haskell and his wife in the

Ernest C. Partridge

[June 9]

June 10 Baccalaureate sermon by Pres King. Dr Barton made missionary address of evening. I made the invocation.

June 11 Winona and I called on Dr Barton & decided that I am to go to Tiflis for relief work. A social for Dr B 1–3.

June 12 I spent the forenoon in Cleveland. Dinner at Chas Adams's. Mrs. Jack & Edith Roberts for supper.

June 13 Commencement Day. Hugh Black spoke on the War. Polly was given a M.A. degree. Alumni dinner. Reunion concert.

June 14 Forenoon in Cleveland. Brought Mrs Greene home from hospital on noon train.

[June 15–16]

June 17 Frances and Alfred baptized at 1st Ch Oberlin. Evening Union Service Cong - Pres. Sandusky

June 18 All day in Sandusky working for a Committee.

[June 19–27]

evening. Armen & Nazeli finished cleaning the kitchen. I did the usual round of washing, cooking etc. I made some doughnuts with sour cream. They were good.

June 16 Sat. Called on Mrs. Hurst whose husband has just died. She is so brave & lonely. Then Mr. P. & I went to the Bosworth's but they were not at home, then to the Wright's. We took supper there, Johnnycake, sauce, toast & cake. The playground on Prospect St. was opened. The children went there twice.

June 17 Sunday. Frances & Alfred were christened this morning by Mr. Van der Pyl. Dr. Husted assisted. Mr. P. held Frances & I, Alfred. Frances wore a white dress with blue ribbon and Alfred a blue Russian blouse suit trimmed with white. Both behaved well. In the evening a meeting for Red Cross. Mr. P. went to Sandusky in the P.M.

June 18 Mon. The great event of the day was the fact that Billo lost his first tooth, lower right. His eyes shone like diamonds when he announced the fact. The four younger children went barefooted towards evening. Mr. Partridge did not return from Sandusky. Miss Webb called.

June 19 Tues. Armen & Nazeli cleaned the parlor. I did a big washing and housework. In the evening when we were all tired and dirty Mrs. Williams telephoned that she was coming to take us out in her auto. In fifteen minutes we were ready & the seven of us went.

June 20 Wed. This was the easiest day that I have had in a long time. I did not wash. Armen did most of the ironing. Mr. P. & I went to the library and to call on the Jameses. In the evening Mrs. Wright called.

June 21 Thurs. Cleaned the pantry. It took the extra time of the three of us all day.

June 22 Fri. Edward went to the Lake, Ruggles, with Herman Giles. He is to visit them in their cottage for a week. Letter from Mrs. Clark saying she is not coming for the present & a card from Samuel saying he is not coming this week. Cleaned the dining and beat the rug "minchev irigum."

June 23 Sat. Warm & showery. Did a large washing in the morning, went down town. Ironed in the evening and washed the porch.

June 24 Sunday. Cooler. Went to church with Mr. P. Mr. Van der Pyl spoke on what we should think about, "Whatever things are true etc." All went to Mrs. Martin's in the afternoon. In the evening Mr. Cummings took our whole family for an auto ride out beyond Elyria. Alfred went to sleep.

June 25 Mon. Cool & lovely. Armen mended nearly all day. Mr. P. & I were invited to supper at Mrs. Greene's. I washed Alfred's hair. Mr. Van der Pyl called.

June 26 Tues. Showery. Mr. Auten took Mr. P., George, Billo & me to Cleveland in his auto. We had a splendid ride. We saw a model of the battleship Pennsylvania. Everything was worked by electricity, flags, anchor, search lights, band & guns. We went to Kaitha but did not see anything of importance.

Ernest C. Partridge

June 28 Frances and I started East. Spent several hours in office at Cleveland. 6:20 train to Albany.

June 29 Reached Albany at 6:30AM. Over to Troy and out for Rutland at 7:45. Burlington 1:30PM. Lunch; a little dental work.

June 30 Had three teeth filled. A short auto ride. George and I went to movie in evening. Read a good deal. (George Partridge, papa's cousin - dentist)

July 1 Rested and took auto ride. Attended church in morning with George.

July 2 George finished my dental work and we took PM boat to Plattsburgh. Drove out to WC [West Chazy] in buggy. Night at Goeweys.

July 3 Frances and I drove out to Olney's to see mother [stepmother, Mary Atwood Goewey Partridge]. Took evening train west.

June 27 Wed. Armen went to Jamestown to visit Marguerite Weatherup for a little and then will go to Chatauqua [NY] where she will wait on table at Carey Cottage. Ernest & I called on Prof. & Mrs. Hutchins in the evening.

June 28 Thurs. Muggy & cloudy. Mr. P. and Frances started for Burlington and West Chazy. We are only five and feel very lonely. The two small ones left went to bed early and George & I took a walk around the block. Nazeli is very helpful, quick & energetic.

June 29 Fri. Another lonesome day, but the weather has been good. I went down to the noon train to see Mrs. Greene and Theodore off for Frankfort. Afterwards I went down town, then sewed a little, made doughnuts and corn bread, ironed in the evening. A card from Armen & a note from Mr. P.

June 30 Sat. I went to Elyria and bought two pairs of curtains for the parlor for $2. I bought a common skirt for $1.35, two waists one for 48 cts and one for 98 cts. In the afternoon, Edward & Herman came form the Lake. Herman stayed to supper.

July 1 Sunday. George & I went to church in the morning & heard Prof. Fullerton. He preached on Jacob & Esau, his real theme being "sacrificing the future to the present, the eternal for temporal." In the afternoon John Schuyler Husted stayed with us while his father & mother went to Miss Jackson's funeral.

July 2 Mon. George, Billo, Carroll Shaw & I went strawberrying and got about 10 cts worth of strawberries in 2 ½ hours. It does not pay. Mrs. Day called about her cottage.

July 3 Tues. Susie Zearing called in the evening. We went down town to buy fire-crackers and things for the fourth. Took a picture of Edward driving the three children & then one of Alfred as Captain Kidd.

July 4 Wed. The glorious fourth. Alfred and Billo and I got up and dressed quickly and went over to Carroll's house. Then the big boys got up. Frances and Mr. P. came on the noon train. Alfred and Frances were so glad to see each other that they couldn't stop hugging & kissing. Picnic on the campus in the afternoon. A few fireworks at home in the evening. A good day!

July 5 Thurs. A big washing. Called on Mr. Adams, then a porch call on Mrs. Moore, took her some of our lovely roses.

July 6 Fri. Had supper at Mrs. Martin's. Mr. James and his wife & mother were there, Miss Cold, Miss Noyes & Miss Webb, cream potatoes, tuna fish, jelly, olives. Jessie played various selections. In the morning we had the family group taken while we were altogether as a family.

July 7 Sat. Ernest went to Cleveland. His traveling money, order for a ticket from Chicago to Vladivostok came. In the afternoon we went to the library and down town. Called on Mr. & Mrs. Bowers in the evening.

July 8 Sunday. Attended church twice to hear Mr. Bowers. In the morning Edward, George and Billo went with us. Mr. James left for Russia on the evening train. I had a long nap in the afternoon.

July 9 Mon. Took lunch at the hotel with Mr. & Mrs. Bowers. Called on Capt. & Mrs. Garland, Mrs. Haskell, Mr. Brand and Dr. & Mrs. Lyman.

July 10 Tues. Called on Mrs. Anderegg & Miscovsky's. These awful preparations for going are very sad.

Ernest C. Partridge

[July 4–11]

July 12 Spent day packing, calling, etc. Mr. Metcalf took my baggage and the family to the train 8:27 to Chicago. A number of people at depot.

July 13 Reached Chicago 8AM (323m). Spoke at W.B.M. meeting. Lunched with Pye. Dinner at Belorian's with Paul & Levon M. 10:00PM train west.

July 14 Short day on train preparing Ethics exam and answering the questions 3–5 PM. Compton's came on train.

July 15 A quiet Sunday. Reading. James joined us at Ogden [Utah]. Came into my sleeper. (1000 m from Chicago)

July 16 Reached San F[rancisco] at 7:50. Evening to Ramona Hotel. James & I went to a show. Ogden–San Francisco 783m

July 17 Spent all day on passport work. Dr Kelsey had us all at luncheon at Hotel.

July 11 Wed. Made some more calls on Mrs. Irving Metcalf, Mrs. Miller, Mrs. Pond & Mrs. Hall & Prof. Hall. In the evening we called on Mr. & Mrs. Andrus & Prof. & Mrs. Andrews.

July 12 Thurs. A busy day with a dreadful ending. Mr. P. left us on the 9:27 train for Russia. Mr. Metcalf took us to the train in his Ford. All except Alfred went. He was asleep. Billo was much affected. He said, "Did papa have to go? Did you want him to go? I didn't. I hope he won't get hurt." The poor boy thought he was going to war.

July 13 Fri. Lonesome, more lonesome, most lonesome. I am thankful that the children are no less than five and want no less attention. I do not have time to think. Mrs. Wright, dear lady, came to see me in the evening. I had to begin accounts today. I do not know how I shall come out.

July 14 Sat. Showery. A sad wedding anniversary, a week of sad anniversaries, our departure from Sivas, Bobbie's death, our 19th with the bridegroom gone. Papa's 71st birthday was this week too, so our minds have been filled with memories & forebodings. We had a letter from Mr. P. from Chicago. It made it seem less as though he were dead.

July 15 Sunday. Nazeli went to church in the morning and I in the evening. In a union service I did not see a single person to speak with. It was a hard lonesome day. Miss Davis came over in the evening.

July 16 Mon. I went to over to Mrs. Martin's to make currant jelly. She made it. We had fourteen tumblers. I had a letter and a postal from Mr. P. from Omaha. Mrs. [?] came over in the evening. Mr. Metcalf started for New York, thence to France.

July 17 Tues. Mrs. Clark and David and Constance came. It seems so good to see them. All of us, except Edward, went to the station to meet them. We were quite a procession coming back, with a baby carriage, a go-cart and cart.

July 18 Wed. Mr. P. is to sail from San Francisco today. I have felt a kind of dread of something all day and when I analyze my feelings I find that it is that that troubles me. I wish I might have had a letter from him today but I did not. I enjoyed the day with Mrs. C. in spite of it all.

July 19 Thurs. Alfred has been a little sick today so I have held him every minute that I could get. I have had quite a little time to visit with Mrs. Clark. Miss Cold and Miss Webb called, also Mrs. Barnard for a few minutes.

July 20 Fri. Alfred asked me where his father had gone and when I told him to Russia he asked "Why?" I told him that he was going to help the poor people there. The he said, "What did the Germans do to them?" Went down town with Mrs. Clark.

July 21 Sat. Always a hard day, washing, ironing, cleaning up. I went down town to buy a present for Alfred. Billo went with me.

July 22 Sunday. Alfred's third birthday. He had a velocipede, a set of garden tools, a rubber ball & some gum. The velocipede was very satisfactory to him but it made trouble because Billo & Frances both wanted it. We had ice-cream, chocolate cake & three candles. Went to church in the evening.

July 23 Mon. Frances was sick all day. At 11:30 at night we gave her a bath and she seemed some better. She also took castoria. Mr. Bohn said that he went out in the country to marry someone. After he went Billy said "What will Auntie Bohn do if Uncle Bohn has married someone else?" Letter from San Francisco.

July 24 Tues. Very, very hot. Mrs. Clark and her children went home. We had a lovely visit with them & were very sorry to have them go so soon. Billo was sick all day. A package of California jewelry came form Mr. P. I went to see Mr. Wirkler about Hampartsoom.

Ernest C. Partridge

July 18 Did some shopping and financial matters. Steamer did not sail till 10PM. So took a ride around city.

July 19 A whole day of absolute rest. A little rough. Read a little bit, slept and talked most of the time.

July 20 Worked part of the day on King's first paper.

July 21 Finished writing King's paper on Corona. I like the machine very well.

July 22 Sunday on shipboard. Dr Pedley of Japan conducted the morning service. Finished "The World of Russia."

[July 23]

July 24 Wrote a good many cards to mail at Honolulu. Also some letters. (2100m San F to Honolulu)

July's 25 Reached Honolulu about 8:30AM. Mr Bowen met us and gave our party a fine day: auto rides, lunch, museum & swimming. Sailed at 4:30PM. (2091m)

July 26 A good deal of motion of the boat but no seasickness. Played shuffleboard & studied Russian.

[July 27]

July 28 Heard by wireless that Russian frontier closed till Aug 15. This will not delay us much unless continued longer.

July 25 Wed. Still hotter. We had a picnic of Turkey people at the arboretum, just got home when there was a tremendous shower, but it was just as hot afterwards. Billo was better but complained of a sore throat some. A letter from Dr. White.

July 26 Thurs. Very hot. Tremendous rain so that the cellar was flooded. The children went out in their bathing suits, that is Billo & George and Frances. Alfred said, "Will you get me a bathing suit?" Mrs. Wright called. I was ironing and had not changed my clothes.

July 27 Fri. Heavy showers in the night cooled the air, so today is comfortable. I was invited to Mrs. Lyman's for dinner with Madame and Mrs. James, Mrs. Martin & Jessie. Mrs. Donaldson was visiting there. In the evening I went to a lecture by Prof. Sherman on Walter Scott. I took a picture of Alfred in George's new khaki trousers. He was sitting on a bicycle. (Ate lemon pie at Lyman's, patriotic duty.)

July 28 Sat. Warm but rather comfortable. Washed, ironed, went to the library & downtown. I bought a map of the world to learn Geography while Mr. P. is traveling. Prof. Andrews walked home with me to carry my books. I made chocolate cookies by Marguerite's recipe.

July 29 Sunday. Went to church twice to hear Mr. Bowers, in the morning on "The individual" and in the evening on "King Lemuel's mother's sermon," last chapter of Proverbs, "Be pure, be efficient, be on the square." We all went to call on Mrs. Martin in the afternoon.

July 30 Mon. Very hot but endurable because there is a breeze. Yesterday Mrs. Wright said she would like Billo. All our children have been spoken for now. Mr. Aldifer wants Edward, George Partridge, George, Mrs. Wright, Billo, Will Olney, Frances, and Mr. Bohn & Mrs. Upton, Alfred. Alfred's picture was taken for the baby show.

July 31 Tues. Hot, very. The photographer came around for some more baby pictures and took Billy and Frances. The baby that takes the prize will have a diamond ring. What a suitable prize!

August 1 Wed. Cooler, a blessed relief. Samuel came as we were eating dinner. He has a vacation for three days. He brought chocolate and gum. Then he bought ice-cream, water-melon, peaches and more chocolate, a baseball mitt for George.

August 2 Thurs. Worked & visited with Samuel. Went to prayer meeting in the evening and then down to call on Mrs. James.

August 3 Fri. Samuel went home. Edward & I went down town to do some shopping and pay some monthly bills.

August 4 Sat. Cooler. Just an ordinary Saturday only we had a good big post from Honolulu from Mr. P. The letters and cards were written on the steamer. They had a good trip, not very rough. Miss Frey, a Swiss lady who once expected to go to Sivas was on the boat.

August 5 Sunday. First warm & then hot and hotter. Nazeli did not feel like going to church, so I went. Mr. Bowers preached. In the afternoon we went down to the water-works but we did not enjoy it very much. In the evening Edward & I went to church. Mr. Buckler brought us home.

August 6 Mon. A little cooler. I washed etc. and then worked in the attic the rest of the day. I had slept in four different beds the night before in an attempt to take care of all the children.

Ernest C. Partridge

July 29 Sunday. A strange day. I had charge of morning service on Juo I. Then in PM as we crossed 180 line dropped a day & called it Monday. Play of crew in evening.

July 30 Day dropped out.

July 31 A very quiet day, rather hot. Am reading Coe Psych of R and studying Russian.

August 1 A very hot night on our side of the boat, a windy day with frequent showers. We met the Korea [ship] about 4:30PM. A dance on deck in the evening.

August 2 A very comfortable day. Fairly smooth and a good breeze. Have read most of the day.

[August 3]

August 4 Increasingly rough. Little seasickness but most people do not feel well.

August 5 Sunday. It got so rough that no one wanted to go to church so we gave up the service. I had a headache and was sick all day.

August 6 Landed at Yokohama about 11AM. Lunched there. Up to Res. Asano's house for a reception. By trolley to Tohio Tokyo Hotel. Honolulu to Yokohama 3445m

August 7 Elmer, James & I with Dr Pedley went to Yokohama. Looked up ticket offices. Found Dr Macallum & visited with him & Mrs Apcar. Cable to Boston. Y–T 18 round T 36 [Yokohama to Tokyo]

August 8 Spent the day doing Tokyo. Went to order a thin suit $7.50 Dr M. came up & we saw the sights. A Japanese lunch, rickshaws etc, ending with an English dinner.

August 7 Tues. Hot but a breeze in the evening. Telephoned to Mrs. Day and find that we cannot have her cottage because the health commissioner has condemned the sanitary arrangements. Edward complains of headaches, stomach ache etc. Dr. Thatcher thinks it is only indigestion. He has no fever.

August 8 Wed. Edward still ailing. We had a queer day, sometimes cool, sometimes hot, rain, sunshine, thunder, lightning.

August 9 Thurs. Cloudy, rainy, cooler. We intended to go to the Lake, all except Edward and Nazeli, to try to make arrangements with Mrs. Day to stay there, but it was too rainy. I worked more in the attic, made a large mess of poor doughnuts, poor because I forgot the sugar until after the flour.

August 10 Fri. Cool. Mrs. Martin and the four younger children and I went to the Lake. Mrs. M. & George went without us because we missed the car. We had a good day and arranged to go to the lake. Coming back we missed the car in Elyria. It has been a pleasant day but hard for one alone with four, although George is a great help.

August 11 Sat. Working, but went to the library and stores in the afternoon and the picture show in the evening where they showed pictures of Oberlin children, six & under. We had three taken but for some reason Frances did not appear. We thought none was cuter than Alfred & we voted for him.

August 12 Sunday. Nazeli went to church. In the afternoon we went to the water-works and feasted on some candy that Armen made and sent. It was fine. In the evening Edward and I went to church. Mr. Whittaker of the Methodist church preached.

August 13 Mon. Tried to get ready to go to the Lake. Word came from the Board that Mr. McCallum had telegraphed that the Partridge party had been indefinitely detained in Russia. I cannot help wishing that he might come back. I feel as though I "really can't" manage this family.

August 14 Tues. At last we got ready and caught the 3:28 car. I came to the conclusion that if it is so hard to get ready to go to the lake, that as for me, I will stay in this country until Mr. P. comes after us.

August 15 Wed. At the Lake. I had a sick headache. The children wanted me to do everything. Both Alfred and Frances cried themselves to sleep because I could not do everything for them. Alfred cried because he wanted me to put on his stockings & after he waked up he began again.

August 16 Thurs. Prof. & Mrs. Hall, three nephews and another lady visited us, bringing a picnic lunch with them. We enjoyed them very much. The boys all had a good time in the water.

Ernest C. Partridge

August 9 Called at the embassy & had telegrams sent to Tiflis Consul. Train to Karuizawa 5 hrs in PM. Stopped at Austen house. T to K 88m

August 10 Bean called and took us for a walk up to his house. Baseball in PM. James played with the Whites.

August 11 Tea in PM at Dr Learneds. Evening called on Mr Caldwell and talked about Vladivostok.

August 12 Went to auditorium for morning service. PM an American Board social for us at Newells.

[August 13]

August 14 Trip to lava beds. A few miles by train which ran off track; 7 miles walk there; too late for train; 12 mile walk down. Got in 11:15. Very hard day for ladies. Lava beds immense.

August 15 Everybody stiff. James and Compton played baseball. Saw some good tennis.

August 16 Lunch at Newells. Three Elmers, Corey's, Scudders, Cozad & Beans. Chocolate dressing. Played a set of tennis. Evening games.

August 17 Oberlin breakfast about 15 persons on hilltop. Saw some fine tennis. Whites beat Blues 4–2, rain. Hata beat Yamashi. Okada beat Spencer.

August 18 Saw some fine tennis, the finals. Hata beat Okada in singles. Altman and Andrews beat Yamasaki & [blank] in doubles. Hata & Kurinanya, Japan champions, played 2 exhibition sets.

August 19 Sunday, a cold rainy day. Dr Dremus Scudder preached The Courage of Jesus. Vesper Bauminga of India, tea afterwards. Evening Elmer, Miss Orvis & I spoke on Turkey at Austin house.

August 17 Fri. Today Edward and Arthur went to Oberlin and I went to Lorain to buy some things. It was too cold for bathing so the children did not enjoy life as much as usual. I washed in cold water with naptha soap.

August 18 Sat. Edward came back but had not played his match because they were not ready for him. I went down town and took Alfred and Billo with me. The result was that I did not get my errands done.

August 19 Sunday. We had a day of eating, breakfast, then pop-corn, dinner, cracker-jack, lemonade and cookies and then supper. As usual I was "all in" when the day was over.

August 20 Mon. Warm. Nothing special to record except a ride with Mrs. Day and her mother. Alfred was asleep and Edward and Nazeli stayed with him.

August 21 Tues. Windy. The lake was very rough and noone went bathing until afternoon when the three boys went in. I went down town and finally got the hammer fixed and a pair of corsets.

August 22 Wed. Water was very rough but everyone went in. Nothing special happened, no mail even for excitement.

August 23 Thurs. The Threshers came & that amused the children for some time. With the help of Edward & Nazeli I did a big washing in cold cistern water with naptha soap. Then all except me went in bathing. We all ate dinner at the Days'.

August 24 Fri. Weather almost cold, lake very rough. Only George and Nazeli went in for about fifteen minutes. We all went blackberrying and got about six quarts. The children behaved very well in spite of scratches etc. Even Alfred tried to pick a few.

August 25 Sat. Very rainy and very cold. No one could bathe. We could hardly stay in the house. In fact the children spent a good deal of time in Mrs. Day's house where they had a fire in the fireplace. I went down town and bought Sunday provisions etc. Made blackberry jam, five pints, very good.

August 26 Sunday. Warmer, pleasant. Spent the day with the children as usual. They went in bathing a few minutes in the afternoon. Alfred has a habit now of punishing himself. If he feels cross he goes to bed and then thinks that I punished him and waits for permission to get up.

August 27 Mon. Pleasant. It was the third strenuous day in succession. We packed up and came back home. Edward came on his bicycle and we on the car. Reached Oberlin at 4:10. It did seem good to be back to a clean, varnished house, where there were no flies.

August 28 Tues. Rainy. Washed clothes, unpacked, cooked etc. Had the first letters from Japan, also letters from Nishan Bekhian & Armen. Mr. P's probably at the summer resort of the Japanese missionaries. Had a fine trip, was not seasick etc. and slept well, read, studied etc.

August 29 Wed. Again washed lake clothes.

August 30 Thurs. Washed three spreads, 10 sheets and several pillowcases in Mrs. Shaw's electric washer. Just fun.

Ernest C. Partridge

August 20 Called on Moran about Asana trip. Engaged horses & guides. Whites won bb championship, James playing 1st. Started up Asana at 6. Our 8, Miss Kenneston, Nusbaum's & Moran.

August 21 Slept one hour at teahouse and started up at 12 night, 3 ½ miles, 3 ½ hrs to top. Volcano fine, sunrise above clouds, saw Fuji. Home at 11:00. The hardest hike I ever saw.

August 22 Very stiff. James & I played 3 tennis matches and won all in House tournament. All-star team beat Japs. Dr Pedley came and we talked Nikko trip.

August 23 All-stars and Japs again, we beat. Garden party 4–6. We invited the missionaries. A letter from Post Wheeler, nothing special in it. We think to go to Habarovsk [Khabarovsk, Russia] after Sept 1.

August 24 Played some tennis. Acted as judge in annual field day. White's 1st anniversary with dinner for our party & a good time evening.

August 25 Miss Orvis & I played our match in tournament. Foxley and Miss Cozad beat us 6–1, 6–3.

August 26 Sunday. Mr Martin of Union church Yokohama preached. I called on Learneds in afternoon.

August 27 A Hartford hike turned into a corn roast on the Waterhouse veranda. Fifteen present.

August 28 Started about 9 o'clock for Kazu farm. Six in party, Miss Cozad with us. Walked 11 miles. Lunched on mountain. Slept Japanese fashion.

August 29 Had fine food with milk & ice cream; walked back 14 miles in four hours. Semi finals in tennis at Austen House.

August 30 I got a blister on my foot from the hike and have had to sit still. Westons beat James and Miss L[?] won finals tennis.

I went to prayer meeting in the evening. Mr. Van der Pyl led for the first time since his vacation. I walked down with the Wrights & home with the Andrewses.

August 31 Fri. A great day. Edward played a tennis match with Evart Buckler and won, then with Arthur and won, so he was presented with a racket as champion of the playgrounds. Prof. & Mrs. Wright called.

September 1 Sat. Armen returned from Chatauqua. Mrs. Clark telephoned from Detroit that she wanted a house. I found a good one by accident. Armen & I went over to the Wirklers' to tell them she would come to work for them.

September 2 Sunday. Armen and I took the children to Sunday School. It was Alfred's first Sunday in the regular primary S.S. Frances took care of him so thoroughly that she is not pay attention to anything else. When Mrs. Richards was teaching them a song he said, "I can't sing that."

September 3 Mon. Cool. Washed as usual. Armen went to the Wirkler's. Mrs. Haas and her four children and Miss Webb called on their way from the arboretum. We had post cards from Ernest in Japan.

September 4 Tues. Went to school with Billo & George. Billo is in the first grade again, with Miss Haynes as teacher. George is in the sixth. Spent the rest of the day mostly getting cloth for a blue dress. I finally found something I liked. Mrs. Jordan is making it.

September 5 Wed. Almost cold or really cold. I lighted the furnace for the first time. Went to missionary meeting. Mrs. Stapleton spoke, very interesting.

September 6 Thurs. Cool. Thunder showers early in the morning, during which a horse became frightened and a milk wagon tipped over in front of our house. Went to have my dress fitted. Called on Mrs. Haskell and Mrs. Haas. Also attended prayer meeting.

September 7 Fri. Went to have my dress tried on and got caught in the rain. It rained & rained & rained.

September 8 Sat. Called on Mrs. Stapleton and Mrs. Greene. Postal from Mrs. Clark saying that she will wait to hear from the Doctor before deciding when to come.

September 9 Sunday. Cold. Edward, Billo & I have bad colds. All except Billo & me went to Sunday School. Ed. and I tried to go in the evening to church but found the churches dark, so called at the Wright's. Armen came in the P.M. & stayed to supper. Telegram from Hampartsoom saying "Not now, but Christmas I will come home."

September 10 Mon. We all had colds. I went to the dress makers for a last try-on.

September 11 Tues. At home all day. The children's colds are not much worse. Billo did not go to school.

Ernest C. Partridge

August 31 A social at Cobbs for all. American Boarders at noon with lap dinners. I told Stone rescue story. Boys vs Over 40s Baseball. I caught, got beat 8–4.

[September 1]

September 2 Sunday. A quiet rainy day. Called on Newells in PM. I spoke in auditorium in evening. T[urkey] present & Future.

September 3 Left Karuizawa at 8:44; about 20 down to see us off. Dr Pedley met us at Takaschi. Reached Nikko 4:18; to Nikko hotel. (K to Nikko 115m)

September 4 A stormy day. Walked to Kirifuri Falls; 4 miles each way. Back to lunch. Dr Pedley left us at 2.

September 5 A ride of 5 miles by trolley and about 8 miles walk to Lake Chuzenji. Lunch there; a motor boat ride & back. A very pretty trip.

September 6 Spent forenoon visiting the Nikko Temple and Museum. Rested, shopped & packed in PM.

September 7 Morning train to Tokyo & Yokohama. Three men stopped & called at Embassy. Had a telegram from Tiflis & waiting for answer. Reached Y about 6 PM. (N to Y 109m)

September 8 Met Korea Niacu.[?], Christians, Cross, Heiningers, Colsons, Miss Husted, Miss Palmerlee, Miss Bellville etc. Tea at Asova. James and I went to Bean's for supper (36m).

September 9 Sunday in Yokohama. Tea at Royal Fisher's and vespers at Union Church.

September 10 I spent most of day getting tickets and arranging for leaving. Comptons & Miss Orvis to Kyoto. Whites, Elmer & I to Kobe. James stays at Tokyo for present.

September 11 Took 9:08 train for Kyoto & Kobe. Compton's & Miss O left us at 7:22 at Kyoto. Miss Cozad met us at 9 at Kobe. All at her house. (Y to Kobe 357m)

September 12 Wed. At house all day. Billo was very naughty in the morning so I kept him in the bedroom all the forenoon until the children came home from the lower grades. Letter from the Board, saying that a letter from Constantinople says that Polly is all right, well & comfortable.

September 13 Thurs. Edward for the first time donned his foot ball suit and went out to play with the Krescent Club which he joined. Mrs. Clark and David & Constance came.

September 14 Fri. Edward got his foot hurt a little. We were expecting Dr. Clark but he didn't come.

September 15 Sat. Warmer. Dr. Clark, James, Stephen & Ruth came. Mrs. Haas and Miss Webb and Mrs. Stapleton called on Mrs. Clark. All our family went to the movies in the afternoon.

September 16 Sunday. All except Alfred and me went to Sunday school. Edward made fudge. Armen made scones in the afternoon for supper. We went to the waterworks for a while. In the evening Edward & I went to church, heard Chester Ralston on "Faith."

September 17 Mon. Had a big washing. Mrs. Clark and I went down town and got my new dress. Everyone admires it. In the evening Dr. & Mrs. Clark came over, also Armen. Had a letter from Dr. Barton, also from Miss Seebury asking to write out some incident about some Armenian child.

September 18 Tues. A red letter day, letters from Ernest in Japan, and a letter from Polly, the first in more than six months. She speaks very encouragingly of herself and the girls who are nurses. They have won for themselves responsible positions in the Turkish hospitals.

September 19 Wed. Warm. Went down town with Edward to get him shoes. Bought some very pretty ones for $4.50, no 7. Afterwards I took the three little ones up to the "Clarks." Dr. had gone to Lorain.

September 20 Thurs. Warm. Doctor is thinking of moving to Elyria to practice. Went with Dr. & Mrs. Clark to the first lecture in the Seminary, given by Pres. King. Mrs. Stapleton called and the Clarks were here too.

[September 21]

September 22 Sat. Work, work, work, but letters from Japan helped out, although they made me sad. Mr. P. is probably in Siberia studying the Russian language. I called on Mrs. & Mrs. James. They had just had letters from Mr. James. The Clarks came over, have decided to go to Elyria.

Ernest C. Partridge

September 12 Wrote letters and accounts AM. After dinner went to Ex-prisoners house and to suburban cottage for supper.

September 13 Kobe College for prayers. Visited Kindergarten School & Bible school. Out to Korea. Supper & social together at college.

September 14 Called on Walker & Russian consul. Saw Ifantides. Left Miss Cozad's after lunch, to steamer to see China party. Train to Kyoto. At Dr Cary's. (46m)

September 15 Rained all day. Miss Alice Cary took 3 of us to temple and damascene & Croissone works. Yunabi supper with a crowd. WGP(1) [first letter to Winona]

September 16 Sunday in Kyoto. Dr Cary took me to a SS & 2 churches. Evening 5 o'clock service at Cary house. Bauminga spoke about India.

September 17 Visit Doshisha. Prayers at Preparatory Dept. First service at Theological Dept. Called on Pres Haradas. Compton & Lombards called in evening.

September 18 Left Kyoto 8:15 for Tsuruga. Arrived there about 1. No trouble in Customs house. Sailed at 6 PM to Tsuruga 120 m (2) [2nd letter to Winona]

September 19 A quiet day on steamer Renza RVS. Jordan party along. Nearly finished T & Soc course [for] King['s class].

September 20 Landed at Vladivostok about 10AM. Customs house easy. Visited consul, no room obtainable. Temporary quarters in consulate. 490 m.

September 21 Spent the day trying to find rooms and studying Russian. City crowded, hard to find places.

September 22 Studied Russian most of the day. Talked with Mr Caldwell about plans. Went to a movie in the evening.

September 23 Sunday in Russia. After breakfast took a walk, went to Cathedral, heard of rooms to rent. Read most of day. Ate breakfast late and no lunch. (3)

September 23 Sunday. An awful morning, Billo & Alfred both naughty. Dr. and Mrs. Clark, Dr. & Mrs. Clawson and all the children came over. We went to church in the evening, Armen & I. Mr. Van der Pyl spoke about "shallow calls."

September 24 Mon. Called on the Clarks. Went to Prof. Rausenbusch's [Rauschenbusch] lecture, about the social qualities of Christianity.

September 25 Tues. I was so tired when the time for Prof. R's lecture that I was afraid I would be too sleepy to listen, so I went to see Mrs. Clark and we went down town. In the evening she and the Doctor came over.

September 26 Wed. The Clarks went today and we feel quite lonely. I am very sorry to have them go but probably they know what is best. I did not go to Thank-offering meeting nor church social.

September 27 Thurs. Went down town to get a few things for the children, to give them on my birthday.

September 28 Fri. My birthday. I made a cake. Armen came over to supper. Mrs. Shaw came to congratulate me. Armen & Nazeli gave me a dozen handkerchiefs, Edward a lovely collar and George some little blue pins.

September 29 Sat. Work, work, work, washing, washing floors, washing heads until four o'clock, then went to call on Mrs. Atkinson. Poor lady, she is very homesick. I am sorry for her. I wish I could find her a house on this side of the town. Edward played in his first real game of football. Crescents vs Elyria Club, score 19 to 0.

September 30 Sunday. Went to church early in the evening. Mr. Van der Pyl spoke on the "Tragedy of a double life," based on Dr. Jekyl and Mr. Hyde. Mrs. Atkinson called in the afternoon.

October 1 Mon. Attended a lecture by Prof. Rausenbush but was too sleepy to be much profited. After the lecture Mrs. Atkinson and I went to look at a house for her. Armen came over and she and I mended stockings in the evening.

October 2 Tues. Another lecture by Prof. R. Again Mrs. Atkinson and I went to look at a house.

October 3 Wed. Stayed at home and got to the bottom of the stocking basket, the first time for a long time.

October 4 Thurs. With Edwards and George I attended a church supper. In order to get away from home I sent out for ice-cream for the children and invited Armen over. But even after they had all agreed to it, it was a sad parting at the corner where they went with me.

Ernest C. Partridge

September 24 Rented two rooms, bought a blanket & quilt, ordered sheets made. In evening went to a concert by the Urkutzk Military Band. Very good.

September 25 Had a headache most of day. Read & studied some, settled room. Went to a Russian bath and to bed early.

September 26 Wrote letters one hour, Russian most of the rest of day. 1st real lesson with Mr Fomenco. Tea at Mrs Newhard's. Golden Horn Restaurant for dinner. Out late. Good music. (4)

September 27 Up late. Studied all day. At night took a walk and dinner at Georgian's place on pilaf & kvas. FW Smith, White. (5)

September 28 Breakfast at 10:30. Dinner at 6:30 at new place. Movies. Studied Russian all day except on hour P[hilosophy] of R[eligion].

September 29 Breakfast at 9:30. Lunch at Cafe by sea. All a little off on food. Coffee & sweets for supper. Read one hour P & R, rest of day on Russian.

September 30 Sunday. Rose late, after breakfast went to the Cathedral for an hour. Read and wrote most of the day. Ed (6)

October 1 Put in a hard day on Russian.

October 2 Wrote a long letter to Dr Barton. Movie 8–10. Dinner at Golden Horn 10–12. JLB, WGP (7)

October 3 Russian till 3:30. Nardae[?] Day dinner with Fomenco's. Bath at 5. Tea at 8. 2 hours study in evening.

October 4 Worked all day on language. Called on Mrs Newhard & got some English reading.

October 5 Spent the day as usual. Tried to buy pillows & found only one. Went to movie and late dinner at Golden Horn. Call from Jamgotchian.

October 5 Fri. I had lots of work to do but went to see Mrs. Greene who hasn't been very well. She seemed better today. I also went to the library and got some more children's books. Letters from Mr. P. from Yokohama, no Kobe.

October 6 Sat. A busy day as usual and no gas to use. Edward & I went down town in the evening and bought some odds and ends, ball bearings for the cart, electric bulb, hearth broom, shovel, tongs, comb, clothes brush, lampshade etc. Edward & the Krescents played against Elyria 4–6.

October 7 Sunday. Mrs. Haas and Miss Webb called. In the evening Edward and I went to church. Mr. Van der Pyl spoke about Kiplings "They," the next world, saying that one had penetrated the other world and brought in news. Kipling wrote this about the loss of his daughter.

October 8 Mon. I went to Seminary lecture by Prof. Rauschenbusch, sat beside Mrs. Haskell who knitted Red Cross stockings all the time. Alfred lives in imagination. He is now Constance, now Richard, now James, and when he wants to comb his hair he is George. When he wants to please me especially he becomes Alfred again.

October 9 Tues. I got fixtures for the cart wheel and ball bearings for Edward's coaster brake. Something always needs fixing. Attended Prof R's lecture. His great word is "solidarity." Walked down town with Mrs. Gulick.

October 10 Wed. Three letters of Sept. 15, 17 & 18 from Mr. P. He was on the boat going to Vladivostok, but without much hope that they would get through to Tiflis very soon. Mrs. Hall and I called on Mrs. Carroll Churchill of India and then I called on Mrs. Buddington in her new house.

October 11 Thurs. After washing cooking etc. I went down town & did heaps of errands, shoes $3.50 & trousers $1.25 for Billo, a tablecloth $3.13, sweet apples, a new cereal "Granola," went to the library, to see if Mr. Brown could mend our chairs, bought gum etc.etc. Billo had a rash on his arms, face, and legs today.

October 12 Fri. An awful day, snowy, windy, cold, damp, no gas, all winter clothes immediately necessary. We lighted the fireplace and kept from freezing, cooked what we could down cellar where the gas is a little better.

October 13 Sat. Again cold, again no gas, but the gas was good in the night and I turned it on full force to heat up the house. The house was warm until noon and the water. A letter from Vahan. Billo and Frances have a rash. I called Dr. Thatcher. Oberlin-Haidelberg game 7–7.

October 14 Sunday. The house was in dreadful confusion. I swept from the front side-walk to the back door and picked up hundreds of things that the children had been playing with. Armen cooked marshmallow candy & salad dressing. Gas good all day.

October 15 Mon. I attended Mr. Rausenbush's lecture but was so sleepy that I decided that it was not worth while to go.

Ernest C. Partridge

October 6 Rose late & on return from breakfast found Goodsell. Spent some hours with him, saw him off on steamer. Sent letters to WGP (8), Barton, White & Compton by him.

October 7 Sunday. Rose late, breakfast 10:30 & dinner at 7. Read some Lyman & Fosdick. Wrote George a letter about my room & conditions of life.

October 8 Worked on Russian till 3PM when Anderson party arrived. We took in 4 and dinner with them, movies.

October 9 A holiday and as I had a headache I did not study. Found 2 rooms for our friends. Francis to stay with me. News of murder of Enver, Talaat & D Javit. [This news was a rumor.]

October 10 Work on language till 4:30 excepting time to write CCC and HHW. Sent letters by Mrs Carter. RR strike settled & trains started again. 3 letters from WGP & one from Dr Barton.

October 11 Called on British consul to ask about Turkey. Nothing new. Spent an hour and a half with my landlord on language.

October 12 Several hours on Russian. Wrote Winona. Went with Elmer's teacher to call with him on my new teacher, a young lady out in the suburbs. Am to have an hour a day E & R alternating. (11)

October 13 Breakfast with Fomenco's 1st time. Wrote letter most of forenoon and sent by a traveller. 1st lesson with young lady 4:30–6:00, 6–7 Fomenco, 9–11 with him and a friend. CCC, HHW, Barton (12)

October 14 Sunday. Only diversion lunch with Mr & Mrs Newhard. Wrote a letter to Edward.

October 15 Studied most of day; lesson in English 4:30–6. Some Russian in it.

[October 16]

October 17 Wed. In the afternoon I was invited to Prof. Wright's house to meet Mrs. Lybeyer(?). I had a very pleasant time and wore my new blue dress. In the evening while we were eating supper Samuel came.

October 18 Thurs. I attended a meeting of the First Church ladies of this section at Mrs. A. G. Cummings's. In the evening Mrs. Greene gave me word that Dr. & Mrs. McCallum were here for a short time, so I went down there. Dr. McC. had seen Mr. Partridge in Japan. Package came from Japan, beads, pin box, tray, paper knife.

October 19 Fri. Went down town and then to call on Mrs. Lybeyer with Armen.

October 20 Sat. Samuel, George, Billo, Frances, Alfred & I went to Elyria and called on the Clarks. We also had a picture taken, like stairs, two dollars a dozen. The children were especially dreadful, clinging to me all the time. Edward & Geo. played in the same team against Norwalk. Edward made his first touch down.

October 21 Sunday. Samuel left at noon, only the train was late and left at about half past two. Mrs. Haas and her children and Miss Webb called. In the evening Edward and Armen and I went to church and then went home with Mrs. McCallum.

October 22 Mon. The chief event of the day was three letters from Mr. P. from Vladivostok. He is settling down to study Russian, waiting for word from Tiflis which he doesn't really expect to get. The next event of importance was that I went to sleep in the afternoon.

October 23 Tues. Stayed at house all day and did all sorts of things, washing in the morning as usual. Mrs. Buddington asked me to go to the Artist Recital with her, but it is so hard to get away from them all that I decided not to go. We got again to the bottom of the stocking basket.

October 24 Wed. Did not wash, decided to write lots of letters, but Mrs. Wright called in the morning. Then after dinner I gave the little ones a bath and then was so tired that I put on my best clothes and went to call on Mrs. Van der Pyl. Mrs. Martin & the Misses Webb called. Allies gained 2 miles on the western front.

Ernest C. Partridge

October 16 Wrote Winona and sent by Mrs Draper to Japan. Russian lesson 5–6, 7–9 movie, dinner 9–11 Pochin (13)

October 17 A batch of mail. Letter from Winona quoting telegram from Tiflis asking for workers. Scuba[?] cipher message to consul S. 2 ½ hours of Russian with Mr. F.

October 18 Anderson party got off tonight. Studied some and had lesson. Bill Francis took us to dinner. Went to depot for 10:30 train.

October 19 A confirmation letter from Smith. Telegram answered [on] Sept 24 never came. He calls us. Went to movie & late supper. (14)

October 20 A wire from Whites. They are coming next week. Sent him an answer.

October 21 A very quiet Sunday, read, wrote, ate and slept.

October 22 Worked hard on lessons.

October 23 Sick all night and had a very unpleasant day. Caught cold. Slept & loafed all day, eating nothing till night. Read a little in evening.

October 24 About sick all day with light grip. Did not go to lessons.

October 25 Whites & a party of 25 YM [young men] & 2 YW [young women] got in. Whites in upstairs room. All but 4 went on Evening Express. Movie and late dinner with Whites.

October 26 Called on DeWitt & companions. He pays us for 3 rooms downtown. Tried to find shoes without success.

October 25 Thurs. Big washing & ironing. I went to Dr. Thatcher's with Edward and the Dr. found that he has water on the knee. He can ride his wheel but must keep his leg stiff. Poor Edward.

October 26 Fri. Armen spent the day at our house and I went to Cleveland to get a suit for Billo at Baker's. I found the store had been burned the night before. I bought a suit at Taylor's but it was too small.

October 27 Sat. Regular program, a confused day, went down town to get some materials for George's Halloween costume. Rented some crutches for Edward. Mended stockings & ironed in the evening.

October 28 Sunday. Only George and Billo went to S.S. Frances had a bad cough and is quite deaf and Edward took care of his knee. But in the evening he went with Armen & me to hear Prof. Hannah on the 400th anniversary of Luther. Mrs. Atkinson & her children, Mrs. Stapleton and Dr. [Ruth] Parmalee called.

[October 29]

October 30 Tues. Mrs. Clark came to attend the meeting of the W.BM.I. and also Miss Loughridge. It is lovely to have them here. I took Billo to the Young People's rally and in the evening he and I went to a Halloween celebration at George's school where he was a fairy.

October 31 Wed. Alfred nearly got strangled with a strap. He was playing that he was a dog. Nazeli and Armen & Carroll rescued him. Mr. Henry Riggs called. I attended two sessions of the meeting, heard Miss Webb, Mr. Riggs & Pres. King.

November 1 Thurs. Attended the afternoon session of the meetings, heard Mrs. Pye of China, Mrs. Marden, Mrs. Thompson of Africa and Miss Pavlova. Miss Loughridge left in the evening. We had such a good time with her. I hope she will come back here to stay.

November 2 Fri. Edward had such a bad cold that he did not go to school. I was invited to Mrs. McCullough's to see Dr. Ruth Parmalee. All the Turkey missionaries nearly were there. In the evening I ironed until after eleven.

November 3 Sat. Usual routine but went to call on Mrs. Marden, had a pleasant call. Two letters from Mr. P., one written Oct. 1 & 5 and the other Oct. 9. He thought to go on with Mr. Anderson but was to send word if he went. I have received no word.

November 4 Sunday. The children were engaged with a toy telegraph nearly all day. Mr. Van der Pyl preached on Locksley Hall, or a young man's prospect. Mrs. Haas and her children came for a little while. It was not so hard a Sunday as usual. Went to the station to meet Asdghig but she did not come.

November 5 Mon. Went down town intending to pay all my bills but forgot the meat bill. Called on Mrs. Marden a few minutes to ask about Vartevae.

November 6 Tues. Letters from Mr. P. or copies of letters to Dr. Barton etc. sent by Mr. Goodsell from California. Today is the day that they are trying to vote Ohio dry. The reports are county dry, probably state. Heard Sergeant [unreadable] about trench warfare.

November 7 Wed. Wet or dry voted yesterday but even today the result is uncertain. Probably drys will win. Italians retreated again but Haig got a victory on the western front. I attended a missionary meeting. Reports from Mansfield & Columbus. Miss Elizabeth Webb spoke very interestingly.

Ernest C. Partridge

October 27 Wrote a short letter to Winona and sent it by a traveller. Studied & had Russian lesson.

October 28 Another Sunday. Ate all meals by invitations with Fomenco's. Read in soc. Cons. and a story.

October 29 Received wire from Compton that coming Thursday; also one from Smith Maynard etc calling us at once. We have reservation for Nov 15th.

October 30 JLB (17)

October 31 Received a telegram from Consul Smith calling for whole party.

November 1 Worked on Russian all day except an hour in morning when I bought a pair of boots, 145 rubles. Compton's came in evening.

November 2 Had a headache and did not work very hard. Gave an English lesson. Went to movie and dined at Golden Horn. Wired Sec O to come at once.

November 3 Worked all day on Russian lesson.

November 4 Sunday. Went to Cathedral. Read till 1:30. Coffee at Compton's room all together. A long walk.

November 5 Received two letters from Winona; one each from Edward & Billo. (19)

November 6 Received wire from Miss Orvis that she is coming probably Monday. Another from Erivan. Studied most of day. Movies & Golden Horn.

November 7 Tried to shop a little. Went to bath. A long lesson; an hour of Berlitz.

November 8 Thurs. Ohio went dry by 3,000 majority, but the Italians retreated again. If they can only stand now until reinforcements came up. I went to the afternoon tea at Mrs. Greene's to meet Mr. & Mrs. Van der Pyl. Present were Prof. & Mrs. Wright, Mr. & Mrs. Shaw, Miss Metcalf, Dr. & Mrs. Taylor, Madame & Mrs. James, Prof. Currier, Mrs. Willard.

November 9 Fri. Called on Mrs. MacCullough and Mrs. White. Went to the lecture by Wesley Frost, consul to Greenstrom. He lectured about the Lusitania and the other victims of the U-boat, most gruesome. Alfred had crayons and "vote drys" in the paper bag and asked me to tie them up.

November 10 Sat. Only Saturday.

November 11 Sunday. I did not go out all day. In the evening they had a union service under the auspices of the Y.M.C.A. Nazeli went. We didn't have any callers either.

November 12 Mon. Warm and pleasant as it has been for two weeks, no, rainy in the morning. Edward and Billo & I went to see Mary Pickford in "A romance of the Redlands," rotten as the boys say. Russia is in revolution & Italians retiring.

November 13 Tues. Warm. Seventeen years today since we reached Sivas. I was invited to Mrs. Pond's for supper. Today they had no sugar at the store. I found one pound at another store. Russia seems more hopeful today. Called on Mrs. Ohly.

November 14 Wed. Warm.

November 15 Thurs. Warm. Went to prayer meeting for the first time in a long time. British & French troops arrived in Italy. I hope they are not too late.

November 16 Fri. Warm. Called on Mrs. Tucker and Mrs. Clark, both new neighbors. One day I asked Alfred what made him so lonely and he said, "Because I love you so much." Mrs. Martin & the Misses Webb called.

November 17 Sat. Usual routine, only in the evening Miss Noyes called. News came this morning that Mr. Partridge has started on to Tiflis. I wish he had stayed where he was until things settled down. Mrs. Bohn brought over some brown bread. George got up and helped the three little ones dress, so I could rest and at night read Billo to sleep.

November 18 Sunday. A little colder at night. I was on my feet nearly all day, but went to church at night with Mrs. Moore. Mr. Van der Pyl preached on "An old man's retrospect" based on "Lockley Hall sixty years after."

Ernest C. Partridge

November 8 Steamer a day late. Worked on Soc Cons & Russian. Tried to shop a little.

November 9 Worked some on Soc Cons paper. Studied some Russian.

November 10 Steamer came in early this morning. 15 YMCA men on it. One bunks with me. Had a lesson; went to movie & Golden Horn. Telegram from Miss Orvis.

November 11 Sunday. Morning service at Cathedral, English at Lutheran Church at 4PM under YMCA men. Visited at Compton's. Dinner together. (George and Billo)

November 12 Finished S. Cons. paper for Pres King.

November 13 Last lesson in Russian.

November 14 A Thanksgiving dinner at the Golden Horn with the 16 YM fellows. Turkey before starting on journey.

November 15 A busy day doing last things and packing. Wrote some. Dined with Fomencos and got on train about 10PM. 11 YM men on train. (Ed, T 21)

November 16 A comfortable night after we got settled. Elmer & I are together. James & White in second. The rest of us 1st class. Reached Harbin at 9:10 & changed to a better car.

November 17 Train running very well & on time. Diner serves good meals reasonably. Stopped about 5PM to repair baggage car. Started at 11. Customs 3–5AM. No trouble.

November 18 Sunday. Read some Fosdick, King and Tarkington seventeen.

November 19 Running 16 hrs late. Reached Urkutzk at 9:30PM. Several hours along the end of Lake Baikal. We have decided to go to Moscow. (22) (1525m)

November 19 Mon. Warm. I was invited to supper at Mrs. Martin's with Miss Noyes. I did quite a little knitting on my wristlets which I am making for the soldiers. Letters from Mr. P. about his starting for Tiflis. He's not going to Moscow so that is not so dangerous.

November 20 Tues. Another letter from Mr. Partridge. I called on Mrs. James, Mrs. Haas and Mrs. Greene. Frances is still a little afraid of Alfred. I think. Perhaps he has a little more sense about when and where to strike, but he is a real tease.

November 21 Wed. Warm & Rainy.

November 22 Thurs. Went to prayer meeting.

[November 23]

November 24 Sat. All the Clarks came. We gave them bulgure pilaf and oranges for dinner. Mrs. Clark, James, David & Constance stayed over Sunday. George's grade, 6th, played against Elyria sixth and beat them 14–8. George & James got shut [in?] a shed & called for help by telegraph.

November 25 Sunday. George's twelfth birthday. We had a chicken but it took until three o'clock because the gas was so low. George received a combination game board, some little Japanese trinkets, a picture of his club, a checker board, turn over (upside down)[gift list not continued] 50 cts & 25 cts.

November 26 Mon. No gas. I have to saw and split wood for the fireplace. There is no dry wood, no coal except dust, and no gas. What we shall do, I do not know. Mrs. Martin gets up at four o'clock and does her cooking. Armen & I went to see the Garden of Allah.

November 27 Tues. No gas but not very cold. Alfred woke up at 4:30 and refused to sleep any more. I sat down and wrote a letter to Mr. P. and got behind in everything, so much so that I could not get dinner ready for George on the low gas. Dr. & Mrs. Marden called in the morning.

November 28 Wed. Warm. I got up at half past five and made mince pies for Thanksgiving, so to use the gas before it went off. The result was that it did not go off at all and now they say we are to have plenty.

November 29 Thurs. Thanksgiving. We were invited to Tank Home and also to the Clarks' so we went to the Clarks's. Dr. came with his auto for us. We took mince pies, pumpkin pies, scones & jelly. Mrs. Clark had cooked a fine turkey. We had a good dinner and a fine time. We came back by car.

November 30 Fri. Letters from papa, Nishan Eff. and Hampartsoom. Nishan Eff. writes that 31 more Sivas people have arrived at Ezroom, among them Arpiné. I wonder who the others were. Armen came over for supper. George went to Mr. Wood's shack with the Krescents.

Ernest C. Partridge

November 20 Cut off my beard which had a six week start. Read and played 42.

November 21 Mr Simmons got on early and we had a visit with him.

[November 22]

November 23 Passed Omsk at 3AM. 36 hours late. Gradually coming up to the Ural Mountains. Whites & James & I are eating one meal a day in our rooms. (1526m)

November 24 Read and played flinch and 42. YM quartette came back and had a sing in evening. Passed Ekaterinburg at 5AM. (557m)

November 25 Sunday. We had a very nice service in our apartments with the YM men. I had charge of it.

November 26 Reached Vologda at 10AM. Had a special car on 11 o'clock train to Moscow but could not make it because of the baggage. Got a special car on 11PM train. (929m)

November 27 Reached Moscow at 3PM. Met by Cavass from YMCA who brought us all to headquarters where we are being royally entertained. (358m)

November 28 Called on Consul general who thinks we should go on alone. Food here about 20% higher than the Vlad. prices. Wrote Winona. Saw evidence of recent riots. (23)

November 29 YMCA had Thanksgiving reception which was very pleasant. Not many outside people but Consul Gen Summers & Prof Ross were there.

November 30 Spent day making plans and getting ready to go. Mr Gaylord YMCA secretary from Petrograd spoke to us in evening.

December 1 Left house at 9AM to take train. Finally got off at 3PM. Seated in 3 cars which do not go thru.

December 1 Sat. A hard day for Edward, the third holiday to get through without being able to go out. He went to the movies in self defence in the P.M. I went to a reception at Keep Cottage as the guest of Helene Lenthi, of Key West, Fla. whose mother was a school mate of Mr. P.

December 2 Sunday. Plenty of gas all the time now. A most distracting day. I feel as though my bringing up children is a failure. The three little ones are very unruly. Edward and George are all right but take very little responsibility. Heard Sanctus, Unfold ye Portals and Thy rebuke hath broken his heart.

December 3 Mon. I tried to telephone to Dr. Clark to ask him to put Nazeli on the train in Elyria but found that they were both out of town. They went to Detroit to attend Edith's funeral. She died very suddenly. I went with Nazeli.

December 4 Tues. My first day without anyone to help me. I tried to do just the ordinary everyday work, when the circumstances were most propitious, weather warm, noone sick, no extra cooking, small washing. I got through between three and four and when I sat down I went to sleep in my chair. Then supper, dishes and kids and ironing.

December 5 Wed. About like yesterday. Armen came over and stayed so I could go down town to buy something for Billo's birthday. We had four letters from Ernest, still from Vladivostok. Mrs. Metcalf presented us with two tickets for the Messiah.

December 6 Thurs. Billo's birthday again. We had no party for him, but he had several presents, a little milk cart and horse game, "Peter Coddle's journey to Chicago," a weather prophet, and stick craft. We had a cake. I made a cake and Armen the frosting. While I was putting the children to bed she came over and washed the dishes, like a fairy.

December 7 Fri. Colder & snowy. Yesterday Billo fell in the mud just before school & could not go because he had no second shoes, an indication of our poverty. I had to buy some for George. I got "Trotmock" again. Armen had a letter from Marie, promising $200 a year for two years so she could study. Edward was sick & did not go to school.

December 8 Sat. Nothing but work. Armen helped out in the evening. The weather turned cold and stormy very suddenly while George and Billo and the two little ones went for the milk. Alfred cried all the way from the cold.

December 9 Sunday. Very cold and windy. Noone went out. With all over efforts the thermometer stayed a little above fifty most of the day. Toward evening the wind died down and the house got thoroughly warm.

[December 10]

December 11 Tues. I sewed on Edward's "S.K.," his first letter won in athletics, that was in football. Jerusalem fell into the hands of the English after [incomplete]

December 12 Wed. George went to Warner Gymnasium with the Krescents to practice his first basketball. He too is growing up. I had a woman to wash as I had a hoarse cold and did not want to get worse.

Ernest C. Partridge

December 2 Sunday. A long day on the train. James and I paid a fee to keep others out and are very comfortable. We have eaten out of lunch baskets today.

December 3 Reached Rostov about noon. Got order from Commandant for places. Military officers put us on train at 10PM. 4 people crowded into our 4 berth room. (772m)

December 4 Reached mineral waters Junction about 8PM. Half way to Baku. Train very very crowded. 4 extra people in our coupe all the time. Plenty of food and hot water.

December 5 Reached Baku about 9AM. Breakfast in station. Got permission to board train early and got on about noon. Left at 2; very crowded.

December 6 Our party of 8 (7) and one Russian lady in 2 two-berth coupes opening together. Terrible crowd. Slept by turns. Reached Tiflis about 3PM. International hotel. (343m)

December 7 Spent day at Consulate and shopping. Mr Heald who has charge of work at Alexandropol met us and is to tow us out. Miss O., Compton & I to A[lexandropol]. James goes to Trebizond. Rest to Erivan.

[December 8]

December 9 Sunday. Called on Mr Montesanto who is here from Trebizond.

December 10 Spent day shopping & getting ready to go to Alexandropol.

December 11 Wrote Winona and a card to Anderson; finished up business at Consulate. Wrote Wiggins and prepared to ex account. Went to depot at 8 & were put on train. (24)

December 12 A very crowded and uncomfortable journey from 11PM to 4PM. Mr Heald, 5 Americans, one Armenian and 6 Russians in a 4 berth coupe. From A at 4 met by workers to Hotel New York. (150m)

December 13 Thurs. Cold all the week. Edward cannot rise on his bicycle so George draws him to school and back on a sled. Edward & I went to the Messiah on tickets which Mrs. Metcalf gave us. Mrs. Clark and James came from Elyria and stayed one night. Word from the Board that Mr. P. has reached Tiflis.

December 14 Fri. Armen came over in the afternoon and I went down town and bought Billo some trousers $2.00, shoes $3.15, union suits $1.25 a pair. I had no time for Christmas shopping. The days are too short. Ironed until eleven.

December 15 Sat. Cold but gas is good. I did not even have a minute between the after dinner work and getting supper except long enough to curl Alfred's hair. Saturday is always hard but today I was not very well anyway. Letter from Mikran Eff.

December 16 Sunday. Not quite so cold. Another Sunday gone. I had a lame ankle so did not even go to church in the evening. Armen made brown bread and scones. She and George went to the Sacred Concert at the First Church.

December 17 Mon. Warmer. Armen came over and I went down town to do some shopping. She stayed to supper but had to go home to stay with the children in the evening. She got supper and washed the dishes.

[December 18]

December 19 Wed. Billo, Frances & Alfred went with me to the sixth grade play, "Santa's allies." George was Major of the post card artillery. It was very, very good, but Alfred was afraid of Santa Claus. Six of us joined the Red Cross and got one big cross & five small ones for six dollars.

December 20 Thurs. Wed. morning Alfred & I went to the kindergarten party.

December 21 Fri. Primary S.S. party. I took the three little ones. They had ice-cream, cookies, candy & a Christmas tree with a present for each one. Frances got a box of tiny clothes pins. Billo a stocking with lots of things in it & Alfred a whistle.

December 22 Sat. Carroll was here with our children all day. They raced & ran & did things up generally. Edward's marks for this two months were English 90, Latin 90, Math solid geom. 96, History 91. The boys wrapped up Christmas things.

December 23 Sunday. At home with Alfred all day. The S.S. concert came in the evening. Armen went with the children. I wrote to Mr. P. and Baidzar.

December 24 Mon. The day before Christmas. I was very busy all day but had to go down [town] the last part of the evening to get a few last things.

Ernest C. Partridge

December 13 A very dirty hotel. Spent day visiting industries. Rented 3 rooms for a month and I am staying with Mr Heald. Hope to get better arrangement soon.

December 14 Did some shopping, made rounds of work. Toward evening wrote some on Final 2 papers.

December 15 Spent forenoon getting Comptons fitted out for house-keeping. I bought a wardrobe and unpacked my baggage.

December 16 Sunday. A quiet day reading. Took a long walk with Mr Heald. Wrote Winona. (25)

December 17 Began work a little regularly by commencing stock taking, preparatory to taking over things on Jan 1st. Weighed up about 3500 pounds of stocking yarn.

December 18 Made rounds twice morning and afternoon with Mr Heald. Hovsek began work as repair carpenter. More stock taking.

December 19 Spent whole day stock taking. Made one round of works. Visited an Armenian industry for lace and loom work. Tea with Comptons.

December 20 Went rounds of work. Inventoried some, made one call, tea at Compton's, read the in evening.

December 21 Wrote Winona. Made round of work, had dinner a little early. Mr Heald and I went to train early and got a compartment. Train left about 5, Junction at 10. (26)

December 22 Reached Erivan about 2AM; in a big fire. I stopped at Yarrows. Visited a good deal of work. Evening committee meeting at Whites. (83m)

December 23 Sunday. I took all meals today with Maynards. Preached first time in Armenian in the morning service. Had a Xmas service in PM. James speaking.

December 24 Spent forenoon with Yarrow at works. After dinner trimmed tree and toward evening had celebration. P party gave me 2 neckties.

December 25 Tues. Christmas. We had stockings for all, but little white baby stockings because it is war time & we could not fill such big stockings. The boys fixed the tree. The great thing was the electric train toward which Miss Gage gave five dollars and I $2.25. Edward had a bicycle seat, necktie, clasp, [?] Japan, gloves etc, pencil sharpener. See Memoranda.

December 26 Wed. A hard, confined, tired day. Mrs. Clark's two sisters called in the afternoon with James. Mrs. Stapleton also came.December 27 Thurs. Another hard day. Started to wash a little before four, but was called over to Mrs. Metcalf's to see Mrs. Greene, so the washing remained.

December 27 Thurs. Another hard day. Started to wash a little before four, but was called over to Mrs. Metcalf's to see Mrs. Greene, so the washing remained.

December 28 Fri. Colder. Same program. Hermann Giles came in the afternoon and took supper with us. I washed until 5:30, then put Alfred to bed and then began to get supper. We had popovers, warmed up potatoes, pineapple sauce, graham crackers and coffee.

December 29 Sat. Edward spent the day with Hermann and George, also took dinner with them. Then Edward and George were invited to Mrs. Martin's with other missionary children. My present from George, an electric toaster, came today and we had electrified toast for supper.

December 30 Sunday. Same as usual only George did not get up in time to go to S.S. so the little ones could not go. Edward does not go on account of his knee. After Armen came I called on Mrs. James and little Albert at the hospital. He is a lovely baby, seems already to have intelligence.

December 31 Mon. I did not feel very well so I did not

Ernest C. Partridge

December 25 Christmas day in Erivan. Dinner at Maynard's in Whites room. James, singing & supper at Yarrow's.

December 26 Every one spent forenoon getting over effects of Xmas. I put in a good part of day at the works, picking up information. A committee meeting in evening.

December 27 Spent whole day with Maynard and Yarrow getting facts about conduct of the work.

December 28 Went to station but found it very difficult to get on train. So Commandant arranged for us to go tomorrow on a private car. PM at works.

December 29 Waited an hour for Commandant's car and then went to station at 11 where we waited till 5 before we got on a small private car of the Chief Engineer group to Tiflis.

December 30 Sunday. A very slow, tedious journey up to Alexandropol. Mr. Heald and Haigaz meet us train at 12 noon. All dined with H. Slept most of PM. (83m)

December 31 A busy day going the rounds of work and picking up loose ends.

have any "pep" to work. Mrs. Whiteside washed. Mrs. Wirkler called in the afternoon. Mrs. Atkinson and Miss McLaren called in the morning. A postal from Samuel says that he is to go immediately to France and cannot even come to see us.

Memoranda. Christmas presents. George had special interest in the train, tinker toy, pin from Japan, gloves from Grandpa etc. Billo had various toys, a pin from his father from Japan, wonder blocks. Frances had a doll, doll house, a flat iron, handkerchiefs, hair ribbons, pocket book. Alfred had two toy trains, big ball, telephone, soap baby, a boy doll. Then Mrs. Johnston gave them five dollars & Uncle R. ten (over)

Memoranda. Mrs. May Williams sent six pinks [?], Prof. & Mrs. Wright sent six pinks [?], Mrs. Metcalf sent a basket of beautiful apples.

Diaries of Winona & Ernest Partridge 1918

January 1 Tues. New Years. Mrs. Martin and Miss Elizabeth Webb were the only callers. Armen came to supper and in the evening did part of the ironing and sent me to the movies, Marguerite Clark in the "Goose Girl."
Dinner—rice pilaf
Supper—beans & scones, cherry pie

January 2 Wed. Very cold, about 10° below. Frances tried to sweep while I was washing and swept the inside of the fireplace, the walls. Dear little girl. She thought she was helping mama. I tried to appreciate her effort but I had to wash the floor. Letter from Baidzar and Miss Gage.
Dinner—potato chowder
Supper—corn bread & jam, cherry pie.

January 3 Thurs. Very cold. Susie Zearing called in the afternoon and we sat in front of the open fire trying to keep warm, while the children raised Cain.
Dinner—bean soup (thick), fruit jelly with whipped cream
Supper—toast & chocolate

January 4 Fri. Cold & low gas. We all stayed in all day except to go for the milk and Edward rode up to Hermann's house but he was not at home.
Dinner—leftover bean soup (thinned) and leftover potato chowder, leftover jelly & bananas
Supper—Gibson's cinnamon rolls, tuna fish, pear sauce, peanut butter (spoiled)

Ernest C. Partridge

January 1 My first day in charge of work. Spent forenoon in office. Dinner about 2 with Comptons. Played 42 for a time. Stayed to supper.

January 2 Prospect of new buildings for work. Called on Dr Derderian about our men being taken for soldiers. City orphans clothed.

January 3 Bought a new desk. City orphans clothed. Discussed effort to get rice & potatoes for distribution. Enoch Kizarian began work as CC's secretary.

January 4 First A. volunteers in town. Fortress given up to them.

January 5 A busy day at office. Mr H finished work and turned over everything. Ashod Papazian came. Reception to Heald & us by officials of our work.

January 6 Sunday. Helped Mr Heald pack till noon, dinner at Compton's. Carl and I went to station w. H. but as train very late not wait. Much snow & colder. My last night in H's room.

January 7 First day in absolute charge. Compton settled at Mr H's desk till we get better quarters. Wrote children about vacation trip.

January 5 Sat. Warmer & good gas. The great event was George's return from the shack. He had a fine time, grew fat, took cold, skated five miles on the river. Everyone was delighted to see him, for he had been gone four whole days.
Dinner—soup, apple pie
Supper—leftover cocoa, scones

January 6 Sunday. Warm & rainy. We were generally used up with various ailments. But we had a second Christmas tree on two dollars that Baidzar sent for the children. I bought some tablets, pencils, tracing books and card.
Dinner—cabbage sarmas, coffee, jelly & whipped cream
Supper—corn bread, jam, peanut butter, coffee

January 7 Mon. Colder, very slippery. I fell on the corner of Elm & Professor, just in front of Mr. Horner. I had gone down town to pay monthly bills. Mrs. Fullerton said that I was not to try to break my ankle so I could get a rest, but I did not break anything.

Dinner—baked beans, leftover sarmas, bananas
Supper—warmed up potato cabbage à la Turque sauce, graham crackers

January 8 Tues. Colder and the gas low, but not low enough to require the fireplace. The children had a fine time sliding on our walk which is glare ice. Even Frances and Alfred slide on their stomachs or any place.
Dinner—Wiltshire sausage, potatoes, gravy, figs & apples
Supper—No gas so toast & chocolate

January 9 Wed. Cold, snowy and windy, gas low. Alfred said, "I guess I'd better do something, bettern't I?" He is very good at inventing new expressions.

January 10 Thurs. Cold, no wind, gas low. Armen came over and stayed with the children and I called on Mrs. Greene and Mrs. Haskell.
Dinner—potatoes, [unreadable], gravy, corn
Supper—leftover macaroni & beans; Armen made scones.

January 11 Fri. Cold & low gas. A very confused day. Alfred and Billo were a little sick and it has been a day where the three little ones had many demands, but they all got to sleep by seven o'clock.
Dinner—potato chowder (not enough to go around), apple pie
Supper—corn bread, jam, sauce, cheese

January 12 Sat. Colder & lower gas. We were shut up in the parlor where in front of the fire place we could get the temperature up to 50°. Our friends telephoned occasionally to see if we were frozen. But nothing happened.
Dinner—potato chowder again, bananas
Supper—toast & cocoa

January 13 Sunday. Very cold & low gas. The same program as Saturday, but we stuck it out without changing our furnace to coal. Mr. Metcalf concerned for our comfort offers to send wood from his own cellar but we did not need it.
Dinner or lunch—graham cracker sandwiches sitting by the grate
Supper—baked beans, coffee, jelly

January 14 Mon. Warmer and the gas very strong in the afternoon. I cleaned up the house all the forenoon, worked until four and then took the three little ones to call on Mrs. Atkinson who was not at home.
Dinner—Wiltshire sausage & potatoes, oranges
Supper—warmed up potatoes, Gibson's biscuit's, pineapple sauce

January 15 Tues. I did nothing but work until four and then I was too tired to do anything else.
Dinner—macaroni & beans, gingerbread & milk
Supper—popovers & boiled eggs

Ernest C. Partridge

January 8 Moved to new room opposite Comptons. Very cold & uncomfortable.

January 9 Called on General Autranik. A very pleasant man, seems able. Asked about our making stockings for soldiers. Talked over work with CCC and agreed that he be treasurer.

January 10 Turned over treasury work to Compton. Went to see barracks bldg for industrial work.

January 11 Went to see No 1 building for headquarters or hospital. A good place for either. If we can get it.

January 12 Worked on material for a report of work. Went to see building of our bank director for hospital and residence. Called on him. I had tea. Com. meet decided to take over Darandarupan work.

January 13 Sunday. Rose late. Read some, wrote Winona. Worked on Prof B's paper. Took a long walk in PM.

January 14 Armenian New Year's Day. Went to SS exercises in AM. Wrote report to Vickrey, letter to Yarrow about D & D work. YM & YWCA social evening.

January 15 Went to Bank to introduce CC. Asked for No 1 & Barracks for Industries & got immediate consent. Talk w Hagop Eff about D & D work which we will take over.

January 16 Wed. I took the three little folks down town while I went to the bank. They were cold before they got back, although the weather is not very cold.
Dinner—potato chowder, oranges
Supper—corn bread, salmon

January 17 Thurs. Good winter weather, good gas. Armen came over and stayed to supper so that I could go to the annual supper at the first church. I sat by Miss Hinman, opposite Mrs. Birdseye & Miss Strong. Good reports, best financial condition for years.
Dinner—potato chowder, cherry pie
Supper—warmed up potato biscuit, snow ice-cream

January 18 Fri. Colder. Nothing special happened. The children went to school & Alfred and I stayed at house. Edward bought a thrift stamp, 25 cts for each stamp, 16 on a card, payable in 1923. George went to Woody's to a meeting. Out of sugar. Mrs. Shaw lent me some.
Dinner—potato gravy & canned corn, apple pie
Supper—toast & cocoa

January 19 Sat. Colder & very low gas. We had a fire in the fire place all day. The children played aeroflame, house, made stocks to put Billo in, had picture show, concert etc. It was too cold to play out of doors. Susie Zearing asked me to go to the N.Y. Sym. Orchestra concert but I could not.
Dinner—bean soup, apple pie
Supper—potato, Parker House rolls from Gibson's

January 20 Sunday. Same as usual. We had only two meals. Edward and I went to church in the evening. Mr. Van der Pyl spoke on "How we may know God." It was very cold but no wind.
Dinner & supper—beans, fruit jelly & whipped cream
Lunch—popcorn & milk

Ernest C. Partridge

January 16 Began cleaning the barracks. I went to see No 2. Began stockings for soldiers. Baron Kafiandb went to Erivan for vacation.

January 17 Spent time over planning work in new buildings. Agreed to give No 1 to Industries. Medical work to begin in old offices until better buildings found for Hospital. (29)

January 18 Barracks cleaned out. Russian soldiers tried to get in. Sent Arshavir & Hovasef to Erzeroom. Deferred Tiflis trip to go with Maynard. (30)

January 19 1st day of Armenian Christmas. Called on B. Garabed, Armenaug, Solak and Hovasef. Also on General Autranik. Toothache most of time. Tried to find a dentist without success.

January 20 Sunday. Toothache continued so stayed in all day. Read and wrote George.

January 21 Last day of Xmas vacation. Went to a dentist who pulled wisdom tooth on right side. Gum sore but ache stopped. Slept little last night.

January 22 Work opened up slowly. Began stocking work & shoes for women. Finished Steiner's book.

January 23 Went to see barracks opposite weaving. Suitable for Ind. hospital & house. Hope to get it soon.

January 21 Mon. Cold again but good gas. Susie Zearing called & Alfred was tired and wanted some milk. He said to me in an audible voice, "I wish everybody wouldn't stay all the time." Susie was greatly amused. Mrs. Clark and Mrs. Miller called.
Dinner—potato salad, gingerbread
Supper—toast & cocoa

January 22 Tues. Not very cold. Took Alfred & Frances on the sled and called on Mrs. Atkinson. They want to walk and slide etc instead of riding demurely. Prof. Powers gave his first lecture. George went & enjoyed it.
Dinner—macaroni & beans, oranges
Supper—corn bread

January 23 Wed. Good winter weather. The second Powers lecture. Edward & Armen went.
Dinner—gravy, potatoes, corn, apple pie
Supper—popovers

January 24 Thurs. Snowed. I went to Dr. Powers lecture on "America & the Orient." He discussed South America a little & Japan and its need of expansion and a place to expand.
Dinner–leftover bean & macaroni, leftover pie
Supper–potatoes, biscuit from Gibson's

January 25 Fri. Cold. I went to Prof. Powers' lecture in the evening with George. The subject was "U.S. and Great Britain." What a wonderful empire. All got their marks. All good. Edward above 90 in everything.
Dinner–bean soup, bananas
Supper–cereals, warmed over biscuits

January 26 Sat. Colder. A letter from Mr. P. from Moscow describing their lively journey. The boys went to a basketball game with the soldiers from Camp Sherman. Score 16 to 7.
Dinner–bulgure pilaf, bananas
Supper–leftover pilaf, corn, macaroni, biscuits

January 27 Sunday. Very cold. My ears nearly froze on the way to church in the eve. Mr. V. spoke on "How to interpret the Bible." It was very sane, sensible and reverent.
No dinner. Lunch of graham cracker sandwiches
Supper–beans, coffee, jelly & whipped cream

January 28 Mon. Warmer, contrary to the weather predictions. I did the ordinary jobs and besides I cleaned the cellar. The boys have no school this week on account of the lack of coal.
Dinner–potato chowder, gingerbread
Supper–graham rolls & cereals

January 29 Tues. I went down to Mrs. Greene's where Mrs. Stapleton, Mrs. Haas and Mrs. Bunker, of Africa, were also invited. A letter came to Dr. Clark asking him to go to Palestine.
Dinner–macaroni & beans, bananas
Supper–corn bread & grape jelly

January 30 Wed. Nothing special.
Dinner–potato soup, bananas

January 31 Thurs. Same program, housework.
Dinner–macaroni & beans, nuts and molasses candy

February 1 Fri. Cold and low gas.
Dinner –bulgure pilaf, bananas
Supper–toast & cocoa

Ernest C. Partridge

January 24 Red barracks given to us. Drew plans on it and figured on its uses.

January 25 Started cleaning Central building. Whitewashing of the No 2 going on. Letters from Erivan.

January 26 Karahdise & Djaporea clothes finished & sent for distribution. Craig passed through to Tiflis.

January 27 Sunday. Went to YMCA meeting. Calls from B Hymayaf, Parsek & later from B. Garabed. Wrote Billo & Winona. Read a good deal. (32)

January 28 Called on Sunupat about our workers. Moved cotton & wool thread & stocking work to Annex. Stoves put up in several rooms.

January 29 Wells of YMCA came early today. Moved offices to Central bdg A. Armenaug and Oriorts came back. Talked with Dr Ohsen about medical work.

January 30 Called on Dr Derderian with Wells. Moving and settling work going along.

January 31 About 30 people cleaning and repairing Central Building. Things begin to look better. Called with Wells on Mayor and Autranik's Adjutant. Ashod went to Tiflis.

February 1 Inventory of Committee lacework finished. Went to see that house for a residence.

February 2 Inventoried Committee Carpenter and iron shops. Soup kitchen opened. Roof repairs in rooms finished. Hovsef came from Erzroom. Hospital whitewash and 1st cleaning finished.

February 2 Sat. Hampartsoom came. It was so good to see him. Then Mrs. Clark came to talk about letting the doctor go to Palestine. She stayed to supper.
Dinner–bean soup, bananas
Supper–warmed up potato, pear sauce, baking powder biscuits

February 3 Sunday. Mild in the morning, growing colder. Armen came back to stay today. In the evening Edward & I went to hear Mr. Van der Pyl on "What we may know of the future life." No dinner.
Supper–beans, scones

February 4 Mon. Cold. Armen went back to help Mrs. Wirkler so I was alone with the work again.
Dinner–potato chowder, oranges

February 5 Tues. Very, very cold, about 13° below. The kitchen was the warmest place & we ate there twice and sat there in the evening.
Dinner –baked beans, nuts & candy
Supper–toast & potato with cheese

February 6 Wed. Warmer. Hampartsoom and I went down town and bought him an overcoat for $28, a beauty, gray chevrot[a leather-type fabric]. Then we went to see Mr. Wirkler and the library.
Dinner–Wiltshire sausage, potato, gingerbread
Supper–corn bread, leftover potato & cheese

February 7 Thurs. I attended missionary meeting for the first time in months. The subject was Africa. Mr. Andrus, Mrs. Richards and Mrs. Bunker took part.
Dinner–vegetable soup, raisins & figs
Supper–dried beef scones, pineapple sauce

February 8 Fri. Mr. Carr telephoned that Dr. Clark is to start for Palestine next Wednesday.
Dinner–Goolash, i.e. meat, potato, tomato cooked together, bananas
supper–biscuits & leftover fruit salad, fine

February 9 Sat. Warm. I went to Elyria to see the Clarks, found Dr. in his office and then we went to the house. Came home at 7:10. The boys met me & took me to a basket ball game. O 23, Case 13.
Dinner–bulgure pilaf, bananas
Supper–biscuits, warmed up potato

Ernest C. Partridge

February 3 Sunday. Went to YMCA meeting. Long walk in PM. (33)

[February 4]

February 5 Went to see a house for us and decided to rent it. Only 5 minutes walk from offices. A fine place. Plenty of room.

February 6 Rented new house. Four rooms in main part, 5 & kitchen etc. and yard. Drywood and some furniture. Clinic opened today.

February 7 First cleanup of Central building finished. Still working on locks, glass, stoves etc.

February 8 Began using basement of annex for warehouse, moving corn, lacework. Report of fall of Constantinople probably considerably aggravated.

February 9 5000 Russian soldiers in town & a good deal of unrest. Yarrow's men are bringing money now.

February 10 Sunday. Spent day taking care of my feet, chillblains bad. Read a good deal. Wrote WGP. Ashod went to Tiflis. Druggist accepted our offer last night.

[February 11]

February 12 Teachers of Girls Industries came & worked getting rooms in shape. Finished moving lace house. Haig is working on moving supplies. Yenook went to Tiflis.

February 10 Sunday. Warm & melting. Got up with a sick headache but got better as the day went on. Went to evening service with Hampartsoom & Edward. Prof. Lyman on "Mary's place in the universe." Telephoned to Dr. Clark about Cairo.
Lunch–graham crackers, peanut butter, cheese, etc. milk
Dinner & supper–[?], coffee, jelly, whipped cream, biscuits

February 11 Mon. Warm. Mrs. Clark and David came over, mostly to see Mr. Metcalf. Alfred, Billo & I went to the station with them & all got ones feet wet. I had a letter from Mr. Peet about Vahan's money.
Dinner–potato chowder, tapioca pudding
Supper–raisin [?] bread, herring, gingersnaps

February 12 Tues. Cleaning up day. The snow was melting. The children got wet again & again. At night there were nine pairs of shoes drying at the register. Dr. Clark was to leave for N.Y. to go to Palestine. Arthur & Herman came to supper.
Dinner–beans, oranges
Supper–potato & cheese scalloped, scones, fruit salad, chocolate cookies & macaroons

February 13 Wed. Warm & drying up fast. In the night Alfred had a stomachache, then an ear ache. Today Frances had a headache & vomited. Edward has a bad cold, but none are really sick. Billo had his hair cut & got a pair of rubbers with Hampartsoom. Mrs. Williams took me to the Phila. Symphony Orchestra. Mrs. Metcalf gave Hampartsoom a ticket. Mrs. James and her little boy were there.
Dinner—potatoes & codfish gravy, leftover salad, cookies, & marshmallows
Supper—cottage cheese with nuts & cream, biscuits

February 14 Thurs. Valentine's day. Warm. Instead of buying valentines we made heart cookies. Billo made red hearts with flags on them for Carroll, Ralph, Allen & William, also for Alfred. Mrs. Shaw sent me her picture with Carroll for a valentine. Alfred was a little sick but no worse at night. Madame James, Mrs. James & the baby called.
Dinner—macaroni, bananas
Supper—warmed up potato, toast, cookies

February 15 Fri. Colder. I went to tack a Red Cross quilt at Mrs. Williams's house. The refreshments cost more than the quilts were worth, I think. The boys went to a basket ball game. O.S.U. 23 Oberlin 14. George played against the Scouts and the Krescents beat.
Dinner—bulgure pilaf, tapioca pudding
Supper—leftover pilaf & macaroni, cornbread

February 16 Sat. Colder. Glee Club concert. Edward & George earned their tickets, but Mr. Wirkler sent another ticket so someone could go with them & then Mrs. Metcalf brought a ticket so Hampartsoom & I went. It was very good, but very long.
Dinner—cabbage sarma, oranges
Supper—warmed up potatoes, scones

Ernest C. Partridge

February 13 Miss Orvis and Wells & I moved to new house. Finished doing Girls Base Rooms.

February 14 Finished moving to new house. Very well fixed. Lace school started today. 42 girls began sewing clothes for old people.

February 15 Moved packing department up to Central Bdg. Began moving new blacksmith shop.

February 16 A busy day with lots of Details. Capt Gracey and Robert McDowell came in PM.

February 17 Sunday. Caught a bad cold in my head. A quiet day visiting and getting the news.

February 18 Capt G & McD left for south at 4AM; slept in cars till 10 & came back. Trouble down line; no trains going down. A hot meeting to encourage enlistment.

February 19 Guests got off for south at 2PM by special train. Mr Craig came about 6PM. Also Prof Hagopian. Craig our guest. (35)

February 20 Had a call from Dr Hagopian. He is in charge of Aid for Soldiers' families. Appeals for work greatly increased.

February 17 Sunday. Cold. Dr. Aked spoke about the Armenians. Armen & Hampartsoom & Edward went. Edward said, "If they don't give after that, they never will." Lenten evening service. Dr. Bitling, Baptist. No dinner.
Lunch—graham crackers, peanut butter
Supper—beans, coffee, jelly & macaroons

February 18 Mon. Cold, warmer in the afternoon. I had a big washing & did not finish until after three. Went down town with Hampartsoom to find out about his lessons etc. Capt. Garland came to offer to take our boys to the father and son banquet.
Dinner—potato chowder, Brazil nuts & raisins
Supper—corn bread, prunes, leftover sarmas

February 19 Tues. Warm. We expected Mrs. Perry but she did not come and no letter. I went to see Miss Hurd about Hampartsoom's English. In the evening I went to see Susie Zearing.
Dinner—macaroni & beans, bananas & oranges, corn bread
Supper—warmed up potatoes, popovers, Armen ate 8-9 popovers

February 20 Wed. Mr. Bohn took Edward and George to the Father & Son banquet. They were also invited by Capt. Garland & Mr. Pond.
Dinner—potato, gravy, corn, gingerbread

February 21 Thurs. Very cold, low gas. These days Alfred talks against his curls. He is fond of wearing a cap of George's with a vizor. He says, "When you wear your brother's cap with a thing out in front, you don't want curls, do you!"
Dinner–bean soup

February 22 Fri. Washington's birthday. Warmer. I did not go out all day. Armen & Hampartsoom went to the chapel to the address by Talcott Williams. The Clarks came from Elyria.
Dinner–potato cheese doughnuts

February 23 Sat. Warmer. All the children except Edward & Alfred went to the Glee Club concert, repeated for children. Billo went to the Basket ball game between High School & Sandusky. The first time this winter that I have hung the clothes out of doors.
Dinner –bulgure pilaf, oranges
Supper–warmed up potato, corn bread

February 24 Sunday. Warm & springlike, gas fine. Edward, George, Hampartsoom & I went to the Union Service at the chapel. Mr. Grant of Elyria spoke. Mrs. Grant told me that the Clarks are going to Detroit tomorrow.
Lunch–graham crackers, cheese, peanut butter, milk
Supper–baked beans, coffee, jelly

February 25 Mon. Lots of gas because it is warm. We expected Mrs. Perry but she did not come. The Clarks were to go to Detroit today. I am sorry to have them leave Elyria.
Dinner–potato chowder, oranges
Supper–beans, corn bread, prunes, gingersnaps

February 26 Tues. Mrs. Perry came at night about nine o'clock. She went to Cleveland and came back. It was not very cold but she felt cold. She had not changed much from Turkey.
Dinner–macaroni

Ernest C. Partridge

February 21 Another conference with Prof Hagopian. He wishes to cooperate with us in his relief work. Committee promised exception for 22 men for us & 4 for Hospital.

February 22 Got promise for 4 cotton carders that volunteered; contracted to buy 160 lbs of tea. Had Prof H & Dr O to dinner.

February 23 Worked hard all day in details. YMCA social at Oriorts' rooms in evening.

February 24 Sunday. A quiet day. Did not put my shoes on because of chillblains. Gen Autranik came in evening from Tiflis. Edward H & W (36)

February 25 Called on Gen Autranik. Sold 2500 pr socks. New edition of money in town from Tiflis. Saw 2500 soldiers start off in evening. Craig went with them to Erzeroom.

February 26 Baron Garabed went to Tiflis. I took first Russian lesson here. Bought 200 pounds of meat and flour yesterday.

[February 27]

February 28 Ruth and I inventoried all lacework materials & divided up sending some to Baron Haig. She & Carl are to supervise the lacework department.

February 27 Wed. Warm. Mrs. Perry & I called on Mrs. Greene and Mrs. Haas. Visited with Mrs. Perry doing as little work as possible.
Dinner–potatoes, dried beef, kidney beans, fruit
Supper–leftover macaroni, beans, corn bread

February 28 Thurs. Warm, rainy. Mrs. Perry received callers in the afternoon. Mrs. Atkinson, Miss Noyes, & Mr. & Mrs. Riggs. Mrs. Perry went away on the 5:30 train. We enjoyed her visit. The news these days is too terrible. The Russians have been entirely deceived and browbeaten by the Germans who broke their armistice and are marching in. The Russians are very much demoralized.
Dinner–potato, codfish gravy, gingerbread
Supper–biscuit, warmed up potato, pineapple cake arrived late.

March 1 Fri. Didn't go anywhere nor do anything but housework. Frances was sick at night and we thought she had measles.
Dinner–bulgure pilaf
Supper–leftovers & potatoes cooked with cheese

March 2 Sat. I washed three floors and washed besides the regular work & finished just in time to go to Miss Curtis's for Leaven Club. Miss Oak spoke about art for children.
Dinner–potato, gravy, corn, bananas & apples
Supper–Gibson biscuit, cocoa

March 3 Sunday. Billo & Frances did not go to S.S. because they had colds. In the evening Edward, Hampartsoom & I went to hear preach - Bishop DuMoulin, Coadjutor of Ohio.
No dinner. Lunch–graham crackers, cheese, jam, peanut butter
Supper–beans, brown bread, coffee, jelly

March 4 Mon. One of the hardest days I have had. I finished washing at 4:30 just in time to get supper. In the evening I did Algebra most of the time.
Dinner–potato chowder, nuts & raisins
Supper–corn bread, beans

March 5 Tues. Warm. I did my ironing in the afternoon so that I might have a whole evening to mend stockings but Mrs. Metcalf came & persuaded me to go to the Artist Recital. William Willeke cellist & Mrs. Bennett pianist.
Dinner–macaroni, oranges
Supper–warmed up potato, prunes, popovers

March 6 Wed. Rainy, muddy, cold. I did nothing remarkable except mend eight pairs of stockings. I feel very rich. Billo spends most of his spare time with Loman on the delivery wagon. I ordered sugar expecting two pounds as usual & they sent me ten.
Dinner–potatoes, corn, pork gravy, gingerbread
Supper–corn bread, peaches (dried & cooked), leftover macaroni

March 7 Thurs. A letter from Mr. P. dated Dec. 9 Tiflis. He wrote of seeing Mr. Montesanto. This is the first letter after reaching Tiflis. I attended a lecture on the Armenians, given by Mrs. Atkinson.
Dinner–bean soup, oranges
Supper–graham bread, potato with cheese

March 8 Fri. Warmer. Billo & I went to Elyria & bought him a suit of clothes and two waists. Bought here a pair of shoes for $4 & rubbers for 85 cts. Billo was very lovely all the way. When he is good, he is very, very good etc. Alfred tries to attract my attention & if he doesn't get me to listen, he says. "Mama I love you," but see this thing or whatever he wants to say. He knows that I cannot stand that.
Dinner–bulgure pilaf, bananas
Supper–scones, warmed up potato, peach sauce

Ernest C. Partridge

March 1 Moved 20 women to annex for officials' thread work. Capt Gracey, Yarrow & Welch came on way to Tiflis. Left 8PM. Saw them off at depot.

March 2 End of a hard week. Work irregular owing to drafting & many complaints about pay. Peace Parleys begun at Trebizond.

March 3 Sunday. Service in old office rooms. Hovasef went to Kara Killesi to buy wheat. Frances & W (37)

March 4 Beginning to find food supplies.

March 5 Bought 2000 pounds of potatoes. Supply Com is to give bread & sugar tickets to all city refugees. Baron G got back from Tiflis.

March 6 Prof Baron Sarkis on food distribution work. Took long walk on Kars road. Mr Craig returned from Sarakamish trip.

March 7 Started 3 new carpenters making looms.

March 8 Made 1st sheet for hospital on wide loam. C & I had a long talk with Baron G about work. Stapleton got in from Erzeroom. City gave us 6 guns for works.

March 9 Sat. Rainy. I spent the afternoon with the three little ones at the Y.W.C.A. circus. They had a fine time eating popcorn & ice-cream, but Alfred got tired. He said, "I am tired all over." In the evening I went with the big boys to the basket ball games, Oberlin 27, Hennfrom[?] 20, and High School 23, Lorain 13. These are the last games of the season. Our cellar is flooded with several inches of water. George went with rubbers on with no shoes & stockings to put out the furnace.
Dinner–Wiltshire sausages, potatoes, oranges & bananas
Supper–potato, biscuit, cake, pineapple

March 10 Sunday. Very cold, gas low. I went to Pres. King's Bible Class with Hampartsoom and sat with Mrs. Greene. In the evening I stayed at home with all the children & had a family time.
No dinner. Lunch–crackers etc.
Supper–beans, biscuit, coffee, jelly

March 11 Mon. Cold, gas almost the lowest this winter until evening. Mrs. Van Der Pyl called and Mrs. Barnard. Mrs. V. kept saying that Alfred is like a big wax doll. He is some lively for a wax doll, I say.
Dinner–potato chowder, bananas
Supper–corn bread, tuna fish, leftover pilaf & potato, gingersnaps

March 12 Tues. Warm & pleasant, plenty of gas, but two things happened to make extra work. Frances & Billo went to Rawdon's Creek to play & got all wet and muddy and Frances & Alfred both had accidents. Then after supper a bird got in the chimney and fluttered & fluttered filling the room with soot through the fireplace. I washed it with five pails of water and then the dining room where it had been tracked through. I finished that & the dishes & the children's baths at ten o'clock, but my ironing had to go over till the next day.
Dinner –macaroni, doughnuts
Supper–warmed up beans, scones

Ernest C. Partridge

March 9 Had office whitewashed & cleaned. Worked on plans for reorganization. Russian lesson.

March 10 Sunday. Mr Stapleton preached in morning and I in PM. Telegram from Yarrow & Ansol coming from Tiflis.

March 11 2000 lots of potatoes moved to Carding basement.

March 12 Capt G, Yarrow, Welch, & Ansol came in the before noon. I joined them for Erivan, left A at 5PM. Halfway down in early morning motorcar train overtook us.

March 13 Our engine jumped track and we changed to flat cars on motors. Tight with Tartars, 2 autos hit. Detrained at Etchmiadzin [headquarters of Armenian Church] & drove to Erivan. I stopped at Bachelor's house. (83m)

March 14 Spent AM at industries and offices. Important Committee meeting in PM. Red Cross proposal & finances considered.

March 15 Part of morning in offices and works. Heald, Gracey, George, & I drove red car down to Gamarlu. Saw work there. Committee meeting. Dinner at Yarrow's. Social evening.

March 13 Wed. I did not do anything remarkable except wash my hair which was black from soot as a second bird too came down the chimney. It was wet and the children had to be looked after all the time. I ironed until half past ten and got to bed some after eleven to be waked up again and again by wind, thunder & lightning.
Dinner–potatoes, gravy, corn, nuts & raisins
Supper–corn bread, leftover macaroni, potato chowder, crackers with frosting

March 14 Thurs. Warm, rainy. When the children went to school it became almost as dark as night and such a green color that it was frightful. I went to hear a Haskell lecture by Dr. Torrey on the relation of the Gentiles and Jews in Palestine. I spoke with him afterwards. He is a fine man, not changed much except his hair, which is quite gray.
Dinner–bean soup, bananas & oranges
Supper–biscuit, prunes, potato, crackers frosted

March 15 Fri. Russia accepts by a large majority Germany's terms of peace. I went to another Haskell lecture. Mrs. Greene, Mrs. Wright & I sat together, all knitting stockings. Afterwards Hampartsoom & I went to buy him some collars.
Dinner–rice pilaff, gingerbread
Supper–cornbread, cereals

March 16 Sat. Pleasant & a little warmer. I went to Mrs. Wright's to dinner with Prof. Torrey and Mrs. Greene. It was very pleasant. Edward went to North Amherst to a Boys' Conference.
Dinner–bulgure pilaf, bananas
Supper–scones, potato, apple sauce

March 17 Sunday. Hampartsoom and I went to Pres. King's Class. He spoke very seriously feeling that we were facing a great crisis in the war. Alfred came to meet me, he and I to meet George, Frances & Billo. Geo. & F. got home first, then came to meet us, Geo. & Alfred went home & then A. came to meet me.

March 18 Mon. I did not do anything out of the ordinary. The weather was good and the children played out of doors all day. Letters from Mrs. Perry.
Dinner–potato chowder, banana
Supper–beans, brown bread, cookies

March 19 Tues. Another warm day. The children were all criss-cross so I did not allow them to go out to play in the morning, except Alfred. He had a nap in the afternoon.
Dinner–macaroni, doughnuts
Supper–potato, apple sauce, corn bread

March 20 Wed. Warm & pleasant. The great events of the day were washing Alfred & Frances's hair and Edward's first tennis this year. He played with Arthur & Hermann. They all won.
Dinner–fish balls, Sally Lunns [a type of yeast bread, originating in Bath, UK], bananas
Supper–leftover macaroni, potato, Sally Lunns, corn bread, apple sauce, prunes, toast new chocolate

March 21 Thurs. Warm. I attended mass meeting for women, addressed by Miss Eleanor Baker. She made the war seem very real, that we must not use white bread, ham over bacon. Armen & the three oldest went to see "Jack & the Beanstalk" in the evening. Billo did not like it, too bloody.
Dinner–Bean soup, huts, raisins
Supper–cereal, [?], potato & cheese

Ernest C. Partridge

March 16 Spent day discussing plans. Com meeting in afternoon. Cafeteria dinner at Whites. Decided to send out women & children probably South.

March 17 Sunday. Visited at Maynards, lunch with Whites. Dinner to Persian consul at Batchelor's. Decided to go up on morning train if it comes. James to go to A while I am in Tiflis.

March 18 On way to station met Craig from Tiflis. Smith calls us all out at once [ordered to evacuate Erivan]. Had a Com. meeting and decided to go. Gracey, Ansol, Heald, & Elden to stay 3–4 days to close up.

March 19 Party left Erivan about 11AM in 3rd class car special. Reached A at 6. Baron G. came down, as several others. Rather crowded but comfortable.

March 20 An uneventful journey to Tiflis where we arrived about 2PM. Most of single men sleeping at Consulate. Others scattered in rooms at hotels.

March 21 A long meeting about journey & Committee work. Yarrow, Maynard, & I with Consul a special meeting to prepare for continuing work.

March 22 Worked on plans for journey. Bath. Another relief committee meeting.

March 23 Our party of 33 with 20 others attached to us left Tiflis at 10PM for Baku. American, English, French, Belgian, Russian, Georgian, Austrian, & Assyrian. Had 2 2nd class cars & comfortable.

March 22 Fri. A little colder, but the children played out all day. The fire whistle blew five times & Alfred ran in and looked at the card and came to me and said "Southwest." He had seen us do that. George at supper at "Woody's" with the 2nd basket ball team.
Dinner–potato, gravy, corn, gingerbread
Supper–corn bread, fruit, salad, potato

March 23 Sat. Pleasant. Work, work, work, but I actually got time to sew on some buttons and run in some new elastic and mend Edward's trousers, clean Frances's coat etc.
Dinner–rice pilaf, bananas
Supper–leftover potato, bean soup, pancakes

March 24 Sunday. Cold but pleasant. Attended Pres. King's class & was glad to be encouraged for the paper said that the Germans had made a wedge in the western front.
No dinner, lunch.
Supper—beans, fruit salad

March 25 Mon. I had to go to Elyria to get George a suit. I finished washing at two, washed the dishes, got ready myself, hunted up Alfred & Frances, got them ready, sent Edward to school to get George out, took the 3:25 car with the three children, got George a suit, came back at 5:10, had supper, got Billo ready & went to the community sing in which George sang with the schools. We were thrilled with the patriotism, and especially the report that 200,000 Germans had been captured. The excitement was great.
Dinner—potato chowder, coffee, jelly
Supper—scones, beans

March 26 Tues. Edward had his first debate in his English class, "Should German be dropped from the schools." He was affirmative. His side won both on the debate and the merits of the question. No mention in the paper of the $200,000, a mistake evidently. The British are losing ground on the western front but hopeful that they may stand.
Dinner—macaroni, bananas
Supper—potato, cornbread, prunes

March 27 Wed. Armen was sick & did not go to laboratory in the afternoon. The news is a little better but not much. The crisis seems to be coming.
Dinner—potatoes, kidney beans, nuts, raisins
Supper—brown bread, potatoes, prunes

March 28 Thurs. Mrs. Greene called. I had a long letter from Nishan Bekhian, including a quotation from Mesrob. Hovsep, Enoch, Krzigian are in Russia. The Russians took back Odessa. On the West no special news. Germans advanced in some places.
Dinner—fishballs, popovers, apple salad
Supper—tomato soup, corn bread

Ernest C. Partridge

March 24 Sunday. A quite comfortable journey to Baku getting in at 10PM. Got permission to sleep in cars. Searching by Tartars. (343m)

March 25 After breakfast on car Craig & I went uptown to investigate. No hope of getting away quickly. Some of ladies and 2 families at hotels. Most of men in Arm. church.

March 26 Comptons, Whites, and Dr R in private housings. Rest of men went to English club where we are very comfortable. Trying to arrange for a special boat.

March 27 Got promise of a boat for party soon. Spent most of day down town on business. Visited hydroplane hangers.

March 28 Spent several hours at SS [steamship company] offices. About 1000 obstacles but finally promised a boat as soon as traffic opened. Taken sick with bowel trouble.

March 29 Telegram from Astrakhan [Russia, on left bank of Volga River] that ready for transportation next Wednesday. SS Co promises to send us out after first passenger steamer. A gang of Bs [Bolsheviks] wanted our boat.

[March 30]

March 31 Sunday. Two services at English church. Yarrow morning. Stapleton afternoon. Fighting between Tartar's & Bs began at 5:45 & continued to 9. My health better tonight.

March 29 Fri. Vacation in College & kindergarten. I went to call on Mrs. Haskell & her family and Mrs. Greene but they were not at home. I visited with Mrs. Haas a few minutes. A telegram announcing the arrival of Garabed Eff. Paelian.
Dinner—bean soup, tapioca pudding
Supper—potato, fruit salad, oat meal [?]

March 30 Sat. Dinner—rice pilaf

March 31 Sunday. Easter, lovely weather. Only George had a new suit, but I cleaned Edward's gray clothes. Frances wore her white coat and Alfred his. Billy wore his new suit, which he got a little while ago. Edward was a jun[?] in the East pageant. We all went, leaving the house alone.

Memoranda. An example of 1918 English, Buster Brown to Tige: "Tige, there was a great big giant named Goliath, who was putting it all over everybody and a little guy named David took a stone and beaned him on the filbert and croaked him."

April 1 Mon. A postal from Garbed Eff. saying he is at Park Ave Hotel in New York waiting to see where his work is to be. He may go to Chicago and then we should see him.
Dinner—macaroni, bananas
Supper—soup, corn bread

April 2 Tues. I went to the bank, took Billo to the movies to see Marguerite Clark in the "Amazons," got Edward a pair of low shoes for $4.50 ($5 shoes). They wanted Alfred for a mascot in the Yale-Princeton basket ball game but he did not want to and did not.
Dinner—potato chowder, bananas
Supper—brown bread, apple sauce

April 3 Wed. Had a copy of a cablegram from Mr. Yarrow, telling of the awful conditions of the Armenians between the Turks & Tartars. He wants money to help them protect themselves. The date of the telegram was March 30.
Dinner—potatoes, gravy, corn, nuts, molasses, candy
Supper—diced beef, oatmeal crackers, corn meal fan cakes

April 4 Thurs. Pleasant but cold. The paper says that the Armenians took Ezroom back from the Turks. I hope it is so. 2 letters from G. P. one from London, one from N.Y. A letter from Samuel saying that he has been sent to Indiana but he does not know what they will do with him.
Dinner—bean soup, tapioca pudding
Supper—corn meal [?], potato cooked with dried beef, apple salad

[April 5]

April 6 Sat. George played base ball against 6th grade in Elyria. He played first base. They were beaten 20–5. Alfred earned his first money, 5 cts for carrying ashes for Mrs. Merrill with a dipper. George earned 20 cts & Billo ten. Edward went on a birthday auto ride & picnic with Horace Mosher. Liberty Loan day. All day the telephone girls said "Liberty Loan number."
Dinner—rice pilaf, bananas
Supper—eggs, scones

April 7 Sunday. Again I went to Easter Vespers & again I was sleepy. A cablegram from Mr. James saying he is coming home. We all wonder why.

April 8 Mon. Cold, a little snow. The cablegram from Mr. James was from another Mr. James, not Walter. A letter and telegram from Garabed Eff. saying he is coming tomorrow. Miss Noyes called.
Dinner—macaroni, doughnuts
Supper—potato, corn bread, syrup

Ernest C. Partridge

April 1 Heavy gun fighting began early. Gunboats engaged. Steady firing all day. T[artar]s evidently driven back some. A bad fire on the dock in evening which burned most of night.

April 2 Fighting continued all day. Walk towards town to the barricade. Stormy. Tartar market burning.

April 3 Fighting stopped about 9AM. Most of us went to town. SS offices closed. A little sporadic fighting but it seems Ts have enough.

April 4 Went down town about steamer. Offices closed. Walked out to no 32 to find boat, not there. No fighting today. Hoped that a settlement being made.

April 5 Craig and I walked thro walled city and burned section. Peace terms signed. Some hope of a boat out tomorrow.

April 6 Funeral of Russians killed in fight. Promise of a boat tomorrow evening. Whites and Comptons came out to club to stay. Dr. Kennedy sick w[ith] malaria.

April 7 Sunday. Several hours at SS offices; promise to start at 6:30. Trouble with crew, false start. James & Catchpool went on board Van as scouts. Several of party stayed up at Club.

April 8 Boat came to pier 6 at 9:30 & we went on board. Most of relatives of crew joined us for a joy ride. Inspection for soldiers & food. Out into harbor about 4.

April 9 Tues. Cold. Garabed Eff. came. He has not changed a bit in ten years. It was so good to see him. His wife stayed to visit her mother.
Dinner—hamburg steak, potatoes, kidney beans
Supper—beans, biscuit, fruit salad

April 10 Wed. Cold, snow, hail. Letter from Mr. P. from Alexandropol. Need to work & visit at the same time. It was so cold the children could not go out to play. Garabed Eff. went at 5:30. I went to Mrs. Wright's to supper with Mrs. Haskell & Mrs. Marsh. We had fried eggs, sauce, cookies.
Dinner—chicken, mashed potato, bananas
Supper at home—corn bread, warmed up potato
Apples came from Mrs. Perry.

April 11 Thurs. Several inches of snow on the ground but a little warmer. After visiting with Garabed Eff. for two days I had to work hard to make up for lost time.
Dinner—warmed up chicken, mashed potato, bananas
Supper—eggs, corn bread, applesauce

April 12 Fri. Cold. Worked all day, cleaned up the bedrooms, finished at half past five.

April 13 Sat. Warmer. A letter from Polly written Feb. 4, containing two photographs of herself. She does not look as though wheat were $250 a bag.

April 14 Sunday. I did not go to church because George did not feel well. Our ash pit got on fire and almost set the house on fire. Mr. Metcalf and Mr. Darling came and cleaned it out so we did not call the fire department. I went down to the water works with the children.

April 15 Mon. Nothing unusual happened except that George was too sick to go to school in the afternoon & I called Dr. Thatcher in the evening. George vomited all day Sunday and so was weak. The doctor gave him some medicine & he slept well but had to starve almost.

April 16 Tues. Rainy. George stayed in bed until about suppertime. He ate only very thin slices of very dry toast, a little malted milk, a cup of chocolate and a glass of milk. He feels empty but has gone to sleep. Tonight's paper says that the Germans have advanced on the western front.

April 17 Wed. Rainy. Miss Phelps came to Mrs. Atkinson's with Miss McLaren and I went over to see them. Mrs. Stevens was there. Then we went to Mrs. Steven's to afternoon tea.

Ernest C. Partridge

April 9 Left gunboat at 9:53AM after superficial search for arms. A quiet & pleasant day, a little rough towards evening. No one sick yet. Slept on deck till 5AM.

April 10 A quiet day growing rougher. We are eating in a hold, some sleeping there. I stayed down.

April 11 Increasingly cold but smoother. Passed up roads and anchored 2 miles below town for night.

April 12 Reached Astrakhan about 9AM. No steamers up Volga yet. Slept on board one night & have arrangements to occupy 1st cabin of Kief [a ship] for a week till she starts for Samara.

April 13 The Nizhin novgorod took us down to the Kief & started for Baku. 1st steamers up river left tonight. Williams, Welch & Catchpool started for Samara by rail. 1st bed for 26 days.

April 14 Sunday. Morning service of the Kief. I preached. Craig, Wells, James, & I started by train to Saratof. Trains started exactly on time. Fighting between Bs and Cossacks began in town.

April 15 A good night in International Sleeper. Reached Volga about 4PM. Spent 4 hours getting on ferry across & up to Saratof by train. Went to hotel, found room but tried to get on night train, failed & slept in station. (411m)

April 16 The commandant put us on a special 3rd cl car for Rteshchevo; left at 9AM. About 3:30PM missed train and slept in station. (120m)

April 17 Spent day waiting for train. At 2PM got on a boxcar which carried 60 people thro night. A terrible experience. Train of 56 cars, ours no 954,608.

April 18 Reached Renza at 4AM & walked half a mile with the baggage, ferried across river, got wagon for luggage to other station. Welch & Catchpool joined us and got special boxcar to Samara. (98m)

April 18 Thurs. A real April day, showery, then cold. I went to prayer-meeting with Mrs. Shaw. The subject was, "What shall we do with delinquent members and what is the least that we should require of them?" It was a good meeting but a few make long speeches.

April 19 Fri. Cold, low gas. I went to a lecture with George & Edward, a lecture on Japan by Dr. Hanna. It was very interesting and the slides were beautiful. Edward was an usher.

April 20 Sat. Cloudy. Nothing but work.

April 21 Sunday. I did not get out at all but slept in the afternoon.

April 22 Mon. Frances five years old. We gave her roller skates again, ball bearing this time. She had some other little things, perfumery, ball, cup & saucer, candlestick. We had ice-cream & cake. Arthur ate with us. I washed spreads & my regular washing at Mrs. Shaw's in her washing machine.

April 23 Tues. A little cold, a little warm, a little pleasant, a little cloudy. The postman passed us both times. The western front in France is quiet but perhaps that portends evil.

April 24 Wed. Medina Conference, Mr. Van der Pyl's installation. I heard the last part of the evening session. I arrived as Mr. Spence was speaking. He is fine, fine perfectly inspiring but Mr. V. is finer. Germany gave an ultimatum to Holland but Holland seems to be somewhat ready.

April 25 Thurs. Pleasant but rather cold. While the little folks were at the tennis court I went to Mrs. Metcalf's to see Mrs. Upton. Mrs. Martin, Miss Webb and Miss Cold called. Billy was very naughty.

April 26 Fri. Rainy, not cold. Mrs. Tucker called, and then Mrs. Atkinson. George went out to Woody's shack to stay over night. We had a quick supper, boiled eggs, toast and pancakes of ready made flour. Mr. Metcalf brought a grate for the parlor fireplace.

April 27 Sat. Edward's birthday. I gave him money & caramels. George gave him a baseball and Billy a pair of pincers. The new lawnmower came from Mr. Hosmer $9. New American, 18 in. cut. George got back, had a fine time.

April 28 Sunday. At home all day until evening, when Hampartsoom, Edward & I went to church. Mr. V. preached on "Socialism as a substitute for the Gospel." Edward's birthday cake was not hard enough, the frosting, so we ate it today. Arthur was here to supper.

Ernest C. Partridge

April 19 Six of us held boxcar all night. Set up 3 beds & were very comfortable. Reached Samara at 6PM. Found a bunch of YMCA men & are staying with them. Prospects of getting on seem good. (240m)

April 20 Forenoon baseball game of YMCA men. Went to station to see Miller's office & Duncan's car. Evening Prof Robertson's lecture on Gyroscopes. Craig decided to stay here for present.

April 21 Sunday. Went to station early & found chances good so took baggage down to Miller's car. Slept night at Cech[?] Information car and waited for our train, the last one carrying the 6th Regiment.

April 22 Waited whole day at station. Slept at Information car. A number of ordinary trains thro, heaviest travel going west.

April 23 Awakened at 6AM to take train. One 3rd cl coach for officers. Found one officer who speaks some English and an orderly who knows more. Started across Siberia at 8AM.

April 24 Comfortably fixed in officers car with a lieutenant who speak some English. Have an orderly. Making fair time. Reached Ufa at 6PM. 1st Eng lesson with 12 officers. Bought five Ural stones.

April 25 A long slow day. Made 151 versts [obsolete Russian unit of length] in 25 hours. Most of day in stations waiting for orders. Another English lesson.

April 26 Made good time today and reached stop 5 versts out of Cheliabinsk at 3:30PM where we stopped. 10 trains in city & we shall not move until they are cleaned out.

April 27 With Lieut Porkonis we walked into town and did some shopping. At lunch, called on Bill Duncan in his car. We ran into the city at 8PM and spent the night on a siding. (628m)

April 28 Sunday. A long stupid day waiting to move. I have taken cold & slept most of day. Took a walk in PM and read some.

April 29 Mon. Nothing doing, except work. I finished washing after four. In the evening I ironed.

April 30 Tues. I took the three little ones & George to a picture show on birds. In the evening I took Billo to a Red Cross benefit vaudeville. George's grade dressed in sailor suits had a flag drill but I was too late for that. It was very good, the colored show, the lost silk hat, the allies, etc.etc.

May 1 Wed. Cold but pleasant. May day again. The children hung & received more or less baskets. I made fudge to put in one. I spent a good deal of the day hunting for Frances. She slips out and disappears down to the tennis court or over to Catherine's or out picking flowers. The most exciting thing was a letter from Mr. Case saying that Mr. Partridge & Mr. James with a company of Y.M.C.A. messrs are at Samara. It will be fine to have him at home but dreadful to think what the reason must be, that he cannot do more relief work.

May 2 Thurs. I went to Prof. Miller's with many others to hear about his war work for foreigners. Very interesting. Mrs. Elmer and Enid called. Mrs. E seems very frail. I do not see how her husband could leave her and go to Russia.

May 3 Fri. Warm, like summer. Winter underwear is a burden to the children. I lost Alfred today, he disappeared from his play place. After I had hunted everywhere I could think of he came back with Billo. They had been to a fire over behind Prospect St. School.

May 4 Sat. Edward went to Mr. Wood's shack. Hermann & Mr. Brace also went, others too, whom I do not know. George played with the 6th Grade team against Wellington. Oberlin won. But the Varsity lost to Case by one point.

May 5 Sunday. Very warm. Again I did not go to church all day. We took our lunch down to the arboretum and that gave the neighbors a little rest. In the evening Alfred had a terrible cry because he still wanted to wear his heavy nightdress.

May 6 Mon. Warm. I took Billo, Frances & Alfred down town on the cart. Edward walked with me & felt that we had too many "flawed kids." We bought sport shirts for Edward, white shoes for Alfred & Frances & got Billo's hair cut.

May 7 Tues. Showery. I realized that Frances is not truthful. She makes up things to tell other people as truth and she tells me things to cover up what she has done. She is the first of our children who was not been absolutely reliable.

Ernest C. Partridge

April 29 Studied and read AM. Walked to town PM. Miller got in with an esc[ort] of 3rd Regiment and called on us. We visited him in evening.

April 30 Went with Miller & James to bath. Lunched in town. Found on return to car they had moved us to a better apartment with Lieut Porkonis.

May 1 Anniversary of new Gov't. Great parade. I studied most of day. Went down to St. John's car. He is with the Serbs, and played 42. Met several Servian officers.

May 2 Took breakfast with St. John and had a phonograph concert. Worked several hours on Turkish & Lyman [Oberlin class]. Called on Miller and St. John. Wrote Winona by carrier to U: our party passed thro in 2 2nd cl cars making good time, all well. Comptons stayed in Samara for Serb relief work.

May 3 Studied most of day. Miller came in PM and played 42. St. John got off with last trains of Serbs for Archangel.

May 4 Spent some time looking at Ural stones. Bought 3 rubies, 3 topaz, 2 opals, 1 moon stone. Report that we may be here 2–3 weeks. We are thinking of going on alone. Miller is waiting for telegram from Vlad.

May 5 Sunday Easter. Bells & shooting all night.

May 6 No hope of break in delay so we have decided to take a passenger train on to Omsk. Went to take train at 11PM but did not get on till 1.

May 7 Started at 2:30 in a 2nd class coach with a couple of Ts who had only 3rd cl tickets and were ordered out but did not go. Fairly comfortable.

May 8 Reached Omsk about 6AM; fairly comfortable. Consul Thompson met train to get funds we brought for YM work. Continuing same train to Urkutz. Left O at 6AM. 14 people in coupe. (498m)

May 8 Wed. Cool. Edward played John Adams in tennis, tryout for High School team and got beaten although he is really a better player. As soon as John got a game or two Edward apparently got nervous and then couldn't succeed.

May 9 Thurs. Cool. Edward played a second match with Powell and got beaten again, poor kid. This throws him off the regular team. Perhaps he can play doubles. Edward & John Adams played doubles with Arthur & Norman & beat them but that doesn't count. Mrs. Atkinson called.

May 10 Fri. Cool & rainy. Alfred had been a little sick but Billo is better of his little fever attack. He slept all the afternoon & night & was better. Alfred has a little fever and has bad dreams.

May 11 Sat. Again Polly's birthday. I made a cake but the frosting did not get hard so we will eat it tomorrow. I did not get my dress changed at all but worked around all day. Mr. Case wrote that Mr. Chambers wrote that Mr. Favre had a letter from Polly in which she says that conditions are getting better all the time and that she would like to have Miss Stucky come if possible.

May 12 Sunday. Rainy. Mothers Day. I was very much surprised to receive from my big boys and Armen & Hampartsoom a potted plant, a box of stationery & two pounds of candy. Edward & George & I went to meeting to hear Mr. Van der Pyl preach on "An Old fashioned mother." Billo was not well & did not go out.

May 13 Mon. Billo is thoroughly broke out with the measles, but the Doctor allows the boys to stay in the house if they do not go into his room or the bathroom. Hampartsoom went to Worcester to sleep as well as to eat.

May 14 Tues. Beautiful day. Billo's second day of measles and he is much better. The hardest work is to keep Frances and Alfred away from the neighbors' children. If they are going to have measles I wish they might have them now, all together.

May 15 Wed. Pleasant & warm. Trot, trot, trot from Billo's room to the windows & doors to see where Frances & Alfred are. Billo does not seem sick a bit and he got up & dressed. It is hard to keep him in two rooms & hard for me too.

Ernest C. Partridge

May 9 Reached Novonikalaiovsk at 4:30AM. Found here Hymphries & Alpine with 1120 Servian refugees. Comptons are to come on to care for them. 12 people this night. (391m)

May 10 Very uncomfortable.

[May 11]

May 12 Sunday. Reached Urkutsk 10:30AM. Had passports vized and got at once on a 1st class car said to be going thro to Habarovsk. Had coupe alone & very comfortable. (1152m)

May 13 Jogged along all day at a fair rate. Passed Chita in the night.

May 14 Passed to the single track beyond the Manchurian line early this morning. Reached Kyenga [Kuenga] at 3:30 & passed on at 5PM.

May 15 Painfully plugging on at 15 miles per hour, road very crooked and grades heavy.

May 16 Another day of same kind. Good food along road excepting butter which cannot be bought. Running through section full of forest fires; finished 1000 versts from Kuenga.

May 17 Reached Bochkareva at 10AM and began last stage of journey to Habarovsk at 11:20. (851m)

May 18 Reached Habarovsk about 10PM. Slept at a table in railroad restaurant. But places in 1st cl sleeper. A bad night.

May 16 Thurs. Warmer. Billo very well even though he was awake a good part of the night with itching. I got some cocoa butter and that seems to work finely.

May 17 Fri. Measles again & again, only in name, for Billo is perfectly well. George went to the shack with "Woody."

May 18 Sat. Norman telephoned to Edward to go to Youngstown to play in the tennis match. They went to Cleveland but there was a mistake and the Rayen boys came here then rushed back to Cleveland and brought our boys back & they played here. Our boys lost all their singles & Edward & Royce Powell won their doubles. Uncle R. sent $100 for "bathing suits."

May 19 Sunday. Baccalaureate, but I am quarantined. We had a fairly comfortable day because we do less housework & I can give more time to the children. Miss Cummings came over and asked Frances to go for an auto ride. She had a fine time.

[May 20]

May 21 Tues. Edward had a very distinct pain in the right side of his abdomen so we consulted the doctor. After seeing him twice he pronounced it appendicitis at half past three. At seven P.M. they operated. Dr. Thatcher assisted by Dr. Colegrove and Dr. Jameson gave the ether. Miss Noyes, Miss Greenwood helped. I stayed until he went to sleep & then came back before he woke.

May 22 Wed. I went four times to see Edward & also attended the Seminary banquet. Billo is out playing so the children do not require so much attention. I neglect the housework all I can. Mrs. Whiteside does the washing.

May 23 Thurs. About the same program. Edward pretty sore but improving, eating only a little broth. Mr. Bohn went in to see him. George went to the circus in Elyria with Prof. Fullerton, had a fine time. Alfred seems sick, very feverish. I attended the anti-saloon league banquet with Mrs. Metcalf.

May 24 Fri. About the same program. Edward seems much better, ate three good meals and ice-cream between. George & Arthur were in to see him. There have been three appendicitis operations in the hospital since Edward.

May 25 Sat. Went to see Edward four times. Francs & Alfred seem measley but it is not evident yet. Very warm & very heavy showers which do not cool the air. Herman sent Edward a potted plant, Easter lilies.

May 26 Sunday. First time to eat strawberries. I made a shortcake because the majority wanted it. Alfred seems very miserable. It is probably measles but it does not seem like Billo. Miss Selover called on Edward and brought him some peonies.

May 27 Mon. Hot. Alfred is thoroughly broke out with measles. His eyes are swollen and his eyes are swollen. He does not talk very much except to say "I love Mammy." Billo went to school, and Edward is getting better, I could not spend much time with him because Armen was away almost all day. I just ran in between times, but George took him some ice-cream.

Ernest C. Partridge

May 19 Sunday. Left Habarovsk at 2PM in reserved coupe of 1st cl car with a buffet car attached. Had a fine sleep.

May 20 Reached Junction at 2:12PM and Vladivostok at 7:40 in the evening. Found Goodsell's room and left our baggage there while we had a bath & supper. Spent the night with him. (478m)

May 21 Found all our party in Vlad. Few steamers badly eroded. Our cruiser Brooklyn in harbor looks fine.

May 22 Heald & Williams left for Japan. Maynard to stay for YM work for present. Reception at Lorey's house. American films evening for Brooklyn sailors.

May 23 Spent most of day getting passports vized etc. & buying tickets to Harbin. 4–6PM Visited the Brooklyn & had a fine time. Chaplain Torrance and Dr. Drum.

May 24 Decided to delay going to hear from Boston. Whites, Dr. K and Miss Orvis went to Harbin. Cable to Dr Barton sent yesterday.

May 25 Elmer, Stapleton & Jensen went to Yokohama today. James and I moved to a room at 67 Svetlanskya. Letters by Elmer to WGP JLB Favre mother & ASL.

May 26 Sunday. Stayed in bed till noon to make up for back sleep. Ate at Golden Horn. Prof Robertson's lecture at 4. Evening service at Doug's. Prof spoke. Stopped for tea.

May 27 Studied Russian until noon. Decided to go to Peking [Bejing] with Yarrows on Wednesday. Took passport for vize to Chinese Consulate. Called on Maynards in evening.

May 28 Made arrangements for trip to Peking. Paid Maynard back 4000 R of 12,000 rec'd on exp[enses]. Went to bath and packed. Telegram from Relief party in Japan to wait.

May 28 Tues. cooler. Frances is broken out with measles and feels pretty sick. She did not want to get up even to sit in my lap. Edward sat up first in his room in a little while and then in the garden. Billo went to see him twice. Herman also went to see him & Mr. Van der Pyl. He received a letter from Mrs. Willard.

May 29 Wed. Frances is still pretty sick. Edward sat up nearly all day and about suppertime George & Billo and I brought him home in a wheel chair. It was very good to have him home. It was so lonesome to come home every day and leave him at the hospital.

May 30 Thurs. I tried to do a few things that had been left but did not succeed. There are too many calls from someone every minute. I made a cake in honor of Edward's coming. We had ice cream for dinner. Only George and Billo went to the parade & they marched in it.

May 31 Fri. I took Edward in a wheel chair to the High School plays, "Land of Heart's Desire" and "The girls over here." He saw several of his teachers who were very cordial.

June 1 Sat. I went with Edward to a tennis match between Oberlin & Wooster. I stayed only through one set. Oberlin won. The High School tennis team got beaten at Youngstown. George, Billo, Armen & Hampartsoom went to the movie for the benefit of athletic assoc. "Treasure Island."

June 2 Sunday. I have been sick with a very bad cold, just able to drag around. It was children's day but out children did not go. We have one week more of measles and then we can take our sign down.

June 3 Mon. A cablegram from Vladivostok says that some of the company are going into Y.M.C.A. work, one probably to Persia, but Partridge "proceeding to America unless otherwise instructed." Edward decided that he did not feel like going to school after all.

June 4 Tues. Nothing special happened except Prof. & Mrs. Wright called in the evening. They are going over to Arkansas where Prof. is to give a week's lectures to some Methodist ministers.

June 5 Wed. Cooler. I went to tea at the tea-room with Miss Zearing, Miss Wolcott, Mrs. Baker, Mr. Seemann told me that Edward is an A No. 1 pupil. They will give him his History and English grades without more study. He took one Latin exam and in his Algebra Miss Selover will help him in two subjects to get through.

[June 6]

June 7 Fri. I went downtown to buy material for a dress but could find nothing. I paid various bills, had an ice-cream soda with Edward. He went to the doctor's and he found there was a blood blister, so he had to put gauze & plaster again.

Ernest C. Partridge

May 29 Talked with James, Goodsell, Yarrow, & Maynard & I decided to go along to Peking. Left with Yarrow and Reitsel at 10:20. Comfortably located in 1st cl car.

May 30 Major Barrows from Philippines, US Army and Consul Mosher of Harbin [Haerbin, China] on train. Reached H at 11PM. Met by Gott and Sherer. I stayed with S. At breakfast long talk with Stevens. (485m)

May 30 Left Harbin at 2:40PM in 1st cl sleeper. Reached Chang Chun at 10PM. Fine train American sleepers. 2 US RR [railroad] engineers with us, Victor and Shields. (150m)

June 1 Reached Muhden at 8:25AM. A good breakfast at station. Train out at 11:40. Good car with coupes and buffet car thru to Peking. (125m) (over)

June 2 Sunday. Reached Peking on time at 10:20AM. Tientsin at 6:30. Stopped at Hotel Peking. Called on Wilder Cross & Heininger. Supper at Wilder. Spoke on work. (Muhden – T 100m T-Peking 84m)

June 3 Started for Taiku [sister Louise was ABCFM missionary here] at 9:20 with Dr Metcalf and Miss Nemager. Reached Junction at 4:20 Chinese Inn. (WGP) (154m)

June 4 Took train about 7:30. Rode till 4PM to Yitza where we found cart waiting for us. Rode 4 hours to a village where we stayed in an opium refuge. (170m)

June 5 Four hours in the cart brought us to Taihuhsien where I found a cordial welcome at the Hemingways. Went over the hospital in PM with Dr H.

June 6 Spent the day at the Flower Garden, riding over on a pony. Saw school, martyr's graves [Louise and nine ABCFM missionaries were killed in the Boxer Rebellion], had lunch with King & Davis, toward evening into city where saw Chapel site.

[June 7-8]

June 8 Sat. I went to Elyria and got material for a thin dress, six yards at 29 cents a yard. There was an eclipse of the sun. The children watched it for about an hour.

June 9 Sunday. Pleasant, a little warm. My cold still continues, worse every morning, better in the evening. Frances Hutchins took Edward and Arthur for an auto ride. Edward, Hampartsoom, and I went to evening service. The last regular service until fall.

June 10 Mon. Cool & pleasant. I went down town and met Edward at the doctor's office. Edward has a little oozing from a vein but nothing serious in connection with the wound.

June 11 Tues. Still cool. I worked on a thin dress. Mrs. Whiteside washed. Edward had a dizzy or faint spell but I think it was from reading in the sun.

June 12 Wed. I led devotions at the W.C.T.U. meeting at Mrs. Peter's. Only about ten were present. Then I went to call on Mrs. Haskell and her daughter and Mrs. Elmer. We had Gibson rolls for supper, the first time in many weeks.

June 13 Thurs. Edward and I went to High School Commencement. His name was read among those who were 90 or above for the year. Edith Brisaker of Africa and Norman Martin of Turkey graduated.

June 14 Fri. I tried to get some time to sew but did not get much as Armen was away all the forenoon and all the evening. Billo was promoted this time. George's marks, Eng. 90, Spelling 100, Pen 70, Grammar 89, Arith. 94, Geog. 89, Music 80. Edward's marks, 2nd semester, Eng. 90, Latin 92, Math 90, Hist. Incomplete

June 15 Sat. I went down town, bought a collar & belt for my new thin dress, a hair ribbon for Frances, tennis shoes for Billo ($1.00), to the library & got some books, to the Administration building for tickets. In the evening Edward & I went to the Commencement plays, "Lonesomelike," "The Lost Silk Hat," "The Florists' Shop."

June 16 Sunday. Baccalaureate Sunday, pretty hot. Edward & I went to the patriotic service in the evening. Helen Blowehard called after service.

June 17 Mon. I went down town to buy a petticoat and Edward went to the doctor's. Then I bought some strawberries and came off and forgot them.

June 18 Tues. I went to the last part of the alumni meeting. Frank Warner presided. Then Mr. Kingsbury spoke about telephones in war time. The new service flag was dedicated, the old one with 528 & the new one with 80 stars.

Ernest C. Partridge

June 9 Most of forenoon visiting with Corbin, lunch there. Went to White Pagoda etc. PM. Missionary supper at ladies. I told story of deportations.

June 8 Read and visited till 3PM. Went with King & Davis & Gray to dinner with a couple of Chinese merchants. A five course dinner with lots of unknown things to eat.

June 9 Sunday. Spoke at Chapel in morning, a collection for relief. Mr Hung translated. Dinner at ladies. I spoke at meeting of missionaries about industrial work.

June 10 Started on Dr H's horse for Fenchow [one of Louise's mission stations] with Mr King's man as guide. Lunch with Falls at Kihsien. Night at Pingya with Gardeners. (33m)

June 11 Guide did not meet me so I went on to Fenchow with a man walking. A rather hot day and very dusty. Sleeping at Hummels and eating with ladies. (26m)

June 12 Visited hospital & boy's school and saw rest of compound. Rode out to the Valley with Hummel and spent night there.

June 13 Spent the day at the Valley where most of the people are. All ate together at noon and visited. Returned to city in evening.

June 14 Dinner at noon with Hummel and Leest with Chinese secretary of YMCA at rooms in city where missionaries used to live in 1900.

June 15 Gave up going back to Taiku on account of heavy rain. Visited Girl's School and went out to Valley in evening as guest of Watson.

June 16 Sunday. Spent day at Camp. I spoke about relief work at meeting of missionaries and returned to city in evening.

June 17 Started for Taiku about 6AM. Lunch with Falls at Kihsien. Got in about 7PM. Ice cream at ladies. (51m)

June 18 Left Taiku about 10AM with Hemingway family on way to Peking. 5 hours by cart to Yitsa. Some rain but a fair trip.

June 19 Wed. Commencement. In the morning Mrs. Clark took me to Wellington in the auto for a ride. I met Mrs. Ford & Helen. Armen & Edward went to Commencement. When I came back George was washing the dishes. I went to alumni dinner. Mr. & Mrs. Adams, Mr. & Mrs. Bowers, Mr. & Mrs. Newcomb were there. Reunion glee concert.

June 20 Thurs. I went to prayer meeting & when I got back found Karakeen Etyemezian (Yetenez) here. He missed his car and stayed all night. He had been very successful in business, owns a hotel in Detroit. He gave the children 2 lbs. choc. peanuts & ice-cream. George & Billo went to Mr. Wood's shack.

June 21 Fri. Heavy showers. I called on Mrs. Fullerton to tell her how to make "tanaboor." In the evening Edward and I went to Prof. Moore's lecture on Ireland. It was very good indeed.

June 22 Sat. Cold. I had a fire in the grate. Gas low. Armen started for Akron at 6:30 A.M. and I felt lost to be alone Sat. I did not get the ironing done at all. George & Billy came home. They had a nice time. Billo got a little homesick and wanted to come and see his mother & go back. He got along well, though & enjoyed it.

June 23 Sunday. Still cold. We had a picnic lunch at the arboretum. Mrs. Haas and her three younger children, the two Stapleton girls and Mrs. Greene called. In the evening Edward & I went to hear Mr. Haskell on Bulgaria and left George in charge of the three little ones. They were all right but George said it was lonesome. This was the first time & I guess it will be the last.

June 24 Mon. A letter from Mrs. Clark. Her children have whooping cough. Perhaps she can visit us later. I bought eight dining room chairs @60 cts and two rocking chairs @$1.50 of Mr. Crafts and it does seem good to have something whole to sit in.

Ernest C. Partridge

June 19 8 hours by train to Junction. Met a group of new missionaries going into Shansi for United Brethren missions. (170m)

June 20 Train at 8:55 reached Paotingfu about 2PM. Hubbard was late so went to house in ricksha. Visited school & Memorial Cemetery.

June 21 A good short visit with Holbrook, Miss Chapin & Miss Breck. Visit Pres hospital & YMCA. A fine work. Reached Peking about 9PM. Dr H met train. (184m)

June 22 Guest at Dr Ingram's in compound. Called on Dr Williams, Drs Raynolds & Goodrich. YMCA ordered clothes, wrote some.

June 23 Sunday. Chinese church morning. English PM. Dr Raynolds spoke. Prof Robertson back from Russia.

June 24 Went with Hemingways to call on Ogilvie's at Pres. compound. Saw Boy's School.

[June 25]

June 26 With Dr Wilder to Bazaar, Lhama Buddhist temple and Confucian Temple. (90m)

[June 27]

June 28 Dr Ingram took me to the Imperial Museum. A fine collection of pottery, cloisonné work, jade. Met Dr & Miss Smith, Porter & Beers. Went to Fungchow to visit Whites. (30m)

June 25 Tues. I did not get as tired as yesterday although I washed three floors as an extra. Mrs. Haas came this morning while Hector was having his tonsils removed. Billo was invited to Laurence White's house & he and his mother called in the evening. Mrs. Whiteside washed.

June 26 Wed. In the morning we had five letters from Mr. P. written in Jan. 1918 from Alexandropol. In the afternoon we had two written from Vladivostok and mailed in Japan. Mrs. James, the mother, called in the evening. Frances had a lame knee nearly all day, so that she would fall when she tried to step on it, but it got well itself.

June 27 Thurs. Hampartsoom's "questionnaire" in regard to his military service came and we spent most of the afternoon filling that out. I lent Mr. P's letters to Mrs. Elmer and Mr. Adams. The three boys went out to the Krescent field in the evening, George to play & the others to watch.

June 28 Fri. Warm. I did not feel well. I hear that they have only one patient in the hospital, so it is just the time for me to go. I had a letter from Dr. Barton who seems to think that Mr. P. is in China. Another letter from Alexandropol, this time to George.

June 29 Sat. Warm. Frances, Alfred and I went up to Mrs. Martin's to see Mrs. Goodsell. We had a good time but I thought we never should get ready. Edward, George & Billo started for the shack a little before two, then I had to bathe and dress the two children & myself. I got Alfred & Frances each a pair of low, select leather shoes & Frances also high shoes for stockings.

June 30 Sunday. Very warm and sticky until we had showers & then it became cooler. We took our lunch in the arboretum & Mrs. Elmer & Hugh came down there. Arthur came twice to see Edward. He is working on a farm this summer. The children all seemed to be crossgrained & it was a hard day on the whole.

Memoranda.
Edward height – 5ft 7 ¼ in weight 109 lbs
George height 4 ft 7 ¼ in weight 77 lbs
Alfred 37 lbs

July 1 Mon. Quite cold, delightful. I didn't do much except sweeping the bedrooms & some ironing. Mrs. Elmer came to read me a letter from Mr. Elmer. Miss Davis called in the evening. Edward, George & Billo went to the movies, Marguerite Clark in Bab's diary. A letter from Samuel saying that he has flat foot & perhaps tuberculosis, will be examined by X-ray.

July 2 Tues. George & Edward went to Mr. Wood's shack in the evening.

July 3 Wed. I went to Missionary Meeting and heard Mr. Olds, very good. Prof. Hall died very suddenly in Birmingham as he was bicycling to a place beyond. A Mrs. Wright, tall angular negro, cleaned Armen's room.

July 4 Thurs. Hot. Mr. & Mrs. Bohn took us all for an auto ride in the morning. The three boys went to the shack in the afternoon, returning about 10 P.M. Alfred, Frances & I took lunch on the campus with Mrs. Shaw & her sister, then community sing, then ice-cream, then home. No firecrackers, no noise.

Ernest C. Partridge

June 29 Dr Wilder took me to Bell tower; largest perfect hung Bell in world.

June 30 Sunday. Finished Shansi letter. Wrote several other letters. PM English service. (WES, WGP)

July 1 Left Peking at 8:35 for Shanghai. Found Prof Robertson at Tientsin and rode with him for 10 hours to Tsinanfu. (84m)

July 2 Rode all day and reached Nanking about 5:30PM. Ferried across river & went to Hotel till train time at 11PM. Sleeper for Shanghai. (631m)

July 3 Reached Shanghai at 7AM. Found Evans Home, had breakfast, went to Consulate, found our party and located with them at Astor hotel. Worked on passport & money. (193m)

July 4 Made two sightseeing trips. Chinese theater. Called on Donald and Gilbert of the Far East Review. Went on "Katori Maru" at 11PM. [The Katori Maru was a Japanese passenger cargo ship built 1913 and torpedoed by the Dutch in 1941.]

July 5 A good start on this part of our trip. Sea quiet and not too warm.

[July 6]

July 7 Sunday. Two days of bowel trouble and discomfort.

July 8 Reached Hong Kong about 8AM. All quartered at Hong Kong Hotel. I am very miserable from bowel trouble. (825m)

July 5 Fri. Hotter. Cleaned out the ice-chest, ironed etc. etc. was nearly dead when night came. Edward hosed the children. Sultan of Turkey died. We had maple nut ice-cream for desert. The children had a little auto ride with Mrs. Robeson.

July 6 Sat. Cool. We hired Mr. Jones's pony for an hour and the children rode around town. They enjoyed it but quarreled more or less about who should drive and who should stand in the back.

July 7 Sun. Cool, almost cold. We had lunch in the arboretum. I made fudge. Edward and I went to church but Fred Comings and Pagi Ferar bothered the children so much that I think I shall not leave them again. Mr. Bernard Mattson is the summer supply.

July 8 Mon. Cold. I called on Mrs. Hall. She is very brave and sensible, wants to find a smaller house. She had lots of callers. I had a letter from Mr. P. written in Pekin June 2. He was about to start for Shansi. Edward had one written from Vladivostok.

July 9 Tues. A little warmer. I expected a call from Mrs. Olds but finally she could not come. Mr. Mattson called. Edward, George & Billo went out to the shack with Mr. Wood. Hampartsoom came over to have me help him with Algebra.

July 10 Wed. Mrs. Clark & three children came at 5:00 P.M. to make us a visit. It is good to see them again. I discovered that my bank account is short. I wrote to Dr. Barton about it.

July 11 Thurs. Cool and a little rainy. Armen sent balloons to the children. They have laughed and cried over them. I ironed all the afternoon nearly. The boys went to the games. The Congregationalists beat the Methodists.

July 12 Fri. A year since Mr. P. went. It seems short and long. I have been too busy to get lonely very often.

July 13 Sat. Edward and I went down town. I wanted to see Mr. Houghton about Suren Sewny's exemption card. He was not there.

July 14 Sunday. Another anniversary week and today our twentieth with Ernest in China, Japan, Russia or on the sea.

July 15 Mon. The boys went out to the shack with "Woody."

July 16 Tues. Mrs. Martin & the Misses Webb came to call. Edward took an examination in History, which finishes up his work after appendicitis. I went down town with Edward to buy a wrist watch case. He got a black one for 50 cts.

July 17 Wed. We ironed & ironed, Mrs. Clark & I, but did not finish. She has much more energy than I do. After working all day she keeps at stockings & sewing all the evening.

July 18 Thurs. I ironed & ironed again. The boys, three, went to the Thurs. P.M. games & then the news came that the American soldiers had taken twelve towns and 50,000 prisoners. I hope it is true.

July 19 Fri. Americans & French still going on. When I was coming out of the racket store I met Annie Fish McClure just for a minute. It seemed so good to see her but she is very thin. I did a big washing and got very tired. George & I took the cart and the go-cart to be mended & sent a bundle of old clothes to Lewiston. A letter from Mr. P. from Fenchepe [Fenchow].

July 20 Sat. Washed floors, ironed until quarter of six. A cablegram from Mr. P., saying, "Coming Frisco August thirtieth." It was from Hong Kong. We had also a letter from him from Taiku.

Ernest C. Partridge

July 9 Called at Consulate about passport. No word from Washington but can get an emergency passport to Colombo [Sri Lanka].

July 10 Met Albert Telfeyan of New York. Just out of Persia. He dined with us and talked over conditions.

July 11 Dr Cook called in hotel physician, a specialist in hot weather troubles and their decision is that I must not go on now. So am going home.

July 12 Fortunately found passage on Pacific Mail Venezuela going next Wed to S. F.

July 13 Prof Jackson's lecture to Parsees [Zoroastrians who fled Iran to India 10th century]. Tea with them. Chinese YMCA dinner in evening. dft no 54/265 for $250.00 Hong Kong & S Banking Grp 12 mos

July 14 Sunday. Persian party got off about noon. Called on Mr Gregory & he & Telfeyan & I went to call on Manoog. Auto ride in evening.

July 15 Same party with Mr's sister, had tea, and then went to Summit [now called The Peak] but a shower spoiled the view. Got my ticket and police permit.

July 16 Did a little shopping.

July 17 Went aboard Venezuela at 10. Sailed about 1PM. First enjoyable meal tonight for 10 days.

July 18 Very warm. I am slowly improving in health. 28 [days to go]

July 19 Weather cooler, in fact delightful. Sailing along the coast of China. Shore visible most of time. 27 [days to go]

July 20 Reached Shanghai early in morning and spent day and most of night loading freight and then waiting for high tide. 26 (825m)

July 21 Sunday. Left harbor at 5:30AM. A quiet day. No services on board. 25

July 21 Sunday. Another hot and hard day. We went to the water works with our lunch but the little ones were not very happy there and wanted to come home. We shall have to find something new to amuse the children Sundays.

July 22 Mon. Our new old auto came and Edward learned enough so he took everyone to ride, Clarks & Partridges. Alfred's birthday. He had sand pile pail & shovel, two large marbles, a boat & electric car. We had maple nut ice-cream & choc. cake. Alfred had his picture taken with his curls and then went to the barber's and had his curls cut off. He does not look like Alfred.

July 23 Tues. The auto was still in use. I went to Elyria to get a license (No. 393738). It was very hot but it rained in the afternoon and the children went out in their bathing suits. The three oldest & Ruth went to see Mary Pickford in "Rebecca of Sunnybrook Farm." 393738

July 24 Wed. Very hot. Mrs. Clark & Edward went to hear Singer, a Canadian soldier. He was very common, used dreadful language, was a cigar maker. Edward, George & Billo went to the river to swim with "Woody." They used the auto some. Frances & Alfred weighed & measured for the census. They were both above in height & below in weight. I thin the scales are wrong.

July 25 Thurs. Hot. I washed in the morning and Mrs.C. & I ironed in the afternoon, not the same clothes. Edward and Billo went to the games & ate supper very late. Our auto has been up for repairs all day.

July 26 Fri. Hot, but showers & cooler at night. The three boys went out to the shack with "Woody" right after dinner. One of our tires blew out, the first blow out, but probably not the last. Mrs. C. & I again ironed until supper time.

July 27 Sat. Very hot. Washing floors, cleaning bedroom, ironing, cooking, etc. ad infinitum. I was too tired even to walk down town for an ice-cream soda. Mrs. Clark & Edward went.

Ernest C. Partridge

July 22 A cool night and much better weather since we turned east. 24

July 23 Reached Kobe about 5PM. I went ashore after dinner and called on Miss Barrows. Sailed at 5AM. 23

July 24 A rough day, many people undercover most of the day, better toward night. 22

July 25 Reached Yokohama about 8AM. I went ashore morning and afternoon for a little shopping. Dr Lawrence of Empress and Telfeyan here. (800m)

July 26 Sailed again at 10AM. Sea very quiet.

July 27 Ideal sailing. My health is improving all the time. Fair appetite and gaining in weight. Played Jenkins Up in evening. 19 (335m)

July 28 Sunday. Another quiet day. No services on board. 18 (378m)

July 29 17 (247m)

July 30 16 (341m)

July 31 Took a swim in tank at 6AM. 15 (291m)

August 1 Gained a day here so we had two Thursdays. Tank busted, no more swimming. 14 (2 days 276, 304m)

July 28 Sunday. Very heavy showers but no cooler. Not so bad as some Sundays. We ate lunch at the water works but were driven home by the showers, reached home just in time. The children put on their bathing suits and went out in the rain.

July 29 Mon. Hot in morning, shower & cooler. Bought a new auto tire for $18 (Mrs. Clark gave ten). There seems to be something else the matter with it. I had a letter from E.C.P. July 4th from Shanghai, American stamp. George went to "Woody's" to sleep. He is to motor to Toledo with him tomorrow.

July 30 Tues. Cool, almost cold. Mrs. Clark & I were invited to meet Mrs. Haskell's sister-in-law, Mrs. Ring. She is from Texas & very interesting. Mrs. Irving Metcalf, Mrs. Jewett, Mrs. Belden, Mrs. Wright were there, yes & Mrs. Gammon.

July 31 Wed. Cool & beautiful. Again we fixed the auto, a wire was broken, just got it home & the gasoline began to leak. After a long time we got Mr. Parmele & found out how to turn it off. Mrs. Elmer & Pearl called. They heard that probably Mr. P. could not get his passport to go to Persia.

Memoranda. Oct. 1918 E.C.P. 153 ½, Ed. 115, George 83, William 56, Frances 46 ½, Alfred 40 ½.
Alfred reaches the height of affection. He says, "I will love you till you die and I will die when you do."

August 1 Thurs. Cool. They used the auto some. Mrs. Clark and I did the ironing and finished at four o'clock. Mrs. Elmer came to read me a letter from Mrs. Marden.

August 2 Fri. Cool, growing warmer towards night. Mrs. Clark went to Elyria and Ruth & I took care of the children. Mrs. Clark bought me a blue silk poplin skirt, very pretty. Mr. Parmele came to fix the auto again. A letter from Samuel. My allowance came $141.67.

August 3 Sat. Cool & lovely. A usual Saturday for me. The boys went out to get Arthur but got only 1 ½ mi. out when a tire blew out, so they telephoned to me to do something. Finally I got Mr. Parmele and he said to ride in on the rim, which they did very successfully.

August 4 Sunday. Hot. The second Sunday that Alfred has been to Sunday School. We ate our lunch at home but took a walk to the waterworks. But we could not stay long on account of showers.

August 5 Mon. Very hot. I went down town in the morning to do a lot of jobs. I went with Edward to have his eyes examined, then with Frances to the barber's to have her hair bobbed, no first to the dentist's to have her tooth filled, then to the garage to see about the auto.

August 6 Tues. Extremely hot. The Clarks went home at noon and Edward, George and Billo went to the Lake with "Woody," so I was alone with the two little ones. In the evening we went to call on Miss Noyes, Mrs. Elmer & Mrs. Wright. Mrs. W was not at home.

August 7 Wed. Very hot. Scrubbed floors etc. etc. Got three letters from Mr. P. one written from Alexandropol in Feb. & one in March & one in June from Peking, also received my first letter from a soldier in France, Hrant Messaryan.

Ernest C. Partridge

[August 2]

August 3 Red Cross auction of contributed articles netted $791.00 12 (294m)

August 4 Sunday. A brief anniversary service on 4th year of England's entry to war. 11 (298m)

August 5 Reached Honolulu at 5PM. I went uptown and bought a hat & some magazines. 10 (total 3389m)

August 6 Sailed at 7AM. 9 (55m)

August 7 Getting rougher and tiresome. 8 (281m)

August 8 7 (286m)

August 9 6 (290m)

August 10 5

August 11 Sunday. Church of England service in a.m. 4

August 12 Red Cross activities netted $1500.00 for voyage concert this evening. I have gained 7 pounds on this trip. 3

August 8 Thurs. Showers all day but at the end hotter than ever. Getting ready for the Lake and nothing else need to be said. Letters from Mr. Favre & Nishan. Nishan heard from Hampartsoom's father & from Polly in May.

August 9 Fri. A little cooler. Worked like a beaver, all of us, until the 3:25 car. The boys went on their wheels. We got there about five o'clock and got some settled, brought our supper with us. George got a bottle of milk in Lorain. It was good to get to the Lake but a little lonesome. Bless the big boys!

August 10 Sat. Getting settled, going in bathing, ordering and cooking food. The appetites a[re] tremendous. We found two places where we can get milk at 12 & 18 cents a quart.

August 11 Sunday. Hot but heavy showers cooled the air. Not so bad for Sunday. Our kerosene stove gave out and we had to do some cooking at the Day's house. The four youngest went into the water for a few minutes in the morning and Ed. & Geo. took a dip before getting into bed.

August 12 Mon. Very, very hot. The children went into the water morning, afternoon & evening. The Days went to the Day-Austin picnic. I received a hundred dollars from Uncle R. Alfred's diving is very funny. He gets up on the pier, holds his nose and sputters awhile, then lets go of his nose and jumps into about two inches of water on the land side of the pier & swims on his stomach.

August 13 Tues. Still hotter and the night hot and the mosquitoes dreadful. I used disinfectant, cocoabutter & cold water on the children's bites, but they went to sleep late. They went into the water morning, afternoon & evening.

August 14 Wed. Cool and comfortable. The boys helped with the housework & then with their help I did a large washing with cold water & naptha soap. We had a letter from Mr. P. from Hong Kong, saying that he was not very well & the Doctor thought it was not safe for him to go to Persia.

August 15 Thurs. Cool. I did the ironing. Edward & I went down town to buy a few things and look at tires. The children went into the water twice. No mail. War news good but not startling.

August 16 Fri. Cool. The event of the day was a visit from "Woody" and "Pinky." I enjoyed meeting him very much. Fortunately we had plenty of beans and apple sauce, and "Woody" likes coffee. Mr. P's description of his journey from Tiflis to Vladivostok came, very interesting.

August 17 Sat. Armen & Mr. Nigoghosian came from Akron to visit us. Two telegrams from Ernest from San F- saying he would come Sat. night or Sun. morning & one from Chicago saying he would come Sun. morning at seven o'clock.

August 18 Sunday. We all got up and took the seven o'clock car for the station and arrived just after he got off the train. He looked strange in his Khaki suit and leather leggings but we were glad to see him. Armen & Mr. N. went in the afternoon.

August 19 Mon. I had no intention of washing but the weather was so cool and nice that I did. I did not finish until after four in spite of all the help I had. Alfred weighed 37. Frances 45. Billo 53. Edward 111.

August 20 Tues. Warmer. Mr. P., Edward & George went to Oberlin intending to return in the afternoon, but they telephoned that they would come in the morning. I ironed & went in bathing with the children.

August 21 Wed. Warmer. About noon the people came from Oberlin & met Billo and me down near the dairy where we were getting milk. George weighed 79 ½, Edward 109

August 22 Thurs. Very hot, water calm. I ironed a little for Kitty and washed for ourselves a little. The boys were in three times, I once. Mr. P. the little ones and I went to call on the Churchills. Mr. C was not at home.

August 23 Fri. Hot. Mr. P., Edward & George went in and brought out the auto. Mr. Wood came in his with Hermann, Pinkie & Teddy, so we had eleven for supper. At noon Billo & I went down for the milk and brought home ice-cream cones for the children.

August 24 Sat. Cooler. The chief excitement of the day was auto riding. They went after the milk in the morning and at noon with the auto & then down town in the afternoon but the second time down the car stopped & refused to budge. Carroll Churchill came down to help them.

Ernest C. Partridge

August 13 Reached San Francisco about 5:30PM. Garfield hotel lost & found my baggage. Sent a wire to Winona.

August 14 Called at Board Rooms; found letters WGP and EFB. Called on Mr Anderson. Bought suitcase. East on S.P. at 1PM.

August 15 Reached Ogden at 2PM. (783m)

[August 16]

August 17 Reached Omaha at 1AM. Chicago at 4PM. One hour late because of derailed freight car. Left at 8:35PM on Nickel Plate for Lorain. (1000m)

August 18. Sunday. Reached Lorain at 7:30AM. Whole family met me at station. Armen and Nigohosian up from Akron. (323m)

August 19 Rested and read and swam twice with the kids. [Family is vacationing at the lake.]

August 20 Went to Oberlin with two big boys. Worked on car but stayed overnight and decided to return on trolley. Lunch at Wrights & tea at Martins.

August 21 Made several calls in Oberlin and returned to Lorain about noon.

August 22 Called at Churchills.

August 23 E & G & I went to O[berlin]. Varnished kitchen, pantry, & bath room and rode out in bus. Woodie & some boys came out & stayed to tea.

[August 24]

August 25 Sunday. Cool in morning, growing warmer. Rather a lazy day. Alfred Churchill took the boys out in the boat. Mr. P. went to Cleveland to attend a meeting of the Russians with Prof. Wright. Mrs. Roth brought us some ice-cream & cake left from their picnic.

August 26 Mon. Cool. Mr. P. stayed over night in Oberlin and came out in the afternoon. He and Edward went down town to see about the auto. Edward wore a pair of his father's long trousers, the first time. They are a striped cream color & blue. He doesn't look like Edward.

August 27 Tues. Cool. I washed and washed and then washed. The kerosene gave out and I had to get dinner partly in the house. The lake was rough and the weather cool so they bathed only once. Arthur came out and spent the day. Merrill's S.S. class had a picnic & the Mayor & H.S. principal & Roth's had a picnic supper.

August 28 Wed. Rainy. I ironed nearly all day on clothes on which the starch stuck to my irons. The irons did not heat well either. The boys went fishing with Alfred Churchill in his boat but didn't get a bite.

August 29 Thurs. Cool & lovely. Geo. & I went down town & bought him trousers, short waist, unionsuits & stockings. The Churchills came to call in the evening & invited us to lunch Friday before we start.

August 30 Fri. Cold in the morning & rainy but cleared off and grew warmer so we came home, the two little ones & I in the car and the others on the auto. We got home first, found the house all upset on account of the varnishing, but we finally got something to eat and went to bed.

August 31 Sat. Tried to clean up a little, made a cake in honor of Mr. P., went down town in the auto, bought

---

Ernest C. Partridge

August 25 Sunday. Went in to Cleveland in PM to attend a Russian rally. Out to Oberlin at night. Slept at hotel room.

August 26 Spent forenoon in Oberlin varnishing & went out to Lorain after lunch at hotel with Mattson, Jones, & Harrows. Ed's 1st long trousers [16 yrs old].

August 27 Arthur rode out & spent the day with us.

[August 28–29]

August 30 Returned to Oberlin. Three boys & I in bus, others by trolley.

August 31 Straightened house out some. Fitted Edward out with long trousers, etc.

September 1 Sunday. Heard Mr Van der Pyle in morning and in evening at Union service gave his talk to employers.

September 2 Worked hard all day. All went out to movies, Douglas Fairbanks in "Down to Earth."

September 3 Evening to Fauk Home to see Miss Ward. I brought her home for night. School begins.

[September 4]

Edward's first long trousers, shirts, sock, shoes, collars, cap, necktie, then trousers waists, cap & shoes for Billo, shoes for George.

September 1 Sunday. I went to church in the evening to hear Mr. Van der Pyl give his talk to the employers. In the afternoon we went to the water works and Hermann came. Also Mrs. Haas and her children. Edward's first appearance in long trousers. We took his picture.

September 2 Mon. we went down town to change Edward's suit which was too small. Got a larger size of the same thing. Then I washed until four o'clock. We all went to the picture show, Douglas Fairbanks in "Down to Earth" and Mutt & Jeff.

September 3 Tues. I did a big ironing. Miss Ward came to Tank Home and we went down in the evening and brought her home to spend the night. It seems good to see her again. She seems thin. She is on her way to S. Dakota to teach in Ward Academy. School commenced.

September 4 Wed. Rainy & cool. Miss Ward was here until noon. Miss Noyes and Mrs. Elmer spent a good deal of time here. I got dinner for Miss Ward, then for the three school boys, then for Mr. P. & the little ones who went to the station. In the afternoon I washed & finished the ironing. Mr. P. spoke at the Miss. Meeting.

September 5 Thurs. Rainy & cold. George was elected Captain of the Seventh Grade football team. Mr. P. & I went downtown and he bought a gray striped suit and a blue suit and an overcoat, $30 apiece.

September 6 Fri. Cool & pleasant. Washed again, went down town in the "bus." Mrs. Giles & Hermann called. She seems young enough to be his sister and a younger sister at that.

September 7 Sat. Mr. P. & I went to Prof. Andrews' for supper. In the evening Prof. & Mrs. Forster came in and two other ladies. Mr. P. talked continuously for three hours, of course about his stay in Russia.

September 8 Sunday. Ernest was to preach for Mr. Van der Pyl but finally he was here so preached. E. spoke to the men's class at the Second Church. Mrs. Haas came in the afternoon and we all went down to the water works, ten children.

September 9 Mon. Warmer. E. varnished another bedroom floor so we moved around again. I tried making stuffed tomatoes but they were not good. I could not wash until afternoon so did only the colored clothes. Madame James called in the evening.

September 10 Tues. Ernest & I were invited to dine at Prof. Hutchins. Besides us there were Prof. & Mrs. Swing & Herbert & Prof. Shaw. We had a fine time and splendid supper, chicken, salad, ice-cream, cake, coffee. We left the children alone, the little ones with the older ones for the first time.

September 11 Wed. Cold & rainy. E. & I went to Mrs. Martin's to a Turkey missionary social as some are leaving soon, Miss Cold for Chicago, Mrs. Stapleton, & the Misses Webb for Hartford, Mrs. Haskell & daughter Mary for Kansas City. George took care of the children & Ed. took us up & brought us back in the auto first time.

Ernest C. Partridge

September 5 George elected capt of 7th grade football team. I bought two suits & an overcoat at $30.00 each.

[September 6]

September 7 Supper at Prof Andrews. Prof and Mrs Foster & others came in and I talked about Russia.

September 8 Sunday. Heard Mr Van der Pyl in morning & Dr Williams evening. Spoke to a large crowd at 2nd ch men's class.

Spetember 9 Varnished a floor, canned tomatoes. Letter from Vickrey about meeting September 19–20.

September 10 Dinner in evening at Prof Hutchins, Prof & Mrs Swing & Herbert & Prof Shaw.

September 11 A Turkey missionary social at Mrs Martins'. Ed took us up & called for us in the bus.

September 12 Winona and I spent PM cleaning second story.

September 13 Team at Ponds.

[September 14]

September 15 Sunday. Van der Pyle in AM. Prof Root evening on library work at Camp Sherman.

September 16 Frances & I took trolley to E[lyria]. Sleeper to New York. Huelster with us. Annual meeting of Relief Committee.

September 12 Thurs. Cold & rainy. Nothing of importance happened except we cleaned upstairs, separating things to send to Maine and putting the others in order, getting the room ready for Armen.

September 13 Fri. Cold & cloudy. I washed & ironed all day until I had to get ready to go to Mr. Pond's to supper.

September 14 Sat. Washed 2 floors, swept, and ironed until quarter of twelve, only going down town in the auto to try to find Frances a hat, which I did not find. Edward has a very bad cold, also Billo, but not so bad.

September 15 Sunday. Rainy, especially in the afternoon when Mrs. Haas and six children were here. In the evening we heard Prof. Root on the library work at Camp Sherman, 45,000 soldiers, 35000 volumes, 40 distributing places, all sorts of magazines, great work.

September 16 Mon. Rainy & cold. The colds are no worse but not much better. Ernest and Frances started off for New York today. Frances does love to go "trabeling" with her father and she is very good to take because she falls in with any plan you make for her and thinks it is fine.

September 17 Tues. Cool but pleasant. I washed until 4:45, and in the meantime had three callers whom I received in my old clothes. In the evening I had to iron some handkerchiefs for Edward, so kept on and did quite a bit of the plain ironing.

September 18 Wed. Cool, some sunshine, some rain. Our hot water tank sprang a leak, so the water was turned of from the house nearly all day until Mr. Metcalf could get a man to fix it. We found out how necessary water is. We brought some from Mrs. Burnett's. Alfred & I went over to see Mrs. Metcalf and Rachel.

September 19 Thurs. All rain. One day where I neither washed nor ironed. I mended some stockings, finished getting the upstairs room ready for Armen. After half past eight I called at Prof. Wrights'.

September 20 Fri. Sunshining, no rain all day. Edward took me up to call on Mrs. Martin. The Misses Webb were just leaving for Hartford. I bought Billo some "trotorvak"[?] shoes for $4.50 & rubbers for $1.25.

September 21 Sat. Frances and her father got home finally at nine o'clock after missing connections in Buffalo and Cleveland. It was good to see Frances and her father too. She began immediately to tell me about the monkeys that she saw at the zoo. Helen Paelian took her.

September 22 Sunday. Had a dreadful cold and felt sick nearly all day, but I went to church in the evening to hear Prof. Miller on the Slav question. Armen finally came about ten o'clock at night.

September 23 Mon. A pleasant day. Armen & I washed clothes but I did not finish mine. Hampartsoom finished his schedule. He is to take French, Physics, English Composition, Mechanical and Free Hand Drawing.

September 24 Tues. We went down town & got a suit, dark blue $32 and a gray and black mackinaw $10 for Edward and helped Hampartsoom select a suit. He bought a brown one with green stripes for $38. Mr. P. & I called on Prof. Andrews in the evening.

Ernest C. Partridge

September 17 Reached New York ½ hour late. Could not find Marian. Visited Board Rooms. Most of day at Committees offices. Lunch at Albino Club, night White P[lains].

September 18 Rainy. Into city forenoon at offices. Helen [Paelian] came down and took F[rances] home. Lunch with GP [Garabed Paelian]. Night with Albert Telfeyan.

September 19 Took suitcase to GP's and saw Frances. Busy day of conferences. Many friends. I spoke 15 min of Caucus. Home with GP.

September 20 A full day; lunch with E.C.W. Supper with Dr Barton. GP brought Frances to train 11:30PM. Sleeper west.

September 21 A good night, train 2 hours late at Buffalo, 3 hours wait; Oberlin 9:30PM.

September 22 Sunday. Spoke in M. E. Church at Oberlin morning. Evening Prof Miller small people of Central Europe.

September 23 Odd jobs all day. 2 sets tennis. Men's Brotherhood 1st church evening.

September 24 Called at Prof Andrews in evening.

September 25 Tried to call on Hutchins and did call on Mrs Shaw.

September 26 Alfred the baby began to go to kindergarten. Edward is a senior in HS. Prof Youtz lecture in evening.

September 27 Took a ride around town in the car.

September 25 Wed. Armen registered in College, also Hampartsoom—Armen Freshman, H. Sophomore. Mr. P. & I went to call on the Hutchinses but they were not at home, so we called on Mrs. Shaw.

September 26 Thurs. Perfect fall weather. I took Alfred and Frances to kindergarten. Today my smallest boy, the baby, begins school. When Edward is a High School Senior Alfred is in the kindergarten. We went to the first lecture in the Seminary by Prof. Youtz, who just came from Auburn.

September 27 Fri. Beautiful weather. We all rode around the town in the auto. It goes very well now. We do not trust it very far out of town yet, but perhaps it would go all right.

September 28 Sat. My birthday. I worked all day but at supper we celebrated with ice-cream & cake. I could not make cake because we could not buy sugar. Mr. P. gave me a silk waist. Armen some stockings, George a box of candy and the little ones some dish towels. The auto gave out to Edward was too busy to get me a present.

September 29 Sunday. Mr. Nigoghosian of Akron called, also Mrs. Haas and some of her children. We went out to Woody's field for a walk and ate chocolates that "Gar Eff" sent. In the evening we went to hear Mr. Van der Pyl on Pres. Wilson's speech in New York on the issues of the war.

September 30 Mon. Rainy–great news. Bulgaria has surrendered. The fire whistle blew and the bells rang. Everyone was excited. We had a committee meeting at Mrs. Greene's. Mrs. Martin, Mrs. Haas and Miss Richmond to plan a Turkey meeting for November.

October 1 Tues. I had to wash again as Alfred was sick in the night and vomited over a good many things. Mrs. Jewett & Mrs. Gulick called. Mr. P. & the three boys went to Lyman Howe's picture show, all sorts of film curiosities, besides travel pictures.

October 2 Wed. Rainy. Thankoffering meeting. Mrs. McCord of South Africa spoke. It was very interesting. In the report of the Miss. Society it came out that for the two previous years the Thankoffering was $134.50, the same to a cent. Last year the contribution was 23 cts more than the year before.

October 3 Thurs. Pleasant. The one day in the week when I have neither washing nor ironing. I called on Mrs. Huntley, a Baptist Missionary from Shanghai.

Ernest C. Partridge

[September 28]

September 29 Sunday. Mr Van der Pyle spoke in evening on Wilson's speech on the issues of the war.

September 30 Bulgaria surrendered unconditionally.

October 1 Took 3 boys to Howe picture show which was very good.

[October 2–3]

October 4 Decided to take 2 courses in Seminary, C of R, Maclennan and Psyc of R, Fiske. Heard Willis on Liberty Loan. Went to Shack with Woody, Ed and Herman.

October 5 Called on Mrs Greene, Mrs Elmer, Miss Richmond and Mrs Hass.

October 6 Sunday. Prof Hutchins preached twice in 1st church.

[October 7–8]

October 9 Winona went to Elyria to Ohio Branch meeting.

October 4 Fri. A beautiful day. I went to hear Ex. Gov. Willis speak about the fourth liberty loan. It was the first time that I had seen the military unit together. In the evening Mr. P. & Edward went to the shack with "Woody" and Hermann.

October 5 Sat. Warm, almost like summer, showers. Mr. P. & I called on Mrs. Greene, Mrs. Elmer, Miss Richmond & Mrs. Haas. Mr. P. had a letter from Dr. Barton, suggesting the possibility of sending missionaries, without their families, back to Turkey soon.

October 6 Sunday. Warm, growing colder. Sunday school before church. Edward, Mr. P. Hampartsoom & I went to church. Prof. Hutchins preached comparing the children of Israel, exiles to Babylon, with the present Christian world. Edward wore suit, shirt, collar, necktie, silk stockings, all given him by Lois Cummings. Her brothers are soldiers so wear uniforms.

October 7 Mon. I tried to see Marguerite Clark in the movies in "Bab's Burglar" but saw instead Uncle Tom's Cabin. It was good for that but I do not like sad plays. George went with me and was disappointed but Mutt & Jeff saved the day for him.

October 8 Tues. A beautiful fall day. I attended the Parent-Teachers association with Mrs. Huntley of Shanghai. They discussed the tardy rule, the movies, midyear promotions, quarantine for contagious diseases etc. a very interesting meeting.

October 9 Wed. Beautiful autumn day. I attended the Ohio Branch meeting in Elyria. Some of the speakers were Mrs. Bunker of Africa, Mrs. Edward Haskell, Miss Richmond, Mrs. Nelson of China. It was a very interesting program. I took dinner with Mrs. Brooks. I bought Billo a drum for school band. Weights today.

October 10 Thurs. Beautiful day. I attended a lecture by a Belgian woman, who had been a Red Cross volunteer in Belgium after 9 days training. She fled with her wounded men from Antwerp to Bruges, then to Ostend, then to England. Later she came to America to study & learned English almost perfectly. She told a story of giving castor oil to a soldier who ran away.

October 11 Fri. No excitement except that we went to see a trophy train, containing all kinds of guns, equipment etc. captured from the Germans, also French and American equipment. We took all the children, had to stand in line a long time, in the rain & then they rushed us through.

October 12 Sat. A real [Armenian words], washing, ironing, washing floors, mending, baths. Frances has a cold and has been vomiting. Billo and Alfred have colds too. The Spanish influenza is coming nearer. I hope Oberlin may escape.

October 13 Sunday. Mr. P & Edward & George went to Sunday school, but the little ones had colds. Mr. P. spoke about Turkey. The evening meeting was called off on account of influenza.

Ernest C. Partridge

Ocober 10 Worked some on bus.; studied some. Lecture by a Belgian girl 1st church PM in evening.

October 11 Took whole family to see a trophy train in evening.

[October 12]

October 13 Sunday. I spoke about Turkey in 1st church SS.

October 14 Schools all closed tight on account of Spanish Flu.

[October 15–23]

October 14 Mon. The schools are all closed. Fortunately Armen was home as I was sick with dizziness & nausea. I think I was never so really sick in my life. The dizziness is dreadful.

October 15 Tues. Mr. P. & I went down town to call on Mr. & Mrs. Haskell in the evening. Mrs. H. was knitting like all the Swiss people. She said that she had nothing to do on the boat coming over because her knitting was in her trunk, while she had six children, one a small baby. Called on Miss Brownback & arranged a physics lesson for Hampartsoom.

October 16 Wed. I did not feel very well again but the weather was so warm that I washed one of the bed spreads and what other clothes were dirty, also mended stockings. Mrs. Greene called, and Mr. Bowen of Honolulu. Although the German peace proposition did not go through. Turkey has not yet surrendered.

October 17 Thurs. Warm & pleasant. I washed two spreads and what else was dirty. Mrs. Elmer & Mrs. Haskell called. Armen went to a picnic with Miss Pinneo, two Russians, a Greek & three Americans.

October 18 Fri. We went to a student volunteer picnic at the waterworks. Mrs. Fullerton called. We went to see Prof. & Mrs. Wright in the evening.

October 19 Sat. Nothing doing. Alfred likes to sing "Glory, glory hallelujah" but he forgot and began singing "Curly, curly hairlehujah." He is very sweet but is often naughty. Miss Sinclair came over to offer the use of her electric washer.

October 20 Sunday. No church nor Sunday School on account of Spanish influenza, and then it rained a good part of the day. We did take a little walk in the afternoon. Miss Richmond of Talas, took supper with us and told us stories of the two Budselis, Nubar and Shamilian.

October 21 Mon. Beautiful weather again. I did not wash and Armen did not have school so I had rather an easy day. Mrs. Clark took the three little ones for an auto ride and Mrs. Murdock and Everet took Alfred down town to have some ice-cream. Edward went to New London with "Woody."

October 22 Tues. Pleasant – Mr. P. & I did the washing with Miss Sinclair's electric washer. It was very easy and quick. I slept for about two hours in the afternoon. Mr. Van der Pyl called in the evening.

October 23 Wed. Warm & pleasant. I was invited to Dr. Husted's to meet Miss Huebner of Taiku, China. She was very interesting. The neighbors were there, Madame & Mrs. Horner, Miss Dickson, Mrs. Van der Pyl, Mrs. Hastings, Mrs. Metcalf, Mrs. Thatcher, with Mrs. Wolfe and Mrs. Husted.

October 24 Thurs. Last year the Allies gained two miles on the western front. Today Pres. Wilson sent word to Germany that their government must be entirely changed or there would be no peace terms except full surrender. I finally went down town and looked for suits for Alfred but found none.

October 25 Fri. A little rainy but warm most of the day. I intended to call in the afternoon but mended stockings instead. We were invited over to Mrs. Greene's in the evening to meet Mrs. Davis of Japan but Alfred did not go to sleep until 9:30 so I did not go. Turkey accepts Pres. Wilson's terms but it is too late for that I guess.

Ernest C. Partridge

October 24 Went to Cleveland for a R Exec Com meeting. Lunch at Union Club. Twing, Maurer, Huelster, Hill, Florimer & I.

October 25 Studied most of day. Evening I went to Mrs Greenes to meet Miss Davis of Japan.

[October 26–December 3]

October 26 Sat. Warm. Cleaned up, ironed etc. Miss Richmond called. Mr. P., Edward & I called on Mrs. Giles and Hermann in the evening. Oberlin played Reserve and was beaten 6–3. They played their coach & he won the game. Dirty playing.

October 27 Sunday. Warm, clear in the P.M. No church, no S.S., a strenuous day. Went to walk twice with the children, played games, read, especially played cat's cradle with Frances. She has just learned it. Miss Richmond & Miss Noyes took supper with us–baked beans, brownbread, coffee, jelly.

October 28 Mon. Cool, cloudy, rainy. I washed with Miss Sinclair's washer. It took 2 ½ hours for a large washing. Austria asks for immediate armistice. The British have taken Aleppo. The Armenians must be happy indeed to be free, what few are left.

October 29 Tues. Pleasant, a little cooler. Baked pies, ironed, called on Mr. & Mrs. Bunker in the evening. Hungary separates from Austria. Our auto was fixed so that it goes very nicely.

October 30 Wed. A little rainy. I had neither washing nor ironing. I made an apron, mended stockings, etc. Mrs. Greene called. Everitt Lamison came to the door with his Halloween lantern.

October 31 Thurs. Halloween and Turkey surrendered. We cannot imagine all that it means. We cannot take it in that the missionaries and Armenians are free, free. We celebrated both occasions with doughnuts, cider & candy. The children had masks, Alfred a skull, Frances a blue half mask, Billo a pumpkin, George an old man. After hours and hours of hard labor Mr. P. & Edward have finally got the car or "bus" into very good condition. They manufactured a muffler which works finely. The car seems really like an auto now.

November 1 Fri. Colder – Turkey surrendered Oct 31, it seems. Austria crumbling, Emperor left Vienna for fear of the mob. How much do the Turkey people know of it all, I wonder. We went down to call on Mrs. Haas and the evening on Miss Huebner of China.

November 2 Sat. Austrian King fled from Vienna. Emperor William will not abdicate. Bulgaria becomes a republic. Things are moving on. I called on Mrs. Lamison and her mother, Mrs. Murdock. A letter from Garabed Eff from Chicago. Perhaps he will visit us on the way back to N.Y.

November 3 Sunday. Now Austria has surrendered. Next? I went to church twice today. This evening Mr. Van der Pyl spoke to a union meeting on the Wet & Dry state. Prof. Root spoke on the present situation and what we should do.

November 4 Mon. A very easy day, no washing, no ironing. We went in the auto to call on Mrs. Caldwell but did not find her. M. P. had a letter from Dr. Barton telling about the intended expedition to Turkey and asking him to go to Detroit to look up Ford tractors.

November 5 Tues. Election day. Mr. P. went to Detroit. In the afternoon I washed with the washing machine, did not finish until about five. We had five tickets offered us for the artist's recital, an organ recital, but did not use one.

November 6 Wed. Cox elected, wets ahead [Ohio voted on restricting alcohol]. A busy day. Morning, down to the church to fix the Turkish things, then afternoon Turkey missionary meeting. Mrs. Haas, Mrs. Caldwell & Miss Richmond. Armen sang three or four songs. Evening, a social of missionaries at Mr. Haskell's.

November 7 Thurs. Oberlin went as wild as possible over the surrender of Germany and then found out that it was a false report. We only hope that it is a forecast of what is coming soon. A letter from Miss Rice about going back. Ohio went dry if nothing happens to change the vote.

November 8 Fri. Today the plenipotentiaries reached Foch. We shall soon have some news. Mr. Partridge came from Detroit. He visited Ford Co. thoroughly, saw Mrs. Clark, Ned Clark, Sherm Callender, Mikran Eff., the Malijarnians, Hranoosh Var., Dr. Konyonmjian etc.

November 9 Sat. In the first place Garabed Eff. came a little after eight. Then about eleven Mr. Manavian came. We had a busy confused day, but very pleasant. We did just as little housework as possible.

November 10 Sunday. Church, visit from the Haas family, evening news of the flight of the Kaiser to Holland. Newsboys were selling papers on the street at ten o'clock even in Oberlin.

November 11 Mon. At four thirty the fire whistle blew, Mr. P. came to my room & said, "There it is, Mrs. P." and it was the peace we had waited for so long. We all joined the procession and then a fine meeting in the chapel. Dr. Williams, Dean Bosworth, Prof. Hutchins, Musical Union orchestra, a packed house. A wonderful day.

November 12 Tues. A drop from yesterday as I spent most of the day washing. I washed in Miss Sinclair's washer but could not finish in the morning, so had to go again in the afternoon.

[November 13]

November 14 Thurs. They had floats to advertise the students' war chest. Armen represented an Armenian mother and Frances, her child. Frances wore a ragged much patched dress. I could not go because it was just noon and I had to get dinner.

November 15 Fri. Everyday program, some washing, some ironing, sweeping, dusting, cooking, washing dishes etc. etc.

November 16 Sat. I went out for the first time since Monday. I just had to do some errands. I had to pay for it by ironing & darning in the evening.

November 17 Sun. I stayed at home all day but Mr. P. spoke twice in the First Church, once on Heroism and once on Reconstruction in Asia Minor. Hermann took super with us and Mrs. Haas and her children called.

November 18 Mon. Washed with the machine. Went down town in the car with Edward to get him some gloves. Got undressed kid, lined for $1.80.

November 19 Tues. Went to the Student Volunteer social at Mrs. Alice Williams's. The Turkey missionaries were especially invited. In the evening Mrs. Metcalf took me to an Artist Recital. Mr. Goerner played the cello and Mr. Breckenridge accompanied.

November 20 Wed. We took Edward, Frances and afterwards Billo and George down town to get shoes. Mr. P also got some for himself and I got rubbers. The bill was $36.85. Mr. P. & I went to a church supper at the second church.

November 21 Thurs. Mr. P. & I went to a church supper at the second church. They unveiled photographs of pictures of Mr. Fairfield and Dr. Hutchins. We sat at Mrs. Andrews' table.

[November 22]

November 23 Sat. We went to Dean Bosworth's to a farewell reception to Prof. Hutchins, who is to go on a tour around the world with Sherwood Eddy. The seminary students, faculty and a few others were there.

November 24 Sunday. A letter from Dr. Barton saying that it would be possible for the families to go as far as Constantinople and be ready to go in as soon as possible. It is the hardest question I ever had to decide.

November 25 Mon. George's birthday. A very mixed up day. George had to have a lunch so he could play football at noon, so no birthday dinner, ice-cream & cake in the afternoon, inviting Johnny & Carroll. Presents were, cart, gloves, knife, Life, Popular Mechanics, book for snapshots.
Mr. P. & I took supper at the tea rooms etc. at Mrs. Greene [invitation]. Others invited were Miss Abbott, Mr. & Mrs. James, Mrs. Haskell, Mrs. Haas.

November 26 Tues. We washed in the morning and had callers nearly all the afternoon, Mrs. Martin, Prof. and Mrs. Jewett, and Miss Marion Metcalf. In the evening Parent-Teachers association. George spoke, "Me & Gott" and "Mud, mud, mud."

November 27 Wed. The day before Thanksgiving. I baked mince & apple pies and made cranberry sauce and then ironed. The other big folks down to George went to a Naval Quintette Concert, thinking it was vocal but found it was string.

November 28 Thurs. Thanksgiving. A letter from Mrs. Sewny. We hoped Samuel would come, but he did not. We asked two soldiers but they were all taken. Hampartsoom and Lawrence Knowlton came, so we were ten. We had a 16 ½ lb. turkey, after exchanging a poor one.

November 29 Fri. Washing etc. etc.

November 30 Sat. I went down town to do more shopping, stockings, underwear etc. These days are dreadful days because I have to decide whether to go back to Sivas now on the transport, whether to take George, what to do with Edward etc. etc.

December 1 Communion Sunday. I have been feeling sick all day but I went to church and hear[d] Mr. Van der Pyl. He is always good. Edward is tending furnace for the first time. He has Mrs. Morrison's & Mrs. Wright's for a few days.

[December 2–3]

December 4 Wed. Samuel came very unexpectedly. Alfred was overjoyed to have a soldier in the family. We all enjoyed his visit.

December 5 Thurs. Took the five o'clock train from Cleveland for Albany.

December 6 Fri. Arrived in Burlington. George [Ernest's cousin the dentist] met me at the station and took me straight to the office. He began on my teeth.

December 7 Sat. George spent almost every minute of the day on my teeth, almost finished.

December 8 Sunday. George took me for a little ride but we did not go to church on account of the "flu."

Ernest C. Partridge

December 4 Samuel blew in without notice. I went to Cleveland to speak at Euclid Ave Cong Ch and returned late.

December 5 Winona left for Burlington about noon.

[December 6]

December 7 Had ulcerated tooth pulled, was vaccinated, and had typhoid serum all at once.

December 8 Sunday. Was sick all day from ulcerated tooth, vaccination and typhoid serum.

December 9 Mon. George finished my teeth – I went with Beth and her mother while they did some shopping. I took the 3:40 train for Shoreham. I reached Mrs. North's about eight in the evening, had supper and then saw old friends.

December 10 Tues. I saw in Shoreham a good many friends, Jim Bush, Mrs. Cook, Nellie and Lyman Tottingham, Mrs. Harvard, Florence, Stowell, Mr. Albert Smith, Mrs. Gene Baldwin, Mr. & Mrs. Burge, Mr. & Mrs. Simmons. Left there at ten to go to Hartford. Mr. P. met me, also Mr. Bohn.

December 11 Wed. We were entertained by Mr. & Mrs. George Hills, who seem to be very rich. They have a beautiful house on Gillett Street. The meetings were good. I met quite a number of old friends.

December 12 Thurs. Mr. Peet was taken sick, so they had to return to Washington. On the Turkey, Bulgaria program, Mr. Holway, Dr. McCallum & Mr. P. spoke. Dr. Zweimer spoke very eloquently in the evening.

December 13 Fri. The meetings closed. Mr. P. went to Brooklyn. I to Springfeld. Visited Nazeli and Miss Gage came to spend the night.

December 14 Sat. Went to New York, stayed at Garabed Eff's house. Helen and Frances [Paelian's daughter] seem very worthy of him.

December 15 Sunday. Garabed & I went to the Armenian Church, saw Marie Baskian & her sister, met Mr. Bedigian, saw Dicran Kalfayan, Kahanian, Hachadon. Called on Marian [Boghosian], Rebecca came to visit us. Saw Hadji Agha's wife.

December 16 Mon. On the train. Arrived in Oberlin about two o'clock. Armen, Edward, Frances & Alfred met me in the "bus." Wasn't I glad to see them!

December 17 Tues. Housework again. I went down town with Edward to get some gym clothes. He joined the gym by paying five dollars.

[December 18]

December 19 Thurs. No electricity in the morning so I washed by hand. The weather was so warm that the first clothes that I put out were dry before the last ones were out.

December 20 Fri. Morning, Kindergarten Christmas tree with Frances & Alfred, afternoon Primary S.S. tree with the three little ones, evening Prospect St. entertainment. George was Jack Frost. He did very well.

December 21 Sat. Mr. P. came a little after noon.

Ernest C. Partridge

December 9 Went to Cleveland about noon. Made application for passport and took evening train East.

December 10 Had a pleasant trip East with Dean Brown. Hartford about 11AM. Entertained at George Hills. Winona came in evening.

December 11 Many Turkey people present. A good meeting.

December 12 In PM Holway spoke for Bulgaria, Dr Macallum, for Turkey & I on war work in Russia. Tweenies[?] in evening.

December 13 PM train to Brooklyn with Mrs Hubbard & Mrs Horton. Guest at Hortons. Spoke in evening at Central Church.

December 14 Spent the day in New York. Dinner with GP and Winona. Night at Miss Wheeler's.

December 15 Sunday. Breakfast with Miss Wheeler, Reconstruction, South Ch, Brooklyn. Dinner E.C.W. Supper with Hortons. Evening Heald & I at Plymouth Church, Brooklyn.

December 16 Called at Board Rooms & Relief Offices. Talked to Mary Hubbard. Noon train to Boston. Reached city at 6. Night at Ross's.

December 17 Spent day at Board Rooms. Major Lowenstein & I spoke in evening at Fremont Temple at a pageant for Armenian Relief. Dr Barton presided.

December 18 Spent the day calling on Avakian, Hampartsoonian, Papazian & at the Board Rooms.

December 19 Did some shopping. Went out to Melrose Highlands for night with Mr & Mrs Leon Smith. Spoke at Brotherhood Meeting.

December 20 Did some last things in Boston. Lunched with Ross & took train west at 2PM.

December 21 Reached home a little after noon.

December 22 Sunday. I did not go to church. The children went to S.S. Mr. P. spoke in Elyria in the P.M. Wrote Christmas notes.

December 23 Mon. Very warm for several days. I did some Christmas shopping. Went to an entertainment in the James Brand House, in which Edward was the son of an Armenian Relief Worker.

December 24 Tues. Busy getting ready for Christmas, made pies in the evening. Armen stuffed the chicken & the others did up their presents. We filled the little white stockings. They insisted upon hanging up one for me.

December 25 Wed. The four younger ones & I got up early and had our stockings. Then Christmas dinner, then the tree. We had a fine time. Everyone was happy and patient and good natured and satisfied. George said again & again, "the happiest or best Christmas yet." See memoranda.

December 26 Thurs. Day after Christmas & wash day!

December 27 Fri. Called at Prof. Jewett's in the evening & met Dr. Sidney Gulick & his daughter.

December 28 Sat. Home all day, except a funeral in the P.M., a Dixon girl died of influenza. They are missionaries in Ceylon.

December 29 Sunday. Home all day.

December 30 Mon. Frances coughs dreadfully.

December 31 Tues. Frances slept better & seems better. Ernest started for Little Rock, Arkansas, where he is to speak.

Ernest C. Partridge

December 22 Sunday a Xmas sermon by Mr Van der Pyle. I spoke on reconstruction at 1st church Elyria in PM.

December 23 Wrote an article for the Congregationalist & drove the car some in PM.

December 24 Drove car a good deal and finished Christmas preparations. Word to work for Campaign in Mid West.

December 25 A good Christmas. Ed got a watch. George a pocket kodak.

[December 26]

December 27 Called at Jewett's in evening. Met Dr. Sidney Gulick.

December 28 Acted as bearer at funeral of Dixon girls.

December 29 Sunday. Hot water tank sprung a leak early this morning & I spent some time fixing it. Very cold.

December 30 Spent day reading for Seminar paper, packing and getting ready for road.

December 31 Noon train to Chicago. Worked most of PM and evening Board of Trade Hotel. (323m)

Memoranda.

Edward, a wrist watch from his father, pen from me, pocket book from Billo, drill from Edward, High School banner from Armen, several little things.

George, camera from papa, sled, bird guide, patriotic pin from Billo, necktie from Armen, etc. etc.

Billo, Baby Phonograph from papa & mama, watch from grandpa, mittens from grandma, neckties, book from George.

Frances, baby carriage from us, hair ribbons, drawing slate, etc. over shoes, mittens.

Alfred, soldier suit, overshoes, picture book, soap bubbles, squeaking dog.

Carroll gave a fire engine to all the kids together.

Ernest had a steel mirror, coat & trousers hanger, Oberlin banner from Hampartsoom, other small things.

I had a diary from E., lace corset cover from Armen, gloves from Hampartsoom, handkerchiefs from Ed., round box that George made himself, etc. etc.

Diaries of Winona & Ernest Partridge 1919

Flyleaf: "Winona G. Partridge with Christmas Greetings 1918 Ernest"

January 1 Wed. Such a mixed up day to begin a new year. We slept late. Armen had a sore foot so I had to do the housework and began to wash at half past eleven, finishing at half past two. Then dinner, then Mrs. Martin and Mrs. Husted called. After they went, after dark, I hung up the clothes, then supper, then baths, beds made up to jump in.

January 2 Thurs. Cold. Went to Mrs. Wrights' for afternoon tea. Mrs. Wright and her sister from Norway were there, also Mrs. Greene, Miss Abbott & her mother, Miss Brownback, Mrs. C.B. Martin, Mrs. Koessler, and Alsatian. We had tea, coffee, cookies, several kinds of candy.

January 3 Fri. Very cold. Tel. from E. from Little Rock. Well. The gas was low and we could get the therm up to 60° only with the fireplace too. The pipes burst in the Prospect St. School so the boys had a vacation but not Edward. For him, school all the forenoon, laboratory, drill, then study until after ten. He did not go to the basket ball practice because his knee hurt.

January 4 Sat. Very cold, low gas. A hard day, day to clean the house, cold, children all home, but it helped a little that they played some over in Carroll's cellar, played soldier, but poor little Alfred was detailed to guard a bridge out of doors and so came home very cold. He cried & cried with cold feet, listened to a story & then cried again.

Ernest C. Partridge

January 1 Early train to St. Louis. Night sleeper to Little Rock Arkansas. (284m)

January 2 Reached Little Rock at 10AM. Marion Hotel. Cleaned up. Called on Sec. Hodges. Saw paper men. Spoke at Rotary Club lunch. Dinner with Jewish club. (349m)

January 3 Dictated some letters & stuff for press. State conference 10–4 with lunch. I had one hour. Night train to St. Louis.

January 4 Breakfast in depot at St. Louis. 9AM train to Des Moines via Moberly. Train late reached Des Moines at 10:30 to Hotel Franklin. (349m)

January 5 Sunday. Morning spoke in Plymouth church. Evening C.E. Missed date outside by late train.

January 6 Wire from Case to be in N Y. Friday to sail. National Com interfering. Have wired Case & Macallum. Spoke at luncheon of workers, evening.

January 5 Sunday. A little warmer, so gas better. A telegram from the Board: First transport for Turkey sails January thirteen, men only, can you go arriving N.Y. not later than Friday night Jan ten. No instructions regarding baggage received but will come later. Another transport expected later for missionary families & others. Wire me collect. Alfred a little sick. Called Dr. Thatcher.

January 6 Mon. Cold, growing warmer. A letter from Dr. Barton in which he says thinks I'd better not go out on the first transport to Turkey. I had already decided so, but I am glad to be justified. Mr. & Mrs. Stapleton called, also Mrs. Haas. A letter came from Mr. P. & Garabed Eff.

January 7 Tues. I could not wash until afternoon because there was no one to stay with the children, so I worked all day and was so tired that I thought I was going to have the "flu" but could get up no temperature. Mrs. Greene and Mrs. Wright called to know if we had heard from Mr. P. I sent another telegram to Des Moines.

January 8 Wed. Missionary meeting, Africa. African missionary children sang the chicks. Mrs. Fuller gave a very interesting talk. I had a telegram from Mr. P. saying he would get to Elyria at 7:10AM. Letters from Mr. Case saying that E. is to go on the 19th, not on the 13th.

January 9 Thurs. E. did not arrive until noon, trains being late, came over from Elyria in a taxi in nineteen minutes, supposing every hour was precious, and that he was to go to New York on Friday.

January 10 Fri. Made doughnuts in the morning to the great joy of the whole family. Mr. P. and I went to a reception of the Leaven Club. Miss Coe and Japanese students acted various scenes representing New Year customs and the fairy story "Tongue-cut Sparrow." Alfred cried and said: "I am so happy. I do not like to be so happy."

January 11 Sat. Mr. P. was intending to go to Indianapolis in the morning but decided to stay and see part of the basket ball game and then go on the sleeper. We had a family group taken in the PM. Then I went to the doctor to see what was the matter with my back. Nothing serious.

January 12 Sunday. Gas low in the morning although it is usually good on Sunday. George, Billo, & Alfred went to S.S. and Edward and I to church. I have felt very tired because the strain was off, I suppose.

January 13 Mon. Warm. I took Frances and Alfred down town to do some errands, took them in George's new cart. A telegram from Ernest saying that he will not be home until Thurs. I read a paper written by Ernest on Normal Conversion, in Prof. Fiske's class, which met at his house. Interesting class, beautiful home, refreshments, ice-cream, macaroons, lady fingers, choc. peppermints, mints, salted almonds.

Ernest C. Partridge

January 7 Wrote some letters and wait for answers to wires. Answer from Macallum to follow Boston instructions so I am going east in the morning.

January 8 Rock Island train to Chicago, 5 hours late. Left Des M[oines] 4:30PM Chicago 2:10AM. Just caught train to Cleveland. (358m)

January 9 Reached Elyria at 10:50. Taxi to Oberlin. Found that I am not to sail till 2nd transport Jan 19th. (341m)

January 10 Am to keep Indianapolis date next Sunday.

January 11 Wrote letters, cleaned things up, and packed & sent by box Xpress. Michigan Aggies basketball. Night sleeper Cleveland to Indiana. (33m)

January 12 Sunday. Reached Indianapolis 8AM. Claypool Hotel Cong church AM. Boys YMCA 2:00 Mess meeting 2:30. Big ME Church Evening. (283m)

January 13 Morning train to Veedersburg. H.S. 3:30. Rally in evening. (65m)

January 14 Morning train to Covington. Worth Rasd. [Acad.?] PM. H.S. Union meeting evening. Night train to Indianapolis. (79m)

January 15 State Conference at Columbia Club, address. Evening State Conference of Episcopal church. Night train to Cleveland. (283m)

January 16 Reached Oberlin at 10:10AM. Packed and got ready to go. Annual supper of 1st church.

January 14 Tues. Warm, cloudy, growing colder. Letters from Ernest enclosing clipping about transport which was to sail Monday. Motorcycles, autos, trucks, food stuffs, cloth, blankets etc. etc. Mrs. Haas called, also Miss Marion Metcalf. George and Billo went to the gym to play basket ball with the Krescents, and they had a shower bath, a "little" one as Billo said.

January15 Wed. A hard day, finished washing at five. Sent a telegram to E. telling him that Mr. Case thinks he'd better go back, as Mr. Fowle wants experienced men with the language.

January 16 Thurs. E. came on the 10:10 car. After long deliberation decided to go Friday night to New York. Tried to get word from New York about exact date of sailing but could not. We attended the 1st church annual supper. Sat with Mrs. Greene, Mrs. Haskell, daughter & d-in-law.

January 17 Fri. E. started for Constantinople via New York at 4:19 from Elyria. The children, except Edward who had drill, Armen & Hampartsoom went to the car. I went to Elyria with him. He telephoned from Cleveland that he got a reservation on the 20th Cent. Limited. So we are without a man again.

January 18 Sat. Our day passed as usual, only I got through better than I expected to. Mr. P. arrived in New York.

January 19 Sunday. The children went to S.S. all except Edward. Armen went to church in the morning and Edward, George, Hampartsoom and I in the evening. Mr. V– spoke on the American Laboring Man. He says he is industrious and conservative, but unintelligent and crude.

January 20 Mon. Warm. A letter from Ernest says that he will probably sail Thurs. He took lunch with G. P. & Mr. Manavian, was to hear Shah Mooradian sing. He [Ernest] was to go with a party of forty of whom he was to be the leader.

January 21 Tues. Very warm & springlike. A tel. from Ernest saying that he is to sail Thurs. Mr. Holoway and Dr. Usher are to go. He wanted his cloth scarf. The children & I took it down and sent it by special delivery. Attended Parent Teachers Ass[n]. Mr. MacMurray says to give the children milk when you don't know what to do.

January 22 Wed. Very warm. A letter from Ernest says that he has seen a number of his Armenian friends. A letter from Miss Putney says that Mihran Toumajian and another Gurun [near Sivas] boy had escaped to Egypt. Mr. Caruf wrote her that he has been transferred to Smyrna. I went to Missionary tea at Mrs. Fitch's.

January 23 Thurs. Rainy. In a 7th grade party the night before they had a spelling match on a certain two pages of words which they had studied. Four stood, George, Marlise Johnston, Virgina Gehrkens & Eleanor Bounard. Today it came down to George & Virginia and then she gave them words which Virginia had happened to study and G hadn't, so George failed on "aquatic", trying to pattern it after "acquit." Virginia got the prize, a big star, or rather her side did. This is George's last day in seventh. We suppose that Ernest sailed today. We got no letter and no telegram. I had a long distance call & thought it was he but it was a man in Wakeman [nearby college town] who wanted me to speak Sunday.

Ernest C. Partridge

January 17 Winona went with me to Elyria to take 4:19 train. Could not get a sleeper so took 7:20 from Cleveland.

January 18 New York 9:40AM. Went to Board and Committee offices. Got passport visa work started. Chak-Murafian concert. Home with Paelians. Park Ave Hotel.

January 19 Sunday. To Armenian church in morning. Paelians & Racoubians & I spent day together at restaurants and hotels.

January 20 A conference with Pensacola party in morning. Got passport from British & finished at French. Evening with Khaladjian at party.

January 21 Worked hard all day buying and at Rooms evening. Swiss reception 45 present. They gave me a Corona.

January 22 Bought uniform and other stuff. Spent some time at Rooms and evening and night at Prof Lyman's.

January 23 Spent day buying and dictating letters at Rooms. Farewell reception at Boat.

January 24 Finished shopping and writing and packed in evening.

January 25 Sailed on Pensacola at 11AM with Dr Ussher, Holway, Kingsbury & Beach & 37 recruits. Quite a carnival down to see us off. [The Pensacola was seized from Germany in May 1917 and commissioned in the United States Navy in October 1917. The ship was then assigned to NOTS in January 1918 to carry supplies for Syrian-Armenian relief. (http://www.history.navy.mil/danfs/p/pensacola.htm)]

January 24 Fri. I attended a mother's club which meets at Mrs. Haskell's house. They read "Over Fool Hill" [Guiding Boys Over Fool Hill, A. McKinney], which represents the time in a boy's life, usually 13 to 16, when he is lawless, rude etc. Edward got over it without me knowing it. George is at the foot. Let's see if he goes over.

January 25 Sat. A telegram from Ernest that he is sailing this morning, later a letter telling of his reception by the Armenians where they gave him a Corona type-writer. They were certainly very cordial & generous. Alfred is sick, high fever, but no sign of a cold so we think it is not the "flu."

January 26 Sunday. Sunny & springlike. Alfred is better, so it is nothing serious. I went to Wakeman and spoke on the Armenians. Mr. Blair is the pastor. I went and came in a taxi and it was very pleasant. The College students were not allowed to go to church on account of the "flu."

January 27 Mon. Warm & pleasant. A letter from Ernest written at 12:30AM Friday before he sailed Sat. Then I had one dictated to a stenographer that same day, but written out the next day. He says that Haig Symabenkian is in Damascus. A card from Nishan Bekhian, saying that he is trying for a passport through British Embassy.

January 28 Tue. A little colder. Miss Noyes received notice to teach N.Y. next Thursday. I worked all day, washing in the afternoon. Armen had an exam in Geometry. Edward was in command of his company for a few minutes. He & G. both had basket ball practice.

January 29 Wed. Snowed, but not very cold. I went to say "Goodbye" to Miss Noyes and telephoned "Goodbye" to Miss Trefethren. Hermann came in the evening and wasted his time & Edwards'. A letter from Garabed Eff. telling of Ernest's stay in N.Y., reception on the boat, dinner with 43 Armenians etc. etc.

Ernest C. Partridge

January 26 Sunday. Dr Wirt preached in the morning and Mr Count in the evening.

January 27 Movies on deck in Evening. Dr Ussher lecture on social customs & diseases.

January 28 A conference on running cars in PM. I spoke on Russia in the evening.

January 29 Due in Beirut tonight. Everybody writing & cleaning up.

[January 30–February 8]

January 30 Thurs. Warm & pleasant. I attended a farewell reception to Mr. & Mrs. Stapleton. There were besides the missionaries, members of the Second Church Bible Class, Dr. & Mrs. Williams, Prof. & Mrs. Williams. I went over to Mrs. Wright's in the evening for a few minutes. She gave me a black crepe skirt.

January 31 Fri. Warm again. I went down with Alfred & Frances to see Mr. and Mrs. Stapleton off on the car. There I met Mr. Martin, a tall, large, fine-looking man. He says there are many Sivas people, women & children, in Aintab. In the evening I went to Mrs. Haas' house for boys club & mothers' meeting. Frances came to me & said, "I say vomiter" and Alfred says "vermometer", which is right? Then Alfred explained that it is what you put in your mouth when you are sick.

Memoranda: George's report, 1st semester, Seventh A, Reading 90, Spelling 95, Grammar 96, Arith 87, Music 84, Physiology 90, Geog.; Edward, Latin 91, Eng. 90, Hist. 88, Physics 93.

February 1 Sat. A little colder but Frances and Billo played out of doors nearly all day. Alfred was a little sick again and drank milk and orange juice mostly. Mrs. Moore brought over two lemon pies and said "to share, that she appreciates her neighbors." I went with the boys to the Ohio State basket ball game, very exciting, tied 16–16, then played five min more & Oberlin made 4 points & State lost.

February 2 Sunday. A little cold. George, Frances & Billo went to Sunday School. Edward & I to church. Mr. Van preached on "the Struggle for Character," a very good sermon. Hampartsoom spent the PM with us. Hermann took supper here. We had long "singing prayers" as Frances calls them.

February 3 Mon. Very warm. I got my bank book and found that they had made a mistake and instead of $33 overdrawn I am $50 to the good. I went down town & Armen bought silk for a skirt. George & I called on Mr. Martin. Report of a wireless from Ernest. "Try Laymans Miss. Movement. Going fine two language lessons educational lectures daily ten agriculturists big shipment next steamer more tractors both caterpillar & Fords on suggest mess kits camp chairs & washbasins for each recruit."

February 4 Tues. Washed.

February 5 Wed. The children more or less ailing. I went down town and back just as fast as I could to see about my bank account.

February 6 Thurs. Armen sick, came home at nine o'clock. I went to get her schedule changed, had to wait until nearly twelve from ten to see Prof. McLennan. Armen then went to bed, grew worse and Edward began to be sick. Called Dr. Thatcher who said she had the "flu." She went to the hospital.

February 7 Fri. Edward genuinely sick as well as the little ones, all "flu." George and I held the fort. Mrs. Burnett sent baked apples and a thin custard and playthings for the children.

February 8 Sat. Everybody some worse. Mrs. Lamson brought soup. Mrs. Wright sent soup and extra sheets. Mrs. Greene sent eggs. Such kind friends as we have. Mrs. Burnett had to go to North Amherst but called up from there to see if she should hurry home.

February 9 Sunday. Some better, temperatures down. Doctor did not come at all. Edward & Frances in bed all day. Mrs. Greene came to see how we were, also Mr. Nieto called. Mrs. Lamson brought books to read, Little Black Sambo, Timothy's Guest & Under the Lilacs. Mrs. Wright brought cookies, biscuits, & marmalade.

February 10 Mon. Armen & little ones have no temperature, dressed & cross and lively, the little ones. Armen still at the hospital. Edward complains of sore lungs etc. etc. Dr. says no disturbance of the lungs. George & I still flu-less.

February 11 Tues. Edward's temperature lower and he feels better. All the little ones better in the morning but Frances felt miserable in the afternoon. I had a letter from Uncle Rufus with a hundred dollar check. What a blessing that man has been to me! Edward will have a sweater now.

Ernest C. Partridge

February 9 Got off at Gibraltar with Captain & visited US Naval base and Consulate. Sent cable to W[inona]. Sailed again about 3PM.

February 10 Sea quite rough but men have got used to it. Warm enough to be on deck.

February 11 Men are working well on Turkish now. 2 lessons a day for each division. Dr Ussher lectured in evening. I took a bath in Captain's tub.

February 12 Our musicians gave a concert in the evening followed by a good prayer meeting led by Bill Hawkes.

February 13 At 3PM Joe Beach gave 1st talk on Paul's Journeys. Evening, I lectured on the Deportations.

February 14 At 3 Holway, a fine lecture on Paul's second journey. Dr Ussher in evening on travels.

February 15 I gave 3rd Journey with Emphasis on Smyrna Ephesus etc. Evening Dr Wirt on Western front.

February 16 Sermon by Macgelhom. Evening a good meeting led by Vroonian, special music.

February 12 Wed. Warm & pleasant. Lincoln's birthday as usual. Armen came home from the hospital and Edward sat up for the first time. At supper we were all seven at the table for the first time in nearly a week. The boys had five invitations to the father & son banquet. Mr. Bohn, Prof. Royce, Mr. Ohly, Mr. Thurston, George Jones son of Lynds Jones.

February 13 Thurs. Warm & rainy. All "flu" cases better. Mrs. Bohn cooked us some chicken which they devoured eagerly. George had another invitation to the banquet, from Prof. Moore. A letter from Yervant Chadurigian from N.Y. He is blind & writes one line right over the other. He is in the hospital for treatment. Great excitement making valentines.

February 14 Fri. Warm & rainy – Valentine's Day and very thoroughly celebrated, candy hearts from Mrs. Metcalf, cooky hearts, Ralph Williams, ice cream for dinner from Spencer Fullerton and heaps of regular valentines from neighbors & others, song book from G.P., bulgure from Samuel. Mr. & Mrs. Martin called. George went to father & son banquet with Mr. Bohn. Miss Tiffle read in N.Y. Times Pensacola [Ernest's ship] reached Gibraltar Feb. 7.

February 15 Sat. Saturday, regular grind. The children were well enough to go out. Billo & George went to the basket ball game. Oberlin 30, Reserve 18. It was Billo's first game and he enjoyed it very much.

February 16 Sunday. Snowed but very cold. All the children except Edward went to Sunday School. Arthur and Lawrence came. Edward made fudge. Billo spent the afternoon with Russell Van der Pyl. He will go to school hereafter probably. To think that they have really had the "flu."

February 17 Mon. Snowy. Billo went to school. Edward went out three times, around the block, down town with me, and up to Woody's to supper. Armen is better too but has not been out yet.

February 18 Tues. Snowing. Armen and Edward started in school today and survived. I went to Parent Teachers Association meeting. Prof. Miller spoke on "Intelligence Tests." He gave tests for various ages. I think they are all up to normal in our family, but I am not sure.

February 19 Wed. Mrs. Haas called. I had not seen her for a long time. She has had a letter and cablegram from her husband. She says she feels twenty years younger.

February 20 Thurs. Warm. I went over to call on Mrs. Wright. She is herself making me a waist, black & green, to go with a black skirt she gave me. She is certainly a good friend. Miss Davis walked home with me.

February 21 Fri. I always work hard Friday to make Saturday easier and so my Friday is hard.

February 22 Sat. Washington's birthday. Lowell's hundredth anniversary. Edward and Armen went to hear "Bob" Millican or Lieutenant Colonel Robert Millican. They liked him very much and thought him very handsome.

February 23 Sunday. I went to church twice. In the morning Mr. Van der Pyl on Foreign Missions, and in the evening, Bishop of Ohio on "Self abnegation and Courage".

February 24 Mon. Warm & sunny. I received two letters back that I had written to China to Ernest, one July 2 & one July 14, a 20th anniversary letter. They had been to Bagdad and sent back. The boys went to see Les Miserables at the movies.

February 25 Tues. Rainy, snowy, blowy, a little colder. Letters from Damascus & Detroit, from the Clarks. Dr. writes that he has seen Haig Symabergakian & Suren Tafedjian. Dr. will be coming home soon.

February 26 Wed. Dr. Fosdick spoke but I did not go.

February 27 Thurs. Day of Prayer. Dr. Fosdick spoke, but I did not go.

February 28 Fri. Shansi Day. Dr. Wm E. Strong spoke but I did not go. In the night Alfred's leg began to pain him. He could not move it without screaming and would not let me, but today played all day.

Ernest C. Partridge

February 17 Movies on deck in evening. Dr Ussher spoke on Social Customs and Diseases.

[February 18]

February 19 Reached Beirut late in evening and anchored outside breakwater.

February 20 Started unloading about noon. Half our men working each day. Supervising work. Major Nicol of Red Cross in charge of our workers.

February 21 Prof Crawford took Urik Ussher & me, Connolley driving, up to Antoura orphanage [College Saint Joseph, Lebanon] 150 Gurun o[rphan]s, 10 from Sivas. Arousig Mooghalian there.

February 22 A reception to our party at the college.

February 23 A dozen of our fellows went to Antoura. Dinner with Col Finley at Prof. Dorman's. Had a visit with Tabit from Sivas.

February 24 Had 2 hours work on cargo. Sailed for Constantinople about 10:30AM. Water rough.

February 25 More of men seasick then on Atlantic.

[February 26–28]

March 1 Reached Ismid Bay about 9:30. Mercurius unloaded and gone. Western Belle finishing. Barton, Moore, Hatch & Washburn down from City to see us.

[The Mercurius was a Dutch ship seized by United States March 1918 and commissioned in US Navy in April 1918. Brought supplies for Syrian-Armenian Relief to Constantinople.]

[The Western Belle was built in 1918 and transferred to the US Navy in November 1918. The ship carried flour and coal to Derindje Turkey.]

March 1 Sat. Armen took the children to the Y.W.C.A. Circus. Alfred again had a very bad night and could not walk during the day. He went to the circus but could not walk much. I had punished Alfred by putting him on a chair to stay for a while. After he went to bed he said, "I love you very much but I wish you wouldn't be so spankable and putable." I said, "Do I ever spank you?" "No, but you put me."

March 2 Sunday. I put a hot water Bottle on Alfred's hip and he slept all night and had no more pain in the day time. It seemed like a miracle really. I went to church in the evening to hear Prof. Shailer Mathews.

March 3 Mon. I washed this morning and in the P.M. took Alfred & Frances and went down town to the bank. Got some material for an apron, picked up Mrs. Caldwell, went Mr. Martin's to take a cable from Dr. Barton, form Constantinople. Edward went to him. Everet hit Alfred with a stone "beer & beans" club and cut his head.

March 4 Tues. Very warm and summerlike. Mary Burnett's birthday. The children ate ice cream with her. Two letters from Ernest from Gibraltar in the morning and this telegram in the P.M.: "Naval Operations reports Pensacola arrived Beirut Feb. 19th sailed 24th due Constantinople March 1st." Billy forgot and went across the lawn at school and was so distressed thinking he might be sent to Miss Askew, the principal. So he and George went to tell her, but she wasn't there, so George told her afterwards and she said, "It will be all right." I think this is the nearest that any of them have come to being disciplined.

March 5 Wed. Colder, snowy. Edward got the proofs of his pictures. Two or three are very good. The fourth is a made-up grin. They are $5 pictures which they get for $2 ½ a dozen. I went over to read Mr. P's letter to the Metcalfs. There has been a series of hurts, Alfred in mouth & back of head, Billy twice in the same eye, Edward in the eye, Frances in various places, George in the eye various times.

March 6 Thurs. Nothing special happened only Mrs. Shaw and I ran off to the movies and saw Mary Pickford in Armadilly of Clothesline Alley.

March 7 Fri. I was invited to Mrs. Belden's but the children did not get to sleep until half past eight so it was too late to go. The High School Basket Ball tournament commenced. Both Edward and George bought tickets.

March 8 Sat. In the morning George did not attend the tournament but beat the rugs and took Frances to the dentist. In the P.M. I went to an afternoon tea given by Mrs. Bunker of Africa. There were present Mrs. Fuller and Mrs. McCord of Africa. Mrs. Greene, Mrs. Haas of Turkey, Mrs. Haskell & her daughter from Bulgaria, Mrs. King, Mrs. Andrews of Oberlin, Mrs. Gulick of Japan, Mrs. Garland of Micronesia.

March 9 Sunday. Morning, Mr. Bohn preached on the Ultimate Program. Evening, Dr. Nieldrum of Cleveland on "What shadow do you cast?" Hermann stayed to supper.

March 10 Mon. I heard Madame Huard, an American who married a French painter. Her story was thrilling, dreadful, interesting, showing what an American woman can do under most extraordinary circumstances.

March 11 Tues. Ironing. Mrs. Wright & Mrs. Greene called.

Ernest C. Partridge

March 2 Worked with Commission on personnel and plans for Interior trips till 11. Remainder of day on cargo & trains for trip. Not much Sunday.

March 3 All our men working 18 hours a day on cargo, warehouse and garage work.

March 5 Dr Barton, Dr Gates and several of the men came down towards evening. Cargo about finished.

March 6 Left Derindje at 10:30AM. Party of 20 Americans, 5 chauffeurs, 3 cooks & one interpreter on a special train of 22 cars; 2 passengers, rest supplies.

March 7 Reached Eski Shehir [southeast of Constantinople, southwest of Ankara] at 2:30AM. Sent telegrams. Afion Kara Hissar [Afyon Kara Hisar, literally black opium castle] about 2PM.

March 8 Reached Konia early in morning. Miss Cushman met train. Unloaded and rearranged cars for two divisions.

March 9 Dr Barton's party left at 7:50AM for Adana. Irwin and I spoke at church service. Six of us dined with Miss Cushman. No work today.

March 10 Unloaded a car of flour and groceries etc. for Konia. Had Miss Cushman, Capt Lee Boviar and Lieut Gordon to dinner.

March 11 Unloaded a car of condensed milk and finished our business. We are ready to move on when our guard comes.

[March 12]

March 13 Thurs. Washing again. Before I finished Mrs. Haas and Miss Marion Metcalf called.

March 14 Fri. Ironing again. The Parents' reception of the High School. I sat beside Mrs. Hutchins. Francis N. is president of the class. The orchestra played, the glee club sang. Mr. Rawdon & Prof. Root spoke about new H.S. building. Ten pupils spoke. The Juniors gave a play about visiting Maggie in the slums.

March 15 Sat. Went to Mrs. Martin's at 9 P.M. to see Mr. Goodsell. Mr. Haas, Mr. & Mrs. James & baby, Mr. Gulick and Mr. Caldwell were there. A rainy Saturday is about the limit in a family of children in a small bungalow.

March 16 Sun. A rainy Sunday after a rainy Saturday. It cleared for a little while so the children went out. George was some better. I went to supper at the men's building with volunteers etc. Mrs. Mailini & I were together, a stereopticon lecture on Africa by Mr. Fuller & a sermon on The Church of the New Era by Kerring.

March 17 Mon. The rainy days really made me sick. I was in bed all day sick all over, tired out. At night I had indigestion so that I could not lie down, just walked the floor for ever so long. George stayed at home feeling sick with a cold.

March 18 Tues. I was better and able to do the housework slowly but sent out the washing. Mrs. Murdock, Mrs. Shaw, Mrs. Hall & Marion Metcalf came to inquire for me. George stayed at home largely to help me but had an earache in the P.M. Edward not well.

March 19 Wed. A pleasant day. The little ones were out all day. Edward is still not well but has improved from morning until evening. I went down town especially to get Alfred some shoes & rubbers. I also did some other errands. In the evening, George put the children to bed and I went to her a French Chaplain speak.

Ernest C. Partridge

March 12 Curt and Custer went down line with Capt Butler to see Bozant's supply stuff.

[March 13–15]

March 16 Sunday.. Attended service by English chaplain in Turkish college. Dinner with Miss Cushman. I conducted English service in evening.

March 17 Dr Washburn's first section got in at 5PM. 20 people bound for Adana. Webb sisters, Miss Cold, Miss Holmes.

March 18 2nd section in charge of Dr Lambert got in at 5:30PM. Mary Hubbard with them. Arranged for her and Miss Larson to be left in Konia.

March 19 Dr Washburn's party left at 7:30. Dropping 4 trucks for our route.

March 20 Dr Washburn could use help. Dr & Mrs Smith for Konia. I left on night train for Constantinople to get workers & supplies.

March 21 Dr Lambert's party was to leave Konia at 7 till morning. Saw Lieut Picthouse at Afion KH. Haymesta rode with me to Ayeland. Capt Brown.

March 22 Reached Direnge [Direndje] about noon. Dr Moore expected down so decided to wait.

March 23 Sunday. I preached in morning Dr Ussher on Caucasus in evening.

March 20 Thurs. Edward went to school although he was really not able. George did not go. He too has a cold and a cough.

March 21 Fri. I finished washing at quarter of five. The worst of that is that after that I cannot rest but have to look after children at the naughtiest time of the day. I am not very patient, I am afraid. Edward stayed at home. Geo. went.

March 22 Sat. Fortunately a pleasant day. I took the children to the Glee Club Concert given especially for the school children. It was good but rather diluted.

March 23 Sunday. Weather good but children all coughing and I have a cold myself. Billy's earache was the worst. Hampartsoom, Hermann, Arthur, Lawrence, Mrs. Haas with five children called. I went to church in the morning. Mr. Van preached on "The True Test of Christian Life."

March 24 Mon. The excitement today has been that Fred Goerner, while out walking on the Ramsey track with Marion Hernick, accidentally shot her. He had been shooting & was just putting up his revolver & it went off. He carried her a mile to the last house in the city. She was taken to a hospital and is recovering, but it was a dreadful experience for them both. Billo had an abcess in his ear which broke last night. They are all coughing.

March 25 Tues. A perfect day as regards weather. From Edward to Alfred they cough, cough, cough. I have it too but mine is not as bad. Billo seems to be not getting along very well.

March 26 Wed. Frances went to the dentist, then to Dr. Thatcher, where he decided to remove her adenoids, Friday. Edward made an appointment with the dentist and Billo has his throat nose and ears examined.

March 27 Thurs. Winter again, snow. Frances took castor oil and starved herself in preparation for her operation. She had a headache, was nauseated, but will be better. Mrs. Wright is sick.

March 28 Fri. Cold but pleasant. Frances had her adenoids and tonsils removed. She was as good as gold, a little scared & overawed but reassured by me being with her. Her throat and nose were in dreadful condition. I brought her home in a wheeled chair. She is very uncomfortable but improving.

March 29 Sat. Frances is better but her throat hurt and she had a headache. She ate only ice-cream. Mary Burnett brought her two books. Mr. Burnett sent her some carnations to the hospital so that she would see them when she woke up. A letter from Polly dated Dec. 29, 1918, first letter since the armistice.

March 30 Sunday. Snow and cold, really like winter. Edward, Billo & Alfred went to S.S. George tired and lame from celebrating Horace Mosher's birthday, with hike & base ball. Lawrence ate supper with us. We had cabbage sarmas, very good, then ice-cream, on Frances' account.

Ernest C. Partridge

March 24 Drs Moore & Richards came down in PM and I had a talk with each.

March 25 Caucasus unit called to Constantinople and I came up to city with them by train, staying at Bible House.

March 26 Put in my time at Bible House and Committee Rooms. Evening at Vortavai's house.

March 27 Spent the day at Hissar visiting with Mrs Irwin, Misses Loughridge, Richmond & Bristol. I spoke in evening to relief workers on organization of work.

March 28 Put in the forenoon talking with Mr Peet, Heck and Admiral Bristol about our work and protection. Dinner with Minister of Records, a friend of Dr Ussher's.

March 29 Called on Col Hobson of British Transportation and on the Armenian Patriarch.

March 30 Sunday. Preached in morning in Scutari. Dinner there. PM to Bible House. To Toumadjian's for night.

March 31 Came down to Derindje [aka Derince] on SC248. Talked with most of Relief workers for Sivas.

April 1 Peltier died at Eski Shekir from being run over in jumping a train. Dr and Mrs Marden came in from Aintab. Mrs Sewny is waiting for me in Konia.

March 31 Mon. Cold. Frances improving some perhaps although she had a bad night, would sit up and cry without knowing why or being able to tell why. I had two letters from Mr. P. from Beyrout this morning, one this afternoon, enclosing two written by Polly to Mr. Tabit. I read these letters to Mrs. Greene and Mrs. Wright. Edward, George, Billo & I went to see Marguerite Clarke in Bab's Burglar. George went on a hike with S.S. class.

April 1 Tues. A real foolish day. I began to wash about eleven o'clock in the washer, found it would not drain, came home for dinner. The boys decided to go to the shack at 2:10, then extra underwear, stockings, blankets, etc. The church people wanted our rugs, I went back to finish the washing, returned, cooked macaroni for the cafeteria supper, then Mrs. Metcalf telephoned that Mr. M was bringing a woman to look at the bungalow. It was in disorder from top to cellar but they looked. Armen & Wm went to the supper. Hermann called.

Edward copied Polly's letter and I sent some copies. Frances fairly well but she does not improve as fast as I hoped. Alfred naughty, especially when he is with Billo. At supper I was talking to Hermann & he ate the top of the cinnamon rolls.

April 2 Wed. Pleasant but rather cold. Frances went out for a while in the middle of the day but cried with earache in the evening. I presume it was her tonsils or the place where they were. She and Alfred were awake a great deal last night and consequently I have felt sick all day. College opened.

April 3 Thurs. Rainy. Frances seems much better. Russell came over. They played delivery wagon in the dining room, then airplane down cellar, then looked at magazines in the attic, then disk turning in the parlor. Frances spent several hours at Mary Burnett's and took lunch there.

April 4 Fri. Usual rainy Friday. Swept, cleaned, washed and now everything is muddy. Frances is better, eats quite a number of things. George came home. It was good to see him again. He had a fine time. Edward gained 4 pounds during the week of vacation.

April 5 Sat. And a usual Saturday, work, clean up. It was muddy outside and as fast as I cleaned someone got it muddy. Of course that someone was usually Alfred, but he always has such pressing business when he comes in.

April 6 Sunday. Pleasant & warm, but in the morning showery looking, so Alfred & Frances did not go to Sunday School. Mrs. Haas came in the afternoon. Mr. & Mrs. Martin stayed to supper and then Edward & I went to church with them to hear Mr. Van on Raymond Robins views on Russia.

April 7 Mon. Sunday night I saw a girl in the choir who has a striking resemblance to Alfred. Today Rachel told me that her name is Miss Peterson of Gray Gables. I want to meet her. Edward played tennis for the first time this season. School parade today to advertise the need of a new H.S. building.

April 8 Tues. No mail at all today. Warm & lovely, thunder

Ernest C. Partridge

April 2 Have to wait a week for transportation to Konia.

[April 3–4]

April 5 Went up to C[onstantinople] on sub chaser. Had a talk with Dr Peet and Dr White. Spent night at B. H. visiting with Yarrow who just got in from Cairo.

April 6 Sunday. Went on steamer to Hissar with Talas ladies to spend day at Irwin's. Dr. Stanley White preached at Robert College. Evening at Alexandrian's.

April 7 Back to Deringe [Derindje]. Work on loading cars.

April 8 Finishing loading. Conference with Dr Moore. Left at 7PM. With 4 cars and 5 people for Konia on Smyrna unit train.

April 9 Reached Eski Shehir at 9:30AM. Remained till 5PM. Reached Afion KH at 11AM. Found Smyrna crowd there. Konia at 11PM.

April 10 Left Konia at 7AM with my party for Ooloo Kishla. Arrived at 7PM.

April 11 Dr Washburn came in from South. Unloaded train of 18 cars and loaded ten trucks for trip to Cesarea and Sivas.

and a few drops of rain. I did not get through until half past five, then I was too tired to move. The town voted to erect a new H.S. building. To celebrate the boys brought bugles, cymbals, etc. to our front porch, beautiful music.

April 9 Wed. Warm & lovely. At noon George came home and asked me if I know that Edward was tied up on S. Main St. I got Mr. Metcalf and we started out. Mr. M. went ahead on the bicycle and found the crowd at the waterworks. Part of the H.S. pupils had wanted a holiday on account of the new building and walked out. Because Ed and others did not join them they tied them up, threatening to throw them into the creek. Mr. M. cut the ropes and let Edward free. Arthur and Frances Hutchins were also tied up. Some said that I broke the strike. Others thought it was Mr. Partridge, others that it was the Marshall, those that did not know Mr. Metcalf, I suppose. Capt. Garland, Mrs. Metcalf and Marion Metcalf came.

April 10 Thurs. Rainy. Last night a heavy thunder shower. The H.S. pupils were back in school but were not allowed to recite, and are not to recite tomorrow. Three days of zeroes will mean failure for some but they deserve it. Today Edward is on the winning side. Letter from Nishan Eff.

April 11 Fri. International night. Hampartsoom was Vartan the Brave. Mr. Jantz the priest and George presented the sword to Vartan. Frances, Alfred and I stayed at home. Letter from E.C.P. from Ismid Bay, one from Polly Feb 23. I was just wild with delight.

April 12 Sat. The same kind of a Sat. as usual only I had to go downtown and get Billo some shoes ($2.90) and stockings for all three (50 cts a pair).

April 13 Sunday. Mrs. Haas came. I went to answer some questions about Turkey for Mrs. Lydia Lord Davis. Russell ate supper with us, Arthur desert only. The S.S. Easter entertainment was given. Edward was Roman Guard, George spirit of brotherhood, the three little ones sang.

April 14 Mon. Wash day. I have been trying to write some letters but I do not get anywhere with them. Alfred and Frances started in kindergarten today after several months of absence, but Alfred did not feel well and went to sleep after he came home. He is extra sweet when he is sick.

April 15 Tues. Mrs. Wright came in the morning and I had a skirt that needed a apron to cover it. I said I was going to make a new skirt so she thought of a skirt she had afterwards brought two, one heavy and one light. In the afternoon took Frances to the dentist and did a few errands. In the evening Parent-Teachers meeting.

April 16 Wed. Rainy cold, disagreeable. I tried to do some extra cleaning up and got awfully tired. Mrs. Burnett ran in for a few minutes and I was almost too tired to talk with her. Mrs. Greene & Mrs. Wright came for a minute in the evening.

April 17 Thurs. I was invited to Mrs. Andrews' with Mrs. Bunker, Mrs. McCord, Mrs. Huntley & her aunt, Mrs. Gammon, Mrs. Fitch and Mrs. Channon. I went over to see Mrs. Johnston a few minutes in the evening.

April 18 Fri. A pleasant day, no rain. I made a none-such mince pie, which was pretty good. Today Alfred rushed into the house for something while I was washing in the cellar. As he ran out he called, "I love you, mama, but I haven't time to love you now." I walked down town with Mrs. Greene.

April 19 Sat. Pleasant & warm. Frances has a very bad cold. Edward earned a dollar working for Mrs. Morrison this morning, three hours. George worked for me nearly all day, cleaning up the yard, beating rugs, mending screens and he got no pay. The three boys went to see Marguerite Clark in "Seven Swans."

April 20 Sunday. Easter, but rather wet. Good for me because I have no spring coat. The Easter Concert at the First Church was splendid. Miss Bradt sang the solo parts. She looks like Mr. Giles, sings beautifully. The children went to the Van der Pyl's to eat fudge, to play.

April 21 Mon. A beautiful day. While I was washing at Miss Sinclair's Billo came home from school with an earache. I had to drop the washing and stay with him until it got better. Mrs. Greene & I called on Mrs. Caldwell. Then I went to buy some presents for Frances. I met Miss Zearing. She stopped to gossip & among other things said that Mrs. Hutchins calls her husband, "Sun-kissed boy."

Ernest C. Partridge

[April 12]

April 13 Sunday. Left Ooloo Kishla at 7 with 2 Fords, 10 trucks. Mrs Sewny, Mary H, Dr. Washburn and Linn, Sutherland, Custer, Curt Irwin & Browning. One truck wrecked on the road.

[J.C. Linn, Jr. published an article about M.L. Graffam, Saw Armenians Suffer and Die, The Evening Post Magazine, New York, Saturday, July 12, 1919.]

April 14 A hard day. Night at empty khan on road.

April 15 Fords went ahead and reached Talas about 4PM. I was sick on road with malaria.

April 16 Spend a day in Talas waiting for truck which came in about 3PM.

April 17 Two Fords started from Talas about 8:20 & reached Sivas at 5PM. I drove half the way. Met by Polly & a crowd beyond bridge,Vali etc. at Gas Khan.

April 18 Trucks came in PM and we all went to a dinner in Semm[?] School by City authorities. Vali present.

April 19 Took Curt and Linn to Fabrica and had a busy day with callers.

[April 20]

April 21 Sunday. First Sunday in Sivas. Started a service in G.S. Obliged to move to yard 500 people present. Greek orphans sang 8 pieces and made a prayer.

April 22 Tues. Pleasant. Frances's birthday, six years old. She received a doll that could open & shut its eyes, a Bubble book containing three records, painting books, paints, candy, a hair ribbon, two hand kerchiefs, a flat iron. We had ice cream & cake. Mary Burnett, Russell Van der Pyl, Carroll Shaw & Betty Johnston came. We all went to the movies Mary Pickford in the Little Princess.

April 23 Wed. Nothing special happened. Mrs. Wright called up "just to let me know she was thinking of me," she said. It rained in the afternoon. I got permission to keep the car in Miss Peterson's driveway.

April 24 Thurs. Very cold. Two letters from Mr. P. one to me & one to George. He was in Afion Kara Hissai on his way back from Konia to Con[stantinople] to get some more workers & to wait for the guard. He got Mary Hubbard away from Dr. Washburn who was taking her to Adana.

April 25 Fri. Very cold, wintry. A letter came from Miss Babson announcing the receipt of a cablegram from Mr. Peet, saying "Partridge & Washburn reached Sivas, Graffam well. Inform Oberlin." A whippet tank performed for the benefit of the victory loan. We all went but Alfred was afraid of the gun and very cold besides. We had three tickets given us to the vaudeville for the firemen. Edward, Geroge & I went. The play "A case of suspension" was funny.

April 26 Sat. A typical Saturday or a little more so from 7 A.M. till 11:45P.M. I had to go down town to buy something for Edward's birthday and so had to make up the time after bedtime.

April 27 Sunday. Warmer. Anti-saloon League speaker. Edward's 17th birthday. He had B.V.D.'s, silk stockings, razor, chocolates, gum, peanuts from Alfred, clove candy, cookies from Lawrence. We had a small chicken.

April 28 Mon. Rainy. Notice from school that Billo has been exposed to mumps. Letter and $100 for Polly from Sivas Armenians of California & Chicago. Telegram from Garbis that he is coming Thursday. Frances played with Mary all the afternoon and Everet played here. He is very rough. Box of locum from Samuel.

April 29 Tues. Letter from Mr. P. from Constantinople, very interesting. He had seen Levon, Khachadoor, Zabel, Vartenan, Hymymak, Tourfuerda. Garbis came for a two hour visit this evening. I was very glad to see him, but it was short.

April 30 Wed. Showery but Mrs. Haas and her two youngest and Frances, Alfred and I, also Albert Heydenburg went to Lorain to see about getting the Day's cottage for the Haas family for the summer. We enjoyed it but I was car sick after I got home. We saw two airplanes in motion, one Lieutenant Liff's that was wrecked.

May 1 Thurs. Showery again. Of course after yesterday I did not go out anywhere, because I had work to do. Edward went with Mr. Bohn to Sec. Jones to enter his name for College next year. He drove the "bus" around the block. Mrs. Haas called for a few min. to show me a snap shot of her husband. Alfred, Frances & Billo made May baskets for me. Alfred also hung one for Everet and Billo for Alfred & Frances. George & Billo went to see Marguerite Clark in "Prunella." Mr. & Mrs. Metcalf returned from New York with Norman's wife who has come from England.

Frances's report 7th & 8 th month 1A. Reading & Lit. –A B+ Penmanship B+ B+ Arith. B+ B+ Music B B Drawing B B

Ernest C. Partridge

[April 22]

April 23 Spent half a day going over Fabrica farm. In PM drove out to meet Sutherland who did not come.

April 24 Dr Marvin has returned to Derindge presumably to bring unit to Sivas. Sutherland waiting in Talas.

April 25 Spent some time visiting buildings that we might need for our work.

April 26 Visited Turkish industries with Hairi Bey and began plans to take over Belorian big house and Nvarts factory for 100 looms.

April 27 Sunday. A rather quiet day. Afternoon service at GS Hall; badly crowded. Shall go to Chapel hereafter.

April 28 Started digging to bring water to city compound. Glazier begins work on our houses.

[April 29]

April 30 Drove out to farm in Mercedes and afterward accepted Antaram's resignation and she & her sister left in evening. Put Mary H in charge.

May 1 Went to college and shook up orphans. White washer began on our house; glazier working on GO [Girls Orphanage] new bdg.

Alfred 2nd & 3rd month 1B. R & L B+ B+ Music C+ B Drawing C+ C+
Billo 7 th & 8th month Arith C B Language C A Spelling A A

May 2 Fri. Pleasant. I went down town to get something for Sarah's birthday. I found a pretty collar and a birthday card. Edward & Prof. Wright carried out their ashes & cinders and made a walk.

May 3 Sat. Showery. Very busy but I got most of my jobs done and went to the movies with the boys. We saw Fatty Arbuckle and "Marriages are Made," a play illustrating German spy system. A letter from Mrs. Clark saying that the Dr. arrived Apr. 26. George played ball at Wellington O 8 W 10.

May 4 Sunday. A real spring day, with torrents of rain for a few minutes. Prof. Foster preached on "Immortality." It was very good indeed but long. Armen went to Wellington to speak. A Jarf and Miss Ullam and Mr. Richards were to speak. Edward ate supper at Lawrence's.

May 5 Mon. George was invited to the Bosworth's to supper, together with the other men on the base ball team of the eighth grade who went to Wellington. They had a good time, sat on the floor to eat potato salad, sandwiches, cocoa, ice-cream & cake. Uncle Rufus sent $100.

May 6 Tues. I worked until supper time and then called after supper on Mrs. Andrews, to make a party call and pay my missionary subscription. I had a sudden idea today that it would be good for Edward to study stenography and typewriting this summer.

May 7 Wed. I cleaned one corner of the kitchen, also cleaned off the pantry shelf and did some sewing for myself. Alfred is so frightened at night that he can hardly sleep, even when he is sleeping with me.

Ernest C. Partridge

May 2 Signed contract for rent of Arm. Hospital Bdgs for 120 notes to be used for Girls Orphanage.

May 3 6 Americans and 3 men went to farm for picnic. Inspected all the work. Our house whitewash well along.

May 4 Sunday. First service in Chapel. About 500 present 32 men, same no [number] women, rest orphans. Visited Greek orphanage at Bostangolu.

May 5 Browning, Sutherland & Warden with 8 trunks came at noon with supplies. Unloaded all before night.

May 6 Sutherland is to stay here for present. Browning gets 3 trucks from Govt and will take passengers down for pay.

May 7 Truck train started off at 8AM.

May 8 Telegram from Barton party on way from Harpoot.

May 9 Went out to meet people in PM but did not come.

May 10 Went out about 10AM and stayed till dark in Mercedes in rain. Roads bad and did not come.

May 11 Sunday. Preached on God as Father. Sarkis Julesarian died. Some went out on road. Party came about 3PM. Dr Barton, Dr Dodd, Bartlett of SSs & Farnsworth.

May 8 Thurs. Having a call from Mrs. Burnett and Miss Marion Metcalf and a long conversation with Mrs. Bowen about Hampartsoom's working on the Lake. I finished washing at quarter of six and went to a Chop Suey supper with Mrs. Greene at six. Then she and I called at the Martin's.

May 9 Fri. Rain, rain, rain. William Ohly spent the afternoon and part of the evening with us. His mother was cleaning house. Alfred and Frances brought home "clean-up" books that they had made in Kinder 9. Edward's S.S. class was entertained by a girl's class today. They had surpassed in attendance and contribution.

May 10 Sat. Again rain. A rainy Saturday with five children in a bungalow is fierce but it did not rain every minute. I went to see Miss Kirkpatrick about making a dress for me. In the evening Mrs. Andrews and I went to see Mr. Henderson about summer school in business college.

May 11 Sunday. Cloudy. Mother's day, Polly's birthday, Communion Sunday. The children gave me a box of correspondence cards and a geranium, very pretty pink. George went to the woods to get flowers for the children to wear. We ate a birthday cake for Polly. Lawrence ate with us. Mrs. Haas called.

May 12 Mon. We all, seven of us, went to see Charlie Chaplin in Shoulder Arms. It was certainly very amusing. I do not wonder that the children like to see him. The play with him was "Opportunity," not so bad. A letter from Mr. P. in Derinje. Told of the escape of several, Mesrob's sister, Toumadjians.

May 13 Tues. A perfect day as regards weather. Armen went to the symphony orchestra concert but the rest of us did not, nor to the May Festival concerts. This was my ironing day. I finished at 5:45. Mrs. Wirkler brought over some very pretty dresses that Sarah had outgrown. Frances was delighted.

May 14 Wed. Mrs. Haas started for North Carolina and the Martins & I with two little ones went to the car to see her off. Armen went to the Baldwin May Day party with Lois Cummings.

May 15 Thurs. Mrs. Worcester came & stayed an hour in the morning, just at ordering time, so I had to have codfish gravy & potatoes, but I did have material for custard pies. Mrs. Greene called. I went over to the Wright's in the evening to read a letter from Mr. P.

May 16 Friday. Edward went to the movies and then to Dick Bosworth's wireless shack to play cards and eat together with Seebury Ford, Hermann, Sidney Gulick, and Frances Hutchins. Edward came home at half past ten or so, but some of them stayed until one or two.

May 17 Sat. George & Billo went to the movies, The Fox Kiddies in "Tell it to the Marines." They liked it so much they stayed through twice. About twelve at night Samuel came. He telephoned from Norwalk but the telephone girl said there was no car, so we went to bed & then he came.

May 18 Sunday. Seminary baccalaureate. Samuel, Hampartsoom & I went in the evening. They went with Edward to Y.M.C.A. because they were going to discuss dancing & smoking. It seems that they are going to remove the ban.

Ernest C. Partridge

May 12 Spent the day showing Dr Barton our work and talking over plans.

May 13 Dr Barton & Dodd went to Talas for one day's stop.

May 14 Polly, Linn, & Sutherland left for Ooloo Kishla in Mercedes. Moved Bindes Fabrica to very old GO Building.

May 15 Called on Kadi about several matters. Got money from Bank. Went to Idadie School to get our furniture & school desks. Barton party came in 8:30PM.

May 16 Barton party left in 2 Fords for Marsovan in the rain.

May 17 Called on Kadi about unrest in city over Smyrna incident. Repairs & readjustment going very well now. City water ran today in compound.

May 18 Sunday. Preached in morning to large audience on Sin. Worked most of PM sorting books in our attic.

May 19 Mrs Sewny opened the Mohajir Khan in Seraiderian house.

May 20 Armenian Hospital property turned over to us by military and began whitewashing work.

May 21 Urasden[?] came in with eight trucks bringing water pipe, milk and flour. Roads very muddy.

May 22 Took in new boys in the ambar[?] house for present. City restless over Smyrna incident.

May 19 Mon. Samuel went back to Detroit in the afternoon. Armen had a letter from her brother Armenag from New York, saying that he was coming here.

May 20 Tues. Showery but did not actually rain. I washed & did not get the clothes out until about three. A letter from Ernest from Derinje, April 7. He says Mrs. Sewny was in Konia. He will be so glad to have her, so will we all.

May 21 Wed. Seminary Commencement. When Armen came home from the exercises she announced that Mr. P. was given a degree. I had no word of it at all, Master of Divinity. [ECP had been working on his S.T.M. degree while traveling.]

May 22 Thurs. The second grade pupils and teachers cam home with Billo to see the mourning dove's nest in our tree. Mrs. Greene walked down town with me but we hurried home on account of a shower, which struck the town just as we arrived at her house.

May 23 Fri. I took Armen's brother over to Mrs. Morrison's to work. In the P.M. I took Alfred & Frances to Billy's school because they are members of the 2nd Grade Audubon Society. I called on Mrs. Wright a few minutes and talked dresses.

May 24 Sat. Rainy. Saturday with all it carries with it. Frances nearly sick with a cold. The notable event was that Edward took Ruth Terborgh to the movies, "I'll say so," hero George Walsh. It was the first time Edward took a girl anywhere. Mrs. Wright presented me with the material for a gray wool & silk crepe dress, perfectly beautiful, too good for me.

May 25 Memorial Sunday. Weather beautiful. Armen and her brother and Edward went to church in the morning, then they all went to walk in the afternoon. I slept about three hours. Hampartsoom & I went to memorial service in the eve. Mr. McAlpine spoke to the G.A.R.

May 26 Mon. Pleasant. A letter from Polly written March 31st. She thinks that she'd better not come home until I can go out. I wonder when that will be. Edward worked for Miss Brownback today. Boys of his size are in quite demand.

May 27 Tues. Mrs. Payne cleaned the bathroom today in seven hours at 30 cts an hour. It is very clean. Mrs. Burnett and I went to the dressmaker's and decided on a style for my dress. In the evening Mrs. Metcalf and I called on a lady from Baltimore who knows the Kbachadorians.

May 28 Wed. Another pleasant day, the fourth without rain. Mrs. Payne cleaned the pantry in six hours and Hampartsoom and Armen & I washed the tin dishes to be put back. Mr. & Mrs. Martin called for a few minutes. They are looking for a house for next year.

Ernest C. Partridge

[May 23–24]

May 25 A wire from Mr Peet which I understand to mean that British soldiers are on way from Samsoun. Truck train left today.

May 26 Govt has word the British troops left Samsoun for Sivas.

May 27 Repairing, cleaning etc. at a great rate in Arm[enian] Hospital. First kiln of lime burned at Fabrica.

May 28 Browning came in in PM in Mercedes with Dr Smith. Misses Spalding and Flynn to stay here.

May 29 Spent day taking new people over plans etc.

May 30 Browning started at 9 & broke a spring just outside the city.

May 31 Broke both bones of right arm above wrist cranking Ford. Went to bed for 20 hours.

June 1 Sunday. HK preached.

[June 2–4]

May 29 Thurs. I went to the movies all alone because it was for the benefit of the High School, but the play was no good. It was "Mile a Minute Kendall." Jack Pickford was the hero and Louise Huff the heroine.

May 30 Fri. Memorial Day. We were late for the parade but we went to the chapel and stayed through the singing by the public schools. Armenag left for Detroit on the noon train. Hampartsoom ate dinner with us. We had cabbage dolmas. Alfred fell from the round towerlike place at the waterworks. Hurt is ear and elbow.

May 31 Sat. Anniversary of Mamma's death. Saturday and hot and a children's day rehearsal at 3 o'clock where the kids have to go clean. Then Armen had a picnic supper with a crowd of girls. George and Billo had a picnic super. Edward left his supper to play tennis & Miss Davis called just as I was beginning, so the little ones & I did not finish. Miss Cummings brought us some ice-cream that they had left over.

June 1 Sunday. Children's Day. The three little ones sang in the Primary department. Billy enters the highest class now. In the evening we went to hear Ellis Van der Pyl and Hans Anderegg speak. I took all the children & we six occupied one seat.

June 2 Mon. Hot. Ellis & Doris Van der Pyl came over. Miss Lois Cummings also came over and sat on the porch until the mosquitoes nearly ate us up. I had a tremendous washing. First letter from Sivas from Ernest Apr. 18.

June 3 Tues. Am ironing the same size as the washing. I went over to the Wright's a little while to read Ernest's letter. Mrs. Caldwell called. The boys' went out to the shack to take a swim.

June 4 Wed. Hot. Mr. & Mrs. Martin came over after prayer meeting to hear Ernest's letter.

June 5 Thurs. Washing again, finished about four. Went to try on my dress at five. Frances broke her new doll, dropped it on the sidewalk. I took Alfred & Frances down town to get Alfred's hair cut. Shops were closed, saw the wall of the town hall fall, gave them some ice-cream.

June 6 Fri. Cooler. Edward's class day. Edward and Natalie Stapleton had a bartering scene in Armenian. Edward sold carpets. They prophesied that Edward was to be a pirate. Then Edward was in a group showing how the Juniors do. We selected a suit for him, dark green.

June 7 Sat. Senior play. Character, Hermann, Seebury Ford, Lawrence Knowlton, John Hill, Martha Haskell, Louise Harlow, Dorothy Beard, Rex Huntley. Edward was costume manager but did not have much to do. Billo is captain & pitcher of the base ball team of Grade 2A. They played the B's & beat them 8 to 0. Billo says that he tried to hit the bat.

Ernest C. Partridge

June 5 Delco light started.

[June 6–7]

June 8 Sunday. I preached.

June 9 Girls Orphanage moved from College building to Armenian hospital plant.

[June 10–14]

June 15 Sunday. Preached in Chapel.

[June 16–August 2]

June 8 Sunday. Maurice Kinnear shot & killed himself last night because Dorothy Landis would not marry him. A terrible thing. The last Sunday evening service. Mr. Van der Pyl spoke on "If I were young today." They sang the Sanctus & Benedictus.

June 9 Mon. Maurice Kinnear was buried from the Metcalf's today and I had to get the children away so we went to the library. I washed but did not put the clothes out on account of the funeral.

June 10 Tues. Hot. Edward shaved his upper lip, first time, then donned his new green $40 suit and went to a class party at Miss Payne's. A postal from Nishan Eff. saying that he was about to start for Sivas. Mrs. Burnett & I went to try on my new dress. I went down town to pay bills.

June 11 Wed. Hot. Trying on dress, ironing, making shortcake for the eighth grade. Van der Pyl reception where Edward and Natalie gave their stunt again, bartering scene. Saw D. Bliss of Beyrout, also Mrs. Crafts.

June 12 Thurs. Word that Polly is on the way home. Edward's Commencement Day. Excersices at 8 P.M., address by Prof. Root on "By-products of Education." Ruth Terborgh, Edward and Gladys Berry were above 90 for their whole course, Edward 91. Arthur & Sydney Gulick each won a prize in English.

June 13 Fri. Very hot. Heaps of work to do, and nothing finished. George was wanted by two women for work before he was up. Everyone is cleaning up for commencement.

June 14 Sat. Edward & Belle Blanchard came to be here through commencement. Edward and Armen went to the Commencement play, "Prunella," not together.

June 15 Baccalaureate Sunday. I went to the service with Edward & Billo. Prof. Bosworth preached. What he says is splendid but he does not have an impressive delivery so we have to just make ourselves listen. It was just too hot to stand two services.

June 16 Mon. I did not finish washing until 4:30 so did not go out to anything. Edward began working in the library. He is to work 7 ½ hours a day and get 25 cts an hour. He is called a page and puts books in their places, hunts up what is wanted in the stacks etc.

June 17 Tues. Illumination night. I had a ticket to the Alumni Peace Celebration but did not go because Armen was sick. I ironed until 5:45, then got supper, bathed the children & went to the parade. George put up the candles for lanterns for us & the neighbors.

June 18 Wed. Commencement. I went at 10 A.M. and returned from alumni dinner about 4:30 P.M. Then reunion concert in the evening. Helen graduated. Ernest's degree was read. Wayne Wheeler was given an LLD. There were six 95ers, Mr. & Mrs. Adams, Mr. & Mrs. Newcomb, Mr. Bowers & I.

June 19 Thurs. Still hot. Edward and Billo went home and Miss Ward came to supper. Edward took Isabel to the picture show, Stella Mavis. George & Armen also went. Miss Sinclair's electric washer was brought over to our house for the summer.

June 20 Fri. A little cooler. I was delayed with the washing and did not finish until 4:30. Nazeli came. A letter from Polly written May 7.

June 21 Sat. Edward was invited to supper with Hermann, Martha Haskell & Isabel Martin by Grandma Giles. Four letters from Mr. P. He thinks we can come out this fall.

June 22 Sunday. Much cooler. I went to church in the morning but no more. In the afternoon & evening I read the letters from Sivas three times, to the Wrights, Martins & Metcalfs.

June 23 Mon. Still cool but growing warmer. I did not do much, a little housework, a little airing clothes, doughnuts etc. I took a nap in the afternoon & felt sick after that. Mrs. Caldwell came in the evening.

June 24 Tues. Most exciting letters from Mr. P. He persuades me to let Edward go out and help him for a year, using almost the same arguments that I used when I wrote to him. He seems to think that we can come in the fall at the latest. Our boiler sprang a leak.

June 25 Wed. A rainy day at last. Yesterday Edward went out to Ruggles to Mrs. Giles' cottage. Hermann started with him but came back for his violin. Then he disappeared while his mother was away. While George & I were searching for his bicycle down town Hermann appeared before us. June 26 Thurs. A letter from Mr. Case enclosing a copy of a letter from Polly to Miss Lamson, asking that they send us out quickly. Nazeli picked the currants & we started some jelly. I fell from a chair in which I was standing and hurt my side & scraped my shin.

June 27 Fri. Cool. I washed in spite of Mrs. Wright's protest on account of my sore arm. In the evening I went to the conservatory concert given for the summer school people. Mrs. William's play Kreister's Fantasie venoral or something like that which we have on the phonograph.

[June 28]

June 29 Sunday. Mr. Van der Pyl's last Sunday until September, communion Sunday. Mr. Woodruff of Bulgaria spoke in the evening. He was good but slow & so long and he had too many ideas on Wilson and politics, I thought.

June 30 Mon. Letters from Mr. P. in which he says there is some unrest but he hopes it will settle down all right. Polly was in Constantinople. The things that he is attending to just makes your head swim. I wish I were there to help. Washed our clothes & Mrs. Elmer's.

July 1 Tues. Another letter from Mr. P. dated before the other saying that he hopes we will get started by July 1st. He thinks Dr. Barton telegraphed about the first of June but the Board received nothing about us.

July 2 Wed. Missionary meeting. Mrs. Fenn, Mrs. Clark and Miss Hinman read about women writers in Turkey, Japan & India. In the evening I actually sat out in the park & read a story.

July 3 Thurs. washed, washed floors, went down town, called on Mrs. Caldwell a few minutes. Mrs. Wright brought over and presented to me an $85 coat, black with kind of an old gold silk lining.

July 4 Fri. Edward went to Cleveland with Hermann, found that the theater car did not come to Oberlin. We had a yard full of people firing off fireworks. Ellis helped as he always does. The children were happy and tired.

July 5 Sat. We tried to go to the movies but after waiting an hour or so for the electricity we got discouraged and came home. It came on afterwards.

July 6 Sunday. It rained and turned cooler to our great relief. I went to church to hear the summer pastor, Mr. Sanderson of Sandusky. A letter from Polly containing a check of $105 to help us out. Mrs. Caldwell called & Doris Van der Pyl.

July 7 Mon. Washing, etc.

July 8 Tues. I took the children to the movies. Billie Burke in The Pursuit of Polly. Frances had a headache caused by looking at the pictures, I think. She and I came home early.

July 9 Wed. Called on Mrs. Elmer and found a lovely piece of silk poplin at the Oriental Bazaar, a lovely blue, at $1 a yard. I called on Mrs. Johnston a few minutes and also on Mrs. Caldwell.

July 10 Thurs. Washing again. So many showers in the night, and then so many today. It thundered, lightened, hailed and poured. About ten or twelve, [the] children put on bathing suits and went down to the corner and played in the water which was knee deep.

July 11 Fri. Nazeli helped with the ironing but still we did not finish until evening. Edward and I and Mrs. Caldwell went to hear Prof. Martin lecture on Constantinople. It was very interesting and instructive.

July 12 Sat. Papa's birthday. He is 74, he says. I thought he was born in '46. [Actually born in '48, so he's 71!] Edward, George & Nazeli went to the movies and saw Ali Baba and the Forty Thieves, played by children. Verne Johnston asked me to take an auto ride with them, but I could not leave the little ones.

July 13 Sunday. I let the children decide about S.S. & church this vacation. This time the three little ones wanted to go to church so Nazeli and I both went. The boys stayed in bed. In the evening Edward and I went to hear Dr. Weddell's funeral sermon on the death of John Barleycorn.

July 14 Mon. Our 21st anniversary. I celebrated only by having an ice-cream cone with Mrs. Hall and Billo. I bought some gingham for a dress for Frances, 3 yds at 35 cts a yard. It rained very hard & the children put on their bathing suits to play in the street.

July 15 Tues. A letter from Polly from Constantinople with an order for $100 to help us out. I read it to the Wrights.

July 16 Wed. Letter from Sivas. Mr. P. broke his wrist so Mary Hubbard wrote for him. I wrote to the Board to engage passage for August 19 if possible.

July 17 Thurs. A telegram from Dr. MacCallum saying that they would send Edward to Sivas, so he is settled. I went down town to get a few things to sew on.

July 18 Fri. Ironing. Alfred weighed 41 ½ lbs. Frances weighed 47 ½ lbs. I weighed 140.

July 19 Sat. We went to the movies in the evening, Tan Mix in "Hell-roarin reform." The best was his beautiful trained horse. He slept beside him, pulled the blanket off, went into a saloon & kicked everything over, etc.

July 20 Sunday. Heard Mr. Sanderson on "Clouds after Rain." He cited Polly as an example of one who does things with no hope of reward.

July 21 Mon. Bobbie's birthday, also James Moore's. Letters from Mr. P. Also a letter from the Board, Mr. Bell, saying that the cabinet decided to advise the Clarks & Partridges not to go at present. The Raymonds called.

July 22 Tues. Alfred's 5th birthday. He had little things given him all through the day. Everet, Helen & Herbert Caldwell, Mrs. Cummings, Carroll, Nazeli & all our family. I made a cake. We all went to the movies, "Hitting the Trail Holiday," and afterwards I took the little ones to have an ice-cream cone.

July 23 Wed. A telegram from the Board saying: "Serious uncertainties Asia Minor. Committee postpones sailing with family."

July 24 Thurs. A letter confirming the telegram saying that there were reports of trouble in Marsovan and Dr. Washburn felt it was not wise for families to go to Sivas at present but Mr. Bell hopes we may go sometime this fall.

July 25 Fri. Letters from Miss Rice & Miss Gage. Miss K. will be ready to sail with me August 19. She has changed her mind now, I suppose. I reckoned up my accounts and found that I am $25 behind and six days to go.

July 26 Sat. A hundred dollars from Uncle Rufus just in time to help out my bank account. Mrs. Haskell called, told me of the trials of her son in not being allowed to go back immediately.

July 27 Sunday. Very hot. Alfred & Frances went to Sunday School, Nazeli to church, & I in the evening. Mr. James spoke in the evening on "Russia finding her way out."

July 28 Mon. Even hotter. A strange day for me. All except Edward and me went for a picnic, both dinner & supper, so Edward and I ate alone and I was here alone the rest of the time. No one called nor even called me on the telephone. Mrs. Metcalf came for just a minute.

July 29 Tues. I went to Elyria to see if I could find a hat for Frances and one for me but did not. I did not find a skirt either.

Ernest C. Partridge

August 3 Sunday. A very miserable day indigestion & no sleep until 5AM.

August 4 Dr Smith & I with Weinberg driving, went to Cesarea for a vacation trip to Constan[tinople].

August 5 Spent the day in Talas resting and visiting with people.

August 6 Weinberg sick so we took Custer in with those down to Ooloo Kishla.

August 7 Took morning train to Konia where Custer met his wife & a party on way to C & Sivas.

July 30 Wed. Warmer. A mixed up day. I went to the Administration building to see Mr. Bohn & Mr. Wirkler about Hampartsoom. I bought a hat, marked down from $10 to $3. The children went for a picnic for supper, Edward played tennis, so Mrs. Caldwell ate supper with me. Dr. Haas came to town.

July 31 Thurs. I bought a hat for Frances, brown.

August 1 Fri. Lecture by Mr. MacLennan in "John Bell," very good indeed. A letter from Howard Wells asking for pictures of Alexandropol. Letter from Garabis saying that he is coming to Oberlin for a visit. Mr. Moore came over to tell me that they are going to move to Buffalo.

August 2 Sat. Mrs. Caldwell & I went down town and did some errands. In the evening I sewed on buttons, mended stockings etc.

August 3 Sunday. Nazeli & the two little ones & I went to church. Mr. Sanderson preached a very good sermon on "The present day heresy." In the afternoon Mr. Nigosian from Akron came & stayed over night. Mr. Elmer, Mr. James and his mother called. I took him to see Prof. Miller. Word came that Ed is to sail Sept. 26.

August 4 Mon. In spite of rainy weather I washed & then the sun came out. Mrs. Caldwell & I went to call on Dr. & Mrs. Haas. Dr. H. tells such dreadful stories of the relief workers in Adana. It makes you sick to think of it.

August 5 Tues. Alfred was sick, had fever all day. It thundered & lightened all night and nearly all day. The lights were off most of the time. I ironed until the electricity went off. Mrs. Caldwell came over. Edward went to Miss Chase's to play cards.

August 6 Wed. A letter from Mr. P. by way of Mrs. Greene. He thinks I am on the way to Turkey and I wish I were. Dr. Haas says that if it were his case he would go. I think I will write to the Board and see if they will let me go.

August 7 Thurs. Samuel came. He is about to start for Wyoming to look up the Government claim lands for himself and some others. I wrote to the Board asking if I might go at my own risk. I rec'd a letter from Mr. Bell saying they had telegraphed to Turkey to ask if we are necessary in Sivas.

August 8 Fri. Samuel went and Hampartsoom came.

August 9 Sat. Hampartsoom and I looked up work for him for next year to earn his board. Edward was invited to Miss Helyer's with Mildred Layman and several other couples. They played cards and other games.

August 10 Sunday. Cool & lovely. Hampartsoom, Edward & I went to church. Mr. Sanderson preached a fine sermon on "We are indispensable." I like him better the more I hear him. Sarkis Andouian came and he & H went. Mrs. Caldwell and Herbert & my family went to the waterworks.

August 11 Mon. Washing. Edward, George, Billo, and Nazeli went to the picture show, Douglas Fairbanks as Mr. Fix It. Frances had queer spasmodic pains in her throat and I took her to the Doctor. He swabbed it out but could find no real trouble.

August 12 Tues. I took Frances to the same picture show but she did not like it very well. Alfred does not like it anyway so George took him down town and gave him an ice-cream cone.

August 13 Wed. I finished the ironing, made pies, wrote six letters & darned stockings, besides general house work. A letter from Mr. Raymond saying that they hoped to give me teaching work in Berea if I do not go to Turkey.

August 14 Thurs. Washing again. George & Billo went to the shack with "Woody" just long enough for a good swim. I went down town and bought some cloth for night dresses, 6 yds at 40 cts a yard, cotton crepe de chine. Nazeli & I cut them out. Edward and Hermann played tennis.

August 15 Fri. I expected Yeranoohi but she did not come.

August 16 Sat. Not only Yeranoohi came but also Mrs. Clark. I was surprised to see the latter. She was persuaded, I think, to take both James & Stephen back to Turkey.

August 17 Sunday. Mrs. Clark, Yeranoohi, Edward & I went to church.

August 18 Mon. Washing. Went down to Tank Home and Mrs. Elmer's with Mrs. Clark.

Ernest C. Partridge

August 8 Dr Smith and I are having a comfortable ride in a boxcar up the Haider Pasha.

August 9 Reached C about 6PM. Two ACRNE ladies joined us at Derindge. Went to Bible House Annex.

August 10 Sunday. Lunch at Astoria. Called on Pres King at Girls College. Dinner at Locatlian's.

August 11 I have been rusticated [domiciled] out at Robert College.

[August 12]

August 13 Polly, Dr Smith, Dr Hekimian and a new nurse started for Sivas this morning. Poor me. They would not let me go with them.

August 14 Began to play tennis with Misses Jillson and Putney.

August 15 Received several calls. Tea at Miss Mannings; tennis. A call from two of Pres King's staff.

August 16 Went to city and did various errands at BH. Called on Major Lane, lunch with Montgomery & Moore of King Commission at Pera Palace.

August 17 Sunday. Church Robert College. Vickrey at dinner. PM to headquarters for talk by V and tea.

[August 18–19]

August 20 Part of day in city visiting & writing. Tea at Prof Anderson's. Tennis with Miss Jillson & Prof Morgan.

[August 21]

August 19 Tues. Mrs. Clark went at 11:56 and Yeranoohi at 12:25. I went to Cleveland with her to put her on the train. We enjoyed her visit very much. It is a long time since I had seen her. Mr. Caldwell arrived.

August 20 Wed. Letters from Mr. P. He has been rather used up. They were written July 6 & July 13. He thinks we should come out there immediately.

August 21 Thurs. Washed in the afternoon because Mrs. Caldwell used the washer in the morning. A letter from Mr. Bell saying that the Com. would not consent to me going to Turkey until they get an answer to their cable.

[August 22]

August 23 Sat. Went to the picture show, Catherine & Jane Lee, very good.

August 24 Sunday. I went in the morning alone. Mr. Sanderson preached on the "Keys of the Kingdom." In the evening Verne Johnston took Edward, Alfred, Frances & me to North Amherst for a ride.

August 25 Mon. Picture show for the benefit of the Boys' Work Com., Jack Pickford as Tom Sawyer, and Fatty Arbuckle.

August 26 Tues. Went to Cleveland with the Johnstons but did not find the suit that I wanted.

August 27 Wed. Worked all day but did not accomplish very much. Mr. & Mrs. Haskell & Eldora called. Letter from the Board saying that they had received no answer from Turkey but would telegraph again.

August 28 Thurs. Washed in the morning and then went out in the afternoon to collect dues for the W.C.T.U. Called on Mrs. Ohly, Mrs. Bohn, Mrs. Rice and Mrs. Cargill.

August 29 Fri. George & I went to Cleveland and I bought a $90 suit for myself which had been marked down to $16.50. It is a beautiful suit but has to be fixed a little. I bought a few things for the children. Geo. had a good time. We went to Keith's.

August 30 Sat. My suit is too small around the hips. Perhaps I will send it to Mrs. Sewny. I had to work hard all day to make up for being away on Friday, ironing, mending etc. I also went down town, bought Billo khaki trousers 1.00, 2 pairs of shoes 3.50 & 4, 2 sport waists @72 cts, stockings @ 55 cts.

August 31 Sunday. Heard Mr. Sanderson. Alfred & Frances went but wanted it to be through all the time. In the morning I said to Alfred, "Your papa would like to

Ernest C. Partridge

August 22 Spent forenoon in city doing errands and planning to return. Tea at Mrs Mannings. Tennis with Prof Morgan and two English Colonels.

August 23 Came down to city early. Arranged to go. Saw Dr Barton. Spent evening at Peet with them & Dr Barton. Tea at Gedik Pasha.

August 24 Sunday. Left Haider Pasha at 8:30 with Seting[?] off the Aleppo Courier. Reached Eski Shehir at 1AM.

August 25 Left Eski Shehir at 4:05 in a 1st-class coup reserved. Afion KH 1PM. Konia about 8. Most of Americans waiting for mail.

August 26 Left Konia at 5AM. OK[Ooloo Kishla] at noon. Found Newell and Duer. Starting for Sivas, I joined them. Night at Nigde.

August 27 On to Talas.

August 28 Reached Sivas about 7PM. Took party up to Cottages.

August 29 Found things in good shape and went to work.

[August 30–31]

September 1 First heard of gossip in circulation about me.

[September 2–20]

see you." He said, "Let's just bust through those old boarders," meaning the Board who do not give us permission to go.

September 1 Mon. Labor day, so I labored, washed floors, made pies & doughnuts etc. etc. Mrs. Wright called, also Doris, also Ned Whipple & his wife. Mrs. Wright gave me 2 ½ yds of beautiful cloth for a skirt, black with a little white stripe. Mrs. Caldwell & I called on the Martins.

September 2 Tues. Schools began. I took Frances to first grade and Billo to third, to Miss Brady and Miss Peck. They have new desks in the first grade and they are fine, adjustable in every way, drawer under the seat and a little rack beside it.

September 3 Wed. The Metcalfs came back. I saw them for a minute. Alfred is so lonely without the children. He asked if he could ride down to the school building in his cart, when I asked him what he was going to do he said, "Just look at the building. It housed his brother & sister."

September 4 Thurs. Mrs. Caldwell and I went to hear Edith Metcalf talk about her work in France and Palestine. A letter from Mr. Partridge written July 3rd. He hopes that we are on the way. I wish we were. George had sore throat & went to the doctor.

September 5 Fri. George did not go to school, but was getting better all day. He and Billo went to Bellevue with "Woody" for an auto ride. Edward and Hermann went to the Lake for a few days, using their cottage. Mrs. Giles to go tomorrow.

September 6 Sat. Mr. & Mrs. Raymond, Dorothy and Ruth arrived in town and spent the evening with us.

September 7 Sunday. Heard Mr. Van der Pyl once more on, "From the Mountain to the Plain." The Raymonds came again for a few minutes.

September 8 Mon. Washed at Miss Sinclair's again as the machine went home. Received permission from Mr. Case to get our passports on the chance that we may go. Had George's picture taken alone and the little ones with me.

Ernest C. Partridge

September 21 I preached in Mother church first time. A good audience.

[September 22–27]

September 9 Tues. George and I went to Elyria to start our passports. We watched the alligators, ate ice-cream soda, went through the ten cent store and other stores.

September 10 Wed. Mrs. Caldwell went to St. Paul to see her sister. She left Helen and Herbert with us. Alfred has acquired the ability to trill with his tongue. He has practiced for months but has only now become able to do it without spitting on every one.

September 11 Thurs. A letter from Mr. P. by way of Mrs. Martin, Mrs. Greene and Armen. He thinks I am on the way, hopes I am but in one way he will be reconciled if I am not because things have not settled down as he hoped they would.

September 12 Fri. Our family with the Caldwell children went to Ruggles Beach to occupy the Giles Cottage. We took the 6:10 car, had a crowded ride but not very uncomfortable.

September 13 Sat. They all bathed in the morning and afternoon. In the evening Hampartsoom came to spend Sunday with us.

September 14 Sunday. Not a bit like Sunday. George and Helen so forgot the day that they began to play cards. We started home at about six o'clock and reached Oberlin at 7:25.

September 15 Mon. Mrs. Caldwell came home so her children went back home. Armen also came.

September 16 Tues. Ironed some, but had to go down town with Edward to buy a trunk. Hampartsoom began eating at the Men's Commons.

September 17 Wed. Armen began eating at Gray Gables, and Hampartsoom moved his room to Mr. Stetson's house.

September 18 Thurs. Our most important question was settled. Mr. P. wrote that he and Dr. Peet and Dr. Barton agreed that we'd better stay in Oberlin. Edward is all upset. We cannot decide just what he'd better do. Billo went up in an airplane, the first of the family.

September 19 Fri. Mrs. Caldwell and I went to see Nazimova in Out of the Fog.

September 20 Sat. Miss Rice arrived. Her sailing is postponed until Oct. 14.

September 21 Sunday. I did not go to church because I did not feel able to. The little folks went to S.S. and Miss Rice went twice.

September 22 Mon. The washing machine did not work so I did not get through until about four.

September 23 Tues. Nazeli went back to Springfield on the 5:38 train. I went to Cleveland and got home on the 10:10. Her ticket cost $20.03 and sleeper three dollars. Edward began working at Tobin's to wait until Business College opens.

September 24 Wed. Frances read her first sentence, "all by herself," as she said. The sentence was, "Fly to the tall tree." George told her "fly," "tall" and "tree" and she read the rest. Ironed until after ten.

September 25 Thurs. Washed again. Gas very low, so that we cooked down cellar.

September 26 Fri. Frances reads and reads. Keeps her books with her all the time.

September 27 Sat. We had a weiner roast at the arboretum, the Caldwells and our family. We had also biscuits, pickles, doughnuts, coffee, cider & grapes. George was captain of the football team and was beaten 6 to 0 by Amherst team. Oberlin beat Heidelberg.

September 28 Sunday. My birthday. Mrs. Caldwell sent over a birthday cake which she sat up to bake while the gas was good. Miss Gage sent two pounds of lovely candy. Armen gave me handkerchiefs, also Miss Rice, George an apron, Billo a comb, Frances two little pins, a bird's nest and some wild flowers, Alfred a thimble.

September 29 Mon. Washing as usual. Miss Rice did the morning work but I got back in time to make some bulgure pilaf. Letter from E.C.P. dated Aug. 22. We went over to see Mrs. Wright.

September 30 Tues. Took all the children to see Lyman Hine's pictures. They enjoyed them and were very good. Miss Rice went to the Martin's for supper with the Caldwell's.

Ernest C. Partridge

September 28 I preached in Chapel. Bad [Badvilli] Krikore at Monastery.

[September 29–October 4]

October 5 Sunday. I preached in the Mother church. Also at an English service in evening at West House.

[October 6–10]

October 11 In company with Miss Dixon, Dr Smith, Brown, HK & Bailag went to Tocat in a Reo [auto]. I drove to top of Chamli Bel. Entertained at Vartouhi's house.

October 1 Wed. Miss Rice and I called on Mrs. MacLennon who was Miss R's S.S. teacher in Des Moines.

October 2 Thurs. Miss R. & I called on Mrs. Elmer at Tank Home. She was not well at all but is slowly improving.

October 3 Fri. Miss Rice and I went to see Mrs. Greene.

October 4 Sat. Miss Rice went to Detroit to visit the Clarks. The children were weighed at the station, Alfred 41 lbs, Frances 49, Billo 58. We roasted wieners again at the arboretum and stayed until nearly 5. I bought some stockings, ties & belt for Mr. P.

October 5 Sunday. I went to S.S. with the children and attended Miss Metcalf's class. Edward and I went in the evening. Mr. Van der Pyl spoke on the Power of Propaganda.

October 6 Mon. Miss Rice did not return from Detroit, although we went to meet her.

October 7 Tues. Miss Rice did come and we all except Ed went to the movies to see Douglas Fairbanks in The Modern Muscateer. We all enjoyed it very much. Luther Fowle called on me & Mr. & Mrs. Caldwell called on him at our house. Mrs. Bohn & her mother called.

October 8 Wed. I finished the ironing I know and did various other things.

October 9 Thurs. Letters from Garbis & Nishan Eff. this week, one saying that he was disappointed in finding a life partner and the other that he had found one.

October 10 Fri. Miss Rice and I went to a meeting of the Leaven Club at Mrs. Fullerton's. Mrs. Hanna read two sketches that she had written, one about "Our cousins-in-law twice removed." They were Maria & Sophia, and the other "Straight Roads through Ireland." Miss R. left in evening. I went to Elyria with her.

October 11 Sat. A rainy Saturday in a bungalow with three small children and a neighbor does not need to be described. It is one of the hardest days I ever spent. George & I went down town and got him some shoes for school $4.00.

October 12 Sunday. Went to Sunday School with the children. In the afternoon we went to walk out to the Krescent field, then over near the big tree where we found lots of hickory nuts. I intended to go in the evening but Alfred screamed so much that I did not go.

October 13 Mon. A notable event, I made creamed potatoes for supper, also French toast, and they ate everything up.

October 14 Tues. I cleaned the ice-chest and under it. It is so old that it is almost impossible to clean it. Bought another pair of shoes for George black, for $4.00. Mr. Cooley says that he could not buy them himself now for less than seven.

October 15 Wed. It was Herbert Caldwell's birthday and he got a new bicycle or rather a second hand one. The chil-

Ernest C. Partridge

October 12 Sunday. Visited Armenian orphanage and churches. Went to Chapel with Commission. Some calls 3–9. Drove to Torkel and back. Picnic supper on the road.

October 13 Returned to Sivas. A good trip. I drove half the way coming and going. Reached Sivas about 9PM.

[October 14–November 6]

dren were invited over there for a party. They had crackers, cocoa, pop-corn, ice-cream, cake and candy. Alfred definitely decided that he would never marry but would always live with his mother.

October 16 Thurs. We paired off and all went to church supper, Ed & Billo, Geo. & Alfred, Frances & I. They had tableaux of different nationalities. Frances posed as Slav and also as Armenian.

October 17 Fri. A letter from Mr. Bell announcing a cable from Sivas to the effect that we are wanted in Turkey, but the Prudential committee refuses to consider our going.

October 18 Sat. Dicran Eff. telephoned from Cleveland that he would come in the afternoon. We met the 4:10 car and then he came at 5:10. It was so good to see him. We visited every minute we could. Bryan spoke in the evening but we did not go.

October 19 Sunday. Dicran Eff. & I went to church and Armen did most of the work. We had pork chops for a treat for dinner. Dicran Eff. went at 3:25 to Cleveland. We called on Mrs. Elmer.

October 20 Mon. I was sick all day, in bed all the forenoon. Edward stayed at home and did all the work, just as well as though he had been trained from babyhood. George did the dishes at night. The children were fine.

October 21 Tues. I was better and worked all day, sitting down only long enough to eat. I took Alfred to the dentist who filled a tooth. It was the first time for him. He was very lovely, but he wanted to kiss me when there was an intermission. He is very sweet.

October 22 Wed. Washed in the afternoon. A telegram from Mr. Bell instigated by Mr. Bohn saying, "Please let your mind rest. Ernest well (Turkey telegram)." Nothing said about Edward.

October 23 Thurs. Mrs. Caldwell and I attended a meeting of the American College Alumnae Association at Miss Sinclair's. A letter from Dr. Barton says that the cable is "Partridge's coming desired." He does not understand why Mr. P. changed his mind.

October 24 Fri. A most discouraging day. I worked all day to catch up and make up for the two hours lost the day before.

October 25 Sat. I got too tired the day before and felt just numbed. The children had sore throat and fever in the night so we did not sleep very well but were all right in the morning and they played out of doors all day. I bought Frances 2 pr. of shoes for $7, a pair of rubbers 75 cts.

October 26 Sunday. I went to S.S. as though with the children but really George rode Frances, Billo rode Alfred & I walked alone. Alfred makes a dreadful fuss about going but prefers to go with me rather than to stay at home without me. Lawrence ate supper with us. Saw Mrs. Crawford at Mrs. Greene's.

October 27 Mon. A rainy day and wash day, really a blue Monday, but it ended finally.

October 28 Tues. I went to school with the children and stayed a while in the first grade to hear Frances read. Miss Brady said that she was doing very well and was "such a dear child." Billo is having a hard time with the tables.

October 29 Wed. I took Alfred to the dentist and he had his tooth filled. Billo had his hair cut. I took my bicycle to have the chain fixed.

October 30 Thurs. I had such a good time at Mr. Irving Metcalf's visiting with Mr. & Mrs. House and their daughter Ruth. I should like to grow old as they are, they are so lively and interesting and everything that is lovely. Ruth is lovely but is not old yet.

October 31 Fri. Hallowe'en. All wanted to have masks lanterns etc. and they all went out but some big boys frightened them and they were glad to be in with mama. George went to a party at Mr. P.G. Worcester's. On all these occasions we appreciate George. He does everything for everybody.

November 1 Sat. rainy. We expected Samuel but he did not come. The missionaries were invited to Mrs. Baldwin's

---

Ernest C. Partridge

November 7 With Misses Thompson & Knopf and Mary, Passimian driving, started for Samsoun. Drove to Chengal. Good weather and a good time.

November 8 Reached Marsovan about 3PM. I joined Nicine[?] party at coal mine. Mary and I guests at Whites. (180m)

November 9 Sunday. A busy day. I preached & helped Dr W in a communion service. Preached at college evening.

November 10 Drove to Samsoun. Stopped at hotel Mautika. Saw relief work. Some shopping. (70m)

November 11 Spent day shopping, visiting institutions.

---

but I could not go. Armen thought she must study for an exam. It takes so long to get the children into bed and asleep that one can hardly do a thing before nine.

November 2 Sunday. A beautiful day. I went to S.S. with the children or rather they went on bicycles and I walked. In the evening Edward and I went to hear Frank Warner on his observation of missionary work in India & Ceylon.

November 3 Mon. In the morning I left Alfred with Mrs. Shaw and went with Edward to join business college. He is to have Jessie Martin as a teacher in short-hand, type-writing & spelling. He takes penmanship with Mr. Henderson. I bought Edward two pairs of gloves and Alfred a jersey. Mrs. Greene called, Mrs. Wright brought me silk for a silk waist.

November 4 Tues. Colder. Billo had a tooth ache and did not go to school in the afternoon. George and Edward rode on the motor wheel which they bought of Sydney Gulick for $35.

November 5 Wed. Again Billo had a toothache and did not go to school in the afternoon. We went to the dentist's and he had it filled. The poor little fellow was awfully scared and I was sorry for him. Dr. Barnard put cocaine in and it did not hurt much, nor did it ache afterwards.

November 6 Thurs. Mrs. Wright came over to see about frogs for Frances's coat.

November 7 Fri. Again Mrs. Wright came over to bring a pattern for the silk waist that she bought for me. What should I do without Mrs. Wright?

November 8 Sat. I went with Edward and Billo to a football game, the first time since I was in college. Oberlin beat Hiram 47–0. It was a much less frightful game than it used to be.

November 9 A pleasant Sunday. In the afternoon we went for a walk, got some hickory nuts, went over to the Krescent field and ate it (Sunday candy), saw a snake. Frances climbed up on a shed roof and pretended she was slipping. Geo. & Billo rescued her.

November 10 Mon. A hard day as usual. Alfred & Frances fussy, Billo quarrelsome. Geo. has a bad cold. Edward may. Everything looks to "mamma" and she is tired.

November 11 Tues. Armistice Day. The children paraded around the streets at recess and Edward was dismissed an hour early but it was very quiet on the whole.

November 12 Wed. Mrs. Duftee called.

November 13 Thurs. The nineteenth anniversary of our reaching Sivas.

November 14 Fri. I attended at Mrs. Merrill's invitation, a concert given for the D.A.R. and their guests. Mrs. Lottie Demuth Williams played five selections, accompanied by Mrs. Bennett. Mrs. Adams sang twice. Mr. Goerner and someone else played on the violin and harp.

November 15 Sat. Oberlin–Case football game, 67–0. Edward and George went at 7:10 and have not returned yet at 11:10 P.M.

November 16 Sunday. Edward & I skipped church in the evening and went to the Martin's to see Dr. Haas but he did not come.

November 17 Mon. Nothing but washing.

November 18 Tues. Dried the clothes, began the ironing.

November 19 Wed. Mrs. Caldwell's birthday, No, it is Nov.20th.

November 20 Thurs. Frances was invited to a birthday party at Ida Welch's, and Alfred to Ervel MacCullough's. Frances was sick at night with ear ache and headache and nausea.

[November 21]

November 22 Sat. With Billy to the dentist's at 8 A.M. and to oculist's at 9:30. Dr. Jameson found that Billo has the same amount of astigmatism exactly that Edward had. They are alike even in their defects.

November 23 Sunday. I felt "rotten" and did not go out all day, but in the evening about 9:30 Vahan telephones from the hotel. He came down and we sat up until midnight talking. He is very interesting indeed.

November 24 Mon. Vahan left on the 10:25 car for Cleveland. I was completely used up after I finished washing in the afternoon but felt some better after I slept a minute or two in my chair.

Ernest C. Partridge

Dinner with English officers.

November 12 Back to Marsovan.

November 13 Dr Marden thinks I have chronic appendicitis and need an operation.

November 14 Decided to have operation tomorrow morning. A musical in evening.

November 15 Changed my mind and started for Sivas. Drove 80 miles to Chengel.

November 16 Sunday. Started out for Tocabor Yeni Khan but decided to keep on & reached Sivas at 10:30PM. 110 miles. (180m)

November 17 Found Major Lance had "spent" 2 days in Sivas, stirring up a dense grudge & finding little new. Mgr administration severely criticized.

November 18 He has wired Constan[tinople] that I be removed for a health vacation and that Miss Graffam be director.

November 19 Worked on accounts & reports. Conducted Unit meetings and at end presented my resignation.

November 20 Have decided to go to the U.S. for at least a short vacation. Winona is very tired. If necessary, shall have operation there.

[November 21–23]

November 24 A farewell reception to me by the Armenians at orphanage. I received a fine rug as a gift.

November 25 Busy packing and saying goodbye. A social at cottage in evening for all Americans. I bought 50 lira rug, a beauty.

November 25 Tues. George's birthday, rather a mixed up day. I had already given him a trip to Cleveland to see the Case game. I gave him some gloves, Edward a season ticket to the Hospital Fair, including chicken supper. The little ones gave him eats. He went to a lecture by Stefannson [possibly Vihjalmur Stefannson, Hunters of the Great North, published 1922] in the evening.

November 26 Wed. I was invited to afternoon tea at Mrs. Greene's with Mrs. Wright and a Dr. Wright, a lady friend of Mrs. W. Rec'd a letter from Dr. Clark enclosing one from Mrs. Sewny written Oct. 12, the very latest from Sivas. She does not mention Mr. P. Polly was going to Harpoot.

November 27 Thurs. Thanksgiving. The first Thanksgiving that we were alone, I think and the first one where I prepared the dinner alone and washed the dishes alone. Armen helped stuff the turkey the night before. Mrs. Greene & her sister called, Mrs. Caldwell and her children also.

November 28 Fri. George and Billo went to the shack with "Woody" to stay until Saturday night. Alfred and Frances and I went to a concert given for the public schools. The High School orchestra played. Mr. Goerner played the cello and Mrs. Adams sang.

November 29 Sat. The usual Saturday only more so, windy, rainy, increasing to a gale at night. Trees blown down, telephone poles, the 2nd chimney. The electric lights on our street were off all the evening and night.

November 30 Sunday. I went to church in the morning, but only Frances and George went to S.S. The wind was very strong. Edward went to Y.M.C.A. in the evening. It was led by Steller and the varsity men spoke.

December 1 Mon. I farmed out my children with Mrs. Caldwell while I washed. I went along Oak St. carrying a tub of dirty clothes with Prof. Jelliff.

December 2 Tues. Ironing

December 3 Wed. Ironing. The weather was very cold. Decided to change from gas to coal in the furnace.

December 4 Thurs. Again washing.

December 5 Fri. I went down town with Ed. Got him trousers ($7.50), 4 collars ($1.), 2 prs stockings (.60 & .75), Billo gloves (.60), prints of passport photos ($4), some little birthday things for Billo. Edward & Geo. went to the Hospital Fair & chicken supper. Frances got angry with me and gathered her things to go down to the Kelsey's to live, and then decided not to go.

December 6 Sat. Billo's ninth birthday. He had some toys, a pair of glasses, a pound of chocolates. We all, except Ed, went to the picture show to see Tom Mix, then ice-cream cones at Tobins, then the three big (!) boys went to the hospital fair to supper & evening program.

Ernest C. Partridge

November 26 Larcombe drove "the gang" down to Talas. Rainy early but a fine day and pleasant run.

November 27 Thanksgiving Day in Talas. A splendid day well arranged. 28 Americans at table. A visit with "the same old gang" in evening.

November 28 Farnum drove me down to OK in a light truck. I drove part of the time. A fine time. A good night with the fellows, Duer & Gilbert. (115m)

November 29 Left OK at 6:30AM. 20 miles out of Konia, a car jumped the track & ditched half the train. One woman killed. Slept in a compartment with no glass.

November 30 Sunday. At 11AM track was cleared. Reached Konia at 2:30PM. Guest for 24 hours at Miss Cushman's.

December 1 Spent day visiting. Left on Express at 4:30 with Major Lance in from Aleppo. A very good night.

December 2 Joined at Derenji by two workers. Reached Constan[tinople] about 8PM. Dinner at G.H.I. Stopping at personnel H.Q. (600m)

December 3 Major Arnold will pay my t[rip] exp home. Hope to get away soon.

December 4 Saw Dr Hoover and think I will delay operation until Oberlin.

December 5 Called on Mr Raindals. A Com-ad-I & station meeting at Gedik Pasha with supper in between.

[December 6]

December 7 A very quiet and all day, reading.

December 8 Decided to go on Italian boat to New York. Regina D'Italia sailing 11th, 25 days to NY. Dined at Astoria with Dr White. Lunch with Lanis & Murchigian.

December 7 Sunday. Cold, drizzly, slushy, slippery. Children in the house all day, crazy to go sliding. Perhaps I should let them but I cannot quite make up my mind to it.

December 8 Mon. Washed. Ed had exam. & got home early to look after the children.

December 9 Tues. Mrs. Shaw & I went to hear Prof. Clark of Chicago read Drinkwater's Lincoln. It was very fine but two silly College people talked all through it just behind us, laughed all through the scene of Lincoln's assassination.

December 10 Wed. Alfred had a tooth ache and I took him to the Dentist in the morning.

December 11 Thurs. Washed again. Mrs. Wright called for a few minutes. Have been ordering Christmas presents all the week. Billo did not feel well in the afternoon, so stayed at home from school.

December 12 Fri. Mrs. Miller invited me to be her guest at their Club dinner. We had a fine dinner and a very interesting play, The Rainbow Kimona Club. Billo not well, coughs, has headache etc. Better towards night.

December 13 Sat. Alfred and I went again to Dentist's. Billo better, probably not whooping cough.

December 14 Sunday. Frances and Alfred and I went to S.S. and A & I were just frozen when we got home but not Frances. She does not mind the cold at all as the others do. I went to the Second Church Christmas concert in the afternoon. It was wonderfully fine.

December 15 Mon. The washing machine refused to work so I washed out some by hand, brought some home dirty. George went to a S.S. party and had a fine time. Someone arranged a very definite & interesting program.

December 16 Tues. Finished my washing after ten at night. Mrs. Van der Pyl asked me to go to the Christmas Concert with her but I had no one to leave with the children. Edward was at Tobins, George at the Gym, & Armen at the Library, I suppose.

December 17 Wed. Samuel came in the evening.

December 18 Thurs. College and Business College closed. We went to a Christmas entertainment at the Prospect Street School. George represented the sun, only less than Santa Claus, greater than all the others.

December 19 Fri. Public Schools closed. Frances was not able to go. Billo seems to have escaped whooping cough. I went to Elyria to do Christmas shopping, not very successful.

December 20 Sat. Armen went to Detroit.

December 21 Sunday. I stayed at home all day as Frances was not able to go. After church in the evening which was a Christmas concert, Samuel brought home peach pie & ice-cream.

December 22 Mon. Samuel went to Detroit and I washed.

Ernest C. Partridge

December 9 Finished passport vize work & wrote article for Orient about Sivas. Lunch at Tocatlians with Yervant Eff.

December 11 Sailed at 4PM on Regina d Italia with Dr Cullen. 3 American army officers on board returning from Russia.

December 12 Reached Smyrna about 6PM. Too late to land.

December 13 Left steamer about 8:30. Took carriage to Paradise. Spent day and night at Reeds. Met Hovhan Vartebed and had a long talk with him and in evening with Reed.

December 14 Sunday. Breakfast at Reeds, drove down to city and took boat about 11AM. Sailed at 2PM. Newman joined us on way to U.S. 23 [days to go]

December 15 Reached Pirieus at 8:30AM. A good deal of quarantine trouble on account of bubonic plague in Constan[tinople]. Sailed again about 9PM for Naples. 22 [days to go]

December 16 A fine day and a little warmer. Constant–Athens 545m 21 [days to go]

December 17 Came in sight of Aetna about 8AM. Reached Messina harbor at 2PM. 20 [days to go]

December 18 Sailed out at 4PM for Naples. Athens–Naples 774m

December 19 Came into harbor at Naples about 8AM. Cold & cloudy. Spent 3 hours in Museum but found picture gallery closed. Capt Borese & St Ambler left us for Paris.

December 20 I am not very well. A stupid day on board reading and watching them load.

December 21 Sunday. Went to Herculaneum and Vesuvius starting from city at 11 & getting back about 7. Well worth the trip.

December 22 Did a little shopping and read most of the day. 19 [days to go]

December 23 Tues. I took the three little ones to the Primary S.S. Christmas tree. Mrs. Richards told me that she thought Alfred had a perfectly wonderful voice for singing.

December 24 Wed. Last preparations for Christmas. I made pumpkin and mince pies. Miss Marie Gane came over and fixed the chicken.

December 25 Thurs. Christmas. We had a very successful celebration. I had some lovely presents, radiolite watch to use at night, immersion heater from Ed., safety pins, kid gloves from Hampartsoom, a bag that Geo made in his grade, tel. from Mr. P. at Naples, arriving in N.Y. Jan. 20.

December 26 Fri. We received various Christmas cards, locoom from Mariam.

December 27 Sat. House cleaning and the left over ironing and mending to finish.

December 28 Sunday. I did not feel very well and did not go out. George, Alfred & Frances went to S.S. Billo started out but got left behind and came back. Miss Haskell came in to warm her hands. She was taking flowers to the cemetery. Mrs. Greene & her sister called, also Prof Wright & Prof. Lybyer.

December 29 Mon. I did not feel able to wash even with the machine. I got Mrs. Glanton to take it home. I cleaned up the boys' room, sending all unnecessary clothing etc. upstairs. The boys skated. There has been skating for a week or so. They skate on the new reservoir. Edward enjoys skating with the girls.

December 30 Tues. Skating.

December 31 Wed. The last day of a year of varied experiences. Two letters from Mr. P. from Con. saying that he

Ernest C. Partridge

December 23 Major Steves and I went to Pompeii and had a very fine trip. One of the most interesting of my life. 18 [days to go]

December 24 Ship ready to start with full passenger list, 1500 steerage. Gov't requires a third doctor so we are waiting.

December 25 Sailed from Naples at 10AM. A little rough going out of day and few ladies at dinner. 16 [days to go]

[December 26–27]

December 28 Sunday. Running very slow to avoid reaching Gibraltar today. 13 [days to go]

December 29 Anchored in harbor of Gibraltar at 9AM. Naples–Gibraltar 1118m 12 [days to go]

December 30 Another day of idleness. Tried to begin to coal [to load coal] but for some reason did not work. 11 [days to go]

December 31 Coaled [coal loading] slowly. Went into town and shopped a little. Drove over into Spain. Played hearts till midnight to celebrate New Year. 10 [days to go]

has appendicitis but will wait to have the operation until he gets home. He saw Miss Rice before she left for Sivas Dec. 8.

Memoranda:

Edward had for Christmas skates, umbrella, football picture, Life from Vahan, collar button, cuff buttons, three neckties from Hampartsoom, Lawrence & Mr. Tobin, metal mirror, knife, pocket book.

George had ouija board, ping pong set, American Boy, Life from Vahan, pocket book, chocolate, pencils in box, tablet, magnet, kit.

Billo, ladder wagon, telephone set, pocket book, auto race, torpedo boat.

Frances, doll, bed room slippers, bracelet (bangle that said D.E.A.R.), child improvement games, hair ribbons, mittens, toilet set, ring, pocket books, mother goose book.

Alfred had dump cart, liberty blocks, pocket book, play wrist watch, two primers.

Diaries of Winona & Ernest Partridge 1920

January 1 Thurs. New Years, but I forgot that the stores would not be open so I had to have a picked up dinner, bacon, potatoes, corn, choc. bars. For the first time I heard the bells and whistles etc. at midnight, even the North Amherst whistles. Then Alfred woke up at five.

January 2 Fri. Very very cold, 6° below. We fired up the furnace to the limit all day but were not very hot, very comfortable though. Mrs. Caldwell & I were going to the movies but Alfred made a fuss and Frances was cross. A letter from Mr. P. from Samsoun.

January 3 Sat. Usual program only so cold that I could not ask the boys to beat rugs. Edward swept one. Mrs. Caldwell and I thought of going to the movies but it was too cold.

January 4 Sunday. I went to Sunday school with the fam, then made chocolate pie. Lawrence and Russell ate supper with us and Edward took supper with the Chases.

January 5 Mon. I sent my washing out again. It is very cold. Armen came and brought us all presents. It was like a second Christmas.

January 6 Tues. Business College commenced.

January 7 Wed. Ironing.

January 8 Thurs. Edward & I went to the movies, Norma Talmadge in A Woman's Way. I bought cloth for a pair of sheets.

[January 9]

January 10 Sat. Mr. P. was to arrive in N.Y. today but we received no word. We fixed up the upstairs room for Armen so Mr. P. could have her room. I hope it is the last time that I shall have to clean up such a mess in Oberlin.

January 11 Sunday. Still no word from Mr. P. I went to Sunday School & then with Edward and Lawrence to the evening service. Mr. Van der Pyl gave a talk to young men on "Ideals." They must not think the world owes them a living, must keep sweet and go straight.

Frances. Dec. Reading B, Spelling A, Arith A, Music B, Drawing B+

January 12 Mon. Waited all day for word from Mr. P.

January 13 Tues. Still waiting, no word. Frances had her name put down as the girl in the B class who read the most lines right. Wasn't she proud and weren't we all proud?

Ernest C. Partridge

January 1 In harbor at Gibraltar. No coaling, too stormy. Read, played cards & wrote.

January 2 Coaled all day.

January 3 Tea on British coal boat. Sailed 4:30PM.

January 4 Rather rough and few people around.

January 5 Still rough and cold.

January 6 Quieter but still unpleasant. Some rain.

January 7 Quite smooth and sun is out. Running north of Azores.

January 8 A very quiet day of good weather and good travelling. Finished reading Trevalyan's 1700 pages.

[January 9–10]

January 11 Quite rough and running very slowly; food bad. [Stomach out of order over bad food (1919 diary).]

January 12 Changeable weather, rain only 200 m (1919 diary).

January 13 173m

January 14 Wed. No word. Two boats from Italy due but evidently he was not on them.

January 15 Thurs. No word. Mr. Smith from the Philippines called because he thought that I was the mother of Charlotte Partridge of South Bend.

January 16 Fri. No word. Some women came to sell a book about children, everything, physical, moral, games etc. etc. Dr. Hemingway of China called in the evening.

January 17 Sat. Mr. Nigoghos Nigoghosian and Hermine came to see about her entering the conservatory. Then I went down town and did some very necessary shopping, underwear, stockings, caps etc. etc.

January 18 Sunday. It was very cold and I could not get the house warm, so the children did not get ready for S.S. Edward and Lawrence and I went in the evening. Mr. V. spoke on the Young Men's Associates.

January 19 Mon. At last the silence is broken and a radio message delayed, from the S.S. Regina, says that he is delayed, will reach N.Y. about the 19th. No word of his arrival in N.Y. today.

January 20 Tues. No word from Mr. P.

January 21 Wed. A telegram announced Mr. P's arrival. Mr. Peabody who came in the same boat telephoned to me from the Y.M.C.A office. He told me various things about the poor food, poor boat etc. the boat was not heated at all.

January 22 Thurs. No News.

January 23 Fri. Mr. P. arrived at 1:30 A.M. pounded on the door until I woke up. He is well, but has to have an operation.

January 24 Sat. Talking and trying to work.

January 25 Sunday. Mr. P. and I went to church. Mr. Van der Pyl and Dr. & Mrs. Martin called in the P.M.

January 26 Mon. George started in High School today. His father went with him. He has Mrs. Willard in Latin, Miss Stone in Civics, Mr. Rawdon in Algebra, Mr. Barnhart in English. Billo was promoted to 3A. Frances to 1A. Mr. P. was examined by Dr. Thatcher and he too says he needs an operation for appendicitis.

January 27 Tues. I asked Mr. Rawdon to allow Alfred to go to school even though he is not six until July. He promised to see Miss Brady and decide.

Ernest C. Partridge

January 14 159m

January 16 99m

January 17 203m

January 18 A wireless from Room's asking if I need an ambulance to land with.

January 19 Very cold but heat.

January 20 Landed 3PM. Met by GP and Mr Hewitt, with car, to their house for tea. Out to White Plains for night. Gibraltar to New York 3300 m

January 21 In to city about 10AM. Spent day at Rooms. Banquet of American Armenian Evang Union. Col Finley preached. Dr Barton & I spoke. Night train west. 40m

January 22 Missed connection at Buffalo. Reached Cleveland 10PM. Trolley to Elyria. With another passenger hired last car to come on to Oberlin. Home 1:30AM. 678m

January 23 Reached Oberlin at 1:30AM. 51 days from Sivas, 40 from Constant. A most tedious trip. Called on Wrights and Mrs Greene.

[January 24]

January 25 Sunday. Mrs P and I went to church. Mr Van der Pyle and Martins called in PM.

January 26 George began his HS course today.

[January 27–29]

January 28 Wed. Mrs. Glanton telephoned that the clothes were smoked and she would have to wash them over so I had to do a little washing myself for the next day. Parent-Teachers association, perfect failure. Miss Durham spoke.

January 29 Thurs. Ironed and ironed.

January 30 Fri. Mr. P. & I went to Mr. James's house for supper. Their babies are perfectly lovely. George was not well, did not go to school. When I got home he had gone to bed with the little ones. Mr. P. went to the Cleveland orchestra concert. Alfred started in first grade. I went over with the last of the children. He is so delighted that he does not want Saturday to come.

January 31 Sat. I went down town and bought seven night drawers and dresses for ten dollars. Billo's fit Frances & Frances's fit Alfred. Billo is out of luck.

Frances, 1st semester Conduct A-, Effort A, Reading B+, Spelling A, Penmanship B, Arith A-, Music B, Drawing B+

February 1 Sunday. Cold. Only Frances went to Sunday School, the rest of us more or less under the weather. I did not go out all day. Mr. P. went over to the Wright's in the afternoon. Mr. Nigoghosian and Hermine came to our house and then Hermine went to her room at Mrs. Morrison's.

February 2 Mon. Much warmer. Alfred proudly set off to school with Frances and Billo. George after being a little sick for three or four days, went back to school. He got 100 in Latin and Mrs. Willard said, "You're just like Edward." That pleased George and Edward and especially mamma.

February 3 Tues. Mr. P. & I went down to call on Mrs. Garland and Mrs. Elmer and then to the Martin's. Armen was having a vacation so held the fort while we were gone.

Ernest C. Partridge

January 30 Mrs P and I went to James' for supper. I went to Cleveland Orchestra Concert. Alfred began to go to 1st grade.

[January 31–February 2]

February 3 Called on Mrs Elmer & Martins.

[February 4–7]

February 8 Sunday. Rose early 6:20 car to Medina, where I spoke on Relief Work; also in SS. Dinner with Harts. Evening Mr Van der Pyl on a Young Man's Business. 98m

February 9 Received several '95 letters. Wrote some. Miss Bradt's vocal recital in evening.

February 10 Talked Turkey situation over with Pres King. Called at Wright's.

February 11 Spoke at W.C.T.U. meeting on Intemperance in Turkey. Pres Harada's first lecture.

February 4 Wed. Mrs. Charlotte Demuth Williams, assisted by Mr. Bennett, gave a concert. Mr. P. went but there was no one at home so I could not.

February 5 Thurs. Frances did not go to school, nor Billo, so Alfred was left alone. I went with him and he came back with Herbert. Frances had a cold.

February 6 Fri. Frances again did not go to school, but Billo did.

February 7 Sat. The anniversary of the "flu" and Alfred and I have felt as though we had it. George and his father went to the Glee Club Concert. George distributed invitations for Baldwin Cottage for 3 ½ hours, earned 85 cts. He was dreadfully tired, but game.

February 8 Sunday. The three little ones and I all about sick with colds. We did not go out. Edward and George got up about eleven but went to church in the evening. Mr. P. went on the 6:20 car to Medina to speak, and came back at suppertime. Mrs. Horner, Mrs. Hall & Mrs. Greene telephoned.

February 9 Mon. Mrs. Glanton sent word that she cannot do the washing any more. I conversed with Miss Sinclair about her washing machine. She has adopted two children so has some washing to do herself. I can wash any morning, however.

February 10 Tues. I washed morning & afternoon and did housework between times. I hung up the clothes just in time to begin supper and I was dead tired, too tired to go to a movie which I wanted to see very much.

February 11 Wed. Mr. P. took my place at the W.C.T.U meeting. I was so tired that I could not iron in the afternoon so I went over to see Mrs. Rote and then ironed until eleven at night.

February 12 Thurs. The invitation for Father & Son banquet have begun to come in although their father is here. Prof. Jeliffe asked them. Valentines have been in the making today, such messes and much excitement.

February 13 Fri. The valentines of the schools were distributed. All three of the little ones got a good supply, but Billy has the most, many of them from little girls.

February 14 Sat. Stormy and colder. George & I went to Cleveland and bought him a brown suit with two pairs of "knickers" for $19.95. We went to the movies there, had dinner and came home at 4:10, found Carroll and John & Rachel Kelsey just tearing up the house, playing hide & seek. Basket ball OSU beat Oberlin.

February 15 Sunday. Extremely cold. No one went to S.S. nor church in the morning. Mr. P. went to Ravenna on the 10:25 car. Lawrence took supper with us and went to church with Ed., George and me. Mr. Van spoke on the Young Man and his wife. He should be clean and pure as she is. She should be helpmeet. Make a home not a hotel.

February 16 Mon. Mr. P. came back from Ravenna.

February 17 Tues. I took Alfred and Billo to the Doctor. Billo's ear has been troubling him, but it is all right now. Alfred seems generally run down. Dr. Thatcher gave a prescription for Gevatol, but Alfred does not like it very well.

February 18 Wed. Mrs. Metcalf brought tickets for the Philadelphia Symphony Concert and Mr. P. and I went. It was splendid. The leader is Stokowski.

February 19 Thurs. Mr. P. went to Canton, expecting to return at night but did not.

February 20 Fri. The great event today was that Billo, who took private lessons in the Christmas vacation because he could not spell, stood the longest in a spelling match. Then his teacher tried to stick him but she could not.

February 21 Sat. I went to Cleveland with Mr. P. on his way to Canton to help him buy some clothes. He bought two suits, a gray $49 marked down from $60 and a dark green $33, very much reduced because it was the last one of the kind.

Ernest C. Partridge

February 12 Dr Harada's lecture on Social Regeneration of Japan. He spoke in evening on Missionary Work in Japan.

February 13 Went into Cleveland to see Huelster. Did some shopping. Returned 4:10 car. 66m

February 14 Wrote and did housework. State basketball game, Oberlin got beaten 13–31.

February 15 Sunday. Went down to Ravenna in PM for Union Relief Rally. Dinner at Statler, supper at hotel. A small crowd, very cold but a good meeting. 70m

February 16 6:47 train to Cleveland. Out to Elyria by train on by trolley. Supper at Ponds. 70m

[February 17]

February 18 Philadelphia Orchestra concert.

February 19 Down to Canton by trolley for a noon lunch. Met several ministers. Spoke at Cong Church evening. Night at Washington Hotel. 94m

February 20 Home early in morning.

February 21 Went to Canton for Sunday but finding no appointments started back & spent last part of night in Elyria. Winona to Cleveland, 2 suits for me. 178m

February 22 Sunday. Home from Elyria for breakfast. First Church voted to unite. Bishop Moulin evening.

February 23 W.B. celebration. Dr. Athen's fine address on Americanism.

February 24 Edward & I went to Cleveland to lunch at Moose Club. Bought suit & overcoat Keith's. 66m

February 22 Sunday. Mr. P. came home unexpectedly because he found no appointment made for him in Canton. I heard Mr. V. in the morning on "The religion of a merry heart," and Bishop Moulin in the evening.

February 23 Mon. Washington's Birthday meeting in the Chapel. Dr. Atkins of Detroit spoke on "Americanism, its qualities, and the qualities of the American." The Musical Union sang a song of which the words were composed by Prof. Youtz & the music by Prof. Andrews.

February 24 Tues. Edward and his father went to Cleveland, bought a suit of clothes ($39) and an overcoat ($26.85) for Edward, attended the Moose Club luncheon, went to Keith's and came home at 7:10 or a little after. Billo is a little sick, so very tired, no special pain. Yeats lecture but I could not go.

February 25 Wed. We all went to see Douglas Fairbanks in the Real American. It was very good but Billo was not feeling well and got tired.

February 26 Thurs. Very, very cold. Alfred brought home his first report card.

Frances: Health A, Conduct. A, Effort A, Reading & Lit B+, Penmanship B, Arith B, Music B, Drawing B. Alfred: Penmanship A, Arith A, Music A/C+, Drawing B/C+

February 27 Fri. Dr. Thatcher told me that Mr. P. was to have his operation Saturday. He was to go to the hospital that evening but did not finally.

February 28 Sat. Mr. P.'s operation at 8 A.M. Dr. Clement of Elyria did it, assisted by Dr. Thatcher, Dr. Colegrove and Dr. Jamieson. He had to sleep in the operating room.

February 29 Sunday. Hospital, morning, afternoon & evening. Mr. P. not comfortable but all right. Mr. Nigoghosian called on him a few minutes. He was put into the room with Dr. Foster who has pneumonia. Mrs. Martin & Jesse, Miss Davis & Mrs. Caldwell called.

March 1 Mon. Mr. P. uncomfortable but hungry. Mr. Nigoghosian sent a potted cyclamen, very beautiful white flowers with waxy leaves.

March 2 Tues. Mr. P. improving but not yet comfortable. Mrs. Greene sent potted primrose. Mrs. Caldwell broke her arm.

March 3 Mr. P. much better. Dr. Foster went home and now Mr. P. has room alone, has no one to snore for him or to call the nurse all night.

Ernest C. Partridge

February 25 Douglas Fairbanks in the Real American.

February 26 Alfred brought home his first marks.

[February 27]

February 28 Dr Clement of Elyria and Dr Thatcher operated on me for appendicitis at 8 this morning. Spent day in operating room and slept there.

February 29 Sunday. Moved into room with Dr. Foster.

[March 1–4]

March 5 Set up in a chair most of the day.

March 6 Spent forenoon in my room & dining room and went home about 2PM.

March 7 Sunday. Second Church voted by a barely ⅔ vote to plan of union with First Church.

[March 8]

March 9 I went over to Metcalf's; first time out of house.

[March 10]

March 4 Thurs. Very cold. I washed at Miss Sinclair's in the afternoon. I was wondering how I should get the clothes home when Billo brought the baby carriage to take them home, then Geo. brought an umbrella and Hampartsoon carried them up. Day of Prayer for college.

March 5 Fri. Mr. P. improving fast. Milton Norton's son was brought to the hospital. He had "flu" then tubercular meningitis. No hope of his recovery. The twins and another baby went home form the hospital. Shansi Day.

March 6 Sat. Mr. P. came home in the afternoon. George and Edward brought him home in a wheel chair. Very cold and wintry. There is a student volunteer convention here.

March 7 Sunday. Still colder. Ed & I went to church. Mr. V. preached on The Young Man & his religion, very good. Miss Metcalf called. Mr. Adams, Mr. Nigoghosian & Hermine.

[March 8]

March 9 Tues. Warmer. Mr. P. went over to the Metcalfs, the first time he has been anywhere since his operation. Mrs. Caldwell and Mrs. Greene called. Attended a lecture by Dr. Goddard on Unusual Children. 70% of people not of High School intelligence, 10% of 16 yr. old, etc.

March 10 Warm, melting. Only ice around our house where the sun did not strike. I went to W.C.T.U. meeting with Mrs. Van der Pyl. Dr. Cochran spoke on "Dress & Morals." Then I bought a pair of shoes for $7.95, $12 shoe marked down because there are few left.

March 11 Mr. P. George, Billo & I went to a basket ball game or two rather. O. High School beat Business Col. O All Stars beat Bellevue Giants. I was invited to Mrs. Wrights to meet Mrs. Neil, Prof. O's niece. Mrs. Greene, Mrs. Sam Williams, Mrs. Ward, Mrs. Harris, Mrs. Fullerton were there.

March 12 Fri. Went to Mrs. Beebe's to try on my waist. It was warm and pleasant then but grew very cold by night.

March 13 Sat. Worked hard, but could not have finished if Armen had not come and helped me clean up the bedrooms. I mended and ironed until half past eleven.

March 14 Sunday. Pleasant & a little warm. Communion. Mr. P. and I went, with Hovhan Mocafian. He spent the day with us. He is teaching French in Defiance, Ohio. In the afternoon Hermine, Nigoghosian & Hampartsoom came in.

[March 15]

March 16 Tues. Armen and I went to hear Miss Spinney present the Medea. It was wonderfully done but the play is so sad.

March 17 Went to lunch at 2nd Church with Mrs. Greene, then to Haskell lecture at four, given by Prof. MacIntosh of Edinburgh, then in the evening to Yale (26)–Princeton (21) game with Mrs. Caldwell. Another Mrs. Caldwell did a very small washing in 5 ¼ hrs. @ 35 cts an hour. Bought three pairs of roller skates @$2.50.

March 18 Thurs. Stayed at home to make up for yesterday, especially to iron but my electric iron failed so I could not iron. I tried to mend stockings but used up my darning cotton and had to stop, so I ended with ironing to do & stockings to mend. George went to Krescent banquet at Park Hotel. The white mice died.

March 19 Fri. Washed. Came home at quarter of twelve and found that Mr. P. and I were to go to Wright's for dinner at half past twelve. We went and left the children to go to Mrs. Caldwell's to wait until I came home. When I came home Helen & the children had washed the dishes.

March 20 Sat. Regular jobs. The Woman's Glee Club gave a concert for the school children. We went with the four younger children. It was good but not as good as the men's club.

March 21 Sunday. Edward, Mr. P. and I went to the Second Church and heard Prof. Youtz. In the evening at 6:15 we heard Dr. Elmer Lynn Williams, the "fighting parson" of Chicago. He was representing the Intercollegiate Prohibition Association.

March 22 Mon. Washed. Billy was sick. We tried an auto & Billo vomited in it and several times at home.

March 23 Mrs. Clark came on the afternoon train. Billo still not well and did not go to school. We bought the Ford for $450. Met Mrs. C. with it.

Ernest C. Partridge

March 11 Went to Gym in evening for 2 basketball games with Winona, George & William.

March 12 Walked down town for first time. Called on Dr Thatcher. PM went to Elyria to get a belt. Evening called on Wrights.

[March 13]

March 14 Sunday. A visit from John Mask offices. Calls PM from Martins, Hermine & Nigosian. Winona and I went to church AM.

March 15 Kellers Fellers vs Stellars Hellers, a fine game, latter won 27–25.

March 16 First Haskell lecture by Prof Macintosh very fine.

March 17 Second Haskell lecture. Edward went to banquet of Business College.

March 18 Third Haskell lecture. Edward & I began to look up Ford cars. George went to Krescent Banquet.

March 19 Talked Fords with Clark. Fourth Haskell lecture. Dinner at Wright's.

March 20 Went to Woman's Glee Club Concert for children. Then to indoor track meet.

March 21 Sunday. Prof Youtz in 2nd Church AM. The Fighting Parson at 6:30. Dr Macintosh last Lenten service.

March 22 Tried Pfaffs Ford.

March 23 Bought a Ford for $450. Mrs Clark came.

March 24 Wed. Washed again by hand. Dr. Clark came from Springfield about half past ten. Billo went to school. I ironed at night. It is very easy to iron when there is someone to talk with.

George's first High School report: English B+, Latin A+, Civics B+, Math A+.

March 25 Thurs. The Clarks left on the noon train. We took a long ride in the afternoon and another in the evening. Had a chance to sell the Ford for $500. This is one day in the week that I neither have to wash or iron.

March 26 Fri. Washed but also went out to ride, to the dressmaker's etc.

March 27 Sat. Made doughnuts for W.C.T.U. bake sale. George went to his first class party, that is High School class. It was not a great success, only the refreshments were good. Bought Billo and Alfred shoes @$6.30 and $3.60.

March 28 Sunday. Union service at 2nd Church. Mr. Van der Pyl preached on "Christ or Barabbas?" We took a ride in the Ford out to North Amherst road. I went to a Woman's Mass meeting, Inter-Church World Movement. Mrs. Huntley & Mrs. Davis spoke.

March 29 Mon. I tried to clean house, washed the walls and ceiling of the parlor and then Armen and Hampartsoom cleaned the woodwork, then H. & I the windows. That much used me up entirely.

Ernest C. Partridge

March 24 Dr Clark came late in evening. George 1st HS report English B+ Latin A+ Civics B+ Math A+.

March 25 Had long station meeting with the Clarks. They went on noon train. Took a long ride in PM. 30m

[March 26–27]

March 28 Sunday. Mr. Van der Pyl preached at the union service at 2nd Church. Took a ride on N. Amherst Rd. 20m

[March 29–31]

April 1 Read at library in PM. Took long ride in evening. 25m

[April 2–7]

April 8 Armenag Sharigian came for a visit & brought Alice with him. A Hoover rally in evening.

March 30 Tues. Cafeteria supper at the church. I made doughnuts for it, but the little ones and I stayed at home.

[March 31]

April 1 Thurs. Took a fine ride in the morning, Edward driving. The car goes very well indeed.

April 2 Fri. I cleaned the alcove in the kitchen and the contrast is striking. It was "good Friday" but we did not attend any service. They held services in the Methodist church. We planned to go to Lorain but it was too cold. Armen went to Cleveland.

April 3 Sat. Cold indeed. I cleaned around the house quite superficially, a few windows. Geo. on the outside.

April 4 Sunday. Easter, cold & rainy. The Easter sermon in the morning & the Easter music in the evening were fine. We left the little ones with Geo. & Helen Caldwell.

April 5 Mon. Mrs. Martin & Mrs. Greene and Mrs. Caldwell came in and we read letters from Mr. Lyman and Mr. Crathern about the trouble between the French and Turks in Marash.

April 6 Tues. Cold, snowy & disagreeable. Mr. P & I cleaned the dining room. It took all day with what other things we had to do. Miss Marion Metcalf called right in the midst of it. Mrs. Caldwell wanted me to go to the artist Recital with her, organ, but I was too tired.

April 7 Wed. Cold, but sunshine at intervals and wind so that the clothes dried. I attended missionary meeting, Dr. Bowen of Nankin University spoke very interestingly.

April 8 Thurs. Cold. Mr. P & I spent most of the day cleaning the pantry. We got it nearly finished but one end is still dirty. Armenag and Alice came on the afternoon train.

April 9 Fri. Mr. P. went to Elyria for an Inter-Church World Movement meeting. Armenag went to Cleveland. Alice went to school with Alfred and Frances. All except Alfred, Frances, Edward & me went to the Fireman's benefit. Frances had a toothache so I could not go.

April 10 Sat. Armen took our children and Alice to the Y.W.C.A. frolic. We drove down town afterwards and bought shoes for Frances, low patent leather, $3.00 and low yellow for Alfred $2.70.

April 11 Sunday. Armenag and Alice went home on the noon train. Mr. P. & I went to Cleveland or Lakewood where Mr. P. spoke in Mr. Bowers church. The children invited Helen Caldwell and Lawrence for supper. We came home at 10:10.

April 12 Mon. Washed.

April 13 Tues. Spent the day washing the kitchen walls. I had to scour every inch. Ironed in the evening.

April 14 Wed. Washed at Miss Sinclair's and hung the clothes out. They dried very nicely.

April 15 Thurs. Again a whole day cleaning the kitchen. I can clean only one wall a day. Alfred distinguished himself in school by singing a few notes that the others failed on.

April 16 Fri. Mr. P. and I went to the movies. Mary Miles Minter in "Nurse Marjorie." Billo had a headache and did not go to school.

April 17 Sat. Finally finished the kitchen about 5 o'clock. After supper Mr. P. & Alfred & I went over to call at the Wright's. Hermine stayed over night. Edward & Lawrence went to Cleveland to see Ben Hur. They came home at 1:05.

April 18 Sunday. Went to church twice. "Personal Religion" and "Sky Pilot." Mr. Nigoghosian called, also Dr. & Mrs. Martin. We went to ride a little way, but it was cold. Our cat had four kittens.

April 19 Mon. Washed a little.

Ernest C. Partridge

April 9 Spent day at Elyria and Interchurch World Conference for Lorain Co. Evening Fireman's Benefit.

[April 10]

April 11 Heard Pres. King on Asia Minor. Winona & I went to Lakewood. Short visit with Bowers. I spoke in evening, home by trolley. 60m

[April 12]

April 13 First lecture by Prof Coreybeane on Armenia.

April 14 2nd lecture on Armenia.

April 15 Spoke on Boards work in Turkey at 1st church Elyria. 3rd lecture by Prof Coreybeane on Armenia.

April 16 Mrs P & I went to movies, Mary Miles Minter [silent film actress].

April 17 Finished cleaning kitchen. Called at Wrights in evening.

April 18 Sunday. Mr Van der P "Personal Religion"; evening "Sky Pilot" [silent film].

[April 19]

April 20 Heavy rains. Mrs P & I with Ed & two little ones drove to Bellevue to Association Meeting. Back in PM. George & I drove to Elyria Country Club where I spoke on Mandate to Rotary Club. 85m

[April 21]

April 22 Worked a long time cleaning car & tightening things up. Drove 18 miles in PM. Prayer meeting. Hoover meeting after.

April 20 Tues. Terrific rain, so that we had eight inches of water in our cellar. The third grade teacher did not get to school & there were only 3 in the 1st & 2nd. About noon we started for Bellevue, all except Geo. & Billo. Saw Mr. & Mrs. Breed. Mr. P. spoke. We came home & then Geo. & his father went to Elyria Country Club. Geo. & Billo had dinner at Hobbs. Letter from Polly Mar. 10.

April 21 Wed. Washed, washed all day, then went for a little ride in the evening and came home and went at it again.

April 22 Thurs. Warm, springlike, but showery. Frances birthday, naturally. She had one doll that opens & shuts its eyes and George gave her eight little ones of different sizes. Edith Dufty also gave her some silk hats, coats, dresses, etc. Edward gave her two pendants, Billo box of choc. marshmallows, Alfred a doll, Herbert a record. We took an auto ride, had cake, ice-cream.

[April 23]

April 24 Sat. Mr. P. went to Detroit.

April 25 Sunday. Mr. Irving Metcalf invited me to go to the May Festival Concert, The Spectre's Bride. It was wonderful. The soprano was Miss Lawrence.

April 26 Mon. A dreadful day for Alfred. He had a swollen cheek. He did not want to go to school, but finally George persuaded him to let him take him on the wheel. The he got out of sorts because he wanted more sugar after his cereal was like syrup.

April 27 Tues. Edward's birthday. He had a shirt, Oberlin College Memory book, soap box from Billo, tooth brush holder from Frances, Judge from Alfred, hat & clothes brush from George. Each except Alfred gave 18 candy kisses because we are not allowed to give the other kind. Alfred still is. We had pork roast instead of chicken @40 cts.

April 28 Wed. I went to an Armenian supper at the First Cong. Church of Cleveland and then spoke afterwards in their prayer meeting. I met some very pleasant people, Mrs. Hobbs and her daughter, Mr. & Mrs. Goodenough, Mr. and Mrs. Kedgie. Mr. P. went to Toledo for two meetings.

George weighed 94 ½ lbs. Frances weighed 55 ¼ lbs. Alfred weighed 44 ½ lbs.

April 29 Thurs. Ernest returned from Toledo.

April 30. Fri. Rained nearly all day. I washed at Miss Sinclair's and got drenched going and coming.

May 1 Sat. A pleasant day. May baskets were the order of the day. George and Billo got up early and went to the arboretum to get flowers. George finished the last May basket, one for Billo, about one o'clock.

May 2 Sunday. I did not go to church until evening. Mr. Van der Pyl spoke on the "Discipline of Sorrow," illustrated by George Elliott's Arnon Barton. We rode through North & South Amherst in the P.M. It was pretty cold most of the way.

May 3 Mon. Mr. P. returned from Toledo on the 5:43 train.

May 4 Tues. U.L.A. lecture by Gregory Mason on America's World. Mr. P. went to Painesville to speak to the Plymouth Rock Association.

Ernest C. Partridge

[April 23]

April 24 Noon train to Detroit. Clarks met me at depot. Night with them.

April 25 Sunday. Dr drove me to Highland P Church. Spoke twice. Clawson's for dinner. Callenders supper & night. North Woodside Cong church evening. Armenians of Sivas after. 20m

April 26 Calls on Malejans and Dr Nishan. Home with Dr Mikran, Sivas Alumni, then banquet for Armenian Premier.

April 27 Morning train to Oberlin. Voted for Hoover. Edward's birthday. 160m

April 28 Toledo Association. I spoke on Mandate.

April 29 Women's Foreign meeting. I spoke on our obligation to A. M. [Asia Minor]. Toledo AM. Home 5:43 PM. 85m

[April 30]

May 1 Case-Wooster-Oberlin track meet. Oberlin beat Wooster by 10 points. 8:38 train to Toledo. Night Boody House. 85m

May 2 Sunday. Day at Washington St Church. A.M. Challenge of A. Minor [Asia Minor], SS two classes. Evening Mandate. Dinner & supper at Arnold's. Night at Briggs.

May 3 Spoke an hour to Toledo Ministers on Mandate. Lunch with Luethis. Home at 5:43. 85m

May 4 Went to Painesville to Plymouth Rock Association. Spoke on Challenge of AM [Asia Minor]. Gregory Mason. Evening Oberlin. 130m

May 5 Oberlin vs Wooster baseball beaten 10–5.

May 6 Church prayer meeting. Elected delegate of 1st church in State Association.

May 5 Wed. Missionary meeting. Lecture on Medical missions illustrated by stereoptician.

May 6 Thurs. Great event. We had Alfred's hair cut like a man's. It changes his looks entirely to lose his Bob.

May 7 Fri. Contest concert between Prospect & Pleasant St. schools. The prize, a large American flag was given to Pleasant St. by one point. George sang in the cantata, "The Walrus and the Carpenter."

May 8 A usual Saturday. We drove to Wellington to take Mr. P. to the train to go to Mansfield. George & I went to Dramatic Ass. Plays. The 12 pound look. Back of the Yards. Sir & Lady Sims, Kate Priest, policeman, Michael, mother & girl, suppressed desires, Henrietta, Mabel, psychopathic analysis, Stephen Brewster.

May 9 Sunday. We drove to the shack, a fine place & beautiful drive. It is mother's day & they gave me a potted plant. Mr. Van der Pyl spoke on Browning's Pippa, the Unconscious influence of a happy spirit.

May 10 Mon. Mr. P. came from Mansfield. Monday is busy day, washing, cleaning up etc. In the evening we took a ride to Wellington. We took Mrs. Caldwell & Rachel Kelsey with us. I was very, very lame from climbing down & up at the shack Sunday.

May 11 Tues. Mr. P. went to Akron to attend the State Conference. They could not start the car & had to push it into Mrs. Caldwell's driveway. Edward came home early from the store because Mr. Tobin was away and Ives was sick.

May 12 Wed. Rainy.

May 13 Thurs. Alfred wanted Kellog's Toasted (wheat) biscuit, so he asked for "wheat crossed off biscuit." Mr. P. returned from Akron. I started to clean the bathroom, washing the walls.

May 14 Fri. Finished the bathroom. Mr. P. went to a lecture on "Cancer" by Dr. Clement of Elyria. He said that one woman in eight between the ages of 45 & 55 and one man in 14 die of cancer.

May 15 Sat. I went with Mrs. Caldwell to the Baldwin Mayday party. Scenes from Shakespeare. Miss Bradt and Miss Harter sang several times.

May 16 Sunday. We drove in the P.M. to Ruggles Beach and ate our lunch by the Giles Cottage by the violets, in the sun. Baccalaureate seminar of Seminary by Prof. Hutchins, a sort of farewell seminar on his part too as he goes to Berea.

Ernest C. Partridge

May 7 Singing contest between Prospect & Pleasant schools. Pleasant won.

May 8 A Case game in PM. We beat 3–1. Family drove me to Wellington. Reached Mansfield's 11PM. Guest at Lentens. 50m

May 9 Sunday. Spoke in SS, then in 1st Church. Evening Mayflower Church.

May 10 Home about noon. Drove to Wellington after supper.

May 11 Went to Akron to State Conference. Guest with Mr Van at House's. 70 m

May 12 A very good series of meetings.

May 13 Home from Akron in time for supper. We reported Conference in Union PM. 70m

May 14 A lecture in evening by Dr Clement on "Cancer."

May 15 Heidelberg-Reserve-O track meet. We won easily.

May 16 Sunday. Mr Van in AM. Drove to Ruggles beach for lunch. Mr Hutchins preached Sem. Bac[calaureate] in evening. 44m

May 17 Dr Hume's first lecture on Non-Xu Prob movements in India.

May 18 Dr Hume on Non-Xu Saints in India. PM Political Conditions. Spent evening at Churchill's visiting with Dr H.

May 19 Sem. Com. Dr Gunsalers on " Education of an American." Banquet. Then Gunsalers ill[ustrated] lect[ure] "The Religion of Rembrandt."

May 17 Mon. Dr. Hume spoke on the Non-Christian Protestant movement in India. He was very interesting.

May 18 Tues. Something going on all day. Dr. Hume twice, student volunteer, movies, Polyanna but I did not go to any of them.

May 19 Wed. Seminary Commencement, Dr. Gunsaulers, lecturer, banquet, evening lecture by Dr. G. I went to the banquet only.

May 20 Thurs. Mr. P. & I took Mrs. Harris and Miss Barker to Wellington for a ride. It rained part of the way but we put on the side curtains and did not get a bit wet.

May 21 Fri. Mr. P. took Miss Barker & Prof. & Mrs. Wright to Elyria. In the afternoon, the three little ones, Mr. P. & I went with Mr. Pond out to a school house 3 miles north. It was the last day, they spoke pieces, sang etc. Then Mr. P. and Mr. P & I made speeches, then ate ice-cream & [?] a neighbors house [?].

May 22 Sat. A hard day. Mr. P. went to Lodi. I went to Gray Gables to a house party.

May 23 Sunday. Mr. P. preached at Lodi & Ashland. We, with Lawrence, went to Linwood Park in the afternoon and ate our lunch there. George drove quite a little. In the evening Mr. Van preached on the Ceaseless Urge of Love, Evangeline.

[May 24–26]

May 27 Thurs. Took supper at the hotel with Mrs. Greene. The others were Mrs. Harris, Miss Kaughey, and Mrs. Bunker. George said that in Latin class he did not know the word for "tired" (defenses), but a girl told him without thinking he said it and then when his turn came again on a word that he did know he did not say it, to even up.

Ernest C. Partridge

May 20 Drove to Wellington for a ride with Mrs Harris and Miss Barker.

May 21 Took Miss Barker & Wrights to Elyria. In PM Mr. Pond & W & little kids to schoolhouse for closing exercises. 26m

May 22 5:25 car to Lodi. Guest at parsonage. 55m

May 23 Sunday. Morning Cong Ch Lodi. Spoke to Men's class. Church evening, Ill[ustrated] lecture for Leininger of Ashland. 15m

May 24 Home at noon. Night parade and mock convention with George. 45m

May 25 Second session of convention. Hughes nominated on 4th ballot.

[May 26–June 11]

May 28 Fri. Edward received his diploma from Business College, no Commencement exercise. The children got their marks this week. Frances & Billo have gone up. Alfred about the same. George up.

May 29 Sat. Samuel & Alexan came about 11:15 P.M. We sat up until almost one. Alexan has so many horrible things to tell.

May 30 Sunday. Mr. P., Edward & George drove to Bellevue where Mr. P. preached for Mr. Breed. I went to a memorial service under the arch. We took our lunch to the arboretum. They came back for supper. Service for G.A.R. Lights went out. Mr. Van — just wonderful.

May 31 Mon. Memorial day parade, three little ones marched. Samuel & Alexan left at noon. Edward took two crowds of people to the lake, $2 & $5 respectively.

Memoranda George weighed 91; Frances 52; Alfred 43; Billo 61; Mr. P. 153; Hampartsoom 175; W.G.P. 148

June 1 Tues. Cleaned up after two days of neglected work on account of company. Mrs. Greene & her sister left on the evening train and we took them down.

June 2 Wed. Got my dress, a pongee silk that Miss Peterson gave me, from Mrs. Galehouse who had made it over some. She wanted to charge a dollar but I gave her $1.50.

June 3 Thurs. Last day of school for George as he had no exams being above 85 in everything.

[June 4]

June 5 Sat. Ernest went to Cincinnati to speak on his way to Berea. We all went to Wellington with him eating our lunch beside the station.

June 6 Sunday. Children's day, which means dressing the children up clean twice. All three spoke, Alfred, standing by Eldora Haskell, said "God made my life a little light, within the world to glow, a little flame that burneth bright, Wherever I may go. God made my life a little flower that giveth joy to all, Content to bloom in native boxes, although the place to small." Frances said "And this were told, 'Tis a pleasant thing that little children call him king." Billo recited with others the Ten Commandments, Beatitude, & Twenty-third Psalm. He received a diploma from the Primary Dept. and a Bible from the First Church. They all deported themselves well. In the afternoon we drove to Kipton, then Wellington, then home. Lawrence & Edward disagreed about some turkeys & chickens.

June 7 Mon. Mr. & Mrs. Getchell called.

June 8 Tues. I tried on my dress, black & white gingham.

June 9 Wed. Went to call on the Getchells after the Conservatory Commencement, which lasted until about nine. Billo went out to the shack with Woody and a lot of small boys, the first time he had gone without George.

June 10 Thurs. We started for Wellington at 7:30 A.M. to meet Mr. P. Saw the Getchells at the station. It is evident that Billo is the noisy one of the family and the one that keeps the little ones stirred up.

Ernest C. Partridge

June 12 Drove to Cincinnati. Spoke in two churches. 225m

June 13 Sunday. Spoke morning for Pratt. Evening another church.

June 14 Morning train to Berea, Ky. 132m

[June 15]

June 16 I spoke on PM program with Dr Warren Wilson. PM train back to Cinn[cinati]. 132m

June 17 Reached Oberlin. 225m

[June 18–19]

June 20 Sunday. This commencement our 25th Reunion. A fine crowd back and a good time.

June 11 Fri. The children all got their reports, all promoted creditably. George, his first semester, had two A's in Math & English & B+ in Latin & Civics. Billo promoted to 4B. Frances to 2B & Alfred to 1A.

June 12 Sat. Mr. & Mrs. Adams, Mr. & Mrs. Hawley, and Mr. Proctor were here for '95 business meeting.

June 13 Sunday. Very hot. I went to the regular service in the morning. They sang the Sanctus. Mr. Swan and Miss Bradt singing the solos. Mr. P. went to the Baccalaureate – the evening service but I did not. We took a drive through Kipton, Brighton & Wellington.

June 14 Mon. A class party at Mr. Adams' house. The Callenders, Raymonds, Mrs. Behr, Mrs. Jack & Mr. Sheffield had arrived. We had a fine time.

June 15 Tues. Class reunion at the James Brand house, present Callenders, Raymonds, Mrs. Behr, Mrs. Jack, Miss Lister, Miss Roberts, Smithkous, Woodmansee, Proctor, Sheffield, Adamses, Bowers, Hawleys & Newcombs, Williamses. A very pleasant reunion with the 95 children present, picture.

June 16 Wed. Commencement – I did not go to the exercises but I went to the dinner and the reunion Glee Club Concert. Armen left for Wilmington, Vermont where she is to be cook for a Geology group.

June 17 Thurs. Rainy. Everything finished, everyone going home. The Callenders stopped to say "goodbye." They are a fine family. I had to clean up the house and do a little housekeeping.

June 18 Fri. I washed and ironed and tried to get ready to go east.

June 19 Sat. More ironing and getting ready. I went down town to take my hat and buy a few things. My hat is the same brown one that I bought in Boston when we first came back for $1.50.

June 20 Sunday. The first service of the United Church, a very impressive communion service. Mr. P. and Ed and I went. As it rained we did not take a ride. In the evening, we called on Mrs. Giles-Kline and took her to the station to meet Hermann.

June 21 Mon. Worked all day to get ready to go. Called on Mr. Pond, Mrs. Hall and the Wrights.

June 22 Tues. Rainy, almost decided not to start, but did start at 10:30. Reached Erie about 7:30. Stayed at the Park View Hotel. Adults $1.25. Children 75 cts. Very comfortable.

June 23 Wed. Erie to Buffalo. Stayed with Mrs. Jack who has a lovely home. Went to call on Prof. & Mrs. Moore. Had a very pleasant time indeed.

June 24 Thurs. Buffalo to Oswego. Our first auto trouble. The hub of the front wheel gave out, $4.30. At Oswego, stayed at the Adams House, very unpretentious but comfortable.

June 25 Friday. After a long day we arrived at Winthrop [St. Lawrence Co. NY] where Aunt Ruby Crane lives. We had a very nice time there on a farm with plenty of room and plenty of good things to eat.

June 26 Sat. Arrived first at Mooers where we hunted up Mrs. Atwood-Bosworth, then Annie Olney's, where we took supper, then at West Chazy. Mr. P.'s mother [stepmother] has grown old very fast, is quite deaf and very disconsolate.

June 27 Sunday. West Chazy. It was Camp Meeting and we did not attend any service. We went to Mrs. Bosworth's for supper and had a nice time.

June 28 Mon. We intended to go beyond Burlington but after driving through the Hero islands we got in after noon. Geo. [cousin the dentist] was alone and wanted us to stay. I worked what I could in that old fashioned house, a lovely place.

June 29 Tues. Breakfast in Burlington. Geo. [cousin] went with us to Montpelier and took us to dinner. We were caught in a terrible rain, tried to dive into a barn, got stuck, were so delayed that we went only to St. Johnsbury.

June 30 Wed. Breakfast in Vermont, lunch in New Hampshire and supper in Lewiston, Maine. We had trouble with a front wheel, the second one, at Danville Junc. But finally we drove very slowly to Lewiston and found papa and his wife waiting for us.

July 1 Thurs. We left Lewiston about half past ten and took lunch in a beautiful woodsy lane where we were eaten up with huge mosquitoes. The car gave us some trouble, the radiator having to be filled often. We also had a puncture. Reached Monson about eight.

July 2 Fri. The children explored everything nearly on the farm. I washed the journey clothes. We have most glorious food. We drove down town.

July 3 Sat. Esther & I ironed and then in the afternoon, she and Ernest & the three little ones and I went strawberrying. The black flies and minges [midges; tiny biting flies] were just dreadful and the little ones soon got discouraged and went home.

Ernest C. Partridge

[June 21]

June 22 Rained but started East. Erie at 7PM. Park View Hotel. 1341/2

June 23 Erie–Buffalo. Guests of Jacks. Called on Moores. 931/2

June 24 Buffalo–Oswego via Rochester. Front hub gave out. Adams house. 1451/2

June 25 Oswego to Potsdam. Stayed night at Aunt Ruby's & Fred's. 165m

June 26 Potsdam to West Chazy. Called at Bosworth. Night with mother. 90m

June 27 Sunday. Bosworth's drove down and we drove up & stayed to supper. 20m

June 28 Drove to Burlington. Spent night with Dr. Partridge [cousin George, the dentist]. 50m

June 29 Burlington to Montpelier. 75m

June 30 Montpelier to Lewiston. Ruined another hub. Changed it in the morning ourselves. 133m

July 1 Lewiston to Monson. A late start. Got to Uncle Gene's about 7PM. 122m

[July 2–10]

July 4 Sunday. We all went to church and Uncle Gene, Ernest & I stayed to Sunday School. Uncle G. was superintendent, Ernest & I both teachers.

July 5 Mon. Esther and I washed & dried our clothes between showers. The children celebrated with cap pistols and fire crackers, then in the evening we had sparklers and pin wheels and colored lights.

July 6 Tues. Ironing & strawberrying.

July 7 Wed. Ironing.

July 8 Thurs. Went strawberrying and got soaked, Mr. P., Esther & I. Uncle Gene got soaked where he worked & the children coming home from swimming. Only Aunt Jennie was dry.

July 9 Fri. Went strawberrying, got scared of rain and came home, then went again & got a lot. Edward went with us. Afterwards he had fever and was really sick.

Ernest C. Partridge

July 11 Reached Monson. True Aim of Life. Evening, Life was Manifested.

[July12–17]

July 18 Sunday. Morning, Monson, Fact of X. Evening, Russia.

[July 19–24]

July 10 Sat. Went to the villages in the evening and got some gingham for a dress for Frances. The others went to Guilford for a pattern.

July 11 Sunday. All went to church except Aunt Jennie.

July 12 Mon. Our family & Esther went to Guilford, bought shoes for George for $4.75, & for Billo $2.50, less Educators[?].

[July 13–14]

July 15 Thurs. Edward, the two little ones and I went to Lewiston. We had a little trouble and then stopped to help another man so we did not get there until about seven o'clock. Found them waiting for us and supper ready.

July 16 Fri. Came with Grandpa and Grandma to Newport [ME] where we stayed over night with Aunt Frank and Cousin Fannie. We saw Fannie's husband, John Grindell.

July 17 Sat. Came to Garland [ME]. We had some auto trouble just before we arrived at Frank's so we had to go out from Garland 2 ½ miles to get a part that was lost. Stayed with Cousin Emma. Her daughter Gladys and the latter's "beau" John Robinson were there.

July 18 Sunday. I spoke in the church. Then Papa and our family drove to Bangor to take dinner with Nellie Graffam Bartlett. The Guilford people came down and Nellie's daughter-in-law were there so we had quite a party.

July 19 Mon. It poured so that we did not dare to start out with the auto without chains. We drove over to Mary McCoomb's house with a horse, stayed there to dinner and supper, then back to Emma's.

July 20 Tues. Came home to Monson. Found Billo had been a fine boy all the time we were gone. Two letters from Polly written in June, quite recent. Esther and I washed in the P.M.

July 21 Wed. Ironed.

July 22 Thurs. Alfred 6th birthday. He had a boat, a knife, a pink comb, and various things to eat. Esther made ice-cream and cake & I frosted it. Uncle Gene fell off a load of hay and broke two ribs but he sat at the table to celebrate Alfred's birthday.

July 23 Fri. Dr. Sampson came to see Uncle Gene and plastered him up. Uncle G. no worse.

July 24 Sat. Rained. Did very little with the hay. My father has been visiting here all week and helping where he could. Uncle Gene thinks he is very strong and capable still.

July 25 Sunday. We went to church. In the evening Mr. P. spoke about Polly. Aunt Jen. & Esther went and I stayed with Uncle Gene. He is much more independent.

July 26 Mon. Edward & I and the little ones took papa to Garland and then both of them to Newport where they took the train for Lewiston. We had lunch and then came back to Monson, reaching here about six o'clock.

July 27 Tues. Washed.

July 28 Wed. Ironed.

July 29 Thurs. Aunt Jennie & the two little ones & I went down to Charlie Weeks's and stayed to supper and until the others came for the mail.

July 30 Fri. Esther & I were going blueberrying but because was not a hay day Mr. P. & Edward took the car to pieces as usual & did not get it together in time for us to go.

July 31 Sat. Mr. P. & Esther, George & I went blueberrying in the afternoon, going about five miles into Elliotsville over terrible roads. We got about twelve quarts. It began to rain so we came home early.

August 1 Sunday. Mr. P. preached in Monson in the morning and we all except Edward drove to Garland in the afternoon where we preached in the evening. The children were very much interested in three cute little Jersey calves.

Ernest C. Partridge

July 25 Sunday. Monson, morning, Juo 14/22. Evening MLG.

[July 26–31]

August 1 Sunday. Monson, morning, Juo12/24. Evening, Garland, Missionary talk. 20m

[August 2–7]

August 8 Monson, morning, Vision of service.

August 9 Committee paid me $72 for summer work.

August 10 Left Monson about 8:30 for Lewiston. Dinner at Newport. Lewiston about 6 PM.

August 11 Lewiston to Laurents Mass via Portland, Portsmouth & Haverhill. Night at Franklin House. 129m

August 2 Mon. Returned from Garland about ten o'clock. They got in four loads of hay. Alfred was sick all day after he got home, had fever & headache.

August 3 Tues. Washed. The mowing machine broke, so they did not do a great amount of haying. Alfred better.

August 4 Wed. We, with Esther, went to Moosehead Lake. Mr. P. called on Mr. Vrooman who had gone to a Missionary picnic in a grove. The auto spring broke & we got home with difficulty. We had a fine view of the lake from the hill as we went in & a hill at the east.

August 5 Thurs. Esther, Billy & I went to Elliotsville blueberrying. We got about twenty quarts. It was very hot but the berries were very thick.

August 6 Fri. Aunt Jennie and Uncle Gene went to Elliotsville berrying & got ten quarts or so. They took a lunch and stayed all day. They were pretty tired but seemed to have enjoyed it.

August 7 Sat. Washed, Washed my hair and then dried it by raking hay with the horse rake to please the children.

August 8 Sunday. All except Aunt Jen. went to church, George, Frances, and I in the buggy with Nell. In the afternoon our family and Esther went to the big falls, took our supper. The three little one all got in & got wet.

August 9 Mon. Uncle Gene and I called on Mrs. Rob and Mrs. Leon Thomas, while Esther and the children went to the quarries. Then we all went up to the Wallace Homer's and saw his stuffed birds and animals.

August 10 Tues. We left the farm after taking our pictures, went to Lewiston, found papa all right. We bought a new radiator, put it on and started along in the morning.

August 11 Wed. Started on, went through Portland, Kennebunkport, York Beach, Portsmouth, took supper in Haverhill, slept in Lawrence. I telephoned to the Blunts and found Sarah was staying at Charlie's recovering from an operation.

August 12 Thurs. Took breakfast with the Blunts, called on Miss Davis and the Riders. Lucy Abbott came to see us. We drove to the cemetery [burial site of Fanny Goodell Graffam], then to Lucy's where we had cold milk. Drove to Concord and Lexington, visited Sleepy Hollow, Lexington Bridge etc. Drove to Worcester.

August 13 Fri. Stayed over night at Zuzu's, called on Mr. Putnam, did a little shopping, stayed with Zuzu for a fine dinner. Nazeli was there, also some Armenian girls who had just come from Aleppo. Drove to Amherst, got stuck in the mud between Ware & Belchertown, terrible thundershower.

August 14 Sat. Amherst, got settled in the parsonage, a beautiful house and surroundings.

August 15 Sunday. I stayed at home from church to keep the children quiet because church is so near.

August 16 Mon. Went to the garden, got corn and beans and a few peas.

August 17 Tues. Drove to Ashfield and took dinner with the Perry's. Mrs. Perry not very well, had very poor help, but getting along. Drove to Mountain Rest, saw Mrs. Riggs, Mr. & Mrs. Ernest Riggs, Mrs. Wingate, Mrs. Christie, Mrs. Mote, Miss Trowbridge.

August 18 Wed. Drove to Barre to see the Blanchards, got stuck on a hill between Pelham and Prescott for lack of gasoline. Walked to the top, found a Mr. Norton who gave us gasoline from his own car. Had a fine dinner & a good time at Barre. Lucile & Alice were at home.

August 19 Thurs. Stayed at home and got ready for Miss Gage! Mr. P. went to Boston to see Mr. Barton.

August 20 Fri. Miss Gage did not come but wrote that she would come Saturday. Mr. P. returned.

August. 21 Sat. She came and we were very glad.

August 22 Sunday. Mr. P. preached but the rest of us did not go to church. In the afternoon, we drove out past Sugar Loaf and stopped in the densest shade we could find and ate some chocolate that Miss Gage brought.

August 23 Mon. Garabed Eff., wife & Frances came about noon. Miss Gage went home in the afternoon and Mrs. Sewny came about six o'clock.

Ernest C. Partridge

August 12 Breakfast at Blunt's, Andover. Called on Davis & Ryders. To Worcester via Concord. 55m

August 13 Worcester to Amherst via Ware & Belchertown, bad rains. 50m

[August 14]

August 15 Sunday. Preached 1st ch Amherst. Juo 12/24.

[August 16]

August 17 Drove to Ashfield for dinner. Visit with Percys. Stopped at Mountain Rest [religious summer retreat in Goshen, MA; built 1902] on way home. 43m

August 18 Drove to Barse for visit with Blanchards. 70m

August 19 Went to Boston early train. A long talk with Dr Barton. Lunched with him. Out to Auburndale for night. Evening with Alden Clark. 99 1/2

August 20 Spent day till four in Board Rooms. Out to Amherst. 117m

August 21 Worked on car part of forenoon.

August 22 Sunday. Spoke in 1st ch Amherst on Americas Response in NE. Evening N. Amherst a nice talk for Gustin. Miss Gage with us. 36m

August 23 Drove to N. Amherst for a carburetor. Miss Gage went. Paelian's came. Mrs Sewny came in PM. 36m

August 24 Mrs Sewny, Paelian, Edward, George, & I drove to Mt Rest & Ashfield. Had a long conference with Wingate & Merrill. 50m

August 25 Mrs Sewny went. Hawleys for dinner PM. Some of family drove to Northfield.

[August 26]

August 24 Tues. Mr. P., Gar Eff, Mrs. Sewny, Edward and George drove to Ashfield and Mountain Rest while Helen and I stayed with the little folks.

August 25 Wed. Mrs. Sewny went home in the morning and we drove to Northfield in the afternoon.

August 26 Thurs. We stayed at home all day because they were working on the car.

August 27 Fri. The Paelians were going in the morning, but they wanted to see the campus etc. and when they got through it was nearly noon so I persuaded them to stay to dinner. They got off about half past three. Then I hustled to clean up the house to start Saturday. Took supper with Mr. Alden Clark, Dr. C's uncle.

August 28 Sat. After lots more hustling on the part of us all we left Amherst about eleven o'clock and drove to Schenectady. We stayed at the Hough House, very comfortable but very noisy. We paid $8½ for three beds in two rooms.

August 29 Sunday. Drove to Auburn, not nearly as beautiful as the northern route by which we went. We found a lodging house that was like the Arnasia Khans, gaudy but dirty, six dollars.

August 30 Mon. Drove to Niagara Falls, found a pretty rooming house, $8, settled down and then went to see the sights. We walked across the bridge to Canada, saw the falls by electricity. It was wonderful and even the little ones were awed.

Ernest C. Partridge

August 27 Amherst–O 665m

[August 28–29]

August 30 Reached Oberlin about ten o'clock AM. Staying at Fauk [Home].

[August 31–September 6]

September 7 Wrote S.T.C. Alumni letters. Also to Dr B about Trebizond. Raymonds called on way thro. Car in shop for repairs.

[September 8–30]

August 31 Tues. Edward and George got up early and walked over to Goat Island, and the little ones and I went partly across that bridge. Then we came back, had breakfast, and started toward home, stopped a few minutes at the Jack's to get a check cashed. Stayed at Ashtabula $9.

September 1 Wed. Our last day of travel. We came to Oberlin about noon, had lunch at home and then found that it was the day the stores are closed, so we had to scramble around to find anything to eat. It is good to be back, but our house seems like a doll house compared with the Amherst parsonage.

September 2 Thurs. Housework, washing.

September 3 Fri. Washing again & ironing.

September 4 Sat. Edward, Hermann and George Landis went to Ruggles Beach for the afternoon and evening.

September 5 Sunday. Mr. P. & George went to church. Edward returned from the Lake after I had worried about him all night and day. We called on Mrs. Greene and the Martins at Tank Home. The boys had stayed at the Giles Cottage.

September 6 Mon. Labor Day. Last day of vacation. Heavy hail storm. We went to the movies to see Marguerite Clark in "Girls," then to Tobin's for ice-cream cones.

September 7 Tues. Took the children to school, Billo to 4B, Frances 2B, Alfred to 1A. Miss Brady is still in the first but Billo has a new teacher. Frances, too, Miss Keflar. The Raymonds called, just for a half hour or so.

September 8 Wed. Washed all day long and Mr. P. did nearly all the housework. Billo's teacher is Miss Campbell.

September 9 Thurs. Frances earned her first wages, two cents an hour, for wheeling Llewelyn Jones.

September 10 Fri. Washed again, but very little. Cleaned up the house mostly.

September 11 Sat. Always a mixed up day and it rained.

September 12 Sunday. Communion service in the Second Church. Drove after dinner to the Lake, the nearest place, about twelve miles from here. The car runs very well, since it is all made over and fixed up.

September 13 Mon. Mr. P. varnished the parlor floor and put up four cans of peaches. I have done nothing out of the ordinary except to take a nap in the afternoon.

September 14 Tues. Washed at Miss Sinclair's. I got through at noon this time. Called on Mrs. Farrell and Mrs. Rader.

September 15 Wed. I had a sick headache all day, was so nauseated that I could do nothing. Mr. P. did all the housework. At eight P.M. I woke up and my headache was gone. When I came out I found Mr. P. ironing. I took his place and did part of it.

September 16 Thurs. I felt very well and commenced cleaning the attic. I went to prayer-meeting with Mr. P. in the evening.

September 17 Fri. Washed again. Mrs. Wright and Prof. W. called. I finished up the attic. Frances got her first marks in the second grade. A on one paper and A+ on the other. Mr. P. varnished the dining room one coat.

Ernest C. Partridge

October 1 Got car back from garage. Called at Fauk Home. Winona & Alfred came in PM from Burlington. I left for Chicago on evening train. 323m

September 18 Sat. Mr. P. varnished the dining room again and the bath room. We took a lunch and all, except Edward, drove out to Lorain to the Days'. We roasted wieners and corn, had biscuit, doughnuts and milk. Mrs. Day invited us to supper, so we stayed.

September 19 Sunday. I did not go to church because all my clothes were out of order and then the top of the molasses can flew out and sprinkled my hair with molasses, so I had to wash it. Mr. P. spoke in Cleveland in the evening. Armen came.

September 20 Mon. Mr. P. came. Hampartsoom came. The Ford was out of order so we could not ride Sunday nor Monday.

September 21 Tues. George sick with a cold. Edward & his father, Mr. Martin, Alec & Lawrence went to Cleveland to see a league base-ball game. I washed under many difficulties. Lucile Day came to call.

September 22 Wed. Dried the clothes. Edward registered in college as a Freshman, French, Mr. Cardery, Chemistry, Prof. Holmes, Bible, Dr. Graham, Trig, Prof. Dortal, Physical Ed. Nelson Metcalf. First chapel at four. Mr. P. spoke in Toledo.

September 23 Thurs. First lessons, French at eight o'clock. Mr. P. went to Ravenna, found that the meeting was postponed until Friday. Saw Miss Trefethren at the Sun. lecture by Dr. Graham. She was in Sivas in July.

September 24 Fri. Mr. P. again went to Ravenna. Got some lovely embroidered waists and handkerchiefs from Polly.

September 25 Sat. Mr. P. took Miss T. to the station. George attempted to drive the car and ran into a telephone post. The steering wheel was loose, so he was not to blame. Cousin Will Day called.

September 26 Sunday. First service of the United Church in the Chapel. I went in the evening. Lucile Day called.

September 27 Mon. Tie-up, great day. They got Edward before the time and were sending him outside of town but a senior interfered. He stayed with a bunch of Freshman, ate down town. He tied up two but did not get tied up himself. He & Frank Huntley came home, dirty, torn & famished.

September 28 Tues. Alfred and I started for Burlington for my dentistry. We had ice-cream & cake in honor of my birthday, for desert at noon, but otherwise we did not celebrate.

September 29 Wed. We reached Burlington at 1:45 and went to the office. George [cousin, the dentist] worked on me from 3:30 until nearly supper time.

September 30 Thurs. Geo. filled three teeth, extracted 11 roots of six teeth, finished me up before noon. We went home to lunch, did a little shopping, took the train at 4:45 for home. Reached Albany about 10:30 & left at 11:45 on the sleeper.

October 1 Friday. Reached Oberlin at about three, train two hours late. No one expected us, only Billo at home. Expenses to Burlington: Fare to B. $17.50, returning about the same.

October 2 Sat. Lots of cleaning up.

October 3 Sunday. Pres. King's class on Mark, evening service, Enfranchisement of Women.

October 4 Mon. Washed, picked grapes & corn from Mrs. Merrill's garden. Took my gray dress down to Mrs. Dulmage, but have to have it dry cleaned. Called on Mrs. Haskell. Letter from E.C.P. Uncle Gene, Aunt Jennie. Alfred took supper with Everet Lamson.

October 5 Tues. Frances's report 2B Conduct B+, Effort A, Reading B+, Spelling A, Arith. B+; Alfred 1A Conduct B, Effort B, Reading C, Penmanship C, Music B

October 6 Wed. Tried to wash in Miss S's washing machine but it did not work so I had to wash out what I had wet by hand. I finished.

October 7 Thurs. Went to try on my blue dress which Mrs. Dulmage is making over, enlarging mostly. Called on Dr. & Mrs. Martin & Jessie.

October 8 Frid. Miss Hagopian from Hadjin came to call. In the P.M. we got the car out, took Miss H's suitcase to her room, got my dress, $2.

October 9 Sat. Cleaned house, talked with Miss Hagopian. Mrs. Wright brought my coat back that she had been mending. Edward went on a hike, the Freshmen invited by the Juniors. He took Miss Chessner. Then the Freshmen men had supper given by the Y.M.C.A.

October 10 Sunday. Evening service "Rise of Bolshevism." Then went to Tank Home to say "Goodbye" to the Martins. In the afternoon with Lawrence we drove to the Lake, 12 miles. The children played in the sand.

October 12 Mon. Alfred went to school but came home on account of a headache. I tried to get ready to go to Marietta to the Board Meeting. I had my blue dress fixed over, Armen's hat made over ($3), rubber heels put on my shoes to straighten them up. Took Alfred to Dr. Colegrove, gave castor oil.

October 13 Tues. Did not go top Marietta because Alfred was not very well. He seemed worse in the afternoon, sores on his lips and his throat swollen. Edward's first Chemistry test A+. Edward's first Math O.K. English Freshman, not sub-Freshman. Mrs. Trowbridge & Mr. Riggs brought madzoon for Alfred.

October 14 Wed. I did not go to Marietta on account of Alfred. I had every hour arranged for but not counting on a sick boy. I went to see Mrs. Wright a while in the afternoon. Alfred better towards night but cannot eat because his lips are so sore.

October 15 Thurs. Alfred still sick with his mouth. It is very hard for him. He cannot eat, and grows thinner and thinner.

Ernest C. Partridge

October 2 Stopping at Hotel Stratford. An afternoon conference of Relief Workers.

October 3 Sunday. 11AM Spoke at Bethlehem Pres Church. 4:30 PM St Stephen's Lutheran Church. 8PM with Kirbye at a German Lutheran church. Chop Sewy afterwards. 12m

October 4 All day sessions of Workers with lunch together.

October 5 Spoke to 750 pupils of Fenger High School. Should be 6th. [Oct 6 entry]

October 6 Went with Dr Littlefield to hear him speak & see film & slides. Spoke part of time.

October 7 Spoke an hour at Chic Evangelistic Inst 1754 West Washington. Went to Hyde Park YM but too late to speak.

October 8 1130 Chi Col of Osteopathy but found a holiday and no opening.

October 9 No speaking. Luncheon with speakers. Evening at Paul Norhadian's.

October 10 Sunday. Unity Ch Oak morning. Dinner at Dr Hemingway's. Evening Xu Ch Harvey.

October 11 Swedish Ministers Meeting 10:30–11. Supper with the Wallers and took evening train to Marietta.

October 12 Reached Marietta at 1:30. Guest at Mrs S. C. Gilman, 305 4th St. Session began this PM. 466m

[October 13]

October 14 Turkey session this AM. A very satisfactory program.

October 15 China session & last very good. Bohn and I left Marietta at 2:35PM on train to Dover, trolley to Cleveland. Bohn stopped off at Akron.

October 16 Friday. I went to an afternoon tea at Mrs. Churchill's. It was her mother's 35th wedding anniversary. Armen came home to stay with Alfred. We expected Mr. P. and went to meet him twice but he did not come. Edward got back his first Bible paper, A, and Miss Metcalf had written "very good."

October 16 Sat. Mr. P. came early in the morning, having been on the way from Murietta since two o'clock the day before. He enjoyed the American Board meeting very much, saw the Clarks, the Getchells, Dr. Haas etc. Mr. P. went back to Chicago in the evening for Sunday appointments.

October. 17 Sunday. Edward and I went to church. Mr. Van der Pyl spoke on "Christianity a man's religion." We did not go to ride because Alfred did not want to. He seems a little better. Edward drove Armen and Mr. Frazier, an Indian & Mr. Curtis, from Japan, to Wellington where they are to speak.

October 18 Mon. Alfred much better. He kissed me for the first time in the week and thought it a most wonderful privilege. Harry caught a mouse.

October 19 Tues. Alfred went to school and seemed all right when he came home. He said that he caught up with Buddy and went ahead of him.

October 20 Wed. I went to a Home Missionary Meeting at Mrs. Andrews's house. Mrs. Hosford, the State President spoke. In the evening Armen came home from 7 to 8. Washed the dishes, and I went to student's recital. Mrs. Maitland sang. Two good letters from Polly, September 4 & 13.

October 21 Thurs. Today Billo was sick and so I was busier than ever. I intended to clean the cellar but could not leave him that long. I had to go down town to get George some shoes ($5.50).

October 22 Fri. Billo still sick.

October 23 Sat. Edward took Ettrick, Lawrence, Frank Huntley and Seemann to Wooster. Met his father there. But Oberlin was beaten 19 to 0. George played with the Crescents & beat the other team. H.S. won against Vermilion. Edward came home about 11:30.

October 24 Sunday. I went morning & evening. We rode to the lake road, then Lorain & back home. Mr. Nigoghosian and Hermine called.

October 25 Mon. Mr. P. came home in the afternoon to wait for his next appointment.

October 26 Tues. Mr. P. still here. I went to the dressmaker's to try on my gray dress. Billo went back to school. Frances has chicken pox.

October 27 Wed. I got the garbage man to take all the rubbish out of the cellar, a great relief. I attended a political meeting to find out how to vote.

Ernest C. Partridge

October 16 Reached Cleveland 1:30 AM. Train to Elyria 4:35. Car to Oberlin 6:20. Spent day getting ready to go again. Oberlin 7. Train to Chicago 8:19. 219m

October 17 Reached Chicago 8:20AM. 11 AM Garfield Park Baptist Ch. 4:30PM Westside Y.W.C.A. 8PM Austin Xu Ch. 10:15 train for Wheeling. 323m

October 18 Reached Wheeling in company with Gen A. at 1:30. Met at depot by Dr Smith. McLures Hotel. Rested rest of day. 476m

October 19 Spoke to 4 groups of children at the Ritchie school. High School at 1:30, 400 pupils. Webster School 3:00, 3 groups.

October 20 Spoke at 9:50 at Jefferson school, 2 groups. 1:30, 2 groups at McKinley school.

October 21 Spoke at 3 groups in Elm Grove HS and at Warwood HS in PM.

October 22 Elm Grove 4, 5–6 grades. 3 times in AM.

October 23 Took a 7AM train to Wooster for Oberlin football game. We got beat 19–0. Edward drove down & took me 11 miles to my train back to Wheeling. 212m

October 24 9:30 United Pres. Ch Men's class. Women's class, Boys class. 11 1st Res Church, 11:30 St Luke Episcopal, 7:30 [?] Pres.

October 25 7AM train to Wellington reached Oberlin at 2:30. 140m

[October 26]

October 27 Dr Rhonda Williams gave a fine address on The League of Nations.

October 28 Thurs. Alfred sick with some intestinal trouble.

[October 29]

October 30 Sat. Hiram game. All went except Alfred & Frances and me. Alfred getting some better.

October 31 Sunday. Alfred did not want me to leave him for a minute so I did not go to church. We took a ride in the afternoon but he sat in my lap all the time.

Memoranda: Billo's report – Health A, Conduct A, Effort B+, Reading B+, Eng B+, Penman B+, Arith C, Geography C, Physiology B. George – English B+, Latin B+, Physiology A, Math A. Frances – Health C (chicken pox), Conduct A, Effort A, Reading A, Spelling A, Arith B+. Alfred – Health B, Conduct B, Effort B+, Reading C+, Writing C, Music B+

November 1 Mon. Worked around the house all the forenoon, then washed in the afternoon, then was tired out. Alfred was better.

November 2 Tues. I voted for President etc. I voted for Cox & Roosevelt. For the four coming Presidential elections I shall have a boy casting his first vote. I hope they will all have more worthy candidates for their first vote than I had.

November 3 Wed. Went down town with Alfred, got two pairs of shoes, 3.50 and &2.00, also rubbers for him and a pair of shoes for myself $10. Harding, not Cox, elected President.

November. 4 Thurs. I washed out some things, called on Mrs. Barnard to see about her house for the Stapletons.

November 5 Fri. The event of the day was Alfred's losing his first tooth. It had been very loose and came out while he was eating an apple. Another event was a letter from Polly, Oct. 3. She is expecting a crisis of some kind and hopes we may see each other before many months.

November 6 Sat. In the afternoon Billo came in from play feeling miserable and we later found a few spots and we

Ernest C. Partridge

October 28 Heard Prof Fullerton on the Peace treaty. Julian candidate for US Senator.

[October 29]

October 30 Hiram beaten 43–0.

October 31 Mr Van der Pyl preached in morning on "A Nations Strength" evening "League of Nations." Took an auto ride in PM. 15m

November 2 Stayed in Oberlin to wrote. Winona & I both voted for Cox. Family drove me to Elyria in PM to take train to New York. Went via Philadelphia.

November 3 At Hotel Albert. Most of day at One Mad Ave. Evening with Miss Wheeler. 622m

November 4 Day at Rooms. 4 PM to White Plains. A good visit with Mrs. Hubbard, Mary & Hugh. 20m

[November 5–6]

November 7 Sunday. A long visit with Auntie Tipple. Spoke at an Armenian Rally to raise funds for Cilician army.

November 8 Forenoon at Rooms. PM to Philadelphia, a call on Carrol's. Night at Kabakjians.

November 9 Morning train to South Jersey. Bridgeton to speak at Minister's Meeting. Back in PM to Jersey City & out to Passaic for a meeting. Reached NY at 2AM. 140m

November 10 Left New York for Oberlin at 2PM. Reached Oberlin at 6:20AM. 11th.

knew he had chicken pox too. Geo. & Ed went to Cleveland to the Reserve Game. O won 20 to 14. They went to Keiths & returned at 1:30.

November 7 Sunday. Communion, the first in the Chapel. I went & when I came home I found Geo. all broken out with chicken-pox. We had thought of sending Ed away but Miss Greenwood said that it would be of no use. Edward & Alfred haven't taken it yet. Billo quite sick.

November 8 Mon. Billo seemed to have complications, sore throat, fever & abcess in the ear. Miss G. said that it should not affect his throat. As I see no spots I did not call a Doctor.

November 9 Tues. Billo still sick. Mr. P. in Philadelphia visiting Dicran Eff.

November 10 Wed. Mama tired as last year. Billo a little better.

November 11 Thurs. None of my family attended Armistice Day celebration. Mr. P. arrived before seven just as we were getting up. He was on his way to Indianapolis, left in the evening. I took occasion to wash at Miss Sinclair's.

November 12 Fri. Billo pretty well. He was to have taken private lessons this week but was not able.

November 13 Sat. Twenty years since we arrived in Sivas. Oberlin–Case game 23 to 0. Ed & Geo. went.

November 14 Sunday. I have not been out since last Sunday. My feet are so sore that I cannot bear to walk more than I have to. Ed & I went to evening service, Mr. V. preached on Blindness, suggested by Maeterlink's "The Blind."

November 15 Mon. I went to Elyria to find some blue dishes but did not find any. I decided to buy some other kind in Oberlin, so that I could replace them easily. Dr. MacIntosh did not allow Frances to go back to school.

November 16 Tues. Frances returned to school in P.M. Mamma's birthday. The first real snow of the season. My foot very bad, like an abcess on the bottom.

November 17 Wed. I bought woolen stockings for four @ 75 cts, no for three, mittens for Alfred & Frances, 60 cts & 75 cts. I bought stockings for myself, like boys, for $1., underwear for Billo $2.

November 18 Thurs. Washed at Miss Sinclair's. Got some new dishes here at the racket store. 12 dinner plates, 12 desert plates, 6 cereal dishes, 6 cups, 6 saucers, fruit dish (glass), 12 fruit saucers, 1 nappy, 1 round dish, 1 milk pitcher, all for $15.04. I made 6 pillow cases.

November 19 Fri. Ironed.

November 20 Sat. I was invited to an old ladies party at Prof. Wrights. Mrs. Van der Pyl and I were the youngest, by far. The guests of honor were Mrs. Clark, of the Presbyterian Board and her friend, Miss Burton. Others were Mrs. Shurtleff, Mrs. Burton, Mrs. Whipple, Mrs. Jewett.

November 21 Sunday. Frances & Alfred went back to Sunday School. I went to church, walked home with Mrs. Kelsay. The children had some goose feathers & dressed up in feathers and paint like Indians.

November 22 Mon. Washed by hand.

November 23 Tues. Mrs. Metcalf offered me a ticket to the Detroit Sym. Orchestra concert but I just had to iron so to have time to get ready for Thanksgiving.

November 24 Wed. made doughnuts, pies, birthday cake, stuffing, etc. Edward, George & I went to Wellington to meet Mr. P at 10:45. The train finally came about one o'clock.

Ernest C. Partridge

November 11 Home at 6:20AM. Left on 8:10 trolley for Cleveland. Big Tous to Indianapolis. 671m

November 12 Reached Indianapolis at 8:20AM. Conference at State office 12:30 train to Terre Haute. Registered at Hotel Deming. 391m

[November 13–14]

November 15 Terre Haute minister's Meeting. Spoke on N.E.R. After train east to Winchester. Night at hotel.

November 16 Morning train to Fort Wayne. Centliore hotel. Spoke 20 minutes Kiwanis luncheon. Spent night. 214m

November 17 Early train to Indianapolis Conference with Dr Royse. PM train to Terre Haute. Stopping at Filbeck Hotel. 192m

November 18 Interurban to Clinton. Call on Rev Geo E Francis local chairman. Laid out a plan for County which promises well. PM to Sullivan but accomplished nothing.70m

November 19 Trip to Sullivan. Called on Mrs Thompson, Rev. Cross and others. 40m

[November 20–21]

November 22 Early trolley to Clinton. Francis and I visited Dana, Cayuga and Newport organization township committees. Left at 8AM. Back at 7PM. 70m

[November 23]

November 24 Left on 12:58PM train 2 hours late for Wellington.

November 25 Thurs. Thanksgiving & George's birthday. We had a good dinner all together. George had some new waists, two phonograph records, a knife, a necktie, a book, a puzzle & a magnet. Armen took him to the movies. Mr. P. & I went too. Marguerite Clark in "Luck in Dawn."

November 26 Fri. Washed at Miss Sinclair's. Mrs. Husted and John Schuyler called. Mr. P. & I called at Mrs. Wright's

November 27 Sat. Mr. P. went back to Indiana. We bought a new coat for Alfred, a Mackinaw, brown ($9.50), some waists for George.

November 28 Sunday. I went to church twice, in the morning with Edward and in the evening with George. Armen went to Elyria with some of the Cosmopolitan Club. They spoke, sang etc. at Mr. Grant's church.

November 29 Mon. Washed. Decided to let Billo have private lessons with Mrs. Wright as he does not seem very well.

November 30 Tues. I went over to school to see Miss Campbell, Billo's teacher, and find out about his lessons.

Alfred: Health C, Conduct A, Effort A, Reading B, Penmanship C+, Music B+.

December 1 Wed. Billo began lessons with Mrs. Wright. He came home with a headache and said that he would never go again, that she talked all the time. He begged to go back to public schools.

December 2 Thurs. Miss Garner came just after dinner and stayed until after supper. Mrs. Metcalf took her down to see something of the College. Billo went to Mrs. Wright and came home delighted. Frances came home because her eyes hurt her. I went to hear Prof. Clark read Shaw's Androclus and the Lion. Mr. Lampson gave me a ticket.

December 3 Fri. I went down town, bought some trousers for George $2.50, gloves for Billo, 90 cts, cloth for sheets $4.50, blackboard 1.25, tablets 37 cts.

December 4 Sat. Elmas Marookian came in the evening.

December 5 Sun. Only George went to S.S. I went to church. Mr. Van – preached a tercentenary sermon.

December 6 Mon. Billo's tenth birthday. He received a pair of slippers, two toys, a ticket to the hospital fair. Edward invited him to the chicken supper. He had also a slate blackboard. We had ice-cream & cake and Russell Van der Pyl for supper.

Ernest C. Partridge

November 25 Arrived W[ellington] 1:30AM. Winona E, & G met me in car. A fine Thanksgiving dinner and day. Also George's birthday. 329m

November 26 Saw a Krescent football game. George playing center. Billo a sub. W & I called at Wright's in evening.

November 27 Co SS Assoc. Cleveland 8:25 trolley, 11:30 train to T.H.

November 28 Sunday. Got in on time at 9:23. A SS rally of T.H. pastors & supt's. I spoke about our work. A representative will be appointed. 391m

November 29 Dr. Royse came. We called on Bogart, Reinbolt, and in evening a meeting of Bogart's Committee. Does not favor drive, will help individually.

November 30 Called on Mrs Shaley. At Reinbolt' office, revise & had duplicated my biog sketch. Tried to see Snively & Co. Supt of Schools. Spoke 20 mins at Women's Miss Inst at Cong Church.

[December 1]

December 2 Called on editor's of three daily papers. Attended lecture on Near East by Mrs Hallie Linn Hill [Mrs Hill wrote Handbook on Citizenship].

December 3. Called on Y.M. Sec Gram Herring, Reinbolt. PM went to Brazil and called on W.E. Carpenter, Supt of largest SS in world, to ask Ed Nanse to talk Chemistry. 52m

December 4 A rainy day. Worked over slides. Prepared for Sunday and read. Elizabeth, William, Ruth, Malcolm, Cayuga Inst.

December 5 Sunday. 8 o'clock to Clinton, Baptist SS 10. Xu SS 10:30. 1stl ME 11. Dinner with Francis at hotel. Union meeting at Pres Church at 2:30. Train to Cayuga. Supper at parsonage. [?] [?] back to T.H. 75m

December 6 PM Went to Brazil but could not see Mr. Nanse. Talked with Mr. Carpenter. 32m

December 7 Tues. I started to wash in the afternoon but the machine was out of order.

December 8 Wed. Washed in the morning. Went down town in the afternoon to see if I could find some clothes for Billo. I did not find anything and decided to send to Mr. Hosmer. Elmas and I went to the Zoological Laboratory and Prof. Budington showed us microscopes.

December 9 Thurs. I took Billo & George to Elyria to make a last effort to find clothes for Alfred, but it was of no use.

December 10 Fri. Billo & Geo. went to the hospital fair, also Armen and Elmas.

December 11 Sat. Billo, Geo., Edward, and I , also Elmas went to the fair, but not all together. We came home together. We heard a play about Scotch life.

December 12 Sun. A miserable day because I did not feel well and everything seemed wrong. Four went to S.S. Billo went on a hike with his class. Geo. & Carroll went in another direction. Edward took the rest of us out for a ride.

[December 13]

December 14 Tues. Edward and I went to hear Roy Chapman Andrews on the Land of Kublai Kahn. It was very good and the pictures taken by his wife were fine.

December 15 Wed. I washed at Miss Sinclair's. It is easy when Elmas is here.

December 16 Thurs. The Elijah given by the Musical Union. For soloists they had only two from outside. Miss Sanderson and Mr. Quait. Prof. Maitland was Elijah, Mrs. Maitland sang, also Mr. Haroun, Mr. Adams, Mrs. Savage, Mrs. Hastings & Patricia McDonald.

December 17 Fri. The children keep saying that it is the last day of school this year. George & Billo went to basket ball practice. Edward is behind in his laboratory work so he is working extra afternoons so has no time to play.

December 18 Sat. A dreadful day because I made mince meat and ironed curtains and washed some windows as extras.

December 19 Sunday. I went to church and heard Mr. Van der Pyl on Wayside Tasks. Billo & I went to the Methodist Christmas Concert in the P.M. Mr. Adams leads them. It was very good. Early in the morning about five, girls & boys sang Christmas Carols around town.

Ernest C. Partridge

December 7 Lunch at Exchange Club as guest of Dr Tyler. Talked with Mrs Miller about Committee work. Evening train to Indianapolis. Night at Lueden Hotel. 73m

December 8 Forenoon in State Office. Train to Lafayette, Hotel Fowler. Called on Dean Coulter & Pres Stone. Lecture night at Bill Aitkinhead's home.64m

December 9 Call on Dean Coulter. Lecture on Baghdad by Dr Banks. A conference with Mrs Bennett Taylor. Trolley to Logansport. Night Barnett hotel.

December 10 Early train to South Bend. Oliver Hotel. Lunch with Father Burns, Pres of Notre Dame. 45 minute talk in Chapel. Visited library & Museum. Reached T. H. 6:25PM. Saw Dr. Royse on train. 249m

December 11 Spent day reading and resting and getting ready for Sunday.

December 12 Sunday. 6:30 train to Rosedale. Frank Jukes met train. Breakfast & dinner with them. Spoke in SS & church of ME church. Evening with M E Church Rockville. Supper with Dr & Mrs Royse. 46m

December 13 Dr Royse called on his way to office between trains. I am almost sick with a cold.

December 14 Guest at Exchange Club at noon. Spoke 20 minutes. Spoke on Heroines at State Normal School Y.W. 35 minutes.

[December 15]

December 16 Took PM train north to Crawfordville. Night at Crawford House. Attending a meeting for the organization for a County committee. 52m

December 17 Spoke 30 minutes at Chapel of Wabash College. Lunch at home of Prof Grave. To T.H. in PM via Indianapolis. 117m

December 18 Read most of day. Wrote a few letters.

December 19 Sunday. Morning at 1st Cong Church. Evening W.T.H. Cong Church. Very cold. 6m

December 20 Mon. I did quite a heap of Christmas shopping, left our packages at Whitney's and my muff at Watson's.

December 21 Tues. I washed again in the washing machine that does not reverse without help. Armenag Sharigian sent us some bulgur so we had pilaf and madzoon.

December 22 Wed. I went to Elyria early to meet Mr. P. and them we went to Cleveland, hoping to find something for Alfred to wear, but did not. We bought a few little things for Christmas. Elmas & Armen went to Detroit.

December 23 Thurs. Again we went to a S.S. entertainment, the first in the United Church. There were tableaux illustrating the Christmas story, very beautiful, music behind the scenes, Mr. Van der Pyl reading, the Christmas tree with candy bags for all.

December 24 Fri. About the same program as last year.

December 25 Sat. Stockings in the morning with a few little things. The Metcalfs brought 4 gold fish. Lucile Day came to the tree. We all fared well. I had community silver 4 knives, forks, & spoons, sugar spoon. Edward rain coat, George watch, Billo desk with blackboard, little ones desk. Then mittens from grandma.

December 26 Sunday. Hovsep and Vahan Khacharian came. They know about so many people that we know.

December 27 Mon. A box from Marsovan containing hard gingerbread, butter nuts, a pound of butter, homemade candy, all delicious and make us feel sentimental. Again locoom from Mariam.

December 28 Tues. Very cold, but the children went out sliding.

December 29 Wed. I washed at Miss Sinclair's. Billo went with the Johnstons to Kipton, to slide. They went in a pung[spring cart?]. Edward and Lawrence went to Miss Chase's to supper. Katherine was to be there.

December 30 Thurs. At noon I decided to take a one o'clock train to Detroit, leaving Mr. P. and Hampartsoom to take care of the family. I reached Detroit about four and went to the Hotel Metropole, stayed there with Samuel, calling up Mrs. Clark by telephone.

December 31 Fri. Went home with Mrs. Clark, stayed there to lunch, then she and I went, first with the Doctor to the Kuslarians, then to Mrs. C's home, then to Highland Park, found Josie Beard Heywood not at home, called on Hranoosh Var., Asdghig, then supper with Samuel, the Armenian Club until after midnight.

Ernest C. Partridge

December 20 Minister's Meeting voted to urge church to present NER before March 1st. 4:13PM train to Winchester. 78m

December 21 7:35AM train to Howe. Spent 3–5 at Miss William's home. Drove to Legrange. Supper of 25. Spoke 1½ hours to 50 people. Train down to Kendallville. 143m

December 22 Train at 3:20AM to Elyria. Winona joined me & we shopped in Cleveland. Returned on noon train. 238m

[December 23–24]

December 25 A very good Christmas dinner. H.K. with us. Lucile Day came for tree. We gave George a Watham watch, Winona community silver, Edward a rain coat.

December 26 Sunday. Mr Van der Pyl morning. Dr Beard on China evening. Vahan Khacherian & Hovsep came from Detroit.

December 27 Spent day with guests. They went back at 5:05.

[December 28]

December 29 Wrote letters most of day. Bowled a little with Edward.

December 30 Winona went to Detroit for a short vacation. Ham & I are doing the homework.

December 31 Lawrence came for supper and we played Rook & Pit till 12.

Memoranda

Edward had bill pocket book, 2 neckties, ten dollars from Papa, rain coat, Eversharp pencil, game, toy phonograph, top, pencils, erasers, 2 dollars, Life, Popular Mechanics, O pin, play stick pin, Oberlin stationery, mittens.

George had Waltham wrist watch from the family, 4 neckties, gloves, mittens, Mr. Donley phonograph record, cuff-buttons, book, handy-box, toy automobile, slippers, ten dollars, one dollar.

Frances, doll, dressed by Mrs. Prosser, doll house, furniture for three rooms, doll trunk, desk, painting books, ace cap, mittens, handkerchiefs, sweater, crocheted cap, beads, ring, $5, one dollar, Garden of Fuse cup & saucer

Alfred, desk, mittens, ace cap, $5, one dollar, bank, painting books, slippers, soldier suit, pistol, Bear book, animal book, cup & saucer.

Billo, $5, $1, desk with blackboard, jazz band, mittens, building sticks, painting book

Diaries of Winona & Ernest Partridge 1921

January 1 Sat. Came home at noon. Before I left Hovsep called me. Mrs. C. had stayed overnight with me. The turkey dinner was late. Samuel ordered chicken and that did not arrive so I had dinner on the stage. All the family except George met me including Hampartsoom.

January 2 Sunday. Mr. P & I went to church. The children went to S.S. I called on Mrs. Wright. Mr. P. went back to Terre Haute.

January 3 Mon. Lots of work to catch up. Children went back to school. I went to see Billo's teacher.

[January 4]

January 5 Wed. Edward & I went to Cleveland, got him a green suit for $50, two trousers, went to theatre, Otis Skinner in "At the Villa Rose." Armen came back.

January 6 Thurs. Washed at Miss S's.

January 7 Fri. Went down town to get Billo a jersey ($2.50), stockings (65, 65, 75), trousers for Billo ($1), and Alfred ($1.85). Basket ball practice for Geo. & Billo.

January 8 Sat. I worked hard but got pretty well through. Basket ball game O 3, Hillsdale 16. Billo is to go to the games when he has been good according to the judgement of his big brother.

January 9 Sunday. I did not go out on account of my feet. The children went to S.S. Ed & Geo. to evening service. Mr. V. preached on the Meanest Man in Town.

January 10 Mon. I attended the section meeting, met two women, Miss Spore & Mrs. Farnsworth-Ransom who said they remembered me from college.

January 11 Tues. Frances Dec. Reading B, Spelling A, Arith A, Music B, Drawing B+.

January 12 Wed. A hard day, working against time all day, washed, ironed, cleaned the house.

January 13 Thurs. Davis Van der Pyl's wedding. I was too late for the ceremony. Then we went to the Annual Meeting of the church.

Ernest C. Partridge

January 1 A busy day cooking and writing. Winona came back at 5:43.

January 2 Sunday. Mr Van der Pyl preached in morning. A lecture on Pilgrims in evening. All the boys went but Alfred. Took 11:30 train out of C to Indianapolis.

January 3 Reached I[ndianapolis] at 730. Breaskfast, a conference with Royse. Train to Terre Haute. 391m

January 4 A bad headache all day. Called on Herring.

January 5 Called on several of the ministers. Supper and evening at Men's Club 1st Cong Church.

[January 6]

January 7 Two rainy days in which I accomplished little outside. Considerable trouble from lumbago.

January 8 Made an appointment to speak at Kiwanis Club Jan 20. Called on Pres Parsons, some hope of a date there.

January 9 Sunday. No appointments. A quiet day reading and writing. Heard Dr Leon Harrison at Open Forum on "Marriage & Divorce."

[January 10]

January 11 Calling at houses of the ministers of city. Walked 6 –7 miles. Made about ten calls.

January 12 Continued calling on ministers. Called on Dr. Siebennorgan at Dr Blair's request. Lunch with Herring at Roots.

January 13 Notified Dr Blair of calls and arranged to speak in central Xu Ch next Sunday evening. News of Custer's sentence 6 months.

January 14 Fri. Washed hard to make up for dissipation of the day before.

January 15 Sat. Usual Saturday, fortunately pretty good sliding, Billo was invited to the Johnston's for dinner. Ed. Went to N.Y. Symphony orchestra. Geo. studied all the evening.

January 16 Sunday. Started in to stay at home & rest my feet but got restless & went in the eve to hear Frank Warner on the Southwest, Fisk Jubilee Singers in the afternoon. Four of the children went. I went to sleep.

[January 17]

January 18 Tues. Seamas McManus, Irish humorist, lectured and told stories.

January 19 Wed. Very unexpectedly to us Ernest came home. He finished his work in Indiana and came. Rained & froze, so icy people could hardly walk.

January 20 Thurs. Warmer, wet & muddy. I washed at Miss Sinclair's. Mr. P. did most of the cooking. Alfred was roller skating and fell in a mud puddle.

January 21 Fri. Washed more or less, and ironed in the evening.

January 22 Sat. Mrs. Sewny writes that she is coming to Oberlin to spend the rest of the furlough.

January 23 Sunday. Went to church in the morning with Ernest. In the evening Mr. V. spoke on "The Fatal gift of beauty" so I did not go.

January 24 Mon. I washed and in the afternoon went down town in the auto. I saw Dr. Colegrove about Alfred's nose & my feet. He has abcesses, not adenoids. My arches are broken down because I am stout.

January 25 Tues. Mr. P. and I called at Prof. Andrews's. George wore his first shirt, that is outside shirt, in place of a waist. George finished his exams.

January 26 Wed. I washed at Miss Sinclair's. Mr. P. got a telegram to go to Racine, Wis. next week. George got a permit for the gymnasium for five dollars.

January 27 Thurs. Cold.

Ernest C. Partridge

[January 14]

January 15 Rose 4:45 took 5:30 train to Indianapolis. Spent forenoon in Conference. A slow trip home, delayed by a wreck on track. 146m

January 16 Sunday. Spoke at Central Christians (1) church. Evening service.

January 17 Forenoon Ministers Meeting. PM calling at houses of ministers.

January 18 A telegram from Royse that I may quit in T.H. Took 10:30 train for Cleveland.

January 19 Reached Cleveland at 7:30, Oberlin on 10:10. 391m

[January 20–22]

January 23 Sunday. Heard Mr Van morning & evening" Fatal Gift of Beauty."

[January 24–26]

January 27 Supper & conference of religious workers. Church PM. Mr Labingier spoke on Religious Education. Called at Wright's.

January 28 Winona & George & I went to Cleveland shopping at Bakers at 50% discount. Bought me a suit. Suit, raincoat etc.for George.

January 29 Called on Beards & Mrs. Greene. A very exciting basketball game. Oberlin beat Michigan Aggies 23–21. Winona, Ed, George, Billo & I went.

January 30 Sunday. Winona & I heard Mr Van der P on "To whom shall we go?" Evening went with George "The Enlarging Sphere for Young Women."

January 28 Fri. Mr. P., George & I went to Cleveland, bought $25 suit for Geo. for $12.50, an $85 suit for Mr. P. for $42.50. We went to the Hippodrome & & saw all sorts of dancing. In the evening we went to a program for Parent-Teachers Ass. Billo got sick & vomited in the aisle twice before we got out.

January 29 Sat. Worked some but did not finish. In the P.M. we took the children to see Tom Mix, then called on Dr. Beard and Mrs. Greene, to basket ball in the evening. Michigan Aggies 21, O 23, very exciting.

January 30 Sunday. Went to church in morning (To whom shall we go?).

January 31 Mon. All were promoted. George to Soph B. Billo to 4A. Frances to 2A, Alfred to 1A. It was quite an exciting day. We called on Mrs. P., such resignation, such platitudes. Who could stand it? Mr. P. went on the evening train to Racine, Wis.

February 1 Tues. I intended to wash at Miss Sinclair's but Geo. had planned to go to the gym so I could not go. Ed also went to gym, I think.

February 2 Wed. I tried to wash at Miss Sinclair's but when I was well started Alfred came over & said that he felt sick and wanted me to come home, so I left the clothes in the machine until evening when A was asleep.

February 3 Thurs. Alfred better but did not go to school. I had a nice call from Dr. Floyd Smith. I ironed in the evening but the iron gave out. All sorts of troubles this week.

February 4 Fri. The last of Edward's exams, Physical Ed. & Trig. I attended a meeting of the sixth & fifth sections of the Womans Association.

February 5 Sat. A terrible day. Besides being a very rainy Sat. three feet of water came into our cellar, putting out the furnace fire and cutting off our drain. Our hood & coal were all under water, as everything else.

February 6 Sunday. The water drained off after Mr. Darling & some others succeeded in clearing out the main drainage pipe. I did not get out anywhere and my disposition is worn out.

February 7 Mon. Billo came home from school sick and did not go in he afternoon, probably from the dampness & cold. George also came home sick but went in the P.M.

February 8 Tues. Edward and Hampartsoom put in two tons of coal and then cleaned the cellar, an all day job, is cleaner than ever before. Billo was sick, Dr. Colegrove came, had fever, headache, sore throat.

February 9 Wed. I was miserable but just had to wash in the afternoon. At night I was worse naturally. Edward was also sick, all from the cellar.

February 10 Thurs. Billo much better, I sick until noon, but better in P.M. Alfred came in with his boots half full of water.

[February 11]

February 12 Sat. Went down town with George & bought him some Sunday shoes, $7.00.

Ernest C. Partridge

January 31 Got ready for another trip. Called on Mrs Pond. Ed got A in French, 3 little ones promoted. Ed & G in exams. Evening train to Chicago.

February 1 Reached Chicago 7:30AM. Had visit with Norhadian, Pushman, Mrs Lee, Dr Hitchcock & English. Lunched with Pushman. Train to Racine Wis. Spoke at Knights of Pythias (2).

February 2 Conference with Chairman Fowler & Sec. of local committee. Spoke in evening at 1st M.E. church (3). After that, meeting of Eagles (4). WGP [letter recipient]

February 3 Had a call from Mr Chenowith, one of the Cong pastors. Spoke 25 min. at Kiwanis Club (5) at lunch & half-an-hour in evening at Moose Club (6).

February 4 No appointments today. Called on Fowler. A visit with Oscar Banker [Bauher?] of Talas. He took me to see John Poladian. Movie in evening. Willard, Farnham [letter recipients]

February 5 No appointments, read in Public Library, wrote letters, went to movie. Hosmer, WGP, Dwight, Barton [letter recipients]

February 6 Sunday. Went to Universalist church with John Poladian. Lunch & dinner with him. Spoke to 100 Armenians in PM (7). Visit with Miss Kelly, heard her speak in evening.

February 7 Rode to station with Miss Kelly & thus had a visit. Rest of day reading & writing.

[February 8]

February 9 Lunch at Racine Rotary Club, ¾ hour address (8). Called on Poladian. Met Abraham Khorasanjian & wife, daughter of Harotum Mumjian. To Milwaukee at Wisconsin Hotel. Herring, Farnsworth [letter recipients]

February 10 A very bad day with headaches and nothing to do. WGP, JLB, Dr Doughty, Linn [letter recipients]

[February 11]

February 12 Left Milwaukee on PM train for Appleton, Sherman House.

February 13 Sunday. I went to church in the evening alone, because Edward was not well and George stayed with him.

February 14 Mon. Valentine's day. The children had an abundance, that is the little ones. Ed. & Geo. got one or two. Armen several.

February 15 Tues. Warm & springlike. I worked hard all day, finishing washing just in time to get supper. Billo went to basket ball practice.

February 16 Wed. The event of the day was that Yeranoohi came. I went to a Home Missionary meeting, led devotions, Miss Colcord, Miss Klingerhagen & Miss Sinclair spoke.

February 17 Thurs. Father & son banquet. Edward, Prof. Graham, George, Mr. Bohn, Billo, Prof. Lehmann. I went to see Prof. Root about Aghavni, also bought some cloth for some aprons. Took Yeranoohi & Alfred & Frances to the movies in the evening. At 2 o'clock Samuel call[ed] up from Detroit – A.M. just for a visit.

[February 18]

February 19 Sat. Alfred sick.

February 20 Sunday. Yeranoohi & I went in the morning to hear Mr. Van –.

February 21 Mon. Alfred some better but did not go to school.

February 22 Tues. Washington's birthday. Prof. Graham spoke. Yeranoohi, Armen, Edward & Geo. went. Poor Billo was sick and lost a trip to the Shack which Geo. took; a party at the Kelsay's which Alfred & Fr. attended and movies which Yeranoohi & the little ones attended.

February 23 Wed. Alfred & Billo still sick. I went to the doctors and got medicine for Alfred. I bought a pair of shoes for Geo. ($6.00), two pairs for Billo 4 & 2.50, two for Frances 2.50 each, one for Alfred 1.50, one for myself 7.50. All these except mine were ½ price.

February 24 Thurs. Alfred had a red spot on his cheek so Doctor came to see him, thought it was probably saysipilas [rosacea?] and told us to be careful.

February 25 Fri. Doctor thought that Alfred needed more care or I needed more help, but Mrs. Sewny came on the noon train and Alfred seemed so well that she agreed to take a special case at the hospital. A letter from Polly in French.

Ernest C. Partridge

February 13 Sunday. Sherman House, Dr Peabody asked me to speak briefly at service (9). Made prayer. PM train to Juneau. Night at hotel. 69m

February 14 Session of Dodge Co Ministers meetings 11–3 at Beaver Dam. Lunch. I spoke one hour (10). Drove 14 miles with Harkness to Waupun. A Y.M. supper. I spoke 20 min (11). Volleyball game. Home with H. 25m

February 15 Morning train to Appleton. Called on Homer Smith $100. Walked with Dr Peabody & supper with them.

February 16 Called on Co chairman, Mrs Rosebush. PM train to Waupun. Spoke at Central Europe supper (12). Home with Harkness. 52m

February 17 Spent day reading & visiting. Went over States Prison. Evening a Masonic Ladies night. I spoke (13).

February 18 Spoke 40 minutes at Waupun H S. Train to Oshkosh. Dinner (14) PM train to Appleton. Saw Lawrence (21)–Ripon (18) game, a very good one. 72m

February 19 Morning train to Manitowoc. Mrs Stranthern took me to call on some of the ministers. Spent the evening with the Gatas & Holway's at Two Rivers. 57m

February 20 Sunday. St Paul's M.E. SS 2 addresses. St Paul's church service. 1st Pres church service. 1st Pres Mission PM. Norwegian South evening (20).

February 21 Morning train down to Milwaukee. Found some mail. Thompson not in office. Went to Hotel Wisconsin. Heard lecture on Christian Sciences. WGP [letter recipient] 73m

February 22 A legal holiday, office closed. Saw "Inside of the Cup." CRR, WHR, DVR, Mrs Harkness [letter recipients]

February 23 Jaskins, CEC, HHW, Case, Dwight [letter recipients]

[February 24]

February 25 Left Milwaukee on sleeper for Pembine.

February 26 Sat. Alfred seemed much worse, the redness had spread ever across to his other cheek. Mrs. Sewny came & stayed from 6:30 to eleven, so I could sleep.

February 27 Sunday. Alfred had a better night and was very ambitious and hungry in the morning. The redness is still spreading to his ears neck & even into his hair.

February 28 Mon. Alfred's right eye was closed and the swelling seemed to be spreading. He was not comfortable nor ambitious.

March 1 Tues. Alfred very much better. Dr. says the disease has reached the limit. His face is peeling. He wants to eat, and would like to get up and be dressed. We are very happy. Miss Lampson telephoned to me that Edward was in the Freshman tenth.

March 2 Wed. Alfred improving but in bed.

March 3 Thurs. Alfred peeling all over his face. I read, read, read, and he plays with Miss Gage's blocks.

March 4 Fri. Inauguration of Harding. Ernest came at 9:25 P.M. He slept at Prof. Wright's because we had no room for him.

March 5 Sat. Alfred dressed but in the room.

March 6 Sunday. Alfred free from the room but Frances had 103°+. Edward, George, Mr. P. & I joined the United Church. Mr. Van der Pyl called. Ernest went to Milwaukee.

March 7 Mon. Frances's temperature had been up to 103 but was down today. Alfred was out playing, very happy. Mrs. Sewny & I went down town. I bought underwear for Frances $4.50, shoes for A ($3.60), thermometer $1.75, stockings for myself $2.00.

March 8 Tues. Frances still sick.

March 9 Wed. George & I both sick, fever, sore throat. Frances better.

March 10 Thurs. George & I both improving, France went to school again. Yeranoohi went home, because she has to be in Philadelphia Monday.

Ernest C. Partridge

February 26 Reached Pembine in a snowstorm at 7:20. Missed train to Dunbar, took 11:00 freight. 202m

February 27 Sunday. Taught Bible class, attended M.E. service, spoke an hour in PM and in evening on Heroines. People very attentive (21–23).

February 28 Left Dunbar at 7AM. Reached Fond du Lac at 5PM. Palmer House. Went to bed early. 235m

February 29 Mr Gilroy called early. Spoke HS 1:30. Women's Club 3:00. Twilight Club 7–10 (26).

[March 1]

March 2 Spoke between 10 & 4 at six grade schools and the Normal School at Fond du Lac (33). Lunched with Mr Mendenhall.

March 3 Morning train to West Bend. Spoke 45 minutes at HS. Evening one hour at Commercial Club (35). 34m

March 4 4:30 train to Chicago. Toledo to Oberlin by trolley arriving at 9:10PM. Alfred has erysipelas [strep-toccus bacterial infection] but is better. 408m

March 5 Edward in Freshman Tenth 14 boys & 22 girls out of 360. Frances all A's but one A+ & C+ in music. Billo all A's & B's except C+ arith. Oberlin beat Denison 23–16 State Champions.

March 6 Sunday. Edward & George joined United Church. Winona & I by letter. Sleeper to Chicago.

March 7 Reached Milwaukee at 10:30. Spent day in office. 5:10 train to Oshkosh with Gregory. Athern Hotel. 323m, 165m

March 8 Luncheon at Kiwanis Club at Oshkosh. I spoke 35 minutes (36). A committee was appointed to carry on a campaign.

March 9 Gregory and I went up to Neemah and had a conference with Ruegg of the Cong Ch about work there. Took sleeper for Chicago. 24m

March 10 Reached Chicago at 8:15. Train to Detroit 4 PM. Put up at Metropols with Samuel. Called on Spillane. Dinner at Statler with Spillane & Mrs Watson. 449m

March 11 Fri. About 12:30 A.M. Mr. P. called up from Samuel's hotel in Detroit.

March 12 Sat. I worked very hard, then Dr. Merrill & Mrs. Sewny came to supper. Then we three went to Mrs. Belden's with all the other missionaries.

March 13 Sunday. I went to church twice. Mr. Arnold of Toledo in the morning & Dr. Beebe of Boston in eve. Mrs. Sewny came to supper.

March 14 Mon. After much telephoning I succeeded in getting the missionary children here to meet Dr. Merrill from 6:30 to 8. The three Stapleton girls, Frances MacCallum, Arthur & Isabel Martin.

March 15 Tues. Heavy thunder showers. George just barely got home from the movies without getting wet.

March 16 Wed. Went to Cleveland to get shoes for my broken down arches, from Roy Hane. Bought waists for Alfred, Oliver Twist, waists for Billo.

March 17 Thurs. Went down town and bought four sheets @ $1.50, also white cloth for bloomers. Mrs. Smith did my washing in 4 ¼ hrs at 35 cts an hour. Mrs. Sewny took supper with us.

March 18 Fri. I was at home all day. The weather was warm.

March 19 Sat. Usual round of cleaning up. Mrs. Sewny came over in the evening.

March 20 Sunday. Morning, Palm Sunday sermon, Mr. Van der Pyl, evening, Prof. Graham, both very fine.

March 21 Mon. Mrs. Sewny & I called on the Wrights and read them Dr. Barton's first letter to the missionaries since coming from England, Supreme Council.

March 22 Tues. Mrs. Sewny took me to the Cleveland Symphony orchestra, very fine.

March 23 Wed. I was feeling horrid but I found that the washerwoman that I had for two weeks could not come until Friday so I washed at Miss Sinclair's.

Ernest C. Partridge

March 11 Called on Callender, lunched with him. Saw Dr. Malegian[?] & Ed Baron & Haig Boyagian. Went out to Clarks for supper, a social of church. I spoke (37). WGP [letter recipient] 20m

March 12 Talked with Spillane. Breakfast with Baron. Called on Tarouhi, Malegian's, Yeranouhi, and Ausur's. Dinner at Armenian club with 9 alumni (38). Mrs Nishan and Miss Jorforian. Night at MKD's.

March 13 Attended Armenian Prot service & spoke (39). Dinner with Dermenjians. They took me to train back to Oshkosh. Dinner with Tatoolians. Chicago sleeper to Oshkosh. 449m

March 14 Attended Rotary lunch but got crowded out of speaking. Called on Co chairman. Committee Meeting in evening. WGP [letter recipient]

March 15 A conference with several members of committee. Call in PM on Supt of Schools. Evening "Jackknife Man."

March 16 Call on Supt of Schools and Principal of H.S. Arranged for addresses in HS & at Principals meeting. Trip to Ames. Successful trip. WGP, Howard Jones, Baron, SB, Dwight [letter recipients] 28m

March 17 Trip to Neemah. Called on Clark and Shattuck. Both cordial, promised to help & to give. WGP, Hitchcock, Arnold Bell [letter recipients] 30m

March 18 Spoke 20 minutes at Oshkosh high school to 1000 pupils (40). WGP, GLP, ALRW [letter recipients]

[March 19]

March 20 Sunday. Morning Presbyterian Church at Neemah, also SS. Evening Union meeting at Pres Ch Oshkosh (42). 30m

March 21 Rotary date fell thru. 1:12PM train to Milwaukee at Wisconsin. 81m

March 22 Dictated several letters. Jemjem, JLB, Reo, Peet, Doughty, Fowle, WGP [letter recipients]

March 23 Morning train to Portage. A futile trip this Co Ch away and no way to work. 93m

March 24 Thurs. Letters from Ernest about going back, letter from Dr. Barton about various things, congratulating Edward on being in the Freshman tenth.

March 25 Fri. While I was cleaning off the kitchen shelf to please Mr. P. if he should come, because one of his hobbies is cleaning off the shelf, he stepped into the door.

March 26 Sat. I had cleaned up & done various extras before so I did not have a hard day. Ernest cleaned up the yard, fixed the auto, emptied the ashes and me to Gym. exhibition afternoon & evening. I went to a party that Hermine gave.

March 27 Sunday. Easter, beautiful early but rained most of the day. Mr. P. & I went to church, then Edward brought the children & we drove to Elyria where Ernest took the train for Milwaukee.

March 28 Mon. No school, because the cellar was flooded & the furnace was out. It made a mess at home because it rained all day.

March 29 Tues. No school in the morning. I sent Alfred down town to buy some cakes at Gibson's and told him to tell them to charge it to Mrs. P. He forgot "charge" so after some thinking said, "I am Mrs. Partridge's boy & we don't pay." Some sweet boy.

[March 30]

March 31 Thurs. Raining & cold. Edward and I worked on the bedrooms to look over papers, books & extras. Armen and Hampartsoom did the housework.

Reports. Frances, Reading A-, Spelling A, Writing B, Arith A, Music B, Drawing C+
Alfred Reading C, Spelling A, Arith B, Music A, Drawing C+
Billo Reading B+, Spelling B-, Arith B+ English A, Writing B+, Geog. B, Physiology B

April 1 Fri. Pleasant but rather cold. Alfred & Frances both fooled me. Alfred began to fuss that there was a nail in his shoe & the "April fool." A unique concert to exhibit the Edison phonograph, Marie Morrissey sang with herself, sang a duet with herself. Flute & piano played in unison with the same in the phonograph.

April 2 Sat. Pleasant & warmer. Armen & I went down town and bought me a gingham dress for $5. We went to the movies too. I cough so badly that I cannot go anywhere else.

April 3 Sunday. Warm. We went to Birmingham in the auto. I had to have the doctor twice to stop my nose bleed. Mrs. Sewny took supper with us.

Ernest C. Partridge

March 24 Afternoon train to Chicago. Sleeper to Elyria. 178m

March 25 Reached Elyria at 8:10. Home by trolley. Worked an hour on car opening under pistons. 341m

March 26 Worked on car, found nothing wrong, drove in PM. Athletic field day PM & evening at gym. Took all children in PM.

March 27 Easter sermon AM Oberlin. Family drove me to Elyria for 1:11 train to Chicago. Reached Mil[waukee] at 10:20, Medford. 341m, 85m

March 28 Got mail at office. Out to Waukesha for County Ministers Meeting. Back to city at Miller Hotel.

March 29 Part of forenoon in office. Out to Oconomowoc to see chairman of local committee. NY life, MS, WGP, Malcolm, Preshman [letter recipients] 70m

March 30 Spent day writing and reading and working at office on itinerary. Case, Reed, Irwin [letter recipients]

March 31 Helped move office to 229 Arcade. 3:50 train to S. Germantown. Lecture with slides. Taxi to Thiensville. Interurban to Milwaukee, sleeper to Mondovi. Last day with National Bureau. 43m

April 1 Reached Mondovi in AM. Made some calls with Co Ch Bartlett. Slides lecture to Civic League 60 min (44). Much interested. Apptd committee to work on Co quota. 246m

April 2 Left Mondovi at 9:20. Reached Madison at 5:20. No train to Richland Center. Spent night. Evening called on Howard Jones. 188m

April 3 Sunday. 11:25 train west to Richland Center. 3:40PM Park Hotel. Called on Rev E.E. Clark, M.E. Co Chairman. Spoke for him in evening (45). 60m

April 4 Mon. Warm & pleasant. Edward drove with George, Ettrick, and Hampartsoom to Ruggles Beach. The recreation committee took the students out there.

April 5 Tues. Warm. We, the family & Armen, drove to Lorain and had our dinner on the beach. It was very pleasant.

April 6 Wed. Warmer. The last day of Edward's vacation, also of Armen's so I have the work to do myself hereafter. It has been a fine rest this week.

April 7 Thurs. Billo went to a S.S. party where Mr. Lobengier shared pictures of Porto Rico.

April 8 Fri. Armen & I went to see the "Humoresque," very good.

April 9 Sat. I took the three little ones to the Y.W.C.A. frolics. It was not as funny as usual but interesting, with their bright paper cakes & costumes.

April 10 Sunday. Cold & snowy. Little ones put on their winter flannels again. I did not go anywhere on account of my cough. We had 7 callers. Mrs. Sewny stayed to supper.

April 11 Mon. Cold. Nothing special. Our 7 callers of Sunday were Ettrick, Arthur, Lucile Day and Mr. Huchins, Hermine & Nigoghosian, Mrs. Sewny & Hermann.

April 12 Tues. The boys went to a movie Monday, The Saphead, & liked it so much that I took the little ones but they could not understand it.

April 13 Wed. Mrs. Sewny had word that they want her in Talas right away. She plans to sail on May 12.

April 14 Thurs. The N.E.R. Com. in Con. telegraphed "Partridge come later." Also that Polly is telegraphing for 10,000 liras for unemployed women.

April 15 Fri. Mrs. Sewny and I went to Elyria to apply for her passport. Edward held the fort at home. Bazaar at Prospect St. school in evening.

Ernest C. Partridge

April 4 Spoke 40 min at HS (46) at 2PM. Supper with Thompson's treasurer. They drove me to Ithaca, but no meeting arranged.

April 5 I spoke at Co. Min meeting, a dozen men present. Drove 16m with a Conf min in PM to Lone Rock, a slide lecture (48). Hotel. 16m

April 6 Morning train to Richland Center. Drove to Ash Creek for evening talk & back in a Hudson (49). 12m

April 7 Mr Clark drove me out to Gillingham in PM. Guest at Parsonage. Rev W.E. Caldwell Pres. Spoke at Union meeting in evening (50). 7m

April 8 Cleaned up spark plugs and tightened up car for Caldwell. Drove to Bloom City for service in M.E. Ch (51). I drove car back in evening. 12m

April 9 Rose at 5:15. Taxi to Center. 6:25 train to Madison. Milwaukee & Sheboygan 7PM. Hotel Forster. 214m

April 10 Sunday. Cong church SS. M A Brandt. M.E. morning service & SS. Dinner with Brandts at Hotel. Home with them for a visit. Evening union meeting Baptist church Sheboygan Falls (55). 10m

April 11 Spoke at Sheboygan HS at 8AM. Ministers Meeting at 10:00. Falls HS at 2 (58). Orders from Thompson to go to Superior. 10m

April 12 Spoke at Plymouth HS 8:45. Mr. Brandt went out. Sheboygan HS, Freshman 12:45 (60). Lunch with Brandts. Train to Fon du Lac 2:15–4. Supper at 1st church. Visit at Gilroy's. Sleeper to Superior. 44m

April 13 Reached Superior at 8AM. Called on Co ch Mr J.O. Bach and Bayne Cong minister. WGP, Thompson [letter recipients] 308m

April 14 Mrs Bach took me to High School. Spoke 35 minutes to 850 pupils (61). A fine crowd & gave good attention. Called on Wingate & his partner.

April 15 Called on Stratton Roth and May. Mrs B took me to East End HS. Spoke to two divisions of HS (65). Train to Ashland, Hotel Knight. Merritt called on me. 62m

April 16 Sat. Rainy and cold. The children just tore the house down nearly. Some of the neighbor children came to help out.

April 17 Sunday. A cold, snow, rainy Sunday. What a day we had! My cough is still too bad to go to church. Wallace Carr just spent the day here.

April 18 Mon. Cleared off. We feel better.

April 19 Tues. Pleasant & warmer.

April 20 Wed. Pleasant. Alfred & I went to Elyria to buy a dress for Frances which I did not find and some little things for her birthday. Prof. Wright died about 3 o'clock.

April 21 Thurs. Faculty play. The importance of being E(a) rnest. Prof. Ward or Algemon, Prof. Jelliffe, Jack or Ernest. Frances birthday. Frances had for her birthday electric curling iron, pencil, white dress, golf dish, Bub the Book, handkerchiefs, scissors

April 22 Fri. I went to see Mrs. Wright. She is not seeing very many people.

April 23 Sat. Prof. Wright's funeral. Prof. King, Prof. Root & Prof. Dickinson spoke. Mr. Van der Pyl conducted the funeral.

April 24 Sunday. A beautiful warm day. We drove to Lorain. I was invited with Mrs. Sewny to supper at Mrs. Stapleton's.

April 25 Mon. Mrs. Sewny & I went to a debate on "Should Ireland be independent?" Mr. Mahoney, affirmative and Rev. Dickinson Lewis, negative.

[April 26]

Reports:	Reading	Spelling	Arith	Music	Drawing
Frances	B+	A+	A	B+	C+
Alfred	C-	C-	B	A	C+
Billo	A	A	B+	C	

Billo: English A, Pen. B+, Geog. B+, Physiology A

April 27 Wed. Edward's birthday. He got silk stockings, $10, tennis balls, candy, Ever sharp pencil. Mrs. Sewny & I went to see Kazares, the wolf dog.

April 28 Thurs. Mrs. Sewny & I went to Lorain, saw Mrs. Day, had supper in Elyria.

April 29 Fri. Mrs. Sewny left for N.Y.

April 30 Sat. Mr. P. came in the morning.

Ernest C. Partridge

April 16 Early train to Sheboygan, 13 hours ride, a long day. Heavy snows around Milwaukee. Hotel Toeste Sheboygan. 315m

April 17 Sunday. A quiet day in hotel reading and writing. 1st Pres church in evening (64). WGP, MacMahon [letter recipients]

April 18 Afternoon train to Appleton. Evening called on Dr Peabody. JWT, Lund, AL, PW, WGP [letter recipients] 68m

April 19 Spoke in Appleton HS to 750 pupils. Train to Milwaukee. Hotel Miller. Dictated an article. 100m

April 20 Dictated three articles & several letters. Sleeper to La Crosse. 198m

April 21 Called on Dixon & Rowlinson Cong Minister. Spoke at Rotary (66). Hotel Stoddard. Called on Carrie [Day]. WGP, Ruddock-Holley [letter recipients]

April 22 Spoke at State Normal School (69). 12:40 train to Oconomowoc. 5:40 Hotel Majestic. 165m

April 23 Went in to Milwaukee to take slides. Saw Miller in evening. MH, SB, GLP, Surinab, Clark, Irwin, WGP [letter recipients]

April 24 Sunday] SS Cong church Oconomowoc. M.E. Morning Service. Cong Ixonia PM. Baptist evening (71). 12m

April 25 Spoke at High School. Trolley to Milwaukee. A couple of hours in office. Dinner & movie with Koruber. Sleeper to La Crosse. Fatty Arbuckle "Dollar a Year Man." 32m

April 26 Reached La Crosse at 6:20AM. Stoddard spoke at lunch of Kiwanis (73). Call from Don Webber. Night train to Eau Claire. WGP, Carrots, Sec of State Bartlett [letter recipients] 197m

April 27 Reached Eau Claire at 2:40AM. Hotel Galloway. Miss Shepherdson, Fowle, Bayne, Partch [letter recipients] 151m

April 28 Spoke at Eau Claire Normal School, luncheon of workers. Auditorium evening 400 people (76). "Peace Treaty."

April 29 Left Eau Claire at 11:30 for Chicago. Sleeper to Elyria. 325m

April 30 Reached Oberlin at 9:10AM. Field meet in PM. Worked on car. Mrs Greene called. I called on Mrs Wright. 341m

May 1 Sunday. Communion. Many children joined the church. A cold May day but they got flowers & hung some May baskets.

May 2 Mon. Mr. P, Alfred & I went to Cleveland, bought suit for Mr. P. gray $45, four pr. trousers for Alfred, sweater for Alfred $8.50, sweater for Frances $6.50, hat for Mr. P. $5.00. We went to the Hippodrome.

May 3 Tues. Worked all day, washing ironing, cleaning, cooking. Alfred wore his blue & yellow sweater to school and Frances her brown one.

May 4 Wed. George & I went to see 2 one-act High School plays, A Pot of Broth & Spreading the News.

May 5 Thurs. George & I went to the movies although I was not feeling well. It was "The Snob."

May 6 Fri. I was sick all day but could just drag around. Frances was not well either but she went to school.

May 7 Sat. Frances & I both a little better. Frances & the Kelseys had a circus. Mrs. Kelsey & I were the spectators.

May 8 Sunday. Mother's day. The children gave me a geranium and all wore flowers for mother. Billo & Alfred gathered them from the waterworks. We drove to Lorain and ate our lunch. Lawrence went with us.

May 9 Mon. I should have gone to section meeting & I was also invited to Mrs. Fitch's to meet a lady from Buffalo, but the boys do not get home until four any way and today they thought they were going to play tennis.

[**May 10–12**]

May 13 Fri. Frances & I went to see Jacknife man. Billo & George went in the evening.

May 14 Sat. An easy Saturday. I seemed to have much less work to do than usual. I went to reception at Lord Cottage, invited Hermine & I called on Mrs. Fitch.

Ernest C. Partridge

May 1 Sunday. W & I went to communion in AM. I heard Dr Beard on China in evening.

May 2 Finished work on car & drove a little.

May 3 Winona & I spent day shopping in Cleveland. Alfred with us. I bought a gray suit, raincoat for WW [Billo]. Clothes for Alfred, sweater for F.

May 4 1:11PM train Elyria to Chicago. Sleeper to Spring Valley. 341m

May 5 A visit on train with Dr Gammon from Woodville to Spring Valley. I spoke in evening "Challenge of A[sia] M[inor] to Congregationalists." Spent night in a house. 378m

May 6 Morning train east to Milwaukee 6:35 Hotel Miller. 292m

May 7 Spent forenoon in office writing letters. 4:15 train to Madison. Gaskins, WGP, Bayne, Miss Kelsey, D. of State, Miss Rice, ERK, Fra, Bold, CH.[letter recipients] 83m

May 8 Sunday. A quiet day at Madison. Cardinal Hotel. Heard Dr Peabody preach.

May 9 Called on Mr Warner at Madison & Dr Carter at Cong Headquarters. 9:30 sleeper to Superior.

May 10 Reached Superior at 8AM. Guest at Wingate's. Spent day at Cong Association sessions. Brownell and I spoke in the evening (78). 336m

May 11 Sessions of the Conference morning and afternoon. Spoke at Rotary at noon & Hammon Ave Pres Ch Woman's Miss Soc at 3PM (80).

May 12 Spoke at Kiwanis at noon luncheon (81). 4:03 train to Ashland. Knight Hotel. 64m

May 13 Spent several hours at Northland College, visiting with Brownell. Lunch at college. Evening Cong Men's club (82).

May 14 Spent most of day in my room at Hotel. Very disagreeable weather. Merritt called in PM & Mrs Bell of Bayfield in evening. English [letter recipient]

May 15 Sunday. Sherwood Eddy, evening & P.M. Young People's Conference. I spoke for Turkey. Prof Hanna, a stereoptician lecture on a trip around the world. Prof. Graham.

May 16 Mon. Called on Mrs. Van der Pyl and kept her from the Prayer Circle. Also on Mr. & Mrs. Metcalf. They told me that they want the bungalow next year, so we have to move.

May 17 Tues. Spent my spare time inquiring about houses.

May 18 Wed. George and I went to the movies, "It pays to advertise." The comedy was a man papering his house.

May 19 Thurs. George & I went to a play by High School pupils, Bicycles. Capt. Garland said we could have Tracy Cottage.

May 20 Fri. Called on Mrs. Wright, read Dr. Barton's letter to her & Mrs. Stapleton & Mrs. Greene.

May 21 Sat. Went to Gray Gables porch party.

May 22 Sunday. Took the children to the arboretum & golf links in the afternoon & was nearly ready to drop.

[May 23–24]

May 25 Wed. Mr. P. came at noon.

[May 26]

May 27 Fri. Engaged the Tracy Cottage for next year.

May 28 Sat. Worked all day as usual.

May 29 Sunday. Memorial Sunday. Church morning & evening.

Ernest C. Partridge

May 15 Joint YM, YW meeting of College Men's Class Cong Ch. Ch service Pres Ch in evening (83-6). Dinner at Brownell's with Merritt's. WGP, CRR, HSR [letter recipients] 10m

May 16 Spoke at Northland College Chapel (87). Went around grounds with Brownell. 4:20 train to Superior. Night at Hotel. JWT, CDP, JWT [letter recipients] 62m

May 17 7AM freight Superior to Webster. Co Chairman away nothing arranged. Took train to St Paul. 144m

May 18 Took 11:30 sleeper St Paul to Portage. Missed train at Portage to Randolph 3PM train. I spoke in evening at Cong Assoc meeting (88). 296m

May 19 7:17AM train to Madison. Found Gregory and Koruber. Mr. Warner out of town so we could do nothing today. 80m

May 20 Visited with Miss Kelley. She called on Warner who refuses to do anything.

May 21 Left Madison at 6:05 to Williams Bay. Called on AF Newcombe, Cong min. Looked up houses. Walked out to camps. Train to Lake G., taxi Springfield, train to Milwaukee. 189m

May 22 Sunday. Spent day at Hotel Miller Milwaukee.

May 23 Down to Kenosha & back. Woman's Miss Meeting of Cong Ch at Mrs Tremper's (89). 68m

May 24 Worked in office. PM train to Sheboygan with English. Spoke at Association, back to Chicago with English & on to Oberlin (90). 104m

May 25 Reached Oberlin at 10:10AM. Seminary Com. Ex. Pres. Faunce. Banquet in evening. 170m, 341m

[Mat 26]

May 27 Worked some on car. Drove Mrs Greene and Miss Vaughn to Cemetery. Went to see Tracy Cottage & decided to take it.

May 28 Took car to garage & had a new timer wheel put in and it runs finely.

May 29 Sunday. Morning Service. Drove to Lorain. Memorial service in evening. 40m

May 30 Memorial Day. Parade. We went to the cemetery [Ernest's mother, Eliza Croker, is buried at Westwood Cemetery], later to the shack for lunch, towed the Huntleys in four miles.

May 31 Tues. Washed; ironed, went to see Black Beauty with the children.

Billo Reading A, Eng. A, Spelling A, Writing B, Arith C, Geog. C+, Physiology A

Frances Spelling A+, Drawing C+, Reading A, Arith A, Music B+

Geo. Eng. A, Math A, Latin B+, History B+

Alfred Reading C, Eng. C+, Spelling C, Arith B, Music A, Drawing C+

June 1 Wed. Miss Hagopian spoke at the missionary meeting but I could not go. I cannot go anywhere before four when Geo. or Edward comes home.

June 2 Thurs. I went over to see Mrs. Wright. She says she is going to Turkey with us. That would be fine.

June 3 Fri. Billo is very miserable with an abcess in his ear, temperature etc. etc. We gathered up clothing for the Near East.

[June 4]

June 5 Sunday. Ed & I went to church and the children to S.S. except Billo who was not feeling well. We went to Lorain and ate lunch beside the road. Frances cried all the time we were there because she could not go barefoot.

[June 6]

June 7 Tues. Although I had taken the children to a circus movie in place of the circus, we decided to go to Cleveland to the real circus. Norman Metcalf went with us. We also went to the Wild West Show.

[June 8–10]

June 11 Sat. Went to Elyria & bought a blue plaited skirt.

Ernest C. Partridge

May 30 Memorial Parade. Drove to near shack for swim. Lunch on return. Towed Huntley's in to Oberlin. Sleeper to Chicago. Carnegie Tech [?]. 35m

May 31 Breakfast in Chicago with Dr Fiefield. Train to Milwaukee. Wrote letters. Evening train to Waupaca. WGP, Burney, Vartouhi, NY Life, Hovassian, Papas, Marian, Irwin, Wingate, Kelsey [letter recipients] 131m 408m

June 1 Reached Waupaca at 12:30AM Hotel Delavan. Found Dr Slade out of town. Wrote letters.

June 2 Talked with Mrs Slade & we decided to postpone effort for a week. Went to Wisconsin Rapids to see County chairman there. Hotel. WGP, Thompson [letter recipients] 45m

June 3 Found Mr Mott out of town and went to Wausau. Carroll met me & took me home. Wife Edith, girl Mary Elizabeth. WGP, Talmadge [letter recipients] 42m

June 4 Spent some time in his [Carroll's] office and drove 40 miles with him and also a long drive with his wife. 40m

June 5 Sunday. Spoke at SS of 1st Pres Ch (91); also in a boys class. PM Carroll drove me out in the country to a service. Evening service of 1st Pres Church (94). 15m

June 6 Morning train to Waupaca. From Junction City down found Merritt on train. 68m

June 7 Spent forenoon at Dr Slade's, writing letters and making plans. Thompson called me to Milwaukee. Down on PM train. [Hotel] Miller at 10:30. 131m

June 8 Talked things over with Thompson. Wrote letters. Spoke to Captains of Girl Scouts (95). John B, WGP, Custer, Miss Cain, Mrs Bartlett, Weld [letter recipients]

June 9 Morning train to Waupaca. Hotel Delavan. Talmadge, Baynes, Peabody, CDP Grant, Gilroy, Brandt [letter recipients] 131m

June 10 Conference with Dr Slade. Drove to Weyanwegan with Home Hostess. Placed in Waupaca, groceries. Movie evening. 22m

June 11 Drove to New London. Called on Rector. Dinner at hotel. Arcne of GG with Slades. 42m

June 12 Sunday. Went to Lorain.

June 13 Mon. Reception for Miss Kaughey, went to Elyria, then Alice Caldwell's recital, then reception at Dascourt.

June 14 Tues. Washed some. Went to Mrs. Haskell's for supper.

June 15 Wed. Mr. P. came home.

June 16 Thurs. Armen, Ham, Ed., George & I went to Cleveland. I bought a blue silk dress, a black & white dress.

June 17 Fri. Commencement play, Green Stockings, Whit. Andrews & Alice Lockwood's last play. She was "Poor Celia", Hermine's wedding.

[June 18]

June 19 Sunday. Baccalaureate Seminar. I did not go. We took a ride.

June 20 Mon. Mr. P. went away to speak in Sheboygan.

June 21 Tues. Illumination night. '01 was just crazy. '91 float of flowers was beautiful.

June 22 Wed. Commencement. Hampartsoom received his diploma. Alumni Dinner Glee Club concert, but I stayed with the children. E. came in the evening.

June 23 Thurs. Packed, cleaned, dumped, burned etc.

June 24 Fri. ditto

June 25 Sat. ditto

June 26 Sunday. Mr. Van der Pyl preached.

June 27 Mon. Busy

June 28 Tues. Started for Williams Bay at 11:45. It rained everything in the P.M. Reached Defiance. Went to movies, Honest Hutch. Stayed at Hotel Cunningham.

June 29 Wed. Went 280 miles to Hammond. Followed 9 trails, Yellowstone Trail, TOL Chi T.A.C. 52, J.H., Lincoln Highway, Liberty Way, Ade Way, H.M.C. Chi Motor Club Trail. Majestic Hotel.

Ernest C. Partridge

June 12 Sunday. SS at St Mark's (96). Morning service at St Mark's. 3PM Palace theatre films & slides. 7:30 Baptist Church (99). Dinner & supper at Slade's. 5m

June 13 2:54AM train to Milwaukee. [Hotel] Miller. Wrote some letters. Thompson out of town today. Crooks, Haig, S Allen, Clark, NY Life [letter recipients] 131m

June 14 Spent forenoon in office. PM train to Chicago. Sleeper to Oberlin. 426m

June 15 Reached Oberlin from Elyria at 10:10.

[June 16]

June 17 Wedding service of Hermine Dahessian and Nigohas Nighosian at Mrs Tenney's. Commencement Play. Very fine.

June 18 Waseda game Oberlin 8–1.

June 19 Sunday. Mr Van in morning. Baccalaureate in PM.

June 20 Varsity-Alumni game, Varsity won 7–1. 1:11 train from Elyria to Chicago and Milwaukee. Night at Miller [Hotel]. 426m

June 21 Morning train to Sheboygan. Spoke at noon at Rotary Club (100). PM train back to Chicago. Sleeper to Oberlin. 137m

June 22 Reached Amherst at 8:10. Boys met me in car. Commencement & Alumni dinner. Gusthous & wife, Newcomb & wife, Adams, Winona & I.

June 23 Packed

June 24 Packed

June 25 Packed

[June 26]

June 27 Moved stuff to Fauk Home barn.

June 28 [Family] Left Oberlin in car for Lake Geneva about 11AM to Defiance. Hotel Cunningham. Movies evening rained hard in PM. 131m

June 29 Defiance to Hammond just out of Chicago. Yellowstone Trail, Tol-Chi, TAC 52. JH Lincoln Highway, Liberty Way, Adeway. Majestic Hotel. 210m

June 30 Thurs. Arrived in Williams Bay [WI]. They went in swimming right away.

July 1 Fri. Tried to start housekeeping. Swimming twice.

July 2 Sat. Sherwood Eddy spoke at the Camp. Ed & his father went.

July 3 Sunday. Mr. Mott preached but I did not get ready in time to go.

July 4 Mon. Billo & Alfred woke people up. We celebrated all day. Florence Baldwin Lee came in the evening.

July 5 Tues. Swimming. Mr. P. & Ed. Went to Milwaukee, returned in time to swim.

July 6 Wed. Swimming. I washed clothes in the back yard, hard work with no conveniences.

July 7 Thurs. Swimming.

July 8 Fri. Ed. & his father went to an Episcopal Camp above Milwaukee. Slept on hard bunk with no pillow.

July 9 Sat. Geo. took the children swimming in the morning, then the others came at noon & they swam at the camp. All of them, even Frances dive & swim. Called on Mr. & Mrs. Bedikian.

July 10 Sunday. Ernest preached in the little church here. Met Mr. & Mrs. Parkhurst, Mr. Olehim, Prof. Frost. Edward sick, 102°, headache.

July 11 Mon. Edward sick with fever and headache. Called on Mrs. Lee. Met Prof. Bryant of Middlebury and Miss Parsons.

July 12 Tues. Billo sick just like Edward. Edward still sick but we took Ernest to Walworth to take the train to La Crosse.

July 13 Wed. Edward some better. Geo. drove the fliver [the Ford!] alone for the first time. He drove down town three times, took the children bathing twice.

July 14 Thurs. Edward still better, Billo a little better. The Ford got wet and did not go until afternoon. Our 23rd wedding anniversary. I celebrated by washing & taking care of Billo. Ernest away.

[July 15]

Ernest C. Partridge

June 30 Called on Michel in Chicago. Drove on to Williams Bay & went in swimming. 110m

[July 1]

July 2 Heard Sherwood Eddy in evening for 1½ hours.

July 3 Sunday. Dr Mott in morning.

July 4 Edward & I drove to Milwaukee and back for a conference with Thompson. 130m

[July 5–7]

July 8 Ed & I drove to Richfield 22 miles north of Milwaukee to a summer camp of Epis[copal] boys where I spoke in evening (101). 79m

July 9 After breakfast at camp, drove to Milwaukee. Spent half an hour in office then back to Wms [Williams] Bay. 79m

July 10 Sunday. Spoke at Wms Bay Cong Ch morning. "Challenge of Near East to Cong." (102)

[July 11]

July 12 Drove to Walworth in evening. Train to Janesville, Janesville to La Crosse. Spoke in Normal School night. 33m

July 13 Spoke in Normal School (103). Night at Hotel. 158m

July 14 Train to St Paul and River Falls. 159m

July 15 Spoke in Normal School 500 (104). Back to Wms Bay. 78m

July 16 250m

July 17 Sunday. Family drove me to Burlington [WI]. Evening train to Steven's Point to Hotel. 177m

---

July 16 Sat. Ernest came home in the evening. We met him at Walworth.

July 17 Sunday. Edward and I went to hear Marion Lawrence at Conference Point. The children went along & stayed on the shore. Papa went to Burlington to take the train.

July 18 Mon. Ernest came back in evening. Edward began working at the Observatory, as a recorder for the Parallax Dep't, working with Prof. Lee, Florence Baldwin's husband.

July 19 Tues. George went to work for Prof. Barrett, mowing lawns, pruning etc. Alfred got sick after swimming.

July 20 Wed. Mrs. Ulchin(?) called to sell tickets for Marie Bashian's concert. Ernest went to Chetek. Alfred sick but a little better toward night. The Lees & Prof. Bryant called.

July 21 Thurs. Alfred quite sick. Frances also sick.

July 22 Fri. Alfred better in the morning but worse at night. Marie Bashian Bedekian gave her concert. Edward & George went.

July 23 Sat. Alfred quite sick. Mr. P. came home. The boys went to meet him but missed him, had a blowout, trouble with fan belt etc. I went to Mrs. Lee's in the P.M.

July 24 Sunday. The ladies I met at Mrs. Lee's were Mrs. Frost, Mrs. Sullivan, Mrs. Michel & her sister-in-law, Miss Calvert, Mrs. Parkhurst, Mrs. Ulchin, Marie, Miss Brock, Miss Parsons, Miss Willard. Alfred better. Went to church.

July 25 Mon. Alfred still better. Frances was not much sick, soon got better.

July 26 Tues. Alfred still better, only in the morning he had a sore throat until he found out his mother was not going to Milwaukee. Geo. Billo & Mr. P. went, returning a little after supper time.

July 27 Wed. Ed., Alfred & I took Mr. P. to Elkhorn for the 6:30 train to Milwaukee. I went to Mrs. Sullivan's to a ladies party. Mr. P. returned. We took a ride. Three girls from Eleanor Camp came for a drink, were lost.

[July 28]

July 29 Fri. Picture show, Mary Pickford in Daddy-Long Legs. Film broke ever so many times.

[July 30]

July 31 Sunday. Pastor Jensen preached.

Memoranda

[before August 1] June 19 Alfred weighed 50, Frances 57, Billo 70, George 115, Ed 129, Mama 163

August 1 Mon. Y.W.C.A. employees stunt night.

[August 2]

August 3 Wed. Was invited to Mr. Michel's and spoke to the ladies there about Turkey.

[August 4]

August 5 Fri. Movie: Douglas Fairbanks in "The Mask of Zorr."

Ernest C. Partridge

July 18 Spoke in Chapel at Normal School and in two classes (105-7). Back to Burlington at 8PM family met me. 177m, 38m

[July 19]

July 20 Went to Madison, night at Hotel. 67m

July 21 Early train to Chetek. Evening address at West Wis[consin] Epworth conference [Epworth Leagues were part of United Methodist Church history]. Night at Conf. 225m

July 22 Morning train to Wisconsin Rapids. Night at Hotel. 149m

July 23 Early train to Green Lake, across lake to Presb. camp. I spoke at noon (109). Taxi to Ripon, train to Burlington. Winona & boys walked to Lake G, home by boat. 205m

[July 24–25]

July 26 George & Bill & I drove to Milwaukee. 120m

July 27 Ed took me to Elkhorn to take 6:30 train to Mil[waukee]. Back in PM. Went to State Normal but did not speak. 120m

[July 28–August 1]

August 2 Miss. Ed. Conference began.

August 3 Lecture 1 (110) on near East.

August 4 Lecture 2 (111).

August 5 Mr & Mrs Wood, teacher in Elyria H.S., camped in our yard. Lecture 3 (112).

August 6 Sat. Mr. & Mrs. Welles, Dorothy & Lester came and occupied the upstairs rooms. We all ate in the kitchen, some mess.

August 7 Sunday. Mr. Newsome preached. Marie sang twice. Alfred nearly laughed aloud. Her singing was beautiful.

August 8 Mon. George & his father went to see Dr. MacDonald of Geneva. He advised that Geo. have his tonsils removed immediately.

August 9 Tues.We took Geo. to the hospital at Harvard, Ill. Seelye removed tonsils & adenoids. I stayed all day with him. He took the anaesthetics well and was not nauseated.

August 10 Wed. We went over & brought George home about noon. He was pretty miserable but glad to come home.

August 11 Thurs. George very miserable.

August 12 Fri. Geo. miserable but braced up in the evening & went to the movies with Edward.

August 13 Sat. We went to the little library and got some books. Geo. could not get breath through his nose, so I telephoned to Dr. Seelye. He said that it was unusual.

August 14 Sunday. Dr. Tittle of Evanston preached on The Wise & Foolish Virgins. In the evening Mr. Ruegg spoke at the Williams Bay church.

August 15 Mon. All except Frances & Alfred went to the Observatory to hear a lecture on Comets by Dr. Barnard. The little ones stayed with Florence Lee.

August 16 Tues. Mr. P. had lumbago. We all, except him, went to the movies, Dinty. I was sorry the children went, too sad.

August 17 Wed. Ed, George & I went to Milwaukee. I bought some dresses for Frances, but found nothing for me. Bought melons at Buckmans.

[August 18]

August 19 Fri. A terrible storm, trees blown down, all lights off. Before the storm the children went down the Lake to Geneva & we brought them home in the fliver [the Ford].

August 20 Sat. Lights or electricity of until towards night. Children went to a party at the Van Briesbarcks. We called at the Barretts.

August 21 Sunday. We heard Richard Roberts in the morning and saw pictures of The Life of Christ in the evening.

August 22 Mon. Took Geo. to Geneva to have Dr. Seelye look at his throat. We saw lots of trees blown down. Called on the Parkhurst in the evening. I washed but it rained before the clothes got dry.

August 23 Tues. Took our three Turkish neighbor children to ride to Fontana.

Ernest C. Partridge

August 6 The Welles family stopped with us over Sunday. Lecture 4 (113).

August 7 Prof Richardson preached 11 Soares in evening.

August 8 Lectured on near East (114). Lecture 5 (115). George & I went to see Dr McDonald at Lake Geneva. Lead Servants of King (116).

August 9 Took George to Hospital at Harvard [IL] where he had tonsils & adenoids out. Bill $62. Lecture 6 (117).

August 10 Brought George home in the rain. Lecture 7 (118). Dramatics "Girls of Van."

August 11 Lecture 8 (119). Drove Corbins around Lake. 20m

August 12 Took Corbins to train. Drove Elyria ladies around Lake. 25m

[August 13]

August 14 Dr Tittle of Evanston at College Conf. Mr Ruegg in evening in village.

August 15 A lecture by Dr Barnard on comets.

August 16 I had lumbago quite bad.

August 17 Winona, Ed & George went to Milwaukee to shop.

[August 18–20]

August 21 Sunday. Heard Richard Roberts in morning and saw pictures of life of X in evening.

[August 22–25]

August 24 Wed. Washed.

August 25 Thurs. I attended a tea with Mrs. Parkhurst where I spoke about our work, no about Polly mostly.

August 26 Fri. News from the Board of a cable saying "Seven days after an operation (Miss) Graffam died Aug. 17."

August 27 Sat. About noon we started for Oberlin, so that I could be ready to go East. Stayed at Gary, Ind. at Commercial Hotel $7½ for three rooms.

August 28 Sunday. Our auto began to knock, had a cylinder fixed at Westville, then the spring broke and Mr. P. & Ed. fixed that. Stayed at Ligonier in a rooming house.

August 29 Mon. Had the auto fixed again at Toledo. Stayed in Fremont at the Colonial Hotel.

August 30 Tues. Arrived in Oberlin and stayed at Tank House, ate at the Hotel at noon, but afterwards at Tank.

August 31 Wed. Rec'd letter about Polly from Mr. Case, the Clarks, Miss Dwight & Sara Blunt. She probably had a cancer according to reports from Con[stantinople].

September 1 Thurs. Rec'd letters from Papa, poor man, Armen, Florence, Dr. Merrill.

September 2 Fri. We moved into Tracy Cottage.

September 3 Sat. Tried to do some settling, called on Mrs. Wright.

September 4 Sunday. Went to church in the morning to hear Mr. Van der Pyl. Drove to Lorain in the P.M.

September 5 Mon. A letter from a Mr. Fuller who was returning from Turkey, said he was writing for Polly to tell us of her operation. She fully expected to recover.

September 6 Tues. Schools began. I went to Pleasant St. school with the little ones. Alfred has Miss Lancashire in 2nd. He knew her before. Frances has Mrs. McKie & Billo, Miss Brinker.

September 7 Wed. Ed & his father, Norman and Elaine Metcalf went to Cleveland. Ed bought a suit. They went to a ball game and then the fliver would not go. They put it in a garage & Mr. P. stayed in Cleveland. Ed came home on the car.

September 8 Thurs. I went to Cleveland on the car and came out with Mr. P. I bought an $8 pòngee waist for $3.85. I ripped and pieced my blue dress & took it to Mrs. Dulmage.

September 9 Fri. Washed at Mrs. Wright's. Just as we got to the stockings the electricity went off. Then the car would not work & we walked home. Children went to movie "Too Much Johnson."

September 10 Sat. I ironed all day.

September 11 Sunday. Communion in the morning. Took a ride to Elyria. Frances was naughty & her father stayed at home with her.

September 12 Mon. In the night Billo had toothache & Alfred had fever & vomited. Alfred did not go to school. We put up ten quarts of peaches.

September 13 Tues. Alfred went back to school. Ed. & his father finished the garage. Mrs. Greene called.

September 14 Wed. Washed & ironed and got ready to go East.

Ernest C. Partridge

August 26 A telegram from Boston, "Seven days after operation Graffam died August 17th."

August 27 Started for Oberlin about noon. Commenced Hotel Gary [Indiana]. 150m

August 28 Sunday. Burned out a piston rod bearing & had a new one put in at Westville. We put in new front spring. Night at Ligonier, Ind. 120m

August 29 At Toledo found oil passage clogged. I had to have it fixed. Stayed at Colonial, Fremont. 182m

August 30 51½ m

[August 31–September 31]

September 15 Thurs. Mr. P. drove me to Elyria to take the train, but after all I had to change in Cleveland.

September 16 Fri. I reached Boston with Rachel Metcalf about eleven o'clock by fast time. Bought a waist, black trimmed with blue. Went to the Board rooms and then out to Somerville to stay with Miss Gage.

September 17 Sat. Left Boston at 7:25. Papa came to the station in Lewiston but did not go to Monson. Had to wait in Newport, so went to see Aunt Frank and had dinner there. Esther met me at the station in Monson and we drove down to the farm.

September 18 Sun. Uncle Gene, Esther & I went to church with Nell. We had a good sermon and I saw some old friends. We drove over to the Baptist church & saw Sara Mathews. Esther went to Dover.

Ernest C. Partridge

October 1 First College Football game beat Wittenberg 14–0.

[October 2–7]

September 19 Mon. I just enjoyed being with Uncle Gene & Aunt Jennie & Violet and the baby on that lovely farm. Charlie & Ella Weeks drove up.

September 20 Tues. Mrs. Rufus Drake drove me to Dover & I took the train there for Lewiston. After a long walk from the station with a heavy suit case I reached the house & found my father and mother well.

September 21 Wed. I sewed, pressed my plaited skirt, wrote letters, called on Jennie Tambling Fields.

September 22 Thurs. Papa and I left Lewiston about four o'clock, went to Portland on the trolley, had supper there & then took the boat to Boston.

September 23 Fri. My father and I called on the Board people. They had had letters from Miss Rice about Polly's last days. Went out to Andover.

September 24 Sat. Visited at the Blunt's, went to the cemetery, called on Miss Davis. Mr. Bigelow called.

September 25 Sunday. Memorial Service for Polly. It was about the hardest service I ever attended, although suitable and impressive. I saw many, many friends, took dinner with papa at the Hills'.

September 26 Mon. Started with Sara Mathews for New York. Papa went to Maine. Garabed Eff. met me. We had a nice evening together. It was tie-up day in Oberlin. The Sophomores, Edward's class won.

September 27 Tues. I stayed in N.Y. Muggerditch Odabashian spent the afternoon with me. Mrs. Hubbard & Mary came to supper.

September 28 Wed. Mrs. Hubbard & I went to Philadelphia & spent the day at Dicran Eff., my birthday. They gave me two boxes of candy. We went to see Independence Hall. Took a long drive in Fairmont Park.

September 29 Thurs. Reached Oberlin at 11:10. Frances, her father & Armen met me at the car. It was good to get home. Called on Mrs. Wright.

September 30 Fri. Worked around in the house, trying to get accustomed to things again.

October 1 Sat. Washed in the morning & ironed in the afternoon.

October 2 Sunday. Went to church, heard Mr. Van der Pyl on The Business Man's religion. Took a ride in the P. M. Then all stayed home in the evening.

October 3 Mon. I cleaned the upstairs bathroom etc. and washed the kitchen floor, swept the cellar way stairs & cleaned up generally. Mrs. Wright called.

October 4 Tues. I went to Thank Offering Meeting [Missionary meeting]

Alfred's grades 2B Conduct B+, Reading B+, Spelling B+, Writing C+, Arith B, Music B+, Drawing B.

[October 5–7]

October 8 Sat. Oberlin beat O.S.U. 7 to 6 at Columbus. The team returned at 11:15 and the three men of my family went to help them celebrate.

[October 9]

October 10 Mon. Billo's report, Reading B, English B+, Spelling B, Writing A, Arith C, Hist B+, Physiology A. Frances: Reading B+, Spelling B+, Arith B

October 11 Tues. Went with Mrs. Van der Pyl to the Sorosis Club. Prof. Moore spoke on "Our Foreign Policy." Billo sick. Dr. gave him medicine for intestines.

October 12 Wed. Columbus Day, no school. It was cold and rainy. I called on Mrs. Bankhardt.

October 13 Thurs. Billo got five dollars for furnishing the mission work in Morris's adventure event. It was to be the final comer but finally one drew lots and it fell to Billo.

October 14 Fri. Alfred got an Arith. paper with three A+'s on it. A letter from Nishan Eff. about Polly's death and funeral, in French. We called on Mrs. Andrews who has a sprained ankle.

October 15 Sat. Edward & his father went to Alliance to see the game, Oberlin 13, Meth. Union. They took four boys with them. George went with the H.S. team to Bellevue but did not play. Oberlin 0, B. 6. The rest of us had a wiener roast in the arboretum.

Ernest C. Partridge

October 8 OHS beat Fremont 14–0. College beat OSU there 7–6. A great celebration after return of team.

[October 9–14]

October 15 Ed & I with four fellows drove to Alliance & back 160m to see Oberlin beat Mt Union 13–0. Started at 7:30 and got home at 10PM. George went to Bellevue got beat 6–0. 160m

October 16 Drove to Lorain in PM. 40m

[October 17–19]

October 20 Sale of Strauss store started. I clerked there 8–8.

October 21 Spent part of day at Strauss store.

October 22 OHS beat Norwalk 21–6 in AM. Varsity beat Hiram 38–6. Billo played between halves on Krescents. Played well. I worked in Strauss safe 5–10.

[October 23]

October 16 Sunday. Service in honor of 100th anniversary of Finney's conversion. It was very warm & pleasant and we drove to Lorain.

October 17 Mon. I did not do any great stunt. We had supper with wieners & cider & doughnuts again at the arboretum, this time with George. We put in two tons of coal.

October 18 Tues. Fussed with washing & ironing all day. We put the clothes out, then it rained & we took them in, then it cleared & we put them out.

October 19 Wed. Finished the ironing and went to Home Miss meeting in the afternoon. A student, Mr. Jones, spoke about his work in South Dakota & Miss Groves read about different missionary fields.

October 20 Thurs. Mr. P. helped Mr. Whitney tend store, culling out Strauss's goods. Ed. got his first grade in economics A+ & Geo. an A+ in Latin.

October 21 Fri. Mr. P. worked in the forenoon at the store. I cleaned the down stairs.

October 22 Sat. High School game with Norwalk 21–6. Afternoon, Oberlin College & Hiram 38 to 6, all the family went because Billy's team played between halves. Billy plays right guard. He was quite a star. I had been to the Hiram game two years before and nothing between.

October 23 Sun. Ed., his father & I went to church in the morning and Geo. & his father in the evening. The little folks went to S.S. We went for a ride but came back early as it was cold.

October 24 Mon. Raymond Robins & Norman Thomas debated on Socialism. George & his father went. I called on Mrs. Wright & Mrs. Howard was there. Letters from Miss Rice, Mrs. Crawford, Miss Noyes. Miss W. gave me letter from Mrs. Greene to send.

October 25 Tues. The children are all so busy. Today, for instance, Billo had a violin lesson after school, then went to sell some bluine. Alfred joined him at five. Frances had music lesson this morning, then practice after school, then an appointment with the dentist. George has football practice every day from four to six.

October 26 Wed. League of Women Voters meeting at Mrs. King's. Mrs. Martin presided. Mrs. Fullerton & Mrs. Andrews & Mrs. Peabody spoke. School session in the evening in place of Parent-Teachers.

October 27 Thurs. Ironed. Billo had two back teeth extracted. He came home in the morning with a toothache.

October 28 Fri. No school on account of Teachers' Institute. Evening Halloween party at Tank Home. Edward dressed in soldier's uniform. Billo as cowboy, Frances a witch, Alfred as soldier. Geo. had athletic meetings. Children went on a picnic & Mr. P. & I went to Campus View and had a banana split & coffee & rolls.

Ernest C. Partridge

October 24 Raymond Robin & Norman Thomas debate on Socialism. George & I went.

[October 25]

October 26 An exhibition school session at Pleasant School.

[October 27–28]

October 29 Billo & I went to Delaware with Woody to see Wesleyan game. Started at 5. Back at midnight. We beat 21–0. OHS beat Elyria 24–0. 150m

[October 30–November 4]

November 5 We beat Wooster 14–6 at Home Coming game over 5000 present. Many Alumni back. H.S. beat Lorain 15–0. Ed went to Elyria to play indoor baseball.

October 29 Sat. Billo & his father went with Woody to Delaware to see Wesleyan game, starting at 4:30AM, returning at midnight. Geo. & Edward went to H.S. game in Elyria. Oberlin won in both games.

October 30 Sunday. Morning service, "Seek you first the Kingdom of God." We took a lovely ride in the country. Got lost in the back roads & came out in Wakeman.

October 31 Mon. Halloween. George went to a party at the Collins Studio, Billo to Mr. Locke's. The rest of us stayed at home & ate chestnuts.

George: Eng. A-, Lat. A+, Hist. A, Math. B
Billo: Conduct B, Effort C, Reading B, Eng. A, Spelling B, Penmanship B, Arith. C, Hist. B, Music B+, Phys. A
Frances: Conduct A, Effort A, Reading B+, Spelling A, Arith. B

November 1 Tues. I ironed nearly all day and got very tired in the knees. In the evening Edward studied very comfortably on French & Chemistry. I try to help him in French but he knows really more than I do.

November 2 Wed. I took Frances to one dentist & Mr. P. took Billo to another. We bought them both shoes, brown.

November 3 Thurs. Miss Metcalf called while I was making doughnuts. I bought Alfred some shoes. Church supper. Mr. P. & George went.

November 4 Fri. Mrs. Root invited me to go to the Alumnae meeting at Mrs. Harrow's. Prof. Morrison spoke of his trip abroad. I met Eleanor Jones Seemann, the mother of Bill Seemann, Edward's friend.

November 5 Sat. H.S. against Lorain 15 to 0; College against Wooster 14 to 0. In the evening Edward & a bunch of the boys went to Elyria to play indoor baseball with a church team. They were beaten 44 to 11. We washed in the morning and I ironed in the afternoon & evening, finished at eleven o'clock.

November 6 Sunday. Home-coming Sunday and the chapel was filled. The choir sang Sanctus. In the evening all except the little ones & me went to church. Then, some boys kept ringing the door-bell. Later Mrs. Wright came & I thought it was one of the boys, so I did not go some twice.

November 7 Mon. I had rather an easy day. Word came that they want Mr. P to come to Constantinople anyway. They will decide very soon. I called on Mrs. Cook, one of my neighbors.

[November 8]

November 9 Wed. I went to Mrs. Wright's to supper with Susie Zearing, Harriet Chamberlain, Miss Rockwell & Miss Brownback.

[November 10]

November 11 Fri. Armistice Day. The children were home after ten o'clock. Cold & snowy.

November 12 Sat. Migration Day. All migrated to Cleveland except the little ones & me. Case 7, Oberlin 7. George stayed in Lakewood with Carroll. The others got home a little after eleven. The Board decided to have Mr. P. go back.

November 13 Sunday. Morning service. Mr. V, The Shining Face.

November 14 Mon. Billy came home sick, fever, headache.

November 15 Tues. Mrs. Taylor & Mrs. Wright called. A letter from Dr. Clark. They wait for him in Turkey.

November 16 Wed. Home Miss. Meeting at Mrs. Sam Williams's. I saw a number of my old neighbors, Mrs. Roeder, Miss Leonard, Mrs. Robeson. Mrs. Van der Pyl brought me home.

November 17 Thurs. With Mrs. Wright we all except

Ernest C. Partridge

November 7 Word from Dr Merrill that they want me to go to Constan[tinople] this fall.

[November 8–10]

November 11 Armistice Day. A program to Chapel. Dan Bradley spoke.

November 12 Ed & George & I went to Cleveland to Case game, a tie 7–7. An Oberlin program at State theater. 72m

[November 13–16]

November 17 Went to Elyria to find a dog but found nothing. 18m

November 18 H.S. played Alumni and won 13–0. George went to H.S. football banquet in evening.

November 19 Last game of season, Reserve. We won 7–0 with McPhee out and Wheeler limping.

November 20 Communion Sunday. A large number united with church. W & I went to Miss Zearing's for supper. Miss Chamberlain, Mrs Wright, & Miss Brownback there.

November 21 Ed & I went to Annual football banquet at Gym. 500 people present. Prof Bosworth, Amant, & Frank Burke spoke.

[November 22]

George, drove to Elyria to hunt for a little dog to buy. Took Billo to the Doctor. He said that nervousness caused those bilious spells.

November 18 Fri. As Billo has been sick all the week I went to see his teacher about his lessons. The High School played the Alumni, 13 to 0. George went to their foot-ball banquet given by the girls of the High School.

November 19 Sat. Oberlin–Reserve, 7 to 0, the last game of the season.

November 20 Sunday. Communion Sunday, a large number joined the church. Mr. P. & I went to supper at Miss Zearing's. We had fruit salad, toast sandwiches, coffee & cookies served in the parlor. Mrs. Wright & Miss Brownback were there.

November 21 Mon. I called on Mrs. Wright. Mrs. Murdock came in. I went to Mrs. Metcalf's but she was not at home. We washed & the bother got dry actually. Football banquet, Mr. P. & Ed. went.

November 22 Tues. Ironed for house. In the evening Mrs. Wright was alone so she asked me to come to spend the evening with her.

November 23 Wed. Getting ready for Thanksgiving. We called on Mr. & Mrs. Hummel. Billo with a girl from his grade and two children from the first grade sang Thanksgiving songs in the sixth grade.

November 24 Thurs. Thanksgiving. Edward was at Grey Gables. Lawrence Knowlton and Kenneth Taylor ate with us. Mrs. Wright and Harriet Chamberlain called. Ed, George & Mr. P. went to the movies.

November 25 Fri. A holiday for all except Edward. Frances had pains in her feet and hands like rheumatism.

November 26 Sat. Another holiday. Edward and I went to see Ibsen's Doll House, very fine, so many good sermons played. Frances some better but not able to walk.

November 27 Sunday. The fourth day of "no school" but we survived better than I expected. The weather has been bad nearly all the time. We took a little ride to get Frances out.

November 28 Mon. Frances just screamed every time she moved. The Dr. came, gave her some tablets and toward night she got well like a miracle, so she could walk even without it hurting her.

November 29 Tues. Frances still better, the stiffness passing. Geo. & Edward went to see Douglas Fairbanks in The Three Musketeers. Edward took Lois Walton.

November 30 Wed. Frances all right, no ache nor pains. We had a letter from Helen Wright saying that there was a little dog & a brown one, at the Humane Society, so Geo. & his father went to Cleveland & bought the little, white Snoopie. It is for Billo's birthday.

Alfred: Spelling B+, Writing B, Arith. B+, Drawing B
Billo: Reading B, Eng. B, Spelling B, Writing B+, Arith C, History C+, Music A, Physiology A
Frances: Reading B+, Spelling A, Arith. B+, Music B

December 1 Thurs. The children & all of us are so fond of the little dog. Armen & Mrs. Wright came to see her.

[December 2–5]

December 6 Tues. Billo's birthday. Russell came over to supper. Dog, collar, chain, two tops, 5 balloons, ticket to hospital fair & chicken dinner.

[December 7]

December 8 Thurs. Papa's birthday. I made a leopard cake. He had tickets for the hospital fair etc. etc.

December 9 Fri. Hospital Fair. Billo, Geo & their father went, the first two to supper. I made apple pies for the Fair.

December 10 Sat. Frances had music in the morning & then she & Billo both had a play & party in the P.M. & Alfred & I went too. We had a photo taken. Then we all went to the Hospital Fair. Two plays, "Shawn", "Fourteen for Dinner"

December 11 Sunday. Cousin Will Day and Lucille were here to supper.

December 12 Mon. Cousin Will called, also Mrs. Wright.

December 13 Tues. I went to a play given by our section, called Honeymoon Flats.

December 14 Wed. We went again to have our picture taken, dreadful stunt.

December 15 Thurs. Nothing much, music for Frances, basket ball for Alfred and Billo at 5:30 every day & George at 6:30.

December 16 Fri. Called on Susie Zearing in the evening.

Ernest C. Partridge

November 23 Called on the Hummels.

November 24 Thanksgiving. Ed at Grey Gables. Lawrence & Taylor ate with us.

[November 25–December 27]

December 17 Sat. Geo. & Alfred and I went to Elyria and did a very little Christmas shopping. Mr. P. took supper at the Faculty Club with Mr. Bohn & Mr. Van der Pyl & Clarence Graham.

December 18 Sunday. Christmas concerts. I stayed at home with the children.

[December 19]

December 20 Tues. Edward did taxi work bringing children to a Christmas party at Gray Gables.

December 21 Wed. George's marks: Eng. A, Latin A+, Hist [?], Math A

Edward came home to stay and Armen came. I went to Home Miss. meeting. Mrs. Shauffer spoke.

[December 22]

December 23 Fri. Alfred was Little Boy Blue in a play at school. Billo went to a Christmas party.

December 24 Sat. We had the Christmas tree. All fared well.

Ed: silk stockings, Chemistry book, flash light, mittens from Grandma, Eversharp from Miss Gage, record.
George: football, camera case, Eversharp, H.S. pin, 4 neckties, silk socks from Carroll, Parchesi board, $2
Billo: Cowboy suit, Eversharp, flinch cards, 2 musical instruments, handkerchiefs, $2.
Frances. Several small dolls, hair ribbon, handkerchiefs, wash stand, trunk, petticoats, mittens.
Alfred: Cowboy suit, mittens, bank, gun

December 25 Sunday. In the evening a Nativity Play, arranged by Prof. Ward, Wise Men, Shepherds, Mary, Joseph, Gabriel, Jesus, very impressive, beautiful music.

December 26 Mon. Official Christmas day. We received a box of candy from Haig. Skating on Gayter's. Ed. & George went.

December 27 Tues. Armen took me to the movies. Just out of college, Jack Pickford. A story about pickles.

December 28 Wed. Mr. P., Ed., Geo. & I went to Cleveland today to buy George's first long trouser suit. Incidentally we bought a new mackinaw for Billo, a dress for Frances & waists for all.

December 29 Thurs. Washed. Hung the sheets out doors and they froze as fast as I put them out but dried before night. Ed played basket ball against the High School 12 to 15.

December 30 Fri. Mrs. Martin invited me to her house to meet Laura Shurtleff. Those present were Mrs. Andrews, Mrs. Caskey, Mrs. Lawrence, Mrs. Haroun, Miss May, Miss Swift, Mrs. Chase & Miss Chase, Mrs. Carne. George came back. Ed. played at Kipton, 57 to 25.

December 31 Sat. Ed. played cards until nearly midnight, then we talked until the New Year. We had heaps of things to do, [?], ironing, letters to write etc.

Alfred: Reading B+, Spelling B+, Writing B+, Arith B, Music A, Drawing B
Frances: Reading B+, Spelling A, Arith B
Billo: Reading B, Eng. B, Spelling A, Writing B+, Arith D, Geog. C, History C-, Music B+

Ernest C. Partridge

December 28 Mrs P, Ed, George & I drove to Cleveland to buy clothes.

[December 29–31]

Diaries of Winona & Ernest Partridge 1922

Flyleaf: "Winona G. Partridge, Oberlin, Ohio Christmas 1921 ECP "

January 1 Sunday. George's first appearance in long trousers. He does not look older but like a kid dressed up like a man. Hermine & Nigoghos and Lucile took supper with us.

[January 2–4]

January 5 Thurs. Edward started in school again.

[January 6–13]

January 14 Sat. Frances had her tonsils removed for the second time, also adenoids. Dr. Colegrove & Miss Greenwood were along. Frances did not take ether easily this time as she did before but it came out all right and we brought her home in the evening, although it was very cold. I spent the whole day with her and her father kept house and did all sorts of extras, varnishing floors etc.

January 15 Sunday. I stayed with Frances all day while the others went to church, S.S. etc.

January 16 Mon. Frances much better, throat very little sore. We washed. Mr. P. varnished the other half of the kitchen linoleum.

January 17 Tues. Mrs. Stapleton invited me to a Club Meeting, but the time was wrong, so we went to the library and then to Campus View for refreshments. Frances much better, but not in school.

January 18 Wed. Rainy afternoon, very wet weather & very slippery. Mr. P. had the third injection for typhoid & is sick from it. Billo's violin troubles never end. Today the tail broke. The D string went bad from a poor budget.

January 19 Thurs. I went to call on Mrs. Wright, but she

Ernest C. Partridge

January 1 Hermine, Nigoghas & Lucille took supper with us. George put on long trousers.

January 2 Had New Year's Dinner with Maynard family, Miss Shane and Mr Northcote at our house.

[January 3]

January 4 1st typhoid serum injection.

[January 5]

January 6 O.H.S. beat Sandusky 24–19.

January 7 Ober basketball team beat Hiram, here, in a slow game 23–18.

[January 8–10]

January 11 Second typhoid serum. Makes me about sick for 2–3 days.

[January 12–13]

January 14 Frances had operation for tonsils & adenoids. Brought her home in evening. Reserve beat us at basketball in Cleveland. I varnished ½ kitchen floor.

[January 15]

January 16 Varnished rest of floor.

[January 17]

January 18 My third typhoid injection. Also vaccinated.

[January 19]

was not at home so I visited with Etta and Wright McCullom. Mr. P. was feeling miserable from his third shot of anti-typhoid serum.

January 20 Fri. Mrs. Wright went to Auburn and we went to see her off. I took Frances to see Dr. Colegrove. He says her throat is doing finely, but she must stay in until Sunday. H.S. vs. Bellevue.

[**January 21**]

January 22 Sunday. Mr. P & I went to Cleveland at 10:25, took dinner with Mr. & Mrs. James. Then we went to an Armenian Meeting, where Mr. P. spoke. Weather turned very cold.

January 23 Mon. Took supper at Gray Gables, although it seemed too cold to go out. Had a fine supper. Armen & Edward sat at our table, Mr. & Mrs. Van der Pyl too.

January 24 Tues. Very cold. Took supper at Lord Cottage with Lucile Day. We sat with Miss Farwell and the Bowen girls. One is about to start for China.

January 25 Wed. Mr. P and I went to hear James Matt Osborne on Politics and Prisons. He told the story of his persecution by politicians.

January 26 Thurs. Still cold. Schools closed for mid-semester vacation. Mr. P. & I went to church supper and then to trolley station where he took the car, starting for Constantinople.

January 27 Fri. Ed had exams in Chemistry and Economics. George got his semester report. Latin A+, Eng. B+, Geom. A, History A.

January 28 Sat. The Clarks came at 10:30AM. Papa was supposed to arrive in New York and then leave for Andover.

January 29 Sunday. I stayed at home all day. The children went to S.S. & the others to church. Mrs. Stapleton and Eleanor called.

January 30 Mon. Dr. Clark went. Reports, all promoted.

Billo: Reading B+, Eng. C+, Spelling C, Arith B, Geog. C, Physiology A, Music B+, Writing B+
Frances: Reading B+, Spelling A, Arith B+, Music B
Alfred: Reading B+, Spelling B+, Writing B-, Arith B, Music A-

[**January 31**]

Memoranda
Alfred weighs 50 lbs height 3.11
W.G.P.   160
E.C.P.   158
Edward   129
George   127
Frances   60

Ernest C. Partridge

January 20 Mrs Wright went off for a visit. Bellevue beat O.H.S.

January 21 We beat Kenyon 34–22 in a fast, interesting game. Wheeler ma[d]e 26 points out of 34.

January 22 Mrs P & I went to Cleveland, dinner with James and I spoke at a gathering of 125 Armenians. Dr Bradley also spoke & they showed "Alice in Hungerland" [film portraying work being done in orphanages etc in Near East].

January 23 Mrs P & I took dinner at Grey Gables. Mr & Mrs Van der P also invited. 1st cold serum.

[**January 24–25**]

January 26 Finished up last things. Winona & I went to Annual Supper of United Church. I took 8:25 car to Cleveland. Sleeper to Pittsburgh. 34m

January 27 Breakfast and a visit with Custer in Pittsburgh, on to Phil. Spent night at D.H.K.'s, Yeranouhi & Tatarian, Raphaelian's. George's marks Eng B+ Latin A+ Hist A+ Geom A. 2nd cold serum.

January 28 Tried to find Miss Spalding in morning but failed. In to New York and out to Boston & Andover. Guest at Bigelow's. 588m, 232, 23

January 29 Sunday. Spoke Old South morning SS 3 times. Dinner at Blunts. Called on Stackpole and Twitchell's. Lawrence church in evening. 8m

January 30 Morning train into Boston. Ministers Meeting, noon prayer meeting. Saw Gaskins. 4PM train to Hartford. Night at Sem. Vrooman & Anak. 22m

January 31 Reached New York about 10. Saw Fowle, Miss Dwight, Vickrey. A supper evening 23 present, given a briefcase. Night with GP. Ed got A++ in Calculus & 98 in Chem exam. 232, 10

February 1 Wed. George was sick with a cold. It settled above his eyes so that he could not read and could hardly see.

February 2 Thurs. George still sick. He asked John W. to find out about his lesson. He came over and just guessed at what his lessons would probably be.

February 3 Fri. George better but stayed at home. H.S. basket ball, H.S. 26, Elyria 14. Frances went on her father's ticket.

February 4 Sat. Frances played in her first recital, two pieces, Froggie Wee & ?. Armen, Alfred & I went. Basket-ball, H.S. beat State High of Cleveland, 19 to 18. Alfred went.

February 5 Sunday. I went to church in the evening. Mr. V. spoke on the popular fallacy that people outside the church are just as good as those inside.

February 6 Mon. We all went to see Mary Pickford in Little Lord Fauntleroy. She played both Cedric & Dearest.

February 7 Tues. We registered Frances and Ruth in the Conservatory for $37.50 apiece. Ruth is to have Mrs. Morrison and Frances, Miss Swanson again.

February 8 Wed. Washed. Went down town to pay some bills etc. Mrs. Clark & I went to the movies to see Bebe Daniels in Speed Girl.

February 9 Thurs. We ironed and cleaned up the house. Mrs. C. & I went to hear Prof. Bosworth on Revelation.

February 10 Fri. Dr. Jameson examined Frances's eyes and found them very bad. At first she could see only the very coarse ones but gradually began to see more, showing that it is the nerves, as the Dr. said.

February 11 Sat. Oberlin–Reserve basketball 26 to 21. Billo played between halves and was quite the star as a guard, although his team lost 2 to 0. Frances went to a valentine party at Phyllis Ohly's.

February 12 Sunday. Mrs. Clark, Edward & I went to church. In the afternoon I went to see Mrs. Wright, who had returned from Indianapolis sick with a bad cold & cough.

February 13 Mon. Spent the forenoon putting drops into Frances's eyes, going to the oculist, incidentally doing a little housework.

February 14 Tues. I had a lame foot so that I could walk only with difficulty. Mrs. Clark did the walking work and I tended the washing machine.

Ernest C. Partridge

February 1 Called on Hyrabed & Bedikians; passport work. Lunch with Kurkjian. Spoke at Woman's Meeting Arm[enian] church. Saw Shuorig. Out to White Plains, my cousin Edna, Mrs H V May & I talked till 12. 22m

February 2 Miss Tipple came on in the night & we had breakfast & lunch together & a good visit. Packed & sent trunks to NER warehouse. Called on MacLaughlin & spent evening with Miss Wheeler. Sleeper to Boston. 40m

February 3 I spoke in W.B.M. Meeting. Saw many friends. Finished passport work. Saw Gaskins. Night with Hal Ross. 232m

February 4 Last day in Boston. Hal Ross gave me $10.00 for sightseeing. Spent day in rooms. Had long talk with Dr Barton & Riggs. Sailed about 5 for Liverpool. Dr White, Nazeli at boat.

February 5 Sunday. Journey starts out well. Not too rough. I had morning service, on "Worship." WGP1 [first letter to Winona] 203m

February 6 3rd cold serum. WGP2 248m

February 7 Colder & rougher. Reading Wells history, writing letter. WGP3 Goshins, Hawley, Gilroy 282m

February 8 Dr & I began to talk Turkish. WGP4 George, Lamkin 245m

February 9 Frengul., Perry, Edna W. 284m

February 10 Rough and unpleasantly cold. Carrots, Roghos, Billo WGP5 educat 301m

February 11 A dull day of reading. Went to bed with a headache early. Mrs Greene, Ed. 4th cold serum. 269m

February 12 I had charge of service again. Spoke on Heb 1/1. WGP6 272m

February 13 English, Moore 244m

February 14 WGP7, Linn 291m

February 15 Wed. Mrs. Clark & I went to a lecture by Hamilton Holt on the Disarmament Conference. Sat up with Edward until after twelve to finish his French. I had Billo's Arith & George's Algebra & Latin to help with.

February 16 Thurs. Very, very cold. Stoking the furnace all day. Frances got her glasses, tortoise shell over steel. They magnify quite a little.

February 17 Fri. Billo had a tooth-ache & came home from school. I went to a reception at Mrs. Lord's house. Nearly all of my old friends were there.

Memoranda
1922 People present at Mrs. Lord's reception, Feb. 17.

Mrs. Viola Partridge	Miss May
Mrs. Caskey	Miss Brugger
Mrs. Jameson	Miss Dean
Mrs. Upton	Miss Nickerson
Mrs. C.B. Martin & daughter	Mrs. Wirkler
Mrs. Buddington	Mrs. Haroun
Mrs. Sam Williams	Ms. Cargill
Mrs. Griswold & son	Mrs. Barnard
Miss Sinclair	Miss Fitch
Susie Zearing	Mrs. Wager
Mrs. Vernon Johnston	Mrs. Lampson
Mrs. Dickinson	Mrs. Nicol
Mrs. Alexander	Mrs. Carr
Mrs. King	Mrs. Rogers
Mrs. Fullerton	Mrs. Ward
Mrs. Taft	Mrs. Jelliff
Mrs. Kramer, Mrs. Partridge's sister	

February 18 Sat. We worked hard all day, went up town long enough to buy Billo some underwear which proved to be too small. Ed & Isabel, George, James, & Stephen went to Glee Club Concert.

February 19 Sunday. I felt too tired and miserable to go anywhere. The children were very noisy but not very quarrelsome.

February 20 Mon. Went to the college movie with all except Edward. It was a variety, Heidi of the Alps, and then views of fish at the bottom of the sea, devil fish, angel fish, cuttle fish.

[February 21–22]

February 23 Thurs. Mrs. Clark & I went to a stereoptician lecture by Dr. Palmer of Honolulu and then to Mr. Stetson's class. He talked about the gang spirit in boys from 9 to 13.

Ernest C. Partridge

February 15 Reached the harbor about 2PM and after a stupid lot of backing & shifting got off the steamer about 5. Lord Nelson Hotel. 268m

February 16 Left Liverpool with Dr Clark, Benham and Folen at 9:40 for London. Lunch on train. In at 2PM. Went to Penn Club. 9 Faers Stock Sq [an address] where we found good quarters. Barrie's Quality Street in evening. 220m

February 17 Called on Gentle-Cachett, Gracey & W.J. Childs, shopped some, sat in gallery of House of Commons a few minutes. Spent three hours in National Gallery.

February 18 Bought tickets to Paris. Visited St Paul's, Westminster Abbey, Wallace & Tate Galleries. Several Murillos [Bartholome Esteban], annunciation [painting] very fine. Rubens Holy Family. At Tate many modern works of Reynolds, Turner & Millar's.

February 19 Sunday. AM went to City Temple & heard a good sermon by McClelland of Trinity Glasgow on Church of Future. 3:15 St Paul's. 7 Heard Stuart Holden on "Christ unchanging and unchangeable." WGP8

February 20 Left London at 8:20 for Paris. A pleasant trip on Channel. Reached Paris at 4:25. Hotel du Louvre. Saw Monna Vanna at National Opera House, Maeterlincks. London-Paris 262m

February 21 Went to Panorama of War. Spent several hours in Louvre, Renaissance pictures, Millars & Corot, Mona Lisa, Winged Victory, Venus de Milo, Notre Dame. Sleeper on Simplon to Lausanne.

February 22 Reached Geneva at 10AM. Miss Stucky met train. Mr Favre not well. Lunched there with him & Mrs Naville & Miss Stucky. Tea with Mr & Mrs Naville. Jemjemian came in evening. WGP9 Paris-Geneva 388m

February 23 12:20AM train to Lausanne & Milan. Saw "Lords Supper" Brera, Ambrosiana Cathedral. 2:05 train to Florence. Arrived at 11:20 at Hotel de la Ville. Geneva-Milan 171m

[February 24]

February 25 Sat. Case 20, Oberlin 18.

February 26 Sunday. I saw June Merriam at church. It was so good to see him. I went to see Mrs. Wright for a little while in the P.M. The children had a party for themselves & us & Ruth.

February 27 Mon. Ten letters from Liverpool & London. The passage across was pleasant but took ten or eleven days. They are hopeful now about a settlement in Turkey. Father & son banquet. Edward & Mr. Bohn, George & Dr. Husted, Billo & Mr. McKee.

February 28 Tues. Alfred's eyes were examined for glasses. Dr. Jameson said that one eye was 1/10 of normal & the other less than 1/3. I went to hear Dr. Raymond Calkins on "Can I believe in a personal God?" Then I went to see Mrs. Wright and read her seven letters from Mr. P.

March 1 Wed. Ruth has the flu and is over here. Connie is cranky too. Yesterday a letter from Florence B. Lee says that they are going to Rome for an Astronomical Meeting, sailing April 6. I made candy for Pleasant St. sale in Ruth's place.

Alfred: Reading B-, Spelling B, Penmanship C+, Arith B, Music A-, Drawing C+
Frances: Literature B, Eng. C+, Spelling C-, Arith C, Geog. B, (She was absent ¼ of the time)
Billo: Conduct A+, Effort A, Reading B+, English B+, Spelling B+, Writing B, Arith A, Geog B, History B+

March 2 Thurs. Mrs. Clark took me to the "Sheik." It was very good indeed. Ruth is better but has a rash. It seems like three-day measles.

March 3 Fri. Alfred got his glasses & got them broken the same day. Dorothy came over to play. David & Alfred quarreled and the game stopped.

March 4 Sat. When we looked at Alfred's glasses after they were cleaned we found they were not broken. Oberlin-Miami 34–28.

March 5 Sunday. I stayed with the children in the morning & went in the evening, to the first of the Lenten services, Dr. Graham. Armen came down in the afternoon.

March 6 Mon. We had six washers full of washing but the weather was good and we dried some out of doors.

March 7 Tues. Mrs. Clark & I went to Leaven Club meeting at Mr. Fullerton's. Mrs. Clark spoke about Turkey. Mrs. King, Mrs. Fiske, Mrs. Ned Bosworth & three theologue ladies.

Ernest C. Partridge

February 24 Visited Cathedral & Campanile. Academy saw Angelo's David. Ufffizi & Pitti galleries.

February 25 6:40 train to Venice reaching there at 3:20PM. Hotel Victoria. Strolled around to St Marks and looked at shops. The most charming place in the world. 217m

February 26 Went to St Marks for mass, then to Methodist Italian service. In PM to St Lazzaro to Mekhitarist Monastery [Armenian Monastery founded in Vienna 1810], on to Leido & back to city.

February 27 Had a guide for day with Dr from New York & a couple, to St. Marks. Doges Palace, Santa Marie della Salute, St John & St Paul, Frari [also a church] & exhibition of glasswork. WGP11

February 28 Went to Murano to glass factory and then to S Lazar where we spent some very interesting hours with a monk and the head of the monastery. Simplon-Orient at 8pm.

March 1 Travel very light, only one other passenger in our sleeper.

[March 2]

March 3 Reached Constantinople at 3PM. Went to Bible House where we saw a number of people. Over to Scutari to stay with MacCallums at Language School. 1237m

March 4 Spent forenoon at Bible House. Went to a meeting in Pera of Xu Workers in PM. Am having long talks with Miss McLean about Sivas. WGP12

March 5 Sunday. A quiet day of rest. Heard HH Riggs in Armenian at Scutari service. WGP13

March 6 Attended language school lesson. Went to Bible house. Night here with Goodsell.

March 7 Edward's marks Econ. A Cal. A+ Fr A B+ Chem. Spent day at Bible House. Out to Scutari for night.

March 8 Wed. I went to see Dr. Colegrove about my goiter. He thinks it will disappear. He weighed me. I weighed 157 lbs., three less than six weeks.

March 9 Thurs. Lecture on the first eleven chaps. of Genesis by Miss Fitch and lecture on the savage age of children by Prof. Stetson.

March 10 Fri. Mrs. Seeman died very suddenly of heart failure after attending a Freshman class party.

March 11 Sat. Rainy. We suffered & died in the morning, but took the children to the movies in the afternoon, Jack Pickford in "The man who had everything."

March 12 Sunday. I did not go to church in the morning, nor George nor Edward but Ed. & I went in the evening. Prof. Youtz preached.

March 13 Washed & hung the clothes all out of doors.

March 14 Tues. We finished all our ironing and felt complacent.

March 15 Wed. Henry the Magician gave an exhibition. I did not go, but the three oldest boys did and enjoyed it very much.

March 16 Thurs. Lecture by Mr. Van der Pyl on Ecclesiastes, Vanity of Vanitees. He shocked Mr. Childs by saying that "Remember now thy creator in the days of thy youth" was an interpretation.

March 17 Fri. Mrs. C. & I took our five little ones or four to see Hansel & Gretel in which Frances & Ruth took part. The play was fine. When we came home I worked on French with Edward until twelve.

March 18 Sat. I got lots of work piled up, mending etc. so I worked until after eleven, partly because I took the children to Peck's Bad Boy, Edward took Laura King to The Girls' Glee Club Concert.

March 19 Sunday. I was quite dissipated, going twice to church. In the evening Dr. Fitch of Amherst College preached. He said that goodness in a college student is learning is his lessons and is any one doing his job. I read to the children nearly all the P.M.

March 20 Mon. Mrs. Clark and I have adopted the universal washing day, but this time it was very cold. Letters from Constantinople, announcing their safe arrival but no definite plans.

March 21 Tues. Letters from Florence for Mrs. C. & cards and letters from Venice for the Partridges. It looks as though Mr. P. would go to Erivan but it is not sure.

Ernest C. Partridge

March 8 Spent day at Bible House. Night at Kadi-Keoui with Markham.

March 9 Came into Stamboul in morning, dinner with Yani Ifandides. Com-ad-I meeting decided Erivan for me. Dr C to stay here a few weeks, then to Sivas. WGP14

March 10 Lunch at American Men's club. Consul Mosher spoke on Caucasus. Mr Pearce held S.S. conference in PM.

March 11 Spent day in Stamboul, forenoon in office, writing letters & working over accounts. PM SS Conference. WGP15

March 12 I preached morning at Scutari church 1 Jus1/2. PM at Miss Burgess' chapel. Heard Dr Pearce at Langa Church SS.

March 13 Spent day at Bible House. Saw Proestahi & wife. GK Bible woman Elenie. WGP16

March 14 Spent day with Boghosian's at Makri Keoui.

March 15 Day at Bible House. Night with Toumadjians.

March 16 Forenoon at Bible House. Station meeting at Gedik Pasha.

March 17 Spent forenoon at Bible House. Luncheon at American Club. Tea at Nvart Aivazians. Played Rook in evening. A disagreeable rainy day. WGP17

March 18 Forenoon at Bible House. Lunch at Sailor's Club. Our house attended a play "General Post" by British officers. Very good.

March 19 Sunday. Preached at Vlanga church in morning Jno 4,24. Dinner with Nvart Aivazian. PM visited one of Central Com. Orphanages at Keoluli, Dr Der Stefaman. I spoke.

March 20 George's semester marks Latin A+ Eng B+ Math A History A. WGP18

March 21 Spent forenoon at Bible House PM called on new Greek Patriarch with Dr Peet.

March 22 Wed. One more card from Florence, this time for Billo. A letter from Miss Rice, saying that Mr. P. could probably not go into the interior [Sivas]. Alfred, Frances, & I took dinner with Mrs. Stapleton.

March 23 Thurs. As George was away in the evening I did not go to hear Pres. King on the Gospel of John. Mrs. C. went. I did quite a bit of washing.

March 24 Fri. Alfred came home from school because his ear hurt. He had been hit by a bat, nothing serious.

March 25 Sat. I had a very bad sick headache and was in bed nearly all the afternoon and until about eight when it began to improve. I had overworked & underslept. The children were very thoughtful.

March 26 Sunday. Wayne Wheeler spoke on the Prohibition situation. He was good as he always is. I was sorry that the boys did not hear him because they went in the evening, Lenten service.

March 27 Mon. Billo sick with a headache. I went to hear Dr. Breasted on the Egyptian ideas about the dead, inscriptions in the coffins, balancing the heart with a feather, magic spells for everything. All College Vaudeville tonight. I stayed & read Ed's French lesson & took care of five while the others went.

March 28 Tues. Letters from Con. Mr. P. is to go to Erivan to look up the possibility of starting a Teachers College.

March 29 Wed. Billy still sick.

March 30 Thurs. Mrs. C. & I went to hear Prof. Fullerton on Jonah. He says that it represents the exile of the children of Israel, 'they were swallowed up by the exile in the wilderness.'

March 31 Fri. The last day of school. Billo absent. I went to see his teacher. She thinks he needs to study only a little Geography. Armen came to stay a day or two.

Frances: Health A, conduct A, Effort A, Reading B+, Eng. B, Spelling A+, Writing C+, Arith C+, Geog. B, Music B+
Billo: Reading B, Eng A, Spelling A, Writing B, Arith A, Geog C+, Hist B, Music C+

April 1 Sat. The Clarks went to Detroit. James & some others went camping although it was cold & wet.

April 2 Sunday. Mr. Van – spoke on the Spirit of Lent, not eating nor fasting, putting off or taking on but deepening the spiritual life. Armen went to Cleveland.

April 3 Mon. Washed, swept, etc. etc. Went to pay Mr. Metcalf Harris' interest. Mrs. Harding called in the evening. Then I ironed.

April 4 Tues. I attended Miss Metcalf's Review Lesson for the Home Department. It was about Elijah, Elisha, Ahab etc. and the Children of Israel. Very enlightening.

Ernest C. Partridge

[March 22]

March 23 Station meeting at Dr Peet's. I led devotions. Dr Peet made a statement about Commissionership of League. WGP19

[March 24] W 20

March 25 Forenoon at Bible House. PM at Dr Kennedy's place. They drove us home in car.

March 26 Morning preached Scutari Girls' Schools, dinner there. Called on Goodsells & Fowles. Concert at Robert College, spoke at Sailor's Club. Night with Flints.

March 27 W 21

[March 28]

March 29 Dinner with Miss Maynard. Called on Dr Wallace at Constantinople College. Saw Yeranouhi Kevorkian. Tea & night at Lawson Chambers.

March 30 Rode to city with Dr Hoover & station meeting at Gedik Pasha. A Turk spoke on Movements in Islam.

March 31 Day at Bible House. Lunch at American Club. W22

April 1 Worked at B.H. [Bible House] till 2:30. Back to Scutari for tea.

[April 2-3]

April 4 W23

April 5 Wed. I went to Missionary Meeting, Africa, Dr. Richards, India, Mrs. Jeffrey, Turkey, Mrs. Stapleton. The children intended to drive out to the Tank House camp but could not find Stephen & Edward Ohly to take them.

April 6 Thurs. Prof. Fullerton on Daniel & Prof. Stetson on the late adolescent period, from 15 to 20.

April 7 Fri. Jackie Coogan in My Boy. All except Edward saw it, very good. We went to the Lake & had a weiner roast, our family except Ed, and Ruth Clark.

April 8 Sat. The Stream of Life, a film given by the Child Conservation League, good but somewhat sad. The Clarks came back in the evening.

April 9 Sun. Mr. Van der Pyl on Liberty & License. The last Lenten service in the evening.

April 10 Mon. Warm as summer. I took my mending over to Mrs. Wright's. George went to see Tol'able David, a bloody film. Hail in the afternoon, thunder, etc.

April 11 Tues. Cold, had to start the furnace again. The last U.L.A. lecture, Akelay on African game. Edward and George went.

[April 12]

April 13 Thurs. Prof. Graham on Religious Significance of the Bible. Mr. Stetson's last lecture was very good, sort of a resumé of the children's progress.

April 14 Fri. Letters from Mr. P. & Mrs. Maynard, the latter urging me to come, the former saying that I probably should. I went to see Mrs. Wright in the pouring rain.

April 15 Sat. Fortunately a pleasant day and the children played out of doors. I bought Frances low shoes for $2. Also trousers for Alfred for $3.50.

April 16 Sun. Easter, I went to the morning service as usual but not to the Easter Concert.

April 17 Mon. Washed and put the clothes out between showers. They actually dried. Frances forgot her music lesson.

April 18 Tues. Cleaned up the house and ironed. A letter from E.C.P. saying that he had no doubt that I should go out this summer.

[April 19]

April 20 Thurs. I went to a Junior S.S. party with Billo. They had some simple plays, worthy of Sivas school girls.

April 21 Fri. Annual Glee Club Concert for the school children. "Looking for a job" by Skidmore, Wood and the janitor, was fine.

Ernest C. Partridge

April 5 Worked most of the day at B.H. Lunched at noon at Hotel de Loudre with University Club.

April 6 Lunched at American Club.

[April 7–8]

April 9 Sunday. I preached at Scutari Chapel in morning on Jno 12/19, "The world has gone after Him" and taught Bible Class in PM.

[April 10–11]

April 12 Worked at Bible House in forenoon. Dr & I took affidavit to Consulate General in PM. CRR, HBR, AMG, Aspinwall [letters written]

April 13 Fixed up a couple of more affidavits. Station meeting & Com-ad-Int in PM. Dr Peet made another statement about League of N. Commissionership. He is disposed to accept now. W26

[April 14]

April 15 Finished Sivas affidavits and wrote Winona about those for her & Mrs Clark. EFB, Edward [letters written]

April 16 Sunday. Easter Sunday attended Communion Service at Scutari church and took it easy rest of day to get over a cold.

[April 17]

April 18 Heard Fred Smith on The Church & International Peace.

[April 19]

April 20 Left Scutari for good. Finished packing, wrote last letters. WGP, JLB, EWR, ECW, SWGL. Station meeting and Com-at-I. Went on board Adria. Supper in Goleta, Night at Gedik Pasha. W29

April 21 Sailed at noon Mr & Mrs Archer, Miss Hardcastle & Miss Legge. NER on board. A very quiet start, few passengers, a good boat. W30

April 22 Sat. Frances's ninth birthday. She invited Rachel & Guy, Barbara, Phyllis, Sara and Anna. We served ice-cream, cake, candy. Thirteen sat down, good luck.

April 23 Sunday. Mr. Van der Pyl on "Unconditional Surrender." We drove nearly to the beach. The children picked flowers and had a good time.

April 24 Mon. Mr. Ryan on the Near East questions, very good.

April 25 Tues. Mr. Ryan brought his lecture up to date, giving more recent history of Constantinople. He certainly has no use for the Turks.

April 26 Wed. Mrs. Clark, Miss Trefethren, Mrs. Stapleton and I took dinner at the Hi-O-Hi tea rooms with Mr. Ryan. He gave us two hours of his precious time.

April 27 Thurs. Mrs. Wright sent for me to come and see her as she had sprained her ankle. The first ball game lost to Hiram, 13 to 11.

[April 28–29]

April 30 Sunday. I went to the hotel to dinner with Mrs. Root, Miss Metcalf and Mrs. Harding. We drove to the Lake straight out and the children played a little while.

Frances: Reading B+, Eng A, SP. B+, Writing C+, Arith B, Geog. B+, Music B+
Alfred: Reading B, Sp. B, writing C+, Arith B, Music A, Drawing C+
Billo: Health C-, Conduct A, Effort A, Reading B, Eng. B, Sp. B, Arith B+, Geog. C-, Music B+, Physiology C

May 1 Mon. Mrs. C. & I call on Mrs. Burkhardt. She told us about traveling on the river in China, so much worse than any araba journeys. Letters from Constantinople.

May 2 Tues. We did the ironing & called on Mrs. Stapleton and her boarder baby. It is very thin and little.

May 3 Wed. Letter from Mr. P. I went to see Mrs. Wright. Miss Brownback was there. Mrs. C. & I went to hear Louise Stallings sing. She was fine.

May 4 Thurs. Sara Plumb's birthday. Alfred was very sad because he was out with George and me when we brought Stallings and Meyer in from the Athletic field. We heard Dr. Bosworth on prayer calling on the mind energy of food to give in something that we can share with another in need.

Ernest C. Partridge

[April 22]

April 23 Sunday. Reached Trebizond about 9AM. Went off to visit NER people and Mrs Crawford and Mrs Stapleton. Sailed on about dark.

April 24 Reached Batoum 9AM. A NER man met boat. Went to Personnel House Capt Ekman, Phelp & Rowland. Went on train at 9PM in Phelp's private car to start for Tiflis. W31

April 25 Still standing on sidetrack this morning. No engine yet.

April 26 Left Batoum early and finally started from a freight depot about 8AM.

[April 27]

April 28 Reached Tiflis early in morning. Spent day at Personnel House. W32 Batoum-Tiflis 218m

April 29 Went on board Courier Car for Alexandropol at 11AM but did not start till 6PM attached to a freight train.

April 30 Sunday. A slow trip with long waits for engines. Finally reached Alex[andropol] about 9PM. Met with cars and taken to Kazachi Post. W33 137m

[May 1]

May 2 Spent most of day going around Kazachi Post. Evening went to a dance at Seversky Post.

May 3 Spent forenoon seeing industrial work & educational work at Kazachy Post. PM visited orphanages and drove over to Polygon for tea. Saw industrial work there.

May 4 Crothers & I took morning train down to Erivan. Found Mrs Powers on courier car. Reached Erivan at 3PM. To Maynard's house. W34 97m

[May 5–6]

May 5 Fri. Some of the children went to a High school concert. I went over to see Mrs. Wright in the evening, took her some eggs.

May 6 Sat. Five letters from Mr. P. about to start for Erivan. George, James, Stephen and I went to Cleveland to get some things for George. We bought shirts, stockings, shoes, cap, and for Edward, BVD's and shirts.

May 7 Sunday. Communion Sunday. A group of children joined the church, like Helen Ward. In the evening Mrs. Swift gave an illustrated lecture on the Passion Play of Oberammergau.

May 8 Mon. A perfect wash day, cool & pleasant. I paid bills in the afternoon and had a dope ["to figure out or calculate a plan"] with Miss Trefethren. In the evening Mrs. C & I took the bunch and two girls besides to see Charlie Chaplin & Jackie Coogan in the "Kid."

May 9 Tues. Ironing practically all day.

May 10 Wed. Cleaned the paint in the parlor and there is no doubt that it needed it. I was very tired, but the improvement was wonderful.

May 11 Thurs. Washing again, but little. They had the movie "The Stream of Life," in place of prayer meeting, but I had seen it before. Polly's birthday.

May 12 Fri. George went to Junior-Senior reception and danced with five girls, but in various ways was refused by others. We cleaned the hall, swept the house, vacuum cleaned the carpet etc. Ironed.

May 13 Sat. Did more cleaning up, fixed a room for Samuel, who came in the P.M. We went to the Gray Gables porch party for 9 to 10. Mrs. Haggerty spoke very nicely about the boys.

May 14 Sunday. Mother's day. The children gave me a potted plant & Edward a ticket to May Festival. We drove Samuel to Norwalk. Had meat loaf made by Mrs. C. & strawberry short-cake.

May 15 Mon. The great event, aside from washing & a letter from Mr. P. from Batoum, was that Edward played three sets of tennis with Marvin, was beaten, but one was a deuce set.

May 16 Tues. Stephen is very sick. They got a nurse for the night. Edward played Gearhart today and was beaten. Frances got stung in both eyes and could not see this morning, but was getting gradually better all day.

[**May 17**]

May 18 Thurs. Mrs. C. went to prayer meeting but as usual I did not. We had a big washing because we had clothes for Stephen & Armen.

May 19 Fri. Mrs. Clark, James, Armen & I went to the May Festival. The Children's Crusade. There were three outside soloists, Miss Adams, Mrs. Hastings, Mrs. Savage, Daphne Kimbal, Mrs. Haroun.

Ernest C. Partridge

May 7 Sunday. Communion service at Armenian church. PM church meeting. I preached on 1 Juo 1/2 in PM service.

[**May 8**]

May 9 William 35 W36

May 10 Called with Maynard on the Archbishop, who said he had suggested that I teach some in the College at Etchmiadztin to be opened in the fall.

May 11 Called on Prof Manvandian, Dean of Literature Dept of University and taught my English class for 1st time.

May 12 Went to government for passports and visited some of NER work. W37

[**May 13**]

May 14 Sunday. Two sermons Sunday. I taught young people's class. To Rusts' for tea after PM service. W38

May 15 Maynard & I drove over to Etchmiadztin to call on the Catholicos. Found him very cordial. Visited the church with Vartan Vartabed. 24m

May 16 Mr Maynard, Sister Bodil & I called on the Commissaire of Education, found him & his assistant McGintsian & Evanguelian, very hospitable. W39

May 17 Spent 3 hours with Supt & Asst Supt of Education visiting orphanages in search of a suitable building. Posted acc[oun]ts to ledger.

May 18 Wrote letters and worked with Maynard settling up acc[oun]ts. Taught two English classes. 1st one of 7 men & one woman very good. W40, 41

May 19 Wrote a lot of letters, 12-15 for this mail.

May 20 Sat. A rainy Saturday and a confused day. I took the children to the movies, then to supper at Gray Gables, except Alfred who broke out with the measles. I was to sleep at Gray Gables in Mrs. Haggerty's absence but stayed with Alfred.

May 21 Sunday. Alfred had measles & did not go to church at all. It was Seminary baccalaureate. It was rainy so we could not ride. In the morning they sang Sanctus, so I wanted Geo. to go.

May 22 Mon. Washing under difficulties, but we got the clothes dry finally.

May 23 Tues. Ironed. Mrs. Clark has to sit with Stephen so she cannot read "If Winter Comes," while I iron. Sat. Sun. Mon. & Tues. I was matron for Gray Gables.

May 24 Wed. Seminary banquet. I was not invited this year but Mrs. Clark went.

May 25 Thurs. Mrs. Clark went to Michigan to find a summer place for her boys. Stephen's temperature was down to 99°. I washed again.

May 26 Fri. Ironed.

May 27 Sat. Edward brought home his gym clothes so I washed again. Oberlin won the big six track meet, although they did not get any firsts.

May 28 Sunday. Dr. Blanchard preached. Edward drove the Metcalfs to Elyria for a funeral. Afterwards we drove to Lorain. George shaved for the first time, no Saturday.

May 29 Mon. Washing as usual but less because I washed Saturday, so by 11 o'clock at night I had finished the ironing so to be free Memorial Day.

May 30 Tues. Parade in the morning. Alfred helped carry the big flag, elected by his class. Frances & Billo also paraded. I marched with Mrs. Miller to represent the League of Women Voters. Armen made sarmas and we with Terry & Linda Belle ate at the waterworks. Then we went to the Lake and came back for a late supper and to bed.

May 31 Wed. Mrs. Clark came back to find that Stephen had been much worse and was not in a good condition.

George: Eng. A, Latin A+, Civics B+, Alg. A+
Billo: Con. A, Effort A, Reading B+, Eng. B, Spelling A, Writing B, Arith C, Geog B, Music B-, Phys. B
Alfred: Reading B-, Spelling B, Writing B-, Arith B+, Music B+, Drawing C+
Frances: Reading B, English A, Spelling A, Writing C+, Arith B, Geog. A, Music B

Ernest C. Partridge

May 20 Spent day with Maynard finishing up odds & ends. Went to train with him about 8PM. Much rain. W42

May 21 Sunday. Pastor Vahan is in the villages on a tour. I preached on Rom 14/12 and taught my SS class of 27 young people. Wrote Edward.

May 22 Worked on account in AM. Had advanced English class at house. Called at N.E.R offices. Church Com meeting 5–7.

May 23 Lower English class.

May 24 Called on Rust at his office. Went to his house in PM to take Crothers money. I had a long visit. Advanced English class. W43

May 25 A holiday. Worked in office till 10, walked out to the Work and had lunch with Miss Shane. Schools out for a picnic.

May 26 Baron Hagop & I took a phyton to Samaghar 4 miles beyond Etchmiadztin. Spent night there and preached in Chapel. W44

May 27 With Bad[villi] Didos we walked 4 miles to Frankanots. Stopped at Asadoors house. Had examination of school.

May 28 Sunday. I preached at 10. School exercises 11–12:30. In PM we three with Bad Puznooni walked over to Hagigana and I preached there. A fine service of 75 people, good interest &fine singing.

May 29 A phyton came from Etchmiadztin for us & Bad Didos came to city with us. Went to Kindergarten exercises. 40m

[May 30–June 8]

June 1 Thurs. Stephen worse. They drew off fluid from his lung.

June 2 Fri. Stephen much worse and they decided to take him to Lakeside Hospital. I took Constance to see the school field day. Alfred led the whole Pleasant St. School. He tends strictly to business.

June 3 Sat. Dr. Colegrove took Stephen to Cleveland. Mrs. C. went on the train. Dr. Crile(?) operated with local anaesthetics, found nothing tubercular. Mrs. Clark stayed. I find five little ones a great many more than three. Edward went to the Lake Ruggles with the sophomore class.

June 4 Sunday. We did not go to the Lake in the afternoon because they were all so naughty. We took a short drive in the evening.

June 5 Mon. Mrs. Clark came back in the evening. Stephen is very sick but a little better. I got the washing out alone. Letter from Mr. P. urging us to get to Con- by the last of August.

June 6 Tues. Mrs. C. is to go every day to Cleveland for the present. I finished the ironing.

June 7 Wed. I was really intending to go to the Missionary meeting but there was no one to stay with the children. Alfred feels sure there are two girls that he could have for the asking, Dorothy Williams & Marguerite Spellbrook.

June 8 Thurs. George and I went over to Norman's to see the room that the boys are to have. Mr. Metcalf came there too.

June 9 Fri. I went down town to pay the bills and call on Mrs. Haskell. I wrote to Mr. Riggs to engage our passage. I am burning my bridges behind me.

Ernest C. Partridge

June 9 Spent evening at Dr Evan's calling on Archers and Miss Hardcastle.

June 10 Had two English classes. Called on Archbishop. Called on Miss Seribuer and Mrs Archer.

June 11 Sunday. Church. SS class. I made closing remarks. PM Oriort Aznive talk about David Livingstone.

[June12–June 14]

June 15 Had last English letters at University. Mr & Mrs Archer, Miss Hardcastle and Mr Lewis to dinner and for evening.

June 16 Had a call from Miss Vancover and a nurse from Alex. Advanced English class. Bought a cow with calf for $31.20.

[June 17–20]

June 10 Sat. We got our plans all made to go to Lorain for a swim and picnic dinner when Geo. found that he had to play off a tennis match. He really did not find a court to play on until late in the afternoon. He was sick in the evening although he won his match.

June 11 Sunday. Children's Day. Frances graduated from the Primary Dep't, said her Beatitudes and received a Bible from the United Church. We drove to Lorain in the afternoon and had a late supper. Mrs. Giles-Kline was here. Edward and Lawrence visited her in the P.M. Stanton Hobbs wanted Geo. to play off his match with him but G. told him he did not play tennis on Sunday.

June 12 Mon. Washing, all dried nicely. Mrs. C. went to Cleveland at 11:25, so she helped in the morning. Billy fell on the cinders and hurt himself so he did not go to school in the morning. Ed had economics exam, long but easy.

June 13 Tues. Edward had chemistry exam.

June 14 Wed. Ed had no exams but studied on French. George is not having exams, no final exams in H.S. this time.

June 15 Thurs. French exam & the last. Mrs. C. & Geo. & I took the children to the Lake, had dinner there and got home for Alfred to rehearse a mock wedding. He was best man at a wedding given for Miss Parsons at Miss Prince's house. It was a shower as Miss P. is to be married soon.

June 16 Fri. I went over to Ruth's recital but did not stay through. I had lots to do but I took time for a few errands. The boys cleaned the parlor carpet with a vacuum cleaner.

June 17 Sat. Mrs. C. & I went down & bought a wrist watch for Armen. I worked cleaning until half past four, then, of course, mending in the evening.

June 18 Sunday. Heard Mr. Van der Pyl, then lunch at the hotel with Antranig Nigoghosian and Mr. Tasgian, baccalaureate sermon by Pres. King on Life as a Whole.

June 19 Mon. Mrs. Clark had to go to Cleveland a little early to take Ruth and James who were to meet their grandfather and go to Detroit by boat.

June 20 Tues. Alumni Day. I went to the meeting for a few minutes and heard Mr. Schermerhorn of the Detroit Times. He told story after story, but the point was that Oberlin was honored by being out of the headlines & she'd better keep out. Illumination Night, cousin Will Day came. Edward ran into a boy but did not seriously hurt him.

June 21 Wed. Commencement. I sat with Armen at dinner. Mr. Adams sat alone. Mr. Jack was there but sat with Sidian who was graduating. The weather was cool and comfortable. Armen & I went to the Art Gallery. Her drawings were fine. The Glee Club Concert was especially good, father & son quartette, Metcalf & Gurney's. I went with Edward.

June 22 Thurs. We had our passport pictures taken and a group picture. Edward began his work at Geroish's. George is helping him as usual. Cool weather helps a lot. The Raymond's stopped in a few minutes in their new Buick.

June 23 Fri. We went to Elyria to get our passports but the offices closed at four.

June 24 Sat. We took our dinner out to Lorain, also our rugs and washed them. It is lovely to have people like the Days to visit.

June 25 Sunday. I went to Sunday School instead of church. Miss Hosford taught the class. After lunch we went to Lorain for a ride & brought back our rugs. Edward went to Cleveland with Mrs. Haggerty.

Ernest C. Partridge

June 21 Balanced Semiannual accounts and worked on paper for Constant[inople].

June 22 Called on Capt & Mrs. Yarrow and Mr. Harris at No 21.

[June 23–24]

June 25 Sunday. Communion. Bad Puznooni preached. I assisted. PM bimonthly church meeting. Reports on Evangelistic work. Severely criticized.

June 26 Sent 1st American Mission mail to Tiflis according to suggestion of Capt Yarrow. Hope it gets out all right.

June 27 Had Lewis & Keller to dinner and for evening.

[June 28]

June 29 Farewell dinner at Rusts for Lewis & Keller, all Americans & Mr Northcote & Miss Tucker present. Mr Horn at beginning but had to leave to catch train.

June 30 Farewell banquet of employees of N.E.R. to Mess'rs Lewis and Keller in our Chapel. About 120 people present.

[July 1]

June 26 Mon. Mrs. Clark & I went to Elyria. I applied for a passport and she got James's trousers. We looked at summer coats and slip over sweaters.

June 27 Tues. I went to the Treasurer's Office and made an affadavit for Vartoohi Oubashian, that she might get her brother's life insurance for her sisters and nephew.

June 28 Wed. Mrs. Clark did not go to Cleveland and we had a family picture taken once more.

June 29 Thurs. The washing machine did not work very well so I did not wash until a man came and told me it would be all right. Finally I did but I got lumbago or something while I was hanging out the clothes.

June 30 Fri. I had the inoculation, first dose for typhoid. I felt miserable before and it affected me very little. I was supposed to be very quiet but I ironed, made cherry pies etc. Letter from Mr. Riggs suggesting that I sail Aug. 25 on the Megali Hellas.

July 1 Sat. Letter from Uncle Gene saying that Esther is very sick. I felt just horrid all day but we took the children to the lake for a swim, also Dorothy.

July 2 Sunday. Still miserable, no church, just a little ride in the evening.

July 3 Mon. A postal & telegram saying that Esther is failing. I telegraphed that I would come but they misunderstood & told me not to come.

July 4 Tues. Because Oberlin was safe & sane we went to Lorain, buying fire crackers on the way. In the evening, we had pin wheels etc. Mrs. Beard & Marjorie came over.

[July 5]

July 6 Thurs. Preston Stubbs visiting us. Armen & Mrs. Clark very much impressed by him & I am quite fond of him.

July 7 Fri. Left Oberlin at 5:43 to go to Boston & Monson. Mrs. Haggerty lent me a dress. Mrs. Clark gave me a hat and lent me a suitcase and handbag.

July 8 Sat. Reached Boston and found no train out to Maine, so went to Andover. Jean and Joe were very cordial.

July 9 Sunday. Attended church at Old South. Sarah and Lucy came to dinner. I called on Miss Davis. Mr. Hill & Marion called on me.

July 10 Mon. Arrived in Monson on the morning train. I walked up to Charlie Weeks's and they got Dr. Holt to carry me up to Uncle Gene's.

July 11 Tues. Helped Mrs. Backer, the nurse.

July 12 Wed. Helped take care of Esther.

July 13 Thurs. I went to the village with Dan Warriner, to see Dr. Holt about Esther. He thinks that she may walk, at least will be able to go on crutches.

Ernest C. Partridge

July 2 Sunday. Badvilli Vahan is away on his vacation and I preached in morning. Karchin Varzhabed led PM. In evening Davis & Lewis called & invited me to be Supt of Ed[ucation] in Er[ivan].

[July 3–4]

July 5 Went to Central School and had a long talk with Principal Tigramian and Assistant.

[July 6–13]

July 14 Mr Tigramian and I went to Dari Chichak to visit the school. Left at 7:15 got home at 6:55PM.

July 15 Began an English Class with Central teachers. Had 2 classes in PM.

July 16 Sunday. Preached in morning on Sabbath Mark 2/27.

[July 17–19]

July 20 Mr Vickrey came and went today; brought me a suit of clothes & a note from H.A.M. saying family sailing about August 1st. Lots of mail but no letters.

[July 21]

July 14 Fri. Our wedding day. Prof. Calvin Clark, who married us, spent the afternoon with me, and Tavie Mathews (a guest) and her mother called.

July 15 Sat. I left Monson at 9:30. Aunt Jennie went to Dover with me. We took dinner with Mrs. L.K. Lee. Prof Clark's son came to the train to see me. He is to preach in Dover.

July 16 Sunday. A good day in Lewiston, though I was very tired. I washed my hair and did almost nothing else. A very good day with my father.

July 17 Mon. Left Lewiston about 4:20 with papa, went to Portland, had supper and took the boat to Boston.

July 18 Tues. Spent the day in Boston, waiting most of the day around the Board Rooms for Miss Gage. Consulted Dr. Hall about Esther. Saw papa off on the Portland boat at six o'clock.

July 19 Wed. Reached Burlington about nine o'clock. Geo. [cousin, the dentist] met me & in the afternoon nearly finished my dentistry, besides taking an x-ray of my teeth. Nothing serious there.

July 20 Thurs. Left Burlington about noon, went to Albany & got a sleeper. Forgot to take my change from my ticket at Burlington.

July 21 Fri. I reached home earlier than they expected me so I surprised them. The house was lovely & clean & the children in fine order. Stephen had returned from the hospital.

July 22 Sat. Alfred's birthday. His principal present was a tennis racket from the boys. We took our supper to the Lake and had a good visit with Mrs. Day. I got the change from Burlington, paid George $4.20.

July 23 Sunday. Mrs. C. & Stephen, Ed & I went to church. Dr. F.H. Foster preached. We drove out on the Elyria road and turned off to "explore," as Geo. says, & found a lovely country road.

July 24 Mon. Tried to wash but the machine gave out, went to Elyria but the tire got a puncture. Mrs. Wright went with us. She helped me borrow $250 from the bank. I had the second typhoid serum.

Ernest C. Partridge

July 22 Another big grist of mail but no letters; a dozen books from Boston.

July 23 Badvilli Puznooni preached in morning. I went after church to Surp Lusavorich.

[July 24–August 19]

July 25 Tues. I was real sick with typhoid. If the real disease is worse I do not want it.

July 26 Wed. Still miserable but getting better. I went over to see Mrs. Wright and then in the evening to a lecture on Syracuse and Palermo by Prof. Martin.

July 27 Thurs. I did a very large washing, all our lines and two of the next house. I went to Elyria & got a better piece for the washer.

July 28 Fri. Ironed & had callers all day. Mr. Irving Metcalf, Dr. & Mrs. Charles McClure, Mr. Jones & Miss Hosford, Mr. & Mrs. Charles Riggs, Mrs. Wright. I called on Bertha Cann.

July 29 Sat. Cleaned the house.

July 30 Sunday. Ed & I went to church. Mr. Wetzel preached. I nearly went to sleep but the trouble was in me.

July 31 Mon. Armen, Edward, Frances & I went to Cleveland. I bought a coat $8.95, a coat for Frances $5, hat $2.95, hat for F. 45 cts, silk dress for F. for $4.85, blue skirt, shirts for boys at $1.65. George said the children were good and Ed said Frances was good. He took care of her in the P.M.

August 1 Tues. Telegram from Aunt Jennie saying that Uncle Gene had a shock and probably could not live through the day. I went over to Mrs. Wright's. Took the children to a free vaudeville in Layter's rink of advertising Indian medicines.

August 2 Wed. Went to a Missionary Social at the James Brand House, then called on Mrs. Fitch. I met Mrs. Cady at both places. Mr. Ohly came to see the puppies, says he will find a home for them all or take them himself.

August 3 Thurs. I sold the washing machine for $50 to a Mrs. Betts(?). The boys washed blankets, quilts and spreads.

August 4 Fri. A telegram came announcing Uncle Gene's death and a sad letter from my father, mourning over my going [to Turkey again].

August 5 Sat. Mr. Hawkes came in the morning. We visited all day and it was hard to get anything done. Alfred had three teeth filled and Frances two out. Mr. Hawkes and I went to Mrs. Wright's for supper. Hampartsoom came. Mrs. Black's sister came for a few minutes.

August 6 Sunday. I was too sleepy to go to church but the others went. We took Ham to Norwalk, Billo got sick there, probably from his vaccination. The others are taking [the vaccination] too.

August 7 Mon. Mr. Hawkes went away and the boys took him to Elyria. Mrs. Clark walked in unexpectedly, to hunt for her old passport.

August 8 Tues. Washed. It took me nearly all day. Mrs. Clark went. The boys took her to Elyria.

August 9 Wed. I took three boys & a girl to Cleveland shopping. We bought suits for the three boys, Alfred's first. His and Billo's are alike, a brown check.

August 10 Thurs. Ironed, but my iron gave out and I had to fuss around to get it fixed.

August 11 Fri. I packed quite a lot. Went to Susie's to supper with Mrs. Wright & Mrs. Murdock.

August 12 Sat. Packed & cleaned up the house, then called on Irving Metcalf and his wife.

August 13 Sunday. Edward, George and I went to church. Edward and I both slept in the afternoon, while Armen and the children went to the waterworks.

August 14 Mon. Packing.

August 15 Tues. Washing & packing. The boys did the washing.

August 16 Wed. The boys worked so hard and were so tired, but so good. We never knew how much they could do.

[August 17–18]

August 19 Sat. Samuel came. I did the last shopping in the evening.

August 20 Sunday. Drove to Lorain, all but Armen, saw the Days. In the afternoon we had some callers.

August 21 Mon. Our last day at home. We all had dinner with Mrs. Haggerty. Called on Mrs. Wright, Mrs. Pond, Mrs. Ohly. Geo. drove the Ford, Ed the Templer. Mrs. H. went with us. Took the 6:5[50] train from Cleveland. Said "Goodbye" to the boys in the station. [Ed and George are staying in Oberlin.]

August 22 Tues. Arrived in Philadelphia. We took a car and Armen met us at the end of the car-line. We went to Independence Hall, to the top of City Hall and in the afternoon to the zoo. Oh the smells and the crawly things. Preston called in the evening.

August 23 Wed. Went to N.Y. Garabed Eff. met us at the station. He took us to the Board Rooms, then to the station to go to White Plains. Frances had a stiff neck.

August 24 Thurs. Mary [Mary Hubbard] took care of the children & Mr. H. and I went shopping. We bought a coat for me, two dresses for Frances, sweaters for Alfred & Frances, a large doll for Frances.

August 25 Fri. Went in to N.Y. with Mr. H. and Mary, to the Hotel, then Mariam came, lunch all together, then in taxi's to the boat. We had quite a little trouble with baggage etc, but G. Eff. & a Mr. Bridgman helped us out. Sailed at 6:50.

August 26 Sat. Frances was sick all day, Billy part of the time. At our table are the Clarks, Miss Bridgeman, Colonel Lowe and ourselves.

August 27 Sunday. Frances sick part of the day but revived by night. Almost everyone out to dinner, sea calm. We had a big dinner and anyway. We have too much to eat.

August 28 Mon. Calm sea, everyone well. The children played all day together pushing steamer chairs; cowboy or some such game. They played spoof in the evening. Two boats passed.

August 29 Tues. A four masted schooner appeared and passed. No other excitement.

August 30 Wed. Not a sail, only a few flying fish to look at. The sea as calm as a small pond.

Ernest C. Partridge

August 20 Sunday. Preached in Erivan morning. Juo 1/18. A53. Went to Surp L. Evening service Chapel. Letters from WGP dated June 29.

[August 21–October 26 Winona, William, Frances and Alfred arrived during this time period. Ernest continued keeping diaries through 1934.]

August 31 Thurs. A spouting whale for excitement.

Memoranda

The hardest month of my life nearly, leaving two boys for so long a time, so far away.

September 1 Fri. Read Under the Lilacs to our children, to Effie Post & Louis Georgis.

September 2 Sat. We saw a sail in the distance, a spouting whale too. I write five letters every morning. I let down Frances' dress.

September 3 Sunday. Dr. Post led an English service. We saw a steamer very close. The sea has been very rough, but very few seasick. I finished Under the Lilacs to the children & read from King Arthur's Court.

September 4 Mon. I got up at six o'clock, the first woman up, the first American to see land after ten days. We saw Gibraltar very indistinctly and also the shores of Morocco.

September 5 Tues. No land except a very hazy outline on the African side. A very uneventful day after the excitement of Gibraltar and the rough sea of the day before.

September 6 Wed. Algiers. "Jake" Bassler took the Clarks and the Partridges ashore. We took a long train ride, then a walk, another ride, and then lunch of bread grapes etc. in the park. Then back to a boat covered with coal dust. Sailed away about eight o'clock.

September 7 Thurs. Once today we saw land on both sides at the same time. Africa on one side and perhaps an island on the other side. I wrote only four letters instead of five.

[September 8]

September 9 Sat. We heard that probably the Megali Hellas would be taken by the government at Piraeus. News from Smyrna that the Turks had taken the city.

September 10 Sunday. Arrived in Piraeus early but our families stayed on the boat, intending to go sightseeing the next day.

September 11 Mon. We were obliged to leave our boat. After great effort our five men got our baggage off, got tickets for the Katian Adria and got us all on the boat. We sailed late in the afternoon.

September 12 Tues. Jake and Lewis had left us so we were more subdued. We saw land most of the time, many boats, warships etc in the Dardanelles.

September 13 Wed. Arrived in Constantinople early, before any one met us. Later Dr. Clark, Mr. Fowle, Dr. Maynard arrived. We stayed until noon to get our baggage off & on again. We engaged passage on the same steamer to Batoum. Went to Hotel de Loudres.

September 14 Thurs. Went to Bible House where I saw Messia Agaran(?), a friend of Polly's, Armen's mother, Paradseen Hanum. Went out to buy some things with Paradseen Hanum, then to tea at Gedik Pasha. When we got to the hotel Alfred had 103° temperature.

September 15 Fri. Paid our bills and went to the boat to find it gone, taken by the Italian government, hunted up our baggage and went back to the hotel. The Maynards came to the hotel too. Alfred better but fever again in evening.

September 16 Sat. Mrs. Maynard, Hrant & I took our children & David to Floria where they had their bathing suits on about 2 ½ hours. It was very lovely.

September 17 Sunday. Went to Dutch Chapel, in the afternoon to Seraglio point a park(?), then to Sailor's Club to supper, then service, then movies. Billo was sick & had to leave.

September 18 Mon. I took a dreadful cold, had indigestion and was miserable generally. We stayed in the hotel except when we went to meals. Vosgian Moonijian, Yeghia Sahagian & Uynyala[?] called.

September 19 Tues. Mr. Maynard, Frances & I started to the Bible House, but found that the Adria had come and was leaving for Batoum in the afternoon. We got ready and got on. Levon Lucigian came to the boat & helped us.

September 20 Wed. We passed Sinope and were near the shore nearly all day. The sea was not rough & we had a good day. Frances was a little seasick.

September 21 Thurs. We reached Trebizond about one o'clock and stayed until eight, but we could not see the Americans. Mr. Maynard thought it was best not even to send word to them.

September 22 Fri. After a very rough night we reached Batoum in the rain. Mr. Martin met us and did everything to help us. Dr. Marden and Mr. Roland were there. We were very comfortable in the personnel house.

September 23 Sat. It was very rainy so we spent the day at home expecting to leave in the evening but finally word came that the special train would not go until Sunday night.

September 24 Sunday. Dr. Marden took the whole company in two trucks up to the summer house. Such wonderful views of mountains and sea, much vegetation, flowers, fruit etc. I have ever seen.

September 25 Mon. After a rather uncomfortable night we arrived in Tiflis, where Mr. P. & Mrs. Marden met us. We found the personnel house there most comfortable and were not sorry to stay until Wednesday. Mrs. Elmer called again and again, took us shopping. We bought mostly candy. Went up a mountain on the singular road.

September 26 Tues. We were invited to the minister's to dinner and also to Mrs. Harris's. We ate well at both places and did not suffer from it.

September 27 Left Tiflis about eight o'clock on a courier car, that is a freight car fitted up with bunks, windows etc. The beds were hard but the car was clean and we had quite a comfortable trip.

September 28 Thurs. The day travel was easier than the night. We passed Ami, Alexandropol, Etchmiadzin and reached Erivan about 6:30 P.M. Dr. Evans was with us from Alex. A Ford came down & took us to the Maynard's house.

September 29 Fri. We went around to some of the orphanages and schools. Agneeve and some of her orphans called, brought flowers & a piece of handiwork. The house is very large and very pleasant. We cannot find a house yet. Miss Silliman & Miss Kaye came.

September 30 Sat. We went to the offices, met some of the Americans, went to the warehouse, bought some napkins and dish towels, two cups, some prints, coffee

[Winona continued writing in diaries until 1955.]

Letters of Ernest C. Partridge 1922

New York-Boston train
Saturday P.M.
Jan. 28th

Dear Winona:–

    I had a comfortable night to Pittsburg and Custer & I had breakfast together and visited a couple of hours. It seems he was, entirely acquitted of any fault in his trial in Sivas. He says he remembers very well Polly's coming to the table one day before he left and saying that she had got all her Board accounts cleaned up in good shape. He says she also said one day that she had a lot of personal money tied up in the accounts. He got the idea that it was 2 or 3 thousand dollars. I had a nice visit with the Kabakjians, Yeranoohi, the Raphaelian's and Krikore Tatarian. Miss Spalding had moved and I could not find her. Stubbs has an office at 220 West Coulter St., Germantown, but I could not get him on the phone. It was noon when I got to New York so I did not try to do anything but came right along. I shall go to Andover about 8:30. I saw a bill board outside of New York. "Ohio has a treat in store for you. It's Tellings Eskimo Pie."

    I lost the Oberlin pin the first night on the sleeper and left my rubbers on the train last night. I hope I shan't sow away more property before sailing. Dr. Dag speaks at Ministers Meeting, Boston, Monday morning so I shall try to see him then.

Love to all, Ernest

❁

THE AMERICAN BOARD
Boston [letterhead]

Leaving Boston for New York
Noon, 4 P.M.
[ca 31 Jan 1922]

Dear Winona:–

I have been on the go since I reached Andover and now find my pen empty so I shall have to write with a pencil.

I had a very pleasant time in Andover. Mr. Bigelow introduced me as the man who had persuaded Mary Graffam to go to Turkey by nearying up her sister.

I saw Miss Gage and Miss Davis at church, spoke three times in S.S. and went home with Sarah to dinner. They were all very cordial. In the PM I called on Stackpole and at Miss Twitchell's. Nellie Cole had arrived Saturday night & I saw quite a little of her. After a visit at Miss Twitchell's with her & her sister Mrs. Hall, her daughter and Miss Cole, we all went over to Dr. Crawford's son's to have a cup of tea. Then I went to Lawrence and spoke for Dr. Marsh. Saw a dozen or twenty old friends, the Ashtons and Mrs. Freeman and Maud. I spent both nights at the Bigelow's.

At once after breakfast this morning I came into Boston and have been meeting people until I took the train. Fred Budd has an idea of trying to get up a Mary Graffam Memorial fund all over the country, starting with the Andover nucleus. He is going to see Dr. Barton about it this week. Their idea is a fund the income of which we could use for some work in the future which would be a memorial. I did not see much I could do in Boston tonight so I took the train to Hartford, arrive there at 7:12 so I shall have the evening to see people and get out early in the morning so as to put my day in on passport work in New York. I took lunch with Dr. White and had a good talk with him about things.

He is of the opinion that the powers will patch up some settlement of Turkey in the early spring.

Miss Cole is determined that I should go to Trebizond and she has told the Board people that our Constantinople people have given up trying to get me to Sivas for the present. Miss Cole may stop off in Oberlin to see you. She says she wants to do so and I imagine she intends to get in a little preparing work with you for Trebizond. Dr. White says he has not given up carrying on the college at Marsovan but in the meantime he's keeping his mind open to other places in case Marsovan proves impossible. He asked me if I had thot [sic] of the possibility of combining our educational work with another institution and said, for example Euphrates College has lost its President and most of its faculty. I told him that I all felt disposed to stand for was a real effort to have an institution that would be a Teachers College. Custer told me they had tried to get him to New York for receive his medal for Relief Services, so they are evidently handing them out.

I am going to try to get my passport work as far along tomorrow as I can so as to have more time for calling. I shall spend one night with the Paelians and one at White Plains and hope to get back to Boston Thursday. Miss Gage gave me ten dollars, five for something for myself and five for our work.

I will try to write again tomorrow.

Love, Ernest

VAHAN KURKJIAN [letterhead]
ATTORNEY AT LAW
287 Fourth Avenue
New York, N.Y.
Phone Grammercy 1160

Feb 1st 1922

Dear Winona:–

I spent the night Monday at Hartford. Called on Ambrookian and had a good visit with Vrooman. Got into New York about ten Tuesday morning and put in a busy day. Called at the Board Rooms, & Mr. R.

Had a long visit with Van [hole in page] who got in last week having left Sivas about the middle of October. He was the treasury man who was there a while. He told me a good deal about finances. Said that he had gone over carefully the form question of finances, that Polly had considerable personal money in that, and he had recommended that the Committee pay her estate who [sic] she had put in. Miss Phelps had typhus but is getting better. Dr. Van & two ladies at Harput had typhoid.

I finished up my passport work this morning. Last night we had 23 at the dinner. Mrs. Hubbard & Mary, Paelian, Ambrookian, Pashyan Hyrabed, Vosgan Boyagian, Vakabadian, Borg Dicran, Tahel, Elbis Mazian's brother, Khachadoor, Haep Surmabegulian, and Vahan Vartanian, Hay Effs' stupid nephew and last but not least my cousin Edna Crane, Aunt Ruby's daughter who teaches in Yonkers. Mary [Hubbard] was speaking there last Sunday and was invited to dinner where she was and they got into conversation about me, so Mary invited her to the dinner. They gave me a fine black manuscript case and this morning Hyrabed gave me a five dollar gold Eversharp pencil. I spent the night, what was left [at] the Paelians. Called this morning [on] Hyrabed and the Bedikians's, did some passport work and am now going out to dinner with Mr. Kushjian.

After that I am going to a ladies meeting at the Armenian church and then to White Plains. Dr. McLaughlin got in yesterday and I have an appointment to see him tomorrow at the house of Mrs. John Stewart Kennedy. Then I hope to run out and see Marian, perhaps take supper with Miss Wheeler and then take a late train or sleeper to Boston.

Love to all, Ernest

❀

ANATOLIA COLLEGE
Marsovan, Turkey in Asia
14 Beacon Street, Boston, Mass.
[letterhead]

3 P.M. Saturday

[Feb 4, 1922]

Dear Winona:–

We are on the way to the steamer. Your letter to the Rooms came this morning. I spent the night with Hal Ross and we called on Dr. Smith. Took lunch with several of the Secretaries.

Ross gave me $10.00 for sightseeing. I am enclosing $4.00 which you can use for Frances' lessons or for your father as you think best. This is personal money.

Nazeli is to come down to the boat to see me. I will write on the steamer about my talks at the Rooms.

Love to all, Ernest

❈

ANCHOR LINE [letterhead]
S.S. Assyria

Feb 6th 1922

Dear Billo;–

I am glad you passed in all your lessons and were promoted. Your average for the semester is about the same as for January, showing that you are not falling behind. I hope you can get some help at home on Arithmetic, Geography, and history and bring up those marks. I see your Arithmetic for January is a B, better than C for this semester.

I do not like to think of your dropping either, basketball which will soon be over, or violin lessons. I think if you hang on in the violin the rest of the year, you will find it easier and will want to go on.

Please try to learn self-control and patience and get enough help at home so that you will be able to carry along all your work with success.

It will be a great thing for you all your life to be able to play an instrument. It is a pleasure for one and can be a means of giving pleasure to others.

Nazeli came to the boat to see us sail. She tried to keep my new family group [photo], but I told her it was the only one I had, that she must get one from mamma. I found today another one in my suitcase, which I shall send to Miss Rice if I do not get to Sivas at once.

Lots of love, Papa

❈

ANCHOR LINE [letterhead]
S.S. Assyria

No. 2
Feb 6ᵗʰ 1922

Dear Winona;–

I will write down in this letter scraps of disconnected things that occur to me out of the past days, as they come to me. I have a couple of stamps which I can no longer use.

I enclose a picture of the new building which the New York Armenians have just bought for a church. It was a buck and with little expense can be well fitted to their use. It's conveniently located on East 30ᵗʰ St. Bedikian and Marie treated me as tho they had lived in Sivas all their lives.

I intended to balance up some accounts in leaving Boston. You can figure these items out of the $40.00 I sent as I sailed and count the rest for Frances's lessons if you want or you can use it for your father, only write me which you do. I will try to send something more from Constantinople, both for your father & personally.

The items that occur to me are
Colgrove 8.00
expenses 4.78
George taxi for teachers .50
13.28

I shall collect these in my expenses account.

They had a big time in the New York Relief Rooms lately and hung decorations on a lot of old relief workers, but it looks as tho there were no missionaries there. Anyway a decoration that is given to several hundred people for one year of work, in some cases indifferently done, would not add anything to me especially. The U.S. government asked the Committee to have their men discontinue the use of the uniform, so they are wearing civilian clothes. If I had my trunks in Boston, I would have taken out my stuff & left it. I think however by a change of buttons I can wear these clothes in the future for riding and interior travel. Capt. Gracey, who was with us in Erivan is now Secretary of the Friends of Armenia and our old architect Childs is in the London Near East foreign department of the British government so we shall try to see them both.

Dr. White thinks that Childs trip thro Asia Minor was taken primarily to gather information for this job rather than for a book.

[missing pages]

last Missionary Herald on the Melhonian legacy. Dr. Barton says none of that money comes to the Board directly but with three missionaries on the Education Board it will likely be spent so as to help us and save us money.

Rockerfellow, Jr. [sic] is going to finance a survey on the Near East and Dr. Barton is chairman of the Committee. A group of experts are to be sent out before long to spend several months in gathering material and when they get it in shape the Commission will go out to Constantinople to work over the results and form conclusions as the basis of future work. Dr. Barton says our long deferred All-T Conference may be held conjointly with the Commission. I called on Dr. Weston of the Pilgrim Press who urged us to send him stuff for his "Church School" magazine. If you can find, in my drawer, the story of Makroohi send it to him, with a note for use. If it is not there it is packed and you can't find it.

Miss Wheeler and Miss Fuller, Bell's associate, were both clamorous for "copy" and I hope to do better in the future.

Mr. Van told me in New York that it was to be regretted that Polly kept so much to herself and in her own hands and head because it made the situation hard for those who remained. He praised her very highly but said she was so nervous that she was hard to work with. Custer told me that she had trouble with every member of the Unit after I left, of course her way was different from mine, and that some of those who helped in getting me out were sorry for their influence. I do not know to whom he referred unless it was either Dr. Smith or Miss McLean.

Lots of love, Ernest

❁

ANCHOR LINE [letterhead]
S.S. Assyria

No. 3
Feb 7th 1922

Dear Winona;–

I want to write you my notes on my visit with Dr. MacLaughlin. He was the guest of Mrs. John Stewart Kennedy, where I went to see him, and I assure you it was some house. I never saw anything like it. I sat in his bathroom & bedroom while Dr. Mac was shaving & dressing for dinner because there was no other time when we could get together. He has spent some time in Paris and London and was told by British statesman about their professed settlement for Turkey. He says things never looked so near settled since the armistice and that in 3-4 months this settlement will be completed. Of course he says this may all go wrong and nothing be settled. The British believe the French will be much more difficult to treat with than the Turks. The general plan is for the Greeks to evacuate the Smyrna district and for it to be put under Inter-Allied Control, Great Britain, France, Italy and the U.S. If we do not go in, then they propose to appoint an Armenian as a private citizen as a member of the Commission.

Either the above plan or a Commission appointed by the League of Nations. A strip of Thrace along Galipoli to be treated in the same way in order to get the Greeks a little farther from Constantinople.

The whole British attitude on Turkey has changed, they think the Greeks can do nothing more and favor letting the Turks back into Constantinople. He says the only guarantee we can have from the Ts is to take them into the League on their good behaviour. The French are pushing their propaganda in Constantinople, and are more active than the British. He thinks it possible that we may get right into Sivas and that things will settle so that you can come by summer or fall. He says that Kemal will be taken into the Constantinople government as prime minister or minister of war and that he will dominate the situation, but that his whole attitude towards us will change favorably.

Dr. White says he still believes the Armenians will have a national home somewhere presumably in the Caucasus and that the Turk if he gets the Greeks out of Smyrna and a strip of Thrace and gets back into Constantinople, maybe induced to be decent in giving the Armenians a strip on the East. It seems to me they are likely to be more cocky than ever, unless the allied forces make that a condition.

Dr. Mac says the Turks are trying hard to conciliate the Armenians in Cilicia and that with all the world looking at them, they will commit no atrocities now, but the fact remains that all the Armenians have left Cilicia, in spite of Bristol's efforts to force them to stay, and that Turks have occupied their houses.

The report that Miss Allen died in Sivas, probably of typhus is unconfirmed, but believed in Boston. Tell Mrs. Clark that doctor is behaving himself well so far. He hasn't danced with any of the ladies yet.

We spent 3 hours yesterday talking finances and he got some fine figures on paper. "If we took in so much in deposits & so much has been paid back, and the Bank pays or does not pay that item and the Board has made so much in interest by the use of this money, how much on a % basis can we afford to pay the rest." But of course that gets us nowhere.

We must get down to business with Peet & be ready for a basis of settlement when one of us gets to Sivas.

Love, Ernest

❧

ANCHOR LINE [letterhead]
S.S. Assyria

No. 4
Feb 8th 1922

You had better number your letters also. E.C.P.

Dear Winona;–
    I am going to read all your letters in order and refer to anything in them.
    I am glad the boys got their watches and hope they will prove satisfactory. I got an unbreakable crystal in my wrist watch in Boston and the first night in my bunk hit it against the wall and knocked it out. I cannot get it in but suppose a jeweler can do it when I land.

I am sorry I did not see Azneeve. I am afraid I have hurt some people in New York and Boston, but I worked as hard as I could and did not get around. I saw no Armenians in Boston but Nazeli. It was a choice of cutting out time with the Secretaries or that. And I think the time I spent in Barton & Riggs & White was well worth while.

I wrote you I think that Miss Phelps is getting better. The quit claim deed came & I will write Nazaret before I land.

I could not get a rain coat on discount in New York and did not get around to it in Boston. Perhaps I can get one in London, or order from America. I bought an Oxford gray, ulster with a high color in Boston.

I left the heavy under wear on purpose. Now I shall throw away a half worn suit I have, and carry that. No, I do not think Dr. White has any idea of any combination for Anatolia. He talks of relocation but not with reference to Armenians. He has thought of Tiflis and Trebizond, but says he still believes they will be in Marsovan.

I got all your letters, one at the Board Rooms and two on the steamer, but did not get the paper. As I was passing the desk to mail a bunch of letters in the Board rooms, the young lady handed me your letter, the last I was to receive, I suppose. I've the corridor first by the letter chute. I met some one and while talking I stuck the letters in, including yours. I chased down the elevator, waited for the postman and got the letter, tho I suppose it was illegal for him to give it to me.

I can't say I had a very good time in New York or Boston. I was so rushed and so sorry to miss people who wanted to see me but of course I enjoyed those whom I saw. I spent 3-4 hrs going out to Brooklyn for a call on Miss Wheeler, partly for policy's sake and largely because Mrs. Hubbard said she was very blue and lonesome. She is sending us now $65.00 each for 55 orphans and we ought to do more to help her, when it is possible.

She is entirely out with Father Fowle, and Mr. Goshins seems about the same towards him. He is a little Smart Alek and I do not look with confidence to his succeeding Peet.

I do not believe that any amount of Polly's money is in the farm. I think it more likely that it is old Armenian & Syrian Relief money. Mr. Belcher told us that our families would be cut $750.00 and that we would get the regular (one person allowance) which he said was more than that now. I think this covers anything I want to say suggested by your letters.

I shall write a letter about my talks with Dr. Barton, Riggs and Dr. White. I am going to try to see Childs and Heathcomb Smith whom I met in Constantinople at the London Foreign Office, Gracey at Friends of Armenia and Mr. Gentle-Cachett as well as some museums in London.

Lot of love, Ernest
Give my love to Armen and Azneeve.
I had a stenographer in the rooms Friday P.M. and dictated 20 letters so that I cleaned things up nicely.

ANCHOR LINE [letterhead]
S.S. Assyria

No. 5
Feb 10, 1922

Dear Winona:–

I think I have written you everything that occurs to me about my days in New York and Boston, except about the hour that Dr. Clark and I had with Dr. Barton and Mr. Riggs. We talked quite freely about the future work, evangelistic, educational & medical. They both seemed to agree with my feeling that it was hopeless to try to resurrect dead Protestant churches, tho probably any fairly strong ones left ought to be continued as leaven.

Mr. Riggs made quite a statement of his views on the future educational work. He feels that the future of Sivas, Harput, Van and Tarsus, educationally is an open one, because all these institutions were exclusively Armenian. That probably the places at Harput ought to be used for Kurdish-Turkish work, while conserving the endowment and traditions of Euphrates College for future work for Armenians. He said he did not see why what was left of Euphrates College, Teachers College & Van should not be united in the most suitable place for Armenians.

Nothing was said about personnel but with him in Boston & Harry committed to the Kurdish work the way there seems open unless they should decide to try to make Euphrates College a cosmopolitan institution. Dr. Barton said regarding Van that he understood that Yarrow considered his connection with Van a closed chapter and Dr. B. said, "I do not think Yarrow will ever settle down to missionary work affairs." Dr. White said again to me on Saturday more plainly then he had said before, and raising the question himself, "I think the thing to do, is to conserve under your direction what is left of these Armenian institutions for Armenians." I said to him, that is what I would like but of course I cannot advocate that. He seems to have come to this attitude of his own accord. I hope he will contaminate Dr. Barton and Mr. Riggs with the same idea. I am afraid however they will want a trained educator.

Well we shall wait and see what we shall see. I am convinced of one thing and that is that if things politically settle down so there is safety of life and freedom of work, we are going to have some very vital and interesting problems to help settle.

Ernest

❀

ANCHOR LINE [letterhead]
S.S. Assyria

No. 6
Sunday P.M.

Feb 12, 1922

Dear Winona:—

We are pretty well along on our journey across the pond and are having quite satisfactory weather for winter, I suppose, but I hope I shall never have to cross in winter again. It is raw and disagreeable, even at its best.

I had to get one of my sick headaches yesterday and went to bed at night feeling very miserable and was not much better when I woke up, but it has gradually worked off thro the day. An hour before the service I was asked to take charge again, but I was rather expecting it so was prepared.

As I brought no notes with me I have had to prepare two sermons, which may come in handy later on. Dr. Clark sang a solo in the service which helped out.

We have been singing gospel hymns for an hour or more this afternoon. It seems that one of the ladies who took Dr. & Susie and me out to lunch in Boston was Kittie Perkins' mother, she said she knew you but I did not locate her until talking to Dr. this afternoon.

The farther I get from home the less I like it. [Armenian or Turkish words] I hope to enjoy the trip across Europe and when I get somewhere and get to work, I shall doubtless feel differently.

Our baggage does not leave New York until the 15th and so will not get to Constantinople until March 15th, and we shall certainly have to wait for it before going on. This will give us time to talk things over quite thoroughly in Constantinople.

Tavie Mathews and her mother were at church in Andover when I spoke there. I left a film with 4 pictures in the Board Rooms to be mailed to you. I have no idea what the pictures are but thought it best to get them developed with no longer delay.

Dr. & I have been talking Turkish an hour or so a day. He seems to have forgotten a good many words some of which I know, but of course, he knows the verb better than I do.

I am about half way thro Wells and may get it finished before I leave London or Geneva and mail it someway.

I suppose you are having a "quiet Sabbath." Do take your kids too seriously and make them do something for their selves and each other. I think you ought to make yourself get out more.

Lots of love to all, Ernest

❄

ANCHOR LINE [letterhead]
S.S. Assyria
Feb 12, 1922

Dear George;—

I was glad to get your brief and unfinished letter just before we left Boston. I think you probably did the right thing in deciding to stick by Woodie, in spite of Stiffler's invitation. I do not expect much from your high school teams until some drastic discipline is administered and there does not seem to be any one with nerve enough to do it. So I guess things will have to wriggle along about as present until the present bunch graduates. I am glad that you did so well in your marks and hope you will not have any serious trouble in keeping up the extra lesson this semester.

My pictures of Snoopy have helped me to relieve a few tired mothers on shipboard by telling kids stories about Snoopy and Tommy.

Our trip is as smooth and warm as we have any right to expect for mid-winter and yet it is not entirely pleasant. The passengers are almost all Irish, English or Scotch going home; some of them American citizens going for a visit. I doubt if there are six native Americans on board. We started out the first day with a smooth sea so the people got their feet and altho it gets pretty rough, there has been little seasickness.

I conducted service this morning with the book rocking so I could hardly keep my feet some of the time.

I wish you would try to write me occasionally and tell some of the news that mama doesn't write.

Sincerely Your Dad

ANCHOR LINE [letterhead]
S.S. Assyria

No. 7
Feb 14, 1922

Dear Winona:–

We are in sight of the north coast of Ireland gradually rounding south to stop before night at the Irish port of Londonderry where we drop a few passengers with their baggage and then go on to Liverpool, where we hope to arrive tomorrow in time to take a train to London, that will get us in not too late.

I have had my last dose of cold serum, and it remains to be seen how effective it is. Tell Edward it had no effect on me except a slight soreness of the arm for 48 hours, which amounted to nothing. I think if I were in his place I would try it.

My seminary class-mate Greeley was in audience at the W.B.M. in Boston and had with him a couple of his church ladies whom he had prepared to meet me. He was very cordial.

I had forgotten, in my plans for this trip that the great Armenian Monastery is at Venice. I shall certainly want to go there. Dr. thinks we had better run down to Florence from Venice. We will see how much we spend before we get that far along.

I hope you and Mrs. Clark are foresighted enough to have your housekeeping up to date when the mail from this steamer reaches the house.

This my 10th letter counting three to the boys and I presume Dr. Clark has about as many to send.

I have been writing about three letters a day to various friends so that I am fairly well caught up. We are studying and talking Turkish everyday and Dr. thinks I ought to limber up in speaking if I got into a Turkish speaking atmosphere for a little while. If I stay in Constan any length of time I shall try to get some chance to talk.

[no closing]

❈

G° HOTEL E LA VILLE
FLORENCE [letterhead]

Feb. 24, 1922

Dear Winona;-
    In Geneva where I wrote last, Jemjemian stayed with us until midnight and helped us on the train. We rode an hour to Lausanne and got on the sleeper getting into Milan at 9:40 in the morning. We got breakfast on the train, left our baggage in the depot and went to Cook's, got some money and tickets for Florence. There we took a carriage to see Da Vinci's Lords' Supper. It is certainly a wonderful piece of art, which no photos properly represent. It is worth a trip across Europe just to see that.
    We visited the Cathedral and two galleries. Not much by the few artists I was looking for but a good deal of unknown material of Da Vinci's. Some very pretty pictures by Correggio.
    We got dinner in the station and took a 2:05 train to Florence, reaching here at 11:15 in the night. Today we have done things rather superficially and are going out to Venice early in the morning.
    We have visited the Cathedral, one of the largest in Italy and with many interesting features, the Campanile, The Academy where the only object that pleased us was Angelo's David. The Uffizi and Pitti Galleries, I was disappointed in both. Of course we tried simply to see the same artists. The Cathedral was designed by Brunelleschi and much of the art work there and in Campanile was done by Giotto.
    The things in the Uffizi I liked best were Raphael's Madonna of the Goldfinch and his The Young St John and Correggio's Flight into Egypt. Of course the Uffizi is one of the richest art collections in the world but it contains less of the work of the 5 or 6 I was looking for than some other collections. Both this and the Pitti were palaces of the Medici and are wonderful buildings apart from the collections, the Pitti especially. Here I liked best the Corrina Madonna of Murillo, and Raphael's Madonna of the Chair and the Grand Dukes Del Sailor's Assumption.
    We shall reach Venice about 3 tomorrow P.M. and I think to leave there Monday or Tuesday reaching Constantinople the 2nd or 3rd of March.
    I have accumulated about five dollars worth of pictures suitable to hang about two that I liked the best in each gallery which will help to decorate a house if we ever have one again that we want to fix up.

This trip since we landed has been pretty strenuous. Mr. Favre was so poorly that his people did not want him to entertain us and were glad to have us stop a short time, tho they were very cordial, so we stayed in Geneva from 10 P.M. to 12 P.M. This cut out a rest that we had counted on.

With lots of love to all, Ernest

❁

HÔTEL VICTORIA [letterhead]
Venise

Sunday P.M.
Feb 26, 1922

Dear Winona;–

We have reached the last stop on our journey to Constantinople and are taking a long breath today preparatory to two strenuous days here.

We came down from Florence yesterday second class reaching here at 3:15. It was a very pretty ride and we had part of the way a physician from New York, as companion.

We are still well satisfied with our trip and especially pleased with Venice. St Marks is a dream. The colors are wonderful. Our hotel is only two minutes walk from St Marks Square where everything centers and distances are very short.

We are paying $2.87 ½ a day at this fine hotel for room, board and service, including everything.

Our bill at Florence was quite high as they wrote on us a lot of extras that we did not understand about. It cost us about $15.00 for two nights and three meals and Dr. Clark insisted on paying the whole bill. When I protested he said his sister had given him some money to spend on the trip and he wanted to do this; that he had got much more out of the museums because I was with him. I answered, then you are paying me as a guide and he said yes. He has been a very good companion and I could not have found a better one, only I wish you might have been with me and enjoyed these beautiful things. Anyway our trip to Palestine and Egypt we will make together after the kids get back to America.

This morning we dropped into St Marks for a few minutes of the morning mass. It is simply wonderful inside & out. I think there is no painting but all the pictures & decorations are mosaic. We attended service at a Methodist Mission where there was supposed to be an English service but the preacher was away and the service was in Italian. If I was going to stay here ten days I would get a book and learn Italian. It is very easy and I think with Latin & English to start with one could get a little of it easily.

In the afternoon we took a steamer over to the Armenian monastery of the Mechitorists [Mekhitarist Monastery]. The porter was Italian and knew no other language. He showed us around the place. After we got around we found some Armenian students in the garden and found that the monks were all in the city for some entertainment, so we saw no one but these boys. We may go out again before we leave.

Tuesday P.M.

Monday we had a Cook guide all day in a party with three others, a couple from Minnesota and a surgeon from New York City. We saw quite satisfactorily St. Marks, The Doges Palace, several churches with fine paintings, mostly by Titian and Tintoretto, and a splendid exhibit of the glassware made here.

This morning we went across to an Island to see the glass ware made and then over to the Mechetarian monastery again where we found a monk to guide us and had a fine time.

We met four or five of the vartabeds, including the head of the institution and saw it much more satisfactorily than on Sunday with the door keeper.

Since that we have been to Cook's for money and tickets, had afternoon tea and done a little shopping. I have accumulated a couple more good pictures, one a water color. I have a few presents to send home from Constantinople.

We leave here at 8 P.M. on the Simplon-Orient Express for Constantinople reaching there Friday P.M. I am going to try to prepare on the train a description of our trip for a few who would be interested.

Lots of love to all, Ernest

❁

GRAND HOTEL DU LOUVRE [letterhead]

Venice, Feb 27/22

Dear Billo;–

I am sending you a postcard of an interesting clock on St. Mark's Square here in Venice. It was built in 1496. The face of the clock has 24 numbers on it as they figure time in Italy from 1 in the morning till 24 at midnight. The dial begins on the right side as you look at it right opposite the knee of the horse. This horse is one of four on the front of St. Marks church. A story above the face of the clock is two squares that tell time by our method. You can see in the center of the squares V 10, that is 5:10 P.M. These numbers are on two rolls and turn every five minutes V 5, V 10 etc. The two figures on top are bronze and one of the other strikes the bell every fifteen minutes.

I hope sometime you may visit Venice as it is a very interesting place.

Love Papa.

❁

OFFICE OF W. W. PEET
Treasurer of American Missions in Turkey
5, American Bible House, Findjandjilar Yocoushou
Constantinople
Telegraphic Address PEET-STAMBOUL
Telephone STAMBOUL 1845-1846 [letterhead]

March 4, 1922

Dear Winona;–

We left Venice Tuesday night at 8 o'clock by Simplon-Orient express and got here yesterday at 3:30 P.M. The train was nearly empty from Sophia on, we were the only passengers for a while and when we got here there were three others on the whole train besides us.

We are staying at the Language School in Scutari which Mrs. MacCallum is running. We saw here last night Dr. Ussher who just got in from Tiflis on his way home. Also, Dr. Peet, Fowle, Regan, two Riggs brothers, Goodsell and Papazian & Mardinos. At the house last night we saw the MacCallums and Miss McLean who is studying Turkish and in the evening Miss Kinney, Miss Riggs & Miss Thirden came in for a time.

We have not talked officially with any one about our future & shall not probably do so until Thursday when the Com-Ad-Int meets. Those who have expressed any opinions seem to fell that there is a much greater call for workers in the Caucasus than at either Sivas or Trebizond.

Mr. Thurber the Sivas Director is getting over typhus and Joe Beach has gone to Sivas as Director. We understand that Dr. Peet has authorized the payment of deposits in the gold equivalent so that problem is easier. I found here a bunch of letters for Sivas (Armenian) which have accumulated, and a dozen so for Polly. The only one of importance is a long one from Rebecca expressing their appreciation of the news her mother had brought and offering her a home with them. It would have been interesting had Polly lived would it not?

I understand the box Miss Rice sent is here. I suppose they would have left it for five years if I had not happened along.

I think I shall start in in [sic] the Language School forenoons and get what I can while I am here. I will write again soon.

Love, Ernest

HÔTEL VICTORIA
VENISE [letterhead]

No. 13
Scutari, Saturday

March 5, 1922

Dear Winona;–

We are quite surprised not to find any mail here for us. They tell us the mail is quite irregular but comes frequently as a rule and I hope to get some letters soon. I had a very quiet day today going to the church near by to hear Harry Riggs in Armenian this morning and visiting with people the rest of the day. I have three preaching appointments for next Sunday two in Armenian and one in English.

Miss McLean and I have talked Sivas by the hour. The box of clothes Miss Rice sent is here and I may send it by Dr. Ussher this week if he will take it. Mr. Thurber the Sivas Director had typhus and Joe Beach has gone in to take his place. Miss Willard is expected tomorrow and has permission to go to Marsovan and Miss Thirden hopes to go with her. I think the most probable thing is that Dr. Clark will go to Sivas and I to Erivan but we may know more definitely after the meeting Thursday. Mrs. Crawford seems to somewhat changed her mind in the last months and doubts now whether we would be allowed to open schools or to do much else. Mr. Stapleton is evidently willing to stay on and she is willing to have him and that may be the way the question will be settled. Ryan is expecting to make a flying trip to America starting in about three weeks and being gone three months. He expects to lecture a couple of times in the Oberlin Seminary about April 27th. So far I have found the Armenians with whom I have talked very pessimistic as to future missionary possibilities in Asia Minor. And yet I do not see how they can allow French Schools and close ours.

Goodsell and Henry Riggs seem to have injected some new life into the city work here. I never saw so much evangelistic activity as now. Riggs preached four times last Sunday in four languages, Armenian, Turkish, Kurdish & English. Miss McLean is a regular new missionary expecting to be with Dr. Dodd in Konia and Dr. & Mrs. Phillip Greene, Fred Greene's son, are very promising candidates and delightful people. These three constitute the language school this year.

Dr. MacCallum is the agent here in Constantinople of the Caucasus Relief work and gives half his time to that work. He is of the opinion that the need of workers is greater there than in either Sivas or Trebizond and he wants me to go to Erivan. I have not talked to Dr. Peet about it yet. Miss McLean says Miss Rice has developed a wonderful executive ability since she had to take so much responsibility after Polly's death, and has done an immense amount of work. She says that in spite of all that Polly wrote and talked about her good health, she was really in very bad condition, but she would listen to no one. Miss Allen was the same. Every one tried his best to prevent her making this trip to Harput in winter but she would go. She had typhus on the journey and died of collapse in Sivas very soon after getting in from Harput.

I caught a disagreeable cold the nights on the sleeper from Venice here, so you may understand that my cold serum, evidently is not effective with me.

I have not sent my traveling account yet but intend to in a day or two and I shall send a copy to you with a statement of how I spent personal money. I spent very little, no more than 25 dollars of personal money. I may send you some for debts when I get things written down so that I am sure.

Dr. Clark is going to the city to see Dr. Marden so I will send this. I am going to talk language study with Goodsell and see if it is best to take some Turkish lessons while I am writing.

Lots of love to all, Ernest

MISSIONS IN TURKEY OF THE AMERICAN BOARD
Office of Treasurer
American Bible House,
Stamboul – Constantinople.
[letterhead]

No. 14
March 9, 1922.

Dear Winona;–

Your first letter to me addressed to Constantinople came this morning. We are still in uncertainty about our future but may know tonight after the meeting today. Monday night I went home with Goodsell to spend the night and we talked till midnight. Last night Dr. & I went down to Kaki Keoui, beyond Haidor Pasha to stay over night with the MacNaughtons and Markham's. They have bought a fine old palace on the shore of the Bosphorus and have a school of 100 boys, 65 of them boarders. They are doing very well and made me homesick for Sivas and old times to see them try to adjust a growing school to unsuitable residences, tho as things go they are quite comfortable. Bill Hawkes is coming out from Sivas they say for a short vacation in about two weeks, when we may be able to get a good deal of information about things. I wish we could get the books out, or at least a list of deposit accounts. The Megali Helas is expected and I hope our trunks are on it. It is a little difficult to get clothes pressed when one has only one suit. I did it myself the other day in my room. I shall be glad also to have my typewriter.

Mr. Van Velson the accountant who was in Sivas told me that he had balanced and carefully examined the farm accounts in Sivas and that he had recommend that Miss G's heirs be paid a balance due her. I have asked Mr. Jaquith to have the matter looked up so that we can understand how it stands. Miss Loughridge is in Sivas helping out during Miss Phelps illness. I will answer your letter and write tomorrow the news about the Committee meeting.

I will try to talk to Fowle soon about Polly's account and I think that I can send a little money, if he's reasonable about it. Of course I have got to get back the $90.00 I spent to pay people to help here and if he is arbitrary I am up against it.

I am sorry to hear about Frances' eyes & hope she may find relief from the glasses. Alfred had better be thankful that he does not need them. They are a great nuisance. I wish Billo could hang on to his violin a little longer for I believe it would get easier. I would not be at all surprised if Dr. Clark stays here in Constantinople as he may do, if he would want his family by summer and in that case it would be hard for you. I am going to sound Miss Kinney as to the possibility of your doing some teaching for her if a suitable place for you to live can be found where it would be safe & comfortable near the girls' school in Scutari. Nothing definite can be decided now anyway.

Brand is President and I am secretary of our class but Bowers ought to be secretary now. I shall be glad if you succeed in getting a piano. I received one copy of the News.

Your letters of the 9th & 11th were forwarded here from Geneva and the one of the 13th came direct this morning.

I am very happy to hear of the success of Billo and Alfred in basketball.

There was a very interesting article in the Outlook of Feb 8th page 228 about the poetry of Charles Ryder.

Miss Loughridge and Mr. Plimpton the Talas director are in Sivas helping out because of the sickness there.

I will write again tomorrow.

Love, Ernest

❊

MISSIONS IN TURKEY OF THE AMERICAN BOARD
Office of Treasurer
American Bible House,
Stamboul – Constantinople.
[letterhead]

March 10, 1922.

Dear Winona;–

I called on Jaquith yesterday morning and talked the situation over with him. He said that if Dr. Peet should ask him to get permission for me to go to Sivas, he should have to decline, because he did not believe I ought to try to go in to Sivas at present. That as Dr. Clark was a physician and spoke Turkish his problem was much different. He said moreover that if I wished to go to the Caucasus he would be glad to do anything he could and would gladly have me in their work if the Mission wanted me to do that.

Yesterday afternoon we had a Committee-ad-Interim meeting and the following decisions were made. First that Mr. Stapleton be asked to stay in Trebizond and have his wife come out to hold things down until the situation changes. This decision was taken in light of the last letters from Mrs. Crawford in which she expresses the belief that any new work like a boys' school will be impossible, and that she is perfectly willing, now that Miss Cole has gone home, to stay on with Mr. and Mrs. Stapleton as associates. I have learned today from Dr. Marden that Mauamer Bey is the Vali in Trebizond, which in itself would make my going there impossible.

In the second place they voted for me to go to Erivan. Dr. MacCallum engineered this through the meeting in very nice shape. I have had long talks with him and Goodsell about things and also Harry Riggs. Maynard is in Erivan and Miss Shane also both doing a regular line of missionary work, super-vising church and school work. The prospect seems to be very good and people seem much interested in that work. After talking at length here we feel that the thing for me to do is to go to Erivan and work in an independent way among the Gregorians and study the school situation from the standpoint of the opening for a teachers college work. I am not very optimistic about what I can accomplish but shall like much better to try this than either the Sivas or Trebizond proposition at present.

In the third place they voted that Dr. Clark stay here for six weeks or two months, at the request of the NER to do Dr. Marden's work while he makes a tour of inspection of the medical work in the Caucasus. It is likely that Dr. Marden and I will go as far as Tiflis together, leaving here in about a week. I cannot go until our baggage comes, the Megali Helas is in today but I have not yet found out whether our stuff is on it or not. Miss Willard came this morning. They voted that it was desirable as soon as Dr. Marden came back for Dr. Clark to go to Sivas. We are going to try to get accounts etc., in as good shape as we can before Dr. goes or before I go. There is not however much that we can do here, although if Hawkes comes as we hear he is, for a short vacation here, we may get a good deal of information out of him.

Yeranoohi Kevorkian is here in the Constantinople College, her second year studying but I have not seen her yet. I have looked through the old accounts and found every item of Miss Wheeler's remittances for some years back in the monthly statements to Sivas, so that I can write her that the money has all been sent in, even if she has had no acknowledgement of it. In looking over these accounts I found that Polly has had a continuous stream of gifts from America for relief from many personal friends and churches. I saw one item of one thousand dollars from the Red Cross in Oberlin for her or in case of her absence for me. I think if things ever straighten out we might write such donors about our future work, or about her memorial.

When she came to bring her books up to date she evidently found 31 monthly statements lacking and had to have duplicates from the office here. They have just sent from here the last list of Sivas remittances, those that were unbalanced and I hope this finishes up that business. I think it very necessary that I hang around the office here for a week or so, because many things come up, that it is wise to talk over and we cannot do everything in a day or two. Dr. Peet approves of having the balance of Polly sent to Boston, and Mr. Fowle, while not liking to pay me on her account the ninety dollars I have sent you, is willing to pay it and charge it to my account in Sivas, and let them there put it on her account. I think Dr. Clark and Miss Rice will undoubtedly fix this up and I hope that money will get to Mr. Gaskins before long tho you know there is not regular mail to Sivas and little hope of any prompt return. I will write Dr. Barton and see if he cannot get Mr. Gaskins to do something at once.

Love to all, Ernest

❀

MISSIONS IN TURKEY OF THE AMERICAN BOARD
Office of the Treasurer
American Bible House
Stamboul – Constantinople
[letterhead]

March 13, 1922.

Dear Winona;–

Mr. Pearce secretary of the World's S.S. Association has spent three days in Constantinople and we had conferences Friday afternoon and Saturday afternoon with him, that were very interesting and profitable. We have asked for a secretary to represent the Association in this section of the world, and there seems to be hope of getting one. Yesterday Mr. Pearce visited several Sunday Schools and I heard him speak at the Langa Church.

I preached in the morning at the Scutari church and in the afternoon at Miss Burgess's chapel, both times in Armenian. Next Sunday if I am here I am to speak in the morning at the Langa Church and in the evening at the American sailor's club. I saw yesterday at the afternoon service quite a few old friends. Mrs. Koyunian, Levon Budakian who was for three years a prisoner of war in India, Yervant Eff. the water engineer who helped Polly a good deal just before I got to Sivas and in the last years of the war.

I think in my last letter about my plans I did not refer to family questions. After they had decided that I should go to the Caucasus, I said something like this on that subject. That you were a teacher and preferred that kind of work to housekeeping and that I should be very glad next summer to get you out here where you could keep a servant and do some school work.

Miss Kinney said to me at once that she would be very glad to have your help, if some arrangement could be made for living that would be acceptable to you. The Markhams said to me later that they should be glad to have you out with them, but nothing was said about a place to live. I imagine that they will raise the question before I leave and if so I will write about it.

Mr. Maynard expects to come down next month to take his family back with him and it may be by fall that I should be convinced that it was safe and proper to have you in Erivan. The difficulty is the same as you had about Berea; we do not want to be tied for a school year when the possibility may open up of getting together. Dr. Ussher says Maynard takes several American papers and that the mail goes regularly tho somewhat slow perhaps.

We expect our trunks and boxes in on a steamer that comes about Thursday so I shall hope to get off within a week or so.

I had a visit with Mrs. Austin yesterday who was in Sivas a year following Miss Thompson in the Armenian orphanage. There is a letter from Mrs. C for Dr. this morning but nothing from you. Address my mail here, American Bible House, via British Military Post box 213.

Love Ernest.

✿

MISSIONS IN TURKEY OF THE AMERICAN BOARD
American Bible House [letterhead]

Address until further notice Bible House care of British Post Office Box 213

No.17

March 17, 1922

Dear Winona;-

I am still waiting for trunks which may come in a couple of days. The boat that is bringing them has been ordered to go on to Batoum so that I may not be able to get my things off as they are likely in the bottom. This will not be so bad for me as for Dr. Clark, if it turns out that way, tho he will be here when the boat brings them back. However, this is all seeing the worst side. As a matter of fact there does not seem to be any good side here now except the fact that there is opportunity to work for people who need our help.

There is no use writing anything political because no one knows anything. The Greek Turkish offensive seems just about to begin again in fact last night's papers say it has begun. We had a telegram from Bekhian Sunday saying that with his family he is well. We do not understand why he wired or what it means. So far as we can judge the Armenians in the Sivas section are not being much bothered just now, tho they may be collecting soldiers. We have had a feeling that perhaps on this account Dr. Clark's going in might make Dr. H. trouble but we learned yesterday that they had asked a month ago from Sivas for an American doctor so they do not seem to feel that way.

I had a long talk with Krikore Boghosian the other day when we visited his school and home and he says we will not have trouble in finding the kind of teachers we want for the College. He mentioned Bekian, Jemjemian, of whom he and Bekian think highly, Kaloyan, and Avakian who make a good Armenian teacher.

The station authorized Dr. MacNaughton yesterday to buy a house adjoining his new property and he told me if this was accomplished they would like to give you a suite of rooms in that building and have you teach what you could. I told him the question was just like the Bera teaching business, that if you could come to Erivan, if I stayed there, of course you would not be willing to stay here. Maynard is coming down next month, if nothing happens to change his mind, to get his family.

You may be interested in the two accounts I am enclosing. The personal account shows that I bought 30.42 worth of pictures presents and personal things and that the actual extra cost of our sightseeing was 20.84. In this account is charged as personal everything that I spent except what I charged to the Board and the 16.65 was charged to them. There are some items in this account like barder laundry that should go against that item but about half of it was gain. We charge to ourselves all expenses while sightseeing except the time we stopped in London which we had to do to get laundry done.

I have half a dozen very nice pictures that will decorate our house, if we ever have one again. The Last Supper is the best but the Madonnas and the Venice pictures are very fine. I got a very pretty pitcher of the Venice glass work and a dish of spun glass for Frances. The collar button box for Edward is leather covered and has a bronze plaque of Dante on the top. George's purse is green leather and Venice stamped work.

I shall send a small package with Mr. Ryan who starts in a few days.

Love to all, Ernest

❀

AMERICAN COMMITTEE FOR RELIEF IN THE NEAR EAST
Bible House, Stamboul, Constantinople [letterhead]

No. 18
March 20, 1922

Dear Winona;-

This is an old letter head but the officers of the NER make no difference to you. Yesterday I preached in the morning in the Gedik Pasha church and in the afternoon went over to one of the Armenian Central Committee's orphanages to speak to 900 boys. I found there Koyunian who was very glad to see me. Guler has gone to America and is at present in Chicago with Vartenush Manendian. I have seen lately the Greek Bible woman who worked in Kara Hissar for us for some years. I saw Levon Lucigian also yesterday and hope to see him again and to find out how he is doing in Robert College.

The papers you send come regularly and I like to have them. I think it is worth while to continue to send them tho how regularly they will get to me in Erivan I do not know. You had better leave off Dr. Peet's name from my address and send, American Bible House, via British Military Post box 213.

Your last letter is dated Feb 19th and contains a eulogy of Mrs. Clark. She certainly has many good qualities which I have no doubt the doctor fully appreciates, as for me I have long since ceased to think of making you over, and am very well satisfied as things are. I never have approved of all your methods in bringing up a family but the boys seem to be all that I desire so why should I criticize as long especially as I shirk my share of the responsibility.

I wish that you would telephone Louis Lord and tell him I visited practically all and only the galleries he recommended from London to Venice and am thoroughly pleased with my trip. Dr. Clark also is well satisfied that we saw for our money just what we wanted to see and at a reasonable cost.

As to '95 officers, Brand is President and I am secretary. I wish you would send Bowers my list of the class from my drawer and I will write him asking that he act as secretary in my absence. I will answer George sometime and hope he or Edward will let me know the scores once in a while. I will write Dr. Barton today about Polly's business.

I called on the Consul-General this morning and he says it is best that someone here be appointed administrator to settle things from this end. I am going to request that he designate Dr. Clark and Miss Rice to make an inventory of her Sivas property and send it in and then the Consul-General will appoint an administrator here to settle the estate in Turkey. This is going to drag along a year or two, even at best and if the inventory does not come out promptly it may be longer. And then any day we may lose the rest of our staff in Sivas so that there will be no need of an inventory. It is my conviction that unless some settlement is speedily made acceptable to Turkey, the rest of the Americans in the interior will be rejected and things will be finished for good.

Dr. Barton has had very emphatic assurances from the State Dept that all American rights here will be protected to the limit. But we are living from day to day with no feeling of confidence as to the future, so far as our work or rights are concerned.

Love, Ernest

✿

MISSIONS IN TURKEY OF THE AMERICAN BOARD
Office of the Treasurer
American Bible House
Stamboul – Constantinople [letterhead]

No. 20
March 24, 1922

Dear Winona;-

Yours of Feb 27th just came and I will answer it at once as I have a little time to write while waiting for a man. I have some good news, very insignificant to the world but of importance to me. Our trunks and boxes came off the boat yesterday and I have just had them open and overhauled things as to get out some of the things I need. I think I shall leave my military stuff here in my small trunk and take only one trunk to Erivan. I can get all I have into the big trunk if I leave that part of it and having cut out the things I brought for Miss Rice and Mrs. Crawford. The trunks were boxed and iron hoped and seem not have been opened.

Last night I went home with Goodsell to spend the night again and had another good visit with him. He asked my opinion about their trying to do some teacher training in connection with the proposed school of religious education which they are thinking of starting next fall. I told him there was no doubt need for that sort of thing but that I shall rather see them start without that and add it later if it seemed best. That I was afraid that if they started with too may departments the thing would break down. He says Cass Reed is urging it all the time from Smyrna and Goodsell thinks he has an idea of being the head of that branch. It seems that Smyrna station invited him back only on condition that he be a member of the station and not dean of the College. He came back having accepted these conditions and now McLaughlin has gone to America and left him as acting President again.

I am probably to preach at Constantinople College next Sunday morning and at the American Sailors Club in Pera in the evening. Now that my trunks are here I shall get away as soon as I can get this paper for losses etc., fixed up, but that is slow work and may take days or weeks. I have to guess at all the values, and then after my work is all done the stuff has to be copied and certified to by a Consul.

I think your idea for George is probably a good one, at any rate it is no harm for him to have it in mind. There is going to be a lot of headache and backache over the Sivas accounts before they are finished. People are very nice until they do not see their money coming and then they begin to rip and tear.

Love, Ernest.

❈

MISSIONS IN TURKEY OF THE AMERICAN BOARD
Office of the Treasurer
American Bible House
Stamboul – Constantinople [letterhead]

No. 21
March 27, 1922

Dear Winona;-

I have been working all the forenoon on accounts and will now write to you and then go back to Scutari for the last part of the afternoon. Saturday afternoon we went over to Haidar Pasha and cut into the country some miles to visit the Kennedys. They are the people who almost came to Talas some years ago as medical missionaries. He was our doctor in Erivan the year I was in the Caucasus, and they are back here now in Lord Mayor's Fund orphanage work. He is a member of the League of Nations Committee on deported women. She is the Miss Robinson, who was with us on the Singh from Marseilles to Athens, an English nurse coming to Athens for work. We had a very pleasant afternoon and then they drove us back to Scutari.

Yesterday morning I preached in Armenian at Miss Kinney's School and in the evening in English at the American sailor's Club. I spent the night in Pera with the Flints. Mr. F. is the office secretary for Dr. Peet here and his wife is a very hard worker in the Sailor's Club. They are American Congregationalists and delightful people. In the afternoon yesterday we went over to Hissar and called on the Goodsells and Fowles and attended an organ recital at the College.

I saw Levon Lucigian, Yeranoohi Kevorkian and Mrs. Maynard. She is very anxious that you should come out and go to Erivan and I told her I was also, but that it would have to depend on later information as to conditions.

I do not know that to do about the box of clothing that Miss Rice sent here for you. If you are coming out soon it seems hardly worth while to ship it to America, if you will not want it there.

I go to the American Club dinner every Friday noon and meet 60 to 75 American men, mostly business men and it seems queer to see so many young Americans here. Heck is away now so I have not seen him.

Lots of Love, Ernest

❊

MISSIONS IN TURKEY OF THE AMERICAN BOARD
Office of the Treasurer
American Bible House
Stamboul – Constantinople [letterhead]

March 31, 1922

Dear Winona;-

Wednesday I went to Hissar and took dinner with Mrs. Maynard, and had a talk with her about Erivan and her plans. She does not seem to know much about things there at present. She is naturally very anxious to get back there and expects Mr. Maynard here in about two or three weeks to pack her up and take the family back. I shall not decide anything until after I get to Erivan, or until I see Maynard, if he comes here before I leave. But it looks to me as tho there is prospect of your coming out this summer. I do not think you ought to spend the whole summer there just to be with the big boys, for that would mean no regular arrangement for the three small children for some time in the fall.

Mr. Ryan is starting for the States today and carries a small package containing a purse got George, a collar button box for Edward and a small spun glass dish and a necklace for Frances. I spent considerable time the other day trying to get something suitable for William and Alfred but did not succeed. Mr. Ryan will be in Oberlin in about three weeks and I hope you can have him to a meal and visit with him. He will give you the latest news. There is nothing definite. The three ministers have proposed a plan by which Turkey comes out of the war better than any nation engaged in it and by which [missing pages/no closing]

❊

ca Apr 1922

To Winona;-

I had a talk with Dr. Wallace, the Dean, acting in Dr. Patrick's place, about Yeranoohi Kevorkian, who is in her second year there. She is doing very well, not a strong student but a fine character and gives great promise of being a useful teacher. I had a long visit with her in the evening.

I was just called out for a talk with Lucigian who came to say that he was ready to serve his people as a teacher with us if we got established anywhere and wanted his help. I like his appearance and he is very well spoken of by his teachers at Robert College. I think he graduates this year.

It seems to me very important that the big boys begin while you are there to write to me, or else I fear they will never get the habit and we shall seldom hear from them after you come back.

Love Ernest

❉

MISSIONS IN TURKEY OF THE AMERICAN BOARD
Office of the Treasurer
American Bible House
Stamboul – Constantinople [letterhead]

April 10, 1922

Dear Winona;-

I have three letters of yours to answer, the last one of which came yesterday and was handed to me at the breakfast table. The Riggs had been in the office yesterday (Sunday) afternoon and brought it home late last night.

Dr. Barton's letter sounds good and I hope it may produce the proper results. I made a mistake in that I did not take time when in Boston to have him understand the situation, in which case he would have kept after Mr. Gaskins until something was done. I took Mr. G.'s word that he would attend to the matter as final. Mr. Belcher is expected here within a few days and it is hoped that he will understand the situation and produce a settlement. Dr. Peet has little to do with accounts and Fowle is rather uppish at times. Personally he and I seem to get on all right.

As to the Sivas accounts, I do not think there is so very much to do, if we could get at the books for a time. Miss Rice has written here that Polly's accounts were all balanced up in good shape up to Jan 1921 and she intended with Mr. Van Velson's help to keep them up to date which was done as far as she could. And of course the bulk of treasury work for the Board accounts in Sivas was very small in 1921. Polly seems to have paid back much of the deposit money so that what remains to be done is to bring these accounts up to date, then make a balance sheet of Bills Payable and Receivable, so as to get exactly the items of deposits left unpaid. Then there are twenty or forty items that people have been after here and in America. After these clamorers are stopped the treasury work will come down to an occasional item to be paid. But before any more sums are paid it is essential that a balance sheet be found, that we know exactly how we stand, and have an idea as to how much, if not all, of these deposits we can pay. There has been so much fluctuation in the value of money in the past years that it is hard to know where we stand until a careful analysis is made. Dr. Clark is willing to do this and I do not think it will take a great amount of time. If Dr. Hekimyan continues to help him, he can do this easily, and this leaves me free to begin a new work for the training of teachers, if we find conditions suitable in Erivan.

I am surprised and pleased at Frances' letter which came this morning. It is very well written. I am answering Billo herewith and will write her soon.

There is no one in Constantinople who knows more about present conditions in the Caucasus than Dr. MacCallum and I have talked with him by the hour about things. There is a scarcity of food in Erivan, but Americans do not suffer. The fact that Mr. Maynard is coming within a few days expecting to take his family back is conclusive on this point, I should say. The Near East has at present large orphanages in Erivan with a number of workers, among them an American physician, a woman I know fairly well. There will be doubtless things we should want that we cannot get in Erivan, but the difference between Erivan and Sivas would be that we can order from Erivan with fair hope of getting stuff, while in Sivas you would never

[missing pages/no closing]

❀

AMERICAN BIBLE HOUSE
Constantinople

April 15, 1922

Dear Edward;-

You may be interested in hearing some of my impressions of Constantinople this time as compared with my first visit twenty-one years ago.

The city, which used to seem very cosmopolitan, is now even more so owing to Allied occupation. There are soldiers from all kinds of colonies and races, Sikhs & Punjabis, Moroccans and Abbysinians, Algerians, besides any type of European born British and French soldiers. There are about 40,000 Russian refugees, many of them with distinctly mongol faces, which adds to the picturesqueness of the place.

One fact that an old resident notices is that the dogs are still conspicuous by their absence, tho few of them are creeping in. The increase in street cars, autos, trucks and busses has somewhat speeded up the rate of travel and makes the Galata bridge even more of a mess than before. Imagine these motor vehicles mixed in with horse vehicles, and then a few ox-carts and buffalo carts thrown in, with an occasional camel carrying a piano box or a bundle of iron pipe 12 feet long, trying to wedge his way through, and you have a situation that is always interesting. Allied occupation has forced the cleaning up of the streets and in this respect the city is better than I have ever seen it. Of course it does not still compare with Oberlin with its traffic laws about crossing the street between corners, etc. I hold my breath most of the time when riding in an auto, but as a matter of fact I have not seen an accident in the month I have been here. They do have traffic-cops on the busiest corners, to flag autos and streetcars, but the pedestrians pay little attention to them, and scoot across the street in all directions.

There has been a saying here that when a Mohammedan walks across Galata Bridge arm in arm with his wife, the millenium will have come, but this must be wrong for this not infrequently happens and we still wait for the millenium. The veil is still in evidence, tho I should say that half the Turkish women wear it thrown back, and some have discarded it altogether.

I have been living this time over in Scutari on the Asiatic side of Constantinople, whence one can look over on the European city, and up the Bosphorus and down the Sea of Marmora. And is always impressed each time anew with the beauty and extent of the Constantinople harbor. In either respect, I think it has no superior and few equals in the world. It does an American good to see the

Stars and Stripes flying over the building of the Guarrantee Trust Company, and on an increasing number of ships in the harbor. Not so infrequently four or five of the big Shipping Corporation steamers are here at once with food for hungry Russia and Armenia. Of course, business is very slack, owing to political uncertainty and economic instability. One indication of the number of refugees in the city is the great increase in the number of peddlers on the streets. A cake of Austrian-made chocolate, marked Amerka, for sale purposes, retails at 3 ½ cents, which would sell for 10-15 cents at home. The aggressiveness of the Russian refugees is clearly shown by the number who peddle their wares. They are making all kinds of toys and useful articles that sell for a small price and seem to be doing well.

Of course Constantinople is very badly crowded, not only because of the refugee population, and the thousands of Allied troops and officers, but also because, while little building has been done during the past dozen years, in this period some 17,000 houses have been lost thru great fires that have swept various quarters of the city.

One cannot possibly understand the meaning of "filthy lucre" unless he has spent a few days making change here. Of course in the depreciation of currency, Turkey is fortunate as compared with her late allies or with Russia. But there is no silver, nickel or copper in circulation and their place has been taken by paper scrip worth now about 1 and 3 cents, and by stamps worth less than two mills. The paper of these is of poor quality and most people carry a roll of gummed tissue paper to patch up their change sufficiently to get it off on the next person.

One of the new things in Constantinople is the American Mens Club, which meets together for luncheon once a week and where one can meet any week 50 to 75 American men, representing business, diplomatic and philanthropic interests, and hear a live address on The Outlook for American Business Men in Turkey, Commercial Prospects at Home, or Salvaging Russia. Last week I attended a luncheon of the University Club, an organization started by the inspiration of American Y.M. men here, counting in its membership College graduates of several nationalities.

[no closing page]

MISSIONS IN TURKEY OF THE AMERICAN BOARD
Office of Treasurer
American Bible House
Stamboul-Constantinople
[letterhead]

April 20, 1922.

Dear Winona;–

I am to go on the steamer this evening and to sail for Batoum early in the morning. After discussing the matter with a number of my best friends here whom opinion I value, especially Dr.

Peet, Dr. and Mrs. Macallum Mr. Goodsell and Miss Willard, I have decided to advise that you plan to come out as early in the summer as you can get ready after school closes, with the expectation that you will be able to proceed directly on to Batoum and Erivan.

Several Americans, Consuls and business men and one or two philanthropists, have come out of Russia of late and I have heard them speak. All seem to agree that the Americans are and will be perfectly safe in Russia and the Caucasus. I do not know the exact condition at Erivan, but the fact that Mr. Maynard is coming down in a few days to take his family back would indicate that he thinks it a proper place for his wife and children. There are famine conditions in some parts of Russia, but this does not mean an absolute lack of food so much as a lack of means with which to buy food.

I asked Dr. Peet this morning what he would write and he said, "if I were in your place I would write Mrs. Partridge to come along. The odds are all in favor of her being able to go right on to Erivan and if things should suddenly change so that she could not go right on she can stop here, tho that is improbable."

Dr. Macallum says he envies us the opportunity we are to have in the Caucasus of setting up new work. He would very much like to go up there and work for he considers the opportunity far greater than the probable opportunity here in this section of the world. Miss Willard and Mrs. Macallum also think you ought to come out this summer.

Miss Kinney asked me yesterday to tell you, that if Armen has not a job for next year and wants to come out, she would like to hear from you on the subject, as there is every likelihood that they could give her work, and would like to have her help.

It is my very strong opinion that you ought not wait until fall in order to get the big boys started in school. I think it is important that you plan to get out by early fall so that the three can start their school work with the Maynard children. You have certainly done your full duty by Edward and George and should think more now about the others and your poor husband. Unless I find conditions that warrant my cabling you not to come, when I get to Erivan, I shall plan for a house for next fall and for some kind of a building for beginning school work, a normal class, at least.

I shall of course write as soon as I have an opinion to write after I get to Erivan, but you had better begin to make your plans to come along, in the middle of the summer. I shall hope to meet you at Batoum at least and may find it best to come on to Constantinople to talk things over, especially if accounts come out from Sivas before that time.

I am not very enthusiastic about the ladies whom you think may come with you. It is one thing for a woman to come out to Erivan to live with her husband and engage in missionary work, and quite another to tour around the country. At the same time, conditions may be quite satisfactory by that time and it is no great stunt to run down from Batoum to Tiflis and Erivan. I presume you had better plan to bring blankets and bedding enough for the family as such supplies are probably more expensive here than there but I try and write on this subject at once after talking things over with Maynard. I shall try to write from Batoum the first part of the next week before going on from there.

Lots of love, Ernest
I am sending Mr. Riggs a copy of this.

❈

S.S. Adria
Constantinople Harbor

No. 30
April 21, 1922.

Dear Winona;–

I worked hard yesterday all day getting things cleared up and getting on the boat, and still we are here. I wrote letters to Dr. Barton & Mr. Riggs and one to you (no. 29) which I did not number, then from 3:30 to 5:30 I attended a station meeting and a Com-Ad-Int meeting. People were all very cordial and said they were sorry to have me leave. Goodsell asked me to write him once a month. After I got my stuff on boat and got settled I went off for dinner and then called at Gedick Pasha to get a letter to take to Dr. Marden, who is on a medical inspection trip in the Caucasus. Mrs. Marden urged me to stay over night so I did not come aboard right after breakfast. We are to sail in an hour or so they say.

The ladies at Gedick Pasha say you ought to bring what you need in the way of blankets, sheets, pillow cases, table-linen towels, etc., as such stuff will be cheaper in the U.S. than here. I have bought a folding bedstead, a thin mattress, three blankets, 3 sheets, 2 pillows

[missing pages/no closing]

❈

NEAR EAST RELIEF [letterhead]
25 Rue Taxim, Constantinople

No. 36
Erivan, Armenia,
May 10, 1922

Dear Winona;–

I have been in Erivan now five days and we have got fairly well settled. Over Sunday we had as guests three NER ladies here from Alexandropol on their way to Tabriz for a short vacation, and also a Persian missionary on his way thro. Our regular family at present consists of Miss Shane, Mr. Maynard, Sister Bodil a Norwegian nurse here to start a small orphanage on her own hook and myself. We have a cook, two other women servants, a boy to do the buying and errands and a secretary for the station, so you see we are well cared for. Mr. Maynard is getting his accounts up and expects to go to Constantinople with a couple of weeks to stay until about the middle of August. The heat here is intense and it would not do to bring his children here so late in the summer. I wish you could get out in time to come back with them, but that may hurry you too much.

My job until September first seems to be to teach a class in English in the Armenian University which Mr. Maynard has started, to do the station treasury work, preach occasionally, and study the whole situation with reference to the future. I have attended once the English class but have not yet taught it. It consists of 24 pupils, all grown, some of them middle aged but mostly young men, two women, who are nearly all very eager to learn and seem to be making good progress. The University is largely on paper, in fact entirely so so far as any University or college or even high school work is concerned. The institution is a kind of Cooper Institute. Its hours are from four to seven in the afternoon and most of the students are people who have jobs and regular work thro the days until four P.M. It looks as tho we could teach about three classes in English next year and Maynard and I agree that we ought to do it. There has been a suggestion on the part of the archbishop here that I teach a class in the seminary at Etchmiadzin next year. Probably nothing will come of this but it would be very interesting if something of that kind should develop. I should then have to have a car, for Etchmiadzin is twelve miles away but we really need a car anyway and must plan in some way to get one when our stay here seems definite.

Maynard is a very good treasurer and is willing to do the business work and supervise the church work. He does not like to preach tho he does it, and he wants me to do the educational work, more than my share of the public speaking, and the government work. Last Sunday we had communion in the morning, and I preached in the afternoon. The courier makes the trip from Tiflis here and back every four days and I shall write every time after I get my machine down from Alexandropol.

Under this system I do not see why you should not get my letters very regularly, tho there may not be boats from Batoum as often as that.

With lots of love, Ernest

❁

NEAR EAST RELIEF
25 Rue Taxim, Constantinople

No. 35
Erivan, Armenia,
May 10, 1922

Dear William, & Frances & Alfred;--
    You will be glad, I am sure to hear something about the conditions of life here in Erivan. Erivan is a city of 130,000 people now, many of them refugees. Before the war its population was only 40,000. It is located on the edge of a great plain and at the foot of a mountain. It is very warm in summer and has a good deal of malaria. There is lots of fruit and food is not expensive when bought

with American money. The NER allows us to buy anything they have on hand, canned goods, flour, rice, cheese and anything else they have so that they [there] does not seem to be much danger of being uncomfortable from lack of things we need. There are about fifteen American relief workers here with the NER, besides the missionaries and a few English relief workers. Mr. Maynard and Miss Shane and I are all the missionaries at present. The Maynards have four boys ages 12, 10, 5 and 2. The oldest boy is farther along in school than Billo, but I think the 10 year old boy might be in a class with Frances.

Most of the Americans here ride horseback and horses are not very expensive, from $20.00 to $60.00. There seems to be plenty of good dogs in this country of a number of kinds. The people who go down to Tabriz for their vacations all bring back canaries with them, which cost down there about $2.00 each. I do not see how I can get along here and do my work without a car and hope when things get settles, if we are to stay here, that I can some way get a Ford.

Mr. Maynard is going to Constantinople in a few days to spend some weeks with his family and bring them back here about the last of August. I hope you will get out to Constantinople in time to come on with them, but if you do not, I shall have to come as far as Batoum and perhaps Constantinople to meet you. From Batoum to Erivan it is about three days ride and we shall probably get, thro the NER, a freight car and put cot beds and a table and chairs in it it [sic] with a primus cook stove and a box of canned goods. This is the most comfortable way to travel and I am sure you will enjoy it. Mr. Maynard has a very comfortable house and I am sure we can find one that will be satisfactory. It is possible to buy very good second hand furniture here cheap. And Mr. Maynard says we can find a good piano, cheap either to buy or to rent.

I certainly hope you will be able to come out in the summer. I ought to hear from mama before long as to what she thinks about coming here.

Lots of love from Papa

MISSIONS IN TURKEY OF THE AMERICAN BOARD
Office of Treasurer
American Bible House
Stamboul – Constantinople

No. 37
Erivan, Armenia,
May 12, 1922

My dear Winona:–
The mail just came in, which means that the courier is in and starts back tonight. I hope that he brought my typewriter and that this is the last time I have to write on this toy, which is not bad for traveling, but which falls far short of being a regular machine.

The courier now comes and goes every four days so you will get that many letters, but they may bunch up at Batoum or Constantinople. I called on the dean of the literary department of the University yesterday and taught my English class for the first time. It contains 22 pupils, three young ladies and nineteen men. I am thinking of dividing the class for the rest of the year, about 15 lessons, for two reasons, one is that we have two kinds of books, about enough of each kind for half the class, and also some of them have studied a little English and could go faster than the rest. We called on the Armenian Archbishop yesterday and had a pleasant visit. He was very cordial. Some weeks ago Maynard called on him and told him that I was coming and he said to him then, "I will arrange for him to teach some in the school at Etchmiadtzin." Yesterday he told us that they had decided to open the school next fall and that in the meeting he had proposed that I be invited to teach there. It is to be a three or four years course probably of college grade. I do not know what they will want me to teach but I should like to have a course in Ethics to start with. The Dean of the University yesterday asked Mr. Maynard to take a letter to the Patriarch in Constant asking him to send English, French and other books for next year and Maynard and I are going to list what we want for English and see that we get them. There will probably be three different classes next year and you may draw one of them.

The present government takes the attitude that it is the function of the government to provide education and so far our school here is not officially recognized. Miss Shane has 350 pupils doing good work under difficult building conditions. Officially they do not allow religious education in the schools because that is the function of the church, which does not do it either. We have come to no issue with them on either of these problems yet and we hope to avoid it and keep going. I am going to write George a letter about money soon. The rate today between Armenian money and the dollar is one dollar buys 9,800.00 roubles.

Love to all, Ernest

Endnotes

1 Winona G. Partridge, *Letters* and *Diaries*, unpublished, Partridge Family Collection. Ernest C. Partridge, *Letters* and *Diaries*,unpublished, Partridge Family Collection. Mary L. Graffam, *Letters*, unpublished, Partridge Family Collection. Edward G. Partridge, *Diary*, unpublished, Partridge Family Collection.

2 Winona G. Partridge, *Letters* and *Diaries*, (Unpublished, Partridge Family Collection).

3 Rev. L. Woods, D.D., *History of the Andover Theological Seminary* (Boston: James R. Osgood and Company, 1885), 199.

4 The National Cathedral School (NCS) was opened on October 1, 1900 in Washington, DC to "educate young women to embrace the core values of excellence, service, courage, and conscience." The education offered was atypical of the time and included both modern and classical languages, English, mathematics, history, science, and physical activity. accessed May 15, 2014, http://www.ncs.cathedral.org/podium/default.aspx?t= 12847; http://www.ncs.cathedral.org/podium/default.aspx?t=112456. Mary Graffam excelled in many of these subjects.

5 The American Missionary Association (AMA) was established in 1846 by abolitionists whose goals were, after abolishing slavery, to educate African Americans, to encourage Christian values, to promote racial equality, and to provide economic independence and opportunities for higher education, accessed May 15, 2014, http://www.amistadresearchcenter.org/archon/?p=creators/creator&id=27.

6 The American Board of Commissioners of Foreign Missions was the first American missionary society formed by Congregationalists in 1810. The ABCFM was based in Boston, Massachusetts and the founding committee determined that the missionary activity would focus on the following peoples—ancient civilizations, primitive cultures, ancient Christian churches and Islamic faith. accessed May 15,2014 http://www.14beacon.org/resources/efg/efg-abcfm1. By 2000, the ABCFM had evolved into the Wider Church Ministries of the United Church of Christ, accessed May 15, 20124, http://globalministries.org/resources/mission-study/abcfm-200.html. Rev. J.K. Greene, Leaving the Levant (Boston: the Pilgrim Press, 1916), 199.

7 Peter Balakian, *The Burning Tigris, The Armenian Genocide and America's Response* (New York: HarperCollins Publishers Inc., 2003), 23.

8 Rev. J.K. Greene, *Leaving the Levant* (Boston: The Pilgrim Press, 1916) 200.

9 *Ibid.*

10 *Ibid.*

11 *Ibid.*, 199-200.

12 Rev. C. Henry Holbrook, "Impressions of Sivas 1912," *Journal of Armenian Studies*, 1(1990-91): 37–71.

13 *Ibid.*, 62.

14 *Ibid.*

15 Winona G. Partridge, *Autobiography*, (unpublished, Partridge Family Collection) 1947).

16 Rev. C. Henry Holbrook, "Impressions of Sivas 1912," *Journal of Armenian Studies*, 1(1990-91): 65.

17 Grigoris Balakian, *Armenian Golgotha, A Memoir of the Armenian Genocide, 1915-1918* (New York: Alfred A. Knopf, 2009). Grigoris Balakian was a high ranking priest in the Armenian Apostolic Church in Constantinople and a respected leader of the Armenian community. Balakian was arrested and confined on April 15, 1915. He eventually escaped and was able to reach safety after which he wrote of his experiences as well as the experiences of fellow Armenians. His memoirs were made available in English in 2009.

18 Armenia - Beginnings to 1915 This historical account of world events is intended to be introductory in nature, thereby providing the reader with a basic outline of events that took place in Turkey during the years that Ernest and Winona lived in Sivas, Turkey and Alexandropol/Leninakan, Russia and Polly's years in Sivas during the war. Readers interested in more depth and detail are directed to the bibliography at the end of this book as well as respected sources on World War I. Additionally, several institutions in the United States (Harvard University, Oberlin College, United Church of Christ) hold the collections of the American Board of Commissioners of Foreign Missions, American Committee for Relief in the Near East, and Near East Relief. These collections contain documents and letters to and from the Partridges and Mary Graffam; materials that lay outside the scope of this project but without doubt hold value and interest regarding the individuals discussed in this book.

19 Abraham D. Krikorian, Professor Emeritus, Department of Biochemistry and Cell Biology, SUNY at Stony Brook, personal correspondence with the author, February 2014.

20 Julius Richter, D.D., *A History of Protestant Missions in the Near East* (New York: Fleming H. Revell Company, 1910), 112.

21 *Ibid.*, 113.

22 Peter Balakian, *The Burning Tigris, The Armenian Genocide and America's Response* (New York: HarperCollins Publishers Inc., 2003), 27.

23 *Ibid.*, 29.

24 *Ibid.*, 36.

25 Abraham D. Krikorian, Professor Emeritus, Department of Biochemistry and Cell Biology, SUNY at Stony Brook, personal correspondence with the author, February 2014.

26 *Ibid.*

27 Peter Balakian, *The Burning Tigris, The Armenian Genocide and America's Response* (New York: HarperCollins Publishers Inc., 2003), 157.

28 Julius Richter, D.D., *A History of Protestant Missions in the Near East* (New York: Fleming H. Revell Company, 1910), 135.

29 Peter Balakian, *The Burning Tigris, The Armenian Genocide and America's Response* (New York: HarperCollins Publishers Inc., 2003), 145, 165.

30 *Ibid.,* 211.

31 *Ibid.,* 305, 364.

32 This city in northwestern Turkey was known as Alexandropol (1837-1924) when the Partridges first went to Turkey. Alexandropol became Leninakan in 1924 while they were living there, and in 1990 the earlier name of Gyumri was reinstated.

33 Peter Balakian, *The Burning Tigris, The Armenian Genocide and America's Response* (New York: HarperCollins Publishers Inc., 2003), 323.

34 *Ibid.,* 349-352.

35 *Ibid.,* 350.

36 *Ibid.,* 354-356.

37 Henry Morgenthau, *Ambassador Morgenthau's Story* (Garden City, NY: Doubleday, Page and Company, 1918), 333.

38 Peter Balakian, *The Burning Tigris, The Armenian Genocide and America's Response* (New York: HarperCollins Publishers Inc., 2003), 181.

39 Ibid., 180, 350.

40 The Layman's Missionary Movement was a men's organization begun in 1906 to support the concept of foreign missions. An educational campaign focused on helping layman and their churches become interested in missions. accessed February, 2014, Library.columbia.edu/content/dam/libraryweb/locations/burke/fa/mrl/ldpd_4492661.pdf; American Committee for Armenian and Syrian Relief was founded in 1915. In 1918 after World War I ended, the organization became the American Committee for Relief in the Near East (ACRNE) and then in 1919 ACRNE was incorporated by an act of Congress to become Near East Relief (NER). accessed June 2014, http://www.armenian-genocide.org/ner.html

41 Ernest C. Partridge, "The Pensacola Party," *Armenian Affairs,* 1(1950): 293–297.

42 Ernest C. Partridge, "Mary Louise Graffam," *Armenian Affairs,* 1(1949-50): 62.

43 Ernest C. Partridge, "The Pensacola Party," *Armenian Affairs,* 1(1950): 293–297.

44 Rev. C. Henry Holbrook, "Impressions of Sivas 1912," *Journal of Armenian Studies,* 1(1990-91): 37–71.

45 Richard Kloian, "April 24, 2009 Tribute for Mary Graffam and Rev. Ernest Partridge: *Unsung Heroes of the Armenian Genocide,*" speech delivered at 94th Commemoration of the Armenian Genocide, Saroyan Hall, San Francisco, CA.

46 Partridge was spelled without an "r" for this generation only.

47 Fred A. Torrance, "Mallory's Bush Article 5," *The Record-Post,* July 22, 1947.

48 Hiram Patridge will probated 15 Sept 1853, New York Probate Records, Essex County, 1843-1852, Volume D, 197.

49 Karen Peters, President, Wilmington Historical Society, Wilmington, NY; personal correspondence with the author, July 2010.

50 Wilmington Historical Society, *Images of America, Wilmington and the Whiteface Region* (Charlestown, South Carolina: Arcadia Publishing, 2013), 108.

51 Obituary of Lyman Prindle, *Plattsburgh Sentinel*, April 6, 1888. accessed July 2013, www.Findagrave.com.

52 Excerpts from *The History of the Champlain Conference 1843-2000*. accessed June 2014, www.north-net.org/wesleyanturnpike/distchrs2/disthist.ppt. Cyrus Prindle, Lyman Prindle, John Croker and Lewis C. Partridge participated in the conferences and all served as president.

53 Robert S. Fletcher, *A History of Oberlin College From its Foundation Through the Civil War* (Oberlin: Oberlin College, 1943) Volume I, 88-89.

54 William A. Hallock, *Memoir of Harlan Page: The Power of Prayer and Personal Effort for the Souls of Individuals* (Minneapolis: Curiosmith, 2012). accessed June, 2014, http://www.coventryct.org/DocumentCenter/View/191.

55 Karen Peters, President, Wilmington Historical Society, Wilmington, NY; personal correspondence with the author, July 2010.

56 New York State Archives, accessed May 15, 2014 iarchives.nysed.gov/civilwarweb/soldier detailservlet.

57 Karen Peters, President, Wilmington Historical Society, Wilmington, NY; personal correspondence with the author, July 2010.

58 Although he died in Waitsfield Vermont, Rev. Lyman Prindle was also buried in West Chazy Rural Cemetery near his beloved, first wife and was later joined by his second wife. Obituary of Lyman Prindle, *Plattsburgh Sentinel*, April 6, 1888, photocopy, Partridge Family Collection. accessed July 2013, www.Findagrave.com.

59 Rev. L. C. Partridge, *Memorial of Miss Mary Louise Partridge, One of the Martyrs of China*, ca 1900. Partridge Family Collection.

60 At this time the population of Florida was increasing quickly. Rollins College was formed in 1885 by New England Congregationalists who wanted to bring "their style of liberal arts education to the Florida frontier." accessed July 2011, http://www.rollins.edu/why-rollins/history.html

61 American Missionary Association, Amistad Research Center website, accessed May 15,2014, http://www.amistadresearchcenter.org/archon/?p=creators/creator&id=27

62 *Ibid.*

63 Forty-seventh Annual Report, p. 54 and Forty-eighth Annual Report, p. 58, *American Missionary Association*, Vol. 40-49.

64 Robert S. Fletcher, *A History of Oberlin College From its Foundation Through the Civil War*. Oberlin: Oberlin College, 1943. 1004 pp.

65 *Ibid.*, 119.

66 Forty-eighth Annual Report, *American Missionary Association*, Vol. 40-49, p. 43.

67 Nat Brand, *Massacre in Shansi* (toExcel, 1999), p.24. The Oberlin Band was a group of 12 protestant graduates of Oberlin Seminary and College who requested to be sent by the ABCFM as a group to China or some place where they would be successful in turning people to Christ.

68 *The Ticonderoga Sentinel*, December 1901.

69 Rev. L. C. Partridge, *Memorial of Miss Mary Louise Partridge, One of the Martyrs of China*, ca. 1900, Partridge Family Collection.

70 *Ibid.*

71 Oberlin Shansi continues on campus today aiming "to promote understanding and communication

between Asians and Americans…through individual and group educational and social programs, educational and cultural exchanges, and community projects." accessed May 15, 2014, www. Oberlin.edu/student-life/diversity/shansi.dot.

72 Nat Brand, *Massacre in Shansi* (toExcel, 1999), 288-292.

73 *Ticonderoga Sentinel*, March 20, 1902.

74 Winona G. Partridge, *Autobiography*, (unpublished, Partridge Family Collection, 1947).

75 Winona G. Partridge, *Memories of Mary Louise Graffam*, (unpublished, Partridge Family Collection, 1944).

76 Winona G. Partridge, *Autobiography*, (unpublished, Partridge Family Collection, 1947).

77 Winona G. Partridge, *Memories of Mary Louise Graffam*, (unpublished, Partridge Family Collection, 1944).

78 Rev. L. Woods, D.D., *History of the Andover Theological Seminary* (Boston: James R. Osgood and Company, 1885), 199.

79 *Ibid.*, 200.

80 Winona E. Graffam to Ernest C. Partridge, November 29, 1896, Partridge Family Collection.

81 *Ibid.*

82 *Ibid.*

83 Winona E. Graffam to Ernest C. Partridge, 3 December 1896, Partridge Family Collection.

84 Edna L. Wellman Laird to Winona G. Partridge, 23 June 1956, Partridge Family Collection. Edna was a daughter of Annie Lucille Partridge Wellman.

85 Forty-eighth Annual Report, *American Missionary Association*, Vol. 40-49:p. 43.

86 In the early years of Oberlin, students were encouraged to participate in one of Shipherd's passions, that of teaching Sunday Schools in nearby towns. These Student Volunteers were loosely organized until the Oberlin Sabbath School Association was formed to provide more guidance. Eventually, many student volunteers expanded their horizons to foreign locations. "A teacher in the hamlet of Pittsfield one year might be carrying the Gospel to the Negroes in Africa, to the West Indies, or to the Indians of our own West a year later." in Robert S. Fletcher, *A History of Oberlin College From its Foundation Through the Civil War* (Oberlin: Oberlin College, 1943) Volume I, 213-214.

87 Frances P. Locke, *Biography of Ernest C. Partridge*, unpublished. Partridge Family Collection. Nat Brand, *Massacre in Shansi* (toExcel, 1999), 86.

88 Ernest C. Partridge, *Questionnaire for 1895 Class Reunion*, ca 1940. Partridge Family Collection.

89 American Board of Commissioners for Foreign Missions, *The Missionary Herald*, April 1913, Volume CIX No. 4, 178-180.

90 Frances P. Locke, *Biography of Ernest C. Partridge*, unpublished, Partridge Family Collection.

91 *Ibid.*

92 Ernest C. Partridge, *College Activities of the Class of 1895*, ca 1940, Partridge Family Collection.

93 George L. Partridge, *Auto By Pat* (Amityville, NY: 1985) 5.

94 Ernest's son, George L. Partridge, was known as *Pat* by his students, campers and grandchildren.

95 In President King's biography, Donald M. Love wrote how, as a young student and teacher, King was mentored by Oberlin's President Fairchild. Through his life as professor and college president,

King thought, spoke, and wrote about personal religion, personal values, education, and the role of students in developing their moral and religious goals. It is to be expected that President King filled a mentor role in Ernest's life. Donald M. Love, *Henry Churchill King of Oberlin*, (New Haven: Yale University Press. 1956) 188.

96 Ernest C. Partridge, *College Activities of the Class of 1895*, ca 1940, Partridge Family Collection.

97 Donald M. Love, *Henry Churchill King of Oberlin*, (New Haven: Yale University Press. 1956).

98 Ernest C. Partridge, *Diary, 1920 to 1924*, February 10, 1920, Partridge Family Collection.

99 *Ibid.*, April 11, 1920.

100 Winona E. Graffam to Ernest C. Partridge, 30 March 1896, Partridge Family Collection.

101 *Troy Daily Times*, accessed May 15, 2014, on www.fultonhistory.com.

102 Winona E. Graffam to Ernest C. Partridge, October 4, 1896, Partridge Family Collection.

103 Ernest C. Partridge to Winona G. Partridge, May10, 1922, Partridge Family Collection.

104 *The Ticonderoga Sentinel*, October 12, 1899.

105 Ernest C. Partridge to William W. Partridge, postcard, 1922, Partridge Family Collection.

106 Ernest C. Partridge to Winona G. Partridge, February 12, 1922, Partridge Family Collection.

107 Winona G. Partridge, *Diary, 1922-1926*, December 12-14, 1922 and December 17, 1922, Partridge Family Collection.

108 Winona G. Partridge, *Diary, 1922-1926*, December 4, 1924, Partridge Family Collection.

109 Robert Melson, "Revolution and Genocide: On the Causes of the Armenian Genocide and the Holocaust," *The Armenian Genocide, History, Politics, Ethics* (New York: St. Martin's Press, 1992) 92.

110 Grigoris Balakian, *Armenian Golgotha, A Memoir of the Armenian Genocide, 1915-1918* (New York: Alfred A. Knopf, 2009) 149.
Annette Höss, "The Trial of Perpetrators by the Turkish Tribunals: The Case of Yozgat," *The Armenian Genocide, History, Politics, Ethics* (New York: St. Martin's Press, 1992) 209.

111 Ernest C. Partridge, *Diary, July 1915 to 1919*, Memoranda Page, Partridge Family Collection.

112 John Minassian, *Many Hills Yet to Climb, Memoirs of an Armenian Deportee* (Santa Barbara: Jim Cook Publisher, 1986) 251.

113 Ernest C. Partridge Diary, July 1915 to 1919, Partridge Family Collection.
John Minassian, *Many Hills Yet to Climb, Memoirs of an Armenian Deportee* (Santa Barbara: Jim Cook Publisher, 1986) 209.

114 John Minassian, *Many Hills Yet to Climb, Memoirs of an Armenian Deportee* (Santa Barbara: Jim Cook Publisher, 1986) 238.

115 *Ibid.*, 238.

116 Samuel Boyagian to Winona G. Partridge, May 10, 1955, Partridge Family Collection.

117 Richard and Georgie (from Istanbul) to Winona G. Partridge, May 22, 1955, Partridge Family Collection.

118 Miss Nina E. Rice to Winona G. Partridge, September 20, 1955, Partridge Family Collection.

119 Ernest C. Partridge, *Diary, July 1925 to 1929*, June 14, 1929, Partridge Family Collection.

120 George L. Partridge, *Auto By Pat* (Amityville, NY: 1985) 8.

121 Winona E. Graffam to Mary L. Graffam, October 14, 1894, Partridge Family Collection.

122 Mary L. Graffam to Winona G. Partridge, June 28, 1921, Partridge Family Collection.

123 Winona E. Graffam to Mary L. Graffam, November 18, 1894, Partridge Family Collection.

124 Winona E. Graffam to Ernest C. Partridge, October 4, 1896, Partridge Family Collection.

125 Winona E. Graffam to Ernest C. Partridge, November 29, 1896, Partridge Family Collection.

126 Winona E. Graffam to Ernest C. Partridge, December 3, 1896, Partridge Family Collection.

127 *Ibid.*

128 Winona G. Partridge, *Autobiography*, (unpublished, Partridge Family Collection, 1947).

129 Winona E. Graffam to Ernest C. Partridge, December 1, 1896, Partridge Family Collection.

130 Winona E. Graffam to Ernest C. Partridge, December 5, 1896, Partridge Family Collection.

131 Winona G. Partridge, *Autobiography*, (unpublished, Partridge Family Collection, 1947).

132 Truman Gibson, *The Lord is My Shepherd* (Chicago: Children's Press, 1970) 25–26.

133 Winona E. Graffam to Ernest C. Partridge, December 3, 1896, Partridge Family Collection.

134 Winona E. Graffam to Mary L. Graffam, December 15, 1897, Partridge Family Collection.

135 Winona E. Graffam to Ernest C. Partridge, November 29, 1896, Partridge Family Collection.

136 Winona E. Partridge, *Diary 1916-1918*, March 18, 1916, Partridge Family Collection.

137 Donald M. Love, *Henry Churchill King of Oberlin*, (New Haven: Yale University Press. 1956) 123.

138 The League of Women Voters (LWV) was formed in 1920 at the convention of the National
American Woman Suffrage Association which was held prior to the ratification of the 19th
Amendment to the U.S. Constitution. The purpose of the LWV was to assist women with
their new responsibilities as voters. It began as, and continues as, a nonpartisan organization
that believes citizens should be involved in government and social reform legislation. accessed
February, 2014: http://www.lwv.org/history.

139 Winona G. Partridge, *Diary, 1916-1918*, October 26, 1916, Partridge Family Collection.

140 Winona G. Partridge, *Diary, 1919-1921*, October 27, 1920, Partridge Family Collection.

141 Donald M. Love, *Henry Churchill King of Oberlin*, (New Haven: Yale University Press. 1956) 167-
168.

> Robert S. Fletcher, *A History of Oberlin College From its Foundation Through the Civil War*
> (Oberlin: Oberlin College, 1943) Volume I, 110

142 Elizabeth "Annie" Fish to Winona E. Graffam, August 26, 1895. Partridge Family Collection.

143 Winona G. Partridge, *Autobiography*, (unpublished, Partridge Family Collection, 1947).

144 *Ibid.*

145 Winona G. Partridge to Mary L. Graffam, December 14, 1900, Partridge Family Collection.

146 Winona G. Partridge, *Diary, 1922-1926*, July 6, 1922, Partridge Family Collection.

147 Ernest C. Partridge, *Diary, 1930-1934*, May 6, 1930, Partridge Family Collection.

148 Winona G. Partridge, *Autobiography*, (unpublished, Partridge Family Collection, 1947).

149 Winona E. Graffam to Mary L. Graffam, October 18, 1894, Partridge Family Collection.

150 Winona G. Partridge, *Autobiography*, (unpublished, Partridge Family Collection, 1947).

151 Winona E. Graffam to Ernest C. Partridge, March 27, 1896, Partridge Family Collection.

152 Winona E. Graffam to Ernest C. Partridge, March 30, 1896, Partridge Family Collection.

153 *Ibid.*

154 Winona E. Graffam to Ernest C. Partridge, 29 November 1896, Partridge Family Collection.

155 Winona E. Graffam to Ernest C. Partridge, December 5, 1896, Partridge Family Collection.

156 Winona E. Graffam to Ernest C. Partridge, March 27, 1896, Partridge Family Collection.

157 Winona E. Graffam to Ernest C. Partridge, December 5, 1896, Partridge Family Collection.

158 Frances P. Locke, *Biography of Ernest C. Partridge*, (unpublished, Partridge Family Collection).

159 Winona G. Partridge, *Autobiography*, (unpublished, Partridge Family Collection, 1947).

160 Armen Sharigian Varbedian to Winona G. Partridge, Valentine's Day card, 1959, Partridge Family Collection.

161 George L. Partridge, *Auto By Pat* (Amityville, NY: 1985) 9.

162 The year digit is unreadable on the letter. The 1891 date is based on the content of the letter and the following dates: her mother's death in May 1890, her father's remarriage in Nov 1891, Mary Louise's graduation from Oberlin 1894. The complete letter is printed in Part II.

163 Winona G. Partridge to Mary L. Graffam, December 14, 1900, Partridge Family Collection.

164 Susan B. Harper, "Mary Louise Graffam: Witness to Genocide," *America and the Armenian Genocide of 1915* (New York: Cambridge University Press, 2003) 214–239. The opening sentence of Susan B. Harper's article on Mary Louise Graffam described her as a "shy teacher." The family accounts and many available documents do not agree with the description.

165 Mary L. Graffam to Graffam Family, June 31, 1891, Partridge Family Collection. My interpretation of this letter is that Mary was comparing her host to her father who she and Winona called Parf. "They say when he is well he is just such a teaser as Parf is."

166 Winona G. Partridge, *Memories of Mary Louise Graffam*, (unpublished, Partridge Family Collection, 1944).

167 J.C. Linn, Jr, "Saw Armenians Suffer and Die," *The Evening Post Magazine*, (New York: 12 July 1919). Linn was attached to the American Relief Commission at Sivas. Linn was mentioned several times in Ernest's diary during April and May of 1919.

168 Mary L. Graffam, *Miss Graffam's Own Story*, taken stenographically by Dr. Richards' Secretary, June 28, 1919 (Turkey), typed copy in Partridge Family Collection.

169 Winona G. Partridge, *Sebastia*, unpublished, Partridge Family Collection, July, 1915.

170 Winona G. Partridge, *Memories of Mary Louise Graffam*, (unpublished, Partridge Family Collection, 1944).

171 *Ibid.*

172 *Ibid.*

173 *Ibid.*

174 Winona G. Partridge to Mary L. Graffam, November 30, 1900, Partridge Family Collection.

175 Ernest C. Partridge, *Mary Louise Graffam, Sivas Turkey* (Present Day Worker Series: 1917) 5.

176 Miss Mary E. Brewer returned to the U. S. shortly after Mary Graffam arrived in Sivas. Miss Brewer's grandparents were early missionaries to Turkey where they ran a school for Greek children in Smyrna in the 1830's. Her father Fisk P. Brewer and her uncle Supreme Court Justice David J. Brewer were born in Smyrna. accessed May 15, 2014, www.findagrave.com.

177 Ernest C. Partridge, "Mary Louise Graffam," *Armenian Affairs* (Vol. 1 No. 1 1949-50) 62.

178 Winona G. Partridge, *Memories of Mary Louise Graffam*, (unpublished, Partridge Family Collection, 1944).

179 *Ibid.*

180 Rev. C. Henry Holbrook, "Impressions of Sivas 1912," *Journal of Armenian Studies*, 1(1990-91): 65.

181 Rev. E. Victor Bigelow, "South Church Service for Miss Mary L. Graffam, Famous Missionary is Subject of Sermon by Rev. E. Victor Bigelow," *The Andover Townsman*, 17 Dec 1920.

182 Ernest C. Partridge, *Mary Louise Graffam, Sivas Turkey* (Present Day Worker Series: 1917) 3.

183 Winona E. Graffam to Mary L. Graffam, November 8, 1894, Partridge Family Collection.

184 National Cathedral School website. accessed May 15, 2014: http://www.ncs.cathedral. org/podium/default.aspx?t= 12847 and http://www.ncs.cathedral.org/podium/default. aspx?t=112456.

185 Winona G. Partridge, *Memories of Mary Louise Graffam*, (unpublished, Partridge Family Collection, 1944).

186 Mary L. Graffam to Graffam Family, June 31, 1891, Partridge Family Collection.

187 Winona E. Graffam to Mary L. Graffam, October 14, 1894, Partridge Family Collection.

188 Winona E. Graffam to Mary L. Graffam, November 4, 1894, Partridge Family Collection.

189 Mary L. Graffam to Winona G. Partridge, May 14, 1921, Partridge Family Collection.

190 Winona G. Partridge, *Memories of Mary Louise Graffam*, (unpublished, Partridge Family Collection, 1944).

191 Winona G. Partridge, *Autobiography*, unpublished, Partridge Family Collection, 1947.

192 Ernest C. Partridge, *Mary Louise Graffam, Sivas Turkey* (Present Day Worker Series: 1917) 8.

193 Mary L. Graffam, *Miss Graffam's Own Story*, Taken stenographically by Dr. Richards' Secretary, June 28, 1919 (Turkey), typed copy in Partridge Family Collection.

194 Winona G. Partridge, *Diary, July 1915 to December 1915*, December 31, 1915, Partridge Family Collection.

195 Winona G. Partridge, *Memories of Mary Louise Graffam*, (unpublished, Partridge Family Collection, 1944).

196 Ernest C. Partridge, *Mary Louise Graffam, Sivas Turkey* (Present Day Worker Series: 1917) 3.

197 Edward G. Partridge, Photo in Partridge Family Collection

198 Edward G. Partridge, *Diary, January 1914-July 1915*, July 6, 1915, Partridge Family Collection.

199 Winona G. Partridge, *Memories of Mary Louise Graffam*, (unpublished, Partridge Family Collection, 1944).

200 Mary L. Graffam to Winona G. Partridge, May 14, 1921, Partridge Family Collection.

201 *Ibid.*

202 Miss Nina E. Rice to Dr. W. W. Peet, September 16, 1921, Sivas Turkey, Typed copy in Partridge Family Collection.

203 *Ibid.*

204 Ernest C. Partridge, *Mary Louise Graffam, Sivas Turkey* (Present Day Worker Series: 1917) 10.

205 Winona G. Partridge, *Sebastia*, July 1915, unpublished, Partridge Family Collection.

206 Mary L. Graffam, "On the Road with Exiled Armenians," *The Missionary Herald*, December 1915, 565-568.

207 Ernest C. Partridge, *Mary Louise Graffam, Sivas Turkey* (Present Day Worker Series: 1917) 12.

208 Winona G. Partridge to Mary L. Graffam, November 23, 1900, Partridge Family Collection.

209 Winona G. Partridge, *Diary, July 1915-December 1915*, October 11, 1915, Partridge
    Family Collection.

210 *Ibid.*

211 Winona G. Partridge, *Diary, July 1915-December 1915*, December 31, 1915, Partridge
    Family Collection.

212 Winona G. Partridge, *Diary, 1922-1926*, November 13, 1924, Partridge Family Collection.

213 Winona G. Partridge, *Diary, 1922-1926*, August 9, 1926, Partridge Family Collection.

214 George L. Partridge, *Auto By Pat* (Amityville, NY: 1985) 5.

215 Ernest C. Partridge to Winona G. Partridge, February 10, 1922, Partridge Family Collection.

216 Ernest C. Partridge to Winona G. Partridge, February 14, 1922, Partridge Family Collection.

217 Ernest C. Partridge to Winona G. Partridge, March 13, 1922, Partridge Family Collection.

218 *Ibid.*

219 Ernest C. Partridge to Winona G. Partridge, February 24, 1922, Partridge Family Collection.

220 Winona G. Partridge, *Diary, 1922-1926*, May 2,1923, Partridge Family Collection.

221 *Ibid.*, August 16, 1923.

222 *Ibid.*, June 11, 1925.

223 *Ibid.*, September 5, 1923.

224 *Ibid.*, October 22, 1923.

225 *Ibid.*, June 19, 1924.

226 Mrs. L. M. Freiwald to Winona G. Partridge, May 8, 1955, Partridge Family Collection.

227 Rev. C. Rexford Raymond to Winona G. Partridge, May 7, 1955, Partridge Family Collection.

228 Winona G. Partridge, *Diary, 1916-1918*, July 13-14, 1917, Partridge Family Collection.

229 Winona G. Partridge, *Diary, 1955*, May 4, 1955, Partridge Family Collection.

230 Winona G. Partridge, *Sebastia*, July 1915, unpublished, Partridge Family Collection.

231 Winona G. Partridge, *Diary 1916-1918*, April 19, 1917, Partridge Family Collection.

232 Winona G. Partridge, *Diary, 1922-1926*, May 30, 1924, Partridge Family Collection.

233 Ann Partridge Murdogh, personal communication with the author, January 2014.

234 *Ibid.*

235 *Ibid.*

236 Northfield School for Girls (NSG) was a school founded by Dwight Lyman Moody in his birth
    town of Northfield, Massachusetts, as the Northfield Seminary for Young Ladies in 1879 with
    the purpose of providing education to those ladies who could not afford one. Moody hoped to
    train generations of Christians who would continue his evangelical efforts. Religious instruction
    and manual labor were required parts of the educational program. In 1971, the Northfield School
    for Girls as it came to be called and the Mount Hermon School for Boys became Northfield
    Mount Hermon School (NMH) and in 2005 the schools consolidated onto the Mount Hermon
    campus. Northfield Mount Hermon School website, accessed May 15, 2014, www.nmhschool.
    org/about-nmh-history.

237 Winona G. Partridge, *Diary 1922-1926*, February 27, 1924, Partridge Family Collection.

238 George L. Partridge, *Auto By Pat* (Amityville, NY: 1985) 58.

239 "The Young Man's Christian Association, YMCA, is an international organization founded in 1844 with the intention improving the spiritual and physical health of the young men in major cities. It combined a social ministry with wholesome recreation." YMCA website, accessed May 15, 2014, http://www.ymca.net/history/founding.html. Pres. King of Oberlin and Ernest Partridge both supported YMCA activities. George Everett Ingalls was General Secretary of YMCA in Kansas.

240 George L. Partridge to Partridge Family, August 12, 1960, P. L. Partridge collection.

241 Mount Hermon School for Boys was founded by Dwight L. Moody in 1881 on property on the west side of the Connecticut River from Northfield. The boys were also required to labor in the laundry, kitchen, janitorial service, or on the farm in addition to academics and religious instruction with the intention to continue Moody's evangelical efforts. In 1971, the Northfield School for Girls as it came to be called and the Mount Hermon School for Boys became Northfield Mount Hermon School (NMH) and in 2005 the schools consolidated onto the Mount Hermon campus. Northfield Mount Hermon School website, accessed July 7, 2014, www.nmhschool.org/about-nmh-history.

242 May L. G. Channon (Mrs. I.M.C.) to Winona G. Partridge, May 15, 1955, Partridge Family Collection.

243 George L. Partridge to Winona G. Partridge, June 10, 1958, P. L. Partridge Collection.

244 "Unitarians Labor to Build Church," *The New York Times*, August 20, 1962, 25.

245 Rev. Julia Older, *Memorial Sermon for Rev. Lynn Partridge*, April 30, 2006.

246 Barbara Locke Johnson, personal communication with the author, 2013.

247 John W. Partridge, personal communication with the author, April, 2014.

248 *Ibid.*

Bibliography

Amistad Research Center, http://www.amistadresearchcenter.org, accessed May 24, 2014.

Balakian, Grigoris. *Armenian Golgotha, A Memoir of the Armenian Genocide, 1915-1918.* New York: Alfred A. Knopf, 2009. 509 pp.

Balakian, Peter. *The Black Dog of Fate.* New York: Basic Books, 1997. 304 pp.

Balakian, Peter. *The Burning Tigris, The Armenian Genocide and America's Response.* New York: HarperCollins Publishers Inc, 2003. 528 pp.

Brandt, Nat. *Massacre in Shansi.* New York: toExcel, 1999. 336 pp.

Bryce, James. *The Treatment of Armenians in the Ottoman Empire 1915-1916, Chapter IX Sivas: The City and Parts of the Vilayet.* London: T Fisher Unwin, 1916. 684 pp.

Buxton, Charles R. *Turkey in Revolution.* London: T. Fisher Unwin, 1909. 3 vol.

Davis, Leslie A. *Slaughterhouse Province, An American Diplomat's Report on the Armenian Genocide, 1915-1917.* New Rochelle, NY: Aristide D. Caratzas, Publisher, 1989. 216 pp.

Fletcher, Robert S. *A History of Oberlin College From its Foundation Through the Civil War.* Oberlin: Oberlin College, 1943. 1004 pp.

Greene, Rev. J. K. *Leavening the Levant.* Boston: The Pilgrim Press, 1916. 349 pp.

Griffeth, Bill. *By Faith Alone.* New York: Three Rivers Press, 2007. 288 pp.

Griswold, Courtland Sherman. *Autobiography.* Oneonta, NY: David M. Griswold, 1990.

Harper, Susan B. "Mary Louise Graffam: witness to genocide," *America and the Armenian Genocide of 1915.* New York: Cambridge University Press, 2003: 214–239.

Holbrook, Rev. C. Henry. "Impressions of Sivas 1912." *Journal of Armenian Studies*. 1(1990-91): 37–71.

Höss, Annette. "The Trial of Perpetrators by the Turkish Tribunals: The Case of Yozgat" in Hovannisian, Richard G. ed. *The Armenian Genocide, History, Politics, Ethics*. New York: St. Martin's Press, 1992. 208–221.

Hovannisian, Richard G. ed. *The Armenian Genocide, History, Politics, Ethics*. New York: St. Martin's Press, 1992. 362 pp.

Israel, Henry, ed. *Rural Manhood*. New York: International Committee of Young Men's Christian Associations, Volume 9 No. 2 February, 1918. 467 pp.

Krakauer, Jon. *Under the Banner of Heaven*. New York: Random House, Inc., 2003. 432 pp.

Krikorian, Abraham D., Professor Emeritus. Department of Biochemistry and Cell Biology. SUNY at Stony Brook. personal correspondence. February 2014.

Krikorian, Abraham D and Taylor, E.L. restoration of the map Near East Relief (on page 19 of this book) which originally appeared in New Near East vol.6 February 6, 1921. Pp. 16-17.

Lincoln Historical Society. *Lincoln Vermont History 1780-2007*. Lincoln, VT: Lincoln Historical Society, 2007.

Linn, Jr, J.C. "Saw Armenians Suffer and Die." *The Evening Post Magazine*. New York, 12 July 1919.

Love, Donald M. *Henry Churchill King of Oberlin*. New Haven: Yale University Press, 1956. 300 pp.

Melson, Robert. "Revolution and Genocide: On the Causes of the Armenian Genocide and the Holocaust" in Hovannisian, Richard G. ed. *The Armenian Genocide, History, Politics, Ethics*. New York: St. Martin's Press, 1992. 80–102.

Minassian, John. *Many Hills Yet to Climb, Memoirs of an Armenian Deportee*. Santa Barbara, CA: Jim Cook Publisher, 1986. 255 pp.

Oberlin College Archives, http://www.oberlin.edu/archive/, accessed February 20, 2014.

Page, Jonathan Conant. *Ringing the Gotchnag, Two American Missionary Families in Turkey, 1855-1922*. Boston: New England Historic Genealogical Society, 2009. 340 pp.

Partridge, Ernest C. *Diary 1930-1934*. Partridge Family Collection. unpublished.

Partridge, Ernest C. *Mary Louise Graffam, Sivas Turkey*. Present Day Worker Series: 1917. 12 pp.

Partridge, Ernest C. "Mary Louise Graffam." *Armenian Affairs*. Volume 1 No. 1 1949-50: 62–65.

Partridge, Ernest C. "The Pensacola Party and Relief Work in Turkey." *Armenian Affairs*. Volume 1 No. 3-4 1950: 293–297.

Partridge, Winona G. *Diary 1922-1926*. Partridge Family Collection. unpublished.

Partridge, Winona G. *Autobiography*. unpublished, ca 1947.

Partridge, Winona G. *Memories of Mary Louise Graffam*. unpublished, 1944.

Pierce, Rev. James W. *Story of Turkey and Armenia*. Baltimore: R. H. Woodward Company, 1896, 500 pp.

Reed, Jeanne B., Althea H. French, and Elizabeth E. Davis. *History of Monson, Maine 1822-1972*. Sesquicentennial Committee, 1972. 219 pp.

Richter, Julius, D.D., *A History of Protestant Missions in the Near East*. New York: Fleming H. Revell Company, 1910. 435 pp.

Rollins College website, http://www.rollins.edu/, accessed January 15, 2014.

Schaefer, Inge. *Images of America: Colchester*. Portsmouth, New Hampshire: Arcadia Publishing, 2003. 129 pp.

Watenpaugh, Keith D. "The League of Nations' Rescue of Armenian Genocide Survivors and the Making of Modern Humanitarianism, 1920–1927." *American Historical Review*. December 2010: 1315–1339.

Wilmington Historical Society. *Images of America: Wilmington and the Whiteface Region*. Charleston, South Carolina: Arcadia Publishing, 2013. 127 pp.

Winter, Jay, ed. *America and the Armenian Genocide of 1915*. New York: Cambridge University Press, 2003, 317 pp.

Woods, Leonard, D.D. *History of the Andover Theological Seminary*, Boston: James R. Osgood and Company, 1885. 386 pp.

Acknowledgements

The precious family heirlooms and wonderful memories that my dear cousin Barbara Locke Johnson shared with me were the instigators for this book. Barbara, along with her mother Frances and her grandmother Winona, had kept these letters and diaries safely all these years. Barbara's husband, David Johnson, began the transcribing process in 2011 and I wish to thank him for the jumpstart.

My friend Cathy Gamble helped me at the beginning of this venture as we struggled to decipher Winona's handwriting in order to read and understand the oldest letters.

I am grateful for the support and enthusiasm of cousins Ann Murdogh, Ellen Cleaver, Julia Partridge, and John Partridge. Ann and Ellen shared their father's childhood diary and personal remembrances for this book. John Partridge contributed his insight as well.

Serendipity brought me an introduction to a Partridge cousin, John Becker (a descendant of Harlan Partridge), and his wife Mary Stott, a fellow genealogist, who shared with me Hiram Patridge's will. The will provided a valuable demonstration of the importance of education in the early years of the family, and identified the "missing" children in my family genealogical research.

A huge thank you and heartfelt appreciation go to my friends Abe Krikorian and Gene Taylor who provided me with subject matter expertise and numerous resources invaluable to this endeavor. They generously shared time and energy to various aspects of this project.

I wish to thank Biff Barnes for his evaluation, insight and suggestions on the project, which in turn, enabled me to bring clarity and focus to my writing.

And finally, I wish to thank my family for their inspiration and support. My daughter Caitlin Low used her talents to design the Hiram descendant chart and I drew from the thoughts and experiences of my son Casey Low during his early Naval Academy days.

Without the full support and loving encouragement of my husband, this endeavor would not have been undertaken. His contribution was immeasurable and consisted of diverse and varied roles: camera operator and photographer, research partner, project consultant, all while providing me with regular and delicious nutrition and periodic excursions away. I know he is ready to have me participate in his retirement.

Index

Revised 2017

First names were used when provided by diarists or letter writers. Winona normally used Mr., Mrs., or Miss, and occasionally used Dr. or Prof. Ernest mostly only wrote last names except for the unmarried women who were honored with Miss. In some instances, different people with the same name are indeed together. It will be up to the reader to discern from the text and any personal knowledge of the individuals to assign identity. It is recommended to search both by surname and given/first name as it is not always clear which name was used. The spellings of names varied among the writers and were not always consistent throughout the diaries and letters.

www.ingramcontent.com/pod-product-compliance
Lightning Source LLC
Chambersburg PA
CBHW050637150426
42811CB00052B/857